FORENSIC SCIENCE

AN INTRODUCTION TO CRIMINALISTICS

McGraw-Hill Series in Criminology and Criminal Justice

FORENSIC SCIENCE

AN INTRODUCTION TO CRIMINALISTICS

Peter R. De Forest, D. Crim.

Professor of Criminalistics
John Jay College of Criminal Justice
The City University of New York

R. E. Gaensslen, Ph.D.

Professor of Forensic Science
Director, Forensic Science Program
University of New Haven

Henry C. Lee, Ph.D.

Chief Criminalist
Connecticut State Police
Forensic Science Laboratory
and
Professor of Forensic Science
University of New Haven

McGraw-Hill, Inc.
New York   St. Louis   San Francisco   Auckland   Bogotá
Caracas   Lisbon   London   Madrid   Mexico City   Milan
Montreal   New Delhi   San Juan   Singapore
Sydney   Tokyo   Toronto

This book was set in Times Roman by University Graphics, Inc. (ECU).
The editors were Eric M. Munson, Christina Mediate, and Jo Satloff;
the production supervisor was Leroy A. Young.
The drawings were done by J & R Services, Inc.
The cover was designed by Mark Wieboldt.

FORENSIC SCIENCE

An Introduction to Criminalistics

16 17 18 19 20 21 BRBBRB 99 9 8 7 6 5 4 3 2 1 0

ISBN 0-07-016267-0

Library of Congress Cataloging in Publication Data

De Forest, Peter R.
     Forensic science.

     (McGraw-Hill series in criminology and criminal
justice)
     Includes bibliographies and index.
     1. Criminal investigation. I. Gaensslen, R. E.
(Robert E.) II. Lee, Henry C. III. Title. IV. Series.
HV8073.D38 1983   363.2′5   82-20803
ISBN 0-07-016267-0

To the dedicated forensic science practitioners and educators, past and present, who have contributed so much to the advancement of the field and thereby to the equity and efficacy of our criminal justice system.

CONTENTS

PREFACE

Forensic science has emerged as a significant element in efforts to control crime while maintaining a high quality of justice. The value of physical evidence and its analysis has been demonstrated in many ways on many occasions, and law enforcement officials have become increasingly dependent on laboratory results for evidence not obtainable by other avenues or means of investigation. As science and technology continue to advance, the capabilities and importance of forensic science laboratories will also continue to grow. At present, all fifty states, and many individual cities, towns, and counties, have forensic science laboratories serving them. Many communities without laboratories are exploring ways to develop and staff them, and those that already have laboratories are looking into ways to improve them and increase their level of services.

Forensic Science: An Introduction to Criminalistics was written as a basic textbook for use in college and university forensic science courses at the introductory level. Little or no prior knowledge of science has been assumed. Enough background material is given in each chapter to enable the student to understand and appreciate the laboratory procedures, their underlying principles, and their potential value and limitations.

This book is suitable for any one-semester introductory course in forensic science for police officers, crime-scene investigators, or beginning students in law enforcement, criminal justice, or forensic science. Other criminal-justice practitioners, such as attorneys or judges involved in criminal cases, may also profit from the information contained in these pages.

Although most of the chapters are devoted to particular kinds of physical evidence, we have taken some care to explore different conceptual ways of looking at various classes of physical evidence. Two types of evidence might be very different in nature, for example, but the methods of analyzing them may have a great deal in common or may even be identical. Similarly, various types of patterns are analyzed and interpreted primarily as an aid to the reconstruction of events, although the patterns may have been produced by quite different events involving quite different materials.

Although we have not formally divided the book into sections, many of the chapters may be grouped. The first three chapters are devoted to introductory, conceptual, and background material and to some basic scientific concepts and the methods that are used in examining physical evidence. Subsequent chapters, which deal with methods, techniques, and approaches, contain back-references to the descriptions of the methods. In this way, students can refer back to the appropriate introductory section as necessary. Chapters 4 and 5 cover most of the types of evidence that require chemical analysis primarily, namely, evidence from suspicious fires and explosion cases, and drug and toxicological materials. Chapters 6 through 10 discuss trace and transfer evidence. Those types of evidence that do not need a full chapter of their own are discussed in Chapter 6. Chapters 9 and 10 have to do with forensic serology. Chapters 11 through 14 follow a logic similar to that of Chapters 6 through 10, except that the subject matter is physical pattern evidence. Throughout, we have tried to stress the fundamental concepts of identification, individualization, and reconstruction in the chapters on particular evidence types. Some material and information that is more technically complex than seemed to be warranted in the main text has been included in certain figures and tables for interested readers. The essential points made in the chapters, however, will not be diminished if this material is not covered or studied in great detail.

Another relationship we have tried to develop is the one between the crime scene and the laboratory—between crime-scene investigators and laboratory examiners. Collection, preservation, and packaging of evidence at a crime scene are discussed generally and for each of the different types of evidence.

Likewise, methods of analysis for each type of evidence are discussed in some detail. There seems to be little doubt that crime-scene searches will be carried out more thoroughly and skillfully, and evidence packaged and preserved properly, if investigative officers understand and appreciate what kinds of analyses can be done. The effect of collection and preservation methods on the results that can ultimately be obtained must be understood by crime-scene personnel as well as by laboratory examiners. Recognition, documentation, handling, packaging, and analysis of physical evidence are all parts of a coherent, continuous process that, taken together, make up the overall forensic analysis.

The three appendixes treat topics that are largely self-contained but whose subject matter occurs in a number of different places in the various chapters. Appendix 1 covers basic scientific measurements and the metric system. Appendix 2 is a discussion of crime-scene procedures. It is intended to supplement the material presented elsewhere in the text on specific evidence types and situations, and tie it together conceptually. Instructors wishing to include lessons on photography in their courses can treat Appendix 3 as a chapter. It can be taken up at any point following the study of Chapter 3. Appendix 3 is designed as an aid in acquiring an understanding of fundamental photographic theory and principles rather than being a "how to" treatment of photography. Practical details of specific techniques, methods required by particular cameras, films, and processes as well as "tricks of the trade" can be supplied by the instructor and reinforced by supplemental reading assigned by the instructor. The list of references included at the end of the appendix should prove helpful in making these assignments.

Throughout the book we have tried to illustrate certain specific and general points about forensic science and physical evidence by including descriptions of real-world cases. Some of these are well known, and others come from our collective experience or that of our colleagues and friends.

We hope that these pages will convey some of the excitement about and enthusiasm for our work that the practice and teaching of forensic science have brought us and that we trust some of our readers may share.

The mention of specific products and brand names and the products of specific companies is for information and illustration purposes only; it does not constitute an endorsement of any specific item or product by the authors or by the publishers.

A number of people have assisted us in various ways in the long and sometimes arduous task of preparing this book, and it is with pleasure and gratitude that we acknowledge their assistance and support: Julie K. Bremser, Elaine M. Pagliaro, James J. Horan, Francis X. Sheehan, Philip C. Langellotti, W. Reid Lindsay, Robert A. Hathaway, Marshall Robinson, Marius Venclauskas, and James Behrendt were all extremely helpful in reading and commenting upon the material in its earlier stages of preparation. In this respect, we wish to add a special note of appreciation to Professors W. Jack Cadman, Michael J. Camp, Richard W. Chang, Joseph L. Peterson, and George W. Roche. Doctors Richard Pinder and Joseph Balkon were extremely helpful to us in the preparation of the chapter on drug analysis and forensic toxicology.

A number of our friends and colleagues, as well as other individuals, organizations, and companies, generously contributed data, photographs, details of case materials, artwork, and ideas for artwork. In this regard we wish to thank Dr. Jew-Ming Chao, Burlington County (New Jersey) Forensic Laboratory; Robert J. Mills and others of the Connecticut State Police Forensic Science Laboratory; Skip Palenik, McCrone Associates, Chicago; Captain Vincent Peterson and staff members of the New Jersey State Police Forensic Science Laboratory; Mark Stolorow, Illinois Department of Law Enforcement, Bureau of Scientific Services; Dr. P. H. Whitehead, Home Office Forensic Science Laboratory, Wetherby, England; the New York City Police Department Crime Laboratory; the Forensic Science Laboratory of the Westchester County (New York) Medical Examiner's Office; Dr. Harold E. Edgerton; and Mrs. Paul L. Kirk. We also thank American Optical Corporation, Bausch and Lomb Company, Blackstone-Shelburne, Kjell Carlsson Innovation. Perkin-Elmer Corporation, Polaroid Corporation, Sirchie Laboratories, Smith & Wesson Company, and Unitron Instruments Company.

Finally, we are deeply indebted to our wives and families for their patience and support during the preparation of this book. Jacqueline Gaensslen was additionally helpful to us with much of the editing and typing.

Peter R. De Forest
R. E. Gaensslen
Henry C. Lee

FORENSIC SCIENCE

AN INTRODUCTION TO CRIMINALISTICS

CHAPTER 1

ABOUT
FORENSIC SCIENCE

SCIENCE AND LAW

Forensic science is the application of the natural sciences to matters of the law; it includes a variety of different activities and specialties. In practice, forensic science draws upon the principles and methods of all the traditional sciences, such as physics, chemistry, and biology. At the same time, there are differences between forensic science and traditional sciences. The differences are attributable in part to the fact that forensic science has some unique objectives, and in part to its continuous and necessary interaction with the legal system.

Natural Sciences and the Scientific Method

Science is not easy to define simply. Popular perceptions of what science is, and what scientists do, are often inaccurate. Many people think of scientists as people who use complex (even secret) means that nonscientists do not understand to gain knowledge that will benefit humanity. Another misconception is that scientific results or conclusions represent "absolute truth." If a result or conclusion is "scientific," people are conditioned to believe that it must, therefore, be right. Advertising techniques commonly attempt to exploit this belief.

Although the attainment of "truth" is one of the goals of science, and thus one of the bases for using the so-called scientific method, this ideal is not achieved in actual practice. Actually, science is that area of human endeavor which tries to organize and understand the connections among natural phenomena. Science is concerned only with *natural* phenomena, with things and processes that are subject to observation, measurement, and experimentation. In addition, science can be distinguished from other disciplines on the basis of its combined theoretical and empirical approach, which is usually called the *scientific method.*

The scientific method may be characterized as consisting of several more or less separate steps: observation (collection of data), conjecture, hypothesis, testing, and theory. Most scientists do follow this general procedure without really thinking about it. Observations are made and data collected. The significance of the observations is considered (conjecture), until some reasonable explanation consistent with all the data—a hypothesis—is arrived at. Experiments designed to test the hypothesis are then conceived and carried out. The new data thus obtained are used to refine the initial hypothesis as necessary. A modified hypothesis which has been verified by a good deal of rigorous testing may come to be called a *theory.* Sometimes, theories which have been extensively tested and verified by many scientists working independently may come to be regarded as *natural laws.*

Forensic scientists engaged in reconstruction of events follow the essential principles of the scientific method just outlined. In attempting to reconstruct the events which took place at a crime scene, for example, the first step is careful observation and assembly of all the known facts. Different hypotheses can then be entertained to see how well one or another of them corresponds to all the facts. As additional facts are disclosed by further observation or by experimental testing, it may be possible to arrive at a theory of what took place.

The scientific method is not some strict set of rules by which all scientists proceed. Rather, it is a particular way of going about gathering information about the natural world and of attempting to organize and understand it. Elements of both deductive and inductive logic are used in applying the scientific method.

In *deductive logic,* a conclusion follows inescapably from one or more of the premises. If the premises are true, then the conclusion drawn is valid. Consider the following example of deductive logic. The oxygen carrier and red pigment in the blood of all mammals is hemoglobin. Human beings are mammals; therefore, human blood contains hemoglobin. The conclusion here is a logical consequence of the two premises. Mathematical proofs are examples of deductive logic. The conclusion is based on the facts in the premises.

In the experimental sciences, deductive logic alone would not be adequate. It is often necessary to go beyond the facts, and to draw conclusions that may have predictive value. This type of reasoning is known as *inductive logic,* and leads to the development of hypotheses. The conclusion drawn has not been proved to be true, although in some cases it may be regarded as being true from a practical point of view. A conclusion may be based on such a vast amount of experience that it is unlikely to be false. We have arrived at the conclusion, for example, that fingerprints are individual, but this has never been rigorously proved. The conclusion is reached through inductive logic, and is based upon millions of observations. The reasoning behind the conclusion runs as follows: Tens of millions of fingerprints have been catalogued in national files. Thus far no two people have been found to have the same fingerprints; therefore, fingerprints are (probably) individual. In order to prove this conclusion rigorously, by deductive logic, it would be necessary to compare the fingerprints of every person living on earth! If two sets were found which matched, then the conclusion arrived at inductively would be false. Since it would be impossible to conduct the examination of every person's fingerprints, we must be satisfied with the conclusion arrived at inductively, by extrapolation from limited experience with a few million examples thought to be representative. Even though the inductive conclusion has not been rigorously proved, it seems quite unlikely that it is false. It is, therefore, a probable conclusion. Such conclusions may be drawn from analogies or informed conjecture that is based upon a large amount of representative data. To be useful at a practical level, it is necessary only that they prove to be correct most of the time.

In summary, then, science begins simply with curiosity about some natural phenomenon. A scientist then makes observations on the phenomenon and formulates an "educated guess" to explain the observations. This guess is the *hypothesis*. Since the hypothesis represents an explanation of some phenomenon, it is possible to make some predictions based upon it. In order to be within the realm of science, a hypothesis must be able to generate predictions which are *experimentally testable*. Hypotheses or theories which are not subject to experimental testing are outside the realm of science. Scientific hypotheses are tested by determining experimentally the truth of their predictions. True hypotheses always yield true predictions. The trouble is that false hypotheses can also yield true predictions, as well as false ones. Thus, experiments which show that a prediction is true do not necessarily demonstrate that the hypothesis from which the prediction was derived is true. They merely lend support to the hypothesis.

The experiments which scientists conduct to test hypotheses are designed to be *controlled,* so that there is only one variable at a time. In practice, it is not usually possible to construct experiments with absolute certainty that only one parameter is variable. Unrecognized variables may influence experimental results. As many different experiments are conducted on a particular question, however, the truth or falsity of a hypothesis becomes clearer, since many different predictions are tested over the course of time. If a hypothesis leads to a prediction that is shown experimentally to be false, the hypothesis has to be changed. Hypotheses are thus altered over the course of time as more and more experiments are conducted to test their validity. As they are modified and altered, hypotheses get closer and closer to "the truth." Because of this self-testing and experimental nature, scientific knowledge is always changing. There is no guarantee that yesterday's truth will be the same as tomorrow's. A hypothesis which has been extensively tested, and which generates a large number of true predictions, is often called a *theory.* The body of scientific knowledge that exists at any given time represents the best explanation of natural phenomena which has been formulated up to that time. It is not possible to know how close to the "real truth" scientific knowledge is at any particular time. The history of science has taught us to be skeptical about what we think is true.

Law and Legal Systems

From ancient times, recorded history has been filled with accounts of different codes, or laws. People trying to live together and function harmoniously in an organized society have always tried to regulate their affairs and relationships in some systematic way. Codes are designed to provide an orderly basis for the conduct of human affairs. Some laws and legal systems have a religious basis; others are purely secular. Legal systems operate under many different forms of government. The laws in effect at any given time are usually influenced by or derived from those of previous periods.

Various activities, regarded as contrary to the collective interest or to some generally accepted moral code, are forbidden by laws. The existing authority then provides for sanctions against those who engage in the forbidden activities. The activities involving relationships among people are also subject to certain rules. In a general way, *criminal* codes govern activities in which society as a whole has an interest, and *civil* codes tend to govern relations between individuals or groups. The distinction between criminal and civil matters depends on the social and historical context of the society which created the laws. Legal structures are always reflections of particular societies at particular times. Without exception, however, the dynamics of their operation represent a human activity that depends on decision making. Legal decision making is nearly always vested in some kind of court or tribunal. Codes and legal systems cannot anticipate every possible circumstance under which disputes will arise between people or with the state. The function of the courts or tribunals, therefore, is to make reasoned judgments in particular cases. They try to apply the general principles of the legal code to the particular circumstances of a given situation. To exercise their function responsibly, courts have always sought ways to ascertain the facts surrounding particular cases. The relationship between law and science had developed out of a common interest in factual information. Although the concepts of *scientific fact* and *legal fact* are often quite different, the application of scientific methods can often provide factual information that is relevant to a legal proceeding and would not be available without the intervention of science.

SCOPE OF FORENSIC SCIENCE

The term *forensic science* is sometimes used as a synonym for *criminalistics*. Both terms encompass a diverse range of activities. Forensic science is also defined in a broader sense to include forensic medicine, odontology, anthropology, psychiatry, toxicology, questioned documents examination, and firearm, toolmark, and fingerprint examinations, as well as criminalistics.

Criminalistics is concerned with the recognition, identification, individualization, and evaluation of physical evidence using the methods of the natural sciences in matters of legal significance. It includes all the areas of trace-evidence examination and forensic chemistry. It also includes the reconstruction of events based on physical-evidence analysis. Different forensic scientists would define the scope of the field differently. Some would include firearm and toolmark examination and questioned documents as a part of criminalistics, for example. Despite the implications of the name, criminalistics activities are not limited to criminal matters. They are used in civil law cases and in regulatory matters as well. People who are engaged in criminalistics as a profession are called *criminalists*.

The major specialty areas included in the wider definition of forensic science are described briefly below. Some of them are taken up in more detail in later chapters.

Forensic medicine (legal medicine; medical jurisprudence) is the application of medicine and medical science to legal problems. Practitioners of forensic medicine are doctors of medicine with specialty certification in pathology and forensic pathology. Most of them are medical examiners. They are concerned with determining the cause and circumstances in cases of questioned death. They also become involved in matters having to do with insurance claims, and sometimes in cases of medical malpractice.

Forensic odontology (forensic dentistry) is the application of dentistry to human identification problems. Forensic odontologists are dentists who specialize in the forensic aspects of their field. They are concerned with the identification of persons based upon their dentition, usually in cases of otherwise unrecognizable bodies or in mass disasters. They also analyze and compare bitemark evidence in many types of cases.

Forensic anthropology has to do with personal identification based on bodily (particularly skeletal) remains. Practitioners are physical anthropologists who are interested in forensic problems. Other areas of forensic anthropology include establishing data bases on bodily structures as functions of sex, age, race, stature, and so forth. Interpretation of footprint or shoe-print evidence might also be included.

Forensic toxicology has to do with the determination of toxic substances in human tissues and organs. Much of the work concerns the role toxic agents may have played in causing or contributing to the death of a person. Further discussion is found in Chapter 5.

Criminalistics includes all the areas of trace and transfer evidence (Chapter 6), such as glass and soil (Chapter 7), fibers and hairs (Chapter 8), blood (Chapter 9), and physiological fluids (Chapter 10). It also includes arson accelerant and explosive residues (Chapter 4), drug identification (Chapter 5) and the interpretation of different patterns and imprints (Chapter 11). It is the broadest of the subdivisions of forensic science.

Questioned documents examination includes comparisons and interpretation of handwriting, mechanically produced material (typing, printing), and photocopied material. Analysis of papers, inks, and other materials used to produce documents may also be included. This subject is covered in Chapter 13.

Firearm and toolmark examination has to do with firearm identification, comparison of markings on bullets and other projectiles, cartridge cases, and shell cases, especially for the purpose of determining that a bullet may have been fired from a particular weapon. Toolmark examinations are concerned with the association of particular impressions with particular tools. A detailed discussion is given in Chapter 14.

Fingerprint examination is concerned with the classification of fingerprints and the organization of sets of prints into usable files. Development of latent prints and comparisons of known and unknown fingerprints are a part of the work as well. This material is discussed in Chapter 12.

Some forensic science activities can be classified under more than one of the major subdivisions above. Toolmark comparisons, for example, are sometimes considered part of criminalistics and sometimes as part of the separate *firearms and toolmarks* specialty. Similarly, hair comparison is usually considered a part of criminalistics, but it could just as well be considered a part of forensic anthropology. Any classification scheme for all the different activities is, therefore, somewhat arbitrary. No one person can be expert in all the sciences and their methods, and it is for this reason that forensic science contains subspecialties. The subspecialties develop around a particular type of physical evidence, or around a particular group of methods and procedures. Some forensic scientists are generalists. They have broad training and experience in most of the basic areas of criminalistics, can carry out a variety of different physical-evidence examinations knowledgeably, or more importantly, refer specific aspects of a case to specialists.

This book is concerned primarily with criminalistics, and the emphasis is on criminal-case applications.

The range of human activity is so diverse that almost anything can become *physical evidence* under one circumstance or another. In any criminal, civil, or regulatory matter, there can be physical evidence which, if recognized, properly handled, and knowledgeably interpreted, can contribute importantly to an understanding of the case.

The methods used in forensic science are those of traditional scientific disciplines, like chemistry, biology, physics, geology, or medicine; but forensic science is something more than a "patchwork quilt" of various disciplines and methods. Before any traditional scientific work is done at all, a forensic scientist or investigator must *recognize* physical evidence in a particular case. Something that is extremely important in one case might be part of the background in another one. A forensic scientist must also be able to decide what kinds of tests, measurements, or analyses on a piece of evidence will be informative under the particular circumstances. And, unlike traditional scientists, a forensic scientist has no control over the condition or history of an item of physical evidence. In many cases, the history of the item is unknown.

The dimensions of a forensic science investigation may include any or all of three major activities in analyzing and interpreting physical evidence: (1) identification, (2) individualization, and (3) reconstruction.

Identification is a process common to all the sciences and, in fact, to everyday life. It may be regarded as a classification scheme, in which items are assigned to categories containing like items, and given names. Different items within a given category all have the same generic name. In this way, botanists will identify plants by categorizing and naming them. Likewise, chemists identify chemical compounds. In forensic science, identification usually means the identification of items of physical evidence. Some types of physical evidence require that scientific tests be conducted to identify them. Drugs, arson accelerants, bloodstains, and seminal stains are examples. Objects are identified by comparing their *class characteristics* with those of known standards or previously established criteria. Class characteristics are the properties that all the members of a certain class of objects or substances have in common.

Individualization is unique to forensic science; it refers to the demonstration that a particular sample is unique, even among members of the same class. It may also refer to the demonstration that a questioned piece of physical evidence and a similar known sample have a *common origin*. Thus, in addition to class characteristics, objects and materials possess *individual characteristics* that can be used to distinguish members of the same class. The nature of these individual characteristics varies from one type of evidence to another, but forensic scientists try to take advantage of them in efforts to *individualize* a piece of physical evidence by some type of comparison process. Only a few types of physical evidence (primarily physical pattern evidence) can be truly individualized, but with some other types an approach to the goal of individualization is possible. We refer to these as *partial individualizations,* and in some cases they are nothing more than refined identifications. The term *identification* is sometimes used to mean *personal identification* (the individualization of persons). Fingerprints, for example, can be used to "identify" an individual. The terminology is unfortunate, since this process is really an individualization. Likewise, dental evidence and dental records may be used by a forensic odontologist in making personal individualizations in situations where dead bodies cannot be readily identified otherwise (such as in mass disasters, or in cases of victims of fires or explosions).

Reconstruction refers to the process of putting the "pieces" of a case or situation together with the objective of reaching an understanding of a sequence of past events based on the record of physical evidence that has resulted from the events. Reconstructions are often desirable in criminal cases in which eyewitness evidence is absent or unreliable. They are important in many other types of cases too, such as automobile accidents. Identification and individualization of physical evidence can play important roles in providing data for reconstructions in some cases.

Forensic science, by its very nature, has to do with legal matters and legal questions. One of its main characteristics, therefore, is its interaction with the elements of the justice system. This feature, among the others discussed above (such as individualization), sets it apart from traditional science. Many forensic scientists are concerned almost exclusively with criminal cases, and they deal almost entirely with the criminal justice system. There are many kinds of civil cases, however, in which physical evidence and forensic science have important roles.

Forensic science comes to public attention most often as a result of involvement in major criminal cases. There are more organized forensic science laboratories formally associated with the criminal justice system than there are associated strictly with civil work. The same general methods, approaches, and procedures are used by forensic scientists, however, regardless of whether the case is civil or criminal in nature. From a scientific point of view, the distinction between civil and criminal is artificial—the distinction is a legal one. In this book, we will make a number of references to criminal cases, but it should be kept in mind that the principles, methods, and procedures discussed are equally applicable to any case, whether civil or criminal.

Civil cases usually involve disputes between individuals or organizations, and they can encompass a variety of situations in which physical evidence can play an important role. Questions concerning the authenticity of a last will and testament, for example, might be referred to a questioned document examiner for resolution (Chapter 13). The larger the estate involved, the more complicated the legal proceedings are likely to become. The recent dispute over the several "wills" of the late Howard Hughes represents a spectacular example of this kind of case. In cases involving apparent mechanical or materials failures, various experts may be called upon to look at items of evidence. People who have suffered bodily harm, or the families of people who have been killed, as the apparent result of mechanical or materials defects or failures sometimes sue manufacturers for damages. Tire-failure cases would be an example. In such a case, the plaintiffs must try to establish negligence on the part of the tire manufacturer (defendant), and examination of the failed materials can provide important evidence. Forensic serologists get involved in matrimonial disputes at times. In contested divorce proceedings, one party may engage the services of a private investigator to try to show that the other party has been sexually involved with another person. In these cases, evidence can be submitted to a serologist for semen identification, and sometimes for blood-group determination (Chapter 10). Blood typing in cases of disputed paternity is commonly used in family court cases where a man is sued for the support of a child whose fatherhood he disclaims (Chapter 9). There are many other examples of criminalistics and forensic science involvement in civil cases.

In any type of case, the principles and procedures of the forensic science investigation remain the same. Recognition of physical evidence, its proper preservation, and analysis can often provide important information to courts and to juries in helping them resolve the complexities of cases.

ORIGINS OF FORENSIC SCIENCE

The historical threads of present-day forensic science can be found in the development of a number of different specialty areas, including forensic medicine and toxicology, firearms identification, questioned document examination, anthropometry, and fingerprints. The field has not evolved at the same rate in every country.

Legal medicine is one of the oldest kinds of forensic science recorded in historical documents. A treatise on the subject was written in the 6th century by a Chinese doctor, Hsu Chich'Ts' si. This work has been lost, but a work published in China in 1247 still survives. Legal medicine probably began to flourish around the 16th century, as modern-day medicine and science began to be developed.

The end of the 18th century marked the beginnings of modern chemistry. This opened the way for the birth of toxicology. The most illustrious figure in the history of toxicology was probably M. J. B. Orfila (1787–1853; Figure 1-1). A Spaniard by birth, Orfila went to France in 1807, where he stayed and eventually became dean of the medical faculty in Paris. His studies placed toxicology on a firm scientific basis, and he was probably the first expert to provide convincing scientific evidence in a criminal trial.

In December 1839, a man named Lafarge was on a business trip in Paris, France, several hundred miles away from his home. He became ill after eating a cake sent to him by his

FIGURE 1-1
M. J. B. Orfila, 1787–1853. *(National Library of Medicine, Bethesda, Md.)*

wife, and he complained of symptoms resembling those in arsenic poisoning. Mrs. Lafarge was a young widow, who had married Lafarge through an arrangement by a marriage broker after the death of her first husband. The marriage was an unhappy one. Mr. Lafarge came home, and his condition grew steadily worse, until he died January 13, 1840. Mrs. Lafarge was charged with poisoning her husband, and it could be established that she had bought arsenic from the drug store as far back as mid-December. The postmortem examination of Lafarge was followed by chemical tests that were inconclusive.

The court then consulted Orfila, the best-known forensic toxicologist of the time, and the body was ordered exhumed. Orfila came from Paris personally and showed that Lafarge's internal organs contained arsenic. He testified to his findings at the trial, assuring the jury that the laboratory ware used in the tests, as well as the cemetery earth, were arsenic-free.

The defense had engaged the services of its own expert, Raspail (Figure 1-2). He was going to testify that he could extract arsenic from the judge's own chair using Orfila's methods. His arrival at the trial was delayed by a fall from horseback, however, and Mrs. Lafarge was found guilty before Raspail could testify. She was sentenced to penal servitude.

The Lafarge case, as the above case example is often called, is often cited as the first in which the defense attempted to rebut the state's scientific evidence by calling on opposing expert. Orfila and Raspail engaged in well-publicized disagreements on a number of other occasions as well.

Orfila carried out some of the earliest known studies on blood and semen identification, but his methods have not stood the test of time. In 1827, for example, he concluded that it was difficult, if not impossible, to extract intact spermatozoa from a seminal stain and that a series of chemical tests was the preferred procedure for the identification of these stains. Because of his reputation, his opinion carried great

FIGURE 1-2
Francois Vincent Raspail, 1794–1878. *(National Library of
Medicine, Bethesda, Md.)*

weight at the time. Others thought that the microscopical identification of sperm
cells was the preferred approach to the problem, and they were right (Chapter 10).

One of the first systems of *personal identification* was based upon a series of body
measurements. Its major proponent, Alphonse Bertillon (1853–1914; Figure 1-3),
developed this system of *anthropometry* in order to establish an identification file
suitable for use in criminal investigations. The system is also called *bertillonage,* in
honor of its developer (Figure 1-4). Bertillon devised the system in Paris, but its use
spread throughout the world. There is no doubt now that this system of measurements cannot uniquely define one person as distinct from all others. In theory, it may
have been possible, but errors in measurement reduced the discriminating ability of
the approach in practice. The significance of Bertillon's contribution lies in the fact
that it represented the first example of the use of an individualization technique

FIGURE 1-3
Alphonse Bertillon, 1853–1914. A photograph taken by
his pupil R. A. Reiss. *(Reprinted from Alphonse
Bertillon, by Henry T. F. Rhodes, Abelard-Schuman, Inc.,
Copyright 1956 by Harper & Row, Publishers, Inc., New
York, by permission of the publisher.)*

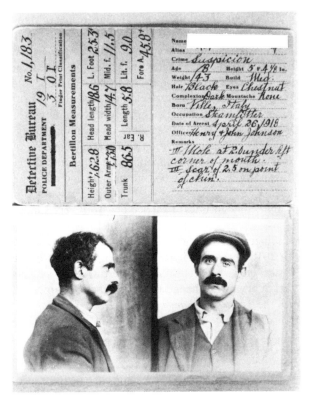

FIGURE 1-4
Cards with bertillonage and identification photographs. The
front of one card and the rear of another are shown.

rooted in sound scientific principles for solving crimes. The system was gradually abandoned as the value of fingerprints became recognized. Bertillon himself actively opposed the introduction of fingerprint systems into police departments, regarding this development as a threat to his own system. Despite this attitude, he was the first person in Europe to utilize latent prints from a crime scene in solving a case. He was also among the first to make use of systematic crime scene photography.

Employment of fingerprints as a device for personal identification grew out of the early efforts of William Herschel, a British civil servant in India in the 1870s, and of Henry Faulds, a Scottish physician who was working in Japan at around the same time. Faulds was the first to recognize explicitly the value of latent prints from a crime scene. The first public proposal that fingerprints might be useful for identifying criminals was actually made by Thomas Taylor, a microscopist with the U.S. Department of Agriculture in Washington, D.C. Taylor's proposal was published in the *American Journal of Microscopy* in July 1877. Another British civil servant in India, Edward Henry, was the first to devise a fingerprint classification scheme (Chapter 12), so that sets of fingerprints could be catalogued and retrieved.

The prototype of today's criminalist was fictional. Sir Arthur Conan Doyle's stories about Sherlock Holmes predicted the existence of the "scientific detective" or criminalist in the real world. Doyle was far ahead of his time in this respect. Many writers have credited the formulation of criminalistics as an operational discipline in reality to Hans Gross of Austria, in part because he coined the term *kriminalistik,* which is translated into English as "criminalistics." There is no doubt that his career deeply influenced the development of the field. Criminalistics was more a concept to Gross than it was a profession, and one which brought scientific knowledge to bear on the analysis and interpretation of physical evidence and involved scientific methods in criminal investigation. Gross was a lawyer and served as an examining magistrate in Graz. He looked upon the criminalistics function as the amalgamation of the expert services of various specialists for the examination of physical evidence which fell within their fields. Gross authored a major text in the field and started a journal devoted to forensic science.

In France, Victor Balthazard and Edmond Locard carried out work very similar to that of Gross. Balthazard was medical examiner for the city of Paris, but he did studies on probability models with fingerprints, bullet comparison, animal hairs, and blood spatter patterns as well. In 1910, Locard (Figure 1-5) set up the first police crime laboratory in Europe, in Lyons. He is well known for his postulate that objects or surfaces which come into contact always exchange trace evidence (Chapter 6). Today, this statement is known as the *Locard exchange principle.*

DEVELOPMENT OF FORENSIC SCIENCE IN THE UNITED STATES

In 1907, August Vollmer was chief of police in Berkeley, California. In the course of a homicide investigation, he enlisted the services of a University of California chemistry professor named Loeb to identify a suspected poison. Professor Loeb did so and presented his results to a grand jury, but no indictment was handed down.

FIGURE 1-5
Edmond Locard, 1877–1966. *(Reprinted from Modern Criminal Investigation, by Harry Söderman and John J. O'Connell, Funk & Wagnalls Company, Copyright 1935, 1940 by Harper & Row, Publishers, Inc., New York, by permission of the publisher.)*

Vollmer attributed this failure to the improper handling of evidence prior to the laboratory examination, and he instituted formal procedures to see that officers were trained in the collection and preservation of evidence. Vollmer called upon scientists at the nearby University of California campus on other occasions, in connection with scientific analysis of evidence in cases. In 1923, Vollmer served a 1-year term as chief of the Los Angeles Police Department and was responsible for setting up a laboratory in the department—the first in the United States. The Los Angeles County Sheriff's Department set up a laboratory in 1930, and a California state laboratory was established at Sacramento in 1931. San Francisco followed in 1932, and San Diego in 1936. Although these laboratories were quite small, the effects of this early start can still be seen today. California has far more criminalistics laboratories than any other state. In addition, Vollmer's efforts in establishing a relationship between the University of California and the Berkeley Police Department resulted in other scientists getting involved in forensic science. Edward Oscar Heinrich was introduced to forensic work in this way, as was Dr. Paul L. Kirk (Figure 1-6). Kirk became so deeply involved in criminalistics that he soon began offering courses in it as part of the biochemistry curriculum. Many of the graduates of this program, and of the criminalistics program established later, have gone on to become criminalists and laboratory directors. The criminalistics program at the University of California at Berkeley also contributed to California's leadership in the field and has fostered the development of other academic programs in California as well as in other parts of the nation.

In Chicago, a wave of public indignation set in following the well-known St. Valentine's Day massacre in 1929. In the course of a special grand jury inquiry into the incident, it was noted that there were no facilities in which to have the numerous bullets and cartridge cases analyzed. As a result, several influential jury members raised funds to establish a permanent crime laboratory. Colonel Calvin Goddard, a retired Army physician, was appointed director of this laboratory, which was set up at the Northwestern University Law School. Goddard was quite conversant with firearms identification and examination, but he had little experience with other kinds of physical-evidence examinations. As background for his new assigment, Goddard toured many European laboratories. He was particularly impressed by the sophistication of police investigators, by the level of their support services, by their use of laboratory services, and by the fact that many police departments had access to the medicolegal institutes to carry out most biological tests. Many of these facilities and police organizations were supported by the national government. He noted that this

FIGURE 1-6
Paul Leland Kirk, 1902–1970. *(Courtesy of Mrs.*
Paul L. Kirk and Blackstone-Shelburne, New York.)

allowed them to establish high standards and to enjoy a broad-based support. The laboratory at Northwestern was transferred to the Chicago police department in 1938.

In 1932, the Federal Bureau of Investigation (FBI) laboratory was established. Other laboratories were set up in Boston, Kansas City, Rochester, New York, Detroit, and New Orleans within a few years. There are now many cities, counties, and states with laboratories or laboratory systems.

In 1937, the criminalistics program was set up at the University of California by Paul Kirk. The program grew to be well known, and Kirk developed a substantial reputation in forensic science, devoting his time to instruction, research, and casework.

At the present time, there are a number of forensic science programs at various colleges and universities throughout the nation.

LABORATORY ORGANIZATION AND SERVICES

Laboratory organization and structure depends to some extent on the nature of the legal system and on the history of forensic science development in the country or jurisdiction.

Forensic pathology and toxicology services are usually provided by medical examiner facilities. Some of these offices also provide odontology and anthropology services when they are required. In European countries, forensic pathology and associated services are often provided by medicolegal institutes. These are often maintained by the central government, and they may be involved in investigations of civil matters, such as disputed paternity and civil liability cases.

Criminalistics laboratories are generally separate from medical examiner facilities, although in some places criminalistics laboratories are maintained within a medical examiner's office. Forensic science laboratories may be organized into a system in which the national government has a central coordinating role. England and Wales, for example, have a centrally coordinated and administered system of forensic science laboratories. A sophisticated research and development facility (the Home Office Central Research Establishment) is part of this system.

In the United States, there is no direct federal coordination of or funding for criminalistics laboratories. The public-sector laboratories are operated and funded by the governments of the jurisdictions which they serve. The development of crime laboratories under a wide variety of jurisdictions has occurred at least in part because of the constitutional sovereignty of the states, the traditional respect states have always had for local autonomy and self-determination, and a general fear of a centralized national police.

Most forensic science laboratories in the United States are publicly operated, and may be part of federal, state, county, or local government. Many laboratories are housed within police or federal law enforcement agencies. Others are operated by state departments of justice or public safety, state and local prosecutors' offices, or state or local health departments. A few laboratories are operated in medical examiners' offices.

In addition to public-sector laboratories, there are a number of private laboratories. Some operate as independent enterprises; others are associated with universities. The services of academic forensic scientists are often available to justice agencies, attorneys, and private investigators for the examination of physical evidence in particular cases. Some independent laboratories provide forensic science services to state or local jurisdictions under contractual arrangements.

There is a tendency for laboratories doing criminal casework to provide services either to police and prosecuting authorities or to the defense. Laboratories which operate under police departments or prosecutors' offices are generally not available to the defense. Laboratories under contract to provide services to police departments or prosecutors are in much the same position. The situation is a reflection of the adversarial nature of the justice system and is also, in part, a reflection of the way in which organized laboratory services have evolved. The adversarial relationship between the state and the defendant tends to place forensic experts engaged by one side or the other into an adversary relationship as well. Most scientists, regardless of who employs them or engages their services, think of their results as entirely objective and try not to allow themselves to be forced into adversarial roles.

Many people have thought about the problems associated with fairness in providing forensic science services to the prosecution as well as to the defense. A great deal has been written on the subject, and a variety of solutions have been proposed. Forensic scientists are inclined toward the view that their function is to employ scientific procedures to unearth factual information about the physical evidence in a case. For the vast majority, this task is one which will yield an objective set of results which is in no way altered by the fact that one side or the other engaged their services or intends to call them as witnesses. Most forensic scientists think of themselves as unprejudiced and make every effort to ensure that their work is objective. They think of their results as a way of providing information to the court, rather than to one side or the other. To do otherwise would subvert the principles of science. It is a fact, however, that the vast majority of cases never get to trial. Most forensic scientists are employed by police and prosecutorial agencies and issue their reports to the submitting police or prosecutorial authority. The *rules of discovery,* under which prosecution and defense are allowed to have access to the details of the other's case (including forensic science reports) vary from state to state. In the short term, it does not seem likely that laboratories will be extensively reorganized so as to be in a more neutral setting (such as directly under the judiciary, as some have suggested), thereby permitting equal access by both sides.

Although the majority of forensic scientists put forth every effort to maintain objectivity, there is no doubt that different ones can disagree about the *meaning* or *interpretation* of results. One scientist might be convinced, for example, that a certain test for blood is only presumptive; in other words, a positive result with the test *indicates* that blood is present, but does not prove it. Another equally competent scientist might disagree. If such a test becomes a major issue in a case that is to be tried, it stands to reason that the attorneys representing the people and the defendant will attempt to find forensic scientists who are prepared to testify in a way that is most advantageous to their presentation of the case.

The complexity and diversity of a laboratory's organization and the range of services provided depend in large part on its size. The larger laboratories, serving populous jurisdictions, tend to be organized into sections according to various subspecialties; there is less opportunity for specialization in smaller laboratories. Some laboratories specialize in particular types of examinations or analyses as a matter of policy (for example, drug testing laboratories). The nation's forensic science laboratories vary considerably in the range of services they can provide. The full-service laboratories tend to be the larger ones. In some jurisdictions, there are several different laboratories providing different kinds of services. A major city, for example, might have a medical examiner facility that does forensic pathology and toxicology and a full-service criminalistics laboratory located within the police department.

There is considerable variation in the internal organization of different laboratories, even among those of similar size and service level. Those who use a laboratory's services should try to become familiar with its organization and with the services it can provide. The laboratory itself has some responsibility for keeping its users informed about its capabilities and organization and for fostering rapport with users.

Criminalistics is a broad and complex field. No individual can hope to become adept in all its aspects. Some type of specialization is necessary. Some laboratory staff members may become expert in the use of certain types of instruments. Others may specialize in the analysis of certain kinds of evidence. Thus, a laboratory might have a specialized serology section in which blood and body fluid stains are analyzed, a chemistry section in which drug and alcohol testing is done, and a trace-evidence section with experts in microscopy who examine hairs, fibers, glass, soil, and so on. Additional sections might be for toolmark and firearm examinations and for questioned documents.

In some laboratories, the responsibilities of specialists within sections can differ. One specialist in a serology section, for example, might work solely on polymorphic enzymes and serum proteins, another might work strictly on blood-group antigens, and still another on immunological techniques. Because of the depth and complexity of criminalistics, the need for specialists is inescapable. There can be serious problems, however, with overspecialization. Persons who have a working knowledge of a broad range of criminalistics problems and techniques are also necessary. These people are called *generalists*. The value of generalists lies in their ability to look at all aspects of a complex case and decide what needs to be done, which specialists should be involved, and in which order to carry out the required examinations. Without such a perspective, tests might be performed that themselves would destroy other, more important evidence.

Ideally, laboratories should not rely exclusively on specialists or generalists. The presence of both is desirable. Large laboratories may be able to a have adequate numbers of generalists and specialists, but in smaller laboratories it is not always possible to do so. Laboratories of modest size might solve this problem by employing several generalists who are at the same time specialists in complementary areas. Each of these individuals could review a case, decide upon what is required, and then pass it on to the one who is most qualified to conduct the specialty examinations. A person can be trained in a specialty after obtaining a broad background in criminalistics, just as physicians are trained in the general aspects of medicine before specializing in more limited areas like psychiatry, neurosurgery, gynecology, and so on.

In some places, laboratory personnel go out to crime scenes to supervise or actually perform the collection and packaging of the evidence. This practice has significant advantages, provided that the laboratory workers who go to scenes have extensive crime-scene experience. Some larger jurisdictions have specialized units which respond to crime scenes, and they are responsible for the documentation and integrity of the scene and for the collection, packaging, and transportation of evidence. Regardless of the division of responsibility, however, the important factor is communication between investigators, scene personnel, and the laboratory.

Everyone has an important role to play, and the value of the results of the overall process is totally dependent upon all participants doing their own part while being aware of the responsibilities and capabilities of the others. Evidence should be recognized, documented, handled, collected, transported, and analyzed in a way that ensures maximum information yield for the case from the effort expended. In addition, recognition, collection, and packaging of evidence must be carried out in a manner consistent with the capabilities of the laboratory to which it will be submitted.

FORENSIC SCIENCE INVOLVEMENT IN CRIMINAL CASES

A number of studies have been done to find out what role forensic science and physical evidence actually play in criminal cases. The studies have focused on the extent to which physical-evidence examinations are used in the various stages of criminal investigation, prosecution, and adjudication.

These stages are indicated diagrammatically in Figure 1-7. There are a number of decision points as a case proceeds. The case can terminate at any one of them. There are also various points at which physical-evidence analysis can terminate and its results cease to be involved, even though the case itself may proceed. The sequence of events in the figure is generalized and oversimplified, but it provides an overall view of the progression of events. A major feature of the involvement of physical-evidence analysis in criminal cases that is not indicated in Figure 1-7 is the dependence of the forensic science role on the nature of the case. First, different types of criminal cases do not receive the same amount of investigative attention. Often, the effort is not even proportional to the level of occurrence of a particular kind of crime. Crimes against persons are usually investigated much more thoroughly than property crimes. Thus, burglaries may occur 50 times more often than homicides, for example, but may command only a small fraction of the investigative time that would be invested in solving a homicide. Second, there are differences in the importance of physical-evidence analysis to different types of cases. Some kinds of cases depend almost solely on physical-evidence analysis if they are to proceed. Drug possession cases provide an example. Without laboratory identification of the substance possessed (and, sometimes, determination of the amount), there is no case. Forcible rape is another example. Normally, a charge of rape cannot be sustained unless evidence of penetration can be found by laboratory analysis. In these situations, therefore, it is expected that forensic analysis will be involved in the majority of cases. Third,

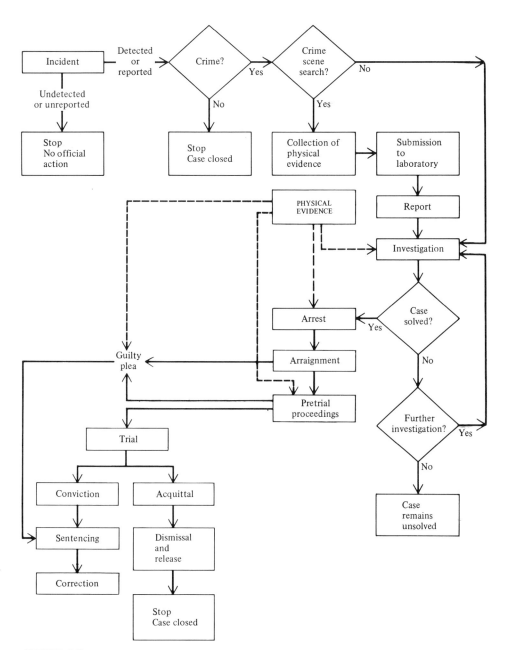

FIGURE 1-7
Physical-evidence flowchart.

certain types of physical evidence are associated with particular crimes much more commonly than with others. Toolmark evidence, for example, is associated much more frequently with burglary than with rape or assault. The opposite is true of blood and body-fluid evidence.

Decisions about the extent of physical-evidence involvement in cases are usually not made by forensic scientists. In the search and investigative stages, they are usually made by police officers and evidence technicians. In the adjudicative stages, the decisions are usually made by attorneys. There is no guarantee that either of these groups will be sufficiently informed about physical evidence to make proper decisions. As more police officers and attorneys acquire special training in forensic sciences, this situation will improve, enabling better use to be made of physical evidence.

The studies which have been conducted confirm the commonsense expectations mentioned above. Without exception, they indicate a substantial degree of underutilization of forensic science and physical evidence in criminal cases. The failure to employ physical-evidence analysis is far more apparent in the evidence collection and investigative stages of a case than in the adjudication stages. Although different studies have been done at different times, in different jurisdictions, and with somewhat differing emphases, the following conclusions are representative of most of the general findings of all of them:

1 Only a small fraction (approximately 1 to 2 percent) of the physical evidence in investigations is collected and submitted for laboratory analysis.

2 Very little use is made of laboratory findings in developing suspects or in directing the investigation; forensic analysis serves primarily to provide the police with confirmations or denials of preexisting investigative theories and to provide legal proof in the courts.

3 Laboratories spend only a small fraction of their time and resources on the analysis of evidence from index crimes (murder, rape, assault, robbery, burglary, larceny involving more than $50, and auto theft); statutory examinations, such as drug identifications and blood-alcohol analyses, make up the majority of most laboratory work loads.

4 In most jurisdictions, there is an almost complete absence of coordinated case investigation and management involving the laboratory; one reflection of this problem is the lack of coordination in record keeping, making it extremely difficult to assemble and review the results of investigative and laboratory efforts in any particular case.

In one way or another, each of these findings reflects an underutilization of physical-evidence analysis in criminal investigation and prosecution.

That such a small fraction of evidence is submitted to the laboratory can be attributed to various causes among which are the following. (1) Investigators may not wish to pursue the investigation with much vigor. The less serious or significant the crime is in the eyes of the police, the less likely it will be vigorously investigated. Police departments are much more likely to allocate limited investigative resources to the crimes they consider more serious. (2) Police investigators may have little or no appreciation of the value of physical evidence. They may not realize what types of information might be obtained from particular kinds of evidence, nor how it might help in the investigation. The laboratory is often used as a last resort in the investigation, and often too late. (3) Police investigators may not have any confidence in the ability of the laboratory to furnish them with information useful to the investigation based upon physical-evidence analysis. Sometimes, this lack of confidence simply reflects a prejudice of the investigator; at other times, it is based upon past experiences with the laboratory. Problems associated with investigator confidence in the laboratory can usually be solved, at least in part, by effective ongoing communication between the two. In this way, investigators come to appreciate the role a laboratory can play at a realistic level.

The laboratory has as much responsibility for keeping its users informed about its capabilities and fostering rapport with them as it does for actually doing the tests. However, most laboratories are saturated with casework and, in some instances, even backlogged. They are not very anxious, therefore, to take steps that will encourage the submission of more evidence. Any substantial increases in the number of cases that can be handled will have to be accompanied by the allocation of additional resources for the laboratories.

The failure of investigators to seek out and utilize physical-evidence examinations comes about for many reasons, some of which were discussed just above. Investigators must realize that physical evidence can be helpful to them, and in what ways. In addition, the laboratory must be able to provide the service requested on a timely basis. A laboratory administrator whose staff is overburdened with drug and blood-alcohol cases, and which is barely managing to complete examinations on evidence from major felony cases, is unlikely to initiate new programs designed to encourage more use of the laboratory's services.

FUTURE DEVELOPMENT OF FORENSIC SCIENCE

There are different ways of looking at the future development of the field, and nobody knows for sure what the future holds. There are a few aspects of development, however, in which current trends or indications may suggest future directions: (1) laboratory organization and structure, (2) research and development, (3) expansion of systems and services, and (4) education.

Laboratory Organization and Structure

It appears unlikely that any major changes in laboratory organization and structure which would measurably affect the delivery of services on a national scale will take place soon. In some parts of the country, statewide laboratory systems are undergoing growth and expansion. There is a tendency in the larger systems to try to locate member laboratories as close as possible to the population areas served. There are some significant advantages in having laboratories close to the jurisdictions they serve.

1 The laboratory can participate more actively in evidence collection, either directly or by coordinating training programs for user agencies.

2 Evidence does not have to be transported over long distances to reach the laboratory, to be returned from the laboratory, or to be moved back and forth to the courts. Transportation of evidence can be costly in terms of the personnel involved, and certain kinds of biological evidence are subject to deterioration if they do not get to the laboratory fairly quickly.

3 A local user has the opportunity to develop a much better cooperative relationship with a local laboratory.

In some cases, state systems are expanded by the construction and staffing of a completely new laboratory facility. In other cases, a laboratory that has been maintained by local government, or by a private concern, may be subsumed by the state system. State assumption of local laboratories tends to come about because of economic pressures on local governmental services.

Another possible trend in the future is a move by local, or even some state, governments to obtain forensic science services on the basis of contractual arrangements with privately operated laboratories. From a government's point of view, such arrangements can be more economical than operating its own laboratories. With a contractual agreement, a governmental agency does not have to employ the people who do the work nor maintain the physical facility. Under most arrangements, the cost to government is also directly proportional to the services actually provided. Pressure from the taxpaying public could make the contract mechanism an attractive alternative for governments in the future.

Many authors in both scientific and legal forums have commented on the need to place the forensic science laboratory on an organizationally more neutral ground in terms of prosecution and defense functions. It has frequently been suggested that laboratories be placed under the control of the judiciary and that services be available under this arrangement to either side. There would undoubtedly be certain advantages under such a system, but there is no indication that it is likely to come about. Contractual agreements, if they should gain in popularity, might lend themselves to these arrangements in that the judicial authority could let the contract for forensic science services. This is disadvantageous in that the laboratory might be perceived as being more remote than one within a given department and communication between laboratory and field personnel might be diminished. Steps taken to foster and maintain investigator-laboratory communication and cooperation would largely neutralize this potential disadvantage.

Research and Development

While forensic scientists take advantage of the findings of research and development projects in traditional scientific areas, there are many problems that are unique to the enterprise. It can be said in a general way that the individualization of physical evidence is the most demanding requirement of forensic science. For most kinds of physical evidence, individualization is an as-yet unrealized objective. The research and development needed for this sort of work is not, for the most part, of much interest to traditional scientists. Advances in methods are required for the detection of very small, but significant, differences among materials that are otherwise the same. In addition, there are almost no statistically significant data bases for physical-evidence types, nor for situations involving physical evidence. This kind of information is essential, because individualization is, in the last analysis, a matter of statistical probability. To say, for example, that a fragment of paint came from a particular source, and no other, is to say that there are no other fragments of paint anywhere that would be expected to be precisely identical to the fragment in question. In order to be able to make statements of that kind, where a physical match is not possible, many thousands of samples must have been studied with respect to all the properties used to draw the conclusion, and it must be certain that the combination of properties in a particular sample differs significantly from that in all other possible specimens.

A related, but somewhat different, issue has to do with the *occurrence* of materials which are encountered as physical evidence. A forensic scientist might, for example, find a glass fragment embedded in the shoe of a suspected burglar which matches the window glass at the site of forced entry in color, fluorescent properties, refractive index, and density. If asked to indicate how many shoes in the random population might be expected to have such a piece embedded in them, however, it is doubtful that the scientist could do so. If such a fact were known, the significance of the finding in the burglary case could be evaluated on a much more objective basis. To cite another example, suppose someone were arrested for having beaten up another person, and a little stain that looked like blood was found on the suspect's slacks. Suppose further that the suspect was group A and the victim group O in the ABO blood group system, and that the laboratory examination of the slacks showed that the stain was indeed human blood of group O. It could be said for certain that the finding was "consistent" with the victim's blood having been transferred to the suspect's clothing. But in order to evaluate the finding on a really sound basis, it would be necessary to know how many people in the general population have a human group O bloodstain on their slacks. We do not know the answer to that question, but the few studies which have been done suggest that the number might be quite a bit higher than one would suspect.

One might speculate that a recent series of homicides in Atlanta might have been solved more quickly if a comprehensive data base on textile fibers were available to the forensic science laboratory. More than half the twenty or so murders occurred *after* the laboratory scientists realized that a certain combination of fiber evidence was common to several of the bodies which had been recovered. This information was valuable in tying the cases together. It would have been even more valuable, however, if a comprehensive and easily accessed data base had been available. Such a resource could have been used to determine when, where, and by whom each of the fiber types had been manufactured. This information might well have assisted the investigation team in identifying a suspect sooner. Compilation of such a data base would be an expensive undertaking and could be accomplished realistically only at a national level. Local laboratories could then have access to the information through computer terminals in their own facilities. The cost of data-base information systems for various kinds of evidence might be high, but it could be a bargain in many cases when compared with the cost of the investigative hours, in addition to the possible prevention of additional crime.

Most research and development efforts are dependent upon funding, usually from the government, and this kind of support has not been adequate in forensic science. The National Institute of Justice (NIJ), which used to be the National Institute of Law Enforcement and Criminal Justice (NILECJ) within the Law Enforcement Assistance Administration (LEAA), is essentially the only source of research and development funds for forensic science in the United States. Some research and development activities are carried out by federal laboratories, such as those of the Federal Bureau of Investigation (FBI), Drug Enforcement Administration (DEA), and Bureau of Alcohol, Tobacco and Firearms (ATF). They tend to have at least some resources whereas the majority of casework laboratories have none.

University-based forensic science programs are of comparatively recent origin, with the exception of a few. University-based researchers are just about solely dependent upon NIJ for funding. There is always fierce competition for relatively small amounts of money. Many of the projects conducted with the help of federal funds during the past decade or so have resulted in significant improvements in a number of areas of forensic science. The fact remains, however, that federal spending for basic and applied research and development in the forensic sciences is in the neighborhood of several hundred thousand dollars per fiscal year, compared with the billions of dollars expended for all basic and applied scientific research and development, principally by the National Institutes of Health, the National Science Foundation, and the Department of Energy.

If the results and findings of research efforts in forensic science are to be meaningful and applicable to casework problems, the work must be done by people who are trained to do research but also have enough experience to appreciate the peculiar nature of the problems at a practical level. There are not many such people. Research and development efforts can sometimes be more effective when there can be good, cooperative relationships between universities and casework laboratories. These arrangements tend to provide the opportunity for researchers and casework specialists to cooperate in finding solutions to aggravating problems. Research and development is the area where improvements would be most acutely felt in enhancing future forensic laboratory capabilities.

Expansion of Systems and Services

Any significant expansion in the number of laboratories in the nation would require massive infusions of tax resources that are unlikely to be forthcoming. It seeems improbable, therefore, that the number of laboratories will increase significantly in the short term, although there will surely be expansion in some places.

Presently, the majority of laboratories are saturated with casework. Additional casework coming into the laboratory simply creates an additional backlog. Increases in services will require at least modest expansion in plant and equipment, as well as some additional personnel. There is no evidence to suggest that these kinds of increases will occur on a massive scale, but some will doubtless be possible. Increases in laboratory services could be of several kinds: (1) the ability to handle more examinations of a certain type; (2) carrying out additional tests which will yield additional or more probative information about the particular evidence; (3) development of better individualization methods as the result of research effort; and (4) further integration of field and laboratory efforts in all cases, so that the laboratory gets involved in the case at the very beginning.

One relatively efficient way of bringing about service expansion, which has not yet been exploited to any significant degree, is the formation of cooperative arrangements among the laboratories in an area, or perhaps among laboratories and a university center. These kinds of arrangements would be particularly useful in making highly specialized services and types of equipment available to more laboratory users. Certain sophisticated techniques, which can be very important in certain kinds of cases, require very expensive and specialized instrumentation, a substantial investment in highly trained personnel, or both. Many laboratories are unable to afford the capital investment required or the operating expenses associated with maintaining highly specialized services, particularly if they are required only in selected cases. Thus, although one medium-sized laboratory might never be able to justify the costs involved in setting up and maintaining an expensive, specialized instrumental procedure, a cooperative arrangement among 5 or 10 laboratories in the area might make complementary services available to all of them. Each of the laboratory organizations might be able to afford its fraction of the costs, and the sum total of work submitted by all the members could make the entire operation cost-effective.

In the past decade or so, forensic scientists in the various regions of the country have become organized in regional associations (the California Association of Criminalists is the oldest regional group, and has existed for over 30 years). It is possible that these associations could assist directly or indirectly in the formation of cooperative arrangements.

Forensic Science Education

Forensic science education may be of several kinds: (1) academic programs leading to bachelor's and graduate degrees in forensic science, (2) continuing education in technical areas for those who are already active in the profession, and (3) educational initiatives directed at various professionals who make use of forensic science or interact with it in their respective fields.

A number of colleges and universities now offer degree programs in forensic science, the majority having initiated them in the past 15 years. The programs vary in their emphases and requirements, but the majority require the equivalent of a chemistry major, and sometimes five or six courses in biological subjects as well, for an undergraduate degree. An important function of these programs, apart from the training of forensic science majors, has been the offering of informational forensic science courses to students in criminal justice programs. In this way, the first steps have been taken toward producing a generation of criminal justice professionals who have a good basic understanding of forensic science, and realistic expectations of the role it can play.

Many faculty members in these programs are actively involved in forensic science casework, either on a consulting basis or by formal arrangement with casework laboratories. Some universities which have forensic science programs are also actively involved in providing continuing education for practitioners in the form of short courses, seminars, or workshops. Some have also taken active roles in trying to provide informational seminars and workshops for practicing attorneys.

Regional associations have also been active in continuing education projects. Some of them regularly provide seminars, workshops, and short courses based upon member-generated interest.

The most neglected areas of forensic science education have been those designed to make user groups and other professionals aware of what forensic science is really all about. These are the areas which will probably require additional attention in the future. Examples are: (1) efforts on the part of laboratory personnel to keep their users informed of their capabilities, (2) active efforts on the part of laboratory staffs to inform investigative personnel in their jurisdiction about the best methods of collecting and submitting evidence, (3) informational seminars in various areas of forensic science for practicing attorneys, (4) informational seminars in various areas of forensic science for judges, (5) introduction of at least a modest exposure to modern forensic science in law school curricula, (6) introduction of at least modest exposure to legal medicine into medical school curricula, and (7) perhaps similar exposure of dental students to forensic odontology.

There are, thus, a number of different aspects of forensic science education, and all of them must be pursued. Every effort should be made to maintain quality programs for the education and training of future scientists. Likewise, continuing education programs must be available for current practitioners. Finally, it is essential that criminal justice and other professionals who may get involved in forensic science problems be made aware of the current state of development of the field.

STUDY QUESTIONS

1 Explain the scientific method.
2 What is a hypothesis, and how is it related to a theory?
3 What is forensic science?
4 What is criminalistics?
5 What are the major specialty areas in forensic science?
6 What are the ways in which forensic science differs from traditional sciences?
7 What are the three major activities involved in analyzing and interpreting physical evidence?
8 What is a class characteristic?
9 What is an individual characteristic?
10 What does *identification* mean?
11 What does *individualization* mean?
12 What does *reconstruction* mean?
13 What is the general difference between criminal and civil cases?
14 How is forensic science involved in criminal cases?
15 How is forensic science involved in civil cases?
16 What is the significance of the Lafarge case in France in 1840?

17 What is bertillonage? What is the significance of Bertillon's contribution to the development of forensic science?

18 What was the contribution of Hans Gross to the development of criminalistics?

19 What were the contributions of M. J. B. Orfila to the early development of forensic science?

20 Where were the first crime laboratories established in the United States?

21 How is the role of the forensic scientist affected by the adversary system of criminal justice?

22 To what extent are forensic science and its findings and results used in criminal investigation and prosecution?

23 What are some of the ways in which forensic science services to the justice system could be improved?

24 What are some of the current problems in forensic science that require further research?

REFERENCES AND FURTHER READING

Conrad, E.: "Landmarks and Hallmarks in Scientific Evidence," in C. Hormachea (ed.), *Sourcebook in Criminalistics,* Reston, Reston, Va, 1974.

Fong, W.: "Criminalistics and the Prosecutor," in *The Prosecutor's Sourcebook,* Chap. 14, vol. I, pp. 323–354, Practicing Law Institute, 1969.

Goddard, C.: "Scientific Crime Detection Laboratories in Europe," *American Journal of Police Sciences,* vol. 1, pp. 14–37, 1930.

Haddad, F. E.: "Admissibility of Expert Testimony," in C. H. Wecht (ed.), *Forensic Science,* Matthew Bender, New York, 1981, vol. 1, chap. 1.

Haddad, F. E.: "Qualification of the Expert Witness," in C. H. Wecht (ed.), *Forensic Science,* Matthew Bender, New York, 1981, vol. 1, chap. 15.

Kingston, C. R.: "Probability and Legal Proceedings," *Journal of Criminal Law, Criminology and Police Science,* vol. 57, pp. 93–98, 1966.

Kingston, C. R.: "Forensic Science," *Standardization News,* vol. 1, no. 4, pp. 1–8, 1973.

Kingston, C. R., and J. L. Peterson: "Forensic Science and the Reduction of Crime," *Journal of Forensic Sciences,* vol. 19, pp. 417–427, 1974.

Kirk, P. L.: "The Ontogeny of Criminalistics," *Journal of Criminal Law, Criminology and Police Science,* vol. 54, pp. 235–238, 1963.

Kirk, P. L.: "The Hybridization of Science," *Journal of the Official Analytical Chemists,* vol. 47, pp. 86–89, 1964.

Kirk, P. L., and L. W. Bradford: *The Crime Laboratory, Organization and Operation,* Charles C Thomas, Springfield, Ill., 1965.

Kirk, P. L., and C. R. Kingston: "Evidence Evaluation and Problems in General Criminalistics," *Journal of Forensic Sciences,* vol. 9, pp. 434–444, 1964.

Kuzmack, N. T.: "Legal Aspects of Forensic Science," in R. Saferstein (ed.), *Forensic Science Handbook,* Prentice-Hall, Englewood Cliffs, N.J., 1982, pp. 1–27.

Lassers, W. J.: "Proof of Guilt in Capital Cases—An Unscience," *Journal of Criminal Law, Criminology and Police Science,* vol. 58, pp. 310–316, 1967.

Lee, H. C.: "Forensic Science—Where Scientific Methods are Utilized to Fight Crime," *Connecticut Journal of Science Education,* vol. 18, pp. 14–19, 1980.

Moenssens, A., E. R. Moses, and F. E. Inbau: *Scientific Evidence in Criminal Cases,* Foundation, Mineola, N.Y. 1973.

Parker, B.: "The Scientific Assessment of Physical Evidence from Criminal Conduct," in D. Glaser (ed.), *Handbook of Criminology,* Rand McNally, New York, 1974, chap. 13.

Peterson, J. L.: *Utilization of Criminalistics Services by the Police—An Analysis of the Physical Evidence Recovery Process,* National Institute of Law Enforcement and Criminal Justice, Law Enforcement Assistance Administration, Washington, D.C., 1974.

Peterson, J. L.: *Forensic Science,* AMS, New York, 1975.

Reichenbach, H.: *The Rise of Scientific Philosophy,* University of California Press, Berkeley, 1951.

Serrill, M. S.: "Forensic Sciences: Overburdened, Underutilized," *Police Magazine,* January, 1979.

Thornton, J. I.: "Criminalistics—Past, Present and Future," *Lex et Scientia,* vol. 11, pp. 1–44, 1975.

Williams, R. L.: "Forensic Science—The Present and Future," *Analytical Chemistry,* vol. 45, pp. 1076A–1089A, 1973.

Wood, D. J.: "Commentary on the Law-Science Relationship in the Admissibility of Scientific Evidence," *Idea* [The PTC Journal of Research and Education], vol. 18, pp. 5–21, 1976.

CHAPTER 2

PHYSICAL EVIDENCE

INFORMATION THAT PHYSICAL EVIDENCE CAN REVEAL

Physical-evidence analysis is concerned with identification of traces of evidence, reconstruction of events from the physical-evidence record, and establishing a common origin of samples of evidence. In every forensic science investigation, the aim is to provide useful information that helps to make the facts of the case clear. Physical-evidence analysis and interpretation can provide a number of different types of information. These are listed next.

1 Information on the Corpus Delicti The *corpus delicti* (literally, the "body of the crime") refers to those essential facts which show that a crime has taken place. Toolmarks, broken doors or windows, ransacked rooms, and missing valuables are all examples of physical evidence that would be important in establishing a burglary. Similarly, in an assault case, the victim's blood, a weapon, or torn clothing could be important pieces of physical evidence.

2 Information on the Modus Operandi Many criminals have a particular *modus operandi* (or method of operation, MO) which consists of their characteristic way of committing a crime. Physical evidence can help in establishing an MO. In burglary cases, for example, the means used to gain entry, tools that were used, types of items taken, and other telltale signs, such as urine left behind at the scene, are all important. In arson cases, the type of accelerant used and the way in which fires are set constitute physical evidence that helps to establish the patterns or "signature" of an arsonist. Cases that have been treated separately can sometimes be connected by careful documentation of similar MO.

3 Linking a Suspect with a Victim This linkage is one of the most common and important that physical evidence can help to establish. It is particularly important in violent crimes. Blood, hairs, clothing fibers, and cosmetics may be transferred from a victim to a perpetrator. Items found in a suspect's possession can sometimes be linked to a victim, such as by comparison of bullets or by analysis of blood found on a knife. It is also possible that trace evidence can be transferred from a perpetrator to a victim. It is important that suspects and their clothing and other belongings be thoroughly searched for trace evidence. Victims and their belongings should be treated similarly.

4 Linking a Person to a Crime Scene This linkage is also a common and significant one provided by physical-evidence analysis. Fingerprints and glove prints, blood, semen, hairs, fibers, soil, bullets, cartridge cases, toolmarks, footprints or shoe prints, tire tracks, and objects that belonged to the criminal are examples of deposited evidence. Depending on the type of crime, various kinds of evidence from the scene may be carried away. Stolen property is the most obvious example, but two-way transfers of trace evidence can be used to link a suspect, a victim, or even a witness, to a crime scene.

5 Disproving or Supporting a Witness's Testimony Physical-evidence analysis can often indicate conclusively whether a person's version of a set of events is credible or whether the person might be lying. An example would be a driver whose car matched the description of a hit-and-run vehicle. An examination of the car might reveal blood on the underside of the bumper. The driver explains the findings by claiming to have hit a dog. Tests on the blood can reveal whether the blood is from a dog or from a human.

6 Identification of a Suspect The best evidence for identifying a suspect is fingerprints. A fingerprint found at a scene, and later identified as belonging to a particular person, results in an unequivocal identification of that person. The term *identification* as used here really means "individualization." Although in common usage people often say "identification of a suspect" or "identification of a fingerprint," this is not strictly correct. The distinction between the terms was mentioned in the previous chapter and is discussed further below.

7 Providing Investigative Leads Physical-evidence analysis can be helpful in directing an investigation along a productive path. In a hit-and-run case, for example, a chip of paint from the vehicle can be used to narrow down the number and kinds of different cars that may have been involved.

A substantial part of the work in a forensic analysis consists of making comparisons between *questioned* and *known* samples. Depending upon the degree of individuality exhibited by the samples, various conclusions can be drawn about the association between the people and the physical evidence in the case.

When questioned and known samples are compared, there are three possible outcomes. (1) They match in all the properties used to compare them. In this case a common origin is possible (or, with a few kinds of evidence, like jigsaw physical fits or fingerprints, can be proven). (2) They do not match. In this case, the possibility of common origin is excluded. Exclusions are unequivocal and provide unimpeachable evidence of nonassociation. Exclusionary findings can be most helpful in the conduct of investigations. (3) In some cases, there is insufficient sample to make a conclusive comparison. In such an instance, class characteristics of the samples would be noted, but a conclusion could not be reached about the possibility of a common origin.

Comparisons which demonstrate exclusions can show that a prime suspect is innocent, that the investigation is proceeding along an unproductive path, or that initial theories about what actually happened are wrong. In other cases, where comparison yields a match, the conclusions depend on the type of evidence involved. Fingerprints are uniquely individualizing if sufficiently detailed. Bullets and cartridge casings can often be unequivocally related to a particular weapon, provided the weapon is recovered. Physical matches can provide proof of common origin with many types of evidence. Tracks and imprints can often be attributed to the object that made them.

With other kinds of evidence, such as glass, blood, hairs, and fibers, it is not usually possible to demonstrate common origin. It is usually possible, however, to indicate the degree of individualization that has been shown by the comparison. In some cases, this indication is *qualitative*; that is, there is no way to evaluate numerically the chance that the compared specimens had a common origin. As an example, consider a hair comparison between a suspect's head hairs and the hairs a victim claims to have pulled out of the attacker's scalp. If the specimens are the same color, then they "match." This finding alone, however, is not a very strong indication of common origin. Suppose that the hair samples are compared for color, diameter, scale pattern, medullary size and pattern, pigment granule structure, and other internal characteristics, and they are still similar. Common sense indicates that the chances of the hairs having had a common origin are now much greater, but how much greater nobody can say.

In other cases, it is possible to be more precise. Suppose that a bloodstain on a suspect's shirt is compared with the blood of a victim. If the bloodstain is human, group B, the victim is group B, and the suspect is O, then the two specimens compare. It is not possible to make very strong statements about the common origin of the stain and the victim's blood, since something like 9 percent of the population has group B. This finding alone would not, therefore, be very compelling evidence that the stain is indeed from the victim's blood. Suppose, however, that we type the blood further for a number of other factors, such as Rh antigens, PGM, ESD, EAP, AK, Gc and Hp, and still find that the victim's blood and the stain match. If we know the distribution of the blood groups in the population, we might be able to say that the chances of finding this particular set of blood types is 1 in 10,000. Obviously, the chances of the bloodstain having come from the victim are now very much greater. The ability to actually do the calculations in the blood case made the conclusions more satisfying than those in the hair case. It must be remembered, though, that for all we know, the hair comparison might be even more potentially individualizing. In that type of case, we just do not have procedures to derive the kind of objective data that were obtainable in the blood case; nor do we have the data bases from which to compute the appropriate population distribution values.

These kinds of considerations need to be kept in mind when evaluating the value of *associative* physical evidence comparisons. In the chapters on specific kinds of physical evidence which follow, we will introduce and discuss the methods and approaches that are applied to identification, establishment of common origin, and reconstruction. Collection, packaging, and preservation of different evidential materials will be discussed, and the relationship between evidence handling and analytical results will be spelled out in more detail.

Properly appreciated and utilized, forensic science can be a powerful and effective tool in the investigation and prosecution of criminal cases. Similarly, it can help to unravel the facts in any kind of case or situation involving physical evidence.

CLASSIFICATION OF PHYSICAL EVIDENCE

Classification Systems

Physical evidence can be classified from several different perspectives. Some of the resulting classifications are more practical than others. However, no single one is completely satisfactory because none can take all the different perspectives into account. Seven different schemes for classifying physical evidence are discussed below: (1) by the type of crime, (2) by the type of material, (3) by the general nature of the evidence, (4) by the physical state of the evidence, (5) by the types of questions to be resolved, (6) according to the way the evidence was produced, and (7) by the analytical approach that is most appropriate. Each is useful in offering a different conceptual perspective for physical evidence, but some are more generally useful than others.

Classification by Type of Crime An obvious way of classifying physical evidence is by the type of crime from which it originates. Thus, we would have homicide evidence, burglary evidence, assault evidence, rape evidence, and so on. This scheme has value in certain situations, but it should be appreciated that *any* type of physical evidence can occur in connection with the investigation of virtually *any* kind of crime. Different physical evidence types are not restricted to legally defined crime classifications. Bloodstain evidence is frequently found in investigations of assault and homicide, but bloodstains can be recovered as important evidence at burglary and other property crime scenes, too. Similarly, semen evidence is frequently found in investigations of rape and other sex crimes, but other kinds of evidence that may not occur with the same regularity could be more important in a given case. Therefore, there is some correlation between the type of crime and the type of evidence, but it is not a perfect one. Understanding the correlations is helpful to investigators in serving as reminders of what to look for at crime scenes, but one should not rely too heavily on this kind of information. Unexpected and unpredictable types of physical evidence could be the most crucial in a particular investigation, and could be overlooked by an investigator with preconceived notions about what to expect and what is likely to be significant.

Classification by Type of Material The second way of classifying evidence is by the type of material of which it is composed. Here, we would have categories such as metallic evidence, glass evidence, paint evidence, plastic evidence, wood evidence, paper evidence, and blood evidence. This kind of scheme, however, is of limited usefulness. A fingerprint found on glass, for example, is handled and examined in essentially the same manner as one found on any nonporous surface, such as plastic, paint, polished metal, or a glossy photograph. Similarly, a toolmark found in metal would be examined and compared in much the same fashion as one found in some other material. In these cases, it is the way in which something has interacted with the material that produced the evidence. The nature of the material itself is less significant. There are some exceptions that are worth mentioning. If it is in the nature of the material to undergo alteration as time passes, proper precautions should be taken to preserve it, or at least to document it. Examples include a footprint in snow, bite marks in perishable food, toolmarks or bite marks in skin, or evidence that might evaporate, such as gasoline.

In cases where it is necessary to try to individualize materials based on subtle differences in their composition, similar laboratory methods are used for materials which have been grouped together in this classification scheme. Microscopic fragments of glass, for example, would be compared using the same techniques, regardless of the kind of object involved (bottle, window, headlight lamp). This classification scheme is generally not too useful, with the exceptions that have been noted.

Classification by General Nature of the Evidence Evidence can be classified as physical, chemical, or biological (or perhaps as animal, vegetable, or mineral). In this scheme, a firearm, tool, toolmark, or cartridge case would be *physical,* whereas a drug sample would be *chemical. Biological* examples would include hair, marijuana, and bloodstains. Such a scheme is of limited value to an investigator, except that it might serve to remind the person in charge of collection and preservation that many items in the biological category are perishable. Accordingly, precautions have to be taken with their packaging and preservation.

Classification by Physical State of the Evidence Evidence, like other matter, can be classified as solid, liquid, or gas. In such a scheme, the *solid* category would include most types of evidence encountered, including articles of clothing, tools, firearms, glass, and paper. Far fewer items would be placed in the *liquid* or *gas* categories. Important liquid evidence would include liquid blood samples (either evidence samples or known controls) and accelerants collected in connection with the investigation of suspected arson. Gas samples may occur as evidence more often than one might think, but they are rarely recognized as such and even more rarely collected. Devices which can be used to sample gases and vapors at crime and fire scenes (Chapter 4) are now becoming available.

This classification scheme is not useful in any general way. However, it can serve to remind investigators of the necessity of packaging liquid samples so that they do not leak from their containers or evaporate. This simple precaution is often overlooked in cases of volatile residues collected at fire scenes. Laboratory personnel are often asked to test for accelerant in samples which have been kept in open or permeable containers for several days. No useful results can be expected from an analysis of such samples.

Classification by the Type of Question to be Resolved   In this scheme, evidence is classified according to whether it will be used as an aid in reconstructing an event, in proving an element of the crime, in linking a suspect to a victim or to a crime scene, in excluding or exonerating a suspect, or in corroborating or disproving an alibi. Similarly, evidence can be grouped according to whether its analysis will be used to provide investigative assistance and leads or as proof for eventual use in a court of law. These schemes are useful during the collection of evidence at a crime scene.

Classification According to the Way Evidence Was Produced   In this scheme, evidence is classified according to how it relates to the act under investigation. An important consideration here is the way the individuals involved have interacted with their environments and with each other, and the type of evidence produced in these interactions. Physical evidence can be looked at as a type of recording medium. Accordingly, examination and interpretation of evidence allows the forensic scientist to offer an opinion as to what has taken place. This activity is similar to that of an archeologist in examining artifacts unearthed at the site of an ancient civilization. Thus, physical evidence is an unintentional and somewhat imperfect record of the interactions of the actors (victim, perpetrator, and so on) and the environment. Considering physical evidence in this way can be very useful and can yield large dividends in an investigation. Within this general scheme, several subclasses of evidence can be distinguished.

Position/Geometric   In this category, the apparent movement or disturbance of objects is documented and interpreted for later use in reconstructing an event.

Imprints and Indentations   Evidence in this category includes fingerprints, footprints, cloth prints, indentations from tools (primer marks, breech face marks, pry marks), tire tracks, and bitemarks. Class and individual characteristics of the device suspected of making the imprint or indentation are compared with the details of the mark made in the recording medium. This comparison is usually accomplished by first producing an *exemplar* mark in a suitable material. The evidence mark and the exemplar mark are then compared.

Striations   Striations are marks consisting of numerous, randomly spaced, parallel lines of varying width that are produced when two surfaces come into sliding contact. These marks result from a dynamic process, as opposed to the static process which results in the production of imprints and indentations. Examples of striation-mark evidence include land and groove markings on bullets, marks made by certain cutting tools (thread cutters, machine tools, wire cutters, bolt cutters, knives, and axes), die marks on wires from the drawing operation, and extrusion marks on certain plastic and metal articles. Striation marks can be produced in any situation where the surface of one object marks the surface of another because one of them is in motion relative to the other one. Certain kinds of marks made by prying tools, such as jimmies and screwdrivers, where the tool slips across the surface, fall in this category. So do some teeth marks, like those made in biting off a piece of cheese, for example. Striation markings can contain both class and individual characteristics (Chapter 14).

Tears, Breaks, and Cuts   Evidence in this category is often of the utmost interest for potential individualization. Here, one or more pieces or fragments of an article are compared with other articles from which they are thought to have originated. If a sufficient number of individual characteristics is present, it is possible to conclude that the items were *one* at an earlier time and, therefore, share a common origin. Thus, a glass fragment could be associated with the particular window from which it was broken by fitting it into the area from which it originated. Physical fits of this kind can be simple with larger pieces, but they are also possible at times with smaller fragments. Such *physical matches* or *jigsaw fits* are applicable to a wide variety of other materials besides glass, including wood, metal, plastics, paper, cloth, and cordage (Chapter 11). At times, evidence such as paint chips can also fit into this category. If the chips recovered are big enough, it may be possible to fit them into position on the object from which they originated.

Breaks and tears normally provide the largest number of details for potential individualization, but success is sometimes possible in cases of cut pieces as well. In some of these cases, the individualization potential depends less on the nature of the cut, broken, or torn surface than on various features on, or within, the body of the article. Examples of such features include writing, printing, designs, surface topography, grain structure, pigmentation patterns, and characteristic irregularities.

Mutual Transfers of Matter   This type of evidence results from contact between two surfaces and involves the transfer of matter across the contact boundary (Chapter 6). Very often, an automobile which scrapes against another will transfer paint to the other vehicle and acquire a paint smear in the process. Other evidence in this category includes dusts, particles, pollens, clothing fibers, vegetation, hairs, soil, and small glass particles.

It is reasonable to assume that a mutual transfer of matter always occurs when two surfaces come into contact, but the amount of material transferred in some circumstances may be too small to be of any practical significance. Thus, in some cases, the transfer may appear to be one-way rather than mutual, or no transfer in either direction may be apparent.

Deposits, Dispersals, and Residues   This category includes transferred matter, but no contact is necessary between the surface on which the matter originated and the surface on which it is found. Examples of this type of evidence include fallen hairs, spattered blood, glass fragments, oil drippings, gunshot residues, explosive residues, and airborne particles. Such evidence may have both class and individual characteristics and may also be useful in reconstructions.

Nature of the Evidential Material   Evidence would be placed in this category when identification is the principal objective. Here, the forensic scientist is called upon to determine the identity of a sample (for example, street drugs, undetonated explosives, or suspected accelerants). Evidence types included in other categories could be placed here as well, for example, bloodstains, seminal stains, gunshot residue, and explosive residue. However, placing them in the sections that pertain to their relationship to the events under investigation is more appropriate. This category is set aside for evidence samples when identification is the sole or primary goal. It is something of a catchall subcategory in the overall scheme in which evidence has been grouped according to the way it was produced.

Classification by the Appropriate Laboratory Approach   In this scheme, evidence is placed into categories according to whether it is simply to be identified, an individualization is sought, or a reconstruction of the event is desired. Looked at in this way, evidence is examined and analyzed in a manner that is relevant to the investigation.

Identification and its dependence on class characteristics was mentioned in Chapter 1. In some cases, an identification of a certain physical-evidence item is all that is required of the laboratory in the investigation. Most of the cases in which the charge is possession of a controlled substance provide an example. Here, the laboratory is used merely to establish an element of the crime. A similar situation is seen in some rape investigations, where the element of *penetration* is established by demonstrating that seminal fluid was present in the vagina of the victim. In other rape investigations, other types of evidence may be found (hairs, fibers, soil), and more analyses may be done on the body-fluid evidence. In these latter cases, individualizations and reconstructions may be attempted.

For a sample to be identified, it must meet certain criteria. The identification is based on a certain combination of *class characteristics.* Samples possessing this combination of properties can be placed in a category with other similar objects or materials, and assigned a name. It is this process of categorizing and naming materials and objects on the basis of common class characteristics that constitutes identification. Criteria for the identification of physical evidence can include morphological, physical, and chemical properties, some of which are indicated in Table 2-1.

Individualization is characteristically attempted with physical evidence such as fingerprints, toolmarks, markings on bullets, broken glass, human hairs, textile fibers, and soil samples. With fingerprints, toolmarks, bullets, and broken glass, direct physical comparisons and physical matches (jigsaw fits) may be possible. These techniques can yield persuasive individualizations under favorable circumstances. With other kinds of evidence, true individualization may not be possible. In these cases, it is possible only to approach an individualization. A number of different criteria are used to characterize the evidence to the greatest extent possible. In some ways, this approach can be looked upon as an extension of identification, and many of the properties shown in Table 2-1 may be used. In addition, other comparative techniques may be applied in evaluating the likelihood of common origin.

Reconstruction would normally be wanted in cases involving gunshot residue patterns, shotgun pellet patterns, bloodstains or blood spatter patterns, and relatively large fragments of broken glass. These are only some of the more obvious examples. Other evidence can also play a major role in reconstruction. For example, a bullet hole through a thin layer of material would probably not provide adequate information about the bullet's trajectory. However, such a hole through a thicker substance, or a series of holes through two or more successive surfaces, could be used to

TABLE 2-1
FEATURES AND PROPERTIES OF MATERIALS—CLASS AND INDIVIDUAL CHARACTERISTICS

Chemical properties
  Chemical composition
  pH
  Reactivity toward known chemical reagents
  Solubility
Miscellaneous physical features and patterns
  Markings
  Inhomogeneities and inclusions
  Morphology
  Size
  Texture
Physical properties (nonoptical)
  Hardness
  Density (mass per unit volume)
  Surface tension (liquids)
  Viscosity (liquids and gases)
  Thermal conductivity
  Dielectric constant
  Electrical conductivity
  Transition temperatures for changes of state
    Melting point (freezing point)
    Boiling point
  Radioactivity
Properties based on interactions with electromagnetic radiation
  Absorption of electromagnetic energy
    Opaque vs. transparent
    Reflectance
    Variation with wavelength
      Color
      Absorption spectra (spectrophotometry)
  Emission of electromagnetic radiation
    Photoluminescence (excitation with short wavelengths
        followed by reemission of longer wavelengths)
      Fluorescence (immediate reemission)
        UV fluorescence
        Infrared luminescence
      Phosphorescence (delayed reemission)
      Fluorescence spectra (spectro-photofluorometry)
  Refractive index
  Dispersion (changes of refractive index with wavelength)
  Birefringence
  Optical rotation
  Turbidity (scattering of light)

Note: This list is not exhaustive. Some of these properties are commonly used in characterizing and comparing physical evidence; others are seldom used. Taken singly, most of these represent class characteristics. However, combinations of several can provide information useful in approaching individualization.

define an accurate trajectory. Similarly, relationships among several items of physical evidence can be useful in reconstruction. Reconstructions are discussed in some detail in Chapter 11.

Workable Classifications

All the classification schemes discussed here have some value, but it is the nature of physical evidence that it does not fit neatly into any one scheme under every circumstance or in every light. Thinking about evidence in all these various ways is helpful in gaining insight into, and an understanding of, physical evidence and its utilization. The last two classification schemes are probably the most generally useful.

STAGES IN PHYSICAL-EVIDENCE ANALYSIS

The initial stages in physical-evidence analysis encompass activities that take place at the crime scene. (In addition to the discussion below, general aspects of crime-scene procedures are discussed in Appendix 2.)

The process used by forensic scientists in their work can be divided into a series of stages: (1) recognition of evidence, (2) documentation of crime scene and evidence, (3) collection and preservation, (4) analysis, (5) interpretation of results, and (6) reporting of results and expert testimony. Every one of the stages is important. The actions that are taken at the earlier stages determine the quality of the final outcome. Discussion of these various stages also points up some of the differences between traditional science and forensic science.

Recognition

The ability to separate important and potentially informative items in a case from all the background things that are simply *there* is an essential skill for forensic scientists and crime-scene investigators. Without it, no amount of scientific analysis is likely to shed much light on the case. There is no one set of rules, no single approach or procedure, that enables one to recognize evidence. It is an ability that develops with training and experience, and one which needs a certain amount of patience. An investigator must be able to entertain, in the mind's eye, various theories about what has taken place in a case. The evidence is then selected on the basis of what is likely to help in distinguishing between the possiblities. In order to make the selection most appropriately, the types of evidence involved must be taken into account, along with what information analysis can be expected to reveal. It is not always possible to reconstruct events in detail from physical evidence and its analysis, but it is nearly always possible to limit the number of possibilities.

Documentation of Crime Scene and Evidence

Documentation is important from two points of view in forensic science: the legal one and the scientific one. Nothing should ever be altered until its original condition, position, and so forth, have been recorded in sufficient detail. Several different means of documentation are available, no single one of which is the best. Each has unique attributes to offer. Generally, the use of more than one method is necessary, and it may be desirable to employ all of them in certain circumstances, because they are complementary. Every major case scene, and the associated evidence, should be thoroughly documented, even if a suspect is in custody and has confessed. In these situations, investigators sometimes assume that the case is solved and conclude that only cursory documentation is needed. During the initial stages of an investigation, there is no such thing as an "open-and-shut case." To assume otherwise is wrong. If incorrect decisions are made at this point, there probably will not be another opportunity to rectify them. Cases in which there is no question about the suspect's identity can become the most difficult to solve, and detailed reconstructions are often crucial for a satisfactory resolution. These reconstructions are impossible without proper documentation.

A successful investigator is more than a mere recorder and observer. An investigator must also be an interpreter—one who knows what less-obvious evidence to seek out, based on what has already been observed, and who anticipates questions that may arise and require resolution later on. To be successful, it is helpful to develop a hypothesis (an educated guess) that explains what has taken place, so that facts tending to support or refute it can be noted and documented. A working hypothesis allows order to be made out of chaos and evidence to be recognized among the numerous unrelated articles at a scene.

The evidence must be critically evaluated, however. As new observations are made, it may be necessary to reevaluate and modify the working hypothesis. Still further modification may be necessary in the days that follow the scene investigation to produce a suitable theory. The formulation of this theory may not be possible unless the scene and the evidence have been thoroughly and properly documented. Among the methods available for documentation are notes, sketches, photography, and audio and video recording.

Notes   Written notes are indispensable in any investigation, even when other means of recording are used. Written notes constitute the core of crime-scene and physical-evidence documentation techniques. Notes should be made in ink in a bound notebook, rather than on looseleaf paper. The pages should be consecutively numbered in advance in case any subsequent allegations are made about pages having been removed or destroyed. Errors made during note taking should be corrected by drawing a line through them, rather than by obliteration or the removal of pages. All entries should be made in strict chronological order, and no blank spaces should be left to allow for out-of-sequence entries.

Notes should contain additional documentation concerning collection, packaging, and labeling of any evidence collected. They should also include a record of the relevant data about any photographs taken, such as photographic conditions, date, time, frame number, subject matter, location, and so forth. This information can be very important for subsequent interpretation of the photographs. In most investigations, it is the written notes that tie together the other forms of documentation.

Sketches   The spatial relationships of objects at crime scenes are best documented by making sketches, with all significant dimensions accurately recorded on the sketch. The sketch itself does not need to be accurately drawn, as long as it contains enough information to allow an accurate rendition to be reproduced at a later time.

Taking photographs at a crime scene does not alleviate the need to make sketches. Photographs are excellent for recording large amounts of fine detail, but they often produce a false sense of perspective and do not normally allow accurate dimensions and spatial relationships to be determined. Recovery of this information might be possible if photogrammetric techniques were used at crime scenes. Photogrammetry has long been used in map making, but has not yet been applied to any great extent in crime-scene work. Another advantage of sketches is that, unlike photographs, they allow the most significant objects and details to be emphasized. The information recorded in sketches and photographs is complementary (Figure 2-1).

Making sketches at a scene has another, often unrealized, advantage. The process of making the sketch focuses the person's powers of observation, and details might thus be recognized that would escape notice if an investigator were just "looking around." The disciplined observation fostered by making a sketch is one of the greatest attributes of this method.

Manuals on crime-scene investigation offer valuable hints on, and suggest different methods of, producing sketches. Investigators should be familiar with a variety of sketching methods, but the particular method is less important than diligence, attention to detail, and investigative outlook. Three-dimensional or cross-projection sketches are generally the most useful for depicting interior crime scenes, but they are not always necessary.

Photography   The importance of photography at crime scenes is recognized by almost everyone, and it is surprising that photography is underutilized or misused at so many scenes. Poor or inadequate photographs are taken with great regularity, even when adequate equipment is readily available.

Photography is a superb means of documenting a vast amount of intricate detail, but, as noted above, it should be used to complement rather than supplant other documentation techniques. Overall photographs can be taken at a crime scene to show the location of items of evidence and their relationship to the scene as a whole. Close-ups can then be used to record the details of specific items of evidence. Such photographs should always contain a scale or, preferably, two scales at right angles to one another. Lighting is very important in crime-scene and evidence photography. In certain circumstances, there is an advantage in taking several shots of a single object under different lighting conditions.

There are obviously advantages in having an experienced crime-scene photographer available during important investigations. Individual crime-scene investigators should also develop and maintain photographic skills, however, because the specialist may not always be available. In these situations, an investigator must be able to produce acceptable photographs without assistance. A good 35-mm camera with a

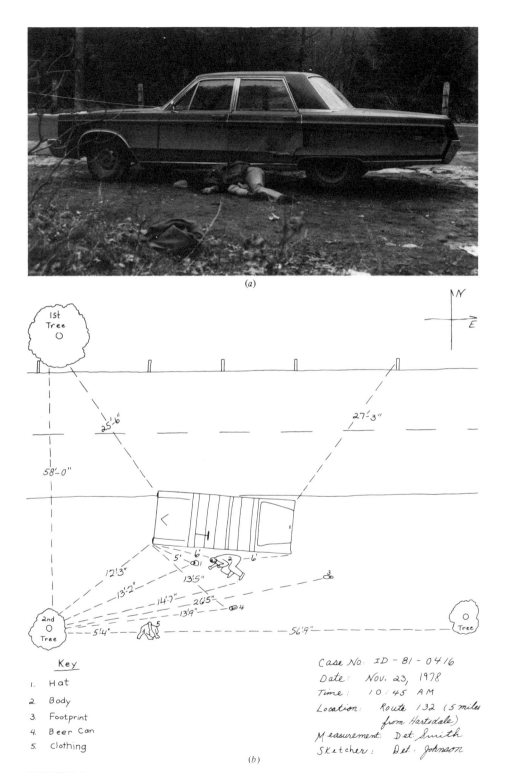

(a)

(b)

Key

1. Hat
2. Body
3. Footprint
4. Beer Can
5. Clothing

Case No. ID - 81 - 0416
Date: Nov. 23, 1978
Time: 10:45 AM
Location: Route 132 (5 miles from Hartsdale)
Measurement: Det. Smith
Sketcher: Det. Johnson

FIGURE 2-1
Crime scene photo and sketch. *(Courtesy of Jerome Drugonis, Forensic Science Laboratory, Connecticut State Police.)*

few modest accessories is adequate in most cases. An investigator has to understand a few simple facts and have a modest interest in photography and a concern for quality in order to produce acceptable photographs. Reference to books and articles on photography and a certain amount of practice will help in learning and using these facts. Crime-scene and evidence photography is a documentation technique rather than a means of artistic expression. For this reason, reference works on scientific photography may be the most appropriate. An investigator should practice photographic skills fairly regularly. No single type of camera or film format is ideal for every purpose. It is good to have a 35-mm outfit and a large-format sheet-film camera. The 35-mm is more versatile and will satisfy most needs. It can be used for overall shots of the scene and for close-ups of particular items. When details of a pattern must be recorded for future comparison and individualization purposes, a sheet-film camera (particularly a view camera) with fine-grain film is a wiser choice, although a 35-mm can often do the job. One should not fail to record such a pattern because a larger-format camera was not available.

The importance of lighting has already been mentioned. Additional attention must be paid to the necessary trade-offs among depth of field, lens opening, shutter speed, film speed, and grain size. When color film is being used, the color temperature, or *color balance,* of the light source must be considered.

When difficult photographic situations are encountered and it is important to know whether a useful result has been obtained, an "instant" camera is useful. Polaroid Corporation markets camera systems for use at crime scenes and in the laboratory. One of these systems, known as the CU-70, includes special attachments for Polaroid's SX-70 cameras which allow them to be used for extreme close-up work (Figure 2-2). The main advantage these confer is the ability to check the final photograph at the scene to confirm whether or not it shows what the investigator wanted to document. A fuller discussion of photography appears in Appendix 3.

Audio and Video Recording   At crime scenes audio- and video-recording methods are less frequently used than other documentation techniques. These newer methods should be used more often, as adjuncts to notes, sketches, and photography, but not as substitutes for them.

Audio recording allows an investigator to document a large number of details without diverting attention from the observational task. This is a valuable advantage at a scene where it is necessary to record a lot of detail of varying or unknown importance. In addition, one or both hands can be left free to make measurements, notes, or sketches, or to take photographs. Perhaps the biggest drawback to this method of crime-scene documentation is a psychological one. Many people are simply not comfortable talking into a tape recorder, especially if other people are within hearing range at the scene. But if this kind of shyness can be overcome, audio recording can be used to great advantage. Soon after leaving a crime scene, the audio notes should be transcribed into written form and integrated with written notes to produce a new set of written notes which focuses on the relevant details. Earlier notes and the tape should be kept until the case has been closed. Some details which did not seem rel-

FIGURE 2-2
The Polaroid CU-70. *(The Polaroid Corporation.)*

evant at the time they were documented might become important as the investigation proceeds.

Inexpensive, portable video recorders and cameras have become available during the past decade. This equipment can be particularly useful at a crime scene, but it should be realized at the outset that the picture quality of these video systems cannot compete with that of conventional photographic methods. Video methods are not a substitute for photography.

The major advantage of video documentation is that it provides the best way to produce an overall record of the scene and the investigation. This record can also include a running narrative on the sound track as an additional aid. The videotape record can also document very effectively the evidence collection process, as well as the sequence and location of each still photograph taken. A good video record allows a subsequent viewer, who was not at the scene, to get the "lay of the land" and to understand the relationships of various pieces of evidence to the scene and to the act being investigated. It can be particularly valuable in communicating details of the case to laboratory examiners. A laboratory scientist cannot be expected to examine the evidence to best advantage in the absence of detailed case information. If an examiner cannot go to a scene, the videotape method is one of the best means of bridging this gap.

Collection and Packaging

Different kinds of evidence are handled differently, and we will describe procedures for each type in the appropriate chapters. Several points are well worth keeping in mind under every circumstance.

1 There is no one set of procedures for any kind of evidence collection that is applicable to every case. Special considerations applicable to specific types of evidence are discussed in individual chapters. As we will see, there are general principles and guidelines to be followed (see Appendix 2), but the approach in a particular case is ultimately based on the circumstances of that particular case.

2 The relationship of an item of evidence to the scene as a whole is often essential; articles should not be touched, moved, tampered with, or collected until the scene has been fully documented by photographs, sketches, and notes.

3 Continuity in the chain of custody is essential to the eventual admissibility of an item of evidence in judicial proceedings; an item whose custody cannot be established at all times from its presence at the scene to its introduction into evidence in court may be ruled inadmissible, no matter how potentially informative it may have been. Care should be taken to record custody information at every stage of evidence handling or transfer from one person to another. The fewer people involved in this process, the easier it will be to keep track of the chain of custody.

Analysis of Evidence

The type of analysis required for an item of evidence depends on what it is, the nature of the case, and what information is required. Many of the different kinds of physical-evidence analysis and their appropriate applications make up most of the rest of this book.

The analytical activities of forensic scientists can be categorized, as we have noted, in terms of identification, individualization, and reconstruction. Identification uses the class characteristics of a material or object; individualization uses the individual characteristics.

Identification usually refers to the identification of an item of evidence. Occasionally, in certain circumstances, one could be talking about the identification of persons. Most kinds of physical evidence have to be identified unequivocally. Sometimes this step may be all that is required, as in the case of controlled-substance possession. In many cases, however, identification is a first step before further analyses are undertaken. Is the red stain blood? Red paint? Strawberry jam? Is this fiber natural or synthetic? Is this hair from an animal or a person? Is this small transparent fragment of material a piece of glass? A piece of plastic? A mineral, like a grain of sand? These kinds of questions usually have to be answered before further tests can be undertaken. The characteristics used to identify various kinds of evidence are discussed in the appropriate subsequent chapters. Identifications are made by comparing the class characteristics of the item or material with those of known members of the class.

Individualization means demonstrating that the origin of a specimen can be uniquely specified. This dimension of forensic science is one that makes it unique among the sciences. It is also the most difficult aspect of a forensic analysis with almost every kind of evidence. Methods and techniques are constantly being sought for the detection of very small differences in very similar materials. In the case of blood, semen, and some other biological materials, we try to exploit the differences inherent in samples from different people. With many kinds of evidence, true individualization is not yet possible. There are different degrees of individualization, however, as we have pointed out and discussed at the beginning of this chapter. Some degree of individualization can be informative, even if it is not absolute. A bloodstain may be known to have come from about 1 in 10,000 people. If the stain compares with the blood of someone involved in the case, this result can be useful and informative even though it is not possible to say that the stain came from the particular person. As was the case in identification above, individualization involves comparison. Here, the individualizing characteristics, rather than the class characteristics, are compared. Examination of individualizing characteristics of evidence can exclude the possiblity of common origin. With most kinds of evidence, these exclusions can often be established, and this kind of information is helpful during an investigation. The methods employed for the individualization of different kinds of evidence are discussed in subsequent chapters in some detail.

Reconstruction can assist in deciding what actually took place in a case and in limiting the different possiblities. Eyewitnesses to events are notoriously unreliable even when they exist. People have trouble accurately remembering what they saw. It is even more of a problem if a complex series of events takes place suddenly and unexpectedly. Recollection of witnesses can change under certain conditions (like stress or interrogation) without the witnesses even realizing it. The passage of time tends to make accurate recollections more difficult, too. What people remember is influenced by their perspective on the incident, their biases and cultural conditioning, their vision, and their ability to remember details and sequences. Even trained observers can disagree about the nature of a series of events.

In many cases, there are no independent witnesses. Victims who survive crimes can give an account of what happened, but they are understandably so upset and traumatized by the events that their versions may not be very accurate. Suspects, if they choose to give an account of what happened, have a vested stake in lying if they are guilty, and may be upset and confused if they are innocent. These accounts can usually not be trusted. Guilty suspects tend to provide stories which, if true, would make them innocent. It is usually informative, therefore, to try to reconstruct the events from the physical evidence involved. Such a reconstruction may provide the only "independent witness" to the events and thus allow different eyewitness accounts to be evaluated for accuracy. The possiblity of a reconstruction is one of the major reasons that the integrity of a crime scene is so important. Anything added to or removed from the scene, anything moved or changed, can and will change the interpretations in a reconstruction. Reconstructions can be very complex tasks based on many types of evidence, stain patterns, analytical results and scene documentation. In other cases, reconstruction can be simple, involving only a single article of evidence.

Many potential reconstructions cannot be accomplished because of a lack of documentation of what took place at the scene, as we have noted above. A good deal of information that might be very useful to the investigation is probably lost in this way. Everybody at the scene has a responsibility for its integrity. If it becomes necessary to move or rearrange anything, there should be documentation of who did what. There is only one opportunity to secure and preserve a crime scene and to document the location and arrangement of all the evidence. Errors made at this stage of the investigation are usually irreparable.

Interpretation of Results

There is a difference between analysis and interpretation, and it should be appreciated. Scientists most often agree on the results of an analysis. If they are going to disagree, it is usually over the *interpretation* of the results. A *reconstruction* of events based upon physical-evidence analysis is always an interpretation and not an analysis as such.

An *analysis,* regardless of how complicated, amounts to a series of observations or measurements of chemical or physical properties and relationships. The measurements can be direct (length, mass, volume), or they can be indirect (spectral properties, refractive index, blood group). *Interpretation* consists of translating the results of the observations into a form that is consistent with all known data and which provides useful information about the situation under investigation.

Sometimes, the distinction between analysis and interpretation is subtle, and the interpretation is obvious once the analysis is finished. A drug-possession case is a good example. Suppose a plastic bag confiscated from a suspect contains a white powder. If analysis shows that the bag contains 2 g of powder, the properties of which indicate 1% by weight heroin and 99% by weight lactose, then it can readily be concluded that the suspect possessed 0.02 g of heroin. In other situations, it is not as obvious. A latent fingerprint developed at a scene may later be shown to belong to a suspect. That fact demonstrates only that the suspect was *present* at the scene at some time. It says nothing about *when* or *why*. Similarly, a bloodstain found at a scene may be exhaustively analyzed, found to be human blood, and to have a set of blood groups possessed by 10 percent of the total population. If a suspect has all those same blood groups, it means only that the blood *may have* come from the suspect.

Reporting Results and Expert Testimony

Most scientists communicate their results and interpretations to colleagues who, among other things, are familiar with the terminology, methods, and approaches that are commonly used in the investigations of such problems and with the state of knowledge in a field. Forensic scientists, however, must communicate their findings to police officers, attorneys, judges, and members of the public who sit on juries. This task often requires that highly technical and complex information be distilled and translated into an understandable set of facts and conclusions. Specialized and technical terminology should be avoided insofar as possible if results and conclusions are to be made clear. Every effort should be made to express the findings in a way that nonspecialists can understand. The simplest possible language in reports and in testimony before the courts tends to be the most informative.

Expert witnesses are given somewhat more latitude in courts of law than other witnesses. It is a general rule of evidence that a witness can testify only to facts known to him or her. Ordinary witnesses may testify to their opinions based on observations of facts, but these impressions have to be amenable to judgment against a background of ordinary experience. Thus, a witness might testify to a person's identity, to the color of an object, or to the distance between two objects. An expert witness, on the other hand, is employed because the issues require analysis and explanation by a person with scientific or specialized knowledge or experience. A qualified expert, who has been demonstrated to the court to have skill, knowledge, or experience beyond that of a lay person, may give an opinion to the court which is relevant to the analyses conducted and to the facts of the case.

Over the years, courts have developed criteria for the admissibility of scientific tests, procedures, and their results. The landmark case in this area is *Frye v. United States,* which took place in 1923. In *Frye,* the court said:

> Just when a scientific principle or discovery crosses the line between the experimental and demonstrable stages is difficult to define. Somewhere in this twilight zone the evidential force of the principle must be recognized, and while courts will go a long way in admitting expert testimony deduced from a well-recognized scientific principle or discovery, the thing from which the deduction is made must be sufficiently established to have gained general acceptance in the particular field in which it belongs.

Subsequent decisions have made it clear that *general* recognition is no longer required as a test of admissibility. In other words, every scientist in the field or specialty does not have to know about a test or be familiar with it in order for it to be recognized. The definition of "the particular field in which it belongs" has been narrowed, too, and is now taken to mean the appropriate specialty or subspecialty within a field of science. On some occasions, the results of experimental procedures, devised to meet the requirements of a particular problem, have been admitted (as in *Coppolino v. State of Florida,* 1968). Such procedures must be based on accepted analytical principles, however, and a proper foundation must be set down for them.

Expert witnesses should remember that they are talking to the jury. Every effort must be made to help the jury understand the physical-evidence analysis and the conclusions which can be drawn from it in terms of the case. Experts can be drawn into complex technical discussions in court, but even under these circumstances, one should take the time to try to explain the answers fully to the jury. Successful presentation of findings in court requires the cooperation of the attorney who has called the expert. Pretrial conferences are essential if the right questions are to be asked and if the presentation is to go smoothly and be informative to the court and the jury.

STUDY QUESTIONS

1 What kind of information about criminal acts and crimes can forensic science help to reveal?
2 What conclusions are possible when known and questioned samples are compared?
3 What degree of individualization can be obtained with the different types of physical evidence?
4 How can comparisons between questioned and known samples that lead to exclusions be used in investigations?
5 What are the different ways of classifying physical evidence?
6 Which are the most useful ways of classifying physical evidence and why?
7 What are the stages in physical evidence analysis?
8 How does one go about recognizing physical evidence at a crime scene?
9 What is documentation of physical evidence at a crime scene, and why it is important?
10 Name the different ways of documenting physical evidence.
11 Is one method of documenting physical evidence better than all the others?
12 What are the main advantages of the different methods for documenting physical evidence?
13 What are the main important principles to keep in mind when collecting and packaging physical evidence at a crime scene?
14 What are the three major activities that can be performed by a forensic scientist in the analysis of physical evidence?
15 How are reconstructions of criminal events related to the preservation of the crime scene?
16 What is the difference between analysis and interpretation of the results?
17 What are the important rules to keep in mind in reporting scientific results in forensic science and in giving expert testimony?
18 What is the landmark case on the admissibility of scientific tests in courts of law, and what did the Supreme Court say in this decision?
19 How has the landmark ruling on admissibility of scientific tests been modified by the courts over the years?
20 What are the important points for the expert witness to keep in mind when testifying on scientific evidence before a jury?

REFERENCES AND FURTHER READING

Beyer, S. C. and W. F. Enos: "Death Scene Checklist," *FBI Law Enforcement Bulletin,* August, 1981.

Darby, W.: "Criminalistics," in C. H. Wecht (ed.), *Forensic Science,* Matthew Bender, New York, 1981, vol. 3, chap. 36.

Federal Bureau of Investigation: *Handbook of Forensic Science,* U.S. Government Printing Office, Washington, D.C., 1975.

Fox, R. H., and C. L. Cunningham: *Crime Scene Search and Physical Evidence Handbook,* U.S. Government Printing Office, Washington, D.C., 1973.

Goddard, K. W.: *Crime Scene Investigation,* Reston, Reston, Va., 1977.

Lee, H. C., et al.: *Physical Evidence and Burglary Investigation Handbook,* University of New Haven, New Haven, Conn., 1980.

Moenssens, A., R. E. Moses, and F. E. Inbau: *Scientific Evidence in Criminal Cases,* Foundation, Mineola, N.Y., 1973.

Peterson, J. L.: *The Utilization of Criminalistics Services by Police,* U.S. Government Printing Office, Washington, D.C., 1974.

Siljander, R. P.: *Applied Police and Fire Photography,* Charles C Thomas, Springfield, Ill. 1976.

Svensson, A., O. Wendel, and B. A. J. Fisher: *Techniques of Crime Scene Investigation,* 3d ed., Elsevier-North Holland, New York, 1981.

Ward, R. H.: *Introduction to Criminal Investigation,* Addison-Wesley, Boston, 1975.

Weston, P. B., and K. M. Wells: *Criminal Investigation,* Prentice-Hall, Englewood Cliffs, N.J., 1974.

CHAPTER 3

METHODS AND TECHNIQUES IN FORENSIC SCIENCE

INTRODUCTION

In this chapter we discuss the underlying principles and the different methods and techniques that are used in forensic science laboratories. This overall view of the various methods will provide an understanding of them and an appreciation of their applications and limitations. Many of the methods are common in all types of scientific laboratories. The application of particular methods to specific forensic problems and evidence types is discussed in detail in appropriate subsequent chapters. Here, a brief explanation of various methods, their underlying principles, and a general description of their uses, is given.

In forensic science, the distinction between methods which are destructive and those which are nondestructive is often important. A *destructive* method is one which destroys the sample being tested in order to analyze it, thereby preventing any further analysis of the same samples. A *nondestructive* method is one which enables the sample to be examined or tested without irreversibly altering it for purposes of subsequent testing. The destructive or nondestructive character of many tests and methods will be pointed out in the subsequent chapters, and the distinction has important implications for the choice of tests or methods to be employed and for the order in which they are to be performed with a particular sample, especially if it is of limited size.

PHYSICAL EXAMINATIONS AND METHODS

Measurement—The Metric System

Scientists express the results of their measurements in a different system than the one commonly used in everyday life in this country. The *metric system,* as it is called, is very important for understanding scientific measurements, and an introduction to it is given in Appendix 1. Readers unfamiliar with metric units or their modern version, *SI units,* should consult the appendix.

Physical Matching

Some of the most definitive individualizations obtained in forensic casework are the result of physical matches. When a piece of an article is broken, torn, or cut away from the article, random processes are involved in the separation, resulting in the production of unique surface configurations at the separation line. If one of the two pieces is carried away in connection with some criminal act, the ability to rely on these random and unique configurations to demonstrate *commonality of origin* at some later time can prove very valuable in the solution of a case. This kind of evidence is fairly common in hit-and-run automobile accidents, burglaries, and crimes of violence. Collisions involving automobiles often provide a wealth of such evidence. The force of impact may fracture several components and dislodge fragments which can remain at the scene. The extensive use of plastics on newer cars contributes significantly to the possibility of finding useful evidence of this type. In addition to plastic fragments, broken glass, paint chips, pieces of metal, and rubber fragments may be separated from the vehicle and deposited at the scene. Additional evidence, which might associate a vehicle with the scene or the victim by physical matching, can be picked up by the car and carried away. The possibilities include fragments of other vehicles, cloth, skin, buttons, and eyeglasses. There could be extensive two-way exchanges of trace evidence, such as oil, grease, hairs, fibers, paint particles, soil, vegetable matter, blood, and tissue, but these types of evidence are not usually amenable to physical matching comparisons.

Physical matches are usually accomplished by bringing the known and questioned pieces into close juxtaposition to try to produce a "jigsaw" fit. It is not good procedure to attempt physical matches in the field, or at a scene. The evidence itself might be damaged in the process, or an exchange of important trace evidence could take place between pieces. Known and questioned pieces should be kept apart and packaged separately. Even the handling of the separate pieces by the same investigator should be avoided if possible. The extent of agreement between the corresponding surfaces of the pieces is ascertained in the laboratory.

There are two types of physical matches: direct and indirect. *Direct* physical matches are obtained when known and questioned pieces of a material or object can be fitted together in a unique manner. Direct physical matches are also called jigsaw fit matches, and conclusively demonstrate a common origin of questioned and known pieces. *Indirect* physical matching is used in those situations where inadequate detail is present to allow a direct match. Examples include cases where a smooth cut separated the pieces, or where an intervening piece is missing. If the inability to get a convincing jigsaw fit is due to a smooth cut, comparison of the continuity of surface features, surface markings, or internal inhomogeneities can be used to indicate or prove a common origin. Here, the pieces would be juxtaposed and examined by various visual, microscopical, and photographic methods. Thus, a piece of cut newspaper might be associated with the particular sheet it came from by comparing surface texture (fiber patterns), crease lines, printing, and inclusions and flaws across the cut line. If the cut extended to one or two edges, the matching of the edges would also be attempted. Similarly, if the evidence consisted of cut cloth, then thread sizes, flaws, dyes, and surface printing would be utilized. Even apparently uniform materials, such as plastic films used in making plastic bags, are often amenable to physical comparison techniques. These films can have surface striations or internal pigmentation variations that can be compared. It is even possible to show that such a bag was made immediately before, or after, another bag by considering these factors. In a recent homicide case, it was possible to prove conclusively that three plastic bags from the scene had come from a box of bags in the suspect's apartment by a physical comparison of pigmentation patterns (see Chapter 11).

If a sample cannot definitely be associated with another one because of surface damage or missing intervening pieces, the continuity of patterns (surface or internal) from one piece to another may be the only way of proving the existence of a common origin. Weave details in fabrics, grain structure in wood, striae or ream marks in sheet glass, scratch marks in paint flakes, die marks on wires, and extrusion marks on extruded items of plastic and metal are the most common examples of these patterns. Physical matching is discussed further in Chapter 11.

Comparison of Markings

Comparison of markings can be used in cases where two surfaces have contacted one another and one or both has received distinctive markings as a result. These markings are of three kinds: imprints, indentations, and striations. *Imprints* are two-dimensional contact markings. Fingerprints and typewriting are good examples of imprints. Other examples would be tire prints, fabric pattern imprints, and foot or shoe prints on hard surfaces. *Indentations* are three-dimensional contact patterns, produced when harder material leaves its impression in a softer one. Tire tracks in soft dirt, firing-pin indentations, and certain pry marks made with tools are examples, and there are many others. *Striations* are produced by processes involving the movement of one or both surfaces. The striation markings on a fired bullet provide a good example, as would certain toolmarks produced by sliding contact. Marking comparisons are discussed in Chapter 11, and specific types of markings are discussed in Chapters 12 to 14.

If a known object is to be associated with an unknown mark, it is common to produce a known, or *exemplar,* mark with the object so that comparison can be made directly between the two marks. Care is required in producing the exemplar, because it must be a realistic representation of the unknown. It should be made in a similar, appropriate material and in a manner similar to that believed to be responsible for the questioned mark. Thus, if an exemplar print is going to be made of a suspect's sneaker, for example, appropriate weight should be applied to it in producing the print.

Determination of Physical Properties

Detailed physical matches or physical comparisons are not always possible, and it may be necessary to determine and compare *physical properties.* Although a combination of these properties can certainly be considered in attempts to diagnose common origin, they are basically *class* characteristics and are commonly used to aid in *identifications.* Their use in attempts to individualize an object is based on the assumption that a given combination of them is rare or unique. This assumption is true only with evidence in which the properties vary independently from each other and in which the range or variation of each property is known to be large in the overall population compared with that in a particular sample. A significant number of properties have to be determined for both the known and questioned samples to obtain a meaningful individualization.

Physical properties are intrinsic to a particular substance and can be measured without reference to any other substance. They are independent of the quantity of the sample. The physical properties of interest in forensic science include density, melting point, boiling point, refractive index, dispersion, birefringence, color, pleochroism, hardness, and tensile strength. Most of them will be discussed further in later chapters.

Most people are familiar with the property of *density,* whether they realize it or not. It is the property that relates to the weight of a given volume of material. Many people would say that lead is *heavier* than aluminum, although they actually mean that it is *more dense.* In more scientific terms, density is defined as the mass per unit volume. In the metric system, density is expressed in grams per cubic centimeter (g/cm^3). In the English system, it is often expressed in pounds per cubic foot (lb/ft^3). Water, for example, has a density of 1 g/cm^3 (at 4°C), or 62.428 lb/ft^3.

The temperature at which a substance makes a transition between solid and liquid states is characteristic for many materials, making it an aid in identification. This transition temperature is called the *freezing point* or *melting point.* This property can also be used to indicate sample purity. In general, pure chemical substances have sharper or more distinct melting points than do mixtures. Mixtures will give sharp melting points only with certain, definite proportions of the two components, known as *eutectics.* The fact that the addition of small amounts of an impurity will lower the melting point below that of the pure chemical substance has an additional use. Knowledge of this behavior can be used to confirm identifications of unknowns by a technique known as *mixed melting points.* If the independent melting points of known and unknown are found to be the same, it is an indication, but not proof, that they are identical. However, if a mixture of the two is found to melt at that same temperature, the two are almost certainly the same material. If they were different, the unknown would be, in effect, an impurity mixed in with the known, and would be expected to lower its melting point substantially.

As a liquid is heated, the pressure caused by its vapor increases. This pressure is known as the *vapor pressure.* When the liquid is heated to the point where its vapor pressure is equal to atmospheric pressure, it has reached its *boiling point.* The boiling point of a pure liquid is quite sharp and is a useful identifying characteristic. Impure compounds or mixtures may have relatively wide boiling ranges.

Other physical properties are discussed in later chapters in connection with particular types of evidence.

Photographic Techniques

Photography has two important and distinct purposes in forensic science. Its use as a means of documenting crime scenes and physical evidence was discussed in Chapter 2 and Appendix 2. Its other purpose is to bring out information that cannot be detected visually.

Photographic films are manufactured which are sensitive to light outside the visible range. Light with somewhat shorter wavelengths than the shortest visible wavelengths is called *ultraviolet,* while light with wavelengths somewhat longer than the longest visible ones is called *infrared.* Ultraviolet (UV) and infrared (IR) light, and their relationship to the electromagnetic spectrum as a whole, will be discussed below in more detail. For the moment, it is enough to realize that these types of light radiation, which are beyond the range of sensitivity of the human eye, can be detected using special photographic films. Photographs taken with UV or IR light can reveal useful information about various types of physical evidence including questioned documents, stained garments, gunshot discharge residue, and certain imprint patterns. Bloodstains are more or less transparent in the infrared region where special IR film is sensitive. One could take advantage of this fact to "see through" bloodstains to photograph gunshot residue patterns, for example (Figure 3-1). Obliterated writing can often be read in a similar fashion.

Visible-light photographic techniques can be used to detect or to accentuate details which are either invisible or very faint. Various lighting techniques, film types, filter combinations, or other contrast-enhancement techniques may be used to achieve the desired goal with different types of evidence problems. Filters are dyed gelatin films or colored glasses which can be placed over the camera lens or the light source. They are often used in black-and-white photography to alter the contrast relationships among differently colored areas of a sample. Areas which have colors similar to that of the filter will appear lighter in the final photograph, whereas those that are very different (for example, complementary colors) will appear darker. A list of colors and their complements is given in Table 3-1.

The contrast of features which differ only with respect to surface contour or relief can be difficult to appreciate visually. These low-contrast features may be encountered with evidence such as indented writing, faint striation marks, undusted fingerprints, and other subtle impressions. They can often be enhanced by the use of oblique lighting and contrast-enhancement techniques. Oblique lighting is obtained when the light strikes the sample surface at a low or grazing angle (that is, almost perpendicular to the camera axis). Considerable care is necessary to get the angle just right, but the quality of the result can make the effort worthwhile. The Polaroid CU-70 camera system, which was mentioned in Chapter 2 (Fig. 2-2), is particularly useful for this purpose.

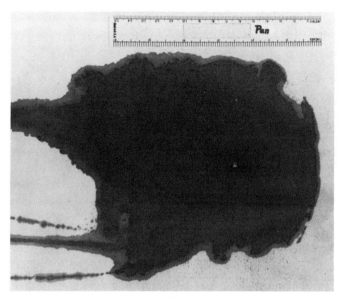

(a)

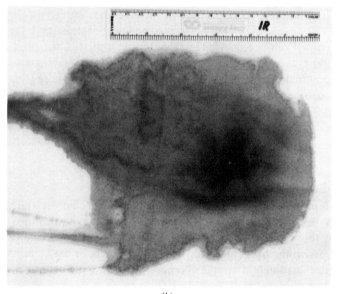

(b)

FIGURE 3-1

(a) Panchromatic photograph of a bloodstain over gunshot residue.
(b) Infrared photograph of a bloodstain over gunshot residue.
(Courtesy of Vincent Crispino and W. Reid Lindsay, Forensic Science
Laboratory, Office of the Medical Examiner, Westchester County, New
York.)

TABLE 3-1
COLORS AND THEIR COMPLEMENTS

Wavelength range (approx.), nm	Color	Complement
400–450	Violet	Yellow-green
450–480	Blue	Yellow
480–490	Green-blue	Orange
490–500	Blue-green	Red
500–560	Green	Purple
560–575	Yellow-green	Violet
575–590	Yellow	Blue
590–625	Orange	Green-blue
625–750	Red	Blue-green

There are several purely photographic contrast-enhancement techniques capable of providing great increases in contrast, but they require some precautions in their use. When contrast is increased, latitude or tonal range is generally reduced. One must be careful to intentionally increase contrast in the sensitivity range that is appropriate for the desired features. It is possible to increase the contrast in the wrong range and produce an image with what appears to be lower contrast than the original. Photographic contrast can be enhanced by selecting appropriate films, printing papers, and developing chemicals. Additional control over contrast can be obtained using various combinations of exposure and development times. These techniques require experience to be used effectively and efficiently and are discussed in Appendix 3.

CHEMICAL METHODS

About the Science of Chemistry

Chemistry is the study of matter and the structural and compositional changes which it undergoes. Different types of matter can be identified and their quantities measured using a branch of this science known as *analytical chemistry*. A sample of matter can be classified according to its physical state (solid, liquid, or gas) and its composition. It is the determination of a sample's composition that is the major concern of analytical chemistry.

Modern laboratories use a wide variety of methods to analyze or determine the composition of samples. Many of these methods, particularly the instrumental ones, have been developed in the last 50 years. Before the advent of chemical instrumentation, it was necessary to rely on measurements of physical properties and on observations of the reactions of samples with special, known chemical preparations called *reagents*. Microchemical (small-scale) adaptations of these classical techniques are still the best for many forensic purposes. Although the distinction between instrumental and noninstrumental methods is somewhat artificial because both may be applied to a given evidence sample, noninstrumental methods are often referred to collectively as *wet chemical* methods.

All samples of matter are composed of *atoms.* It is the type, arrangement, and relationship of the atoms to each other that determines the composition of the sample. The sample may be an element, a compound, or a mixture. A sample of an *element* would consist of atoms all of the same type. There are 92 naturally occurring elements on this planet, plus a dozen or so transuranium elements which are produced in nuclear reactions. The elements, their symbols, and some of their properties are compiled into an organized scheme, called the *periodic table* (Figure 3-2). The symbols for the elements, rather than their full names, are used by chemists for writing formulas, structures, and reactions. Some of the symbols are derived from the Latin names of the elements [for example, Ag stands for silver (Latin *argentum*), and Au stands for gold (Latin *aurum*)].

The smallest unit of matter that is still recognizable as an element is the *atom.* Atoms are made of protons, neutrons, and electrons. They are members of a group of so-called elementary particles, the relationships between which are complex. These are within the province of physics and are not of direct concern to the forensic chemist.

The number of positively charged protons and negatively charged electrons is balanced in all neutral atoms. The number of protons that an atom contains is known as its *atomic number.* Thus, hydrogen has an atomic number of 1, because it has one proton (and one electron). Uranium has 92 protons and 92 electrons, and its atomic number is 92. The atomic number of each of the elements is shown in the periodic table (Figure 3-2). The mass of individual protons and neutrons (uncharged particles) is equivalent and is nearly 2000 times greater than that of the electron. Because the mass of the electron is relatively insignificant, the mass of an atom is overwhelmingly determined by the numbers of protons and neutrons in the nucleus. The sum of the number of protons and the number of neutrons in an atom is the mass number (Z). Different atoms of the same element can sometimes have a different number of neutrons in the nucleus, and these different forms are called *isotopes.* Thus, the deuterium atom shown in Figure 3-3 has one proton and one electron, like hydrogen, but it has a neutron in the nucleus. Another isotope of hydrogen is *tritium,* which has two neutrons (Figure 3-3). Many elements have several known isotopes. Some isotopes are *radioactive.* Radioactive nuclei may emit one or more types of particles or radiation. The radioactivity from a radioactive nucleus can be measured and even used to diagnose the identity of the isotope. Radioactive nuclei are sometimes used as *tracers* in chemical experiments to "label" atoms that one wants to be able to detect later on.

Under certain conditions, atoms can lose or gain electrons. Since there are then unequal numbers of protons and electrons, this results in atoms becoming charged. These charged atoms are known as *ions,* and the process which produces them is called *ionization.* If an atom loses electrons, a positively charged ion is produced,

Periodic table of the elements.

Period	I$_A$	II$_A$	III$_B$	IV$_B$	V$_B$	VI$_B$	VII$_B$	VIII	VIII	VIII	I$_B$	II$_B$	III$_A$	IV$_A$	V$_A$	VI$_A$	VII$_A$	0
1	1 H 1.00797																	2 He 4.003
2	3 Li 6.939	4 Be 9.012											5 B 10.81	6 C 12.011	7 N 14.007	8 O 15.9994	9 F 19.00	10 Ne 20.183
3	11 Na 22.990	12 Mg 24.31											13 Al 26.98	14 Si 28.09	15 P 30.974	16 S 32.064	17 Cl 35.453	18 Ar 39.948
4	19 K 39.102	20 Ca 40.08	21 Sc 44.96	22 Ti 47.90	23 V 50.94	24 Cr 52.00	25 Mn 54.94	26 Fe 55.85	27 Co 58.93	28 Ni 58.71	29 Cu 63.54	30 Zn 65.37	31 Ga 69.72	32 Ge 72.59	33 As 74.92	34 Se 78.96	35 Br 79.909	36 Kr 83.80
5	37 Rb 85.47	38 Sr 87.62	39 Y 88.905	40 Zr 91.22	41 Nb 92.91	42 Mo 95.94	43 Tc [99]	44 Ru 101.1	45 Rh 102.905	46 Pd 106.4	47 Ag 107.870	48 Cd 112.40	49 In 114.82	50 Sn 118.69	51 Sb 121.75	52 Te 127.60	53 I 126.90	54 Xe 131.30
6	55 Cs 132.905	56 Ba 137.34	†	72 Hf 178.49	73 Ta 180.95	74 W 183.85	75 Re 186.2	76 Os 190.2	77 Ir 192.2	78 Pt 195.09	79 Au 196.97	80 Hg 200.59	81 Tl 204.37	82 Pb 207.19	83 Bi 208.98	84 Po [210]	85 At [210]	86 Rn [222]
7	87 Fr [223]	88 Ra [226]	‡															

The values listed are based on $^{12}_{6}C = 12$ u exactly. For radioactive elements, the approximate atomic weight of the most stable isotope is given in brackets.

† Lanthanide series

57 La 138.91	58 Ce 140.12	59 Pr 140.91	60 Nd 144.24	61 Pm [147]	62 Sm 150.35	63 Eu 152.0	64 Gd 157.25	65 Tb 158.92	66 Dy 162.50	67 Ho 164.93	68 Er 167.26	69 Tm 168.93	70 Yb 173.04	71 Lu 174.97

‡ Actinide series

89 Ac [227]	90 Th 232.04	91 Pa [231]	92 U 238.03	93 Np [237]	94 Pu [242]	95 Am [243]	96 Cm [247]	97 Bk [247]	98 Cf [251]	99 Es [254]	100 Fm [253]	101 Md [256]	102 No [254]	103 Lw [257]

FIGURE 3-2
Periodic table of the elements.

58

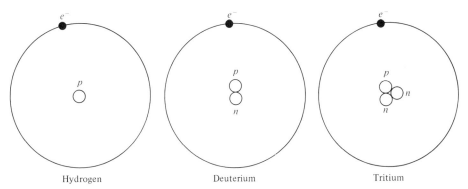

FIGURE 3-3
Simple diagrams of hydrogen, deuterium, and tritium atoms. These are all isotypes of hydrogen.

whereas if electrons are gained, a negative ion results. Hydrogen can lose its one electron to become a positively charged hydrogen ion. The hydrogen ion has a special role in chemistry. The concentration of hydrogen ions in solution is related to the *acidity* of the solution. A special scale, known as the *pH scale* and based on the logarithm of the hydrogen-ion concentration, has been devised to allow chemists to express conveniently the degree of acidity of a solution. The pH scale is illustrated in Figure 3-4, with examples of some common substances positioned on the scale according to their pH values.

A *molecule* is a unit of matter consisting of two or more atoms joined by chemical bonds. Matter composed of identical molecules whose atoms are of two or more elements is called a *pure compound*. Molecules are the smallest units making up compounds in the same way that atoms are the smallest units of elements. A molecule is a specific arrangement of particular kinds of atoms linked together in definite proportions by chemical bonds. Some may contain only two atoms; others may contain hundreds, or even thousands, of atoms. Two general classes of molecules, and thus compounds, are recognized: *inorganic* and *organic*. Originally, these names were assigned to distinguish compounds associated with living organisms (organic) from those of the nonliving world (inorganic). When chemists began synthesizing large numbers of compounds which were formerly thought to be unique to living systems, the meaning of the term *organic* was gradually changed. One common characteristic of molecules derived either directly or indirectly from living processes is the prevalence of carbon atoms linked together. The term *organic* was thus retained and applied to molecules containing carbon atoms in combination with atoms of other elements.

Because of carbon's ability to combine with itself to form long chains, organic molecules can be very large. An infinite number of combinations of atoms is possible in organic chemistry. In fact, about 4 million unique organic compounds are known, and the number is growing all the time! Plastics, paint, synthetic fibers, dyes, drugs, insecticides, and other items of modern civilization are a direct result of discoveries

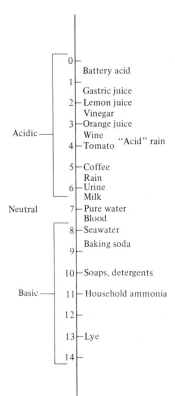

FIGURE 3-4
The pH scale.

in organic chemistry. A few of the most common organic radicals and their chemical formulas are:

Methyl	CH_3-	Ethyl	CH_3CH_2-
Propyl	$CH_3CH_2CH_2-$	Butyl	$CH_3CH_2CH_2CH_2-$
Vinyl	$CH_2=CH-$	Methylene	$-CH_2-$

Examples of common organic compounds and their structural formulas are presented in Table 3-2.

Chemical Identification

Chemical identifications can be made by allowing an unknown to react with a series of reagents. The reactions observed in each case can narrow down the possibilities and lead to an identification of the unknown. The reactions that are used must be observable. Normally, this means that an easily recognizable product must be formed. This product might be a precipitate, a gas, or a distinctively colored compound.

TABLE 3-2
Common Organic Compounds and Their Formulas

Name	Empirical formula	Simplified structural formula
Alkanes (Paraffins)	C_nH_{2n+2}	
methane	CH_4	CH_4
ethane	C_2H_6	CH_3CH_3
propane	C_3H_8	$CH_3CH_2CH_3$
butane	C_4H_{10}	$CH_3CH_2CH_2CH_3$
octane	C_8H_{18}	$CH_3(CH_2)_6CH_3$
Alkenes (Olefins)	C_nH_{2n}	
ethene (ethylene)	C_2H_4	$CH_2{=}CH_2$
propene (propylene)	C_3H_6	$CH_3{-}CH{=}CH_2$
Alkynes (Acetylenes)	C_nH_{2n-2}	
ethyne (acetylene)	C_2H_2	$CH{\equiv}CH$
propyne	C_3H_4	$CH_3C{\equiv}CH$
Alcohols		ROH
methanol (methyl alcohol)	CH_4O	CH_3OH
ethanol (ethyl alcohol)	C_2H_6O	CH_3CH_2OH
n-propanol (propyl alcohol)	C_3H_8O	$CH_3CH_2CH_2OH$
isopropanol (isopropyl alcohol)	C_3H_8O	$(CH_3)_2CHOH$
Acids		RCOOH
methanoic acid (formic acid)	CH_2O_2	HCOOH
ethanoic acid (acetic acid)	$C_2H_4O_2$	CH_3COOH
hexanedioic acid (adipic acid)[a]	$C_6H_{10}O_4$	$HOOC(CH_2)_4COOH$
Primary Amines		$R{-}(NH_2)_n$
methylamine	CH_5N	$CH_3{-}NH_2$
ethylamine	C_2H_7N	$CH_3CH_2{-}NH_2$
ethylenediamine	$C_2H_8N_2$	$NH_2{-}CH_2CH_2{-}NH_2$
hexamethylenediamine[b]	$C_6H_{16}N_2$	$NH_2(CH_2)_6NH_2$
Miscellaneous Halogenated Hydrocarbons		RX_n
methyl chloride (chloromethane)		CH_3Cl
methylene chloride (dichloromethane)		CH_2Cl_2
chloroform (trichloromethane)		$CHCl_3$
carbon tetrachloride		CCl_4
vinyl chloride		$CH_2{=}CHCl$
vinylidine chloride		$CH_2{=}CCl_2$
freon (dichlorodifluoromethane)		CCl_2F_2
Ethers		ROR
methyl ether	C_2H_6O	$CH_3{-}O{-}CH_3$
ethyl ether	$C_4H_{10}O$	$CH_3CH_2{-}O{-}CH_2CH_3$
isopropyl ether	$C_6H_{14}O$	$(CH_3)_2CH{-}O{-}CH(CH_3)_2$
Ketones		R(CO)R′
propanone (dimethyl ketone, acetone)	C_3H_6O	$CH_3{-}\overset{\displaystyle O}{\overset{\|}{C}}{-}CH_3$
butanone (methyl ethyl ketone, MEK)	C_4H_8O	$CH_3{-}\overset{\displaystyle O}{\overset{\|}{C}}{-}CH_2CH_3$

TABLE 3-2 (*Continued*)
Common Organic Compounds and Their Formulas

Name	Empirical formula	Simplified structural formula
Esters		RO(CO)R′
ethyl acetate[c]	$C_4H_8O_2$	$CH_3CH_2-O-\overset{\overset{\displaystyle O}{\|\|}}{C}-CH_3$
methyl propanoate[d]	$C_4H_8O_2$	$CH_3-O-\overset{\overset{\displaystyle O}{\|\|}}{C}-CH_2CH_3$

[a]Adipic acid is a 6-carbon diacid used in nylon 66 (see Chapter 8).
[b]Hexamethylenediamine is used in nylon 66 (see Chapter 8).
[c]Ethyl acetate is an ester of ethyl alcohol and acetic acid.
[d]Methyl propanoate is an ester of methyl alcohol and proponoic acid; note that the empirical formula is the same as that of ethyl acetate.

The term *precipitate* is used to describe an insoluble reaction product that comes out of solution as it is formed and collects at the bottom of the vessel. The fact that a precipitate of a certain color forms with a particular reagent tells the chemist something about the sample being tested. This test, combined with others using different reagents, will generally allow an identification to be made. Some precipitates, particularly those which form slowly, may develop as microscopic crystals with distinctive structures. These can be recognized under the microscope, adding another dimension to the analysis and making the resulting identification more certain. Tests based on the formation and study of these microscopic crystals are known as *microchemical crystal tests*. These and other microchemical methods are particularly useful in forensic science. They are commonly used in testing samples of street drugs, for example (see Chapter 5, Table 5-2), but have other uses as well.

Gases may be formed as a product in reactions between a reagent and the test material. These may be seen as bubbles in the solution or may be allowed to react with yet another reagent to yield a recognizable product. In some microchemical procedures, the gas being evolved in a closed container comes into contact with a single drop of reagent. If it is the gas expected to be produced, it will be trapped and react with the reagent to form a microcrystalline precipitate within the drop. The drop is then examined under the microscope to confirm the identification. The fact that all three steps take place, that is, the gas formation, the gas trapping, and the production of characteristic crystals, makes this elegant but simple method essentially equivalent to a combination of three separate tests.

Some reagents are designed to form colored reaction products with specific elements or compounds. The facts that a color is formed and the color has a particular shade are used to decide whether the substance sought is present. These tests can be scaled down to the microchemical level, where they are commonly known as *spot tests*. There are spot tests for both inorganic and organic compounds. The screening tests used to give preliminary information about the identity of suspected drugs are examples of spot tests that are widely used in forensic science (Chapter 5). Reactions of various drugs with selected reagents are given in Table 5-1.

The measurement of physical properties, such as refractive index, density, melting point, and boiling point, can also be used in connection with wet chemical identifications. These can be determined on samples before the chemical tests are applied or to an untested portion afterwards. Certain physical-property measurements would probably be included as an integral part of an analytical scheme. Meaningful physical-property measurements require relatively pure samples. Thus, unless the sample is reasonably pure as received, preliminary separations and purifications are necessary before they can be carried out.

The various wet chemical identification methods discussed above could be classified as *qualitative* tests or methods. In analytical chemistry, the word *qualitative* is used to describe analyses in which only the identity of a sample or its components is of concern. In situations where *levels* or *amounts* are to be determined, the term *quantitative* is used. Quantitative wet chemical methods can be divided into two types, *gravimetric* and *volumetric*.

In gravimetric methods, the weights of reactants and products such as precipitates are very carefully determined. From these weights, the amount of the component sought can be calculated. Gravimetric methods require considerable care in transferring, drying, and weighing precipitates, and are quite time-consuming. They are not commonly used in modern criminalistics laboratories. Volumetric methods are not as tedious, and are still used to some extent in forensic casework. Here, the volumes of reagents consumed in certain reactions are carefully monitored. In a process known as *titration,* a reagent is added dropwise to the reaction mixture until the reaction is complete. The volume of reagent necessary is recorded and used in calculations to determine the amount of material of interest in the sample. We may note here that the term *titration* as used in analytical chemistry has a somewhat different meaning than it has in serology (Chapter 9) although both are concerned with determining the strength or amount of something.

Chemical Separation Techniques

A sample may be an element, a compound, or a mixture. We have seen that a sample of a pure element would contain individual atoms of only one type and that a pure compound would contain individual molecules of only one type. A *mixture* is comprised of elements and/or compounds in various proportions. Chemical separation methods are applicable to the analysis of mixtures. Such methods can be used to separate a mixture into its various component elements and compounds so that they can be tested separately. With some chemical methods, it is not necessary to perform a preliminary separation in order to analyze a mixture for its constituent components (elements and compounds). The decision as to whether a preliminary separation is necessary depends on what is being tested for and what is present. The principal separation methods available to the chemist include distillation, sublimation, crystallization, solvent extraction, and chromatographic methods. Chromatographic methods will be discussed in the next section. The others are briefly discussed here.

Distillation This process involves heating a sample of liquid to convert it into vapor, which is then allowed to flow to another location where it is cooled, condensing it back into a liquid. In the process of vaporization and condensation, many impurities are left behind and the sample becomes purer. Various modifications of the basic distillation process are used for specific purposes.

Sublimation This technique is similar to distillation, except that the sample is a solid to begin with and is converted directly into vapor and then back into solid. Sublimation is applicable only to solids which will sublime, that is, samples which will go directly from solid to vapor phase without melting and going through the liquid phase. When the sublimed vapor condenses on a cool surface, very pure crystals are formed. The sublimation of iodine is taken advantage of in the *iodine fuming* method of detecting latent fingerprints (Chapter 12).

Crystallization When the concentration of a compound (the *solute*) dissolved in a liquid (the *solvent*) reaches a certain point, no more of the solute will go into solution, and we say that the solution is *saturated*. If some solvent is lost from a saturated solution or some other step is taken to reduce the amount of solute the solvent can hold, crystals of the solute may begin forming. Under properly controlled conditions, these crystals will be purer than the solute material used to make the original solution. Because only very similarly shaped molecules of the appropriate size can be incorporated into a particular crystal while it is growing, crystals tend to be quite pure. This is the basis for purification by crystallization.

Solvent Extraction Not all liquids are mutually soluble. If we shake a mixture of oil and vinegar, a temporary but more or less homogeneous mixture will be formed. If it is allowed to stand undisturbed, however, a separation takes place until the oil is in a uniform layer above the vinegar. We say that the oil and the vinegar are *not miscible,* or that they are *immiscible.* Although some organic solvents such as alcohols and acetone are miscible with water, others such as choloroform and ether are not. Water will float on choloroform, and ether will float on water. A system of two immiscible liquids is required for the purification or separation of materials by *solvent extraction.*

If one of the two liquids contains a solute, and the system is shaken and then allowed to settle, some of the solute will be transferred to the other liquid. Each of the liquids in a mixture of two immiscible liquids of this kind is referred to as a *phase.* Thus, we can say that some of the solute was transferred from one phase to the other in this two-phase system. The amount transferred depends on the relative affinity of the solute for each of the two solvents (relative solubility). Very little or nearly all of it may be transferred depending on the circumstances.

If a particular solvent contains a dissolved compound (solute) of interest in the presence of other solutes which are regarded as impurities, the chemist would like to pick conditions and a solvent pair which would result in a separation of the desired solute from the impurities. Ideally, the impurities would end up in one phase and the substance sought in the other. The relative solubilities of some solutes can be altered by changing the pH of the solution, thus providing the chemist with additional control over the separation conditions. Solvent extraction is a common technique in forensic toxicology (Chapter 5).

Chromatographic Methods

The term *chromatography* applies to a whole family of chemical separation methods. These can be used to purify chemical substances or to aid in identifying them. The term *chromatography* itself may be somewhat misleading. Its Latin roots would indicate that it had something to do with "writing or painting with color." The term was first applied to procedures which resulted in the separation of pigments from natural products. The separation yielded colored streaks or bands. Even though these same separation processes are now commonly used to separate colorless substances, the term chromatography has been kept.

Chromatography involves the separation of substances based on their relative affinities for two phases, one stationary and one mobile. Substances which have higher affinities for the mobile phase are moved, or carried along with it, and are thus separated from those with higher affinities for the stationary phase.

Paper Chromatography   Paper chromatography is one of the simplest types of chromatography. In its most rudimentary form, the separation taking place is like that which occurs when water is accidentally spilled on a document which has been written with a water-soluble multicomponent ink: The ink lines will smear and run. Some of the differently colored dyes in the ink will move at different rates and will look like subtle, colored fringes at the edges of the diffused ink lines. In paper chromatography, this process is more carefully arranged and controlled. Special types of papers, which may have been subjected to pretreatments, are used. In addition, special solvents or mixtures of solvents are used to achieve the desired separation. In paper chromatography, the substances to be separated or analyzed are placed as discrete spots (spotted) at a specified distance from one edge of the paper. This edge is then dipped into the solvent. As the paper is wetted, the solvent migrates along the paper by capillary action. It may move up, down, or horizontally, depending upon the physical arrangement of the apparatus selected.

Thin-Layer Chromatography   Thin-layer chromatography (TLC) is closely analogous to paper chromatography, except that the separation takes place in a thin layer of absorbent material, such as alumina, silica gel, or cellulose, coated onto an inert backing material, such as glass plates or plastic sheets. In most TLC methods, as in paper chromatography, samples are applied as small spots, the plate or sheet is then placed in a chamber, and one edge is dipped into a solvent. The solvent is allowed to migrate up the plate to some predetermined height before the plate is removed from the chamber. If the components are simple dyes or pigments, the analysis may be completed by visual inspection. For other types of components, special visualization methods are necessary. These methods may entail the use of UV light examination, or of special chemical sprays which produce colored reaction products with the invisible compounds. In some cases, several visualization methods may be applied to a single plate. TLC is commonly used in forensic science laboratories for the analysis of drugs (Chapter 5), inks (Chapter 13), and textile dyes (Chapter 8).

In order to standardize the TLC method, a quantity called the R_f has been defined. R_f values apply to any individual components which can be separated by TLC in a defined solvent system under defined conditions. The R_f is the distance which a particular component migrates divided by the distance which the solvent front migrates. Expressed as a formula,

$$R_f = \frac{\text{distance traveled by component (solute)}}{\text{distance traveled by solvent}}$$

The R_f is thus a constant for a particular compound under a defined set of TLC conditions. As a simple example, suppose that a certain compound migrated 4 cm from the origin on a TLC plate under a defined set of conditions and that the solvent front migrated 10 cm on this same plate. The R_f for the compound under this set of conditions would be

$$R_f = \frac{4}{10} = 0.4$$

R_f values range from zero to 1. Published values of R_f for many different compounds under many different TLC conditions may be found in handbooks and standard reference sources.

Column Chromatography   In this technique, a vertical glass tube is filled with a granular absorbent or other substance. This substance is the *stationary phase*. The sample is then added to the top of the column, followed by a special solvent selected as the *mobile phase*. As the solvent flows through the column under the influence of gravity or pressure, various components of the sample mixture will migrate at different rates and thus arrive at the lower end of the column at different times. Fractions collected at various intervals will thus contain the different, separated components. These fractions can then be subjected to futher analysis by other methods.

Column chromatographic methods differ from one another on the basis of the principle involved in the separation, which in turn depends on the substance used to fill the column. Some materials (alumina, diatomaceous earth) bring about separation on the basis of differential adsorption of various molecules in the mixture. The principle involved here is quite similar to that involved in TLC. In *ion-exchange chromatography*, molecules which have a net charge (ions) can be separated. Here, inert matrix materials are chemically bonded to molecules which have a fixed charge. In suitable forms, such *ion-exchange resins* can be packed into columns and used to bind and separate mixtures of molecules which have the opposite charge (because unlike charges attract). In some cases, the net charge on the column material, or on the sample molecules, or both, is dependent upon pH, giving even greater flexibility. Certain types of ion-exchange chromatography are very useful in biochemistry for the separation of protein or nucleic acid molecules. *Gel permeation* (or *molecular sieve*) chromatography is a technique for separating large molecules on the basis of their size. This versatile procedure is commonly used in biochemical studies of proteins and other large molecules.

High-Performance Liquid Chromatography High-performance liquid chromatography (HPLC) is very similar to the column chromatographic methods just discussed. Instead of an open vertical tube and gravity-induced flow, however, it utilizes a closed system and pumps to pressurize the solvent (mobile phase) and force it through the column. The pumps and column are generally contained within an instrument known as a liquid chromatograph. Other components are also included in the instrument, their number depending upon the degree of sophistication of the particular instrument. All instruments, however, have detectors and components for control and readout of the column pressure. Several different types of detectors can be used. These are placed at the end of the column to "recognize," or detect, the components as they emerge from the column. The detector signal is then amplified and displayed on a strip-chart recorder to yield a *liquid chromatogram*. The fractions can also be collected as they are in column chromatography. However, this is not commonly done unless some further analysis of each component is necessary. HPLC can be applied to the analysis of drugs and explosives as well as other samples.

Gas Chromatography Gas chromatography (GC) is similar in many respects to HPLC, although it was developed and perfected earlier. In GC, the mobile phase is a gas, commonly referred to as the *carrier gas*. The stationary phase in one type of GC is an absorbent. This type is particularly useful for the analysis of simple gases. A more commonly used type of GC is known as *gas-partition chromatography* or *gas-liquid chromatography* (GLC). Here, the stationary phase consists of a high-boiling liquid, grossly similar to a heavy oil or grease. The liquid stationary phase must be held in place in the column by some type of support. In a method known as *capillary column* GC, the column consists of a long (10 to 60 m) coil of a very narrow bore (0.2 to 0.5 mm) capillary tubing. In this case, the liquid phase is coated as a thin layer onto the inside wall of the tubing. Capillary column GC is one of the most powerful chromatographic techniques, and it is being used more frequently; but it is not as commonly used as another, somewhat older and established GC method—*packed-column* GC. In a packed column, the liquid phase is coated as a thin layer onto the surface of numerous inert granules. These are then packed into coiled glass or metal tubing (typically with diameters of ⅛ to ¼ in.).

Several factors control the separating power, or efficiency, in GC. Among them are the nature of the liquid phase, carrier-gas flow rate, intrinsic column efficiency, column length, column diameter, and temperature. The temperature of the column is controlled by placing it within an oven in the instrument. Being able to vary the temperature greatly increases the range of molecular weights of compounds which can be analyzed. When the temperature is raised linearly with time during the course of a single run, a very broad range of compounds can be handled. This technique is known as *temperature programming*.

As in HPLC, a detector is placed at the end of the GC column to detect each of the components as it emerges from the column, and a strip chart recorder is used to record and display the data in the form of a *gas chromatogram.* Gases and volatile liquids, such as alcohol and accelerants, are obvious candidates for analysis, but even compounds, such as drugs, which are solids at room temperature can be sufficiently volatilized (converted to vapor) to allow analysis by GC.

Samples which cannot be easily volatilized, such as high-molecular-weight polymers, can be analyzed by an ancillary technique known as *pyrolysis gas chromatography* (PGC). In this procedure, the sample is heated in an inert carrier gas to a temperature high enough to decompose it. The large numbers of small molecules produced in this way can then be separated gas chromatographically to yield a characteristic complex pattern of peaks. Samples of forensic interest which can be analyzed by PGC include paint chips, fibers, plastics, tars, and greases.

Spectroscopic Methods

The methods of chemical analysis in this category take advantage of the interaction of radiation from some portion of the electromagnetic spectrum with the sample.

All the different forms of radiant energy can be considered to be waves and can be arranged in the order of their *wavelengths.* This arrangement is called the *electromagnetic spectrum,* and it is very broad. Visible light is only a very narrow portion of this spectrum. Radiation with wavelengths somewhat longer than those of visible light is known as *infrared* (IR) radiation. Light which has somewhat shorter wavelengths than the shortest visible wavelengths is known as *ultraviolet* (UV) radiation. However, the electromagnetic spectrum extends well beyond these regions in both directions. Beyond the UV, on the short-wavelength side, are the vacuum-ultraviolet, x-ray, and gamma-ray regions. Radiation with wavelengths longer than those of the IR includes far-infrared, microwaves, and a broad range of radio waves. The electromagnetic spectrum is illustrated in Figure 3-5.

The wavelengths of electromagnetic radiation in and around the visible range can be separated to produce spectra by using either *prisms* or *gratings.* Prisms depend on *refraction,* while gratings depend on *diffraction* to bend light. In either case, the various wavelengths of light are bent through different angles. In refraction, the shorter wavelengths are bent the most, whereas in diffraction the amount of bending is greatest for the longer wavelengths.

Prisms can separate light of different wavelengths because materials such as glass have different refracting powers, known as *refractive indices* (RI), for different wavelengths. The amount by which RI varies with wavelength in a given material is known as *dispersion* and is a characteristic property of that material. Dispersion and RI will be discussed in more detail in Chapter 7.

A *grating* designed to produce spectra generally consists of a piece of glass or a mirror ruled with a series of closely spaced parallel lines. The optimal effects are obtained when the spacing between these lines is only slightly greater than the average wavelength of the radiation being used. Diagrams indicating how spectra can be formed using both prisms and diffraction gratings are shown in Figures 3-6 and 3-7.

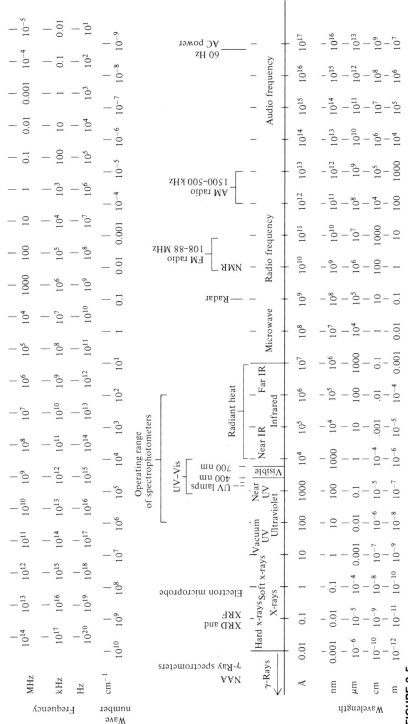

FIGURE 3-5
The electromagnetic spectrum.

69

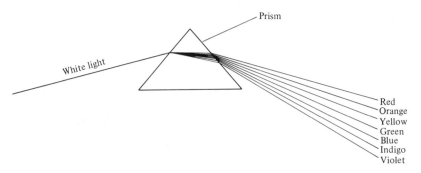

FIGURE 3-6
Dispersing white light into a spectrum using a prism.

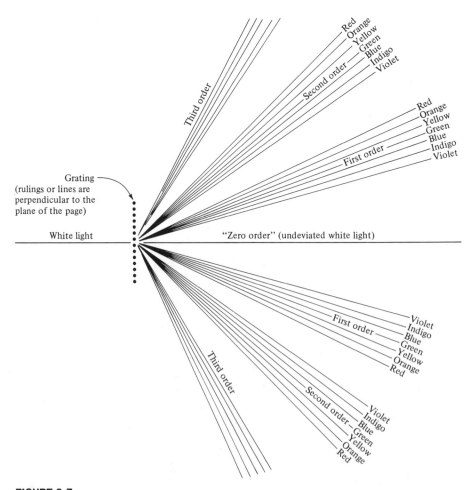

FIGURE 3-7
Dispersing white light into spectra using a diffraction grating. Generally only one of the first or second orders would be used in the spectroscopic instruments.

One other aspect of light waves that deserves mention here is their direction of vibration. Different components of an ordinary light beam can vibrate in any direction perpendicular to the direction of travel. With the use of a polarizing filter, such as those used in the lenses of Polaroid sunglasses, this light can be converted into *plane-polarized light,* in which only light vibrating in a single direction is allowed to pass through. Polarizing filters and plane-polarized light are essential for use in polarized light microscopy (see under Microscopy and Microscopical Methods).

Emission Spectrography Various chemicals can alter the color of a flame. Some of the more common examples of this behavior are: sodium salts, which yield an orange-yellow flame; strontium salts, which yield a red flame; potassium salts, which yield a delicate violet flame; and copper salts, which yield either blue or green flames. If the light from such flames is broken down into a spectrum using either a prism or diffraction grating, much more detail about the change becomes apparent. In fact, many elements which do not appear to alter flame colors in any visually recognizable way can be identified when the light produced is broken down into a spectrum. The characteristic spectra that are produced by breaking down the light from flames or electric arcs containing atoms of a sample are known as *emission spectra.*

The spectrograph is a device for producing and recording emission spectra. It has been used in crime laboratories for many years. In most of these instruments, the sample is vaporized and excited in an electric arc. The resulting spectrum is registered on film or a photographic plate to produce a permanent record (Figure 3-8).

Emission spectrography is a method of analyzing for the presence of atoms of elements, without regard to the molecules(s) of which the atoms are a part. For this reason, it is referred to as an *elemental* analysis method. The chief strength of the method is its capability for simultaneous analysis of a large number of elements at relatively low concentrations. The major drawback for forensic applications is the fact that the quantitative accuracy and reproducibility are relatively poor.

Atomic Absorption Spectrophotometry The availability of atomic absorption (AA) instrumentation is a relatively recent development. AA can be looked upon as the reverse of emission spectrography. Here, the absorption of light by the sample

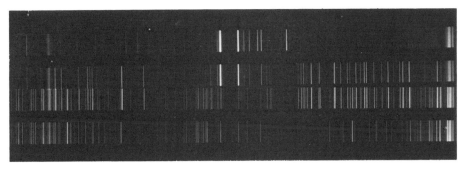

FIGURE 3-8
A spectrogram from an emission spectrograph.

atoms of interest, rather than the emission, is utilized. Absorption and emission are thus, in a way, two sides of the same coin. In AA, the sample is atomized in a flame or furnace through which radiation of a selected wavelength is passed. Atoms of the element sought will absorb their own characteristic radiation in proportion to the amount of the particular element in the sample. The change in intensity of the light, caused by the sample atoms in the beam (the absorption), is measured photometrically using electronic detectors and associated circuitry, rather than photographic film as in the emission spectrograph. The method is extremely sensitive for many elements and has excellent quantitative accuracy. Its major disadvantage is that only one or at most, two elements can be determined at one time. Thus, one must know ahead of time which elements are to be quantitated. AA can be applied to the detection of barium, antimony, and lead levels in samples of suspected gunshot residue (Chapter 14) and to the determination of heavy metal poisons (Chapter 5).

Plasma Emission Spectrophotometry The plasma emission spectrophotometer is a very recent development. It overcomes some of the shortcomings of both the emission spectrograph and the AA spectrophotometer. Like the spectrograph, it utilizes the information contained within the emission spectrum of samples, and like the AA, the light intensities are determined photometrically. A special source, known as a plasma arc, is used to heat and excite the sample. The light produced is broken down into a spectrum and examined by separate electronic detectors placed at preselected "locations" in the spectrum, so that up to 20 or so elements can be accurately quantitated at one time. The forensic applications of this technique are only now being explored.

Ultraviolet-Visible Spectrophotometry Ultraviolet-visible (UV-VIS) spectrophotometers have been available for use in forensic laboratories for over 40 years. This type of instrument is used to obtain absorption spectra from more or less transparent samples (normally solutions). Unlike the AA method, where the light source emitted only certain discrete wavelengths (discontinuous source), the sources usually used with UV-VIS spectrophotometers emit a continuum of radiation over a broad range of wavelengths (continuous source). A continuous source of this kind, emitting light across the entire visible range, would yield the typical rainbow-type spectrum when the light is dispersed (broken up) by a prism or a grating; by contrast, a discontinuous source, such as is used in AA, would yield a series of discrete lines, interspersed with voids, when dispersed by a prism or grating.

The UV-VIS spectrophotometer, as the name indicates, operates in both the UV and visible ranges. Examples of UV-VIS absorption spectra are shown in Figure 3-9. Ultraviolet spectrophotometry is employed in drug identification analysis (Chapter 5), and both VIS and UV spectrophotometry are quite common in quantitative biochemical analyses of blood and body-fluid components.

Infrared Spectrophotometry The IR spectrophotometer is like the UV-VIS instrument, except that it operates in the IR wavelength range. It can be applied to the characterization of both organic and inorganic compounds, although it is most

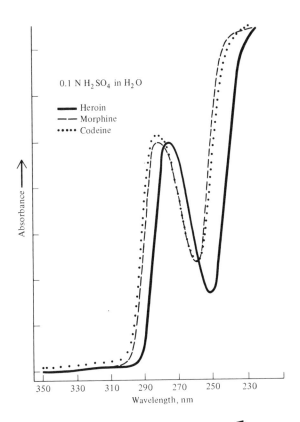

0.1 N H_2SO_4 in H_2O

—— Heroin
— — Morphine
••••• Codeine

Absorbance →

350 330 310 290 270 250 230
Wavelength, nm

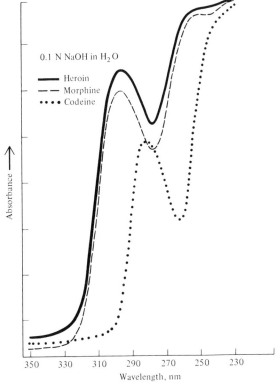

0.1 N NaOH in H_2O

—— Heroin
— — Morphine
••• Codeine

Absorbance →

350 330 310 290 270 250 230
Wavelength, nm

FIGURE 3-9
Ultraviolet absorption spectra of
three opiate drugs at two pH's.
*(Courtesy of Francis X. Sheehan,
John Jay College of Criminal
Justice, The City University of
New York.)*

often used with organic substances. The absorption spectra obtained with the IR are considerably more detailed than UV spectra. The peaks obtained are quite characteristic of the sample. The frequency (or wavelength) of the radiation at the absorption maxima (inverted peaks) can be related to specific chemical groups or bonds within the sample molecule. The spectrum produced is almost like a "fingerprint" for a particular molecule.

IR is employed by forensic scientists in the analysis of drugs, plastics, fibers, paint, and similar substances. It is less effective for identifying mixtures than it is for relatively pure compounds.

Spectrophotofluorometry Spectrophotofluorometry (SPF) is used to produce so-called fluorescence spectra. Most investigators have had some occasion to use a hand-held UV lamp to examine fluorescent "detective dyes" and fingerprint powders and are thus familiar with the phenomenon of fluorescence. Fluorescent substances absorb relatively short wavelength radiation, such as the UV (the exciting radiation), and reemit the energy as longer-wavelength radiation (the fluorescence). In the case of excitation by a UV source, the longer-wavelength radiation emitted is often in the visible range. Excitation in the visible range can produce fluorescence in the longer-wavelength IR (IR luminescence).

In instruments designed for SPF, two wavelength-selecting devices (monochrometers) are used. One is used to select a particular wavelength for excitation, and the other allows each of the emitted wavelengths to be studied individually. As a result, an almost infinite number of two-dimensional emission and excitation spectra can be produced for a single substance. The most complete way to represent this information in a single figure is as a three-dimensional plot of intensity as a function of both emission and excitation wavelengths (Figure 3-10). It is easy to see that this technique provides far more information than could be obtained from a visual examination of fluorescence induced by a hand-held UV lamp.

The SPF technique has been applied to the characterization of many samples of forensic interest. They include tire rubbers, greases, new and used motor oils, and surgical adhesive tapes. In favorable circumstances, the technique is sensitive enough to work with samples as small as crankcase oil drippings or particles of rubber collected from a tire smear or a skid mark.

Neutron Activation Analysis The mechanism of neutron activation analysis (NAA) is somewhat different from that of other spectroscopic methods that we have discussed. However, the method does depend on the production and analysis of a type of electromagnetic radiation (gamma rays) and therefore can properly be included in this section.

NAA is a sensitive elemental-analysis technique that can be applied to a broad range of elements. The sample to be analyzed is placed in a source of slow-moving neutrons (thermal neutrons), such as in the core of a nuclear reactor. The neutrons combine with the nuclei of many of the atoms in the sample to produce unstable, or radioactive, nuclei (radioisotopes). The production of these radioactive atoms is the *activation* step. After a suitable activation period, the sample is removed from the

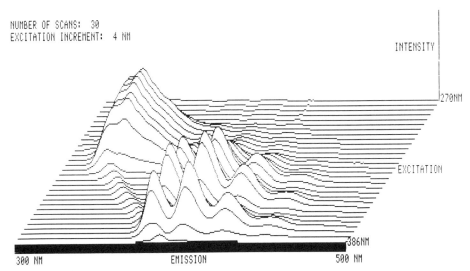

NUMBER OF SCANS: 30
EXCITATION INCREMENT: 4 NM

INTENSITY

270NM

EXCITATION

386NM

300 NM   EMISSION   500 NM

FIGURE 3-10
A three-dimensional plot from a spectrophotofluorometer. (*Perkin-Elmer Corporation, Norwalk, Conn.*)

reactor core and placed in a gamma-ray spectrometer. As the radioactive nuclei that were produced in the activation step decay, they give off gamma rays with energies that are characteristic of the nuclei which produced them. A scientist can determine many of the elements originally present in the sample from a study of the gamma-ray spectrum. Other rays (alpha and beta) are also given off when certain nuclei decay. In some cases, the energy distribution of the beta rays produced may also be studied.

Attempts have been made to apply NAA to forensic problems for about 25 years. In some instances, early optimistic claims made for the technique have not stood the test of time. NAA is a good method of elemental analysis, but problems have been encountered in working with many forensic samples. Most forensic science problems, where compositional individualization is desired, are more difficult than those of ordinary chemical analysis. One of the earliest applications of NAA in forensic science was directed toward the individualization of human hair. Despite earlier optimism, the method has now fallen into disrepute (Chapter 8). The difficulty had more to do with the nature of the hair individualization problem than with shortcomings of NAA as an elemental-analysis technique. NAA can be used much more successfully to characterize samples of metal alloys involved in investigations, such as stolen copper wire or tubing. At times, a close approach to individualization may be possible with these samples. A more common application of NAA has been the determination of barium and antimony levels on the hands of a person suspected of having shot a gun. These two elements are used in the formulation of most cartridge primers, and elevated levels of them on the surfaces of the hands are taken as an indication that the person recently handled or discharged a firearm.

AA has also been used for this purpose, as noted above. Both NAA and AA can provide accurate quantitative results for trace amounts of these two elements, but it is often difficult to interpret what such a finding means. Antimony and barium are not unique to gunshot residue (Chapter 14). NAA can be done only in a few specialized laboratories. NAA methods for gunshot residue determinations require radiochemical separation after activation because of the presence in the skin of high concentrations of sodium which can mask traces of barium and antimony. NAA is very insensitive to lead concentrations, whereas AA is very sensitive for lead determinations. Because of these problems, NAA is now used less frequently for determination of gunshot residue.

X-Ray Fluorescence   Like SPF, x-ray fluorescence (XRF) involves the analysis of radiation emitted when higher-energy (shorter-wavelength) radiation interacts with the specimen. For example, if short-wavelength x-rays strike a sample, longer-wavelength x-rays which are characteristic of elements within the sample material may be emitted. These characteristic x-rays can also be generated when a high-energy electron beam strikes a sample. A spectrum of these x-rays can be produced by "dispersing" them according to their wavelengths or their energies. Spectra of this kind yield information about the elemental composition of the specimen. The term *x-ray fluorescence* applies to instruments or techniques where the emission of x-rays is induced by shorter-wavelength x-rays. An instrument which utilizes a focused electron beam to produce x-rays characteristic of the sample is known as an *electron microprobe*. This technique is excellent for the elemental analysis of individual microsopic particles.

Additional Instrumental Methods

Methods which are, strictly speaking, neither chromatographic nor spectroscopic are discussed in this section.

Scanning Electron Microscopy   The scanning electron microscope (SEM) is a distinctly different instrument from the transmission electron microscope (TEM). The SEM is used to study surface morphology. The images produced are striking and often give the illusion of being three-dimensional. In addition, surface features at various depths within the sample region can all be in clear focus at the same time; in other words, the SEM exhibits excellent *depth of field*. It is far superior in this regard to the optical microscope, where, at high powers, only a narrow zone of sample depth can be in proper focus at one time. If x-ray spectrometers are added to the instrument, the x-rays produced by the impact of the electrons with the sample can be analyzed to give data on the elemental composition of discrete areas of the sample. An SEM so equipped is like the electron microprobe discussed above. An SEM is thus capable of giving both morphological and compositional information from small samples, which is a great advantage with certain forensic problems. A good example is in the analysis of gunshot residue particles (Chapter 14). SEM is further discussed below, in connnection with microscopy.

X-Ray Diffraction   The wavelengths of x-rays are roughly the same as the spacings between the atoms in crystals. Thus, crystals can diffract, or bend, x-rays in much the same way that a series of evenly ruled lines in a diffraction grating can diffract visible light. Crystals can be thought of as three-dimensional diffraction gratings. The term *crystal lattice* is often used to describe this latticework-like arrangement. The angles through which the x-ray beam will be deflected by a crystal depend on the wavelength of the x-rays and on the spacings of the atoms or molecules in the crystal lattice.

Even if a single-wavelength beam (a monochromatic beam) is used with a pure crystalline substance, it is found that several distinct diffraction angles result. This occurs because several sets of planes with unique spacings can exist even in the simplest crystal lattice. A two-dimensional analogy might be helpful in visualizing this point. Consider a piece of graph paper. A dot can be placed at each line intersection to symbolize the atoms in a crystal. The ruled horizontal and vertical lines are analogous to one set of planes in a simple crystal and are one unit apart. Additional sets of parallel lines, with smaller spacings, can also be drawn. One such set would contain the diagonals, connecting the corners of each square. If each of the intersections, or dots, in horizontal rows is connected with every other dot in the vertical column, another set of parallel lines with its own unique spacing is generated. It is clear that a very large number of such *planes* and spacings can be generated simply by using different combinations of vertical and horizontal increments. This idea can be appreciated even better by imagining that hundreds of pins were inserted in the paper at the locations of the dots. If this setup could be brought to eye level and viewed along a line parallel to the plane of the paper, many sets of rows with different spacings would be apparent if the paper were rotated slowly in its own plane. The same effect is observed when riding past a large apple orchard or orange grove.

The ability of X-ray differaction (XRD) to determine the lattice spacings within crystals makes it a useful identification tool for crystalline evidence. Manual and computerized search files have been compiled for thousands of known substances. These files allow the lattice-spacing data of an unknown to be coded and searched for in the file to provide an identification. XRD has been applied to forensic evidence which is crystalline or which contains crystalline materials, including drugs, soil, minerals, and paint pigments.

Mass Spectrometry   In spite of the name, *mass spectrometry* (or *mass spectroscopy*) is not a spectroscopic method. Electromagnetic spectra are not involved. The so-called spectra are arrays of ionized, or otherwise charged, atoms or molecules separated on the basis of their mass-to-charge ratios.

In operation, neutral atoms or molecules from the sample enter an area of the mass spectrometer (MS) known as the ion source. Here, they are ionized and then accelerated by an electric field. Atoms can be ionized in a spark source, whereas molecules are energized by lower-energy processes such as electron impact, chemical ionization, or field desorption techniques. The resulting beam of ions then enters an area where the mass separation takes place. Different means of separation are used with different kinds of instruments. Thus, there are time-of-flight, quadrupole, and magnetic-sector instruments. In the magnetic-sector instrument, the beam of ions enters a magnetic field. The orientation of the beam to the field is such that the charged particles in the beam follow curved paths. Ions with higher charges and lesser masses follow highly curved paths. Those with lower charges and greater masses follow straighter paths. The mass-to-charge ratios of these ions can be determined from the paths they follow.

If a magnetic field of constant strength is used, the paths can be detected from the positions where the ions collide with a detecting surface, such as a photographic plate. When the field is varied in some uniform way with time, all ions can be made to sweep past a slit where a single detector is placed. The strength of the detector signal as a function of field strength, and thus mass-to-charge ratio, is plotted by the instrument.

MS instruments are becoming more widely employed in forensic laboratories for confirming drug identifications and for identifying accelerants in particularly difficult arson cases. For most forensic applications, the MS technique is used in conjunction with GC to yield a very powerful combination known as GC-MS. Here, the samples emerging from the GC are directly introduced into the MS source so that a complete mass spectrum can be obtained on each component of the sample separated by GC. MS also has potential for becoming a valuable individualization tool in criminalistics.

BIOLOGICAL METHODS

Morphological Methods

Since classification systems used in biology are based largely on a detailed consideration and comparison of morphological characteristics, it is not surprising that biological identifications often depend upon morphological observation. These may be macroscopic studies on large specimens using the naked eye, or they may be done with small samples utilizing microscopical observations. If the material under study is itself not microscopic, both approaches may be used. However, for very small organisms or samples, the choice is obviously limited. In difficult identifications, other methods such as staining and chemical tests may be used to augment the morphological observations. Quick, presumptive chemical tests are also sometimes used to screen samples in order to reserve certain time-consuming morphological examinations for those specimens that require them.

Biochemical Methods

Biochemistry can be defined as the chemistry of biological systems or, more simply, as the chemistry of life processes. The reactions, syntheses, and breakdown of biochemicals, such as carbohydrates, lipids, proteins, and nucleic acids, and their organization and function in living systems are the subject of biochemistry. One of the most important aspects of the field is the study of *enzymes* and of enzyme-catalyzed reactions.

Enzymes are proteins which have the special function of serving as biological *cat-*

alysts. Catalysts themselves are not unique to biochemistry. Various catalysts are widely used in other fields of chemistry and in industry. A number of industrial catalysts are used, for example, in petroleum refining. Platinum and palladium metals coated in thin layers on ceramic beads are the basis of catalytic converters used to reduce exhaust emissions from automobiles. In general, catalysts speed up chemical reactions. Thus, a reaction which might take place in days or weeks could be speeded up so that it would occur in only a few minutes if an appropriate catalyst were used. Unlike a reactant, a catalyst is not consumed or altered in the reaction. Although certain reactions can be greatly accelerated by the use of proper catalysts, the reaction has to be possible in the first place. A reaction which will not proceed at all under normal conditions will not be aided by a catalyst. Consider a possible but slow reaction: the oxidation of sugar to carbon dioxide and water, which takes place imperceptibly slowly at normal environmental temperatures. Sugar can be burned at high temperatures to give off energy, however, so the reaction is possible. A sugar cube placed in a flame will burn, but with some difficulty. If a catalyst, like cigarette ash, is added, the cube will burn quite readily. This catalyst seems to have no effect at room temperature. But the room-temperature reaction can be made to take place at appreciably faster rates in the presence of enzymes from yeast or other cells. The enzymes enable this, and other reactions, to take place at high enough rates to maintain life processes.

Enzymes are usually very specific catalysts, most being tailor-made for a particular reaction. Thousands of different enzymes are necessary to make life possible. Each is a highly refined catalyst designed for a specific function. If the only way for our bodies to obtain energy from foods such as sugars were to burn them literally, the cells would have to operate at unrealistically high temperatures. Thus, nature has designed enzymes to make such life-sustaining reactions possible at body temperatures.

Many biochemical methods used in forensic science are designed to test for the presence of particular enzymes, or make use of specific enzymes to test for some other substance. Examples of such tests are found in Chapters 9 and 10 on blood and body fluids.

Certain chromatographic techniques were mentioned previously in connection with column chromatography. These are particularly useful in separating and purifying the very large and complex molecules which are important in biochemistry.

Another important separation technique in biochemistry is *electrophoresis* (Figure 3-11). This procedure can be used to separate large molecules on the basis of their net charge differences. Sample molecules are placed into a stabilizing medium across which an electric field can be applied. They will migrate toward the pole (+ or −) opposite to their own charge. Under a given set of conditions, many of the sample molecules will migrate at different rates, thus bringing about their separation. Most electrophoretic techniques used in forensic science are carried out in stabilizing support media, such as hydrolyzed starch, agarose or polyacrylamide gels, or cellulose acetate. An important application of electrophoresis in forensic science is in isoenzyme and serum-protein typing; this is discussed in Chapter 9.

A somewhat related technique, called *isoelectric focusing,* is now being used in

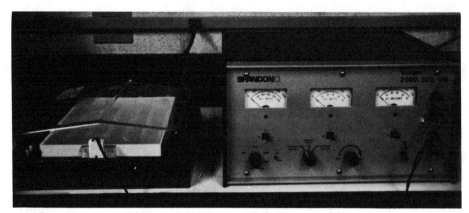

FIGURE 3-11
Electrophoresis apparatus, with tank (left) and power supply (right). *(Courtesy of Julie Bremser, University of New Haven.)*

forensic serology for certain enzyme and serum-protein separations. In this technique, special carrier molecules are added to the medium across which electric current is applied, and separation takes place according to the isoelectric points of the sample molecules. This technique is further discussed in Chapter 9. Sometimes, separations can be obtained using isoelectric focusing which cannot be obtained as readily by conventional electrophoretic procedures.

Immunological Methods

When an individual is exposed to a bacterium or virus which can cause disease, part of the body's defensive response consists of developing *antibodies,* which recognize and disable the foreign organism without harming normal body tissues. Antibodies are special protein molecules which will specifically attach themselves to certain structural configurations on the surface of the invading organism. These configurations are known as *antigenic sites.* In this case, the foreign organism could be called the *antigen.* Antigens can also be large molecules which are recognized by the animal body as "foreign" or "non-self." Antigens, in general, may be defined as agents or molecules which will induce an animal body to elicit antibodies specific for the inducing agent or molecule. The field of study that deals with antigen-antibody reactions is called *immunology.*

The importance of immunology in medical science is clear. Much of the success of modern medicine in almost eliminating the devastating epidemics of recorded history is attributable to: (1) knowledge developed in the wake of the germ theory of disease, which led to a revolution in sanitary practices, and (2) advances in immunology that have led to the development of vaccines for most of the dreaded diseases of the past. Immunology is also important in understanding and treating allergies, and it has a promising role in cancer research.

The aspects of immunology that are of concern in forensic science have little to do with health or the control of diseases, although similar antigen-antibody reactions are involved. Forensic serologists use special antibody preparations known as *antisera* to test for specific antigens in unknown samples. Some kinds of antisera are prepared by injecting a particular antigen into an animal (often, a rabbit). The animal's immune system recognizes the injected antigen as foreign and begins to manufacture antibodies to it. After a period of several weeks, during which one or more "booster" injections of antigen may be given, serum is collected from the animal. It is purified and becomes the reagent antiserum. Such antiserum can then be used to test for the presence, in unknown samples, of the same type of antigen that caused its production. Several methods of using antisera to test unknown specimens are available and are discussed in Chapters 9 and 10. Antibodies prepared in animals are used extensively to determine the species of origin of blood, to identify certain body fluids, and to measure the amounts of hormones and drugs in body fluids and tissues by a technique called *radioimmunoassay* (RIA).

Not all the antibodies used in forensic science are made in animals. Some, particularly the ones used in blood typing, are obtained from human blood. These blood-grouping antisera are discussed further in Chapter 9.

The immunological methods are among the most powerful for dealing with many biological samples. They have the potential of being both very sensitive and very specific. All immunological methods involve tests with, or for, antigens or antibodies.

There are different types of antigens and different types of antibodies. Depending upon which ones are used, different reactions or effects are observed as the result of specific antigen-antibody reactions.

Serology is a term derived from the word *serum,* that part of the blood which contains the antibodies. Serology is a subfield of immunology, and is concerned with studies of human blood groups and various other antigens, particularly those associated with cell surfaces. Many of the methods discussed in Chapters 9 and 10 fall under the general heading of immunological methods.

MICROSCOPY AND MICROSCOPICAL METHODS

General Considerations

Microscopy is a very important tool in forensic science, and this fact is not always appreciated by people who are not forensic scientists. A casual visit to a crime laboratory would probably not change this impression to any great extent. The visitor would be surrounded by a number of modern analytical instruments. The size of some of these instruments and their sophisticated control panels can be quite impressive in comparison with the microscope, which may seem inconspicuous. A closer look at the laboratory operation, however, would probably allow the visitor to appreciate something of the intricate relationship between the microscope and other types of instrumentation employed in forensic practice. Most of the instruments discussed above are essential in a modern forensic science laboratory, but even the most versatile of them cannot rival the microscope in the range of physical-evidence problems for which it is useful.

It may be thought that the term *microscopy* refers only to the use of the microscope, but in fact it has a much broader meaning. Microscopy is an analytical approach in which some type (or types) of microscope is used in conjunction with any and all other types of appropriate analytical instrumentation. At least one kind of microscope plays a central role, even though it may not be used exclusively. In certain types of analysis, the microscope can be the only instrument required.

A surprisingly large number of determinations can be made with a microscope alone. This fact is not widely understood, even by many scientists. Any number of intricate and sophisticated qualitative determinations and quantitative measurements can be made on exceedingly small samples using microscopes. In those cases in which microscopes are used along with other types of instruments, the selection of the other instruments needed and the order in which they will be used often depends on the results of the microscopical examination. One of the major strengths of microscopy is the integration of microscopical and nonmicroscopical instrumentation in solving problems. The only limitation of the microscopical approach is that years of training and experience are required to become an accomplished microscopist. As a result, skilled microscopists are comparatively rare.

Many varieties and types of microscopes exist. Those which find extensive use in forensic laboratories are discussed below.

The Simple Microscope

A simple microscope is little more than a refined magnifying glass. Examples of simple microscopes include hand lenses, linen testers, and fingerprint magnifiers (Figure 3-12). These are small, portable, and easy to use in the field. In simple microscopes, unlike those discussed below, magnification takes place in a single stage. A virtual image, not a real one, is formed. The difference between real and virtual images is explained in the next section.

Nearly all modern simple microscopes are low-power types, although high-magnification designs are possible. More than 300 years ago, the famous Dutch microscopist Anton van Leeuwenhoek designed, built, and used simple microscopes with magnification powers of a few hundred times. The lens used for such a high-power microscope must be highly curved and thus very small. The higher the magnifying power desired, the smaller the lens must be. Some of the lenses used by van Leeuwenhoek were about the size of a pinhead. One major problem with high-power versions of the simple microscope design is that the devices are exceedingly difficult to use. With such designs, it is necessary to view the specimen through a lens placed a few millimeters from the eye. This requires a good deal of practice, patience, and skill. In addition, any minor imperfections in the eye itself are accentuated in attempts to view specimens with one of these small lenses placed so close to the eye.

FIGURE 3-12
A variety of simple microscopes. *1, 9,* transparent-base utility magnifiers. *4, 5,* inexpensive folding pocket magnifiers. Of particular value in forensic practice are: *3,* a fingerprint magnifier with reticle; *5,* a tripod magnifier; *6,* a linen tester for doing thread counts; *7,* a high-quality Coddington type folding pocket magnifier; and *8,* an adjustable-focus magnifier capable of accepting a range of measuring reticles. The latter can be used for making measurements of submillimeter objects at crime scenes. (*Courtesy of Philip C. Langellotti, John Jay College of Criminal Justice, The City University of New York.*)

For practical purposes, simple microscopes with magnifying powers above about 20 are not used.

The Biological Microscope

Most people think of this type of microscope when they hear the term *microscope.* Unlike the simple microscope, this type is a compound microscope, meaning that the magnification takes place in two stages. The enlarged image produced by one lens system (the objective) is magnified further by a second lens system (the ocular, or eyepiece). The objective produces a *real image* of the object; the ocular then treats this real image as an actual object, and forms an enlarged *virtual image* of it (Figure 3-13). This virtual image is like the one produced by a simple microscope. In fact,

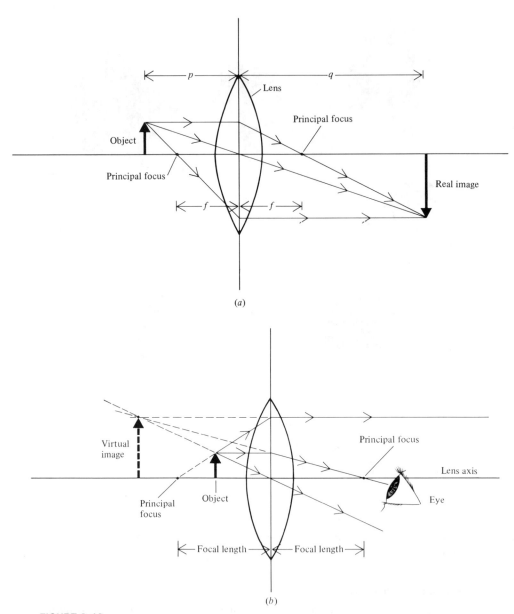

FIGURE 3-13
(*a*) Formation of a real image with a simple lens. This illustrates the principle of a projector or the objective lens of a microscope or telescope. *p* = object distance; *q* = image distance; *f* = focal length. The magnification *m* is given by the equation $m = q/p$. A useful relationship is $1/f = 1/p + 1/q$. (*b*) Formation of a virtual image with a simple lens. This is the principle of a hand lens or magnifier.

the ocular portion of a compound microscope acts like a low-power simple microscope. The real image produced by the objective, like any real image, is inverted and exists at a particular location in space on the opposite side of the lens from the specimen. As is the case with any real image, it can be projected onto a screen. The virtual image produced by a simple microscope, or by the ocular of a compound microscope, cannot be projected. Not being a real image, it does not exist at any location in space but appears to lie on the same side of the lens as the specimen (Figure 3-13).

The compound microscope has a very convenient and versatile design. All the remaining types of optical (light) microscopes discussed in this chapter are compound microscopes. The so-called biological microscope is the most common example of a compound microscope. A modern research biological microscope is illustrated in Figure 3-14.

Serologists may use this type of microscope for reading the results of dried bloodstain typing or for searching for spermatozoa in specimens from a rape case. Hair

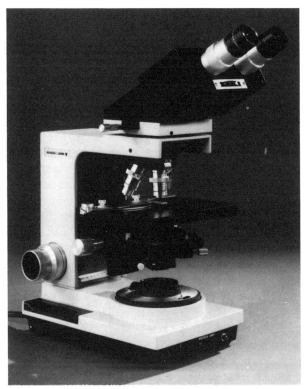

FIGURE 3-14
A compound microscope (biological). *(Bausch and Lomb Optical Company, Scientific Optical Products Division, Rochester, New York.)*

examiners may use it for examinations of scale pattern, medulla, and other comparison characteristics, and drug chemists use this instrument to examine the results of their crystal tests.

The two major types of illumination used with microscopes are *transmitted* and *incident*. For transparent or translucent specimens, the light is shined onto the specimen from below and transmitted through it to the objective lens. This type of illumination is called *transmitted light* illumination. In some instances, a so-called inverted microscope may be encountered. In this design, the objective is placed below the specimen, and therefore the light source must be placed above it for transmitted light illumination. This kind of illumination may work for samples which look opaque because microscopic samples are generally quite thin. Truly opaque specimens cannot be studied in detail by transmitted light. The illumination technique most appropriate for these samples is called *incident light*, or *vertical*, illumination. The light approaches the specimen from the general direction of the objective. A portion of the light striking the specimen is reflected toward the objective and used to form the image.

In normal, everyday life, we view the world around us in incident illumination. For this reason, it is generally easier to relate to the appearance of microscopic objects if incident illumination is employed with the microscope. Transmitted light is normally used to illuminate specimens, however, when the biological microscope is being used. The two types of illumination supply complementary information to the examiner.

The Stereoscopic Binocular Microscope

This type of microscope provides a three-dimensional image. In reality, it consists of two compound microscopes mounted side by side in the same housing. The three-dimensional imaging is possible because each eye is provided with its own individual microscope. This imaging in three dimensions is directly analogous to that employed in the binoculars used by bird watchers and others, in which two telescopes are mounted side by side in the same housing. The stereoscopic binocular microscope, or stereomicroscope, is used for low- to medium-power work only. Such an instrument is illustrated in Figure 3-15.

The stereoscopic binocular microscope should not be confused with binocular versions of biological or other types of compound microscopes. They are very different, and only in the case of the stereomicroscope is the image different in each ocular. In binocular types of compound microscopes, these images are intended to be identical, and the same information is presented to each eye. The extra ocular is provided only for convenience, because some people have difficulty using a single eye at a time. In the stereomicroscope, the two oculars are essential, since a complete compound microscope is required for each eye in order to obtain the three-dimensional image. Each microscope views the specimen from a slightly different perspective, in the same way as the two eyes look at the world with normal three-dimensional vision. With *binocular* compound microscopes, the light beams are split after leaving the single objective and diverted to each ocular. Since the same information from the objective is being relayed to each eyepiece, three-dimensional imaging is not possible.

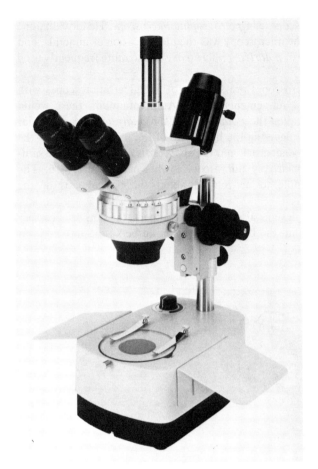

FIGURE 3-15
A stereomicroscope. *(Unitron Instruments, Inc., Plainview, New York.)*

Both transmitted and incident types of illumination (or even both at the same time) can be used with the stereomicroscope, but normally incident illumination is employed in forensic applications.

The stereomicroscope is used by forensic scientists in almost every specialty area, including questioned documents, firearms, toolmarks, trace evidence, and serology. Many preliminary examinations, as well as sorting and sampling operations, are carried out with the stereomicroscope.

The Polarized-Light Microscope

Although stereomicroscopes are applicable to a broad range of forensic problems, the polarized-light microscope is the most versatile of all for obtaining in-depth information from a sample, especially a sample of transfer or trace evidence. Mineralogists refer to this type of microscope as a *petrographic microscope.* Historically, one of the first uses of polarized-light microscopy was the identification of minerals, and of mineral grains in soil. The term *polarizing microscope* is also quite frequently used to refer to the same instrument.

The simplest polarizing microscopes are similar to biological microscopes with certain optical and mechanical refinements added. At a minimum, these would include two polarizing filters, called the *polarizer* and the *analyzer,* and a circular rotating stage. The polarizer is placed in the light path of the microscope below the sample (normally, beneath the condenser), and the analyzer is placed above the sample (above the objective). A polarizing microscope is shown in Figure 3-16. The rotating stage allows the sample to be rotated about the optical axis of the microscope.

Most polarizing microscope designs also include a compensator slot, or accessory slot, and an additional lens within the body tube which can be swung into and out

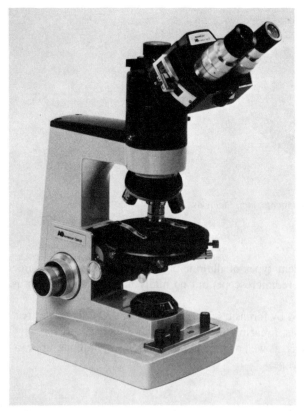

FIGURE 3-16
A polarizing microscope. *(American Optical Corporation, Scientific Instrument Division, Buffalo, New York.)*

of the light path. This extra lens, known as a Bertrand lens, is used in special examinations for studying the paths of rays of light at the rear of the objective. These special examinations are called *conoscopic observations,* and they are used to determine optical properties of crystalline forms of evidence (see Table 3-2). The compensator slot is placed between the objective and the analyzer. This slot allows special test devices to be inserted into the light path of the microscope during the examination of certain specimens. These devices are called *compensators.* They help in determining some of the optical properties of samples. As additional features are added to make even more refined polarizing microscope designs, the resemblance to the biological microscope diminishes.

Some determinations that can be made using the polarizing microscope are listed in Table 3-3. An examination of this list should convey an impression of the power of polarized-light microscopy. The list is not all-inclusive. With some further accessories for the microscope, an even greater number of determinations could be made.

The Comparison Microscope

Two different types of comparison microscopes are used in forensic laboratories. They are similar in optical design and general mechanical construction. They differ in the range of magnifying powers available and in the type of illumination employed. One type is used to compare opaque objects, such as bullets, cartridge cases, and toolmarks. Incident light is used with this type of comparison microscope. The other type of comparison microscope is generally equivalent to having two bio-

---

TABLE 3-3
PROPERTIES DETERMINABLE WITH THE
POLARIZED-LIGHT MICROSCOPE

Morphology
Color
Size
Particle size distribution
Refractive index (isotropic)
Dispersion
Crystal interfacial angles
Isotropic vs. anisotropic (birefringent)
Extinction angle
Uniaxial vs. biaxial
Sign of elongation
Optic sign
Pleochroic vs. nonpleochroic
Sign or absorption
Uniaxial refractive indices (2)
Biaxial refractive indices (3)
Optic angle
Optic axial dispersion

---

logical, or polarized-light, microscopes connected by a prism arrangement known as a comparison bridge. This bridge arrangement, used in both types of comparison microscopes, allows the fields of view from the two separate microscopes to be juxtaposed. They are separated by a fine line which divides the field of view into two semicircles. This line is generally movable, so that the sizes of the two fields can be varied at the expense of one another. Such a microscope can be extremely useful in the comparison of evidence like hairs and fibers. Moderate to high powers are available, and transmitted light is employed for illumination.

These two principal types of comparison microscopes are shown in Figure 3-17.

Electron Microscopes

Electron microscopes exist in two primary types. They differ in a way very roughly analogous to the way light microscopes differ according to the type of illumination used (incident and transmitted).

The first type of electron microscope is known as the *transmission electron microscope* (TEM). Commercial versions of TEMs have been in use for more than 40 years. The sample needed for TEM must be very thin, or a very thin "replica" of the sample must be examined. In a TEM, the electrons used in forming the image pass through the sample, like the light through transparent samples when transmitted light is used with the light microscope.

The other type of electron microscope, which can be used with thick three-dimensional samples, is known as the *scanning electron microscope* (SEM). In this arrangement, the electron beam does not pass through the sample. Instead, the electron beam in the instrument is scanned across the sample in a raster pattern, like that used in television sets. At each point where the electron beam strikes the sample, the electrons may be reflected or scattered off the surface, or may release secondary electrons from just beneath the surface of the specimen. Either back-scattered or secondary electrons can be used in the formation of the image.

Because relatively thick, three-dimensional samples can be examined, the SEM has a number of applications in forensic science. Extensive sample preparation, such as making thin sections or replicas, is not necessary with SEM (as it is for TEM). The only sample preparation that is sometimes required with SEM is the coating of nonmetallic samples with a very thin layer of conductive material (such as gold or carbon). This coating prevents the buildup of electric charge on the nonconductive sample surface. The coating is extremely thin and is applied by one of two vacuum-coating techniques known as vacuum evaporation and sputtering.

FIGURE 3-17
(*a*) A comparison microscope. This instrument is suitable for low-power comparison microscopy of opaque objects such as toolmarks. Note the fiber optic incident light illuminators. This microscope also has provision for low-power illumination of transparent objects. (*Unitron Instruments, Inc., Plainview, New York.*) (*b*) A transmitted-light comparison microscope. This type of comparison microscope is suitable for use with trace evidence such as hairs and fibers. (*American Optical Corporation, Scientific Instrument Division, Buffalo, New York.*)

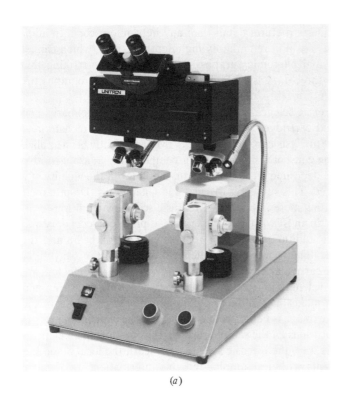

(a)

(b)

The SEM can resolve finer structural detail than any light microscope. In addition, SEM photomicrographs exhibit remarkably high depths of field, which cannot even be approached in normal photomicrographs. The images are so striking that they almost appear to be three-dimensional. Examples of SEM micrographs are shown in Chapter 6, in Figure 6-1(b)–(d).

The uses of SEM in forensic science range from examinations of toolmarks and the markings on bullets and cartridge cases to studies of the surfaces of hairs and small particles. The particle analysis capability of the SEM has recently been applied to the problem of identifying gunshot residue. A major component of gunshot residue is small particles which are deposited on surfaces (skin, clothing) in the vicinity of a firearm when it is discharged. This subject is discussed in Chapter 14. Despite their high cost, SEMs are becoming more important in forensic science laboratories.

When the electron beam in an SEM strikes the sample, it produces secondary and back-scattered electrons. In addition, this interaction of the electron beam and the sample also produces x-rays. The energy (or wavelength) of each of the x-rays produced is characteristic of a particular element in the sample. If special detectors are added to the SEM, the wavelength of all the emitted x-rays can be measured and recorded. This information makes it possible to obtain an elemental analysis of the sample at the same time the image is being produced. In fact, the elemental analysis can be related to specific locations on the sample surface, thus producing an elemental distribution map. In this way, the forensic scientist can learn the location of and the concentration of elements within a sample, and this information can then be correlated with the SEM image. These data are considerably more valuable than having a knowledge of the elemental composition only. The technique has proved to be very valuable in gunshot-residue analysis. Two kinds of attachments for the SEM allow elemental mapping: (1) energy-dispersive x-ray spectrometers and (2) wavelength-dispersive x-ray spectrometers. Either can be added to almost any high-quality SEM. Specially designed SEMs, which include the spectrometers as part of the design, are called *electron microprobes*.

PRESENT-DAY CAPABILITIES

We have mentioned the three primary activities of the forensic laboratory: identification, individualization, and reconstruction. At the present time, the first of these is more highly developed and poses fewer problems than the other two.

True individualizations are possible only in cases involving certain physical matches and patterned markings, such as toolmarks and fingerprints. Available chemical techniques, sophisticated as they are, are not sufficient to individualize evidence based upon composition. More research and development are needed before this can be achieved, and it is not likely that the problems will be solved quickly. In certain areas, such as in individualizing dried bloodstains, much progress has been made in recent years, but hairs, for example, are still compared by the same basic morphological techniques that have been used for over 50 years. These comparisons can yield useful results in experienced and competent hands, but they leave much to be desired.

The number and quality of reconstructions that contribute to solutions at both investigative and adjudicative stages of cases could be greatly improved. More laboratory criminalists need to become involved in reconstructions, and better communication between scene and laboratory personnel is essential.

It is necessary to distinguish between what we sometimes call the "state of the art" in physical-evidence analysis and the practical, real-world analyses that are carried out in an average laboratory. The state of the art refers to the analyses that *could be* conducted, given a completely ideal situation. There are few laboratories that have the resources, trained personnel, and time to carry out state-of-the-art analyses on every different kind of physical evidence.

In the preceding two chapters, we noted that many laboratories are not well supported and are overburdened with large numbers of routine cases. This situation does not allow for appropriate resources to be expended on individualization and reconstruction problems. In addition, reconstructions require effective coordination between crime-scene searches, physical-evidence collection, and laboratory analysis, and this coordination is often inadequate.

The potential value of forensic science in criminal cases is a long way from being realized, even though forensic laboratories have been around for 50 or 60 years. Improvements are possible at every stage—search, recognition, collection, analysis, interpretation, and presentation of findings in court. As these improvements take place, more and more laboratories will be able to provide more and better services for the investigation and disposition of cases.

In the chapters which follow, many different analytical approaches and techniques applicable to a particular type of evidence are described. Not every laboratory has the capability to carry out every technique or procedure. Some laboratories will be much stronger in certain types of analyses than in others.

STUDY QUESTIONS

1 What is a physical match? What kinds of evidence are suited to physical matching?

2 Name the three kinds of markings that can be compared on physical evidence. How do these differ?

3 What is a physical property?

4 Name several physical properties, and explain what each of them is.

5 How can physical properties be used in the analysis of physical evidence?

6 What are the principal applications of photography in forensic science?

7 What is chemistry? What is analytical chemistry?

8 What is an atom? An element? An isotope? A compound? A molecule?

9 What does ionization mean?

10 What is the importance of hydrogen ions in chemistry? What is the pH scale, and how does it work?

11 What is the difference between organic and inorganic chemistry?

12 What are chemical identifications? Name several ways in which these are done.

13 What is the difference between a qualitative and a quantitative test?

14 Name four chemical separation techniques and briefly describe how each works.

15 What is chromatography? Name several different kinds of chromatography, and briefly explain how each works.

16 What are spectroscopic methods? Explain the underlying principle on which they are based.

17 Name four spectroscopic methods and briefly explain how each works.

18 What is neutron activation analysis? How does it work? How is it used in forensic science?

19 What is mass spectrometry? How does it work? Is it a spectroscopic method?

20 What is x-ray diffraction, and how does it work? How is it used in forensic science?

21 Name several biological methods used in forensic sciences.

22 What is an enzyme? How are enzymes used in forensic sciences?

23 What is immunology? Name several immunological methods and explain how they are used in forensic science.

24 Why is microscopy important in forensic science?

25 Name four types of microscopes. Explain briefly how they are different from one another and how each might be used in forensic science.

26 What is a scanning electron microscope? How is it used in forensic science? How does it differ from a transmission electron microscope?

REFERENCES AND FURTHER READING

Bauman, R. P.: *Absorption Spectroscopy,* Wiley, New York, 1962.

Chamot, E. M., and C. W. Mason: *Handbook of Chemical Microscopy,* 3d ed., vol. I, 1958; 2d ed., vol. II, 1940; Wiley, New York.

Conway, E. J.: *Microdiffusion Analysis and Volumetric Error,* Chemical Publishing, New York, 1963.

Ewing, G. W.: *Instrumental Methods of Chemical Analysis,* 4th ed., McGraw-Hill, New York, 1975.

Kirk, P. L.: "Instrumentation in Criminalistics," *Journal of the Forensic Science Society,* vol. 10, pp. 97–107, 1970.

McCrone, W. C., and J. G. Delly: *The Particle Atlas,* 2d ed., vol. 1, Ann Arbor Science, Ann Arbor, Mich. 1973.

Saferstein, R.: *Criminalistics—An Introduction to Forensic Science,* 2d ed., Prentice-Hall, Englewood Cliffs, N.J., 1981.

Schaeffer, H. F.: *Microscopy for Chemists,* Dover, New York, 1966.

Smith, R. N.: "Forensic Applications of High Performance Liquid Chromatography"; R. Saferstein. "Forensic Applications of Mass Spectrometry"; and P. R. De Forest: "Foundations of Forensic Microscopy"; all in R. Saferstein (ed.), *Forensic Science Handbook,* Prentice-Hall, Englewood Cliffs, N.J. 1982.

Walls, H. J.: *Forensic Science—An Introduction to Scientific Crime Detection,* 2d ed., Praeger, New York, 1974.

Willard, H. H., L. L. Merritt, J. A. Dean, and F. Settle: *Instrumental Methods of Analysis,* 6th ed., Van Nostrand, New York, 1981.

Williams, R. L.: "Forensic Science—The Present and Future," *Analytical Chemistry,* vol. 45, pp. 1076A–1089A, 1973.

CHAPTER 4

ARSON ACCELERANTS
AND EXPLOSIVES

INTRODUCTION

Arson has become one of the most expensive crimes in the United States. About one-third of all building fires are attributed to arson, and it may account for losses of more than $1.5 billion a year! The incidence of arson is growing at an ever-increasing rate. It is estimated that there were 1000 deaths and about 10,000 injuries attributable to arson in one recent year.

Arson is a complex crime and often presents difficulties during investigation and prosecution. In 1980, for example, there were 6820 incendiary and suspicious fires in Connecticut, but only 500 arrests were made. Only 72 people were convicted of arson. One of the difficulties is proof of the commission of the offense because of the extensive destruction of the arson scene.

It is a common belief that the forensic scientist's main function in arson investigation is limited to the detection and demonstration of accelerants. There are many types of physical evidence present at arson scenes, however, and the laboratory could play a greater and more active role in arson investigation.

Explosions, like arson fires, often cause extensive destruction and damage to property. It is rather common to find an explosion connected with a fire. The explosion may be the means of setting the fire, or it may be the result of it. The techniques for investigation in arson and explosion cases are, therefore, similar in many ways.

In this chapter, the basic theory of fires and explosions, details of scene investigations, the recognition and collection of various types of physical evidence, and laboratory techniques used in recovering, analyzing, and identifying accelerants and explosive residues will be discussed.

CHEMISTRY OF FIRE AND FUELS

To investigate a fire scene and collect evidence effectively, a fire-scene investigator should have some understanding of the chemistry of fires and of fuels. This knowledge is further essential for the interpretation of the scene and for reconstruction of the events.

Chemistry of Combustion

Fire or *combustion* is a chemical reaction involving the oxidation of a substance known as a *fuel.* The fuel and the substance causing the oxidation (the *oxidant*) combine to release energy and to produce combustion products. A reaction in which energy is given off is called *exothermic,* whereas one which requires the continuous input of energy to sustain it is called *endothermic.*

Fire or combustion is, therefore, an exothermic oxidation reaction of a fuel, in which energy is released in the form of heat and light. The exact nature of the chemical products of combustion depends on the makeup of the fuel and the conditions of combustion. Most of the fuels in common fires are composed primarily of organic molecules containing carbon and hydrogen, and the oxidized forms of these two elements are produced when these fuels are burned. The burning of pure hydrogen produces water, according to the reaction

$$2H_2 \text{ (gas)} + O_2 \text{ (gas)} \rightarrow 2H_2O \text{ (gas)}$$

For the combustion of pure carbon, the product is carbon dioxide as shown in the reaction

$$C \text{ (solid)} + O_2 \text{ (gas)} \rightarrow CO_2 \text{ (gas)}$$

Since most fuels of concern in fire investigation are organic compounds (containing both hydrogen and carbon) or complex mixtures of organic compounds, water and carbon dioxide are the major products of combustion. Methane, the chief constituent of natural gas, has the following structure:

The hydrogen atoms in this molecule are evenly distributed in three-dimensional space about the central carbon atom and can be viewed as being located at the corners of a four-sided pyramid (known as a regular tetrahedron). Methane is the simplest member of a series of hydrocarbons known as *alkanes* (formerly, paraffins). This series contains the common fuels propane and butane. Simplified formulas, called *empirical* formulas, which indicate the proportions of hydrogen and carbon (and other elements where present) in the molecule but do not show the arrangement of atoms in space, can be written for each of these compounds. The empirical formula for methane (whose structural formula is written above) is CH_4, that for propane is C_3H_8, and that for butane is C_4H_{10} (see Table 3-2). Methane burns according to the equation

$$CH_4 + 2O_2 \rightarrow CO_2 + 2H_2O$$

Organic compounds containing atoms in addition to hydrogen and carbon burn in a similar fashion, but oxidized forms of some of the other elements will then appear among the combustion products. If the only element present other than hydrogen and carbon is oxygen, complete oxidation will yield water and carbon dioxide only. The burning of ethyl alcohol, or grain alcohol (C_2H_6O), proceeds according to the equation

$$C_2H_6O + 3O_2 \rightarrow 2CO_2 + 3H_2O$$

Similarly, a balanced equation for the combustion of a carbohydrate, such as the simple sugar glucose ($C_6H_{12}O_6$), is

$$C_6H_{12}O_6 + 6O_2 \rightarrow 6CO_2 + 6H_2O$$

Glucose itself is not a frequent fuel in fires, but cellulose, the major constituent of cotton, wood, and paper, is made up of a large number of glucose molecules attached together. The formation of the linkage between two glucose molecules is accompanied by the loss of a molecule of water for each bond formed. Thus, the empirical formula for cellulose is written $(C_6H_{10}O_5)_n$, where n represents the number of glucose molecules attached to each other. Thousands of them are involved in forming a long-chain cellulose molecule. The exact number depends on the source of the cellulose (cotton, pine, oak, etc.) and is often not known. A balanced equation representing the burning of cellulose can be written as

$$(C_6H_{10}O_5)_n + 6nO_2 \rightarrow 6nCO_2 + 5nH_2O$$

Equations for the oxidation reactions of several other common and simple fuels are shown in Table 4-1.

Most liquid fuels like gasoline, kerosene, and fuel oil are mixtures of many different hydrocarbons, and the exact composition is often not specified. It costs considerably more money to prepare pure hydrocarbons, and their use as fuels would be prohibitively expensive. For the purposes of approximations in certain calculations, gasoline may be assumed to be octane, C_8H_{18} (an alkane). In fact, an isomer of octane known as isooctane is the basis of the *octane* rating system used with gasoline for engines. This compound has an octane number defined as 100.

TABLE 4-1
OXIDATION REACTIONS OF SIMPLE FUELS

Methane	$CH_4 + 2O_2 \rightarrow CO_2 + 2H_2O$
Ethane	$C_2H_6 + 3.5O_2 \rightarrow 2CO_2 + 3H_2O$
Propane	$C_3H_8 + 5O_2 \rightarrow 3CO_2 + 4H_2O$
Butane	$C_4H_{10} + 6.5O_2 \rightarrow 4CO_2 + 5H_2O$
Pentane	$C_5H_{12} + 8O_2 \rightarrow 5CO_2 + 6H_2O$
Hexane	$C_6H_{14} + 9.5O_2 \rightarrow 6CO_2 + 7H_2O$
Heptane	$C_7H_{16} + 11O_2 \rightarrow 7CO_2 + 8H_2O$
Octane	$C_8H_{18} + 12.5O_2 \rightarrow 8CO_2 + 9H_2O$
Ethylene	$C_2H_4 + 3O_2 \rightarrow 2CO_2 + 2H_2O$
Acetylene	$C_2H_2 + 2.5O_2 \rightarrow 2CO_2 + H_2O$
Methanol	$CH_3OH + 1.5O_2 \rightarrow CO_2 + 2H_2O$
Ethanol	$C_2H_5OH + 3O_2 \rightarrow 2CO_2 + 3H_2O$
Propanol	$C_3H_7OH + 4.5O_2 \rightarrow 3CO_2 + 4H_2O$
Ethyl ether	$C_4H_{10}O + 6O_2 \rightarrow 4CO_2 + 5H_2O$
Propyl ether	$C_6H_{14}O + 9O_2 \rightarrow 6CO_2 + 7H_2O$
Acetone	$C_3H_6O + 4O_2 \rightarrow 3CO_2 + 3H_2O$
Methyl ethyl ketone	$C_4H_8O + 5.5O_2 \rightarrow 4CO_2 + 4H_2O$
Ethyl acetate	$C_4H_8O_2 + 5O_2 \rightarrow 4CO_2 + 4H_2O$

Types of Combustion

Two types of combustion can be distinguished, and these are called *flaming* and *glowing*.

Flaming Combustion   In the equation for the oxidation of hydrogen, it can be seen that both the fuel (hydrogen) and the oxidant (oxygen) are in the gaseous state. Thus, the process can be described as a gas-gas or gas-phase reaction. If both components were completely mixed in the right proportions prior to ignition, a very rapid reaction (an explosion) would take place upon ignition. If the rate of supply of fuel were limited in some way, the rate of combustion would be controlled, and an observable flame (like that from a torch) would be noted. A gas explosion and a torch flame are both examples of gas-phase reactions. Flames are produced in both cases. The one in the gas-phase explosion is a spherical flame that spreads outward very rapidly from the point of ignition to the outer boundary of the mixture. Its progress is usually too rapid to be seen. The flame in a torch, or burner, is easy to observe. Flames are a distinguishing characteristic of gas-phase combustion. The combustion reaction is taking place within the flame. The presence of a flame shows that the combustion of a gaseous fuel is taking place, and in fact, flaming combustion cannot take place without a gaseous fuel.

When a liquid fuel like alcohol, lighter fluid, or gasoline is burned, a flame is also observed. Knowing that flaming combustion can take place only with gaseous fuels tells us that such a liquid must be vaporized or volatilized to a gas before it can be burned. Some of the heat produced by a burning liquid fuel is fed back to the liquid to heat it and produce more gaseous fuel (vapor) which supports the flames. If the volatilization is stopped, the combustion ceases. A tactic that is sometimes used in fighting fires in large fuel oil tanks is the recirculation of cold fuel from the bottom of the tank to cool the surface, thus reducing volatilization and the size of the flames. If the fuel in the lower part of the tank is sufficiently cool, and if the circulation process can be continued for a long enough period, the fire can be extinguished.

Flaming combustion with a solid fuel such as wood is harder to understand. Wood does not "evaporate." It cannot be volatilized in the true sense of the word. Yet, there must be some way of supplying gaseous fuel to the flames. When such a solid fuel is heated, irreversible chemical changes take place, resulting in decomposition of the wood. New compounds which did not exist in the unheated sample are produced. Many of these compounds would be gases or liquids at room temperature but are gases at the elevated temperatures at which they are produced. This process, which has variously been called *thermal decomposition, destructive distillation,* or *pyrolysis,* produces the fuel necessary for flaming combustion with solid fuels like wood, cloth, paper, and plastics. Some of the heat of combustion is fed back to the solid to pyrolyze it further, thereby producing a continuing supply of gaseous fuel for the flames.

Glowing Combustion   Solid fuels that cannot be pyrolyzed to produce a sufficient quantity of flammable gases to sustain a flame are not capable of undergoing flaming combustion. Pure carbon (an element) or charcoal (nearly pure carbon) cannot be broken down any further by heat. In addition, carbon cannot be volatilized at reasonable temperatures. When charcoal is raised to a high enough temperature, however, an exothermic oxidation reaction will start (an equation for the oxidation of carbon was shown above). This reaction will take place at the surface of the solid. As one layer of the surface is consumed, a new layer is exposed and the reaction continues until the fuel is exhausted. This is a gas-solid surface reaction between the oxygen of the air and the solid fuel, and it is a good example of *glowing combustion.* The reaction rate is limited by the surface area or surface-to-volume ratio of the fuel and the availability of oxygen. Smaller particles of charcoal will be consumed more rapidly than larger pieces under the same conditions. Extremely rapid reactions are possible when it is finely divided and mixed with air, and this fact explains charcoal dust explosions. If the surface-to-volume ratio is smaller (larger chunks of fuel), the reaction rate can be increased only by providing better access to air. Moving a current of air over a charcoal fire will accelerate the combustion by providing a better exchange of reactants and products at the surface where the reaction is taking place. Thus, blowing on a charcoal fire makes it hotter. Forced-air charcoal fires were the source of heat for smelters, blacksmiths, and other metal workers from antiquity until the industrial revolution.

Pyrolyzable solid fuels such as cloth, wood, and paper may undergo glowing combustion when the conditions are insufficient to support flaming. If the access to air is limited, for example, too little heat may be available to produce a sufficient quantity of pyrolysis products to support flaming combustion. The combustion reaction then takes place at the fuel surface. This form of glowing combustion is often referred to as *smoldering*. If the conditions change so that a smoldering fire has access to a better supply of oxygen, the reaction rate can increase, producing more heat, which may be sufficient to allow for flaming combustion.

Oxidation in a charcoal fire which has an insufficient air supply may take place in two stages, according to the reactions

$$2C + O_2 \rightarrow 2CO$$
$$2CO + O_2 \rightarrow 2CO_2$$

The compound symbolized by the chemical formula CO is carbon monoxide. The carbon monoxide in the first reaction may diffuse away from the surface of the charcoal before it encounters a sufficient supply of oxygen to allow it to be burned further. Small flames seen in pure charcoal fires are the result of burning carbon monoxide. If the carbon monoxide drifts too far away from the heat of the fire before it finds oxygen, the temperature may be inadequate to ignite it. In such a case this highly toxic gas may accumulate. It is for this reason that poorly ventilated charcoal fires are hazardous indoors.

Carbon monoxide produced in structural fires may drift through passageways, sewers, or conduits to locations remote from the fire itself, where it can present a toxic hazard. If an ignition source is present, CO gas may ignite to produce an explosion, or it may ignite and burn with a blue flame if the oxygen supply is limited but continuous. Faint blue flames from this source have been reported at locations some distance away from the main fire on several occasions and have often puzzled fire investigators.

Conditions for Combustion

Several conditions must be met in order to have sustained combustion. Recognition of them is helpful in understanding the behavior of fire and is certainly essential in investigating and evaluating ways of extinguishing fires. Several models have been proposed to illustrate these conditions.

The fire triangle [Figure 4-1(a)] is a model that recognizes three primary factors as necessary for sustained combustion: air (oxygen), fuel, and heat. Removal of any one of these will result in rapid extinguishment of the fire. The effectiveness of water as an extinguishing agent lies in its ability to remove heat.

Water absorbs heat by being warmed up itself by the fire. It takes more heat to raise the temperature of a given quantity of water one degree than it takes for any other common substance. In other words, the *specific heat* of water is higher than it is for most other materials. The specific heat of water is defined as being either 1 Btu/(lb · °F) or as 1 cal/(g · °C). Considerably more heat is absorbed by water if it is vaporized (heat of vaporization). About 540 cal of additional heat is required to vaporize 1 g of water which has already been heated to its boiling point (100 °C). Thus, the *heat of vaporization* of water is about 540 cal/g.

Placing a heavy cloth or a layer of foam over a fire extinguishes it by depriving it

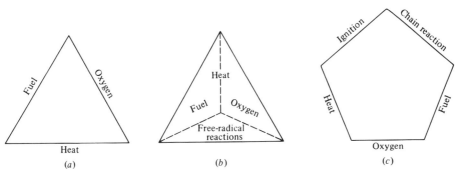

FIGURE 4-1
(*a*) The fire triangle. (*b*) The fire tetrahedron. (*c*) The fire pentagon.

of adequate oxygen. Containing a forest fire by bulldozing a swath around it can contribute to extinguishment by limiting or removing fuel. Similarly, structural fires can be contained by the use of automatic fire doors. Most means of extinguishment can be classified under a heading that corresponds to one of three legs of the fire triangle. However, one more modern means of extinguishment is not adequately explained by any of these three factors.

Certain chemical extinguishing agents, particularly halogenated hydrocarbons (hydrocarbons containing atoms of fluorine, chlorine, bromine, or iodine as part of the molecule) are effective well beyond their ability to cool the fire or to displace oxygen. For this reason, some writers have proposed a fire tetrahedron [Figure 4-1 (*b*)]. Three of the four faces of this solid figure correspond to the three legs of the fire triangle. The fourth has to do with *free-radical chain reactions*. These reactions take place in the flame itself and are necessary for flaming combustion. A free radical is an unstable molecular fragment which serves as an intermediate in the combustion reaction. The equations above which describe the oxidation of various fuels show only reactants and products. Most reactions proceed from reactants to products through one or a series of steps involving intermediates such as free radicals. The free radicals produced in combustion of various fuels collide and react with more stable molecules to form more free radicals, which are then available to attack additional stable molecules and sustain the chain reaction. Chemicals which interfere with the free-radical chain reaction are effective at suppressing flame and thus extinguishing fires.

The fire triangle and the fire tetrahedron explain the factors necessary for sustained combustion, but they ignore factors related to the initiation of a fire. For this reason, a fire pentagon [Figure 4-1(*c*)] has been proposed to take into account the importance of an ignition source.

Types of Fuels

Based on the nature of the chemistry of fire developed above, we can divide fuels into four major categories: *gases, liquids, pyrolyzable solids,* and *nonpyrolyzable sol-*

TABLE 4-2
PROPERTIES OF DIFFERENT CLASSES OF FUELS

Gases	Liquids	Pyrolyzable solids	Nonpyrolyzable solids
Vapor density	Vapor density	Ignition temperature*	Ignition temperature
Ignition temperature	Ignition temperature	Autoignition temperature	Heat of combustion
Heat of combustion	Flash point	Heat of combustion	Surface area
Flammable range	Fire point	Surface area	Porosity
Lower flammable limit	Boiling point	Porosity	Density
Upper flammable limit	Heat of combustion	Density	Moisture content
	Heat of vaporization	Moisture content	
	Flammable range		
	Lower flammable limit		
	Upper flammable limit		

*This term has a different meaning when applied to fuels in this category from what it does when applied to fuels in the other three categories (see text).

ids. Fuels in each of these categories have a set of properties that are of direct relevance to the fire investigator. These properties are summarized in Table 4-2.

Combustion Properties of Fuels

The meaning of a particular term applied to fuels in one category may be quite different from that of the same term when it is applied to fuels in another category. The term *ignition temperature* is a noteworthy example. When applied to a gas, a liquid vapor, or a nonpyrolyzable solid, this term refers to the temperature necessary to get the combustion reaction started. A potentially flammable mixture of methane in air will be stable indefinitely unless it is ignited. There must be initial investment of energy to get the reaction started before the large amounts of chemical energy can be released. In this sense, ignition temperature is similar to a chemical concept known as *activation energy*. Many exothermic chemical reactions require an input of activation energy in order to get started. Once the reaction is going, a small proportion of the energy being released is sufficient to sustain it.

Ignition temperature has a completely different meaning when it is applied to fuels in the pyrolyzable solid class. Here, it refers to the temperature necessary to decompose the fuel to yield ignitable vapor. Such a vapor could be ignited by a spark and start a fire. At a somewhat higher temperature the vapors themselves will ignite and the pyrolyzable solid will burst into flame. This is called the *self-ignition* or *autoignition* temperature.

An important measurable property of liquid fuels is *flash point,* the lowest temperature of the liquid at which enough volatilization will take place to produce an ignitable vapor near its surface. When a liquid is below its flash point, a spark or flame can be brought near its surface and no fire will result. Flash points, boiling points, and ignition temperatures of several representative fuels are given in Table

TABLE 4-3
PROPERTIES OF REPRESENTATIVE FUELS
IN ORDER OF INCREASING BOILING POINT

Material or fuel	Flash point, °F	Boiling point, °F	Flammable range, %	Ingnition temperature, °F
Hydrogen	very low	−423	4.1–74	1075
Carbon monoxide	very low	−313	12–75	1290
Methane	very low	−258	5.5–14	1200
Ethylene (ethene)	very low	−155	3–34	1010
Ethane	very low	−126	3.2–12.5	986
Acetylene (ethyne)	very low	−119	2.5–80	635
n-Propane	very low	−44	2.4–9.5	874
n-Butane	−216	31	1.6–6.5	806
Ethyl ether (diethyl ether)	−49	94	1.8–~50	355
n-Pentane	−40	97	1.4–8.0	588
Petroleum ether (benzine)	−40	95–175*	1.4–5.9	475
Gasoline	−50	102–230*	1.3–~6	495
Acetone	−4	134	2.2–13	1000
Methyl alcohol (methanol)	54	148	6–36.5	880
n-Hexane	−7	156	1.2–6.9	477
Ethyl alcohol (ethanol)	48	173	3.3–19	800
Methylethyl ketone (2-butanone)	35	175	1.8–11.5	960
Benzene	50	176	1.4–8	1075
Isopropanol (2-propanol)	53	180	2–12	852
n-Heptane	30	209	1.1–6.7	~450
Toluene	50	231	1.3–7	1025
Butyl alcohol (n-butanol)	97	243	1.5–11	695
n-Octane	56	258	0.9–~6	450
Cellosolve (2-ethoxyethanol)	111	275	2.6–16	460
Naphtha (Stoddard solvent)	100–110	300–400*	1.1–~6	450
Kerosene	110–185	300–600*	1.2–~6	490
Ethylene glycol	232	388	3.2–?	775

*Liquids which are complex mixtures have a boiling range rather than a boiling point. In addition, mixtures from different sources are often not the same composition. Thus, differences in both boiling range and flash point can be expected with such mixtures.

Note: The data in this table were taken from several sources. These included The Merck Index, Merck and Co., Rahway, N.J.; the Handbook of Chemistry and Physics, Chemical Rubber Co., Cleveland, Ohio; and "Properties of Flammable Liquids, Gases and Solids," Loss Prevention Bulletin No. 36-10, Factory Mutual Engineering Division, Boston, 1950. These figures should be taken as approximations. The various sources did not always agree on the exact values, although agreement on the boiling points of pure compounds was good. Most of the flash-point figures are "closed-cup" values. Others were not specified. Closed-cup values are always somewhat lower than open-cup values.

Notice how flash points roughly parallel boiling points. The correlation is particularly good with chemical compounds within a single class. Generally, deviations from a good correlation are caused by differences in other combustion properties. This is particularly true of the influence of the lower flammable limit. The correlation does not extend to ignition temperature. In fact, within the same family of compounds a negative correlation is seen.

4-3. A container of liquid cannot burn unless at least the portion of the liquid fuel near the surface is raised above the flash point. Lighted matches dropped into a pool of kerosene on a lab bench will be extinguished, because at room temperature kerosene is below its flash point and an ignitable vapor is not present. If a cloth or paper wick is placed in the pool, a match can be used to ignite the kerosene in the wick. In this case the limited volume of liquid fuel in one area of the wick is heated above its flash point, and flaming combustion can take place in this location. The heat produced by the flame will volatilize more fuel as it is drawn into the wick, but the fire will be confined to the wick until all of the fuel is consumed. Kerosene and fuel oil can be burned by spraying or atomizing them into a small flame or spark. This principle is used in domestic and commercial oil burners.

Gasoline, unlike kerosene, has a low flash point ($-50°F$) and therefore always has a flammable mixture associated with the liquid at normal environmental temperatures. A small spark is all that is necessary to trigger a fire or an explosion. A property related to flash point, the *fire point,* is worthy of note. The fire point is a temperature a few degrees above the flash point. At the fire point a spark, if present, will ignite the fuel and produce enough heat to volatilize more fuel and sustain flaming combustion. Ignition of a vapor over a fuel which is at its flash point will result in a momentary flash which consumes the entire vapor. This flame dies out because there is insufficient time and heat to produce an adequate supply of fuel vapor. The flash or fire point of a liquid is somewhat analogous to the ignition temperature of a pyrolyzable solid fuel (discussed above).

Relative vapor density refers to the tendency of a gas or vapor to rise or sink when it is released into air. The vapor density of any gas is directly proportional to its molecular weight. Air is a mixture of gases and, thus, does not have a true molecular weight, but one can calculate an average (mean) molecular weight for it. Assuming that air is 80% nitrogen and 20% oxygen, the calculation yields a value of 28.8. The ratio of the molecular weight of a gas to the mean molecular weight of air is equal to the relative vapor density. For most fuels, this value is greater than 1, indicating that the vapor will sink in air under normal conditions. One should keep in mind, however, that intensely heated vapors, even of fairly high molecular weight compounds, can rise in air.

Information about vapor density is useful in investigating fires and explosions caused by the ignition of gases and vapors. If the source of the fuel and the apparent source of ignition are separated by some distance, it is important to decide whether the gas or vapor could have migrated to the ignition source. Knowledge of the fuel's relative vapor density would be essential in making this decision. In some cases, the nature of the damage produced in a structural explosion is directly related to the relative vapor density of the fuel involved, particularly if there was insufficient time to allow for complete mixing of the fuel with air. Finding that the most extensive damage is near the top of a structure or room suggests that a gas with a relative vapor density smaller than 1 was involved. On the other hand, if the damage is concentrated near the bottom of the structure, a heavier-than-air fuel is implicated. One precaution is necessary, however. Some frame structures are inherently weaker at the base than they are near the roof, and this consideration must be taken into account in any such interpretation.

Mixtures of gases and vapors with air must fall within a certain range of fuel-to-air ratios in order to be ignitable. Mixtures with too little fuel are said to be too *lean* to burn. In this case, the concentration of fuel in air is below the *lower flammable limit*. If the mixture has too high a concentration of fuel to be ignitable, it is above the *upper flammable limit* and is too *rich* to burn. The concentration range between the lower and upper flammable limits is known as the *flammable range* (Table 4-3). At some point near the middle of this range the mixture is in the *optimum proportion,* and the most violent explosion would take place upon ignition. If the fuel is a pure compound, the optimum concentration can be calculated after a balanced equation for the combustion reaction has been written. Explosions taking place in rich mixtures (between the optimum and the upper flammable limit) are less violent than those in somewhat leaner mixtures, but a fire may result because of the excess fuel remaining after the explosion. Explosions in homogeneous leaner mixtures are relatively sharp, but the fuel is consumed and no fire results.

The boiling point of a liquid is related to flash point in that both have to do with the production of a vapor from a liquid. Flash point is the temperature of the liquid at which the vapor pressure is sufficient to produce an ignitable mixture over it; the boiling point is that temperature at which the vapor pressure of the liquid is equal to atmospheric pressure. Boiling point and flash point roughly parallel each other. A fuel that has a relatively high boiling point will tend to have a relatively high flash point, although the flash point is always much lower than the boiling point. The parallelism is more exact when comparing liquid fuels within one chemical class. An additional primary factor influencing flash point is lower flammable limit. At the flash point the partial pressure of the fuel vapor must be high enough for its concentration to reach the lower flammable limit. The fire-point value is influenced by that of the lower flammable limit and by the heats of combustion and vaporization of the fuel.

One factor related to liquid-fuel boiling point is of major importance to fire investigators. It pertains to the behavior of a burning pool, or "puddle," of liquid accelerant on a surface such as a hardwood, linoleum, or vinyl floor. Many investigators erroneously assume that the surface beneath such a puddle of fuel will always become charred or even burn through. On such a smooth surface, charring or burning is rare and can take place only under certain conditions. Thus, a rounded burn hole or charred area on a floor is not necessarily an indication that a liquid accelerant has been used. In fact, other causes of such burn patterns are far more common. Burning curtains or drapes which have fallen to the floor are much more likely to burn through than is a pure liquid-fuel fire. It must be remembered that at atmospheric pressure no liquid can be heated above its boiling point and still remain a liquid. Thus, the surface beneath a burning puddle of fuel will remain relatively cool. As long as there is liquid fuel present, the smooth underlying surface is protected. Once the protective layer of liquid is gone, there is normally no more fuel to feed the fire at this level, and it goes out. However, charring or burning of the floor from a liquid-fuel fire can take place under the following conditions: (1) if the flooring is rough, cracked, or uneven; (2) if holes or raised flammable objects are present; (3) if the surface is porous or covered with a porous covering (like a carpet); or (4) if the liquid contains a very high boiling component.

TABLE 4-4
THERMAL PROPERTIES OF SELECTED BUILDING MATERIALS*

Material	Thermal conductivity†	Specific heat‡	Melting point °F	Melting point °C
Aluminum	1400	0.22	1220	660
Brass	720	0.09	1650	899
Copper	2600	0.09	1980	1082
Cast iron	320	0.13	2460	1349
Steel	310	0.12	2370	1299
Glass	6	0.20	2600	1427
Brick	5	0.22		
Concrete	9–12	0.16–0.25		
Wood	0.8–1.1	0.30–0.55		
Plaster	3–6	0.23		
Plastics	0.7–2.0	0.20–0.35		
Polystyrene foam	0.26	0.32		
Polyurethane foam	0.18	0.38		
Gypsum board	1.5	0.26		

*Values are estimated at control conditions; actual values can vary greatly.
†Thermal conductivity measured by the number of British Thermal Units transmitted in 1 h through 1 ft², 1-in.-thick material for each degree of temperature difference.
‡Specific heat is the number of British Thermal Units required to increase the temperature of 1 lb of the material 1°F.

Some thermal properties of building materials are listed in Table 4-4. Porous solid fuels burn more readily than nonporous ones of the same composition, and high moisture content retards combustion.

FIRE PATTERNS

The path a fire takes is largely determined by the availability of fuel. Ignition taking place in a homogeneous flammable mixture produces a flame front that spreads out equally in all directions, as we have noted. Thus, at a given instant in time, it is in the shape of a sphere. A fire burning on a pool of volatile liquid will conform to the shape of the liquid pool unless an adjacent fuel source becomes involved. Similarly, a fire in a field of evenly distributed dry grass will spread out as an ever-widening circle, unless factors such as uneven terrain or wind intervene.

Structural fire patterns are somewhat more difficult to understand. Most fuel available in a structural fire consists of pyrolyzable solids. For this fuel to be available for flaming combustion, it must first be pyrolyzed. The greatest degree of pyrolysis will take place where the heat is most intense. Since the hot gases from combustion will rise, the greatest amount of pyrolysis will take place above the fire. This process will then provide more fuel for the flames above the fire, further contributing to the production of heat and pyrolysis products above the flames. This cycle results in the very rapid progress of such a fire in an upward direction, with significantly less lateral spread and almost no downward spread. The resulting burn pattern is sometimes referred to as the *inverted cone* or *V pattern,* and it is an idealized pattern for structural fires. Patterns in actual fires can differ significantly from the inverted cone, depending on the circumstances. When a full-scale fire encounters a ceiling, for example, a considerable amount of lateral spread can take place. In addition, stairwells, shaftways, and ducts can produce *chimney effects* which can markedly alter the fire pattern. Fire-fighting tactics can also change the pattern. However, an experienced and knowledgeable investigator can easily recognize these deviations from the inverted cone pattern. By keeping this pattern and possible deviations from it in mind, an investigator can often examine a damaged structure and trace the pattern back to the origin of the fire. The point of origin will be a low point in the burn pattern which is consistent with the overall pattern. The low point can then be scrutinized for possible ignition sources and initial fuel. If arson is suspected, samples from this area would be collected and *tightly sealed* in a proper container for submission to the laboratory and subsequent analysis for volatile liquid accelerants.

RECOGNITION AND COLLECTION OF ARSON EVIDENCE

Fire-Scene Investigation

The primary responsibility of an arson-scene investigation is to determine the cause of the fire. Arson-scene investigation, which is often long and tedious, generally includes:

1 Determination of the point of origin of the fire
2 Examination of electric and mechanical equipment to evaluate the possibility of the fire having been caused by its failure
3 Examination of the burning patterns
4 Recognition and collection of the relevant physical evidence
5 Analysis and reconstruction of the scene
6 Determination of the cause of the fire

It is always better to make a preliminary investigation as early as possible, even before mopping up or the overhauling operation by the fire fighters is finished. Points of origin are more easily established when the scene is intact. Unnecessary moving of burned debris, furniture, and other goods, as well as excessive walking around at the scene, will alter the scene and make the investigation more difficult.

When arriving at a fire scene, the investigator should first examine the building's exterior and surrounding area. Anything unusual in the area around the building, such as a paint or gasoline can, or other container, footprints or other types of impressions (Chapter 11), and other materials, should be noted, documented, and, if possible, collected and sent to the laboratory. Before entering the building, all doors and windows should be checked. If it appears that entry was forced, the investigator should utilize investigative techniques that would be applicable to a breaking and entering, looking for toolmarks (Chapter 14) among other things. If broken glass is found, its location and patterns should be noted, and it should be checked for possible blood and tissue. An arsonist could receive a cut during a break-in if glass were broken in the process. Blood and tissues could be very important as evidence (Chapter 9), as could the glass itself (Chapter 7). Known glass should be collected for future comparison. Often glass chips can be recovered from a suspect's shoes and clothing. Glass broken by mechanical force can readily be distinguished from that broken because of heat. Patterns of both mechanical and thermal glass fractures are shown in Figure 4-2. Latent prints should also be looked for at the point of entry (if there is one) and at other reasonable locations (Chapter 12).

The investigator should begin examining the interior of a building by locating the general area of the origin of the fire. In many cases, a reliable way of finding the area of origin is to remember the general inverted cone pattern typical of structural fires and to follow the path of damage from the least to the greatest amount. Generally, the area that is most heavily burned and severely charred is the area of origin. Occasionally, however, this rule will not apply. If highly flammable material was concentrated in a particular area, then it might be the most heavily burned. Once the point or points of origin are located, the area should be carefully checked. Multiple points of origin are usually indicative of arson, although occasionally a natural or accidental explanation can be offered. If there are several areas of exceptionally heavy burning and charring, any unusual burn patterns should also be noted. These unusual patterns may also indicate arson. Since flammable liquids tend to seek the lowest possible location, the area directly beneath any heavily charred areas must be checked. Anything suspected of containing flammable liquids should be collected in a tightly sealed, clean, and previously unused paint can or canning jar (Figure 4-3) to prevent further evaporation. The container should be labeled with the investigator's name as well as the date, department, location, area from which sample was

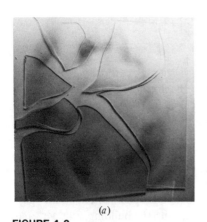
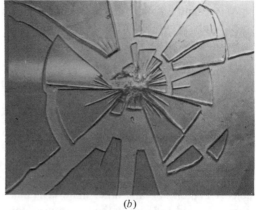

(a)   (b)

FIGURE 4-2
(a) A thermal glass fracture. (b) A mechanical glass fracture. (*Courtesy of Francis X. Sheehan, John Jay College of Criminal Justice, The City University of New York.*)

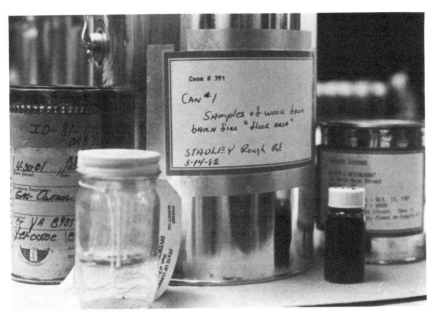

FIGURE 4-3
Containers with labeling information. *(Courtesy of Robert Mills, Forensic Science Laboratory, Connecticut State Police.)*

taken, case number, and a description of the item. If there are any porous or absorbent materials near the origin (paper, carpeting, fabric, books, etc.), these may have retained a substantial amount of volatile accelerant and should be collected. Generally, highly absorbent materials retain more accelerant than hard, nonabsorbent materials, such as glass, ceramics, or metals. If flammable liquid is found, it should be transferred into a small glass vial, tightly sealed, and marked with a label containing the information noted above (Figure 4-3). A photograph of an arson scene is presented in Figure 4-4. It may be possible to compare unburned accelerant samples in the possession of a suspect with residue recovered from a fire scene and say something about their similarity. This would not be possible if the composition of the material in the residue has been extensively altered by the fire or by evaporation due to prolonged delay in collection. Two liquid samples, such as one from a container recovered at the fire scene and one from the gas tank of the suspect's auto, would be expected to yield even more definitive comparisons.

Detection of Accelerant Residues

Many investigators use flammable vapor detectors or chemical tests to help in locating trace amounts of accelerants at the area of origin. There are several types of portable flammable vapor detectors available commercially. In general, field tests for accelerant residues can be placed into five categories, according to their principle of

FIGURE 4-4
A fire scene with burn patterns. *(Courtesy of Walter Anderson, Office of Fire Marshal, Connecticut State Police.)*

detection: (1) chemical color tests, (2) catalytic combustion detectors, (3) flame ionization detectors, (4) portable gas chromatographs, and (5) portable infrared spectrophotometers.

1 *Chemical color test methods* rely on chemical dyes which can be spread around in a suspected area. If the liquid accelerant is present, the dyes will change color in a characteristic way. This method is less sensitive and less specific for flammable liquids than the others which are available.

2 *Catalytic combustion detectors* are popularly known as *sniffers*. In operation, the vapor samples are pumped over a heated, platinum-plated coil of wire, which causes any combustible gas present to oxidize. The heat from this oxidation raises the temperature, and thus the electrical resistance of the coil, and this change can be measured electronically. However, this type of detector is less sensitive to less-volatile accelerants such as turpentine, kerosene, and fuel oils.

3 In a *flame ionization detector,* the sample gas is mixed with hydrogen, and the mixture is burned so that the molecules will be ionized by the flame. The degree of ionization is proportional to the amount of combustible organic gases in the sample.

The degree of ionization is then measured by using an electrometer to determine the resulting increase in the electrical conductivity of the gas. The device is very sensitive, but can yield false positive results with certain pyrolysis products of wood that may be present after the fire is extinguished.

4 A *portable gas chromatograph* allows on-site gas chromatography. In gas chromatography, the sample gas is separated into its components based on differences in retention on a specially selected stationary phase (see Chapter 3). The components are then detected and measured either by a catalytic combustion or a flame ionization detector. This instrument is more sensitive and specific than others. The involved analytical procedures and time required are disadvantages for field investigative use, however. In addition, portable units are not as sophisticated as their laboratory counterparts. The results of the on-site analysis may be useful as an investigative aid, but may not be admissible in court unless the test has been conducted by a qualified forensic chemist at the scene. There is little to recommend the use of portable gas chromatographs at fire scenes. Their use does not eliminate the need for a more definitive subsequent analysis in the laboratory.

5 A *portable infrared spectrophotometer,* like any IR spectrophotometer (see Chapter 3), can give highly specific results with flammable liquids accompanied by a high degree of sensitivity. However, contamination of flammable vapors and the presence of water make this instrument impractical for field investigation.

Collection of Arson-Related Physical Evidence

Besides accelerants, ignition devices may also be present near the point of origin. These devices may be very simple (matchbook, Molotov cocktail, or candle), electrical (electric appliances, flashbulbs, fuses, batteries), mechanical (time clocks, other timing devices), or chemical (rocket fuel, phosphorus, explosives). If an ignition device is found, it should be photographed before collection and then placed in a suitable box with a label. The investigator should avoid touching the device to preserve any possible latent fingerprint evidence.

In the investigation of motor-vehicle fires, the same principles can be applied. Generally, complete destruction of a motor vehicle by an accidental fire is highly unlikely. The location of a burned vehicle usually yields information about possible arson. The pattern of burning can also help in the investigation. If a fire starts (or is started) in front of the fire wall, the engine is usually severely damaged. All plastic and rubber parts will be melted or burned. If a fire was started on the car seat, the interior of the car is usually consumed by fire, while the engine may show little damage. The collection of suspected accelerant residues and searching for other types of physical evidence are just as important for investigators in motor-vehicle fires as in any other kind of fire.

LABORATORY EXAMINATION OF ARSON EVIDENCE

The type of physical evidence at an arson scene depends on the method used by the arsonist to set the fire. However, it generally falls into three categories: (1) ignition devices, (2) flammable liquids, and (3) other associated physical evidence, such as blood, tissue, hairs, fibers, fingerprints, toolmarks, and footprints. The methods for examination of the different types of associated evidence are covered in their specific chapters. Examination of ignition devices is carried out mainly for the purpose of identification. Identification of the type of device and its manufacturer may help in providing useful investigative leads. The most common activity of the forensic scientist is to establish that an accelerant was actually used to set the fire and to determine what type of accelerant it was, although other contributions can be very important.

Types of Accelerants

Various kinds of flammable liquids are used by arsonists for setting fires. Most of them are derived from petroleum distillates. These petroleum distillates are either straight-run products or a mixture of specially processed ones. The following shows the commonly used accelerants:

I Petroleum distillate accelerants
   A Straight-run products
      1 Light petroleum distillate; for example, naphtha, lighter fluid, cleaning fluid
      2 Medium petroleum distillate; for example, paint thinner, charcoal lighter
      3 Heavy petroleum distillate; for example, kerosene, diesel fuel, fuel oil
   B Specially processed petroleum products
      1 Separate aromatics; for example, benzene, toluene, xylene
      2 Blended aromatics and aliphatics; for example, gasoline
      3 Blended or modified products; for example, lubricants and special solvents
II Other types of nonpetroleum accelerants, for example, turpentine, alcohols

The most common flammable liquid encountered in arson cases is gasoline, which is found in about 80 percent of arson cases. Kerosene is found in about 7 percent of them, charcoal lighter in about 4 percent, paint thinner in about 3 percent, lacquer solvent in about 1 percent, with other types of flammable liquids making up the rest. More recently, mixtures of liquids have been detected occasionally.

Methods of Analyzing Accelerants

Recovery of Accelerants from Arson Debris   By far the most useful technique in the laboratory for the detection of accelerants is gas chromatography. However, the process of recovering the accelerant from arson debris is the most crucial step in the analysis. There are four methods available for recovering traces of flammable accelerants from such debris: (1) head space, (2) distillation, (3) solvent extraction, and (4) vapor concentration. Each of them has certain advantages as well as disadvantages.

Head-Space Method   Sampling the vapors from the atmosphere above a specimen in a sealed container is a satisfactory method of recovery of volatile vapors. The simplest procedures are cold head-space techniques. Here, the debris from the fire scene has been placed in a clean, sealed container. Using a syringe, a small portion of the vapor inside the container is withdrawn and injected into a gas chromatograph for analysis. Analysis of the air vapor, collected at room temperature in this way, is called the *cold head-space method*. If the arson debris in its container is heated well above room temperature prior to sampling, the sampling technique is then called the *heated head-space method*. The heated method is preferred when the components of the accelerant are only weakly volatilized at room temperature. In practice, the sealed container holding the fire debris is heated to $100°C$ or just slightly lower. A small portion of the heated vapor is then withdrawn and injected into the gas chromatograph for analysis. Two limitations of this technique are: (1) the concentration of accelerant vapor in the air-diluted head space is limited and (2) discrimination among heavy petroleum distillates is difficult.

Distillation Methods   In the steam distillation method, the fire debris is placed in a boiling flask, heated, and then purged with steam. The distillate is collected using a trap equipped with a cold-water condenser. With this procedure, volatile hydrocarbons present in sufficient quantity can be recovered in liquid form. There are several modifications of this technique, which involve the use of either a different extraction carrier or a different distillation method. These include ethylene glycol distillation, ethanol distillation, and vacuum distillation. The liquid sample recovered in the distillate can then be identified by injecting it into the gas chromatograph or by measuring its density and refractive index or by infrared spectrophotometry (Chapter 3).

Solvent Extraction Method   Here the fire debris is placed in a glass flask and extracted with some known solvent. The volatile hydrocarbons are extracted out of the debris by the solvent and end up dissolved in it as a result. Commonly used solvents are carbon disulfide, methylene chloride, pentane, and hexane. The extract can be evaporated down to a small volume and the sample then injected into a gas chromatograph for analysis.

Vapor Concentration Method   In this procedure, the fire debris is placed in a clean container which may be heated. A small stream of hydrocarbon-free air is passed slowly into the container and out again. The purged mixture (the air and vapor coming out) is then passed through a small tube filled with an adsorbent or trapping material (such as clean charcoal). Volatile hydrocarbon vapors carried in the air stream and adsorbed onto the charcoal are then driven off by heat into a carrier gas stream and directly into the gas chromatograph or are extracted with a small volume of carbon disulfide. The extract can be evaporated down to a suitable volume and injected into a gas chromatograph for analysis.

Identification of Accelerants   Until about 20 years ago, attempts to identify accelerants in arson cases generally utilized physical property differences between the different types of accelerants. Refractive index, density, boiling point, and flash point of the unknown volatile hydrocarbon or other liquid were measured, and these values were then compared with known data to try to make an identification. However, loss of sample through evaporation, the availability of enough liquid sample, and the contamination of fire debris with other materials all made these physical property comparisons difficult.

The most common technique used today in forensic science laboratories to detect and identify accelerants is gas chromatography (GC). The theory and background of GC analysis were discussed in Chapter 3. In this method, volatile hydrocarbon accelerant vapor, or liquid recovered from fire debris, is injected into a gas chromatograph. By the selection of appropriate GC columns and instrumental conditions, the mixture of hydrocarbon is separated into its components, and the peaks, each representing at least one different component, are recorded on the chromatogram. This chromatographic pattern is characteristic of a particular type of hydrocarbon. The unknown accelerant might be identified by a comparison of this pattern and the retention times of individual components with known volatile hydrocarbon standards. For example, Figure 4-5(*a*) shows a GC analysis of a suspected accelerant recovered from fire debris in an arson case. The chromatogram is similar to a known gasoline standard chromatogram [Figure 4-5(*b*)]. This result proves that the fire debris contained a petroleum distillate similar in composition to gasoline. GC is extremely sensitive. Volatile hydrocarbon compounds can be detected in concentrations as low as 10 parts per billion.

Other techniques which have been used for the identification of accelerants, infrared (IR) spectrophotometry and spectrofluorimetry, are less satisfactory in actual practice than GC. All these methods are sensitive and specific, but the production of meaningful spectra requires pure samples. In most arson cases, pure samples are not available. The introduction of GC-IR and GC-MS [GC coupled with IR spectrophotometric or with mass spectrometry (MS) systems] has made it possible to utilize both IR and MS on casework samples. The mixture is first separated by GC, and the components are then individually analyzed by IR spectrophotometry or by MS all in one step. Figure 4-6 illustrates the use of GC-MS in the analysis of residues from arson scenes. Other methods. such as the use of thin-layer chromatographic (TLC) techniques to separate, identify, and compare the mixtures of dyes that are added to gasoline have also been found useful.

EXPLOSIVES AND EXPLOSIONS

Introduction

From a physical standpoint, an *explosion* is a violent outburst, often accompanied by a shock wave, a great deal of heat, and a loud noise. From the chemical point of view, an explosion represents an extremely rapid, exothermic chemical reaction. As noted in Chapter 3, atoms and molecules can join together to form new molecules. At the same time, molecules can break apart, or decompose, into simpler molecules or individual atoms. When these reactions take place, chemical bonds are broken and re-formed and heat energy may be either produced or taken up in the process. If heat is produced, the reaction is *exothermic*. If heat is taken up, it is *endothermic*. When an exothermic explosion occurs, a large amount of energy is released in the form of heat, light, and pressure. The rapid buildup of gas pressure and heat then produces the resulting violent physical disruption.

Explosions can be divided into two broad classes: *diffuse* and *concentrated*. Diffuse

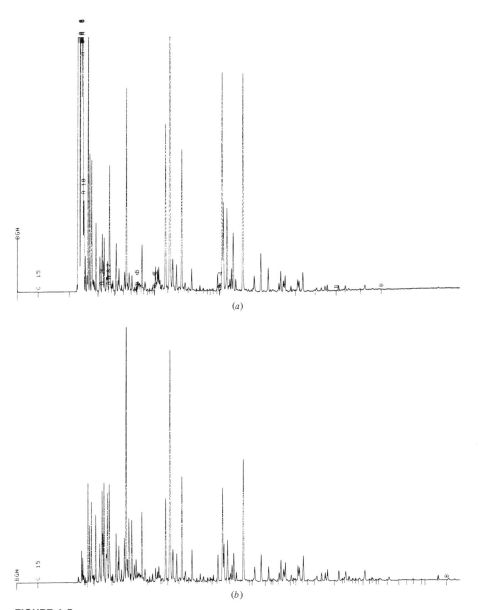

FIGURE 4-5
Gas chromatograms of gasoline. The upper curve is a chromatogram of a known gasoline sample. The lower curve is a chromatogram of a burned gasoline sample recovered from a piece of wood. Note the loss of early emerging peaks (low boilers) in the burned sample. A special high-resolution column known as a capillary column was used for these chromatograms. Note the large number of peaks and their sharpness. *(Courtesy of Christopher P. Chany, Forensic Science Laboratory, Office of the Medical Examiner, Westchester County, New York.)*

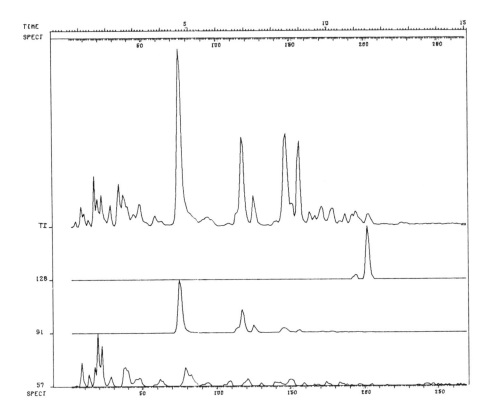

FIGURE 4-6
Accelerant residues and the use of gas chromatography and mass spectrometry. The upper curve is similar to a conventional gas chromatogram. In this case the mass spectrometer merely serves as a detector for the gas chromatograph. All ions produced in the mass spectrometer are detected. In the next curve, only mass number 128 (the molecular ion of naphthalene) is monitored. The presence of naphthalene in an accelerant sample is one characteristic of gasoline. The next two curves show the mass chromatograms where mass numbers 91 and 57 are monitored. Molecular fragments with these mass numbers are also characteristic of gasoline. (Left) Mass spectrum of the naphthalene peak from gasoline. Note the large peak at mass number 128. *(Courtesy of Dr. Howard A. Harris, Director, Crime Laboratory, New York City Police Department.)*

explosions are the type which take place in fuel-air mixtures, such as a dust, gas, or vapor in air. The damage resulting from a diffuse explosion may extend over a wide area but is uniformly distributed as a rule. Concentrated explosions occur with true explosives, such as gunpowder, 2,4,6-trinitrotoluene (TNT), and dynamite. Here, the damage tends to be most severe near the seat of the explosion, and a crater may be formed.

Concentrated explosions generally take place in stepwise, but extremely rapid, reactions. A chain of events occurs when a high explosive is detonated. This chain of events is sometimes referred to as the *explosive train*. The principal events in the sequence for a military explosive are

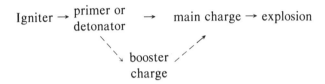

A small initial amount of energy is released by the igniter, which may be electric or mechanical. The energy then produced by the primer or detonator is usually sufficient to initiate the main charge. Sometimes an intermediate booster charge is used. The main charge produces a large amount of energy in a confined space, which results in an explosion. A bomb, for example, is generally a container packed with explosive and a detonating device. When the bomb is exploded, the explosion almost instantaneously produces a large volume of gases that begin to exert extremely high pressures on the interior walls of the container. At the same time, a large amount of heat is produced. The heat and expanding gases may produce several hundred tons of pressure per square inch, causing the container to explode. The sudden release of pressure, and the accompanying rapid expansions, produce the loud noise. It is the sudden release of the rapidly built-up pressure and the resulting exploded debris from the container which cause the destruction of the surrounding areas.

Types of Explosives

In general, explosives are a group of chemical compounds which are not stable in their ordinary forms. When heated, shocked, or struck, they are capable of rapid decomposition, producing an explosion by the liberation of large quantities of heat and gases. The speed with which an explosive compound decomposes (or explodes) normally determines its type and the intensity of the destruction. There are three types of explosives: low, primary high, and secondary high.

Low Explosives   These are primarily propellants, and are sometimes referred to as *burning explosives*. They are relatively easy to initiate and are often used to propel bullets or to project rockets. Examples include black powder, smokeless powder, and solid-fuel rocket propellants. Black powder has been made for centuries and contains charcoal, sulfur, and potassium nitrate. Smokeless powders are more modern and contain organic nitro compounds, such as nitrocellulose and small amounts of nitro-glycerin. These types of explosives are ordinarily stable under normal conditions. If ignited in the open, they will merely burn. However, they will explode violently when ignited under properly confined conditions.

Primary High Explosives   This type of explosive is often referred to as a *primer* or *detonator* and is generally used in blasting caps and firearms cartridge primers. They are extremely sensitive to heat, shock, or friction under normal conditions. In small quantities, they have the potential energy needed to initiate or detonate secondary high explosives. Included in this group are lead azide, lead styphnate, and mercury fulminate.

Secondary High Explosives   This type of explosive, with notable exceptions, is relatively insensitive to heat, shock, or friction under normal circumstances. If ignited, it will usually burn rather than detonate. An intense shock wave from a primary explosive is required for detonation. Such an explosive is used mainly as a booster charge and as a main bursting charge. Some examples of common secondary high explosives are 2,4,6-trinitrotoluene (TNT), ammonium nitrate, pentaerythritol tetranitrate (PETN), cyclotrimethylenetrinitramine (RDX), 2,4,6-trinitrophenyl-methylnitramine (tetryl), nitroglycerin, and dynamite. Dynamite is the most widely found explosive in common explosion cases. Dynamite contains nitroglycerin with other additives to reduce its sensitivity to shock. There are several different types of dynamite, according to which additives are used with the nitroglycerin (ammonium dynamite, gelatin dynamite, and so forth).

Collection and Preservation of Explosion Evidence

The most important aspect of the detection and identification of explosive residue is the collection of appropriate samples from the explosion scene. The scene must be carefully and systematically searched to recover any trace of detonating device and explosive. The first step in locating the remaining traces of explosive and detonating device is location of the origin of the blast. Generally, at the origin of a high-energy or a contained low-energy explosion, a crater is present. Once the crater is found, all the debris and material around that area should be collected and preserved for laboratory analysis. Explosive residues can ordinarily be found on debris near the origin of the detonation.

Some time ago the ATF (Bureau of Alcohol, Tobacco and Firearms) instituted an explosive tagging program to try to assist enforcement agencies in identifying the sources of explosives from residues recovered at explosion scenes. Color-coded taggant particles were added to the explosive material. The average stick of dynamite, for example, contained about 2000 taggant particles. The taggant particle was a nearly microscopic, plastic chip consisting of eight layers. One layer was magnetic to aid in retrieval, and one of the outer layers was fluorescent to aid in visually detecting the particles at a scene using a UV lamp. The other layers were used for color coding. The program did not extend to all samples of dynamite, and it has now been discontinued.

If an unexploded device is found, a special bomb squad should be called in to handle and defuse it.

In addition to the explosive residue itself, all portions of the ignition device and the container must be preserved for laboratory investigation. All wires, tape, electric switches, timing devices, batteries, and fragments must be carefully collected. These items sometimes provide important information that can help in tracing the person who constructed the bomb or device. Ignition devices often contain many parts that are homemade, and many different types of trace evidence, like hairs, fibers, tape, cord, soil, paint, pollens, fingerprints, and toolmarks, might therefore be found. All of these items may be associated with the suspect or with the suspect's environment, and this type of evidence has been used successfully in tracing the origin of explosives.

LABORATORY ANALYSIS OF EXPLOSIVE RESIDUES

Laboratory examination of evidence from explosion scenes is directed toward the identification of the explosive, determination of manufacturer, and tracing of its source. The tagging system for explosives could have made the determination of manufacturer and tracing of the explosive's source a much easier task. A wide variety of chemical and instrumental methods are available for identifying explosive residues.

Microscopical Examination

Much of the debris and soil collected near the origin of the blast contain unexploded or partially burned explosive particles. These particles can be recognized by examination of the debris under a stereomicroscope. When residue particles are found, they should be separated and recovered for further confirmatory tests. Surfaces that are near the seat of the explosion and can be transported should be carefully packaged and taken to the laboratory for detailed microscopic examination. Sometimes, the residues are difficult to find or to separate from the explosive debris because of background color or nearly total consumption of the explosive. To recover these residues, the debris can be extracted with acetone, which will dissolve most of the explosive residue. The acetone–explosive-residue mixture is then filtered to remove debris and can then be evaporated in air to leave the explosive residues behind. Where possible, microscopical examination is preferable to solvent extraction and should be attempted first. Polarized-light microscopy can be used to identify explosive-residue particles.

Chemical Color Tests

There are currently available several reagents for chemical spot tests for explosive residues. The most common are: Griess reagent, diphenylamine, J-acid reagent and alcoholic potassium hydroxide. These reagents are prepared as indicated in the footnotes to Table 4-5. To test for the presence of certain explosive residues, the material must first be dissolved in acetone. A drop of acetone–explosive-residue mixture is then placed on a spot plate and allowed to air dry. A drop of test reagent is added,

TABLE 4-5
COLOR TEST REAGENTS AND REACTIONS FOR EXPLOSIVES

Explosive or component	Color reaction with			
	Griess*	Diphenylamine†	J-acid‡	Alcoholic KOH§
Chlorate	No color	Blue	Orange-brown	No color
Nitrate	Pink to red	Blue	Orange-brown	No color
Nitrite	Red to yellow	Blue-black	Orange-brown	No color
Nitrocellulose	Pink	Blue-black	Orange-brown	No color
Nitroglycerin	Pink to red	Blue	Orange-brown	No color
PETN	Pink to red	Blue	Orange-brown to red	No color
RDX	Pink to red	Blue	Orange-brown	No color
Tetryl	Pink to red	Blue	Yellow to orange	Red
TNT	No color	No color	No color	Red-violet

*Griess reagent: Solution A = 1 g sulfanilic acid in 100 mL 30% acetic acid; Solution B = 1 g α-naphthylamine in 230 mL distilled water.
†Diphenylamine reagent: 1 g diphenylamine in 100 mL conc. sulfuric acid.
‡J-acid reagent: 1 g 6-amino-1-naphthol-3-sulfonic acid in 100 mL conc. sulfuric acid.
§Alcoholic KOH reagent: 10 g potassium hydroxide in 100 mL absolute ethanol.

and any color change is noted. Table 4-5 lists the four common tests and their color reactions. These color reactions are relatively insensitive, but they will give a good indication of the general type of explosive present in the residue.

Microcrystal Tests

Many organic and inorganic components of explosives, such as nitrate, ammonium, sodium, and TNT, can be identified by microscopical methods, including microcrystal tests. Microchemical tests carried out under the light microscope are inexpensive, quick, and reliable. To test for the presence of an element or compound, a drop of reagent is added to the residue, and characteristic crystals or a precipitate will form in a positive test. By examining the color, shape, and other physical properties of these crystals, the unknown can often be identified.

Thin-Layer Chromatography

Thin-layer chromatography (TLC) has been used for screening and comparison tests on explosive residues. The acetone extract of the residue is spotted on a TLC plate, which is then developed with a chloroform solution. R_f values (see Chapter 3) of unknown explosive residue components can then be compared with those of known materials, and a sample might thus be identified.

Instrumental Analysis

Many instrumental techniques have been used to confirm the identity of various explosive-residue components. The organic types of components can be identified by

IR spectrophotometry. An IR spectrum is unique for each type of organic explosive component. By comparing the spectrum with standard ones, an unknown component can be identified. Other appropriate instrumental techniques can also be used. Inorganic explosive components are generally confirmed using x-ray diffraction for crystalline particles, and atomic absorption or emission spectroscopy to identify the elements present in the sample.

Other methods such as scanning electron microscopy (SEM) and neutron activation analysis (NAA) have also been used as aids for the identification of explosive residues.

STUDY QUESTIONS

1 What is fire? What elements are needed to maintain a continuous fire?
2 What is oxidation? How is it related to fire?
3 What is the flash point of a liquid?
4 What is pyrolysis?
5 What are the main objectives of fire-scene investigation?
6 Briefly describe how to go about a fire-scene investigation.
7 Describe some of the field techniques that can be used to detect accelerant residues and describe the proper use of each one.
8 How should suspected accelerant evidence be collected at an arson scene?
9 What kind of evidence besides accelerants might be found at an arson scene and how should it be collected?
10 What are the most commonly encountered accelerants?
11 How is accelerant material recovered from fire debris for laboratory analysis?
12 Name some of the methods used to detect and characterize accelerants.
13 What is an explosion?
14 What is the explosive train, and what are the elements that make it up?
15 Name the different types of explosives and give some examples of each.
16 How would you go about searching an explosion scene? What are the most important things to look for?
17 What are explosive taggants, and how do they help in the investigation of explosions?
18 What laboratory methods are used to examine explosive residues?
19 Name several of the chemical color tests used to detect explosive residues.
20 What is the purpose of using microscopical examination in the analysis of explosive residues?

REFERENCES AND FURTHER READING

Boudreau, J. F., et al.: *Arson and Arson Investigation—Survey and Assessment,* U.S. Government Printing Office, Washington, D.C., 1977.

Camp, M. J.: "Analytical Techniques in Arson Investigation," *Analytical Chemistry,* vol. 52, p. 22A, 1980.

Canfield, D. V., and P. R. De Forest: "The Use of the Gandolfi Camera as a Screening and Confirmation Tool in the Analysis of Explosive Residues," *Journal of Forensic Sciences,* vol. 22, pp. 337–347, 1977.

Carter, R. E.: *Arson Investigation,* Glencoe, Encino, Calif., 1978.

Carroll, J. R.: *Physical and Technical Aspects of Fire and Arson Investigation,* Charles C Thomas, Springfield, Ill., 1979.

Ferrall, R. T.: "Arson Information: Who What Where," *FBI Law Enforcement Bulletin,* May 1981.

Hoffman, C. M., and E. B. Byall, "Identification of Explosive Residues in Bomb Scene Investigations," *Journal of Forensic Sciences,* vol. 19, p. 54, 1974.

Kaplan, M. A., and S. Zitrin: "Identification of Post Explosion Residue," *Journal of the Association of Official Analytical Chemists,* vol. 60, p. 619, 1977.

Kirk, P. L.: *Fire Investigation,* Wiley, New York, 1969.

Lenz, R. R.: *Explosive and Bomb Disposal Guide,* Charles C Thomas, Springfield, Ill., 1973.

Loscalzo, P. J., P. R. De Forest, and J. M. Chao: "A Study to Determine the Limit of Detectability of Gasoline Vapor from Simulated Arson Residues," *Journal of Forensic Sciences,* vol. 25, p. 162, 1980.

Meidl, J. H.: *Explosive and Toxic Hazardous Materials,* Glencoe, Beverly Hills, 1970.

Midkiff, C. R.: "Arson and Explosive Investigation," in R. Saferstein (ed.), *Forensic Science Handbook,* Prentice-Hall, Englewood Cliffs, N.J., 1982.

Peterson, A. A.: "A Report on the Detection and Identification of Explosives by Tagging," *Journal of Forensic Sciences,* vol. 26, p. 313, 1981.

Stoffel, J. F.: *Explosives and Homemade Bombs,* 2d ed., Charles C Thomas, Springfield, Ill., 1972.

U.S. Department of Commerce, National Bureau of Standards, *Fire Investigation Handbook,* F. L. Brannigan (ed.), NBS Handbook 134, Washington, D.C., 1980.

U.S. Department of the Treasury, Bureau of Alcohol, Tobacco and Firearms, *A Field Guide to Recovering Explosives Identification Taggants,* Washington, D.C., 1978.

Yates, C. E.: "Recovery and Identification of Residues of Flammable Liquids from Suspected Arson Debris," in G. Davis (ed.), *Forensic Science,* American Chemical Society, Washington, D.C., 1975.

CHAPTER 5

DRUG ANALYSIS AND FORENSIC TOXICOLOGY

INTRODUCTION

Almost any chemical capable of entering the human body can produce changes in the body's structure or affect its function. The intensity of these changes or effects increases, generally, as the concentration of the chemical increases within the body. Those chemicals that produce beneficial or desirable effects are often used as drugs. Chemicals that produce harmful effects, particularly in low concentrations, are considered poisons.

A *drug* is defined as any natural or synthetic substance that is administered to produce specific physiological or psychological effects. Drugs are useful tools when used properly; however, they are too frequently misused or abused. *Drug abuse* is the nonmedicinal use of a drug in a manner that is not socially acceptable. Although drug abuse may occur with any drug, those with the highest potential for abuse are the ones that affect an individual's mood, physical sensation, or thoughts.

Perhaps the primary hazard of the abusive use of drugs is the likelihood for some persons to develop a "need," or compulsive desire, for their continued use. Such a pattern of drug use is considered *drug dependence* and may occur as a result of a psychological or a physical craving.

The term *addiction* implies a very severe form of dependence, one involving an overwhelming compulsion for the use of a particular drug. It appears that the actual or potential consequences of drug use depend in part on the nature of the drug and in part on the personality of the user.

Beginning in the 1960s, problems associated with drug abuse took on new dimensions in the United States. Today drug abuse has become one of the nation's foremost social problems. It is estimated that more than 10 million Americans are habitual users of amphetamines, barbiturates, cocaine, or heroin. In addition, millions more are users of alcohol and marijuana. To help control the drug-abuse problem, the Comprehensive Drug Abuse Prevention and Control Act was enacted in 1970. Frequently called the *Controlled Substances Act,* this law provides for research into drug-abuse prevention, treatment and rehabilitation of drug addicts, and improvements in law-enforcement techniques. It places control of narcotic, stimulant, hallucinogenic, and depressant drugs under the Drug Enforcement Administration (DEA), U.S. Department of Justice. A "controlled substances list," compiled under the direction of the Attorney General, classifies drugs into five categories (schedules).

Schedule I consists of drugs or substances which currently have no accepted medicinal use in the United States and may be legally possessed only for research purposes. These substances have a high potential for abuse. Common examples of Schedule I substances include marijuana, mescaline, LSD, and heroin.

Schedule II consists of drugs which are currently accepted for medicinal use in the United States. Drugs in this schedule also have a high potential for abuse and, when abused, may lead to severe psychological or physical dependence. Common examples of Schedule II drugs include amphetamine, morphine, methadone, and secobarbital.

Schedules III and IV consist of drugs and drug preparations which are currently accepted for medicinal use in the United States but have less potential for abuse than substances in Schedules I and II. Abuse of drugs in these schedules may lead to moderate psychological or physical dependence. Schedule III includes phencyclidine and phendimetrazine. Schedule IV includes phenobarbital and diazepam (Valium).

Schedule V consists of drugs and drug preparations which are currently accepted for medicinal use in the United States. These drugs have low potential for abuse and may lead only to limited psychological or physical dependence relative to the drugs in Schedule IV. Many Schedule V substances are sold in over-the-counter preparations.

CLASSIFICATION AND DESCRIPTION OF DRUGS

Drugs capable of altering mood or physical sensation, and therefore having a high likelihood for abuse, can be classified as belonging to one of four categories according to their physiological effects in the human body. These categories are: opiates, stimulants, hallucinogens, and depressants.

Opiates

Opiates are natural, semisynthetic or synthetic substances with morphine-like effects in the body. Opiates are primarily employed as analgesics and can be considered narcotic in their effects. A *narcotic,* pharmacologically, is any substance that produces narcosis: a stuporous state resembling sleep, and characterized by loss of sensation. In the past, the term *narcotic* has been associated with any drug or substance that was socially unacceptable, legally prohibited, and likely to produce dependence. It included, for example, marijuana and cocaine, drugs which are not properly classified as narcotics pharmacologically. Because of the popular misuse of the term narcotics, the term *opiate* is best used to describe those substances with morphine-like properties.

Opium Opium is obtained as a milky-white secretion from the unripened seed pods of the poppy plant *(Papaver somniferum)*. When the poppy juice, exuded through cuts made in the pod, is air-dried, it becomes a brown gummy mass which has a distinctive and pungent odor. The principal alkaloids contained in opium are morphine (10%) and codeine (0.5%). They account for the pharmacologic effects of opium, which is usually ingested by smoking in long-stemmed pipes.

Morphine Morphine, one of the naturally occurring alkaloids found in opium, can be extracted with various solvents or by ion-exchange techniques. Morphine is commonly available in the form of its water-soluble salts, morphine sulfate and morphine hydrochloride. These are white, crystalline powders possessing a distinctly bitter taste. Morphine also may appear in tablet, capsule, or liquid form.

Usually administered by hypodermic needle, morphine produces analgesia (relief of pain), drowsiness, decreased physical activity, changes in mood, and the inability to concentrate. Pinpoint pupils and sedation are indicative of opiate use, the suspicion of which may be further supported by the finding of needle marks on the extremities. Most abusers of morphine or heroin describe feelings of tranquility and euphoria (a generalized feeling of well-being); however, tolerance develops rapidly with repeated use.

Heroin Heroin (diacetylmorphine) is prepared synthetically from morphine by allowing it to react with acetic anhydride or acetyl chloride. Usually distributed as heroin hydrochloride, a white or off-white crystalline powder, this water-soluble salt is dissolved and administered by intravenous injection. Heroin is probably the most commonly abused drug among the morphine derivatives. Heroin reaching this country from Europe or Asia may be over 90 percent pure. By the time it reaches the addict, however, it has almost always been diluted, or cut, considerably. Quinine is a common diluent in some parts of the United States, but lactose, mannitol, procaine, and powdered milk are also used to cut heroin.

Heroin is injected directly into the bloodstream where it is rapidly metabolized to morphine. Heroin produces the same effects as morphine on the body; however, it is three times more potent and has a more rapid onset of action. Heroin users describe its euphoric effects as more intense and desirable than those of morphine.

Codeine Codeine may be extracted from opium or prepared synthetically by the methylation of morphine. The common salts of codeine are codeine sulfate and codeine phosphate. Both are available as prescription tablets containing 15, 30, or 60 mg of the drug.

Compared with morphine, codeine is a mild analgesic having no more than one-sixth of the potency of morphine. Codeine is effective taken orally and has been a common ingredient in cough syrups and other pain relief preparations. The abuse potential of codeine is much lower than that of morphine.

Hydromorphone (Dilaudid) and Oxycodone (Percodan) Hydromorphone and oxycodone are both semisynthetic opiates, made by chemically modifying one of the alkaloids obtained from opium. Dilaudid is usually encountered as the hydrochloride salt in tablet form. Percodan, also encountered in tablet form, is a drug preparation containing oxycodone in combination with aspirin, phenacetin, and caffeine.

The semisynthetic opiates produce effects which are qualitatively similar to those produced by morphine. They also have a high potential for being abused and can produce psychological and physical dependence comparable to that produced by morphine.

Meperidine (Demerol) and Methadone (Dolophine) Meperidine and methadone are two common opiates that are totally synthetic. Both may be encountered in tablet form or as aqueous solutions intended for injection. They have considerable analgesic activity and appear to act at the same site in the brain as does morphine.

Meperidine is not as potent as morphine by injection, but it is relatively more effective given orally. The sedation and euphoria produced by meperidine are comparable to that produced by morphine; however, at toxic levels some individuals experience a period of excitement and convulsions rather than sedation.

The analgesic action of methadone is as effective and potent by the oral route as morphine is by subcutaneous injection. Methadone also produces a level of euphoria similar in intensity and duration to that produced by morphine. The medicinal uses of methadone include relief of pain and treatment of withdrawal symptoms resulting from the chronic use of other opiates.

Stimulants

The sympathetic nervous system in humans is involved in the regulation of many peripheral body functions such as heart rate, blood pressure, and smooth muscle tone. It is also involved in regulating centrally controlled functions including respiratory stimulation, psychomotor activity, and appetite level. Normally, stimulation of the sympathetic nervous system occurs in response to physical activity, fear, or other types of physical or psychological stress. However, there are many drugs that can stimulate the sympathetic nervous system. The major effects produced by these drugs include excitement, loss of fatigue, decreased appetite, and increased wakefulness. These effects are considered pleasurable or euphoric by many people. They feel that stimulants prolong and enhance their ability to do work and heighten their enjoyment of recreational activities. The use of stimulants also has peripheral effects including elevation of blood pressure, increased respiratory rate, and nervousness. Excessive use may induce aggressive psychotic behavior, hallucinations, muscular tremor, convulsions, and possibly death. The most commonly abused stimulants are amphetamine, phenmetrazine (Preludin), methylphenidate (Ritalin), cocaine, and caffeine.

Amphetamine (Benzedrine, Dexedrine)   Amphetamine is a drug that is representative of a class of structurally related compounds known as phenethylamines. Included in this class are methamphetamine (Methedrine, Desoxyn), benzphetamine (Didrex), phenmetrazine (Preludin), phendimetrazine, ephedrine, phentermine (Ionamin), and methylphenidate (Ritalin).

The majority of these compounds are prescribed for use as appetite suppressants (diet pills) in weight-loss programs. Ephedrine, amphetamine, and methamphetamine are also used to treat patients with narcolepsy (a disease characterized by an excessive need for sleep); and methylphenidate is used in calming hyperactive children.

Each of these drugs is distributed officially in tablet or capsule form. However, amphetamine, methamphetamine, and methylphenidate are frequently produced illegally in clandestine laboratories and therefore may also be encountered as liquids or powders. Illicit capsules containing a mixture of phenmetrazine or phendimetrazine and caffeine are common on the streets.

Although oral administration of the tablets or capsules is the usual route of ingestion, intravenous injection of dissolved tablets or powders is practiced by some individuals who claim it produces an intensely pleasurable "rush." This, and other subjective effects of amphetamine-like drugs (that is, mood elevation and a sense of increased energy, alertness, and strength) are the major factors contributing to their high likelihood for abuse and physical or psychological dependence.

Cocaine   Cocaine is an alkaloid obtained primarily from the leaves of a South American shrub, *Erythroxylon coca*. It may also be prepared synthetically. Pure cocaine hydrochloride is a fluffy, white crystalline powder. The free base of cocaine is a clear viscous oil. Official preparations include the powder and aqueous solutions which may vary from 1.0 to 10 percent in concentration. Cocaine is usually encountered on the streets as a powder diluted with one or more sugars. Counterfeit cocaine may also be encountered and is frequently composed of one or more of the following compounds: ephedrine, amphetamine, lidocaine, dibucaine, tetracine, caffeine, or benzoic acid. Cocaine is also called *coke, snow,* or *free base.*

Cocaine is used clinically only as a local anesthetic for medical procedures involving the nose, mouth, or throat. It alters sensation in these areas by blocking nerve conduction through a direct action on nerve tissue. Cocaine is also a strong central nervous system (CNS) stimulant. It produces effects in the CNS that are almost identical to those produced by amphetamine.

Ingestion of cocaine is most often accomplished by inhalation of the powder into the nasal passages ("snorting") from which it is absorbed directly into the bloodstream. Inhalation of vapors produced by heating the free base of cocaine is another route of ingestion; it allows a relatively large amount of cocaine to be absorbed in a short period of time. The most dangerous route of cocaine ingestion is by intravenous injection. Direct intravenous injection of cocaine solutions is the most likely cause of death as a result of cocaine use.

Hallucinogens

Hallucinogens are chemicals that are capable of producing psychotic reactions in humans, altering perception of visual or auditory stimuli. The particular effects produced seem to depend on the personality of the subject and on the circumstances under which the drug is taken. Some users may experience effects described as euphoric, with colorful visual illusions and apparent distortions of their bodies and surroundings. Sounds may appear to have greater depth and clarity. Others, however, may experience acute psychotic episodes involving paranoid delusions, intense fear, manic excitement, or depression.

Hallucinogens do not appear to produce significant levels of physical or psychological dependence. Chronic users, however, may suffer memory difficulties, personality changes, difficulty in concentrating, and shortened attention span.

LSD (Lysergic Acid Diethylamide)   LSD was first synthesized in 1938 from lysergic acid, a naturally occurring substance found in the ergot fungus which infects rye and wheat grains. It belongs to a chemical class known as indoleamines, which also includes the hallucinogens psilocyn, psilocybin, dimethyltryptamine (DMT), and diethyltryptamine (DET).

LSD may be encountered as a solution which often is ingested on a lump of sugar. It may also be found in dried form on small paper squares which are meant for ingestion. A dose of 50 μg will result in hallucinations. The user may also suffer mental changes, dilated pupils, a drop in body temperature, and increased heart rate.

Psilocyn and psilocybin are derived from the mushroom *Psilocybe mexicana*. They are both effective when taken orally. DMT is found in the seeds of *Piptadenia peregrinea,* a plant native to the West Indies and South America.

DET is produced synthetically. Both DMT and DET are ineffective taken orally and are relatively short acting. These drugs are usually taken by smoking them in a mixture with tobacco, tea, parsley, or marijuana.

Mescaline (3,4,5-Trimethoxyphenylethylamine) Mescaline is the primary active hallucinogen in the peyote cactus plant. It may also be synthesized in the laboratory. It is usually encountered in powdered form and is effective when taken orally. A dose of 300 mg mescaline will produce hallucinations.

Mescaline is structurally related to amphetamine. Other hallucinogenic compounds that are structurally related to amphetamine include: methylenedioxyamphetamine (MDA), 3-methoxy-4,5-methylenedioxyamphetamine (MMDA), and 2,5-dimethoxy-4-methylamphetamine (DOM), commonly known as STP. Any of these substances may be encountered as powders, tablets, or solutions.

Phencyclidine (Sernyl) Phencyclidine has anesthetic activity and is manufactured legitimately for use as a veterinary anesthetic. It has no legitimate use in humans because of its hallucinogenic actions. A user may experience thought impairment, loss of time sense and comprehension, loss of muscular coordination, dizziness, and double vision. Generally, the effects are considered euphoric, but at times depression or anxiety and aggressive behavior are produced. Often taken by injection, phencyclidine is also "snorted" or smoked. Among its many street names are PCP, peace pill, hog, and angel dust.

Marijuana Marijuana generally refers to an hallucinogenic plant material derived from the flower, seeds, stem, and leaves of the *Cannabis* plant. *Cannabis* is a hardy hemp plant, growing to a height of about 5 ft. It grows well under widely varied climatic conditions. *Cannabis* plants have fluted leaf stalks and narrow, compound palmate leaves containing an odd number of leaflets. The leaves are lance-shaped with serrated edges and are covered with claw-shaped, hairlike fibers. These *cystolithic hairs* are one of the important structural features for the microscopical identification of marijuana.

The chemical substance responsible for the hallucinogenic properties of marijuana is tetrahydrocannabinol (THC). The marijuana plant contains about 0.2 to 2% THC, the majority being found in the flowers, resin, and leaves. Very little THC is found in the stem, root, or seeds. Hashish is the resinous secretion from the flowers of the *Cannabis* plant. It contains from 5 to 12% THC. Hashish oil is a dark, viscous oil extracted from hashish. Its THC content ranges from 20 to 60 percent.

Marijuana has numerous street names (pot, grass, joint, tea, reefer, etc.). It is usually rolled into a cigarette or smoked in a pipe. It is occasionally mixed with some food and eaten. Hashish is most commonly used by being smoked in a pipe. Hashish oil is generally administered by putting a drop of it onto a cigarette or by mixing it with tobacco in a pipe. A smoker usually becomes mildly intoxicated and experiences distortions of space and time. Vision and muscle coordination are temporarily impaired. The basis of any physical or psychological dependence on marijuana is not totally clear, and many studies indicate that there is no evidence of dependency.

Depressants

Ethanol (Ethyl Alcohol) Ethanol ("alcohol") is not ordinarily considered a drug by the public, but it is, in fact, a central-nervous-system (CNS) depressant. More than 85 million Americans consume various alcoholic beverages every year. Ethanol is a colorless, water-soluble, volatile liquid. Its concentration in alcoholic beverages varies from 3 to 6 percent in beer, 9 to 20 percent in wine, and up to or even above 50 percent (100 proof) in "hard" liquor. Ethanol enters the bloodstream unchanged, by diffusion through the walls of the stomach and small intestine. The presence of food in the stomach delays absorption to a degree.

The depressant effects of ethanol are similar to those of general anesthetics. The first mental processes affected are those that depend on training and previous experience. Moderate levels of ethanol cause a loss of inhibition and self-restraint. The user feels increased confidence and may falsely believe that ability to perform manual tasks has improved. At still higher blood levels of ethanol, judgment is affected and there may be depressed motor coordination, slurred speech, dizziness, and reduced visual acuity. Complete loss of consciousness and death from respiratory depression can occur as a result of ethanol ingestion.

Ethanol is metabolized by liver enzymes to acetaldehyde and acetate. The rate of metabolism becomes constant (approximately 10 mL/h) once a moderate blood level has been reached. Approximately 95 percent of ingested alcohol is eliminated by metabolism; the remaining 5 percent is eliminated primarily in urine and expired breath.

Sedative and Hypnotic Drugs Sedatives are drugs intended to produce a calming effect in the user, reducing excitement and activity. A hypnotic drug produces drowsiness and hypnosis, a state resembling natural sleep. All of the sedative and hypnotic drugs are CNS depressants. The effects they produce are indicative of varying levels of CNS depression. Excessive consumption of these agents can cause stupor, coma, and death by respiratory arrest. Included among the sedative-hypnotic drugs are the barbiturates, nonbarbiturate sedative-hypnotic drugs, and the benzodiazepines.

Barbiturates The first barbiturate, Veronal, was introduced in 1903 and a large number of other barbiturate derivatives followed in rapid succession. Barbiturates can be grouped into three general categories based upon the onset and duration of their actions: short-acting barbiturates (pentobarbital, secobarbital), intermediate-acting barbiturates (amobarbital), and long-acting barbiturates (phenobarbital).

The barbiturates are supplied in tablet form and are normally taken orally; however, abusers may dissolve tablets and inject these drugs intravenously. Occasionally, "barbs" are used in combination with ethanol, heroin, or amphetamines.

Long-term use of barbiturates may produce significant levels of physical dependence. Discontinuance under these conditions will cause symptoms of withdrawal characterized by excitement, delirium, vomiting, and convulsions. The consequences of abrupt barbiturate withdrawal may be more severe than those of withdrawal from heroin addiction.

Nonbarbiturate Sedative-Hypnotic Drugs A variety of chemically different compounds can be grouped in this category of CNS depressants. Their effects do not differ greatly from those produced by barbiturates. They are all used to induce sleep and one has very little advantage over the next for this purpose. Several were once believed to be safe substitutes for barbiturates, without addiction potential. However, their potential for abuse and dependence is actually very high. Included among these drugs are: methaqualone (Quaalude, Sopor), ethchlorvynol (Placidyl), chloral hydrate, glutethimide (Doriden), methyprylon (Noludar), and meprobamate (Equanil, Miltown). In recent years, methaqualone has become a major drug of abuse. Deaths and other problems associated with its abuse have increased more rapidly than those with any other single drug.

Benzodiazepines There are numerous benzodiazepine derivatives marketed. Each differs somewhat in the quality of the CNS depressant effects it produces. Their range of therapeutic effects include sedation, decreased anxiety, muscle relaxation, anticonvulsant activity, and hypnosis. Diazepam (Valium) is the most commonly encountered benzodiazepine, because it is the most frequently prescribed and most likely to be abused. Other common benzodiazepines are flurazepam (Dalmane), chlordiazepoxide (Librium), and lorazepam (Ativan). Virtually all benzodiazepines encountered (tablets and capsules) will have been made by an official manufacturer. The abuse potential of the benzodiazepines is high, primarily because of the development of psychological dependence. High doses of these agents can be expected to cause loss of muscular coordination, decreased reaction time, confusion, and lethargy. Use of ethanol in combination with a benzodiazepine is particularly dangerous.

POISONS—TOXIC SUBSTANCES

There are more than 10,000 different kinds of poisons (toxic substances) known. Only a limited number of them, however, are ordinarily found in association with criminal cases, homicides, suicides, and accidents. These substances can be classified broadly into two major categories: inorganic poisons and organic poisons. Within each category, poisons could be found in any of three forms: solid, liquid, and gaseous. Poisons and toxic substances are usually analyzed by a forensic toxicologist. *Forensic toxicology* involves the recognition, analysis, and evaluation of poisons and drugs. Recognition of a poisoning when it occurs, and rapid, reliable diagnosis can be helpful in saving lives in poisoning cases and determining the causes of massive accidental poisoning. It may also help in determining the causes of unknown poisoning deaths. The evaluation of toxicological findings ordinarily includes determination of the amounts of poison present and interpretation of the results in terms of toxic vs. therapeutic dosages.

Inorganic Poisons

The inorganic poisons are frequently heavy metals or metalloids. The most common heavy-metal poisons are antimony, arsenic, barium, beryllium, cadmium, lead, mercury, and thallium. The soluble salts of other metals, such as bismuth, copper, manganese, silver, tin, and zinc, can also cause poisoning.

Arsenic has a long and colorful history as an agent of murder by poisoning, especially in older times. The historically significant forensic case discussed in Chapter 1 was a forensic toxicology case involving arsenic poisoning. Arsenic is commonly encountered in the form of its compounds, including the oxide, arsenites, and arsenates. Arsenic trioxide (As_2O_3) is the best known of these. There are not many homicides caused by arsenic poisoning today, but arsenic is still widely used in various industrial chemicals and in chemicals of agricultural importance such as pesticides and herbicides. These compounds are occasionally encountered as causes of accidental poisonings.

Lead poisoning, although rarely seen in homicide or suicide cases nowadays, is still quite frequent in urban areas because of the presence of lead compounds in wall and water-pipe paints in old buildings. Paints such as these often peel or chip, and pieces of this material are picked up and ingested by small children.

Cyanides are the most important, nonmetallic poisons. Sodium and potassium cyanide are the two most common solid salts of cyanide encountered in poisoning cases. Hydrogen cyanide is an extremely toxic gas, which is widely encountered in some kinds of chemical and metallurgical settings. It is a common cause of accidental industrial poisonings. Cyanide poisoning is very rapid, and death can occur within a very short time after the cyanide enters the body.

Other heavy-metal compounds, such as those of antimony, thallium, and beryllium, are occasionally found in poisoning cases. Potassium antimony tartrate was a common poisoning agent in ancient China. Thallium salts are still used for the poisoning of rodents. Beryllium was once used in some of the phosphors (which, despite the name, are primarily fluorescent, not phosphorescent compounds) which coat the inside of fluorescent lamp tubes.

Many nonmetallic elements—such as phosphorus, fluorine, and iodine—and their compounds are also poisonous. These materials are used in insecticides and rodenticides as well as for various industrial purposes. However, they are infrequently encountered by the toxicologist.

Strong oxidants, inorganic gases (especially carbon monoxide), and strong acids and alkalis are also destructive and sometimes cause deaths. They are therefore considered to be poisons.

Organic Poisons

Organic poisons are commonly classified as *acidic, neutral,* or *basic,* according to the conditions under which they are extracted from aqueous solutions by organic solvents. Barbiturates and aspirin (acetylsalicylic acid), for example, are considered acidic drugs since they are readily extracted from acidic solutions by organic solvents. Morphine, cocaine, and amphetamines are considered basic drugs, because they are more readily extracted from basic solutions. Organic poisons may also be classified as *volatile* or *nonvolatile,* according to their rate of evaporation. Other systems of classification have also been used, as for example by their mode of action (corrosive, irritant, narcotic, etc.), according to their origin (animal, vegetable, etc.) or according to their state (solid, liquid, gaseous).

The large number of opiates and other drugs described in the above sections can be poisonous. Alkaloids and barbiturates are the most important organic poisons commonly encountered by the toxicologist. These drugs are favored by individuals who commit suicide, but they are not very commonly used by murderers. There has recently been an increase in the number of poisoning cases caused by the ingestion of mixtures of opiates, hallucinogens, and other drugs.

Glycosides are a group of naturally occurring substances of plant origin. They are chemically related to sugars and are usually alcoholic or phenolic compounds. The most common glycoside is digitalis, often called a *cardiac glycoside* because it is employed in the treatment of certain kinds of heart conditions. Overdoses of digitalis can be fatal.

Organic pesticides are encountered in many cases of homicidal, suicidal, and accidental poisoning. These substances may be divided into the following groups:

1 Chlorinated benzene derivatives, such as DDT, aldrin, dieldrin, and benzene hexachloride.

2 Coumarin derivatives, such as warfarin (a rat poison)

3 Organophosphate esters, such as parathion

All of these compounds are toxic, and ingestion of or exposure to sufficient quantities can result in fatalities.

There are many other nonvolatile organic poisons, such as ricin, botulin toxin, and snake venoms. These are produced either by plants or animals, and all have very high toxicity.

The most common member of the group of *volatile* organic substances is ethyl alcohol. Other alcohols, too, such as methyl alcohol and isopropyl alcohol, are poisonous, as are aniline, phenol, benzene, gasoline, and many other organic solvents. They are occasionally encountered in poisoning cases and require toxicological identification.

COLLECTION AND PRESERVATION OF DRUGS AND POISONS

Drugs can be found on persons or at scenes. They should be collected with care. Tablets and powders should be collected and packaged in pillbox containers of suitable size. If no suitable container of this kind is available, they should be packaged in clean paper using a druggist's fold (Chapter 6). Liquids should be collected in their original bottles or in tightly sealed jars. Other drug paraphernalia should also be collected.

All evidence collected should be properly labeled with the name of the investigator, the date, time, suspect's name, location of discovery, and the nature and quantity of the evidence. The evidence should be carefully recorded in the log book and then submitted to the laboratory for analysis.

In a case involving a possible poisoning, an investigator should be careful in conducting a search of the scene and preserving physical evidence. Any empty or partially empty container in the vicinity of a victim's body should be collected. Any bottle, envelope, or other container that could have contained poison should also be collected. Any food suspected of containing poison, dishes used by the victim, and any vomitus at the scene should be collected, documented, properly packaged and labeled, and submitted to the laboratory. All containers should be examined for latent fingerprints. Containers should be tightly sealed and placed in properly labeled packages. The finding of a poison container with a trace of the poison remaining in it can make the identification of the poison much easier for the toxicologist. Quick identification of a poison can sometimes result in saving a victim's life. If a victim appears to have died as the result of a homicidal poisoning, the scene should be properly searched for other evidence. Any hairs, fibers, blood, latent fingerprints, or other types of evidence should be collected and preserved according to the procedures discussed elsewhere in this book.

LABORATORY EXAMINATION OF DRUGS AND POISONS

A number of laboratory techniques are commonly used in forensic science for the identification and analysis of drugs and poisons. These techniques may be classified into three categories: (1) isolation and separation procedures, (2) qualitative chemical and microscopical identification procedures, and (3) quantitative determinations, using instruments.

Isolation and Separation Techniques

The major difficulties faced by the forensic chemist or toxicologist are the questionable purity and the limited quantity of the sample to be analyzed. In the case of drugs or poisons requiring toxicological examination, the materials may be present in only trace amounts, and they are contained in body fluids or organs. Although the gross quantities of drugs handled by forensic chemists are usually quite large, they are frequently mixed with various diluting substances that make identification more difficult. The first step in an identification of an unknown drug or toxic substance, therefore, is its separation from various other components in the mixture.

As was noted in Chapter 3, a number of different techniques can be used to separate the components of mixtures. Generally, a solute may be separated from a solvent, or recovered from a mixture, by fractional distillation, evaporation, recrystallization, extraction, centrifugation, or chromatography. The initial separation technique utilized most often in forensic toxicology is solvent extraction.

As mentioned earlier in the chapter, drugs can be categorized as acidic, basic, or neutral, according to the conditions which favor their extraction from an aqueous to an organic liquid phase. A forensic chemist usually first separates an unknown sample of material into several portions. One portion is then dissolved in an aqueous solution. To extract the acidic drugs, the solution is first acidified by adding an acid. (Hydrochloric and acetic acids are commonly used.) Then, an organic solvent (chloroform and ether are common) is added to the solution. These solvents do not mix with water. After addition of the organic solvent, therefore, the extraction mixture contains two separate phases which can easily be seen. The mixture is shaken vigorously, and the acidic drug, which is more soluble in the organic phase in its free-acid form, will be extracted out of the aqueous solution and into the organic solvent. If the mixture is allowed to sit, the organic and aqueous phases will again separate and the organic solvent containing the drug can be recovered. When a basic drug is being extracted, essentially the same procedure is followed, except that in this case the aqueous solution is made basic by the addition of a strong base like sodium or ammonium hydroxide. This treatment converts the drug to its free base form, which is more soluble in the organic liquid phase. Extractions are usually done in a special piece of laboratory ware called a *separatory funnel,* which allows the mixture to be shaken vigorously and then enables easy recovery of the two phases after the shaken mixture has settled.

Extraction of drugs from body fluids or organs is done in the same way as the extraction from aqueous solutions. The tissues or organs must be ground, macerated, or chemically digested first, however, and the mixtures are filtered or centrifuged to remove the debris prior to extraction. Once the aqueous material is separated from the tissue and cell material, the extraction procedures described above can be followed exactly. Volatile drugs or poisons, such as alcohols or phenols, can be separated by steam distillation. The isolated drugs can then be recovered from the distillate by extraction, further distillation, or evaporation and identified by the methods described below.

Methods of Identification

Macroscopic Examination   When drug evidence is submitted to the laboratory, the first step is to log the evidence received into the records. The drugs should then be weighed and a gross description of them recorded (powder, tablets, solution, color, odor, shape, and other characteristics). If tablets are submitted, their shape, size, logo pattern, weight, and the presence of any inclusions should be recorded before dissolving them.

If plant material is involved, it can be examined under a low-power stereomicroscope. Fragments of marijuana leaves can be identified, for example, by the presence of the bear-claw-shaped hairs on the surface (Figure 5-1). These cystolithic hairs contain calcium carbonate at the base. Vegetable material can further be tested by chemical methods to determine whether it is marijuana.

Chemical Tests   Unknown substances can be identified by treating them with various chemical reagents. Certain reagents react with certain drugs to give characteristic color reactions. These color tests are commonly used as screening tests in the laboratory or in the field. Seven common color test reagents, and their uses, are described below.

Cobalt Thiocyanate Reagent   This reagent consists of 2 g cobalt thiocyanate dissolved in 100 mL distilled water. It produces a blue precipitate in the presence of cocaine. It will also give a similar color, however, with many other drugs like Darvon, Demerol, procaine, and chlorpromazine.

Modified Dille-Koppanyi Reagent   Solution A is prepared by dissolving 0.1 g cobalt acetate dihydrate in 100 mL methanol containing 0.2 mL glacial acetic acid. Solution B is made by adding 5 mL isopropylamine to 95 mL methanol. To conduct a test, 2 volumes of solution A is added to the sample, followed by 1 volume of solution B. This is a valuable screening test for barbiturates.

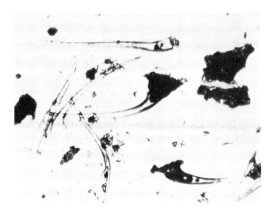

FIGURE 5-1
Marijuana ash showing ''bear-claw''
hairs. (*Courtesy of Detective Nicholas
Petraco, Crime Laboratory, New York
City Police Department.*)

Modified Duquenois-Levine Reagent Solution A consists of 2.5 mL acetaldehyde and 2 g vanillin in 100 mL 95% ethanol. Solution B is concentrated hydrochloric acid, and solution C is chloroform. To do the test, 1 volume of solution A is added to the suspected material, and the mixture shaken gently for 1 min. One volume of solution B is added and gently mixed. Finally, 3 volumes of solution C is added, and the mixture is shaken. A purple color extracted into the chloroform (solution C) layer indicates that the unknown material was marijuana. This is a valuable test for marijuana. Observations should be recorded at each step.

Mandelin Reagent 1 g ammonium vanadate is dissolved in 100 mL concentrated sulfuric acid. This reagent is used as a screening test for codeine (olive color), cocaine (orange color), and heroin (brown color).

Marquis Reagent 100 mL concentrated sulfuric acid is mixed with 5 mL 40% formaldehyde. The reagent gives a purple color with morphine or heroin and with most other opium derivatives. It turns an orange-brown color with amphetamines and methamphetamine.

Nitric Acid Concentrated nitric acid reacts with codeine, doxepin, heroin, LSD, and some other drugs to give a yellow to orange color.

p-DMAB (para-Dimethylaminobenzaldehyde) This is sometimes called Van Urk reagent. To make it, 2 g *p*-DMAB is added to 50 mL 95% ethanol and 50 mL concentrated hydrochloric acid. The reagent turns blue to purple in the presence of LSD.

Table 5-1 lists some of the common color reagents for the identification of drugs, their detection limits, and the final color of their reaction products. All the color tests are more meaningful if carried out under controlled conditions by an experienced forensic chemist.

Microchemical crystal tests are also used. These are considered more specific than color tests. In the procedure, a drop of test reagent is added to a small quantity of the questioned substance, placed on a microscope slide, and then examined under the microscope. Depending upon the drug and the test reagent, specific crystals are then produced by the reaction. These crystals are highly characteristic of certain drugs. These tests are rapid and generally require no purification or isolation of the suspected drug. Hundreds of crystal tests have been developed for the identification of commonly abused drugs and opiates. Figure 5-2 shows a photomicrograph of heroin crystals in the presence of 10% sodium acetate. Table 5-2 gives the most common test reagents for microchemical crystal tests for drugs and their formulations.

Occasionally, forensic toxicologists are requested to test for the presence of heavy-metal poisons. These, as was pointed out above, include arsenic, bismuth, anitmony, and mercury. A Reinsch test is sometimes used to screen these metals. The suspected fluids or organs are first macerated in hydrochloric acid. A clean, new copper strip is inserted into the mixture, which is then boiled. The appearance of a dark-colored deposit on the copper strip is indicative of the presence of heavy metals. The specific metal on the copper strip can then be identified using other laboratory techniques for elemental identification, such as microchemical tests, atomic absorption spectrophotometry (AA), emission spectroscopy, x-ray diffraction, or neutron activation analysis (NAA).

TABLE 5-1
COLOR TESTS FOR COMMON DRUGS

Drug	Reagent	Detection limit, μg	Final color
Amphetamine	Mandelin	10	Bluish green
	Marquis	10	Reddish brown
Barbiturates	Modified Dille-Koppanyi	100	Purple
Cocaine	Cobalt thiocyanate	60	Greenish blue
	Mandelin	100	Orange
Codeine	Mandelin	5	Olive
	Marquis	1	Violet
Heroin	Mandelin	20	Reddish brown
	Marquis	10	Purple
LSD	Marquis	5	Purple-black
	p-DMAB	5	Blue-purple
Marijuana	Modified Duquenois-Levine	100	Deep blue
Methadone	Cobalt thiocyanate	15	Blue
	Marquis	1	Yellow-pink
Mescaline	Marquis	1	Red-orange
	Nitric acid	1	Reddish brown
Morphine	Mandelin	5	Purple

Instrumental Analysis   A variety of instrumental techniques are used to confirm the identity of drugs and toxic substances, and to determine the *amount* of such materials present. These include chromatography, spectrophotometry, mass spectrometry, x-ray fluorescence, and x-ray diffraction.

Thin-layer chromatography (TLC), gas chromatography (GC), and high-perfor-

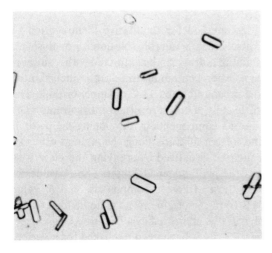

FIGURE 5-2
Heroin crystals produced with sodium acetate. *(Courtesy of Detective Nicholas Petraco, Crime Laboratory, New York City Police Department.)*

TABLE 5-2
CRYSTAL TESTS FOR COMMONLY ABUSED DRUGS

Reagent	Reagent Preparation	Drugs for Which Reagent Is Used	Shape of Crystals
Gold chloride	3 g AuCl₃ dissolved in 100 mL water, and acidified with 0.25 mL hydrochloric acid	Cocaine Procaine	Combs of needles and rosettes of needles Blades in clumps of rosettes
Platinum chloride	5 g PtCl₄ dissolved in 100 mL 1 N hydrochloric acid	Cocaine Benzocaine	Combs of needles Needles
Gold chloride in phosphoric acid	Dissolve 2 parts 5% AuCl₃ in 1 part concentrated phosphoric acid	Methamphetamine D-Amphetamine	Long barbs and long needles Long yellow rods and blades
Platinum iodide	5 g PtCl₄ and 25 g sodium or potassium iodide (NaI or KI) dissolved in 100 mL water	Methamphetamine D-Amphetamine	Blades, some serrated Hexagonal plates
Sodium acetate	10% solution of sodium acetate in water	Heroin Quinine	Hexagonal plates Irregularly shaped "logs"
Mercuric iodide	10% hydrochloric acid solution, saturated with HgI₂	Heroin	Rosettes of dendrites
Mercuric chloride	5 g HgCl₂ dissolved in 100 mL water (5% solution)	Methadone	Small rosettes of rods
Potassium permanganate	2 g potassium permanganate (KMnO₄) and 0.25 mL phosphoric acid to 100 mL with water	Phencyclidine	Purple H-shaped plates

mance liquid chromatography (HPLC) are the commonly used chromatographic techniques. Their basic principles were discussed in Chapter 3. Unknown substances are identified by comparison of their R_f values, retention times, and chromatographic behavior with those of known drug standards.

TLC is an excellent and widely used method for qualitative identification of unknown drugs. An unknown drug is dissolved in a suitable solution for analysis. A bodily tissue or organ suspected of containing a drug can be extracted with a suitable solvent, and the extract analyzed. The solution containing the drug is then spotted onto a TLC plate, which is placed into a preequilibrated TLC chamber or tank. The tank contains the developing solution, usually a mixture of several solvents. The unknown material may be separated into its components by developing the plate, if the different components migrate in the solvent mixture along the plate at different rates. The separated components can then be visualized by spraying the plate with developing reagents or by observation of the plate under UV light. The R_f values of the components are then compared with those of known compounds. The R_f value for a component is the distance it travels from the origin on the plate divided by the distance traveled by the developing solvent; it is expressed as a decimal (Chapter 3). Many drugs have been tested, and their R_f values have been published for a variety of TLC solvent systems. By choosing appropriate solvent systems in which to run the unknown and then comparing the R_f obtained with known values, drugs can usually be screened quite readily. Confirmatory tests can then be applied.

Gas chromatography is widely used as a qualitative and quantitative analytical technique for drugs and alcohol. As mentioned in Chapters 3 and 4, GC separates a mixture into its components on the basis of their different distributions between a stationary phase and a moving gas phase. Different components travel at different rates. As each component emerges from the GC column, it enters a detector. A chromatogram is then produced on a chart recorder connected to the amplified detector signal. Individual components, and the mixture, can be compared to known standards and tentative identifications made. GC, although it is an excellent separation method, is not a technique for making positive identifications, because there are other possible substances which will yield similar chromatograms and comparable retention times. For an absolute identification, therefore, other confirmatory techniques should be used.

Infrared spectrophotometry and UV-VIS spectrophotometry are commonly used in the forensic laboratory for drug analysis. A UV or visible spectrum of an unknown compound could be used to aid in making an identification. UV and visible spectral absorption peaks may show characteristic shifts with certain drugs when these are dissolved in solutions of different pH. These shifts can give important information, therefore, in making qualitative determinations on unknown materials (see Fig. 3.9).

The IR spectrum of each pure substance is unique. An IR spectrum is often referred to by chemists as a "fingerprint" of a compound. This technique can be used for both qualitative and quantitative determination of an unknown drug, provided it is pure. The IR spectrum of heroin is shown in Figure 5-3.

Mass spectrometry (MS) is also used in qualitative and quantitative determination of drugs. This technique, however, like IR spectrometry, is extremely sensitive to the presence of impurities in the sample. The purity of the sample, therefore, is an important factor in determining the quality of the analytical results. Because

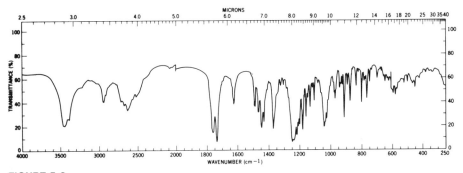

FIGURE 5-3
An infrared absorption spectrum of heroin. (*Drug Enforcement Administration, U.S. Department of Justice.*)

forensic samples are often mixtures and because IR and MS techniques are excellent identification techniques for pure compounds, combined GC-IR and combined GC-MS procedures have now been introduced. Here, a gas chromatograph is interfaced with an IR spectrometer or with a mass spectrometer. Mixtures can be injected into the GC, which separates them into components. As each component comes off the GC column, it is introduced into the IR or MS automatically, without any intervention by the operator. The individual components are then analyzed and can be identified by their spectra. The mass spectra of cocaine and heroin are shown in Figure 5-4.

BREATH-ALCOHOL AND BLOOD-ALCOHOL ANALYSIS

Breath-Alcohol Analysis

The first state law on the admissibility of chemical tests for blood alcohol was passed in Indiana in 1939, shortly after the first model of the Drunkometer was used for breath-alcohol analysis. In early models of breath-alcohol test devices, the concentration of alcohol in breath was determined by measuring the volume of alveolar (deep lung breath) air required to reduce a fixed amount of acidic potassium permanganate solution. The alveolar fraction of the volume of expired breath analyzed was estimated by determining the weight of CO_2 present. However, since the constancy of the CO_2 content of expired breath at rest is questionable, the National Safety Council recommended in 1967 that the use of CO_2 in estimating alveolar breath be discontinued.

Following the federal highway safety program, which requires that states develop specific standards regarding alcohol and driving, various models of breath-alcohol testing devices have become commercially available, such as the Alcometer, photoelectric Intoximeter, Alco-Tester, Alco-Analyzer, Alco-Limiter, Breathalyzer, Alco-Sensor, and Roadside Breath Tester. Table 5-3 lists some of these breath-alcohol testing instruments and briefly describes the principles of their operation. Some of them have types of instruments that utilize a rapid means of measurement which does not involve the classical wet chemical oxidation of ethanol in a breath sample. They rely instead on techniques such as GC, IR spectrometry, and solid state oxidation by means of electrochemical oxidation, fuel cells, catalytic oxidation devices, and metal oxide semiconductor sensors. The principle of all these breath-alcohol testing instruments is measurement of the alcohol vapor in a given volume of alveolar air. The alcohol concentration in a known volume of air is then converted to blood alcohol concentration by the commonly accepted blood-breath ratio. This ratio is 2100:1 (the amount of alcohol in 2100 mL of alveolar breath air is equivalent to that in 1 mL of blood).

One of the most popular breath-alcohol testing devices in use today is the Breathalyzer 1000. It is a modification of the original Breathalyzer. The instrument and a schematic diagram of it are shown in Figure 5-5. The operation has been made more automatic, thus decreasing manipulations required of the operator. The subject is required to blow into a mouthpiece that leads into a metal cylinder, which is in turn

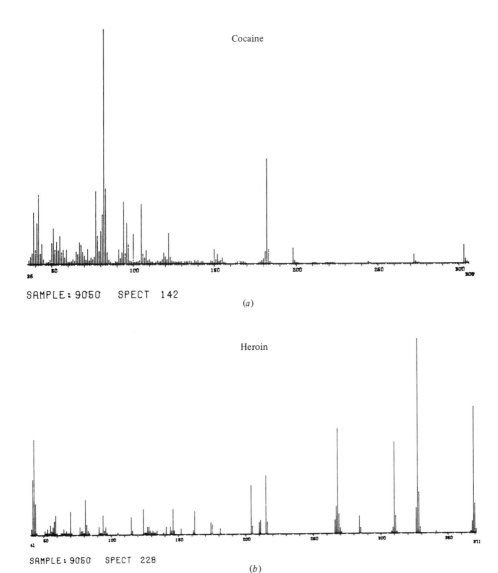

FIGURE 5-4
Mass spectra of cocaine and heroin. *(Courtesy of Dr. Howard A. Harris, Director, Crime Laboratory, New York City Police Department.)*

connected to a second piston-cylinder. The second cylinder collects and discards the first 400 mL of delivered breath. When the last breath has been expired, a predetermined volume of the last portion of alveolar breath (deep lung air) has been trapped in the second cylinder. The amount of breath collected is equivalent to 56.5 mL. This breath is warmed to 50°C, and 55.2 mL of it is bubbled through an ampule con-

TABLE 5-3
BREATH-ALCOHOL INSTRUMENTS

Instrument	Sample	Method
Drunkometer	Mixed expired air	Wet oxidation $KMnO_4$–H_2SO_4
Alcometer	Deep lung air	Wet oxidation iodine pentoxide
Photoelectric Intoximeter	Deep lung air	Wet oxidation—photometry dichromate–H_2SO_4
Breathalyzer	Deep lung air	Wet oxidation—photometry dichromate–H_2SO_4
Alco-Analyzer	Deep lung air	Gas chromatography
GC Intoximeter	Deep lung air	Gas chromatography
Intoxilyzer	Deep lung air	Infrared photometry
Alco-Limiter	Deep lung air	Electrochemical oxidation
Roadside Breath Tester	Deep lung air	Fuel-cell sensing
A.L.E.R.T.	Deep lung air	Sensing (screening test)

taining potassium dichromate and sulfuric acid with silver nitrate as a catalyst. The chemical reaction which occurs is represented by the following equation:

$$2K_2Cr_2O_7 + 3C_2H_5OH + 8H_2SO_4 \xrightarrow[\text{silver nitrate}]{AgNO_3}$$

Potassium dichromate · Ethyl alcohol · Sulfuric acid

$$2Cr_2(SO_4)_3 + 2K_2SO_4 + 3CH_3COOH + 11H_2O$$

Chromium sulfate · Potassium sulfate · Acetic acid · Water

Potassium dichromate solution is yellow and is known to absorb visible light of wavelength 420 nanometers (nm). If alcohol is present in the breath sample, it will have been oxidized to acetic acid by the potassium dichromate. As this reaction takes place, the potassium dichromate solution is changed to chromic sulfate, which is green. The extent of the color change is directly proportional to the amount of potassium dichromate needed to oxidize the alcohol which was present. Thus, the alcohol content of the breath can be calculated by measuring the extent of the color change. The photometric absorbance of the Breathalyzer is first calibrated by equalizing the filtered blue light absorbance of a reference and test ampule (containing potassium dichromate solution). The change in absorbance upon analysis of a breath sample is converted to a digital readout and a printed record of the presumed blood-alcohol concentration, based on the assumption of a blood-breath ratio of 2100:1.

Blood-Alcohol Analysis

In some cases, depending upon the circumstances of the case, and the laws in the particular jurisdiction, blood may be drawn from persons suspected of driving while

(a)

FIGURE 5-5
(a) A Breathalyzer breath alcohol instrument in use. (b) Schematic of the Breathalyzer. (*Courtesy of Lieutenant Robert Horn, Scientific Laboratory, New York State Police.*)

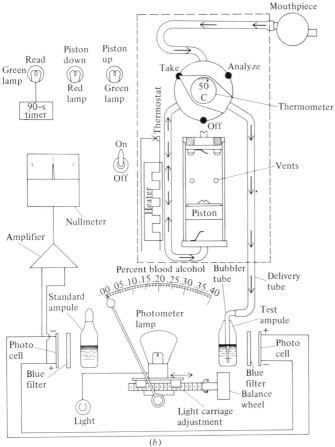

(b)

intoxicated for the purpose of measuring blood-alcohol concentration. In some states, blood-alcohol concentrations in excess of 0.1% are taken as *prima facie* evidence of driving while intoxicated.

There are three major methods for the determination of blood-alcohol concentration: (1) gas chromatography; (2) microdiffusion, followed by chemical analysis; and (3) enzymatic methods using alcohol dehydrogenase.

GC methods take advantage of the fact that alcohol is a volatile substance and can be separated from other substances in blood by GC on a suitable column. Once a standardized GC procedure has been set up, the alcohol concentration in a questioned blood sample can be measured very accurately. This method has the advantage of being relatively fast and of enabling fairly large numbers of samples to be processed in a comparatively short time.

Microdiffusion is a general technique for separating volatile compounds from body fluids, tissues, or other complex mixtures. In one type, small chambers which resemble little dishes are used. These are provided with covers, so that they can be tightly sealed. The sample is placed into an outer well of the dish and may be treated with a reagent that will aid in the release of the volatile compound. The center well of the dish contains another chemical which traps the volatile compound from the resulting vapor. In the case of alcohol analysis, the chemical in the center well causes the alcohol to be oxidized to acetic acid. Microdiffusion thus results in the quantitative transfer of the volatile alcohol from the body-fluid mixture into a simpler solution in which its concentration can be easily determined. In microdiffusion blood-alcohol analysis, the extent of reduction of the chemical in the center well can be determined and is directly proportional to the amount of alcohol that was contained in the sample. The principle is basically the same as the dichromate oxidation principle described above for breath-alcohol analysis.

In the enzymatic method, the sample is treated with an enzyme known as alcohol dehydrogenase (ADH). This enzyme can catalyze the quantitative oxidation of alcohol in the presence of another chemical, nicotinamide adenine dinucleotide (NAD). As the alcohol is oxidized, a like amount of NAD is reduced. By measuring the amount of NAD which was reduced, the amount of alcohol present in the original sample can be determined.

STUDY QUESTIONS

1 What is a drug? A poison? An opiate?
2 Name several important opiate drugs.
3 Name several important stimulants.
4 Name several important depressants.
5 Name several important hallucinogens.
6 What is marijuana? What is the difference between marijuana and hashish?
7 Name several inorganic poisons.
8 Cite two ways of classifying organic poisons.
9 What are glycosides?
10 What precautions and procedures should be used in collecting and packaging drug evidence?

11 Name some of the laboratory isolation and separation procedures used in drug analysis and toxicology.

12 What is extraction? Explain briefly how solvent extraction works.

13 Name some of the chemical tests used for drugs and explain how they are used.

14 What are microcrystal tests and how are they used in drug analysis?

15 What are some of the chromatographic and instrumental techniques used in drug identification? Identify whether each technique is qualitative or quantitative.

16 How can breath alcohol content be related to blood alcohol content?

17 What are the major techniques for measuring blood alcohol concentrations?

REFERENCES AND FURTHER READING

American Medical Association: *Alcohol and the Impaired Driver,* A Manual on the Medicolegal Aspects of Chemical Tests for Intoxication, Chicago, 1970.

Baselt, R. C.: *Disposition of Toxic Drugs and Chemicals in Man,* Biomedical Publications, Irvine, Calif., 1977.

Caplan, Y. H.: "The Determination of Alcohol in Blood and Breath," in R. Saferstein (ed.), *Forensic Science Handbook,* Prentice-Hall, Englewood Cliffs, N.J., 1982.

Clarke, E. G. C.: *Isolation and Identification of Drugs,* Pharmaceutical Press, London, 1969.

Conway, E. J.: *Microdiffusion Analysis and Volumetric Error,* Chemical Publishing, New York, 1963.

Cravey, R. H., and N. C. Jain: "Current Status of Blood Alcohol Methods," *Journal of Chromatographic Science,* vol. 12, p. 209, 1974.

Curry, A. S.: *Advances in Forensic and Clinical Toxicology,* CRC Press, Cleveland, 1972.

Fulton, C. C.: *Modern Microcrystal Tests for Drugs,* Wiley-Interscience, New York, 1969.

Instrumental Applications in Forensic Drug Chemistry, Proceedings of the International Symposium, U.S. Government Printing Office, Washington, D.C., 1979.

Lowry, W. T., and J. C. Garriott: *Forensic Toxicology, Controlled Substances and Dangerous Drugs,* Plenum, New York, 1979.

U.S. Department of Justice, Drug Enforcement Administration: *Narcotics Investigators Manual,* Washington, D.C., 1973.

Winek, C. L.: "Forensic Toxicology," in C. H. Wecht (ed.), *Forensic Science,* vol. 3, chap. 31, Matthew Bender, New York, 1981.

CHAPTER **6**

TRANSFER AND TRACE EVIDENCE

INTRODUCTION

Transfer and trace evidence is very important in forensic investigations. This category of evidence encompasses many diverse types of microscopic or submicroscopic materials as well as some examples that are easily visible to the naked eye. Because of the large number of different materials which may be included, the subject is broad and diverse. Some classes of this kind of evidence are so commonly encountered that they are given separate treatment in this book. Chapter 7 will deal with glass and soil and Chapter 8 with hairs and fibers; blood and body-fluid evidence will be covered in Chapters 9 and 10. The remaining, somewhat less commonly encountered, types of trace and transfer evidence are discussed in this chapter.

Transfer and trace evidence is one of the largest categories of physical evidence, containing numerous types and subcategories of materials. For this reason, there are many examples of materials for which suitable comparison methodologies have not yet been developed to an extent that would enable determinations about common origin. Nevertheless, there are many examples of cases in which trace or transfer evidence can play an important role in determining the facts. The following case exemplifies how trace and transfer evidence can contribute to a reconstruction.

Not too long ago, a police officer was guarding a wounded prisoner in a hospital room during the early morning hours. Five shots were heard, and two nurses saw the prisoner flee. He was recaptured on the hospital grounds with the officer's service revolver in his possession. He claimed that he gained control of the weapon during a struggle which ensued after the officer had tried to strangle him. The officer had been shot three times and died almost instantly. One of the three bullets had perforated his heart. In court, the defendant claimed, as might be expected, that he killed the officer in self-defense during the struggle.

Although the defendant's story did not sound very plausible, little physical evidence that could be used to refute it was uncovered during the initial investigation. During a later investigation, several additional bits of evidence were recognized. A few small, and seemingly unimportant, grease stains were found on one of the bedsheets. Microscopical examination revealed that the grease was similar to that used to lubricate a portion of an intravenous feeding stand which was found on the floor near the victim (Figure 6-1). It appeared that the upper portion of this stand had been separated from its base and used as a clublike weapon. The identity of the grease stains and their pattern on the bedsheet allowed the criminalist to conclude that the top half of the stand had been removed and hidden in the bed prior to the struggle that resulted in the officer's death. This point, coupled with other physical evidence, much of which was not initially recognized, yielded a rather detailed reconstruction which was consistent with premeditation. When confronted with this reconstruction, during the course of his trial, the defendant stopped the proceedings, confessed, and pleaded guilty to first degree murder. The details of his confession confirmed the criminalist's reconstruction. He was sentenced to life imprisonment.

The reconstruction made possible by the trace-evidence analysis here played a crucial role in the investigation. The evidence in this case could easily have been overlooked, and in fact probably would have been overlooked if the investigators had not been especially alert and thoughtful. Even when the quantity of evidence is large enough for it to be seen easily, its significance and relationship to the act being investigated may not be readily recognized.

TRANSFER AND TRACE EVIDENCE: NATURE, DIFFERENCES, DIVERSITY, OCCURRENCE

The terms *transfer evidence* and *trace evidence* are sometimes used synonymously, although they do differ in meaning when carefully considered. Trace evidence can be thought of as evidence occurring in sizes so small that it can be transferred or exchanged between two surfaces without being noticed. Strictly speaking, transfer evidence is evidence which is exchanged between two objects as the result of contact, and trace evidence is often a kind of transfer evidence. Trace evidence can be encountered, however, which was not exchanged as the result of contact. Such contactless exchanges are less common but could include the entrainment of airborne particles or situations in which small amounts of material are projected or fall onto another surface. The deposition of gunshot-residue particles (Chapter 14) is a relatively common example of transfer without contact. Just as trace evidence is not always transferred, all examples of transfer evidence are not trace evidence. Most examples of transfer evidence represent small amounts of finely divided material, but sometimes the amount or color of the material transferred makes it clearly visible and the term *trace* seems inappropriate. An obvious paint transfer is a common example. Even here, however, the amount of material transferred can be deceptively small and may be difficult to analyze.

The diversity of transfer evidence is indicated by the many different varieties

FIGURE 6-1
(*a*) Bloodstains and grease stain on bedsheet. The pattern of the grease stain shows that the sheet was wrinkled when the stain was made by the intravenous stand. (*b*) A scanning electron micrograph (~50×) of an area of the bedsheet containing a grease stain. The individual cotton fibers making up the woven bedsheet have particles adhering to them. (*c*) An SEM micrograph of the stained area of the bedsheet at about twice the magnification of that in (*b*). One single thread dominates the field of view. The particles adhering to the individual cotton fibers can be seen quite well. (*d*) An SEM micrograph (~500×) of the grease-stained area of the bedsheet. The loosely adhering particles of grease seen here were not seen in laundered samples of exemplar stains. This observation helps to show that the questioned grease stain was associated with the crime and was not present following the most recent laundering. (*George Neighbor, Forensic Science Bureau, New Jersey State Police.*)

listed in Table 6-1. Although this list is rather extensive, it is not complete, and there are countless other things that could be encountered in an investigation. A complete list would be nearly impossible to compile since the number of entries would be too great. Any substance or material in a finely divided state could be transferred as the result of contact occurring during a criminal act. Many unusual types of evidence, therefore, could be of great importance in a particular criminal case.

The occurrence and importance of this type of evidence in criminal investigations

TABLE 6-1
VARIETIES OF TRANSFER AND TRACE EVIDENCE

Building materials (concrete, brick, plaster)
Asphalts, tars
Rubber smears and abradings
Lubricants (oils, greases)
Animal stains
Vegetable fats and oils
Food stains
Fingernail scrapings
Blood and other physiological fluid stains (Chapters 9 and 10)
Human and animal hairs (Chapter 8)
Dusts and other airborne particulates
Safe insulation
Paper fibers and sawdust
Textile fibers (Chapter 8)
Miscellaneous plant and vegetable fibers
Feathers
Pollens and spores
Soots and other airborne industrial pollutants
Abrasives
Cosmetics (powders, lipsticks)
Soils and mineral grains (Chapter 7)
Chemicals
Household products (soaps, detergents)
Glass fragments (Chapter 7)
Metal filings and turnings
Plastic fragments (e.g., auto tail-lamp lens)
Gunshot-residue particles (Chapter 14)
Explosive-residue particles (Chapter 4)
Wear products in lubricants

---

has long been realized, examples of its recognition being popularized in the well-known tales of the fictional detective–forensic scientist Sherlock Holmes. The creator of these stories, Sir Arthur Conan Doyle, was remarkably ahead of his time in having an uncannily clear understanding of the basic principles of modern forensic science and of the potential value of physical evidence.

The first nonfictional forensic scientist to formally articulate a philosophical foundation for transfer-evidence occurrence was the Frenchman, Edmond Locard (Figure 1-5). The *Locard exchange principle*, as it is now usually called, states that any time there is contact between two surfaces, there will be a mutual exchange of matter across the contact boundary. Paul L. Kirk (Figure 1-6) of the University of California advanced a somewhat different version of this same basic proposition. He said, "It is virtually impossible for a criminal to commit a crime without leaving evidence behind and carrying evidence away with him." Although this proposition is undoubtedly true in cases where the criminal has interacted with the scene, or directly with the victim, we have not yet reached a stage of development in criminalistics where it can always be demonstrated in practice. A diligent investigator can expect to encounter many cases where no significant trace evidence can be discovered, but this fact should never discourage the effort to collect trace evidence during an investigation. Trace evidence can be extremely valuable in connecting a suspect to a crime scene or to a victim and can also play a crucial role in the reconstruction of a crime (Chapter 11). Clothing is one of the primary sources of and receptors for trace evidence. It is important that the clothing worn by the principals (suspect and victim) at the time of the incident be examined.

COLLECTION AND PRESERVATION OF TRACE AND TRANSFER EVIDENCE

General Considerations

Several different methods are available for collecting trace and transfer evidence. Selection of the appropriate method(s) is not always easy, and depends on a number of factors including: (1) the location of the evidence, (2) the nature and condition of the article to which the traces are adhering, (3) the presence or absence of other evidence and its nature and condition, (4) the type of crime being investigated, (5) the relationship of the trace evidence to the reconstruction of the events, and (6) any other unusual factors or special circumstances affecting the scene or the investigation.

Responsibility for what is collected and the methods to be used in a given situation usually rests with an investigator or evidence technician. The knowledge and skill necessary to make the right decision can be developed only as the result of having extensive experience, general information about trace and transfer evidence, and an appreciation of the ways in which it will be analyzed in the criminalistics laboratory.

In addition to these general considerations, there is another which deserves special comment: the policies and capabilities of the laboratory to which the evidence will be submitted with regard to trace evidence. Different laboratories have different policies, protocols, and capabilities which will influence the choice of collection methods. If the evidence is to be submitted to a local full-service crime laboratory which has well-developed trace-evidence capabilities, an investigator should develop a rapport with the laboratory staff. The knowledge gained from this communication will enhance the investigator's ability to select the most suitable method of evidence collection. If careful, coordinated procedures are followed even in apparently routine cases, investigators are more likely to perform more effectively when major cases develop. Scene-investigation and evidence-collection skills must be kept up to date through frequent discussion with laboratory personnel. In addition, if these good practices are used routinely in all cases, little difficulty will be encountered with scenes and evidence when a major case arises.

Collection Methods

Visual Inspection and Collection The sites where contact is believed to have taken place are closely scrutinized, using a hand lens if necessary. Truly microscopic traces may not be noticed on a visual examination unless they have aggregated to form a larger mass or unless the search is made in the right location. The most significant microscopic trace-evidence samples are usually collected when investigators take the time to formulate and evaluate one or more hypothetical reconstructions of the events prior to making the detailed visual inspection. This approach helps in selecting profitable locations for close scrutiny. If trace evidence is noted, its location is then carefully documented before removal, proper packaging, and forwarding to the laboratory.

Most paper envelopes should be avoided as primary containers because of small openings that exist at the corners. Small particles and fibers, especially stiff fibers like hairs, can work their way out in the course of handling. Glass vials, small plastic bags, or appropriate papers made into druggist folds are suitable containers for particulate evidence. There is no excuse for failing to use proper containers. Druggist folds can be made on the spot, as illustrated in Figure 6-2, with ordinary paper. An investigator should carry a clean pad of paper to be used exclusively for this purpose. Ordinary paper envelopes, although unsuitable as primary containers, are quite useful as outer containers. They are often more convenient to label and seal than primary containers.

The evidential value of the surface on which the traces are found must also be considered. If the traces cannot be removed without altering other valuable evidence, the entire intact surface should be packaged and submitted. It may be desirable to submit the object or surface intact, even if obvious evidence has been collected. Under certain circumstances, large or unwieldy surfaces might be vacuumed after collection of obvious evidence (but see below), and the vacuumings submitted. If the surface is an article (like a garment), consideration must be given to the possibility of transfers taking place during folding and handling, in preparation for packaging. Transfers of trace evidence to other parts of the garment as a result of handling must be avoided, because the interpretation of the findings by a forensic scientist later on will probably be affected. Judgment is often required to determine whether such a potential transfer is significant or not.

Tape Lifts The use of pressure-sensitive or "sticky" tapes as a sampling technique for trace evidence is increasing. A number of techniques for conducting preliminary examinations of the evidence on the tape and then removing the significant evidence for more detailed examination in the laboratory have been developed. Not every laboratory, however, is set up to work with tape, and the investigator should be familiar with the submission policies of the relevant laboratory.

The tape collection method is not meant to supplant but to be used in conjunction with other techniques when appropriate. Tape is often useful when suspected contact areas have been examined and visible evidence has already been removed. Similarly, it can be used to collect microscopic evidence at preselected locations which contain no visible evidence.

A small section of tape can be applied repeatedly to a particular surface area until the tape loses its tackiness. This technique concentrates microscopic evidence into a smaller area. After collection, the tape is usually placed on a card, or folded back upon itself, and placed into a envelope. If the tape has any remaining tackiness, it should *not* be stuck to a card or to itself, since the difficulty in unfolding the tape or separating it from the card without contamination will unnecessarily complicate the analysis. Generally, it is better to place the tape onto a piece of heavy gauge polyethylene plastic and put it into an envelope. If the tape does not stick, it can be placed into a folded piece of polyethylene before being put into the envelope.

Packaging and Submission without Sampling   Under circumstances in which investigators lack experience or are unsure about how to remove and package samples, or if there are no obvious examples of trace evidence, it may be best to package an entire garment or article without removing trace-evidence samples. Trace-evidence transfers from one part of an article or garment to another can take place as the result of folding, handling, and packaging, however.

Some laboratories prefer that garments be packaged in paper, rather than in plastic bags, because particles of trace evidence can adhere to the insides of the plastic bag by electrostatic attraction and be very difficult to remove and because garments which contain incompletely dried blood or physiological fluid stains may mildew if sealed in plastic bags (Chapters 9 and 10). The major advantage of plastic bags is

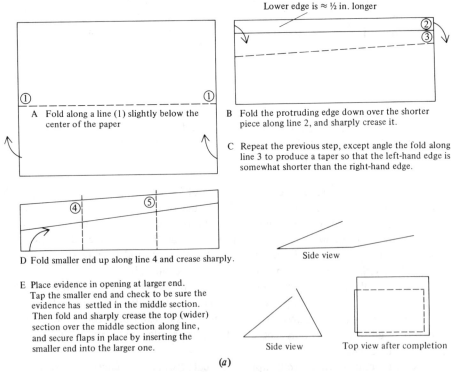

Lower edge is ≈ ½ in. longer

A Fold along a line (1) slightly below the center of the paper

B Fold the protruding edge down over the shorter piece along line 2, and sharply crease it.

C Repeat the previous step, except angle the fold along line 3 to produce a taper so that the left-hand edge is somewhat shorter than the right-hand edge.

D Fold smaller end up along line 4 and crease sharply.

Side view

E Place evidence in opening at larger end. Tap the smaller end and check to be sure the evidence has settled in the middle section. Then fold and sharply crease the top (wider) section over the middle section along line, and secure flaps in place by inserting the smaller end into the larger one.

Side view   Top view after completion

(a)

FIGURE 6-2
(a) How to make a druggist fold from plain paper. (b) A prelabeled druggist fold. The paper is provided with instructions for folding as well as labeled fold lines. An evidence label area is also provided. All of the printing is contained on one side to facilitate copy machine reproduction.

transparency, and unnecessary opening of evidence packages can be reduced if the contents are visible from the outside.

Vacuuming Vacuuming is among the most poorly understood and improperly used methods of trace-evidence collection. It can be very valuable but must be done

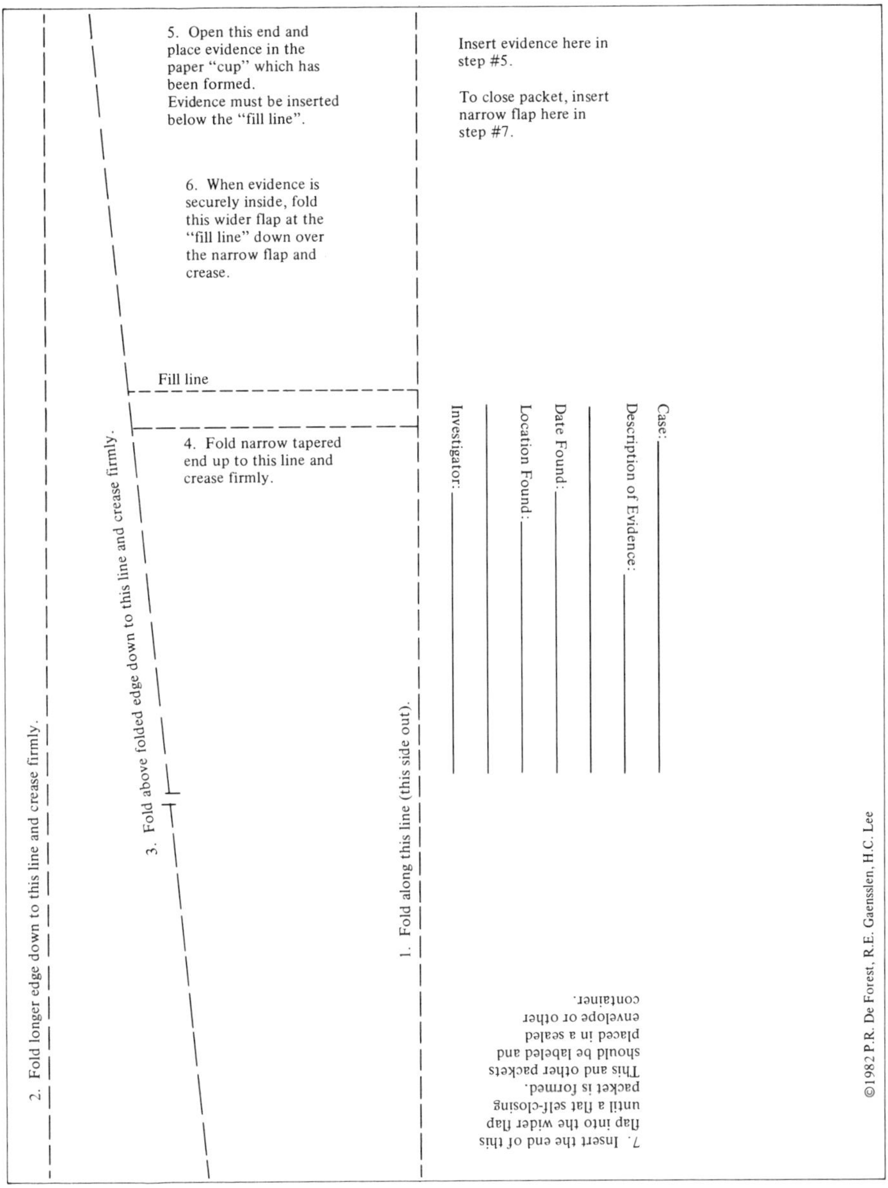

5. Open this end and place evidence in the paper "cup" which has been formed. Evidence must be inserted below the "fill line".

6. When evidence is securely inside, fold this wider flap at the "fill line" down over the narrow flap and crease.

Fill line

4. Fold narrow tapered end up to this line and crease firmly.

Insert evidence here in step #5.

To close packet, insert narrow flap here in step #7.

Case:

Description of Evidence:

Date Found:

Location Found:

Investigator:

2. Fold longer edge down to this line and crease firmly.

3. Fold above folded edge down to this line and crease firmly.

1. Fold along this line (this side out).

7. Insert the end of this flap into the wider flap until a flat self-closing packet is formed. This and other packets should be labeled and placed in a sealed envelope or other container.

© 1982 P.R. De Forest, R.E. Gaensslen, H.C. Lee

(b)

----

1. Fold bottom of page up to here.

EVIDENCE PACKET

I N S T R U C T I O N S

Describe the evidence in the space provided before collecting it. Then follow the folding
instructions step by step. This packet is useful for any small, dry material which does
not have sharp points or edges that will puncture the paper. Do not use staples to close
the packet.

© Travis Owen, 1981

(c)

Figure 6-2 (continued)
(c) Front and (d) reverse views of another prelabeled evidence fold. This is based on a design
that is different from the traditional druggist fold but is also very effective for retaining bits of
trace evidence such as hairs and fibers. It can be sealed with tape in the indicated area or
placed in a sealed envelope. (Courtesy of Travis E. Owen, Director, Acadiana Criminalistics
Laboratory, New Iberia, Louisiana.)

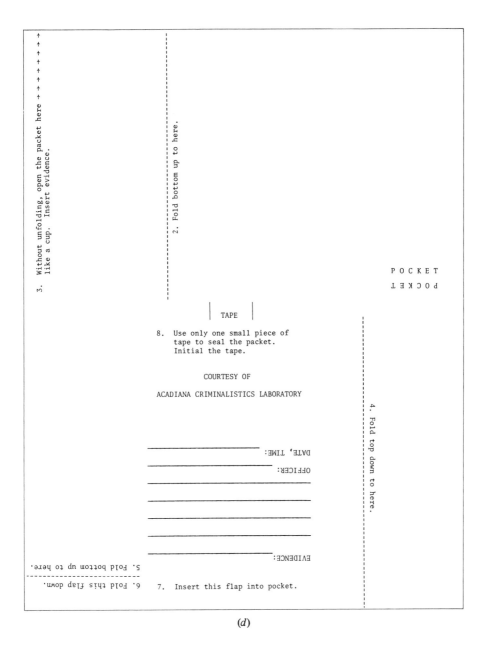

(*d*)

selectively and knowledgeably. Indiscriminate vacuuming results in the collection of large amounts of irrelevant materials, and many hours must be spent by laboratory personnel, laboriously sorting through all of it. In addition, the value of evidence collected in this manner is diminished because specific items of evidence cannot be related to specific locations. Further, there is uncertainty about the time that has elapsed since the evidence was deposited. Consider, for example, the interior of a car.

Fibers and other materials on the tops of surfaces or the top layers of dirt and dust are more likely to have been deposited more recently, and are thus more likely to be related to the incident under investigation. Indiscriminate vacuuming picks up particles and fragments deposited over a long time and mixes them with the most recently deposited samples. Even in a reasonably clean car, vacuuming may collect many items that are years old. If hairs are important, for example, it may be necessary to sort through hundreds of hairs that may have come from any of scores of people who have ridden in the car.

There are two legitimate uses of vacuum collection. The first is selective vacuuming of areas which may contain important evidence, but where none can be seen. Samples from these areas should be separately packaged and appropriately labeled. Second, areas may be vacuumed after other collection procedures have been performed, so that evidence may be picked up which was overlooked in the visual sampling. In favorable situations, the initial collections will yield so much valuable evidence that it will not be necessary to open the package containing the "backup" vacuum sweepings.

Most vacuum cleaners which will accept a hose attachment can be fitted with a device for evidence collection, and several such devices have been used. The main criteria for these devices are evidence integrity and ease of transferring samples to suitable containers. Sample integrity means that any evidence in a sample must not have come from a prior vacuuming. Long tubes or hoses, through which material must pass to reach the collection device, must therefore be avoided. Further, the collection nozzle should be short and transparent.

One of the more elaborate collection devices was designed by Dr. P. L. Kirk, and the design has been marketed by Microchemical Specialties of Berkleley, California, and more recently by Sirchie, Inc., Raleigh, North Carolina [Figure 6-3a]. A very simple device can be improvised by placing a loop of suitable cloth or porous paper between the hose nozzle of a conventional vacuum cleaner and the hose itself [Figure 6-3b].

Control Samples

It is impossible to stress too strongly the importance of collecting control samples. They are crucial to the success of any investigation dependent on trace and transfer evidence. The results obtained with such evidence may become absolutely meaningless if adequate control samples, with which to compare questioned samples, have not been properly collected and submitted. It is futile as well as foolish to spend large amounts of time collecting evidence only to overlook the need for suitable control samples.

There is almost always a need for *known* or *reference* samples in a forensic investigation. The laboratory needs a known sample with which to compare the unknown evidence. The laboratory is not merely identifying something, because identification is not usually informative. The value of the analysis lies in the *comparison*, in trying to establish or to disprove common origin. In many cases, several different known samples may be necessary. Collection of them should never be an afterthought,

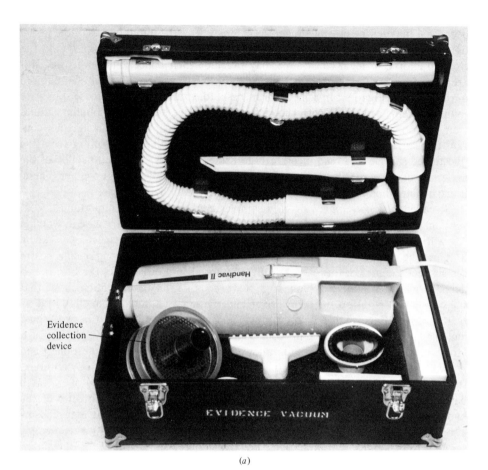

(a)

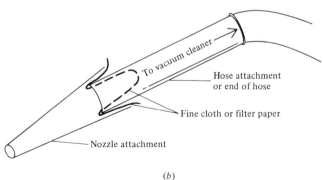

(b)

FIGURE 6-3
(a) A commercially available vacuum collection device. The actual device (see arrow) which was designed by Paul L. Kirk is available separately or as part of a kit as shown. It mounts on most vacuum cleaner hoses and uses regular laboratory filter paper. (*Sirchie Laboratories, Raleigh, North Carolina.*) (b) A simple homemade vacuum collection device. As long as the nozzle is clean, this simple device is perfectly adequate for the vacuum collection of trace evidence. It is certainly far better than collection with an unmodified household vacuum cleaner.

because it may not be possible to get the samples after the initial phases of the investigation have been completed. The samples may deteriorate or be discarded in the cleanup efforts, or legal constraints may preclude their collection even if they still are available. It is best to consider the types of known samples that will be required during the investigation. In a hit-and-run case, for example, where grease stains are found on items associated with the victim, it would be advisable to obtain samples from several areas on the underside of the suspect car. All these areas may not contain the same grease, and if only one sample is collected it might differ from the questioned sample and tend incorrectly to exclude the car. Visual inspection of the underside of the car in this case would help to pinpoint likely areas of contact. These, in particular, should be sampled along with other, less obvious areas.

So-called *alternate known* or *alibi* samples can be at least as important as conventional known control samples. Consider, for example, a burglary case in which a screwdriver which has white paint smears on it is found in the suspect's possession. Suppose the suspect claims that these smears are the result of prying open a box in the suspect's home. In this case, the investigator should either take the box as evidence, or obtain a sample of paint from it. If the laboratory examination shows that the questioned paint on the screwdriver and the known sample from the burglary scene are indistinguishable, a forensic scientist might conclude that the two "could have had a common origin." This conclusion might not carry much weight in court. However, if the laboratory results allowed a conclusion that the questioned and known samples were indistinguishable while the alibi sample was distinctly different, this finding would be considerably more significant. The significance of a match based on chemical composition always depends on the nature and quality of the known reference samples, and any relevant alibi samples. Items that may become alibi samples are not always obvious, but investigators should consider collecting samples from sources that might later be claimed to be the source of the questioned sample. The distinction between this type of alibi sample and many other types of known reference samples other than the primary known sample is often blurred.

When transfer or trace evidence is collected, the need for blank samples is often satisfied, since they usually consist of the surfaces upon which a known or questioned trace is found. If the entire surface or article bearing the trace evidence is collected and submitted, a separate blank is not normally needed. However, if the object or surface is immovable (for example, a concrete wall), the evidence must be removed from the surface. It is best to remove intact the portion of the surface bearing the evidence if possible. If not, a technique such as scraping must be employed, and it may be difficult to collect the evidence without contaminating it with the underlying material. In this case, a forensic scientist will require a reference sample of the surface and the underlying material itself, collected in the same way, so that a determination can be made as to what portion of the evidence sample was contributed by contamination. This reference sample (blank) should be removed from an area close, but not immediately next to the evidence sample area. The blank sample should be labeled, packaged separately, and submitted with the evidence. The laboratory examiner must be informed about any prior handling or treatment of items to be examined for trace evidence. It would not be advisable to dust such items for fingerprints prior to their submission to the laboratory. If they have already been dusted, however, the criminalist must be made aware of it and should be supplied with a known sample of the particular fingerprint powder used.

An explanation of the relationship of any reference, alibi, or blank samples to the evidence samples should accompany the submission, and additional details about the case under investigation should be communicated to the laboratory. It is always important for the laboratory scientist to have a clear understanding of the case. Forensic scientists can usually provide more and better information about the evidence, and can sometimes provide useful investigative leads, if they understand the nature of the case and the specific points at issue.

LABORATORY EXAMINATIONS OF TRANSFER AND TRACE EVIDENCE

Almost any laboratory method or combination of methods may be necessary to deal with transfer- and trace-evidence problems because this type of evidence can consist of such a variety of different things. Since small amounts of material are commonly involved, microscopy plays a major role in examination and analysis. The microscope is almost always the first tool to be employed. In some cases, it may suffice for the entire examination; in other cases, sophisticated laboratory instruments may be applied to the problem once the preliminary microscopical examination has been completed. The microscopical examination is often of crucial importance, because it allows the forensic scientist to select the best subsequent approach or instrument to be used. In cases where only microscopy is used for the examination, it may be employed merely to gather morphological information, or it may be used to make quantitative measurements of physical properties and to collect information concerning the chemical composition of the sample. In summary, the microscope is the single, most important tool for analyzing transfer and trace evidence in the crime laboratory. Microscopy is the only laboratory approach that is common to all the numerous types of evidence in this category.

It is not possible to discuss all the different approaches that could be applied to transfer- and trace-evidence problems in this chapter. Methods for several specialized types of trace and transfer evidence are discussed in other chapters. In the sections that follow, selected, representative examples of transfer and trace evidence that are not treated in other chapters will be presented along with discussion of the appropriate analytical techniques. Types of evidence for which a microscopical morphological approach usually suffices are discussed first, followed by those types that require chemical or compositional methods. The last few examples of evidence types are best analyzed using an integrated approach involving various methods.

Pollens

Pollens can be extremely valuable as physical evidence, although at present they are seldom used. Several properties contribute to their potential value, including small size, great chemical stability, distinct morphology, and a large number of variations

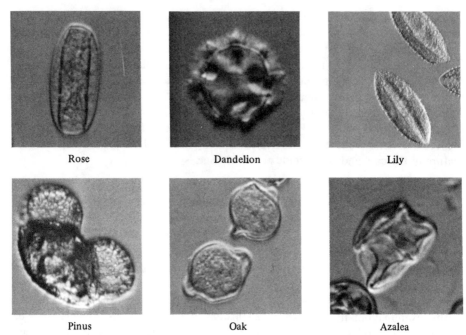

Rose   Dandelion   Lily

Pinus   Oak   Azalea

FIGURE 6-4
Representative species of pollens. These photomicrographs were prepared using a special microscopic contrast-enhancing technique known as Hoffman Modulation Contrast. *(Courtesy of Nicholas Petraco.)*

in shape. Some kinds even have spinelike external structures which help them adhere to other surfaces (Figure 6-4). This feature, and their small size, means that large numbers of them can be transferred unnoticed. Because of their chemical stability, pollens tend to survive for long periods of time, even in certain outdoor environments. Under favorable conditions, they can survive for years; pollen grains thousands of years old have been uncovered in archaeological investigations. The distinctive shapes and structures of these particles often make it possible to determine the species of plant from which they were derived. In some cases, this information, coupled with information about the geographical distribution of the species, allows a determination of the geographical origin of the sample that contained the grains. Such a fact could be very valuable in an investigation.

Pollen grains can be used in two ways in forensic investigations: in determining the geographic origin of an item having pollen on it and in connecting a person to a place. Information on geographic origin might be very helpful as an investigative aid. Pollen found on an article of clothing left behind at a kidnapping scene, for example, might reveal the general area from which the perpetrator came. In other cases, the presence of a certain species of pollen grains on the clothing of a suspect may be useful in linking the suspect to a particular crime scene. The presence of pollen sources at crime scenes should not be overlooked by investigators. An examination of the scene might make it possible to predict the presence and location of a certain species of pollen on the clothes of a perpetrator.

Feathers and Miscellaneous Animal Particulates

Hairs (Chapter 8) are the most commonly encountered examples of animal-derived microscopic physical evidence. Other types of animal traces and particulates, though less common as physical evidence, could play important roles in particular cases. The most noteworthy would be feathers. The particles of dead skin (epithelial cells) which are continuously being shed by many animals (including human beings) can be important as well. Scales of fish, leather particles, and so forth, are additional examples. These evidence types are characterized in the laboratory primarily through microscopical morphological examinations.

Bird feathers exist in a wide variety of shapes and forms. They are often distinct enough on the microscopic scale to enable an expert to identify the species of bird from which they came. Both the light microscope (especially the polarized-light version) and the scanning electron microscope (SEM) can be used for this purpose. The SEM is superior for examining intricate details.

Down, the fine under-feathers of birds, occurs fairly frequently as physical evidence, in part because of its widespread commercial use as a fill, or insulating material, for bedding, pillows, sleeping bags, parkas, and vests. Because it is small, down can work its way out of these articles and be transferred to other surfaces by contact or through the air. Small bits of it can often be found adhering tightly to other surfaces.

Additional types of trace evidence derived from animals can occur as evidence. Epithelial cells are continuously being sloughed off by the skin of animals, including human beings. These may be obvious, as in the case of an abnormality such as dandruff, where many cells make up a single flake, or they may be truly microscopic particles where individual cells have been shed. Epithelial cells are probably present in a large number of cases, but they are not often utilized because methods for their individualization have not been developed. They can be characterized by microscopical morphological techniques, and samples can be treated with special (histological) stains as part of the preparation for examination. Fish scales are characterized by a similar approach, the polarizing microscope often being the best instrument for this purpose.

Wood and Paper Fibers

Since most paper products are composed primarily of wood fibers, it is appropriate to discuss paper and wood fibers together. Many of the techniques used to characterize these materials are similar. Paper and wood fibers occur with a relatively high frequency in criminal investigations. In addition, paper and wood products are also encountered as evidence in larger bulk forms, such as paper documents, wood chips, or wooden articles. Some of the techniques used to examine the larger pieces involve reducing a portion of them to fibers, followed by microscopical and/or microchemical examination. Paper examinations are discussed in Chapter 13.

Plastics and Resins

Plastics are synthetic materials, composed of very large organic molecules known as *polymers.* These large molecules are made up of a large number of smaller molecules (something like putting together beads on a string). The nature of polymers is discussed in detail in Chapter 8. Some of the polymers used for making plastics are modifications or derivatives of natural polymers such as cellulose, the main structural component of plants. Others are totally synthetic and not found in nature (polyethylene, polystyrene, epoxies, etc.). These polymers in raw form are often referred to as *resins,* although the term *resin* can also be applied to natural substances, like the sticky substances which are exuded from certain trees (gum, pine, etc.). Synthetic resins such as epoxies and polyesters are used to bind glass fibers together to form fiberglass articles, like boat hulls and fishing rods. In addition to their uses in making solid and reinforced plastic articles, synthetic resins find many other applications in the manufacture of glues, other adhesives, treated textiles, foamed "rubbers," and plastics, as well as paints. The common feature of plastics and resins is that they are composed of polymers.

Articles and materials composed of plastics and resins represent a wide range of possible evidence types. When they are cut, abraded, or broken, traces of the material can be transferred. In addition, these types of materials may occur as important evidence in bulk forms, like electrical insulation, adhesive tapes (surgical, electrical, transparent), plastic films (packaging materials, plastic wrap, and bags), and articles (buttons). Since these are not examples of trace and transfer evidence, they may seem inappropriate in this discussion. It should be pointed out, however, that if opportunities for obtaining physical matches (Chapter 11) do not exist, a forensic scientist must rely on methods for comparing chemical composition in examining these materials. These methods are similar to most of those used to characterize traces of these materials. Those methods applicable to trace evidence could certainly be applied to larger samples, although the reverse is not necessarily true.

Laboratory techniques which can be applied to traces of materials composed of resins and plastics are numerous. The first step in analyzing such evidence would be microscopical examination. Many of the methods applicable to the study of organic compounds can be adapted to the determination of the chemical composition of plastics and other polymeric materials. These include infrared spectrophotometry, pyrolysis-gas chromatography, pyrolysis–mass spectrometry, and liquid chromatography.

Metallic Fragments and Particles

A variety of metallic particles can occur as physical evidence. Finely divided metals can result from a number of metalworking operations. *Cuttings* and *turnings* are fragments of metals which have been separated from larger pieces by machining operations such as thread cutting, drilling, milling, or turning on a lathe. The shapes of the fragments often indicate the type of operation which produced them. Other metalworking operations, such as brazing, grinding, and polishing, as well as cutting and welding with acetylene torches or direct-current arcs, can produce additional types of metal fragments or metal oxide particles.

Criminal activity can generate metal fragments. Cutting or drilling a safe is a good example. These particles may get into shoes or clothing and be carried away. If a suspect is apprehended, comparison of these particles with those from the scene could produce significant evidence. Similarly, committing a crime in a factory or shop might contaminate the criminal's clothing with such particles. Comparisons could result in associating the suspect with the scene. Alternatively, an article of clothing or similar object from an individual who regularly works in such a shop or factory may shed metallic particles at a crime scene, or the entire piece of clothing may be left behind. A study of the fragments in such a situation might suggest to the forensic scientist that the suspect was employed in an area where certain types of metalworking techniques or fabrications were performed. This information could be useful to investigators in narrowing down the number of leads to be pursued. In addition, analysis of the composition of the metal might show it to be a special alloy, which could limit the possibilities even further, perhaps even to a single factory. Metallic fragments may bear toolmarks (Chapter 14) which might be helpful in establishing common origin.

Gunshot-Residue Particles

Gunshot-residue particles can be considered a kind of trace and transfer evidence. A number of methods have been devised for the analysis of gunshot residue, and they are discussed in detail in Chapter 14 in connection with firearms examinations and reconstructions in shooting cases.

Paint Chips and Smears

There are some kinds of crimes where paint evidence would be expected with a relatively high frequency; these include hit-and-run cases and burglaries. Paint may be important in other cases as well, however. Paint evidence can be in the form of chips or smears. With paint chips, the possibility of obtaining a physical match must be considered. Physical matches are often more convincing than attempts to associate a sample with a particular origin by comparison of color and chemical composition. Another aspect of paint comparisons is layer structure. Many objects (automobiles, for example) have been painted several times, with different types and colors of paint used for each coat. The particular sequence of paint types and colors can be unique and confer individuality onto a sample of paint evidence. The possibility of individualizing a paint sample by a physical match or a unique layer structure does not apply to paint smears. With them, the forensic scientist must look for differences in physical and chemical properties, such as color, solubility, and composition, in attempts to individualize the samples.

Paint chips may be so large that physical matches can be obtained visually, or macroscopically (Chapter 11). In other cases, the use of a stereomicroscope may be required. Layer structure is almost always examined with a microscope, using incident light. Microscopy is also used, initially at least, in attempts to individualize paint samples by unique features or markings as well as by differences in their physical and chemical properties.

Investigators should be careful not to overlook the possibility of physical matches when paint samples are being collected. If an examination of the known or control surface, where the chips are thought to have originated, reveals the presence of fractured edges, these edges should be left intact. Rather than removing chips from these areas, the entire painted article should be submitted as a control. If this action is impossible or impractical, a portion of the article, including the damaged part and the surrounding area, should be carefully removed, packaged, and submitted. If a physical match or layer-structure comparison is not possible because of the nature of the sample, comparison must then be based on physical and chemical properties. The color is carefully compared with standards to try to identify possible sources of the paint. Solubility tests may also be conducted in this determination of class characteristics. Different classes of paint vehicles (or binders—the organic polymer portion of the paint) behave differently when tested with a range of solvent types. The organic or polymeric component of a dried paint film can be studied in more detail by several additional chemical and instrumental techniques, like those used for characterizing or identifying the organic polymers used in plastics. Among the most useful in the forensic comparison of paints are infrared spectrophotometry, pyrolysis-gas chromatography, and mass spectrometry. The inorganic portions of the paint film (pigments, etc.) can be compared by such techniques as emission spectrography, the laser microprobe, neutron activation analysis, x-ray fluorescence, and the electron microprobe. These methods are similar to those used to characterize inorganic specimens, such as metal fragments.

Rubber Smears and Abradings

Rubber can occur as trace evidence in at least three distinct ways. First, rubber particles can be abraded from a larger rubber object such as an automobile tire or a pencil eraser. The particles which result can occur in a range of sizes and can be important evidence in certain cases. Second, contact with a surface can result in some rubber being transferred. The rubber in this case is in the form of a smear or scuff or skid mark. The particles that remain fixed to the second surface are generally smaller than those transferred in the case of rubber abradings. These kinds of marks can be made by tires coming into contact with automobile body finishes, or by black rubber heels from shoes producing scuff marks on a floor or wall. Skid marks produced by tires are another common example. The third kind of transfer is somewhat different from the other two. Here, movement between the rubber surface and the receiving surface is not required. Instead, the rubber material transfer takes place during a period of prolonged contact between the two surfaces. It has recently been found in certain investigations that automobile tires will leave certain, distinctive, invisible tread-mark patterns on certain relatively clean surfaces, such as new concrete floors, when a car has been parked there for a period of time. Diffusion of certain rubber additives out of the tire and into the material making up the second surface is responsible for the production of this type of physical mark. These additives are often colorless and invisible. The patterns produced must be visualized using ultraviolet (UV) light. There have been several cases reported in which it was possible to identify the make and model of a vehicle parked in a garage by scanning the garage floor with UV lamps for evidence of these transfer marks and documenting them with appropriate photographs and measurements (wheel base, front and rear track, etc.). Information about the type and brand of tire also results from the identification of the patterns. Thus, if a suspect automobile is located, it is often possible to find enough individual characteristics in these tire patterns to demonstrate convincingly that the particular automobile left the marks. Whenever it is thought that an automobile involved in a crime has been parked in a location with a fairly clean floor, examination of the floor with UV lamps is certainly warranted.

Laboratory examination of rubber abradings and smears or scuffs is accomplished by a combination of microscopical and other instrumental techniques. Particles in evidence are often identifiable as rubber by the microscopical examination. Preliminary comparison of these with similar particles from a known source can be carried out using the microscope. Additional instrumental techniques which are useful with rubber evidence include pyrolysis-gas chromatography, infrared spectrophotometry, liquid chromatography, and spectrofluorimetry. Traces of rubber from different sources can often be differentiated by one or more of these techniques.

Cosmetics

Cosmetics, particularly lipsticks, are easily transferred and appear regularly as evidence in cases involving crimes ranging from hit-and-run "accidents" to muggings, rapes, and homicides. The evidence stains or smears in these cases may be obvious, but not always.

Face powders and like items are usually characterized by microscopical methods using a polarized-light microscope. Lipstick stains are generally subjected to a preliminary microscopical examination, followed by the application of a selected chemical analysis method to compare the dyes and other components. The dyes, even in a small sample, can be analyzed and compared with those from a known reference sample using thin-layer chromatography. Some of the dyes used in lipsticks are fluorescent and may be compared using spectrophotofluorometric methods. The particular mixture of dyes used is usually characteristic for a certain brand and color of lipstick. At the present time, it is rarely possible to obtain more than a brand and color identification, but this information can be useful as an investigative aid or as corroborative evidence.

Chips of nail polish can be compared in much the same way as paint samples. Nail polishes are really a type of lacquer. The iridescent types contain ground-up

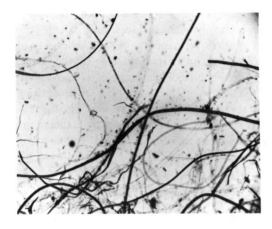

FIGURE 6-5
Household dust. Common household dust contains a surprising variety of particles and fibers. This black-and-white photomicrograph cannot properly reveal this variety.

fish scales. The iridescent and the more conventional pigments can be studied using the polarizing microscope. Additional instrumental techniques are employed as was appropriate with paint samples.

Dusts and Airborne Particles

Dust can be defined as a collection of particles that settle out of the air and accumulate on a variety of surfaces over a period of time. Common household dust, when viewed under the microscope, no longer appears *common*. It is usually, in fact, a complex mixture of many different particles and fibers (Figure 6-5). A relatively small sample of dust may contain hundreds or even thousands of individual particles. All the items listed in Table 6-1 and others not shown in the table or discussed here could occur in various combinations in dust. Some types could be well represented; others might be present as trace constituents. The number of possible combinations is almost infinite. Because of this complexity, dust can be an extraordinarily rich source of information. Dust from a particular locale may be individual, but the individualization will be based less on the uniqueness of the individual components, and more on the uniqueness of the *particular combination* of these components.

The polarized-light microscope is the primary tool used in the characterization of dust particles. Many particles can be identified, and the relative percentages of each estimated, by this kind of examination. Other types of instruments may be employed to identify difficult particles once they have been removed from the rest of the sample. These might include electron microprobe, ion microprobe, x-ray diffractometer, and so forth.

STUDY QUESTIONS

1 What are some of the differences between trace and transfer evidence?
2 What is the Locard exchange principle?

3 Name some of the different types of transfer evidence.

4 What is the importance of microscopy in the examination of trace and transfer evidence?

5 Discuss the different factors involved in the selection of a suitable method for collecting trace or transfer evidence.

6 Name the different methods for collecting trace or transfer evidence. Explain the circumstances under which each method would be appropriate.

7 What are control samples, and why are they important in the analysis of trace and transfer evidence?

8 What are alibi samples, and why are they important in the analysis of trace and transfer evidence?

9 What are pollens, and why are they potentially important as physical evidence?

10 What do plastics and resins have in common with one another?

11 Under what kind of circumstances might metallic fragment evidence be produced and discovered?

12 Explain the different laboratory methods used to compare paint samples.

13 Describe several ways in which rubber marks or abradings can be produced.

14 Name several different cosmetic materials that could be encountered as physical evidence. What laboratory methods would be used to examine the various different ones?

15 What is dust? Name several of the components of dust. Why can dust be important as physical evidence?

REFERENCES AND FURTHER READING

Benedetti-Pichler, A. A.: *Identification of Materials,* Academic, New York, 1964.

Crown, D. A.: *The Forensic Examination of Paints and Pigments,* Charles C Thomas, Springfield, Ill. 1968.

Darby, W.: "Criminalistics," in C. H. Wecht (ed.), *Forensic Sciences,* vol. 3, chap. 36, Matthew Bender, New York, 1981.

Deedrick, D. W., and J. P. Mullery: "Feathers are Not Lightweight Evidence," *FBI Law Enforcement Bulletin,* September 1981.

Kirk, P. L.: *Crime Investigation,* Wiley, New York, 1953.

May, R. W., and J. Porter: "An Evaluation of Common Methods of Paint Analysis," *Journal of the Forensic Science Society,* vol. 15, p. 137, 1975.

McCrone, W. C., L. B. McCrone, and J. G. Delly: *Polarized Light Microscopy,* Ann Arbor Science Publishers, Ann Arbor, Mich., 1978.

Nickolls, L. C.: "The Identification of Stains of Nonbiological Origin," in F. Lundquist (ed.), *Methods of Forensic Science,* vol. 1, p. 335, Wiley-Interscience, New York, 1962.

Pounds, C. A.: "The Recovery of Fibers from the Surface of Clothing for Forensic Examination," *Journal of the Forensic Science Society,* vol. 15, p. 127, 1975.

Ryland, S. C., R. J. Kopec, and P. N. Somerville: "The Evidential Value of Automobile Paint," *Journal of Forensic Sciences,* vol. 26, p. 64, 1981.

Schleuter, G. E., and W. E. Gumpertz: "The Stereomicroscope—Instrumentation and Techniques," *American Laboratory,* vol. 8, p. 61, 1976.

Strelis, I., and R. W. Kennedy: *Identification of North American Commercial Pulp Woods and Pulp Fibers,* University of Toronto Press, Toronto, 1967.

Thornton, J. I.: "Forensic Paint Examination," in R. Saferstein (ed.), *Forensic Science Handbook,* Prentice-Hall, Englewood Cliffs, N.J., 1982.

CHAPTER 7

GLASS AND SOIL

INTRODUCTION

Most experienced investigators can recall cases in which glass and/or soil evidence figured prominently in the solution of a crime. Both types of evidence are encountered quite frequently in a wide variety of crimes. Perhaps the most common kind of case where both could be found in a single investigation is burglary. These two types of evidence are discussed together in this chapter because of the similarity of some of the laboratory approaches used in glass and soil comparisons.

GLASS

What is Glass?

The term *glass* is used to describe a range of materials of varying composition, most of which are synthetic. Naturally occurring glasslike materials are of volcanic origin and include pumice and obsidian. Pumice has a very fragile structure, consisting of numerous elongated gas bubbles trapped in the glass. It is somewhat like plastic foam in appearance. Merely walking repeatedly over many of the forms of pumice will reduce them to a powder. Powdered pumice is used as an abrasive and scouring agent (for example, in Lava soap). Obsidian is compact and generally free of bubbles. It resembles a dark-colored or black glass.

Glass has been made for thousands of years. It is an interesting material with some unusual properties. Unlike most solids, glass is noncrystalline. It is sometimes referred to as a *supercooled liquid*. The major ingredient in most glasses is silicon dioxide (SiO_2). Pure, or nearly pure, silicon dioxide is crystalline and occurs in minerals such as quartz. Common sand is composed primarily of quartz grains and is the source of the silicon dioxide used in the manufacture of glass. In quartz and the other crystalline silica materials, the silicon and oxygen atoms are organized into a highly regular and uniform array or framework known as a *crystal lattice*. In glasses, however, these atoms are irregularly spaced and randomly oriented. Schematic representations of the atomic arrangements for both crystalline and liquid (or amorphous) states are shown in Figure 7-1. If highly purified quartz were melted at a very high temperature (1713°C) and then cooled very slowly, a crystalline material known as cristobalite could be formed. Normally, however, the molten quartz would not have time to crystallize before it cooled below its melting point to form a glassy solid known as *vitreous silica* or *fused quartz*. When quartz sand is mixed with sodium carbonate (soda) and calcium oxide (lime), the resulting mixture will fuse (melt) at a somewhat lower temperature (1400°C) to form molten glass. When this mixture is cooled, even very slowly, it retains the disordered state characteristic of a liquid as it solidifies to form so-called soda-lime glass.

Historically, soda-lime was the first type of synthetic glass. It is still one of the most commonly used glass formulations. Many additional kinds of glass of varying composition exist. Some are used only for special purposes. For example, the addition of significant quantities of lead oxide (PbO) to the melt results in the production of glass with a higher refractive index (or light-bending power), adding to the sparkle of articles made from it. Glasses containing relatively high percentages of PbO, which are used to make decorative articles such as stemware, are commonly referred to as *crystal* or *lead crystal*. Other special types of glasses include the many types of optical glass that are used in the fabrication of complex lenses. Optical glasses are among the most painstakingly produced of all glass types. Various additives are used to provide each of these glasses with the desired optical properties.

The addition of other chemicals to glass can produce modifications of other properties. Normal glasses tend to fracture when heated or cooled rapidly (that is, subjected to thermal shock). However, glasses containing borax (sodium tetraborate)

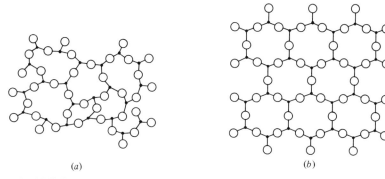

(a)   *(b)*

FIGURE 7-1
(*a*) A two-dimensional representation of a liquid or an amorphous solid. (*b*) A two-dimensional representation of a crystalline substance.

are quite resistant to thermal shock. Formulations of this type are used for the manufacture of laboratory glassware, such as flasks and beakers, and home kitchen utensils, such as baking dishes. Pyrex is one of the most common trade names for borosilicate glasses. The range of variation in composition of several commercially produced glasses can be appreciated from an examination of Table 7-1.

In addition to differences in glass articles resulting from variations in formulation, differences also exist due to variations in glass-working techniques used to form the particular article. For example, glass articles may be formed by various blowing, casting, molding, or rolling techniques. At one time, most flat window glass was made by hand blowing a large quantity of molten glass into the shape of a large cylinder. The cylinder was then cut open while the glass was still warm enough to be fairly soft, and was allowed to unroll, or flatten, itself under the influence of gravity to produce the sheet of glass. Inexpensive window glass is still made by a similar process. Such sheet glass is never completely free of variations in thickness and defects in surface flatness.

Modern, higher quality window glass, known as *plate* glass, is made by one of two primary techniques. The molten glass may be placed between a series of mechanical rollers which form it into a continuous sheet of desired thickness. After annealing and cooling, this type of glass must be mechanically polished to remove the fine imperfections left by the surfaces of the rollers. This polishing step is rather expensive and contributes significantly to the cost of plate glass produced by this process. This polishing step is not necessary in plate glass produced by the recently developed *float* process. In this process, the molten glass is layered over a large bath of molten tin metal. If the bath is effectively isolated from mechanical vibrations, the liquid-liquid interface existing between the glass and the molten metal surface is exceedingly smooth and flat, as is the glass-air surface on the upper side of the glass. The result, after cooling, is a piece of glass with two exceptionally smooth surfaces. This technique has been refined to the extent that large sheets of plate glass can be produced in a continuous process. Molten glass is introduced at one end of a large bath of molten tin, and plate glass is removed from the other end, continuously.

One manufacturing treatment, applied to glass articles after they have been formed, is particularly noteworthy: a heat treatment which strengthens the glass. The

TABLE 7-1
MEAN PERCENTAGE OF ELEMENTAL OXIDES
IN VARIOUS GLASSES

Glass usage	Al_2O_3	CaO	Fe_2O_3	MgO	Na_2O
Window	0.158	8.50	0.123	3.65	13.53
Auto window	0.15	8.10	0.555	3.93	12.90
Headlamps	1.37	0.017	0.06	0.017	5.40
Container	1.416	8.266	0.117	0.283	11.73

Source: Courtesy of Detective Thomas Catalano, Crime Laboratory, New York City Police Department.

glass article is heated until it begins to soften. It is then cooled relatively rapidly and uniformly with streams of compressed air. The outside cools much faster than the inside, creating stresses and a surface-tension effect. Glasses treated in this way are extremely strong and resistant to fracture. However, when fracture does take place, the article disintegrates into thousands of small pieces which are relatively harmless. This type of glass is called *tempered* (or toughened or hardened) glass. It cannot be scored or cut without shattering and, therefore, must be cut to the desired size and shape prior to application of the tempering process. Tempered glass is used as safety glass in automobiles. It has replaced laminated glass in all the windows except for the front windshield. Laminated windshields are still required by law in the United States. In most other countries, tempered glass is used for all automobile glazing requirements. Most local jurisdictions require the use of *safety glass* in glazed doors (for example, storm doors, bathtub and shower enclosures). Tempered glass is also used to make hardened lenses for eyeglasses, although another hardening process can also be used for this process. In this other hardening process, the lens is placed in a molten salt bath at an elevated temperature for several days. Metal ions in the surface layers of the glass lens are slowly removed and replaced by chemically similar but smaller ions from the salt. Thus, for example, sodium may be replaced by lithium. The differences in the amount of space occupied by the two types of atoms result in a slow contraction of the glass in the surface layers during the treatment. This contraction produces a surface-tension effect similar to that arising from the heat-treatment process.

Glass as Evidence

The significance of glass as evidence is attributable to several factors.

1 Glass is very common in our environment because of the very large number of different uses that have been found for it.

2 Glass is normally quite brittle and easily broken, producing fragments of varying size. These fragments are always around in the environment.

3 Glass fragments and particles are commonly produced when glass is intentionally or accidentally broken in the course of committing a criminal act.

4 Small glass particles can be transferred and will often adhere to items of clothing without being noticed.

5 Glass is quite stable and is not altered by a wide range of chemical or physical treatments. Glass thus remains unaffected by normal environmental conditions. Unlike many types of biological evidence, for example, glass evidence does not undergo change or deterioration from the time it is deposited to when it is collected and analyzed in the laboratory.

6 The fact that glass is produced in a range of compositions and by different processes contributes to its value as physical evidence.

7 Besides the range of composition among different types of glass, there is often a range within a given type of glass as well. This compositional variation is unintentional and arises because of uncontrolled differences in the composition of raw materials used to make the glass and because of errors in measuring the amounts of materials used in making up the formulation. Batch-to-batch (interbatch) and intrabatch variation in composition can also result from the contamination of the molten glass during the manufacturing process. Molten glass may, for example, dissolve materials from the walls of the vessel in which it is melted. With the exception of high-quality optical preparations, glasses are not homogeneous mixtures. As a result, articles made from the same batch of glass may have slightly different compositions. Such intrabatch variations can enhance the value of glass as evidence.

Modern manufacturing techniques have reduced the range of inter- and intrabatch variations to be expected in most kinds of glass. In addition, glass manufacturing has become concentrated in the hands of a relatively small number of large manufacturers in the last few decades, contributing to the increased uniformity of modern glass. However, small and sometimes significant differences do exist, even in modern glasses produced under conditions of stringent quality control. Intra-article differences can be troublesome in glass comparisons based upon differences in chemical compositions. The reason for the problem is that matches between samples are meaningful only if the differences between different articles or batches are greater than those within them. Thus, the significance of a match based on chemical composition criteria may be reduced if there are significant differences in composition within the article.

Collection of Glass Evidence

Most of the general considerations regarding the collection of transfer and trace evidence discussed in Chapter 6 apply to the collection of glass evidence. The obvious exception would be samples that are relatively large. It may be helpful to review the evidence-collection section of Chapter 6. The possibilities of a reconstruction of the evidence or of a physical match need to be considered at the time that glass evidence is being collected. These possibilities apply primarily to situations where larger samples are involved, but this kind of work is occasionally possible with relatively small samples. If pieces of glass large enough to contain fingerprints are encountered at a point of entry of a crime scene, the examination of the glass for fingerprints must be the first consideration. If eventual reconstructions or physical matches seem reasonable, the collection needs to be as complete and thorough as possible. In addition, details of the collection should be thoroughly documented before disturbing the evidence. If samples are to be taken from a broken window (at a point of entry, for example), each of the major pieces should be individually identified with a marking pen and photographed prior to removal and packaging. In addition, the notes and photographs should clearly show the orientation of each major piece and indicate directions (up, down, left, right, inside, and outside).

Plastic vials are suitable containers for collecting smaller pieces of glass. Only a single piece should be placed in a vial unless some means of keeping the pieces apart is provided. Very small pieces are unlikely to break in transit and can be grouped together and submitted in druggist folds or plastic vials. Larger pieces should be wrapped separately and securely to prevent damage during transportation to the laboratory. Clothing and similar items thought to contain traces of glass evidence are normally submitted to the laboratory without prior collection, as discussed in Chapter 6, but visual inspection and collection may be useful under certain circumstances. The other trace-evidence collection techniques discussed in Chapter 6 (sticky tape and vacuum collection) may be desirable as backup procedures in other instances. It must be remembered that each case is unique in some way, and rigid rules for evidence collection are not appropriate. The investigator's judgment is the crucial factor in selecting the most suitable technique applicable to the unique aspects of the particular situation being investigated.

When known samples are being collected, the possible need for alibi samples should be considered, although the need is not as common with glass evidence as it is with certain other types of transfer and trace evidence, like hairs, fibers, and soil.

Laboratory Examination of Glass Evidence

Three distinct types of glass examinations are conducted in the forensic laboratory. The first type tries to provide useful information in the reconstruction of a crime; the other two types are concerned with whether questioned and known pieces share a common origin (individualization).

The first step in examining a sample of glass submitted to the laboratory is to perform an inspection and make general observations. During this inspection, the gross characteristics of each sample are studied to determine whether or not certain samples can be excluded from further consideration. If the samples cannot be eliminated, the possibility of obtaining a physical match is considered. When reasonably large pieces of glass are present in both questioned and known samples, there is a reasonable chance of being successful in obtaining a physical match. On the other hand, if one of these samples consists exclusively of small pieces, a physical match is usually much more difficult. If the number of pieces involved is fairly small, the possibility of a physical match is worth exploring (Chapter 11), but if the number of small pieces is very large, the prospects of obtaining a physical match are very poor.

Reconstruction With Glass Evidence

Information useful in reconstructing a crime can be obtained from an examination of the fracture surfaces on larger pieces of glass. An understanding of the way in which glass fractures is required in order to reconstruct events from glass fracture patterns. This subject is discussed in detail in Chapter 11. The possibility of the fracture patterns being useful and important in a reconstruction should be kept in mind when searching a crime scene and documenting and collecting glass evidence.

Individualization of Glass

Physical Matches Glass breaks in a random fashion, resulting in fracture surfaces that are unique, thus providing an ideal situation for physical matches. Individualization of a glass sample is most definitive when a physical match between the questioned sample and a known one can be demonstrated. When reasonably large pieces of glass can be found in both known and questioned samples, it is well worth considering the possibility of a physical match. If either the known or questioned fragments are quite small, the possibility of a physical match is greatly diminished. With very large numbers of small particles to compare, the probability of obtaining a physical match through the expenditure of a reasonable amount of effort is almost zero. In such a case, the comparison must be based on other criteria.

Physical matching is the simplest comparison method for establishing commonality of origin with glass samples. Making physical matches with glass samples is similar to physical matching with other types of evidence. The criminalist simply brings properly identified known and questioned pieces into close juxtaposition and examines the contours of the corresponding edges. If the respective contours are similar, a jigsaw fit is carefully attempted. Such a fit can often provide conclusive evidence of common origin. The process of physical matching is often aided by a preliminary reconstruction. Physical matching is discussed further in Chapter 11.

With glass samples, the fracture surfaces are dimensionally stable and often have a considerable amount of detail. In order to obtain an exact fit, it is necessary to have more than simple two-dimensional correspondence of the edges of the fracture. A glass fracture surface is three-dimensional, and the overall contours as well as the rib marks on the fracture surfaces must correspond. In addition, the smaller marks on the fracture surface which run perpendicular to the rib marks must also agree. These smaller marks are referred to as *hackle marks* (Figure 11-17). A glass fracture, therefore, offers a considerable number of points of comparison, even in a fracture of limited size. As was noted above, the time to first consider the possibility of a physical match is when the samples are being collected.

Other Physical Features and Properties for Comparison If a physical match is unlikely, the comparison of other physical features can be very useful, especially in demonstrating that the samples differ. Some of them are quite obvious. Thus, one could eliminate from further consideration fragments of glass which are representative of the overall sample and which have grossly different surface textures. A sample from a clear glass window would not be compared with a sample from a textured, pebbled, or frosted piece of glass. Similarly, a piece of wire-reinforced glass would not be compared with a known sample from a nonreinforced window. A piece of flat or plate glass would not be considered for further comparison with a curved piece, such as may have come from a bottle, jar, or other container. A surprisingly useful feature is thickness. If samples of glass from broken windows are submitted and fragments within the samples contain both of the original parallel plane surfaces, a measurement of thickness of the original pieces of glass can be made. These measurements can be made so accurately using screw micrometers that it is often possible to exclude samples of otherwise very similar glass. It has to be kept in mind, however, that the original sample of glass may not have had a uniform thickness. Thus, it is necessary to obtain representative measurements, if possible, for both the known and questioned samples.

Glass is not completely uniform when it is examined critically. Sheet glass may exhibit subtle compositional inhomogeneities which can be useful in attempts at individualization. Some inhomogeneities appear as a pattern of parallel striations (called *ream markings*) when they are visualized by certain optical or photographic methods. The patterns can allow for or facilitate reconstructions of glass articles where the intervening pieces are missing. Additional features for making physical comparisons are markings on the surface of the glass or the presence of paint, putty, or other contaminants. Surface markings can be used to orient and position pieces in reconstructions. The adhering materials could be useful in two ways: (1) the *pattern* of the adhering matter may be helpful or (2) the material itself may be analyzed and compared. Paint and putty, for example, could be compared by various chemical methods.

Comparisons Based On Differences in Composition   Glass is a chemically complex material. It exists in many different formulations, and there are variations within a given formulation. Very subtle chemical differences in glass samples are often reflected in their physical properties. It is often easier to detect subtle differences in composition by making careful measurements of selected physical properties than by chemical analysis. This approach might appear to be an indirect one, but it can be better for two reasons: First, it is often very difficult to analyze trace chemical constituents with a high degree of quantitative accuracy. The range of error in the chemical measurements can exceed the range of variation in the samples being compared. Second, physical-property measurements can be made with a very high degree of accuracy and reproducibility and can therefore be used to detect small differences. Physical properties that are useful or diagnostic with glass samples can be divided into two categories: optical properties and nonoptical properties.

Nonoptical Physical Properties   Two nonoptical physical properties are very important in comparing glass specimens: hardness and density.

The *hardness* of materials can be measured on a number of different scales. Geologists or mineralogists may use a different scale from that used by metallurgists. The Mohs scale is used to compare the hardness of known and unknown minerals. The unknown is tested by comparing its "scratching power" with that of a series of known minerals of increasing hardness. The sequence of minerals in this series is shown in Figure 7-2. The unknown sample's position in the series is assigned by determining whether or not it can be scratched by various minerals in the known series and by finding which ones it is capable of scratching. It is placed below the lowest member which is capable of scratching it, and above the highest member which it is capable of scratching.

Most glass samples fall within a narrow range on this scale, and it is therefore not a useful scale in the forensic comparison of glass. There is, in fact, no standard scale which is particularly useful for this purpose, but fortunately, none is really necessary. The criminalist can obtain useful comparative data by evaluating the mutual scratching powers of the known and questioned samples in comparison with samples of glass in the laboratory collection.

The second significant nonoptical physical property in the forensic comparison of glass is *density*. The density of any material is its mass per unit volume (Chapter 3). Water has a density of 1 g/cm^3 (at 4°C). Glass is more dense than water, which

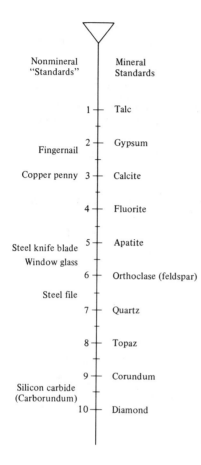

FIGURE 7-2
The Mohs hardness scale. This mineralogical hardness scale was devised by the German mineralogist Friedrich Mohs in 1822 and is still widely used today. Although it relates only relative hardnesses and thus is not a linear scale, it covers a broad range and is easy to use. Modern measurements made with refined instruments show that diamond is much harder than its position on the Mohs scale might indicate. On a 10-point linear scale where diamond would be assigned a value of 10, corundum would be only 2.5 and topaz 1.6. The bulk of the other minerals would be smaller than 1 on such a scale.

accounts for the fact that it sinks when placed in water. Although glass has a fairly broad density range, all glasses have densities of 2 or greater. In other words, if equal volumes of glass and water are weighed, the glass sample will be at least twice as heavy as the water. The densities of two small fragments of glass can be compared quite accurately by placing one of the fragments in a liquid having a density greater than glass, so that the sample will actually float. A liquid with a density less than that of glass is then added gradually, with thorough mixing, until the fragment is suspended in the mixture of liquids. When the glass is exactly suspended, it will show no tendency to rise or to sink. At this point, the other sample is added, and its behavior is studied relative to the first sample. If the liquids are thoroughly mixed, it should be possible to distinguish samples of slightly different density. The first sample should remain suspended, and the second sample should slowly rise or sink if it is different. If both samples remain suspended for a long period of time at any points in the homogeneous liquid mixture, they have virtually identical densities.

Glass specimens with the same densities *may* have come from the same source, but there are many glass specimens which have the same densities, and identical density values alone are not very strong evidence of common origin. If the temperature of the testing liquid is held precisely constant, very fine discriminations can be made between particles differing only slightly in density. If a measurement of the density value is desired, it can be obtained by weighing a known volume of the liquid which exactly suspends the sample and calculating the mass per unit volume. Making separate density measurements for each of two particles is less sensitive than the comparative method just described.

Another useful comparison technique is the density-gradient method. In this procedure, a long glass tube containing layers of liquids differing in density is prepared. The mixing of two liquids of different densities in different proportions gives a series of mixtures with densities in between those of either pure liquid. The bottom layer of the density gradient is designed to have a density greater than that of glass, whereas the top layer is chosen to have a density less than that of glass. The intermediate layers have densities which vary in uniform increments between the two extremes. The gradient tube prepared in this fashion is allowed to equilibrate for about 24 h before use. During this equilibration time, the initially discrete layers begin to blend into one another to form a uniform gradient. When glass samples are placed in the tube, each will settle to the level that corresponds to its own density. If the gradient is prepared in the appropriate density range and is quite sensitive, fairly subtle discriminations can be made by this method. Two of the most commonly used liquids for density-gradient work are bromoform (density = 2.890) and brombenzene (density = 1.499).

Optical Physical Properties   The ways in which a substance can interact with and affect light can be measured in terms of what are called *optical properties*. One of the most common is absorption. An opaque substance will absorb the light falling on it, whereas a transparent one will allow light to pass through it.

Some materials may absorb only a part of the light falling upon them, allowing the remainder to pass through or be *transmitted*. This behavior can be measured in several different ways. A sample which absorbs the majority of light falling onto it is said to have a high *absorption* or a low *transmittance*. The absorption or transmittance of a sample, such as glass, can vary with the wavelength (color) of the light passing through it. White light contains all the wavelengths of visible light. A piece of glass which absorbs all the wavelengths equally would look clear (low absorption) or some shade of gray (higher absorption).

If some wavelengths of white light were absorbed more than others, the glass would look colored. For example, a sample of glass which absorbs the majority of the longer wavelength (red) light but allows other wavelengths to pass through would have a blue-green appearance when viewed in white light. Thus, the color of a piece of colored glass is due to the variation of its absorption with wavelength. With glass, color is the most important result of the differential absorption of light. Glass samples which absorb all wavelengths to approximately the same extent appear gray in color. These are used for tinted glass in architectural applications. Those which absorb all visible wavelengths to the same extent are said to be *neutral*, and these are relatively uncommon as physical evidence. They are used for special optical applications where this behavior is important, such as in the manufacture of neutral-density filters for photography. In comparing glass samples, we can look at the shade of color the glass exhibits as well as the depth of the color (degree of absorption). If known and questioned samples are very different either in shade of color or degree of absorption, they would be excluded as having a possible common origin by this simple physical inspection. Detection of more subtle color differences requires a more complicated comparison.

Another way in which light can interact with matter is seen in the phenomenon of fluorescence. *Fluorescence* occurs when light of a shorter wavelength interacts with a sample to produce light of a longer wavelength. In many cases, the shorter-wavelength light falling on the sample is UV (wavelengths shorter than visible violet). The light which falls on the sample and produces the fluorescence is called the *exciting radiation;* the light given off by the sample is called the *emitted radiation.* If the exciting radiation is in the UV range, the emitted light may be in the visible range. This is the most commonly observed kind of fluorescence with glass.

Fluorescence may be studied visually, photographically, or instrumentally. For a visual study, the excitation source (normally a UV lamp) is shined on the sample, and the color of the emitted light is examined visually. Fluorescence can also be examined using a fluorescence microscope or an instrument known as a spectrophotofluorometer (Chapter 3). It allows the optimum excitation and emission wavelengths to be measured. These are often characteristic of a particular substance. Most often, simple visual fluorescence can be used for exclusions. Float glass has one interesting fluorescence property. Only one of the two plane surfaces of the original glass, the one that was in contact with the molten tin, will fluoresce. Thus, if one finds a piece of glass which exhibits a visual fluorescence on only one side of the two plane surfaces, it is an indication that the sample is float glass.

It is well known that glass (as well as other transparent mediums) will bend light that passes through it. Everyone has observed the effect of an uneven or curved piece of window glass on an image viewed through it. The bending of light by a sample of glass can be measured easily when the sample is in the shape of a triangular prism. The amount of bending which takes place is a function of the shape of the prism and of the composition of the particular sample of glass used to make the prism. If identically shaped prisms are made from several different samples of glass, the differences in the bending of light produced by each will be attributable to the glass alone. The property of glass that is responsible for the amount of bending is called *refractive index* (RI).

Fortunately, it is not necessary to shape a piece of glass into a prism to measure its RI, as this would be impossible in the case of the small particles encountered in forensic casework. If a microscopic fragment or chip of glass is immersed in a liquid of the same RI, it will be nearly invisible when viewed under the microscope. The same effect can be observed on a macro scale by placing a glass rod in a liquid of the same RI (Figure 7-3). The methods used in the forensic laboratory to compare and measure RIs of small particles of glass take advantage of this phenomenon. The unknown sample is placed in a liquid of known RI. Then a determination is made as to whether the RI of the unknown is above or below that of the liquid. If it is noted

FIGURE 7-3
A glass rod partially immersed in a liquid of a similar refractive index. The same liquid and glass rod were used for each of the three photographs; only the illumination was varied. The more diffuse the illumination is, the more difficult it is to see the glass rod where it has been immersed.

that the RI of the sample is above that of the liquid, a higher-RI liquid would be mixed with the original liquid to raise its refractive index. Alternatively, the sample could be removed and placed in another liquid of known but higher RI. In this way, the correct liquid or mixture can be found by trial and error. When the closest match is found, the sample will be all but invisible and the RI of the liquid is equal to that of the glass. The RI of a liquid can be determined using an instrument known as a refractometer.

Actual numerical RI values of samples are not always required. The relative difference in RI between two samples can often be more sensitively detected and is, in general, more important forensically. For very critical discriminations, a comparative RI technique is used. For this, chips of questioned and known samples are placed side by side in the same liquid. Their relative appearances and behaviors are noted when the RI of the liquid is very close to that of one or both samples. The observation of the RI match between the two samples of glass and the liquid is made under the microscope.

The RI of any sample is not the same for all wavelengths of visible light. The RI of glass samples (and of most substances) increases as the wavelength of light used decreases. The variation of RI with wavelength is given the name *dispersion*. The dispersions of different kinds of glasses can be significantly different. Dispersions can also vary within a particular type of glass.

Because of dispersion, accurate RI measurements cannot be made with white light (which contains all the wavelengths), but must be made with light of a single wavelength (monochromatic light). Dispersion itself can be measured on small particles of glass and is also a useful parameter for comparing glass samples. It is usually measured by determining the unknown's RI at three or four different wavelengths.

Chemical Properties   Glass specimens can be compared by instrumental methods of chemical analysis. Many sophisticated instruments have been applied to this problem. From the forensic viewpoint, however, none of them has been found sufficiently superior to the methods based on the comparison of the physical properties discussed above. Despite their sophistication, the applicable instrumental methods do not yield results with the required combination of sensitivity and reproducibility. It should be realized that the chemical differences between similar glass samples are often very slight and may be due to components present at extremely low levels. In recent years, plasma emission spectroscopy and energy-dispersive x-ray spectrometry have both shown promise in the comparison of glass samples.

SOIL

What Is Soil?

Soil is a very rich and complex mixture of diverse particles. It contains mineral grains derived from rock over eons of weathering. It may also contain decayed or decaying organic matter derived from plants. This mixture of inorganic materials and decayed organic matter is what is traditionally thought of as soil. From the forensic point of view, however, soil must be defined broadly enough to include particles created by human activity. Only soils in very remote areas would not have them, and the soils most commonly encountered in criminal investigations are from areas close to human habitation. For this reason, soils considered in crime investigations may contain paint particles, glass, airborne particulate pollutants from factories, bits of concrete, asphalt, tire-rubber abradings, and numerous other trace evidence items such as were mentioned in Chapter 6. Nearly any of the items in Table 6-1 could, in fact, be found in a soil sample. Soils may also contain insect parts and fragments of plants that have yet to decay, as well as living microorganisms.

Soil As Evidence

Soil can be potentially very valuable evidence. Many types of crimes take place under circumstances and conditions which are conducive to the transfer of considerable quantities of soil. It is thus fairly common as evidence.

Its value is enhanced by the fact that there is an extremely large variation among different samples of soil. The large number of possible components of soil can be present in varying amounts. Many essentially random physical, chemical, biological, and human processes contribute to the production of soils, giving rise to a very large number of possible combinations. Even within restricted geographic areas where soils are of the same general type, considerable variation exists. Significant differences can even be found in soil samples taken just a few feet apart. In addition to the individual characteristics just mentioned, soil also has useful class characteristcs. An examination of an unknown soil sample by a microscopist knowledgeable in geology may reveal the area from which the soil originated. This information can be useful as an investigative aid. Additional clues about local conditions at the point of origin of a soil sample can be gotten from an examination of biological evidence. The presence of fragments of certain mosses, for example, may indicate a shaded area. Other biological clues, such as the presence of pollens or morphologically identifiable plant fragments, can yield similar interpretations. The individualizations possible with soil evidence are probably more definitive than those based on compositional variation in any other kind of transfer evidence. The very great potential value of soil as evidence is not widely appreciated by investigators. As we will see in the next section, properly collected soil samples can be the most valuable evidence in a significant number of investigations. The phrase *properly collected* has been used advisedly because the value of soil evidence is almost completely dependent on the knowledge and presence of mind of the investigator charged with its collection.

Collection of Soil Evidence

General Considerations   It is of the utmost importance for investigators to realize that the significance of a soil comparison is dependent on the quality of the sample collection. No amount of sophisticated laboratory work can compensate for improperly collected samples. Control samples (see below) are particularly important with soil evidence, and they are often overlooked or improperly collected. The significance of the results of a comparison between a known and a questioned sample is evaluated in terms of the variations observed among known samples. The general collection methods discussed in Chapter 6 can be used with soil evidence. The most useful of these are (1) packaging and submission without sampling and (2) visual inspection and collection. The vacuuming and tape-lift methods are a last resort in collecting soils.

Collection of Questioned Soil Samples   Questioned or unknown soil samples are generally found on shoes and clothing or on other objects associated with the suspect. They may also be found on a victim who does not remain at the primary crime scene, but whose presence at the scene needs to be proved.

Soil on a suspect's shoes may have been deposited in discrete layers. A study of these layers may indicate to the criminalist that the suspect has accumulated these different layers by walking through areas containing different kinds of soils either before or after the incident being investigated. This layer structure should be disturbed as little as possible prior to examination in the laboratory. For this reason, it is a good general rule to submit articles bearing soil evidence directly to the laboratory without prior sampling. Soil on larger articles, which cannot be conveniently transported, can be collected by cutting out the portion of the object which contains the soil, or alternatively, by employing the visual inspection and collection technique. This should be employed with the utmost care.

The area to be sampled should be studied carefully before any soil is removed. If areas of different color or texture are noted, these should be sampled, packaged, and submitted separately. Documentation of the original appearance of the soil using color photography might be appropriate. In this case the collected samples would be labeled in such a way that they could be related to the areas in the photograph. The visual inspection and collection method would be employed in sampling areas on immovable objects which would be expected to have soil from many different sources present (for example, the fender wells of a suspect's automobile).

Collection of Known and Known-Control Samples The success of an investigation involving soil evidence may well depend on the collection of proper and adequate known and known-control soil samples. The *known* sample is from the point where the questioned samples are thought to have originated. The *known-control* samples are taken from various points in the area around the point where the known was taken. Soil can be excellent evidence, but the significance of a match between questioned and known samples must be interpreted in terms of the degree of variation observed among the known and the known-control samples. It should be clear that a match between questioned and known samples will be most significant when both known and questioned samples can be shown to be distinctly different from the known controls collected from the same general location as the primary known sample. Showing a jury that the known sample is more similar to the questioned sample than it is to other known samples taken in that area can have a great impact.

The collection of known samples is not as simple as it might seem. The precise sites selected for sampling must be given careful consideration. Because of the local variations which exist in soils, known samples should be taken from points as close to the suspected area of origin of the questioned sample as possible. If there is uncertainty, several known samples may be taken. These additional samples may serve the dual purpose of being both known and known-control samples, and additional known controls would probably be necessary. Disturbed areas in the soil at the scene are logical candidate areas to be sampled for knowns. If the disturbed area exhibits any detailed form or pattern, such as a footprint or knee impression, these *must be* thoroughly documented by the use of procedures like photography and casting (Chapter 11) prior to the removal of any known samples. The imprints, if present, are likely to be more important in terms of their value to the case than the soil. Even if this is not true, they are considerably easier to analyze for associative value than soil. It must be remembered that local variation in soil occurs in vertical as well as horizontal directions. Thus, if it appears that the deeper layers of the soil have been disturbed in the course of the crime, both surface and subsurface known samples should be taken. The origin of each of the samples should be carefully documented, and they should be packaged and labeled separately.

The best locations for taking known controls depend on the general configuration or layout of the crime scene. If the scene is an open field or lawn with no distinctive features, the use of a preselected geometric collection scheme, such as the triangular

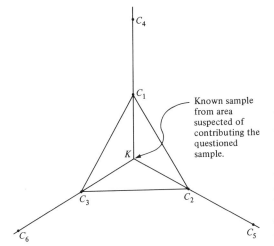

FIGURE 7-4
A triangular collection pattern. This is a suitable pattern for use in collecting soil samples in open terrain. Modifications may be necessary in other situations. This is designed to be used only as an aid in the collection of known and known-control soil samples. Other schemes that assure the collection of samples that are representative of variations in the area of the crime scene are equally valid. The scale used depends on the situation. Control locations C_1 to C_3 might be a few feet from K, whereas C_4 to C_6 might be 50 ft or more away.

pattern shown in Figure 7-4, might be indicated. In wooded areas, small yards, or areas broken up by roads, fences, rocks, streams, etc., such a fixed collection pattern would be inappropriate. In such a circumstance, some knowledge of the way in which the crime took place can be very helpful in selecting points for collecting control samples. A carefully thought-out preliminary reconstruction can greatly facilitate a scene investigation and the evidence collection. Thus, in the case of collecting soil controls, samples would be taken at various points along paths leading to or from the crime scene.

Collection of Alternative Known or Alibi Samples   "Alibi" samples can be extremely important in cases involving soil evidence. Whenever a suspect chooses to offer an explanation for the presence of mud or other forms of soil on shoes or clothing, every effort should be made to obtain samples from the area from which it is claimed that the soil originated. The following case illustrates the potential value of alibi soil samples.

A suspect in a rape-homicide investigation was arrested shortly after the crime was reported. The clothing he was wearing when arrested contained several mud-stained areas. In addition, the work boots he was wearing had considerable quantities of mud in the welt area. He explained the presence of mud on his clothing by stating that he had fallen in an area of his own yard. The alert investigators asked to be shown the area where he claimed to have fallen and received permission to take alibi samples from this area. The scene of the crime was about two blocks away from the suspect's residence. Known samples were taken from disturbed areas near the body, and control samples were taken at various distances away, as well as along a path leading to the site of the rape. Subsequent laboratory examination revealed a high degree of similarity between the questioned samples from the shoes and clothing of the suspect and the known samples from the area near the body. The known control samples removed from the general area where the crime took place were similar, but could be shown to be different. The alibi sample was dissimilar to either the known or questioned samples. These findings together with those derived from some less significant physical evidence were instrumental in obtaining a conviction.

A conviction in this case might have been more difficult to obtain if the alibi sample had not been collected. It was the dissimilarity of the alibi and questioned samples, coupled with the similarity of the questioned sample to the known from the scene, that convinced the jury of the suspect's presence at the scene. The similarity of known and questioned samples was more significant because of the notable degree of local variation at the scene, which was demonstrated by examining known controls. Without the alibi sample analysis, however, the defendant could have argued convincingly that he acquired the questioned samples from some other location in the general vicinity. The data from the alibi sample eliminated the need for the jury to weigh this possibility.

Laboratory Approaches to Soil Comparison

General Considerations   As discussed above, the uniqueness of a particular soil sample depends on the complexity of its mixture as well as on the degree of local variation in the immediate area where the sample is found. The more complex a given soil sample, and the greater the local variation in the area where it is taken, the more likely it is that it can be individualized to the extent where a strong opinion concerning commonality of origin can be offered. Because of the extreme complexity of soil, it can be looked at in many different ways and, thus, there are a number of methods which can be used to analyze and compare soil samples. No single method is superior. Many supply complementary information. The best analytical approach is one which is suited to the strengths of the particular laboratory and which draws upon several different techniques.

In some situations, soil may be encountered as dried mud. Pieces of this material may break off, and physical matches may be possible.

Sample Preparation and Low-Power Examination   Soil samples are rarely ready for comparison as received. Some preparation, such as drying and "coning and quartering," is usually necessary. These steps are taken to ensure that the portion of the sample which is analyzed will represent the overall sample, and to provide for setting aside a part of the sample. The first step in any soil comparison is a preliminary low-power microscopical examination using the stereoscopic microscope. The stereomicroscopical examination and the sample-preparation phases are often combined. During examination with the stereomicroscope, certain gross features or characteristics of the soil are noted, such as the presence of plant fragments or insect parts. Once documented, they can be placed in separate containers. Other debris or obvious gross constituents are treated similarly. The final opinion rendered will be based on an evaluation of the presence of such extraneous materials as well as on comparisons of the constituents which are normally thought of as making up soil.

Once the larger constituents have been removed and properly preserved, the soil sample is ready to be *coned and quartered*. This term describes a process in which the sample is thoroughly mixed and then formed into a conical (cone-shaped) pile on a clean surface. The mixing is necessary to be certain that any portion taken from the overall sample will be representative of it. Any large aggregates of caked soil are gently broken up in this process. The pile is then divided into fourths (quartered) using a small straight edge like a ruler, microscope slide, or laboratory spatula. If the sample is reasonably large, a single quarter of it may be adequate for the remainder of the laboratory analysis. More than one quarter of the cone may be used if the sample is small or if the criminalist plans to use two or more general analytical schemes requiring fresh samples. In any case, it is wise to avoid using all of the sample. The unused quarters can be packaged and saved for presentation in court or for examination by another expert.

Color An obvious but surprisingly useful parameter for comparing soils is their color. Soils exist in a wide range of colors. When critically examined, soils can be divided into hundreds of distinct categories based on their color alone. In order for a color comparison to be valid, all the samples being compared must be treated in the same fashion. They are commonly dried and gently crushed to a uniform consistency before any color comparisons are attempted. The crushing breaks up lumps and loose aggregates of particles. Some laboratories maintain extensive reference collections of soil samples. The color of an unknown soil sample might be compared with the colors of those in the reference collection to limit the range of soil types that the sample could represent. This information could be useful as an investigative aid or in evaluating and interpreting the significance of the color comparison between the questioned and known samples. In color comparisons of this kind, the type of lighting used is often very critical. Comparisons conducted under incandescent, fluorescent, or daylight illumination may yield different results. It may be desirable to routinely employ two or three standardized types of illumination for each color comparison. Color comparisons are particularly useful in preliminary examinations to exclude soils that may have come from different sources. Because of the relatively high degree of discrimination potential of color comparisons, data derived from them and subsequent tests can be combined to add weight to an individualization.

Particle Size Distribution The many different kinds of mineral grains which may be present in a soil sample can exist in a considerable range of particle sizes. The relative abundance of particles in different size ranges is often characteristic for a particular sample of soil. The degree of discrimination which can be expected from particle size distribution determinations depends on the number of size ranges included. With very small samples, the particle size distribution can be estimated using the microscope. With larger samples, this type of data can be obtained by using a stack of carefully graded laboratory sieves. The sieve at the bottom of such a stack has the finest mesh, and the one at the top has the coarsest. The soil sample is placed on the screen in the upper sieve and agitated until all the particles in the soil have found the levels corresponding to their respective size ranges. At this point, the stack is taken apart, and the amount contained within each fraction is determined by noting its volume or by actually weighing each fraction separately. The particle size distribution data obtained in this way are often best presented graphically, by means of a histogram (bar graph). Each bar would represent a particle size range, and the height of the bar would represent the amount of material in that range.

Color comparisons and determinations of particle size distributions for soil samples can be carried out quite easily without expensive laboratory facilities. The combined data can be quite useful in discriminating among similar soil samples.

You can appreciate the potential value of soil as evidence by conducting a simple experiment using a combination of the two approaches just discussed. The experimenter should collect soil samples from several widely separated areas and include several samples taken at different locations near the center of each area. It will be found that it is difficult to find two samples that are not distinguishable, even in this limited experiment. Thus, although the application of more refined laboratory techniques can greatly increase the discriminating power of such a soil comparison, the results of the experiment will show that quite a bit of discrimination is possible using the two fairly simple approaches mentioned above (color and particle size distribution).

Density Gradient Many additional laboratory approaches can be applied to the problem of comparing soils, but two in particular are used often and are discussed here. They are the density-gradient and mineralogical methods. The results of a comparison using either of these can be combined with those used in the preliminary examination to yield a definitive comparison. Some forensic scientists may advocate one of these techniques over the other, but there are no compelling data to suggest that either is superior, and they may supply complementary information. It could be argued that both methods should be used in comparing soils that are not easily distinguished by one or the other, but the use of both methods is probably not necessary. The number of tests that *could be* performed in connection with a particular soil comparison is very large, but there has to be a practical limit so that the examination does not go on forever. More research is needed to compare methods, to determine the extent of overlap in the discriminating power, and to see whether more discrimination is achieved when various combinations are used.

The *density-gradient* technique used with soil is similar to that described for glass earlier in the chapter. In this case, a density gradient is prepared which covers a somewhat broader range of densities than would be appropriate for glass comparisons. A single density gradient tube was sufficient with glass, because unknown and known samples were individually recognizable by their microscopic morphologies and could be added to the same tube. In the case of soil comparisons, however, each sample is composed of numerous small particles which could not be distinguished if the samples were mixed. For this reason, soil comparisons by the density-gradient method require that one gradient tube be used for each separate sample, and it is important that each of these gradients be made in exactly the same way. A special type of rack is usually used to hold these nearly identical gradient tubes. Each is held in a vertical position at the same height, and all the tubes are evenly spaced in the rack. The rack arrangement helps considerably in making visual and photographic comparisons. Once the gradient tubes have been set up and allowed to equilibrate for about 24 h, the soil samples are added to each. Various kinds of pretreatments may be applied to the soils before they are added to their respective tubes. Normally the soil sample is dried and gently crushed or pulverized to remove aggregates or caked soil as part of the coning and quartering step. More elaborate pretreatments may involve the use of washing, sieving, and other preliminary fractionation techniques. In any case, it is clearly imperative that all the soil samples being compared be treated in exactly the same way. A photograph of a typical density-gradient comparison of soil is presented in Figure 7-5. Some of the uniqueness of density-gradient patterns of soil is attributable to the fact that they represent more than just the

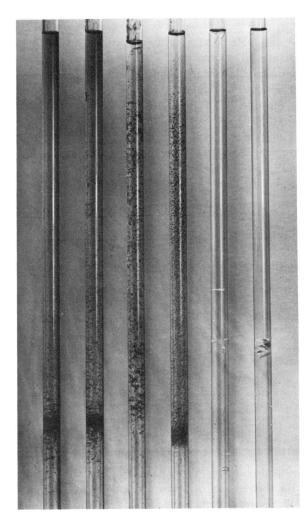

FIGURE 7-5
Comparison of soil samples by density gradient. Note that two of the tubes contain soil sample. Left to right: unknown; three known soil samples; two glass comparisons. *(Courtesy of Beryl Novitch, Forensic Science Laboratory, Connecticut State Police.)*

density distributions of the individual particles making up the sample. Small aggregates of individual mineral grains and clays are present in most soils. Single grains may also be coated with clays. Thus, a range of intermediate densities is possible in such a sample, and this contributes to the complexity of the density-gradient pattern. The exact nature of the mineral grain–clay composites is determined by the history of the interaction of the particular sample with water. Density-gradient patterns characteristic of the specific combination of mineral grains present can be obtained if the soil sample is washed to remove the clay fraction before the gradient is prepared. Certain detergents are especially useful for this purpose.

Mineralogical Profile   The *mineralogical* approach to the forensic comparison of soils is basically a sophisticated microscopical one, which utilizes the polarizing microscope. An attempt is made to identify and determine the frequency of occurrence of each of the types of particles represented in the two samples being compared. A rigorous identification of each particle would be too time-consuming, but fortunately it is not necessary. An estimate of the frequency distribution of the particles in each sample usually suffices. The polarizing microscope can be used to obtain an approximate mineralogical profile for each sample and, in addition, provide information about the frequency of occurrence of nonmineral particles. The polarizing microscope is an extremely versatile tool. Table 3-2 lists many of the properties that can be observed and measured using the polarizing microscope. Most of them are optical properties which are particularly useful for identifying mineral grains. The information provided by observing the optical properties of crystalline particles at the same time that the morphology of these and other particles is being studied allows a skilled forensic microscopist to identify the mineral grains and other particles in the soil sample quickly.

Among the properties that can be determined with the polarizing microscope is refractive index (Table 3-2). When we discussed refractive index measurements on glass fragments earlier in the chapter, we were considering only materials which are *isotropic* (that is, they have a single refractive index at any given wavelength). Most crystals, including most mineral grains, are not isotropic. They may have two or three principal refractive indices and are referred to as being *anisotropic,* or *birefringent.* With these, the refractive index observed depends upon the orientation of the sample with respect to the direction of vibration of the light traveling through it. Anisotropic materials have at least one optic axis along which light can be propagated and behave as though it were traveling in an isotropic material. Those materials with two principal refractive indices have a single optic axis and are classified as *uniaxial* substances, whereas those possessing three principal refractive indices have two optic axes and are called *biaxial.*

If a mineral grain in a soil sample is oriented properly under the polarizing microscope, the distinction between uniaxial and biaxial crystals can be made within a few seconds. If the crystal is not oriented properly, the microscopist may decide that the amount of effort necessary to reorient it is not worthwhile considering the large number of grains to be examined. For this reason, the mineralogical profiles most frequently obtained with soil samples involve making some estimations, as noted above.

A rigorous identification of each of the numerous particles in such a complex mixture is sacrificed to allow tentative identifications and counting of a large number of particles.

The mineralogical approach in the hands of a skilled microscopist can be exceedingly useful in the forensic comparison of soils. It would probably be the best approach for completely characterizing a soil sample if time constraints did not prevent a complete and rigorous identification and tallying of each particle. Because of these practical limitations, there is some argument as to the best approach to be used. The large number of particles to be identified in a reasonable period of time makes recourse to the use of estimates necessary. It can also be argued that since the complexity of soil affords the analyst the opportunity to find subtle differences among soils from nearly the same location, such efforts are unnecessary. Thus, when slight differences between two soil samples are found, some interpretation is necessary to evaluate their significance.

Other Methods of Soil Comparison   Elemental analysis of soils using such techniques as emission spectrography or neutron activation analysis has met with limited success. The elemental composition of a sample is not as diagnostic as the mineralogical profile. X-ray diffractometry has also been applied to the forensic comparison of soils. It is an ideal technique for identifying samples composed of pure or nearly pure crystalline materials or for identifying simple mixtures of them, but it is less useful with complex mixtures such as soil. In addition, the effect of the trace constituents can be lost in the diffraction pattern produced by the major constituents. The particle analysis approach using polarized-light microscopy is a better way of observing and studying minor crystalline components in such a complex mixture. Generally speaking, bulk analysis techniques such as those discussed in this paragraph are less useful forensically than are particle analysis or compositional mapping techniques (Chapter 3). This observation applies to many types of physical evidence besides soil.

Two approaches to the characterization of soil based on its organic composition have been explored. Both involve the use of gas chromatography (GC). In one technique, the soil is extracted with a solvent which is then analyzed using a gas chromatograph. In the other approach, a portion of the soil sample is heated in an inert gas atmosphere to *pyrolyze* the organic components. The pyrolyzate (mixture of gases produced) is examined immediately with the GC. The pyrolysis and the GC separations are carried out in a coordinated way as part of a single technique known as pyrolysis–gas chromatography (PGC), which was discussed in Chapter 3. Both these approaches have shown promise, but further work is needed to evaluate their potential for discriminations in soil comparisons. A newer technique, high-performance liquid chromatography (HPLC) would appear to be potentially applicable to the characterization and comparison of the organic fraction of soils, but it has not yet been applied to this problem. Most of the organic compounds found in soil are derived from the decay of living matter, but they also come from industrial wastes and air pollution.

Biochemical and biological methods for soil characterization have the advantage that they can exploit characteristics unique to the environment of a particular soil sample. This advantage is shared to a lesser extent by the organic approach described above. Biochemical methods applied thus far to the forensic characterization of soil have involved the identification and characterization of enzymes produced by the organisms living in the soil. The enzymes found show considerable variation among soils from different sources. This approach has been studied quite extensively and has shown a good deal of promise. Biological methods for the identification of traces of plants and animals can be used in soil characterization. Insect parts, pollens, seeds, and plant fragments are examples of things that can be of value in soil comparisons. The presence of certain things in a soil sample can also be useful as an investigative aid. For example, the finding of a certain moss in a sample would suggest that the soil came from a damp, shaded area. As discussed in Chapter 6, pollens can be particularly useful for developing investigative information. Microbiological methods can be used to detect the presence and abundance of microscopic plants and animals in the soil. If a detailed microbiological profile could be constructed for the sample, preliminary evidence indicates that it would be unique for a particular soil sample.

STUDY QUESTIONS

1 What is glass?
2 How are different kinds of glass made?
3 What factors contribute to the significance of glass as physical evidence?
4 What factors should be considered when collecting glass evidence?
5 What are the proper procedures to be followed in collecting glass evidence at a crime scene?
6 What methods are used to individualize glass samples? What are the advantages and limitations of each? Which method should be applied first?
7 What are important nonoptical physical properties of glass, and how are they measured?
8 What are the important optical physical properties of glass, and how are they measured?
9 What is soil?
10 Why is soil important as physical evidence?
11 What are the methods of collecting soil evidence? What are the advantages and disadvantages of each method?
12 Which principles should be kept in mind when collecting soil evidence?
13 How is a soil sample prepared for detailed analysis in the forensic science laboratory?
14 What are main properties of soil that can be used for comparison in a forensic laboratory?
15 What is a density gradient analysis of a soil sample, and what information can be obtained from it?
16 What is a mineralogical profile of a soil sample, and what information can be obtained from it?
17 What are some of the biological and biochemical techniques that can be used to compare soil samples?

REFERENCES AND FURTHER READING

Bear, F. E. (ed.): *Chemistry of Soil,* American Chemical Society, Reinhold, New York, 1964.

Cobb, P. G. W.: "A Survey of the Variation in the Physical Properties of Glass," *Journal of Forensic Sciences,* vol. 8, p. 29, 1968.

Dabbs, M. D. G., and E. F. Pearson: "Some Physical Properties of a Large Number of Window Glass Specimens," *Journal of Forensic Sciences,* vol. 17, pp. 70–78, 1972.

Dudley, R. J., and K. Smalldon: "The Evaluation of Methods for Soil Analysis under Simulated Scenes of Crime Conditions," *Forensic Science International,* vol. 12, pp. 49–60, 1978.

Jackson, M. L.: *Soil Chemical Analysis,* Prentice-Hall, Englewood Cliffs, N.J., 1958.

McJunkins, S. P., and J. I. Thornton: "Glass Fracture Analysis—A Review," *Forensic Science,* vol. 2, pp. 1–27, 1973.

Miller, E. T.: "Forensic Glass Comparisons," in R. Saferstein (ed.), *Forensic Science Handbook,* Prentice-Hall, Englewood Cliffs, N.J., 1982.

Murray, R. C. "Forensic Examination of Soil," in R. Saferstein (ed.), *Forensic Science Handbook,* Prentice-Hall, Englewood Cliffs, N.J., 1982.

Murray, R. C., and J. C. F. Tedrow: *Forensic Geology,* Rutgers University Press, New Brunswick, N.J., 1975.

Nelson, D. F.: "The Examination of Glass Fragments," in A. S. Curry (ed.), *Methods of Forensic Science,* vol. 4, Wiley, New York, 1965.

Ojena, S. M., and P. R. De Forest: "A Study of Refractive Index Variations Within and Between Sealed-Beam Headlights Using a Precise Method," *Journal of Forensic Sciences,* vol. 17, pp. 409–425, 1972.

Ojena, S. M., and P. R. De Forest: "Precise Refractive Index Determination by the Immersion Method Using Phase Contrast Microscopy and the Mettler Hot Stage," *Journal of the Forensic Science Society,* vol. 12, pp. 315–329, 1972.

Thornton, J. I., and P. J. Cashman: "Reconstruction of Fractured Glass by Laser Beam Interferometry," *Journal of Forensic Sciences,* vol. 24, pp. 101–108, 1979.

Thornton, J. I., and A. D. McLaren: "Enzymatic Characterization of Soil Evidence," *Journal of Forensic Sciences,* vol. 20, pp. 674–692, 1975.

Von Bremen, U.: "Shadowgraphs of Bulbs, Bottles and Panes," *Journal of Forensic Sciences,* vol. 20, pp. 109–118, 1975.

Winchell, A. N, and H. Winchell: *The Microscopical Character of Artificial Inorganic Soil Substances,* Academic, New York, 1964.

CHAPTER 8

FIBERS AND HAIRS

INTRODUCTION

Fibers and hairs are among the most common and most important types of physical evidence encountered in criminal investigations. Large numbers can be shed from a surface and may be transferred to another one in accordance with the Locard exchange principle (Chapter 6). Fibers or hairs often adhere strongly to the second surface (as anyone who has tried to keep a dark suit lint-free knows well), although just how tightly depends upon a number of conditions. These include the nature of the surface (weave, fiber type, etc.), atmospheric conditions (for example, humidity), the nature of the transfer process, and the type of fiber which has been transferred.

Hairs are actually a special type of fiber. They are discussed separately in this chapter, however, because they have a special importance and are often treated differently. In some laboratories, hairs may be examined in a different section from the one in which fibers are examined.

FIBERS

Fibers can be divided into three main categories: natural, derived (including regenerated), and synthetic. Before the turn of the century, all commercial textile fibers were natural. Derived and synthetic fibers are a product of 20th century technology and can be grouped together as artificial (or man-made) fibers.

Natural Fibers

Natural fibers can be grouped according to whether they are animal, vegetable, or mineral. Some natural fibers have no commercial value but may be important as physical evidence. Many vegetable fibers fall into this category.

Mineral Fibers The major mineral fibers are various kinds of asbestos. Asbestos has been used for a long time as an insulating material as well as in the manufacture of fire-resistant textiles such as gloves, suits, and curtains. It is also used with binders to make such products as asbestos board and pipe. The use of asbestos has decreased in recent years because it has been implicated as a cause of a particular type of lung cancer and other disease.

Asbestos minerals have one important characteristic that makes them useful as fibers. All are crystalline materials in which the chemical bonds are much stronger in one direction (along the fiber axis) than in the other two directions. Thus, solid asbestos minerals fracture, or cleave, to form long thin rods, or fibers, and this process can be continued until extremely thin fibers have been produced. Many of these fibers are so small that they are truly submicroscopic, and as a result they can be carried for considerable distances in the air. The inhalation of these extremely small airborne asbestos particles accounts for the major health problem posed by these materials. The particles are so small that they can easily get into the deepest recesses of the lungs and can be retained in lung tissue, producing irritation and thus possibly contributing to disease.

Asbestos fibers can be valuable as physical evidence. They are easily transferred from one surface to another. Forensic microscopists can group those fibers which are large enough to be examined according to the type of asbestos from which they were derived. The principal kinds of asbestos are crysotile, a form of the mineral serpentine, and crocidolite, a form of amphibole. Commercial asbestos is primarily crysotile.

Vegetable Fibers Although they constitute by far the largest class of natural fibers, many vegetable fibers have no commercial importance. However, some are used in manufacturing textiles and other items. Any vegetable fiber can be important physical evidence in a particular case. The major constituent of vegetable fibers is cellulose. *Cellulose* is a natural polymer, a large molecule consisting of many smaller units bonded together (see under Artificial Fibers).

Cotton is the most common vegetable fiber, and no other textile runs a close second to it in frequency of use. Cotton fibers are the seed hairs of the cotton plant, and are composed of almost pure cellulose. In nature, they help the wind disperse the seeds of the plant. There are other kinds of plants that have similar seed-dispersal devices, but no other fiber of this type has achieved the commercial importance of cotton. The seed hairs of the kapok plant have been used for filling (insulation) in sleeping bags and to provide buoyancy in marine life jackets.

Cotton fibers have a distinctive flattened, twisted microscopic appearance, which is quite characteristic (Figure 8-1). The fibers resemble a twisted ribbon. Certain treatments, such as mercerizing, can change this appearance, but the fibers are still recognizable as cotton by a microscopist. In the *mercerizing* process, the fibers are treated with alkali, making them swell up and become more rounded and less twisted in appearance. This process gives fabrics made from these fibers an improved texture and feel.

Undyed cotton fibers are so common that they have little value as physical evi-

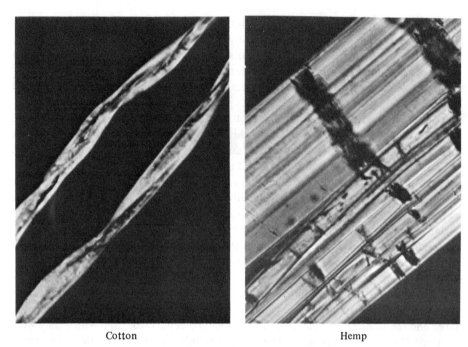

Cotton   Hemp

FIGURE 8-1
Photomicrographs of two natural fibers, cotton and hemp. *(Courtesy of Nicholas Petraco.)*

dence. Almost any surface or dust sample, if examined carefully, will be found to contain white cotton fibers. The only exceptions might be in samples from uninhabited wilderness areas. Certain shades of dyed cotton, however, can be valuable as physical evidence.

Kapok is less common than cotton and consequently can be of more evidential value if found. Kapok fibers, like cotton, are seed hairs composed of almost 100% cellulose.

Forensic microscopists can easily differentiate cotton from kapok fibers. Kapok fibers have a uniform cylindrical appearance and a very large air-filled canal which runs the length of the fiber. It is the air trapped in the canal *(lumen)* which accounts for the buoyancy (ability to float) of kapok-filled articles.

The presence of many kapok fibers on a person's clothing could be taken to mean that the clothing had come in contact with a kapok-filled article having a damaged outer covering. Such a finding might prove valuable in an investigation.

Linen has been used as a textile fiber for a long time. Linen is also primarily cellulose, like cotton and kapok, but it differs from them in an important respect: linen is a *bast,* or *stem,* fiber rather than a seed hair. It comes from the flax plant.

Linen fibers have a distinctive microscopic appearance, looking something like bamboo in that nodes are present at more-or-less regular intervals along the length of each fiber.

A number of fibers that are unsuitable for use in textile manufacturing, because of their coarseness and stiffness, are used in different kinds of *cordage*. These include manila, hemp (Figure 8-1), sisal, coir (coconut), and jute. A skilled forensic microscopist can readily identify these fibers. Since they are not extremely common, they can be valuable as physical evidence. Other types of cordage may be made of cotton (discussed above) or of synthetic fibers (discussed below).

A number of *other vegetable fibers,* though they are without commercial value, may have evidential importance. This category includes the leaf hairs (trichomes) of many species. Although microscopic in size, many trichomes can be characterized in terms of the plant from which they came. They may be able to be associated with particular geographical areas in this way if the plant of origin has a limited habitat. The airborne dust which settles in an area often contains characteristic trichomes and other vegetable fibers, as well as particles such as pollen grains and minerals which are typical of the area. The potential value of this kind of evidence is very great. Although many laboratories do not exploit it yet, there are indications that more use will be made of such evidence in the future.

Animal Fibers The majority of animal fibers of forensic interest are hairs, although fibers such as silk, or even catgut, are sometimes encountered. Human and animal hairs are discussed in detail below. One animal hair deserves special mention here, however, because of its importance in textile manufacturing; this fiber is wool, the hair of the sheep.

Wool has a microscopic structure that is characteristic of hair. The *cuticle,* or outer covering, of the wool fiber is made of flattened cells, commonly called scales. These resemble the scales of fish or the shingles of a roof and are one of the most useful features in identifying an unknown textile fiber as wool. Internal details, which are discussed in connection with hair, can be useful, too. Other animal hairs have uses similar to those of wool, but these are not as frequently encountered as evidence. They include goat hair (common goat, cashmere, and mohair), llama (including alpaca, vicuna, and guanaco), and camel hair. They can be quite valuable if they do occur as evidence. Rabbit hair may be encountered occasionally as part of a blend in knitted textiles.

Cattle and rabbit hair, although not commonly used in making woven or knitted textiles, are found in the manufacture of certain kinds of *felts*. Felts are made from water suspensions of randomly arranged fibers. When the fibers settle out, the water is removed and the mass of fibers is rolled or pressed to form the felt. One property of hairs that makes them especially useful in felt manufacture is the presence of scales on the hair surfaces, causing them to show a ratchet-like effect. It is more difficult for one hair to move in relation to another one if the movement is against the scale direction. Some modern felts are no longer made exclusively from hairs but are mixtures of certain hairs and other fibers. There are even felts with no wool or hair of any kind. These are made entirely from synthetic fibers, like rayon or nylon, although binders are generally required to hold the fibers together.

Silk places a distant second to wool as an animal fiber used in woven textiles. Its use has decreased steadily since the development of artificial fibers. *Silk* fibers are composed of a protein (fibroin) and are spun as long double filaments by the common silkworm *(Bombyx mori)* and a few other species. In processing raw silk to yield the single fibers used in textiles, a gumlike substance (seracin), which holds the two filaments together, is removed. Silk fibers are not very often encountered in criminal investigations, probably because silk fabrics do not shed very easily. In this respect, silk is like the filament type of artificial fibers discussed next.

Artificial Fibers

Most fibers are *polymers,* very large molecules formed by the bonding together of smaller molecules. The small molecules that form the units of a polymer are called *monomers* (*mono,* "one"; *poly,* "many"). The primary polymer making up vegetable fibers is cellulose, which is composed of a single type of monomer, one form of the sugar glucose (Figure 8-2A). Polymers can also be composed of molecules of two or more different monomers, which bond together in a *copolymerization* reaction.

Artificial fibers can be divided into two classes according to the *source* of the polymer used to make them. They can be obtained from *regenerated* natural polymers or materials *derived* from chemically modified natural polymers such as cellulose or proteins, or they can be spun from purely *synthetic* polymers, such as nylon.

Derived and Regenerated Fibers   The first commercially successful artificial fiber was *rayon;* it was produced by the viscose process in 1913. The cuprammonium process has also been used to make rayons. The basic principle underlying either process amounts to dissolving cellulose from cotton or wood and then resolidifying (regenerating) it after extrusion through a small orifice to form a fiber. In certain textile applications, the long filaments are woven to yield smooth fabrics. They can also be cut up into smaller segments, called *staple,* which are twisted together (spun) to form yarns. The yarns can then be woven into fabrics which look and feel more like those made from natural staple fibers. The only natural fiber which occurs in a filament form is silk, and fabrics made from filament rayons are often intended to have a silklike appearance.

Fabrics made from filament-type rayons are less likely to shed fibers than those made from staple. Thus, filament-type fabrics are less likely to contribute to the fiber transfers that often provide valuable physical evidence in criminal investigations. Rayons can be identified using microscopical techniques, and different types of rayons can be differentiated in this way as well. Rayons are marketed under a variety of trade names, some examples of which appear in Table 8-1.

Another class of artificial fibers, although not cellulose as such, are *derived* from cellulose and are called *acetates.* These consist of a chemically modified cellulose known as cellulose acetate. Acetates are ordinarily used in the filament form and are not very common in fiber transfers. Some of the trade names of acetate fibers are included in Table 8-1. Cellulose acetate in a form with a significantly higher percentage of acetate groups is used to produce a fiber type known as *triacetate,* which is marketed under the trade name Arnel.

A number of natural polymers other than cellulose have been tried as raw materials for the production of fibers, but there has been limited commercial success. Fibers have been made from proteins, including milk casein, egg albumin, soybean protein, peanut and corn proteins, feathers, and gelatin. Carbohydrates from seaweed and certain shellfish (especially arthropod shells, which are composed of chitin) have been used as fiber-forming polymers in the past. These fibers have been almost completely superseded by true synthetic fibers and are rare or nonexistent today. The chance of finding one of them in a criminal investigation is remote. Because the polymers for synthetic fibers are manufactured from petrochemicals (chemicals obtained from crude oil), it is possible that a continuing reduction in the availability of petroleum could contribute to a reversal of this trend. Rayon, for example, is enjoying something of a resurgence, and active research on developing commercially profitable fibers from the chitin of shells (lobster, crab, shrimp, etc.) is ongoing. The structure of chitin and its relationship to cellulose can be seen in Figure 8-2B.

Synthetic Fibers   We define synthetic fibers as those made by human beings and where the polymer is chemically synthesized. A large number and variety of synthetic fibers are in use today. Many of them are frequently encountered in criminal investigations, especially the ones that are commonly used as staple, rather than filament. This statement applies primarily to contact transfers of fibers; fiber evidence from filament fabrics is common if the fabric has been torn or snagged.

The first truly synthetic fiber was developed by the Du Pont Company in the 1930s. Its name, Nylon, was dedicated to the public domain in 1938, and became the generic name for a broad class of polyamide fibers. In 1939, women's hosiery made from nylon was introduced and became an immediate success, heralding the beginnings of the synthetic fiber age. Synthetic fibers have completely replaced the natural ones for many applications. The production volume of synthetic fibers is now of the order of billions of pounds every year.

Nylons are *polyamide* fibers, which means that they are polymers made of monomers bonded together by amide linkages (bonds). An amide bond forms when a carboxylic acid reacts with an amine. In making some of the more common polyamides, a monomer with two acid groups is usually polymerized with another monomer having two amine groups. In the reaction of Figure 8-2C, if $R = (—CH_2—)_4$, the diacid is adipic acid, and if $R' = (—CH_2—)_6$, the diamine is hexamethylenediamine.

The polymer produced by linking two six-carbon monomers is known as Nylon 66. Different nylons are obtained by varying the nature of the monomers. For example, Nylon 610 is made up of the same six-carbon diamine (hexamethylenediamine) as Nylon 66, but a 10-carbon diacid (sebacic acid) is used instead of the six-carbon acid (adipic acid). In some cases a single monomer molecule containing an acid group on one end and an amine group on the other, known generally as an amino acid, can be joined with other identical molecules to form the polymer (Figure 8-2D). In Nylon 6, for example, $R = R' = (—CH_2—)_5$, and the monomer is a cyclic (ring) form of 6-aminocaproic acid known as caprolactam. Each monomer ring opens up as it is added to the polymer. The generalized reaction is given Figure 8-2D.

I Natural Polymers

A

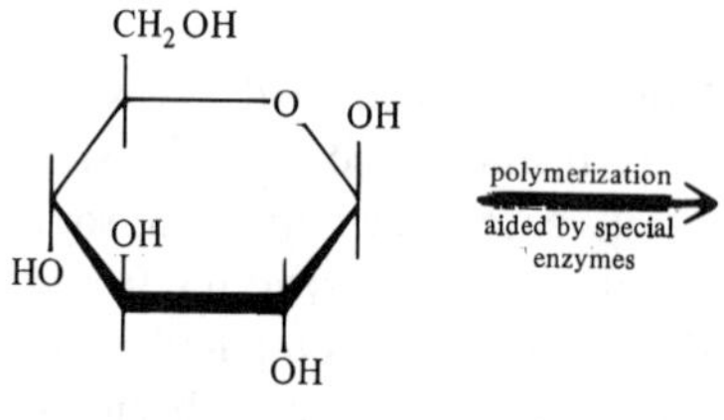

β-Glucose

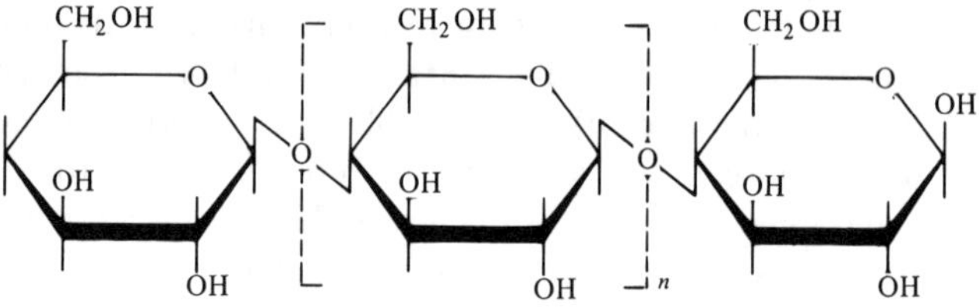

polymerization aided by special enzymes

Cellulose (cotton, rayon)

B

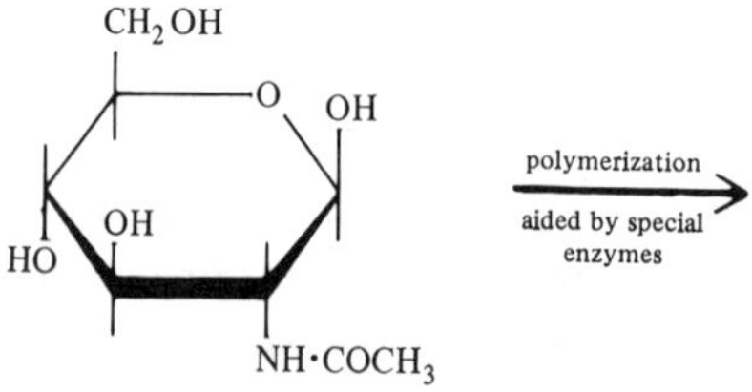

N–Acetylglucosamine

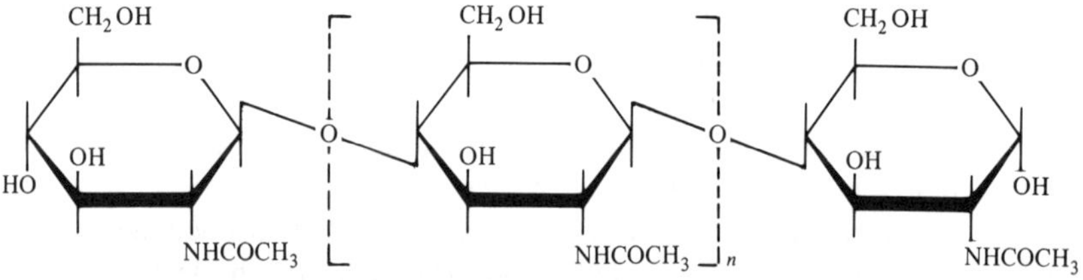

polymerization aided by special enzymes

β (1 → 4)–Poly-N-acetylglucosamine (chitin)

II Synthetic Polymers
Condensation type

C

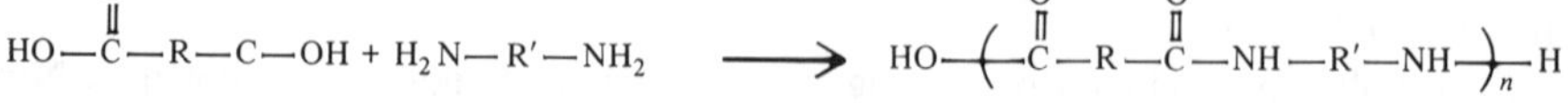

$$HO-\overset{O}{\underset{\|}{C}}-R-\overset{O}{\underset{\|}{C}}-OH + H_2N-R'-NH_2 \longrightarrow HO\left(\overset{O}{\underset{\|}{C}}-R-\overset{O}{\underset{\|}{C}}-NH-R'-NH\right)_n H$$

A difunctional acid (diacid) A difunctional amine (diamine)   Polyamide (e.g., nylon 66, nylon 610)

D

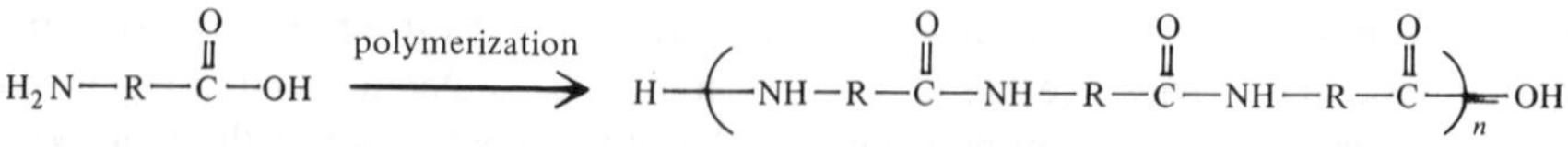

$$H_2N-R-\overset{O}{\underset{\|}{C}}-OH \xrightarrow{\text{polymerization}} H\left(NH-R-\overset{O}{\underset{\|}{C}}-NH-R-\overset{O}{\underset{\|}{C}}-NH-R-\overset{O}{\underset{\|}{C}}\right)_n OH$$

Amino acid   Polyamide (e.g., nylon 6)

E

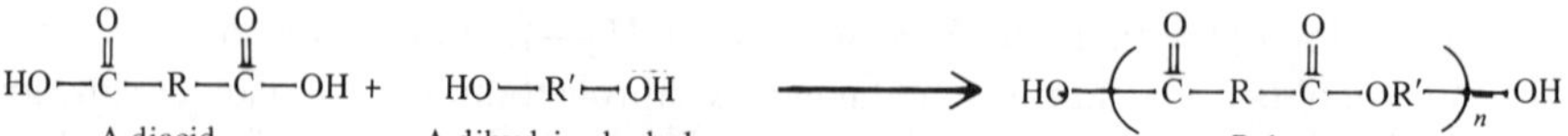

$$HO-\overset{O}{\underset{\|}{C}}-R-\overset{O}{\underset{\|}{C}}-OH + HO-R'-OH \longrightarrow HO\left(\overset{O}{\underset{\|}{C}}-R-\overset{O}{\underset{\|}{C}}-OR'\right)_n OH$$

A diacid (for terephthalic acid, R = —⟨O⟩—) A dihydric alcohol (glycol) [for ethylene glycol, R' = (—CH_2—)_2]   Polyester (e.g., Dacron, Kodel)

198

II Synthetic Polymers (Cont.)
Addition type

F

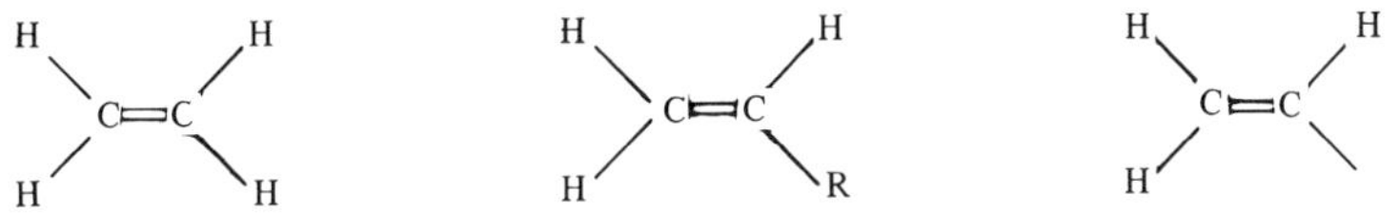

Ethylene $\qquad$ A mono substituted ethylene $\qquad$ Vinyl radical

G

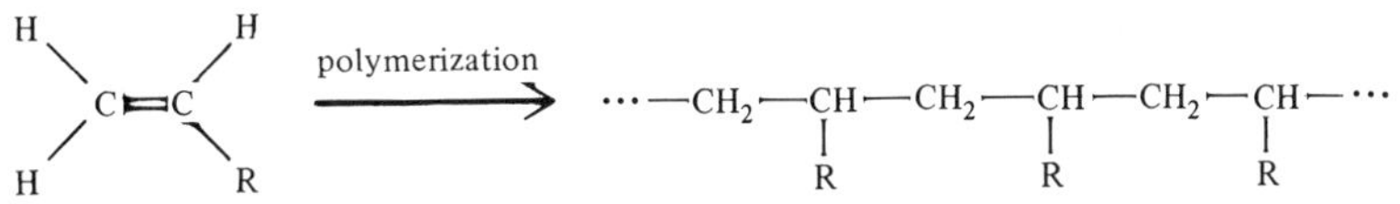

A long-chain repeating polymer

H $H\!-\!\!\left(\!CH_2\!-\!CH\!\right)_{\!n}\!\!-\!H$

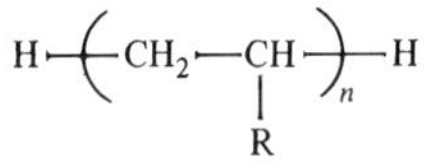

I

$H_2C = CH_2$ $\xrightarrow{\text{polymerization}}$ $H\!-\!\!\left(\!CH_2\!-\!CH_2\!\right)_{\!n}\!\!-\!H$

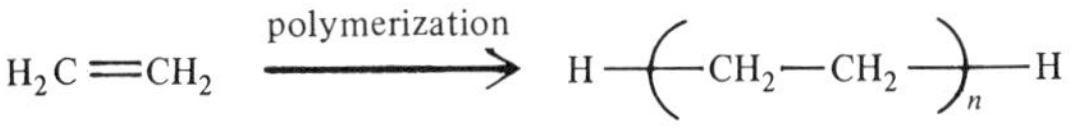

Ethylene $\qquad\qquad$ Polyethylene

J

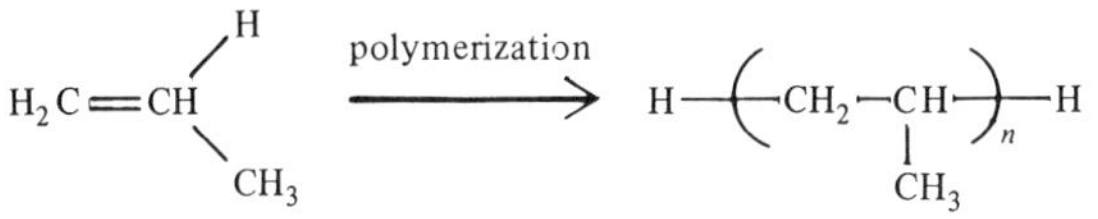

$H_2C = CH$ $\xrightarrow{\text{polymerization}}$ $H\!-\!\!\left(\!CH_2\!-\!CH\!\right)_{\!n}\!\!-\!H$

Propylene $\qquad\qquad$ Polypropylene (isotactic)

K

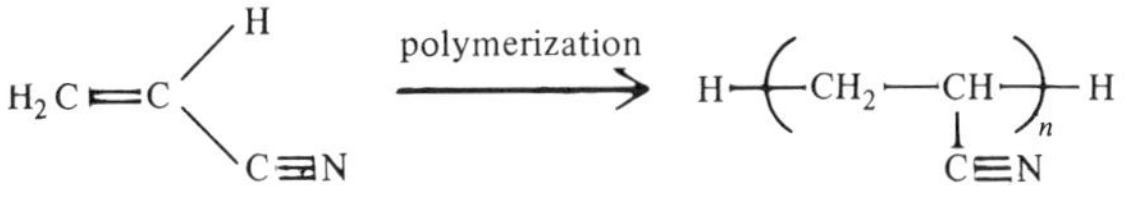

$H_2C = C$ $\xrightarrow{\text{polymerization}}$ $H\!-\!\!\left(\!CH_2\!-\!CH\!\right)_{\!n}\!\!-\!H$

Acrylonitrile
(vinyl cyanide,
cyanoethylene) $\qquad$ Polyacrylonitrile
(Orlon, Creslan, etc.)

L

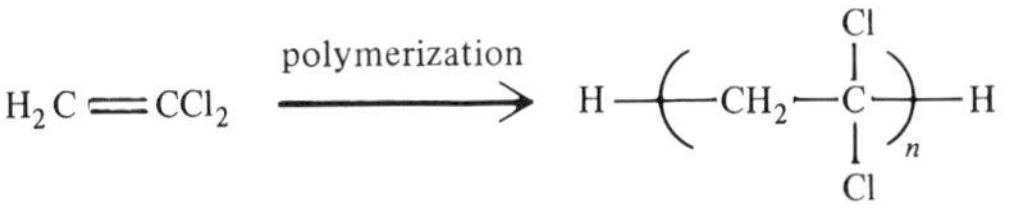

$H_2C = CCl_2$ $\xrightarrow{\text{polymerization}}$ $H\!-\!\!\left(\!CH_2\!-\!C\!\right)_{\!n}\!\!-\!H$

Vinylidene
chloride $\qquad$ Polyvinylidene chloride
(Saran)

FIGURE 8-2

TABLE 8-1
MAJOR ARTIFICIAL (MAN-MADE) POLYMERS

Generic name or class	Polymer and manufacturing process	Examples of trade names
Regenerated or derived from natural polymers		
Rayon	Regenerated cellulose	Beau Grip
	Viscose processed from cotton and wool	Coloray; Enkrome; Fibro
	Modified viscose to give higher wet strength (also called polynosic rayons)	Avril; SM 27; Tufcel; Xena; Zantrel
	Cuprammonium process: more expensive than viscose; relatively small quantities made; also called Bemberg	Bemsilkie; Cuprama; Cupresa
	Cellulose acetate fiber, spun first then converted back to cellulose (strongest of cellulose fibers; not used in apparel)	Fortisan
Acetate	Cellulose acetate derived from cellulose from cotton and wool (soluble in acetone)	Acele; Aceta; Ariloft; Celacloud; Celanese*; Chromspun; Estron; Lanese*; Loftura
Triacetate	Cellulose acetate where more than 92% of hydroxyl groups are acetylated (insoluble in acetone)	Avrel; Courpleta
Azlon	Regenerated protein fibers from milk, corn, soybeans, and peanuts (obsolete in U.S. at present)	Avalac (milk casein); Ardil (peanut); Soylan (soybean); Vicara (zein from corn)
Synthetics—from synthetic polymers		
Nylon	Polyamides: monomers linked together by amide linkages; many subtypes depending on monomers used; many synthesized; a few produced in vast quantities	
	Nylon 66: copolymer of a 6-carbon diacid (adipic acid) and a 6-carbon diamine (hexamethylenediamine)	Antron; Blue C Nylon; Cadon; Cumuloft; Perlon T; Super Amilan; Woolie Amilan Nylon 610 (DuPont)
	Nylon 610: copolymer of a 10-carbon acid (sebacic acid) and a 6-carbon diamine (hexamethylenediamine)	
	Nylon 6: a single monomer (6-amino caproic acid) condenses with itself; monomer most stable in ring form known as caprolactam	Amilan; Caprolan*; Enkalon; Grillon; Nylenka; Nyloft; Perlon
	Quiana: copolymer of bis-*p*-aminocyclohexyl methane and dodecanoic acid	Quiana (DuPont)

TABLE 8-1

(*Continued*)

Generic name or class	Polymer and manufacturing process	Examples of trade names
	Synthetics—from synthetic polymers	
Aramid	Polyamide with more than 85% amide linkages between two aromatic rings	Nomex (DuPont); Kevlar (DuPont)
Polyester	A polymer formed by linking dihydric alcohols (glycols) and difunctional acids, commonly ethylene glycol and terephthalic acid to yield poly(ethylene terephthalate)	Dacron; Encron; Fortrel; Vycron Terylene
	Eastman Kodak producer of a somewhat different polyester from terephthalic acid and 1,4-cyclohexane dimethanol	Kodel
Olefins (polyolefins)	Vinyl-type addition polymers of olefins, ethylene, and propylene	
	Polyethylene	Courlene; Marlex; Vectra;
	Polypropylene	Herculon; Marvess; Merkalon; Vistron
Acrylics	Vinyl-type addition polymers of more than 85% acrylonitrile	Acrilan*; Biloft; Creslan; Fina; Orlon
Modacrylics	Vinyl-type addition polymers containing between 35 and 85% acrylonitrile monomer	Acrilan*; Dynel; Elura; Kanekalon; SEF; Teklan; Verel
Saran	Vinyl-type addition polymers containing at least 80% vinylidene chloride	Krehalon; Permalon; Saran; Velon
Vinyon	Vinyl-type addition polymer containing at least 85% vinyl chloride; copolymer often vinyl acetate	Vinyon CF; Vinyon E; Vinyon HH
Spandex	Polymers containing at least 85% segmented polyurethanes (polyurethane segments linked at intervals to other polymers)	Blue C Elura; Glospan; Lycra; Monvelle (bicomfort); Spandelle; Unel; Vyrene
Anidex	An elastic fiber containing not less than 50% of a polymer of acrylic acid and a monofunctional alcohol; not made in U.S.	Anim 18
Glass	Drawn or spun glass	Beta glass; Fiberglas; PPG; Vitron
Metallic	Decorative filaments which are metal, polymer-coated metal, or metallized polymer	Chromoflex; Durastran; Nylmet; Lamé; Lurex

*Denotes use of trade name for more than one generic type.

201

In the structural formulas the subscript n shows how many times the same monomer structure is repeated in one polymer molecule. In Nylon 66 it is about 100, whereas in Nylon 6 it is about 200.

Nylon fibers have many uses, including hosiery, lingerie, outerwear, tents, tarpaulins, parachutes, bristles, carpets, cordage (string, rope, tire cord), and straps (for example, seat belts). Some of the many trade names under which nylons are sold are shown in Table 8-1. Some of them are difficult to identify as to brand name, although those in the Nylon 66, Nylon 6, or Nylon 610 classes can usually be placed into the correct subclass by a forensic microscopist. A few of the fibers have distinctive structures, and can be identified easily. One type of Antron fiber, for example, has a cross-sectional structure which looks like a rounded square containing four cylindrical canals running the length of the fiber (see Fig. 8-3). The canals are filled with air, giving the fiber additional bulk without adding much weight. This property is desirable in carpets. Other types of Antron have triangular cross sections.

Nylon is also manufactured in films or sheets. Bulk nylon may be cast into forms for use in various machines. A particularly important use is in making light-duty self-lubricating bearings.

In recent years, specialized polyamide fibers have been introduced under trade names such as Kevlar and Nomex. Since they are polyamides, they could be included under the general heading of nylon, but their uses are distinct enough to justify considering them separately. They are referred to as *aramid* fibers, the name being derived from the descriptive chemical name *ar*omatic *amide*. The monomers are aromatic hydrocarbons, and aramid fibers have industrial applications in products such as tire cords. Nomex is a fire- and high temperature-resistant fiber used in protective clothing for fire fighters and racing car drivers. Kevlar is an extremely strong fiber; it is used in the construction of lightweight bulletproof vests for police personnel or public figures who fear assassination attempts.

FIGURE 8-3
Micrograph of Antron fibers (type 857), showing both cross sections and longitudinal views.

Proteins are also polyamides. However, unlike a synthetic homopolymer such as Nylon 6 where a single amino acid is used, proteins are composed of certain so-called natural amino acids put together in specific sequences.

Polyester refers to a polymer in which the monomer units are held together by ester bonds formed when a carboxylic acid reacts with an alcohol. The polymer used in polyester fibers is usually made with two different kinds of monomers. One of them contains two carboxylic acid groups (often, it is terephthalic acid); the other contains two alcohol groups (compounds with two alcohol groups are called *glycols*). These are linked together in alternating fashion to form the polymer (Figure 8-2E).

Polyesters are among the most chemically stable synthetic fibers. They are not affected by most solvents and will even resist attack by cold, concentrated sulfuric acid. Their desirability as material for fabric manufacture is based on their quality of making the fabric wrinkle-resistant. Polyester fibers may be used in filament or in staple form, and either form can be used in fabric blends, such as polyester-cotton or polyester-wool, or alone. The staple form is found in polyester double knit apparel. The filament form is seldom used in normal apparel but is extensively employed in making laboratory coats and other types of protective clothing.

Polyester fibers are used in filling to provide insulation (sleeping bags, jackets, etc.), softness (cushions, pillows, etc.) and in cordage (rope or tire cord). Polyesters are marketed under trade names which include Dacron, Enkalene, Fortrel, Kodel, Terylene, Trevira and Vycron. Polyesters can also be produced in sheet form, such as in Mylar.

Polyolefins are the simplest members of a large and diverse group of polymers known as the *vinyls,* and their monomers are ethylene or monosubstituted ethylene. When one hydrogen is removed from the ethylene molecule, the result is the vinyl radical (Figure 8-2F). The monomers in this group are therefore vinyl groups with various R groups attached. The generalized reaction for the formation of a vinyl polymer is shown in Figure 8-2G. The dots in the formula for the polymer molecule indicate that only a portion of its structure is shown. Since it is made up of repeating units, the polymer can be represented by the more simplified formula of Figure 8-2H. This shorthand notation stands for a long polymer chain with n repeating units.

The term *olefin* is used by chemists to describe compounds having double bonds between the carbon atoms, such as in ethylene and propylene. Although during polymerization the double bonds are broken and the polymers have only single bonds, the term *polyolefin* is well established and is still used to describe this class of fibers.

The polymerization of ethylene yields *polyethylene* (Figure 8-2I). If a methyl group is attached to the vinyl group, the result is propylene (see also Figure 3-5). *Polypropylene* results from linking these units together (Figure 8-2J). A special catalyst is used in the industrial production of this polymer for use in fibers. The catalyst ensures that the monomers are oriented in the same way when they are linked together. This nonrandom or uniform linking results in a stronger fiber known as an isotactic polyolefin.

The relationship between the groups attached to vinyl and the names of the resulting monomers and polymers are given in Table 8-1.

Polyolefin fibers are lightweight and nonabsorbent. They are used in upholstery, indoor-outdoor carpeting, and as thermal insulation in quilted pads and linings. Polyolefins have the lowest melting points of all the common fibers. Pure polyolefin fabrics cannot even be ironed; some blended fabrics containing polyolefins can be ironed if the temperature is kept low. Polyolefin fibers are marketed under numerous trade names, some of which are shown in Table 8-1.

Acrylics are one of the most common synthetic fiber types encountered as physical evidence. Like other synthetics, acrylics are produced as long, continuous filaments, but they are normally not used in this form. Acrylic fibers are commonly cut into staple lengths and twisted into bulky yarns or used to form furlike pile. Bulky acrylic yarns are used to make knit garments, like sweaters. These usually resemble wool in appearance and tend to shed fibers quite easily. Acrylics are also used as carpet fibers.

Acrylic polymers are produced in the same general way as other vinyl polymers. The monomer is most commonly called acrylonitrile, but could be called *vinyl cyanide,* since the R in the general formula is a cyanide (CN) group (Figure 8-2K). Small amounts of other monomers can be used in producing acrylic fibers, and the acrylonitrile polymer itself can even be mixed with small amounts of other polymers. Federal Trade Commission (FTC) regulations require that a fiber contain at least 85% acrylonitrile in order to be called an acrylic.

The uses of acrylic fibers are very much the same as those of wool. Trade names under which acrylic fibers are marketed include Acrilan, Creslan, Orlon, and Zefran. Orlon is the only one of these that is entirely composed of polyacrylonitrile.

Fibers containing 35 to 85% acrylonitrile are classified as *modacrylics* (*modified acrylics*) by the FTC. The large range in acrylonitrile content allowed under this category indicates (correctly) that some formulations are quite similar to acrylics, whereas others are quite different. In some cases, other monomers are copolymerized with acrylonitrile to form modacrylic copolymers; in others, completed polyacrylonitriles are mixed with polymers made from other monomers. Modacrylic polymer fibers are sold principally under the trade names Dynel and Verel. They are used in blankets, carpets, furlike pile fabrics, and specialty items, like doll hair and wigs.

Saran fibers are nonabsorbent and are not commonly used in apparel. They are resistant to chemicals and withstand weathering well. For this reason, they are extensively used in outdoor products, like window screens, garden and patio furniture, awnings, and carpeting. They are also used to make automobile upholstery. Chemically, saran is a polymer of vinylidene chloride (Figure 8-2L). Saran fibers are sold under the trade names Lus-Trus, Saran 25S, and Velon.

Vinyon fibers perform poorly when used by themselves. They are not very strong, and are affected by heat (shrinking at temperatures above 150°F). When blended with other fibers, however, they contribute some advantages to the blend. The resulting mixtures are resistant to chemicals and oils. If a blended yarn or fabric is exposed to heat and solvent treatments, the vinyon fibers soften or melt, cementing the other fibers together. This principle is also used in bonding modern nonwoven fabrics and in certain pressed felts.

Elastic (stretch-type) fibers include a number of different kinds of polymers. The earliest type consisted of fibers made from natural rubber. Synthetic rubber is also used in fiber form. Both kinds are called rubber fibers and are sold under various trade names including Lactron and Lastex. In addition, there are two types of synthetic elastic fibers, spandex and anidex. Both are more resistant to chemicals and light than rubber fibers. Spandex is sold under a number of trade names, including Glospan, Lycra, Spandelle, Unel, and Vyrene. A trade name under which anidex fibers were marketed is Anim 18. Elastic fiber blends are used extensively in all types of stretch fabrics, like hosiery, foundation garments, waistbands, and swimwear.

Glass, drawn or spun as fine fibers, has many uses. In certain forms, it is used as thermal insulation. Glass fibers are combined with resins to produce reinforced plastic composites commonly known as *fiberglass.* Glass cloth or matted fibers are used to reinforce composites employed in making boat hulls or car bodies. Fiberglass rods, masts, or poles are made using bundles of aligned glass filaments which are cemented together with a resin.

A more recent use of glass fibers has been in *fiber optics.* Fibers made of specially formulated optical glass act like miniature "light pipes" and can carry a light beam along a desired path for considerable distances. These fibers are now being used in a number of optical systems and in sophisticated communications networks.

In textile applications, glass fibers have been restricted to curtains and draperies. Glass fabrics are unsuitable for apparel because they are heavy, have poor bending strength, and fibers which break loose can cause serious skin irritation. Trade names of glass fibers include Beta Glass, Fiberglas, PPG, and Vitron.

The so-called *metallic* fibers are used primarily for decorative purposes. Although fabrics composed of metal yarns have been made since ancient times, today's metallic fabrics are rarely all metal. Metallized plastics or plastic-coated metals are more common. Metallic fibers are not common as evidence, but when they are found they can be quite useful. Trade names for metallic fibers include Chromoflex, Durastran, Lamé, Lurex, and Nylmet.

HAIRS

Hairs are extremely common as physical evidence and may be found in connection with a wide variety of cases. In fact, human hairs may occur as crucial evidence in almost any type of case. They are understandably of special importance in cases involving personal contact, such as rape and homicide. In some circumstances, animal hairs can be important as well.

Human head and pubic hairs are most common as physical evidence, but hairs from other areas of the body are encountered occasionally. Animal-hair evidence comes from domestic animals (household pets or farm animals), animal pelts used to make fur apparel, and wild or game animals. With animal hairs, it is usually sufficient to identify the species of origin. With human hairs, however, the laboratory is asked to associate the hairs with a particular individual. This task is particularly difficult, and at present cannot be done with a high degree of certainty. Known and questioned hairs can be unequivocally excluded from having a common origin if they are found to be significantly different. If the samples are similar, however, it is common for an examiner to say that the hairs "could have shared a common origin."

This opinion is normally the strongest that can be given in a hair comparison case. Laboratory methods for examining hair evidence are discussed below.

Nature of Hair

Hairs are physically and chemically complex. They are multicellular structures produced by specialized organs in the skin known as hair follicles (Figure 8-4). During its active growth phase, hair is produced at a constant rate by the follicle. Deep within an active follicle, the cells making up the hair shaft in its formative stages are alive and active. Once the hair reaches the skin surface, these cells are no longer living but have become *cornified* or *keratinized*. At this stage, hair is composed mainly of a particularly tough protein, called *keratin*. Animal hairs, horns, and nails are also keratin-rich tissues.

Structure and Chemistry of Hair   The structure and chemistry of hair are only partly understood, and much of what is known comes from research carried out in the wool industry. One of the most noteworthy features of hair is its exceptional resistance to decomposition. Very harsh chemical treatment is necessary to break it down. Strong acids and alkalis have little observable effect on hair, other than causing it to swell, unless the temperature is raised. Even long exposure to sulfuric acid–dichromate cleaning solution will leave hair largely intact. Some of the stability is

FIGURE 8-4
Photomicrograph of a hair follicle.

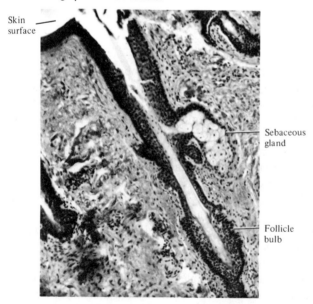

Skin surface

Sebaceous gland

Follicle bulb

attributable to disulfide bonds (sulfur-to-sulfur bonds) that hold the adjacent protein molecules together. By contrast, relatively dilute solutions of household bleach (sodium hypochlorite) dissolve hair quite readily, because they cause oxidation of the disulfide bonds between the proteins. Chemicals which reduce disulfide bonds (like thioglycolic acid and mercaptoethanol) also open up the protein cross-links and leave the hair vulnerable to breakdown by alkalis. This principle is used in making cosmetic depilatories (chemical hair-removing agents).

A few enzymes can degrade hair. Moth larvae use enzymes in their all too familiar attack on wool. The alkaline digestive juices of these larvae contain a substance that reduces the disulfide bonds, thus aiding in the digestion of the protein by protein-degrading enzymes. Another enzyme, a commercially developed keratinase, is used by the tanning industry in dehairing hides. The enzyme does not attack the whole hair. It solubilizes the hair near its root, where the keratin is incompletely developed, so that it floats free of the hide. The remaining hair shaft is not damaged. Hairs removed in this way can then be used in the production of felt. This keratinase enzyme is obtained from a soil microorganism called *Streptomyces fradiae*. The fungus *Microsporum gypseum* has an enzyme system that will degrade hair (wool) as well.

Unlike silk, hair and wool have a cellular structure. Figure 8-5 shows a cutaway sketch of a human hair. Much of the stability of hair and its resistance to chemicals can be attributed to the *cuticular scales* that surround the shaft. These scales are laid down on the hair in much the same way that shingles are laid onto a roof. The unattached ends of the scales point away from the root and toward the tip of the hair shaft. The friction in the root-to-tip direction is accordingly less than it is in the other direction. This difference can be determined by pulling a hair lengthwise, in both directions, between the fingers. This procedure, however, should not ever be done with hairs recovered as evidence. The scales are formed from specialized cells which

FIGURE 8-5
Cutaway view of a human hair. *(Courtesy of Francis X. Sheehan, John Jay College, City University of New York.)*

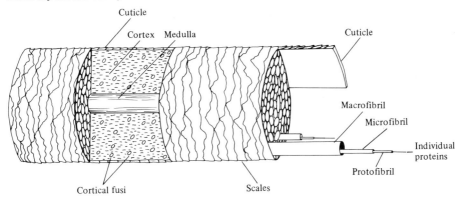

have hardened (keratinized) and flattened in progressing from the lower part of the follicle.

Structural and chemical studies of the scales show that they are somewhat less than 1 μm (one-millionth of a meter) thick and composed of several layers of substances which can be chemically differentiated from one another. The scales themselves are thought to cover the hair to an average thickness of several scales. The outer layer of each scale is highly inert and rich in sulfur. An extremely thin layer that is probably not protein is believed to exist outside the outer layer.

Inside the protective cuticular sheath is the fibrous *cortex,* made up of spindle-shaped *cortical cells;* these are aligned in a regular array and parallel to the length of the hair. The cells are held together by a kind of cement, or by protein fibrils running through adjacent cells, or perhaps both. There is some disagreement about whether the cement actually exists.

The cortical cells contain protein fibrils running parallel to the length of the cell. The largest of them (macrofibrils) are composed of large numbers of smaller ones (microfibrils) embedded in an amorphous protein or cementlike matrix. The matrix protein is rich in the amino acid cystine (which contributes the disulfide bonds to proteins). The microfibrils are in turn made up of still smaller fibrils thought to consist of two or three helical protein chains. Microfibrils as long as 1 μm have been measured, and they may extend the length of the cortical cell. Sophisticated instrumental techniques are required to gather this type of information.

Granules of debris and of pigment (melanin) are dispersed throughout the cortex. Much of the debris consists of cell components that ceased to function when the cortical cells left the nutritive region of the root and became keratinized. Pigment granules are formed by specialized cells in the follicle. Sometimes voids or air spaces known as *vacuoles* or *cortical fusi* are present in the cortex, especially close to the root.

Certain hairs show a central canal (*medulla*) which runs along the length. If the canal is empty (filled with air), it looks dark in transmitted light under the microscope. If it is filled with cells, on the other hand, it may look invisible. A hair which shows the dark streak is said to be *medullated;* the terminology here is quite unfortunate. The presence of this feature varies among individuals, among different hairs from the same person, and even within a hair. The medulla may be continuous, fragmented, or absent. When we say that the medulla is "absent," we mean that it is filled with medullary cells rather than with air, making it transparent and difficult to see. The material in the medulla consists of an unusual kind of keratin, low in sulfur and soluble in alkali, which swells 1000 percent between pH 4 and pH 6. "Medullated" hairs are less dense (because of trapped air) than nonmedullated ones from the same individual.

Growth Phases of Hair   Factors related to hair growth have to be considered when an individualization procedure is being carried out if meaningful results are to be expected.

Human hair follicles go through three distinct growth phases. In the *anagen* phase, the follicle is actively producing hair. In the dormant or resting period, the follicle is said to be in *telogen* phase. The transition period from anagen to telogen is short in human beings and is called the *catagen* phase. After a period of inactivity, the follicle enters the anagen phase again and resumes activity. A telogen hair remaining in the follicle is shed at this point, if it has not been lost already. At the onset of catagen (inactivity), the pigment-producing cells in the follicle contract and cease functioning. The last segment of hair produced before telogen is, therefore, white.

Human hair follicles are independent of one another; each determines its own growth and resting period cycles. Certain animals show hair growth in which many of the follicles are in phase with one another. If samples of hair are removed from the head by cutting, the growth phase cannot be determined, but if they are plucked, an examination of the root enables telogen hairs to be distinguished from anagen hairs. Most hairs coming to the attention of the crime laboratory are fallen (telogen) hairs. Only anagen hairs of equal length can be assumed to represent the same growth period and to be of approximately the same age. This consideration might influence a comparison, especially with factors that are controlled by diet or periodic metabolic changes.

Hair as Physical Evidence

Many of the properties of hair make it almost ideal as physical evidence. It is so abundant that significant amounts can be lost and left behind unwittingly. Compared with other physiological materials, hair is quite stable chemically, being one of the most resistant tissues, in the body to decomposition.

Blood, semen, and hair are the most commonly encountered physiological materials associated with crimes. Hair probably has the greatest potential applicability of all the types of personal physical evidence, even including latent prints. It is undoubtedly overlooked in a large number of cases in which it could be significant; even in cases where it is found, it may not be utilized very much. It is not possible at present to approach anything like the true individualization of hair. Persons whose hair is different enough from the questioned hair to be readily distinguished can be excluded. Hairs found to be similar, however, cannot be said by the examiner to be "identical." It may be reported that the samples were similar in all observable respects. Short of employing neutron activation analysis (which requires unrealistically large sample amounts), nothing more can be said. This situation has been recognized for years; our ability to individualize hair has, in fact, changed very little in the past four decades.

COLLECTION OF FIBER AND HAIR EVIDENCE

Different methods for collecting fiber and hair evidence are used in different situations. Because hairs are a special type of fiber, most of the collection methods for fibers are suitable for hairs. Selection of the most appropriate method depends on a number of factors, and most of the points raised about the collection of transfer and trace evidence in Chapter 6 apply equally well here. It would be useful to review them before finishing this section.

General Collection Methods

All the collection methods used for transfer and trace evidence can be applied to the collection of fibers and hairs. The visual inspection and collection method is commonly used because hairs and fibers are usually visible to the naked eye if one looks carefully. This method affords a knowledgeable investigator the greatest selectivity. The tape-lift method should be used only if the evidence collector knows that the laboratory is equipped to handle such samples. It is less useful with fibers and hairs than with other types of trace and transfer evidence, but it can be important. Tape may be applied, for example, to a selected area which has already been sampled visually to collect any missed fibers and any truly microscopic particles.

Sometimes it is desirable to package an entire article for submission without removing fibers or hairs. It is as important to note and document the location of the evidence in this case as it is if the fibers and hairs are to be removed. Care needs to be exercised in packaging such articles to minimize the transfer of microscopic traces to other parts of the article. Vacuum collection of hairs and fibers should be done with discretion, as discussed in Chapter 6. With hair and fiber evidence, vacuuming is primarily a backup technique.

Special-Purpose Collection Methods

Special collection methods may be required to meet the needs of particular case situations. In collecting pubic hairs from a sexual assault victim, for example, several different samples should be taken. Often a distinction cannot be made between the victim's own hairs and extraneous, or "foreign," hairs at the time of collection, and taking several samples helps to overcome this difficulty. The first sample should consist of loose hairs noted upon visual inspection. These may be found on the victim's underwear or body, even in the vagina. The second sample should consist of hairs observed to be adhering loosely to the pubic area; these can be removed individually. The third sample is obtained by repeated but very superficial combings of the pubic hair. The fourth sample is obtained by vigorous combing. The chances of finding extraneous hairs should be greatest in the first, and lowest in the fourth samples. The last, if taken properly, should be entirely victim's own hair. Sometimes, known specimens of plucked hairs from the victim may be desirable, and these make up a fifth sample. A similar approach should be used in collecting hairs from a suspect if he is apprehended reasonably soon after the incident.

The collection procedure employed is often selected on the basis of the type of commercial evidence collection kit (rape kit) being used. The quality and usefulness of these kits varies. Any commercial kit needs to be evaluated against the collection criteria noted above, as well as others related to body-fluid samples discussed in

Chapter 10. The laboratory staff should be consulted in selecting any such kit. Some laboratories have designed their own.

The availability of evidence collection kits can help in the collection of known and control samples. Instructions accompanying a kit should be followed carefully. No set of instructions can anticipate every situation, however, and investigators should think about each case individually. Collection of particular control samples not called for in the kit's instructions, for example, might be advisable in some cases.

Control Samples

The importance of collecting proper control samples cannot be emphasized too strongly. Without them, the questioned specimens are usually quite worthless, as noted and discussed in Chapter 6.

Known Samples   The requirement for a known sample of fibers can often be met by packaging and submitting an entire garment or other textile. Every precaution must be taken, of course, to ensure that no contact occurs between questioned and known sources of fibers. All the samples must be packaged separately and securely so that the value of the evidence is not compromised. Samples of known fibers from larger articles like carpets can be obtained by cutting or pulling some out. If the article is not uniform in color or texture, the known sample has to be representative of the overall article. Each differently colored area of a multicolored object would have to be sampled, for example, or a representative swatch taken.

Known samples of hair should also be given careful consideration. If questioned head hairs are to be submitted, then the known sample should contain representative samples from different parts of the scalp. Ordinarily, the hairs should not be cut. Vigorous combing or massaging of the scalp will usually yield 30 or 40 telogen hairs. If the questioned sample is thought to contain anagen hairs, then so must the known sample, and these must be plucked. It is advantageous to have both plucked and combed hairs in the known sample in any case, and they should be packaged and labeled separately.

Alternate Known or Alibi Samples   Alibi samples can be as important as conventional known ones, as noted in Chapter 6. In a case where questioned hairs have been removed from the inside of a car, for instance, known samples should be obtained from the people who regularly occupy the car. In the case of fibers, too, possible sources of similar fibers other than the suspected one ought to be considered. If, for example, questioned fibers which look similar to the ones on a victim's clothing are found on a suspect, innocent sources of similar fibers from the suspect's wardrobe or home may have to be considered. Samples of them should be submitted to the laboratory as alibi samples as soon as possible. If an examiner finds that the questioned hairs or fibers are indistinguishable from the knowns, but different from the alibi samples, more weight can be attached to the conclusion of possible common origin. These are really examples of what might be called *anticipated alibi* samples.

A true alibi sample would be one obtained from a source suggested by the suspect's explanation for the presence of the questioned hairs or fibers. Experience and judgment about the peculiarities of each case are necessary in determining the need for alibi samples.

LABORATORY EXAMINATION OF FIBERS AND HAIRS

The primary technique used in the laboratory examination of fibers and hairs is microscopy. The microscope is the only appropriate instrument for hair comparisons at present. Other instrumental techniques may be used in examining fibers, especially synthetic ones, in conjunction with microscopy. Even here, however, microscopy is central to the examination process.

Identification of Natural Fibers

Natural fibers can usually be identified with relative ease solely on the basis of microscopic structure. Some synthetic fibers can at least be tentatively identified in this way, too. Chemical tests are often combined with microscopical examination to provide an even more rigorous identification of natural fibers. Various chemicals or solvents can be used to test solubility. Different fibers will dissolve in one solvent but not in another. Other reagents which will dye or stain a particular fiber type, but not another, are useful as well. Some reagents stain different fibers different colors. The solubilities of some natural and synthetic fibers with various chemical reagents are shown in Figure 8-6. Such a scheme is helpful to the criminalist but is seldom followed exactly. Solubility schemes ignore morphological and optical properties of the fibers. These other properties are an integral part of the approach used by the criminalist or forensic microscopist in identifying fibers. The exact approach used usually incorporates a combination of methods and will differ from case to case.

Identification of Synthetic Fibers

Microscopy is very useful in the examination of synthetic fibers. It can be used to study the morphology of the fiber and to observe the effect of various chemical reagents in the fiber on a small scale. A polarizing microscope (Chapter 6) provides even more valuable information. With this instrument, a forensic microscopist can study and measure several optical properties of a fiber on a very small scale. A single fiber 1 mm long is usually enough, and smaller samples can be studied if necessary. Most fibers behave as if they were crystalline (glass is a notable exception). Fibers are often described as being *pseudocrystalline,* because they do not have the perfect molecular order that is characteristic of true crystals. The order and type of asymmetry shown by most fibers is like that of a uniaxial crystal (see in Chapter 7). They are birefringent and therefore show two indices of refraction. If a ray of light vibrates along the length of such a fiber (parallel to the fiber axis), it will experience a different refractive index than if it vibrates across the fiber axis. These are the directions of the two extreme (principal) refractive indices in the fiber. In a few natural fibers,

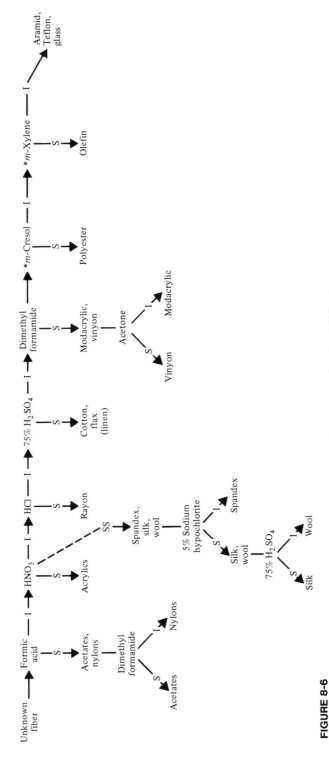

FIGURE 8-6

Solubility chart for common classes of textile fibers. All solvents concentrated and at 25°C unless noted otherwise. (*) Solvent at boiling point. All fiber specimens are placed in solvents for 1 min. S: soluble. SS: slightly soluble. I: insoluble. (*Courtesy of Nicholas Petraco.*)

like cotton, these directions are not parallel and perpendicular to the fiber axis, but in most fibers they are.

In most fibers, the refractive index (RI) along the fiber axis is higher than that perpendicular to it (positive sign of elongation). Acrylic fibers are a noteworthy exception, and the fact that they do have a negative sign of elongation makes them especially easy to identify. Using a polarizing microscope, a good microscopist can determine the sign of elongation of a fiber within a few seconds. The birefringence of the fiber (the numerical difference between the two extreme RI values) can also be determined with the polarizing microscope without knowing the actual value of either RI. Determination of the birefringence and sign of elongation enable a tentative identification of most synthetic fibers. More refined information concerning the identity is obtained by measuring each refractive index separately and comparing both with published values for known fibers. The measurements are done with the polarizing microscope.

The melting points of synthetic fibers may be useful identification criteria. The determination is carried out by placing the fiber within a hot stage, which is then placed onto the stage of a microscope. The fiber is then observed while being heated until it melts, and the melting temperature is noted. The procedure can be refined considerably by observing the birefringence changes that take place during heating, up to the melting point. These observations often provide enough data for identification of a synthetic fiber.

Other identification techniques that can be used include differential thermal analysis, infrared spectrophotometry, and pyrolysis-gas chromatography.

Individualization of Fibers

At present, fibers cannot be truly individualized. It is possible, however, to exclude very similar fibers of the same type from further consideration by the use of increasingly refined comparison techniques. Further, samples of known and questioned fibers found to be indistinguishable after very careful studies with several comparison procedures are more likely to have had a common origin. These approaches to individualization are useful, but are far from being certain. Ordinarily, a forensic scientist can say only that the fibers compared "could have come from the same source." More precise individualization must await research into the development of better methods of discriminating very similar materials.

A forensic scientist comparing fiber samples can approach the problem by setting out to prove that the samples are *not* similar. First, the structures are compared under a low-power stereomicroscope. The sample need not be mounted for this purpose. For more detailed work at higher powers using the polarizing microscope, the fiber must be mounted between a slide and a cover slip. If internal details are to be studied, the refractive index of the mounting medium should be fairly close to one of those of the fiber itself. If external or surface features are more important, a mounting medium of different refractive index will provide better image contrast. It is often advisable to prepare one mount of each kind. These are generally longitudinal mounts (the fiber is lying flat on the slide), although cross sections may be prepared occasionally and can be useful in identifying the manufacturer and generic class of certain synthetics. Features like length, diameter, degree of twist and curl, and surface features such as striations are studied and compared. It may be possible to estimate the cross-sectional structure of the fiber from these studies without actually having to make the cross sections. Figure 8-7 illustrates some of the range of variation in cross-sectional shape of two different generic classes of carpet fibers. Figure 8-3 shows the relationship between the longitudinal appearance and cross-sectional shape for a type of Antron carpet fibers.

Delustering agents are present in some synthetic fibers. They are added to the fiber material prior to fiber formation in order to reduce the sheen. The most common one is finely divided titanium dioxide. It gives the fiber a speckled appearance under the microscope.

Other useful features include waves or crimps. Synthetic fibers are often purposely crimped to provide more bulk in the resulting textile product. Crimping prevents adjacent fibers from lying close to one another, and this feature is often found in fibers used to make pile fabrics.

If all fibers were white, individualization would be more difficult than it already is. The fact that many fibers are dyed, however, gives another dimension to fiber comparisons. In addition to identifying the fiber types, the color of fibers is compared. Identical dyes do not affect different fibers in the same way. The large number of fiber types and different dyes makes visual color comparisons a valid criterion in fiber comparisons. Such comparisons can be refined considerably using a microspectro-photometer attachment on the microscope. In this way, absorption spectra of selected portions of known and questioned fibers can be obtained, and these are more objec-tive than visual color comparisons.

Instrumental techniques, such as pyrolysis-gas chromatography, are sometimes used in fiber individualization; they are normally employed only if a thorough micro-scopical examination has failed to exclude the questioned fibers. Failure to detect differences with the instrumental technique lends further support to a conclusion that the fibers shared a common origin. Results of this kind must be interpreted and pre-sented with great caution, however, because there are no statistically accurate data bases upon which to form an objective opinion (Chapter 1).

Fabric and Cordage Comparisons

Fabric Comparisons Fabric comparisons can be more conclusive than compar-isons of the fibers which compose them. Fiber comparison is but one aspect of fabric comparison. People responsible for evidence collection should keep this point in mind.

The term *fabric* may include weaves, knits, and felts; nets, laces, and plaited (braided) fabrics are sometimes encountered as well. The structure of felt is the sim-plest: the fibers are simply matted and pressed together. There are different kinds of knits, and some are quite complex. Machine-made knits have long been used for hosiery, lingerie, and T-shirts. Knits are now also used in outerwear (double-knit polyester suits). The pattern of the knit is important when comparing two samples of knitted fabric. Woven fabrics are still the most commonly encountered in criminal investigations.

Weaving is an ancient art and has many variations. The simplest weave, called

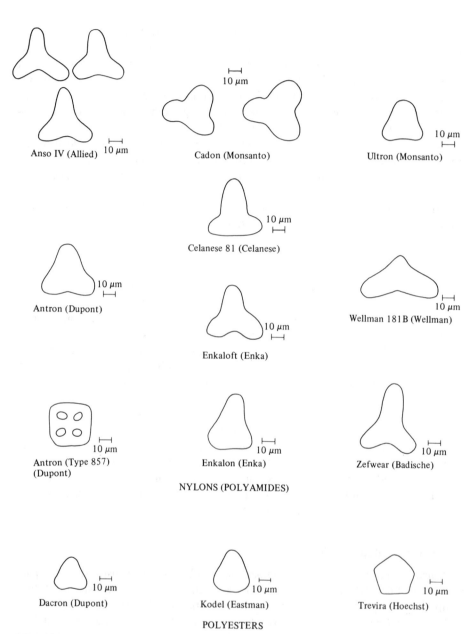

Anso IV (Allied) ⊢⊣ 10 μm

10 μm ⊢⊣
Cadon (Monsanto)

Ultron (Monsanto) 10 μm ⊢⊣

Celanese 81 (Celanese) 10 μm ⊢⊣

Antron (Dupont) 10 μm ⊢⊣

Enkaloft (Enka) 10 μm ⊢⊣

Wellman 181B (Wellman) 10 μm ⊢⊣

Antron (Type 857) 10 μm ⊢⊣
(Dupont)

Enkalon (Enka) 10 μm ⊢⊣

Zefwear (Badische) 10 μm ⊢⊣

NYLONS (POLYAMIDES)

Dacron (Dupont) 10 μm ⊢⊣

Kodel (Eastman) 10 μm ⊢⊣

Trevira (Hoechst) 10 μm ⊢⊣

POLYESTERS

FIGURE 8-7
Representative cross sections of some carpet fibers. *(Courtesy of Skip Palenik, McCrone Associates, Chicago, IL.)*

plain, is familiar to most people. Two types of threads are distinguishable in any weave. These are the *warp* threads, which are aligned with the length of the fabric and are attached to the loom during the weaving process, and the *weft* (or woof) threads, which are at right angles to the warp threads and are woven into the warp to form the fabric. In a plain weave, weft threads alternate over and under one warp thread at a time. A large number of variations in weave patterns can be introduced by (1) altering the number of warp threads the weft goes over and under, (2) using warp and weft threads of different materials, or (3) using warp and weft threads of different diameter or twist. Diagrams of plain and other weave types are shown in Figure 8-8. Weave patterns are useful in comparing known and questioned fabrics and can often be seen in fabric imprints. Either type of evidence can be very important in forensic investigations. It is also possible for the twist of the yarns or threads to be either the Z or S direction, corresponding to the slant of the midportion of each of the two letters. The fabric may contain only Z or S threads or may contain both types in a particular combination or pattern. This information may be of great value in fabric comparisons or even in imprint comparisons if the fabric imprint is sufficiently detailed. Of course, the use of differently colored threads lends an additional dimension to fabric (although not imprint) comparisons.

The forensic comparison of two woven fabrics can be based on a study of many parameters in addition to comparisons of the fibers which make up the yarns. The yarns can be composed of more than one type of fiber, twisted together. Different numbers of yarns can be twisted together to make each thread, and warp and weft threads may have different compositions. The number of threads per inch (thread count) in each direction may be characteristic, and, as noted above, many weave patterns are possible.

The strongest proof of common origin for two pieces of fabric is obtained if one can demonstrate a detailed physical match (Chapter 11). An indirect fabric match of this kind is illustrated in Figure 8-9. Matches between torn edges usually provide a greater number of points of comparison than those between cut edges, although convincing matches can sometimes be obtained with the latter. Physical matches can be important in any type of crime, but are more common in hit-and-run, burglary, and homicide cases. The value of weave patterns, which are shown in Figure 11-7, and their imprints will be discussed in Chapter 11.

Cordage Comparisons   Cordage appears prominently in any list of common evidence types. A list of the fiber types used in cordage is shown in Table 8-2. The successful comparison of cordage depends on much more than comparing the fibers which make up each sample. Cordage can be quite simple or very complex in construction. The simplest types are made by twisting the fibers together to form a yarn-like strand. Some are made by twisting complex strand subunits together, and still other types can have an intricate braided structure or a core and an outer sheath of different construction and fiber types. The complexity and variation in cordage structure add to the significance of cordage comparisons in forensic casework. The strongest evidence of common origin is obtained when a physical match between two broken or cut ends of cordage can be achieved.

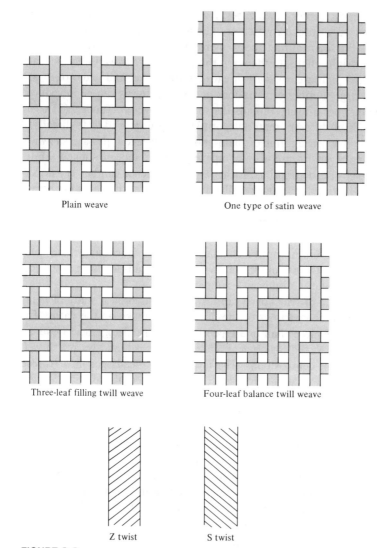

Plain weave

One type of satin weave

Three-leaf filling twill weave

Four-leaf balance twill weave

Z twist

S twist

FIGURE 8-8
Illustrations of some common weaves. Many other variations are
possible. The two principal yarn twists are also shown. In another type of
twist known as *false twist* the yarn consists of alternating regions of S
and Z twist along its length. (*Courtesy of Philip C. Langellotti, John Jay
College of Criminal Justice, The City University of New York.*)

FIGURE 8-9
A physical match of torn fabric. This is a type of indirect physical
match (see Chapter 11). The piece of material on the left came
from a "Molotov cocktail." The one at the right was found in the
suspect's automobile. (*Courtesy of Detective Nicholas Petraco,
Crime Laboratory, New York City Police Department.*)

Laboratory Examination of Hairs

Identification of Human and Nonhuman Hair The first step in laboratory
examination of questioned hairs is the normally simple determination that the sample
is really hair. Based on noteworthy features of hair such as cuticular scales, pigment
granules, and medullary structure, this determination can be done with a quick
microscopical inspection. The next step is determining whether the hair is of human
origin. If the hair is not human, it is possible to determine which species of animal
it came from. Identification of species of origin of animal hairs is not as simple as
distinguishing hairs from other fibers. Most forensic microscopists can distinguish
human and animal hairs easily, but exact species determination requires more
expertise.

Criteria used to determine whether a hair is human include the relative size and

TABLE 8-2
CORDAGE FIBERS*

Natural
  Stem (bast) fibers
    Hemp (marijuana—*Cannabis sativa*)
    Ramie (*Boehmeria nivea*)
    Jute (*Corchorus capsularis* or *C. olitorius*)
    Linen (flax—*Linum usitatissimum*—more commonly used for linen textiles)
  Leaf fibers
    Sisal (*Agave sisalana*)
    Manila (abacá/ *Musa textilis*)
    Phormium fiber (*Phormium tenax*)
  Seed or fruit
    Cotton (*Gossypium*)
    Coir (coconut—*Cocos nucifera*)
Artificial (man-made)
  Cellulosics
    Viscose rayons (tire cords)
    Polynosic rayons (tire cords)
    Fortisan (formerly parachute cords)
  Synthetics
    Nylons (ropes and tire cords)
    Polyesters (ropes and tire cords)
    Polyolefins (ropes)
    Aramids (industrial cordage; bulletproof vests; limited use in tires)

*Cordage fibers are used to make ropes, twine, tire cords, industrial cordage, and sometimes coarse fabrics such as burlap. Inexpensive cordage can also be made from twisted paper or plastic film.

appearance of the medulla, the appearance of the scales, and the diameter of the hair shaft. Most animal hairs have a smaller diameter and a larger medullary index than human hairs, although there are some exceptions. The *medullary index* is defined as the ratio of the diameter of the medulla to that of the overall hair shaft. The value is about ⅓ for human hairs, but is ½ or greater for most animals. In addition, the medulla of animal hairs is more regular, or geometrically patterned, than that of human hair, which usually has no regular structure. The tips of animal hair scales tend to protrude from the hair shaft, and the scales themselves are often more uniform in shape and size. They also tend to be arranged in more regular patterns than is the case with human hairs as well. Photomicrographs of various human and animal hairs are shown in Figure 8-10.

Racial Origin of Hairs Certain gross characteristics of hairs are helpful to the criminalist in making estimates of racial origin. In many cases, however, the considerable overlap of features can make a determination of the race of the donor of a particular hair sample impossible. In addition, in cases of mixed racial background, hairs may have a blend of characteristics, or they may exhibit predominant characteristics of a particular race. For this reason, determinations of racial origin must be

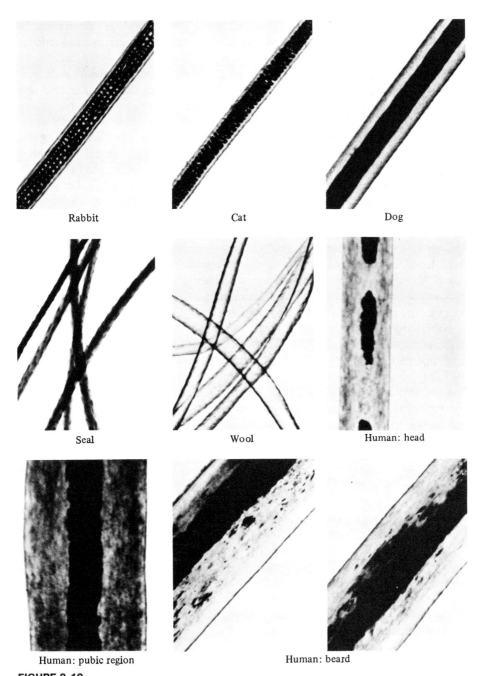

FIGURE 8-10

Human and animal hairs. Cuticular scales are apparent in the photomicrographs of the seal hairs and sheep's wool. *(Courtesy of Nicholas Petraco.)*

approached with a good deal of caution. The characteristics that are most obvious in race determinations are pigmentation, cuticle thickness, diameter, cross-sectional shape, and degree of wave or curl.

The hairs of Orientals (the Mongoloid race, anthropologically speaking) are generally straight with nearly circular cross sections. They are deeply pigmented and tend to have thick cuticles. Hairs from blacks (Negroid) are also deeply pigmented but often exhibit a different shade of color and a coarse clustering of pigment granules when seen in transmitted light under the microscope. They are also tightly curled as a result of having flattened elliptical cross sections. Hairs from whites (Caucasoid) exhibit a broad range of color, pigmentation densities, and shades, all of which are lighter than hairs from either Orientals or blacks. In other general respects, such as cross-sectional shape, degree of wave or curl, and range of diameter, they are intermediate between the other two racial types.

Somatic Origin of Hairs   Hairs from one area of the human body differ from those found in other areas. Some of the differences are obvious; others are quite subtle. An experienced microscopist can usually assign questioned hairs to the proper body region, but this is quite difficult with limb (arm and leg) hairs and those from intermediate or less well-defined body regions.

Head hairs grow to the longest length of human hairs. Because head hair is cut at more-or-less regular intervals, it is relatively rare to find head hairs with a naturally tapered tip. The tips of head hairs are more commonly cut or abraded. Pubic hairs, as compared with head hairs, are generally shorter and curlier with flatter cross sections and often have a continuous medulla. They also tend to show apparent fluctuations in diameter and somewhat tapered but abraded tips. Eyebrow and eyelash hairs are short and curved with finely tapered tips. Beard hair tends to be coarse with triangular or irregular cross sections. The tips may be blunt-cut. Chest hairs are usually fairly long and have tapered tips. Their diameters are thinner and show less fluctuation than pubic hairs. Underarm (axillary) hairs also show less diameter fluctuation than pubic hairs although they are fairly similar in other respects. The differences which allow an experienced microscopist to make other distinctions of this type are quite subtle.

Although there is some correlation among some of the individualizing characteristics between hairs from different body regions, it is important to compare head hairs with head hairs and pubic hairs with pubic hairs in any attempt at individualization. A known head hair sample is of little value for comparison with a questioned sample of pubic hair. When hairs are being collected from a suspect or a victim for comparison with questioned hairs, it is important that they be obtained from the same body region as the questioned hairs.

Individualization of Human Hair

Microscopic Morphological Comparison   The most definitive hair comparison method at present is examination of the microscopic morphology. Although the process is subjective and time-consuming, a forensic microscopist can use it to distinguish many closely related hairs from one another (see Figure 8-11). If differences

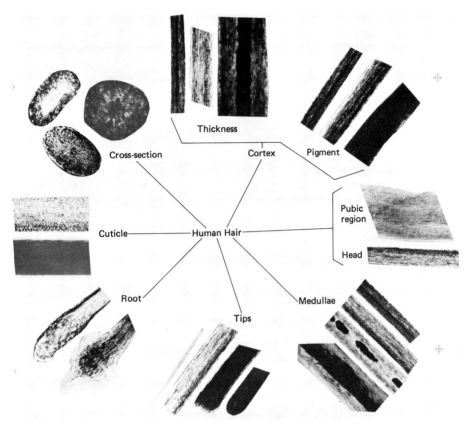

FIGURE 8-11
Microscopic characteristics of human hair. *(Courtesy of Detective Nicholas Petraco, Crime Laboratory, New York City Police Department.)*

cannot be found after a lengthy examination, a report is generally issued that says the hairs "could have had a common origin," not a very satisfactory conclusion in view of the effort required. Various attempts to make hair comparison more objective are discussed below.

Microscopic morphological examination usually includes the comparison of color, diameter range, degree of twist or curl, pigment granule distribution, and size or shape of granules. Table 8-3 gives a more complete list of properties that can be compared. With such a large number of features to compare, one might think that hair comparison results were fairly objective. Nearly all the parameters, however, can vary continuously over a fairly wide range *within a given sample,* and even *within the same hair.* This variation and the fact that objective observations of many of the properties are difficult limit the overall objectivity of the comparison. Combining a large number of essentially subjective observations does not necessarily produce an objective end result. The principal value of a list like the one in Table 8-3 is that it

TABLE 8-3
CHARACTERISTICS FOR INDIVIDUALIZING HUMAN HAIR

Macroscopic characteristics
  Gross characteristics
    Bulk color
    Sheen (reflectivity)
    Texture (degree of wave or curl)
  Measurements
    Length
    Range of lengths
Microscopic characteristics
  General features (normally noted with a stereomicroscope and incident illumination and/or low-power transmitted light microscopy)
    Diameter
    Variations in diameter
      Within a single hair
      Among hairs in sample
    Cross-sectional shape (estimation)
    Color
    Artificial treatment
    Condition of tip
    Root (stage of growth)
    Root (condition)
    Hair shaft abnormalities (knots, disease states, etc.)
  Cuticle (whole longitudinal mount except where otherwise noted)
    Thickness
    Damage to cuticle
    Opacity-transparency
    Color
    Delineation of inner margin
    Degree of scale protrusion
    Scale pattern (as seen in a cast of hair surface)
  Cortex (whole longitudinal mount)
    Color in transmitted light
    Granule shape
    Granule size
    Range of granule sizes
    Clumping or clustering of granules
    Granule distribution
    Cortical inclusions
    Vacuoles (cortical fusi)
    Definition of cortical cells (patent or invisible)
  Medulla (whole longitudinal mount)
    Opaque vs. transparent (i.e., air vs. cellular contents)
    Fluctuations in diameter
    Edge configuration
    Variations in continuity
    Abnormalities (doubling, for example)

TABLE 8-3
(*Continued*)

Microscopic characteristics (*Cont.*)
    Hair shaft cross section (if special cross-sectional mounts are made)
        Shape of cross section (particularly if irregular)
        Measurement of major and minor diameters
        Cuticle thickness
        Radial distribution of pigment granules
        Shape of medulla cross section
Biochemical, cytological, and immunological characteristics
    ABO blood-group substance
    Polymorphic enzymes (root sheath cells)
    Sex chromatin (root sheath cells)
    Y bodies (root sheath cells or proximal cortex)

can be a reminder not to overlook a feature. The list can be a guide in teaching people to do these comparisons too. But there is no direct association between the *number* of different properties which correspond in a comparison and the *probability* that the samples had a *common origin.*

The approach used by experienced examiners, and probably the best one, might be called pattern recognition. Once extensive experience has been gained in observing the range of variation that can exist in most of the diagnostic features, a microscopist can survey a number of hairs and decide whether they look enough alike to have come from the same individual. This process, though subjective, can yield reliable determinations, although the examiner will be unable to give a precise basis for the final conclusion.

The *pattern recognition* process is what all of us do when we recognize a familiar face. We identify the face without knowing how we were able to do it. The process is complex and computerlike; it is programmed into our minds from infancy. It is largely subconscious, and any attempt to produce an objective description of the recognized face will be grossly inadequate in comparison with the subjective and subconscious pattern recognition. You could try to make a list of the features that would describe the face of a friend, but even a meticulously prepared list will not allow someone else to recognize your friend. Hundreds of other faces could be found which would fit the description. However, you could distinguish between any of these faces and that of your friend instantaneously, probably even by looking at photographs of the faces.

The analogy demonstrates that even a subjective determination can give valid results, even though it is not possible to explain how they were obtained. Although such results can be valid, the search for more objective approaches to hair individualization should continue for all the following reasons. (1) The basis for forming a pattern recognition conclusion cannot be explained to anyone else. (2) One person's work cannot be evaluated by another without repeating it. (3) A valid estimate of the probability of samples having a common origin cannot be given. (4) The use of the phrase *could have had a common origin* differs widely in meaning. One forensic scientist could spend 40 h reaching the conclusion, where another might spend 20 min. (5) A properly conducted pattern recognition approach in hair comparisons is very time consuming.

Other Approaches: Past Efforts and Future Potential In the past, several instrumental methods have been explored for individualization of hair, but the results have not been very successful. In some cases, considerable effort has been expended.

Neutron activation analysis (NAA) has been applied to hair individualization by different groups of workers. Many prematurely optimistic claims were made until it was realized that the task was more involved than had been anticipated.

NAA is a superbly sensitive technique for simultaneous analysis of many chemical elements. It is inadequate, however, for the reproducible determination of the quantity of many elements at the parts-per-million level in a short length of a single hair. Further, levels of elements cannot be associated with specific regions of the hair, because NAA is a bulk analysis technique. Another limitation is imposed by the fact that the trace element composition of hair can change as a result of different environmental exposures. NAA is an excellent elemental analysis procedure, but it cannot be employed to solve the problem of individualizing hairs, nor probably can any other bulk analysis technique.

The *ion microprobe mass analyzer* (IMMA) is another very sensitive technique for elemental analysis; unlike NAA it is not a bulk analysis procedure. IMMA can be used to determine the *distribution* of trace elements within a microscopic sample. Concentrations of various elements can be associated with specific locations in a specimen, giving an elemental map of the sample. The technique has the potential of overcoming some of the deficiencies of NAA in this regard. More study will be required before results with this approach can be fully evaluated.

Hair has been studied from the forensic perspective using *pyrolysis–gas chromatography* (PGC). In this procedure, a small sample of hair is heated in an inert atmosphere to a temperature where it decomposes into many gaseous components. Separation of these components by gas chromatography produces a complex curve that can be compared with those produced by other hairs. Initial results obtained with this procedure were encouraging, but it is now clear that more refined PGC techniques will be required if useful information is to be obtained. A similar technique, not yet explored to any extent in hair analysis, is pyrolysis–mass spectrometry (PMS). Here, the gaseous products of the pyrolysis of the hair are analyzed in a mass spectrometer (Chapter 3). This approach is worthy of additional study.

Instrumental techniques applied to hair comparisons ought to meet certain requirements. A large amount of information needs to be extracted from very small samples, and the information should be characteristic. It should also be of a type which allows objective comparison. These criteria are potentially met to varying degrees by NAA, IMMA, PGC, and PMS. Methods which can meet the criteria should be applied to hair analysis in future research in this important field.

Genetic Markers Genetic markers in blood are discussed in Chapter 9, and those in body fluids in Chapter 10. These characteristics are very helpful in the individualization of blood, body fluids, and tissues. Some of them are found in hair as well, and they can be helpful in the comparison of samples.

The ABO blood-group substances (Chapter 10) are present in hair, and thus a person's ABO blood type should be determinable in a hair sample. Some workers have reported success in carrying out this determination reliably, but others have reported conflicting results and do not trust the determination. Perhaps reliable methods for ABO typing in hair samples will be developed in the future.

Some redcell isoenzymes, which make up another class of genetic markers (Chapter 9), are present in the external root sheath cells of human hairs. The isoenzyme type in the hair root cells corresponds exactly to the type that would be found in the red blood cells of the same person. This information can be exploited in helping to individualize hair evidence. The analysis is possible only if external root sheath cells are present on the pieces of hair evidence. Thus, only plucked anagen hairs are of value for these procedures. The fact that the majority of questioned hairs received as evidence are fallen hairs from follicles in the telogen phase limits the applicability of the isoenzyme genetic markers. If pulled anagen hairs are encountered as evidence, it is important that they be collected and preserved so that the adhering tissue (external root sheath cells) is not lost. A person's ABO type can be obtained reliably from the root sheath cells as a rule, just as it can from many other tissues. The red cell enzymes cannot be detected in the keratinized hair shaft as far as we now know. The external root sheath has to be present.

Two methods have been used for determining the sex of an individual from an examination of hairs. The first requires the presence of the external root sheath. The cells are removed from the hair and stained with a special dye. They are then examined microscopically for the presence of *Barr bodies*. These structures are associated with the nuclei of cells from females because of the fact that their sex chromosome makeup is different from that of males (Chapter 9). If Barr bodies are found in a high percentage of the cells, the hair is judged to have come from a female. If none or very few cells contain them, the hair is probably from a male. The determination is neither as clear cut as would be desirable, nor quite as straightforward as it has been made to sound, but if enough cells are present and can be examined, a conclusion is sometimes possible as to the sex of the donor.

The second method also requires anagen hairs but can be carried out on hairs without a root sheath. Here, a fluorescent dye, quinacrine, is used. This dye tends to concentrate in the Y, or male, chromosome of freshly formed cortical cells in the region of the hair root. The appearance of a fluorescing body (the so-called F body, or Y body) in the cells when they are examined under the microscope indicates that the cells are of male origin. The method is not completely accurate, but if a large enough number of cells can be counted and if the material is not too old, a conclusion is sometimes possible. If this technique could be refined to the extent that it would be applicable to telogen hairs (which are far more commonly encountered as evidence), it would be very valuable in many criminal investigations.

There have been some recent investigations into the possibility of detecting individual, genetically determined differences in the matrix proteins of the hair itself.

Although the initial findings do indicate that this approach may turn out to be quite valuable, additional study will be needed for a really complete evaluation of the possibilities.

STUDY QUESTIONS

1 What are the main categories of fibers?
2 How are natural fibers classified? Give examples of each class.
3 What is a polymer?
4 What is a derived or regenerated fiber? Give some examples.
5 What is a synthetic fiber? Give some examples.
6 Give some examples of modern day uses of synthetic fibers.
7 Describe the structure of hair.
8 What are the scales of hair?
9 What is the medulla of hair?
10 What are the growth phases of hair?
11 What characteristics are used to distinguish human from animal hairs?
12 What are the characteristics that help to determine the body region from which a human hair originated?
13 Describe the methods used for hair comparisons.
14 Give some of the methods used to collect hair evidence and describe the reasons for using one or another method.
15 What principles should be kept in mind when collecting hair evidence?
16 What laboratory methods are used to identify natural fibers?
17 What laboratory methods are used to identify and study synthetic fibers?
18 To what extent can fibers be individualized?
19 What principles are involved in fabric comparisons?
20 To what extent can human hairs be individualized?
21 What are some of the advantages and disadvantages of methods other than microscopy that have been used to compare human hairs?

REFERENCES AND FURTHER READING

Appleyard, H. M.: "Fiber Identification and Analysis of Fiber Blends," *Analyst,* vol. 101, p. 595, 1976.

Bisbing, R. E.: "The Forensic Identification and Association of Human Hair," in R. Saferstein (ed.), *Forensic Science Handbook,* Prentice-Hall, Englewood Cliffs, N.J., 1982.

Brunner, H., and B. J. Coman: *The Identification of Mammalian Hair,* Inkata Press Proprietary, Melbourne, Australia, 1974.

Burd, D. Q., and P. L. Kirk: "Clothing Fiber as Evidence," *Journal of Criminal Law and Criminology,* vol. 32, p. 353, 1941.

Gaudette, B. D.: "Some Further Thoughts on Probabilities and Human Hair Comparisons," *Journal of Forensic Sciences,* vol. 23, p. 758, 1978.

Hicks, J. W.: *Microscopy of Hair, A Practical Guide and Manual,* Federal Bureau of Investigation, U.S. Government Printing Office, Washington, D.C., 1977.

Identification of Textile Materials, 7th ed., The Textile Institute, Manchester, England, 1975.

Longhetti, A., and G. Roche: "Microscopic Identification of Man-made Fibers from the Criminalistics Point of View," *Journal of Forensic Sciences,* vol. 3, p. 303, 1958.

Rouen, R. A., and V. C. Reeve: "A Comparison and Evaluation of Techniques for Identification of Synthetic Fibers," *Journal of Forensic Sciences,* vol. 15, p. 410, 1970.

Wingate, I. B.: *Textile Fabrics and Their Selection,* 5th ed., Prentice-Hall, Englewood Cliffs, N.J., 1965.

CHAPTER **9**

BLOOD

INTRODUCTION

Blood evidence can be associated with many different kinds of crimes. Forensic serologists conduct examinations of suspected blood evidence in order to: (1) identify the material positively as blood, (2) establish that it is of human origin, and (3) try to associate it with particular individuals as possible sources. Forensic serology includes the examination of all body-fluid evidence. The examination of body fluids other than blood will be discussed in Chapter 10.

During the Christmas season in 1977, the body of a murdered man was discovered in a small town in New York. The investigation revealed his identity, along with the fact that he had been released from a penitentiary recently. It was further discovered that this victim had often rented cars from commercial car rental agencies and that another recently released man, whom he had known in prison, had sometimes been involved with the victim in the car rentals. Suspicion fell on the second man.

Later, a car which the two had rented was located in another city near the suspect's apartment building. A search of the vehicle revealed a blood clot in the hinge molding of the seat. A search of the suspect's apartment led to the finding of several articles of clothing, one of which bore a sizable stain. The stain on the clothing and the blood clot from the hinge molding were analyzed and shown to be human blood. The blood clot from the car was compared with the blood of the victim, taken at autopsy, for 10 different blood-group systems. The types were found to be consistent with the victim, and not the suspect.

It was possible to calculate that only about 1 person in 30,000 could have the particular combination of blood types of this victim. The suspect could provide no reasonable explanation for this finding. Furthermore, the blood on the clothing matched that of the victim, and not the suspect, for several blood-group systems. The blood evidence in this case, along with several other pieces of evidence, helped to bring about the successful prosecution of the suspect on a charge of murder.

This case illustrates the contribution that forensic blood examination can make to criminal investigation and prosecution.

There are several major aspects of forensic examination of bloodstains: identification, individualization, and reconstruction. Identification and individualization are discussed here. Reconstruction of the events that took place at a scene can be aided by examination of bloodstain patterns. This subject is discussed briefly in a subsequent section of this chapter and in detail in Chapter 11.

Identification of suspected stains is necessary to establish with certainty that they are really blood. Many things look like blood and could be mistaken for it. Most of the time, little is known about the history of samples submitted for examination. They may be fresh or old, relatively pure or contaminated with almost anything, and they may be found on almost any imaginable object. It is essential that a sample be identified as blood before continuing with the forensic analysis of the specimen. If the sample is blood, the next step in the identification is to find out whether the blood is of human or animal origin. Once it is known to be human, analysis can continue to try to associate the specimen with certain persons (*individualization*).

Blood contains many inherited factors. Every person has some of these factors and lacks others. Because many of the factors are inherited independently of one another, there are many different combinations of the factors in different people. The larger the number of factors that can be tested for, the fewer the number of people in the population who are expected to have the particular combination found. Determination of the factors in a person's blood is called *blood grouping, or blood typing.* True individualization of a specimen of blood would mean that a sufficiently large number of factors could be typed so that nobody else in the world would have the particular combination of blood types found. At the present time, this is impossible, and it will probably be impossible for the foreseeable future. Individualization can be *approached,* however, by typing as many factors as possible. The more factors that can be typed, the smaller the number of people whose blood could have the combination of types found.

Blood grouping of *dried* blood is more difficult and time consuming than the grouping of fresh blood. There are not, as yet, reliable methods for typing as many factors in bloodstains as can be typed in fresh blood. As a rule, therefore, not as much individualizing information can be obtained from a stain as from a fresh blood specimen. In the case discussed at the beginning of the chapter, a fairly high degree of individualization was obtained because of the fortunate finding of the fresh blood clot in the hinge molding of the car seat. In this case, the investigators knew exactly how to collect and preserve the blood evidence, and the laboratory was equipped and prepared to analyze wet blood samples for several factors.

THE NATURE OF BLOOD

Blood is a very complicated mixture of different kinds of cells and dissolved substances. Understanding something about blood's composition helps in appreciating the kinds of analyses that forensic serologists can do and the kind of information that can be deduced from the results of the tests.

Blood consists of two phases, or parts: the *cellular* portion, containing red blood cells, white blood cells, and platelets; and the *liquid* portion, containing a large number of dissolved substances and called *plasma.* If blood is drawn from a person's vein, mixed with a chemical to keep it from clotting, and allowed to sit awhile, it will separate into its two parts (Figure 9-1). This separation can be speeded up using a *centrifuge,* which forces the denser, cellular portion to the bottom of the tube faster than it will settle out due to the force of gravity alone.

The cellular portion of the blood contains three kinds of cells; *red blood cells,* or *erythrocytes; white blood cells,* or *leucocytes;* and *platelets,* or *thrombocytes.* Red cells are by far the most numerous. Blood from a healthy person has about 4 to 6 million of these cells in every microliter of blood (about one-fiftieth of a drop). Thus, a drop of blood contains about 200 million red cells, or about as many as there are people in the United States. White blood cells are less numerous, and there are different kinds of them. Normal blood has 4000 to 10,000 white cells per microliter of blood. These cells are involved mainly in fighting infections and in defense against diseases. Platelets, the third kind of cell-like element in blood, are involved in blood clotting.

The liquid portion of blood, plasma, contains a large number of substances, such

FIGURE 9-1
Blood constituents.

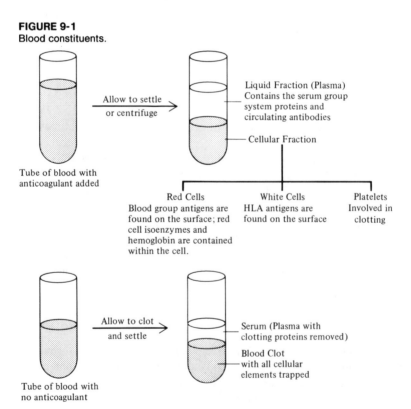

as nutrients, antibodies, proteins, and enzymes. Some of the proteins in plasma are needed for blood clotting. If the clotting proteins are removed from the plasma, the remaining liquid portion is called *serum* (Figure 9-1). An easy way to remove the clotting proteins from blood is to collect blood from a person's vein and not add any chemicals that prevent clotting. The blood will soon clot, and the clot will have all the cells and the clotting proteins in it. Then the serum—the liquid portion remaining—can be collected.

The word *serology* is derived from the word serum, because it is the serum that contains *antibodies*. Much of serology is concerned with the study of specific kinds of antibodies.

RECONSTRUCTIONS FROM BLOODSTAIN PATTERNS AND CHARACTERISTICS

Blood droplet and stain patterns should be examined prior to any evidence collection. The patterns of bloodstains may provide important information about the circumstances of a crime and the movements of the victim, suspect, or both. The shape of blood drops can yield information about the distance from which the blood fell and the angle of impact. The color of a bloodstain, or the consistency of not-yet-dried blood, can give indications about the age of the blood. In shooting cases, the bloodstain patterns can give indications of the relative positions of the shooter and the victim. This kind of information is extremely valuable in determining the conditions that prevailed at the moment the blood was shed and may be useful in reconstructing the events responsible.

In many cases, the blood pattern characteristics can be more important in reconstructing the events and in solving the case than the use of blood grouping. It is very important, therefore, that the patterns be documented before any blood evidence is collected. Reconstructions from bloodstain patterns are discussed in detail in Chapter 11. Bloodstain pattern interpretation and blood grouping to try to associate bloodstains with particular individuals are not mutually exclusive. Both types of analysis can and often should be used in a given case, and both may give important information.

INDIVIDUALIZING CHARACTERISTICS OF BLOOD

The individualizing characteristics, or factors, of blood are found in the red cells, plasma (serum), and white cells (Figure 9-1); they may be conveniently divided into five major categories:

1 The blood-group systems (red cell surface antigen systems)
2 The red cell isoenzymes
3 The serum-group systems
4 The hemoglobin variants
5 The HLA system (histocompatibility antigens of the white cell)

The individualizing characteristics are also called *genetic markers*. They are *genetic* because they are all inherited. They can give information about the genetic makeup of the individual who has them, so they are, therefore, *markers*. All of these are sometimes referred to as blood groups or blood types, but strictly speaking these terms are normally applied to the first class listed above. Each of the above classes of genetic markers has many factors and many systems. A substantial number of them are found to be useful in bloodstain analysis. The genetic marker systems useful in forensic serology all have an important thing in common: in each one, there are a number of different types, and these different types occur in different individuals within the population. Inherited characteristics that have this property are called *polymorphic* traits, or sometimes just *polymorphisms*. All the genetic marker systems discussed in this chapter are examples of polymorphic characteristics. Each of the classes is discussed separately below, except for the *h*uman *l*eucocyte *a*ntigen (HLA) system which consists of a large number of factors. The factors are found on white cells and in tissues, but not on red cells. They are very important in determining whether transplanted tissues or organs will "take" or be rejected. There are not yet any completely reliable techniques for typing the HLA system factors in dried stains, and this is a subject of current research.

Blood-Group Systems

Blood-group systems are the most well known and widely recognized class of genetic markers. ABO is the best known of the blood-group systems. Because of its importance in matching blood for transfusions, almost everyone is familiar with the ABO blood-group system to some extent.

The ABO system, and all the other blood-group systems, are based on antigens and antibodies. With these blood groups, the *antigens* are part of the red cell membrane. When one of these blood-group antigens reacts with its specific antibody, the whole cell participates in the reaction. The results of the reaction between red cells containing specific blood-group antigens and their specific antibodies is a visible clumping of the cells. Groups of red cells become clumped together. This process is called *agglutination*. Agglutination happens because the antibody can react with more than one antigen; the antibody can end up attaching itself to antigens on different cells, causing the cells to be held together. A picture of agglutinated red cells is seen in Figure 9-2. This figure also shows a simplified diagram of what is taking place when agglutination occurs.

Agglutination is the result of specific antibody-antigen reactions. It is not at all the same as clotting and should not be confused with clotting.

The presence of blood-group antigens on the red cell is thus detected by the visible result of their reaction with specific antibodies. Using a series of specific antibodies for blood-group antigens and testing a person's cells with them one by one, we can determine the individual's blood type. The *blood type* is a way of saying which blood-group antigens are present on the person's red cells.

A number of different *blood-group systems* are known. Every person has a *type* in *each* of the systems. Besides ABO, there are the Rh system, the MNSs system, the Kell system, the Duffy system, and so forth. Each person has an ABO type, an Rh type, an MNSs type, etc. The systems are distinguished from each other by the

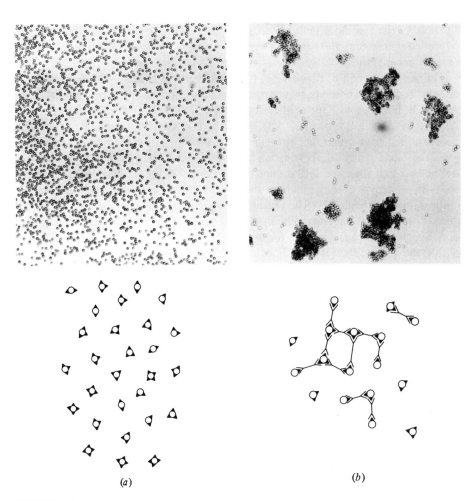

FIGURE 9-2
(*a*) Unagglutinated and (*b*) agglutinated cells. (*Courtesy of Frederick C. Drummond and W. Reid Lindsay, Forensic Science Laboratory, Office of the Medical Examiner, Westchester County, New York.*)

fact that the antigens of any one system are inherited independently from the antigens of the other systems. In other words, the inheritance of the factors determining the type in one blood-group system does not influence and is not influenced by the inheritance of those for any other one. Not everyone has the same set of types for the various systems, and this fact allows us to distinguish between different people on the basis of their blood groups.

The ABO System In 1900, Dr. Karl Landsteiner made a most remarkable discovery about human blood, one for which he was eventually awarded the Nobel prize. He found that the serum of certain people would cause the clumping, or agglutination, of the red blood cells of other people.This did not happen at random, but happened in a systematic manner. These early observations were the first recognition of what became the ABO system.

Human beings can be divided into four major groups based on the ABO antigens on their red cells. There are two antigens, called A and B. A person may have only A, only B, both A and B, or neither one of them. People who have A are called type A; those who have B are called type B; AB people have both antigens; and type O people do not have either one of them. Using specific antisera to the A and B antigens, the blood group of a person can be determined. Group O people are identified by the fact that their red cells do not react with either anti-A or anti-B. Studies on the ABO system over the years have shown that group O red cells *do* have a specific antigen, and it is called H. The reasons for its being called H (and not O) have to do with the current understanding of the biochemistry and genetics of the ABO system. Specific anti-H is available for blood typing and it reacts with O cells. Because of this, the ABO system is sometimes also called the ABH system. The agglutination pattern of the four kinds of red cells with anti-A, anti-B, and anti-H is shown in Table 9-1.

Table 9-1 shows another curious thing about the ABO system: the serum of a person contains specific *antibodies* to the blood-group antigens which the person's red cells lack. Thus, an A person's serum contains anti-B; a B person's serum contains anti-A; an O person's serum contains both anti-A and anti-B; and an AB person's serum contains neither one. The presence of these antibodies in people's sera is interesting for two reasons. (1) Blood transfusions must be between individuals with compatible blood types. If B blood is given to an A person, for example, the anti-A in the donor serum would agglutinate the recipient's cells, and the anti-B in the recipient's serum would agglutinate the donor B cells. The clumped cells in the recipient's blood stream would cause a serious transfusion reaction and possibly even death. (2) It is not well understood *why* antibodies are present. As noted in the discussion of antibodies and antigens in Chapter 3, antibodies are formed because the animal's system has been exposed to an antigen. The ABO system appears to violate this rule

TABLE 9-1
THE ABO SYSTEM

ABO blood type	Antigens on red cell	Antibodies in serum	Agglutination reaction of red cells with		
			Anti-A	Anti-B	Anti-H
A	A	Anti-B	+	−	±
B	B	Anti-A	−	+	−
AB	A and B	Neither anti-A nor anti-B	+	+	−
O	Neither A nor B	Both anti-A and anti-B	−	−	+

of immunology. People have ABO antibodies in their serum from early fetal life, yet there has been no apparent exposure to the antigens. None of the other blood-group systems show this kind of behavior, and the reason for the presence of ABO antibodies in human serum remains a puzzle.

Other Blood-Group Systems   In addition to the ABO system, there are about 15 other well-established blood-group systems. Those which have been usefully applied in forensic serology so far include the Rh system, the MNSs system, and the Kell, Duffy, and Kidd systems. Some systems which have not yet been applied to bloodstain analysis include the Lutheran, Colton, and Dombrock system.

Most people are somewhat familiar with Rh. When blood is taken for transfusion from blood donors, the blood bank usually types it for the major Rh antigen in addition to typing it for ABO. On the basis of this typing, people are classified as Rh-positive or Rh-negative. Rh-positive people have the major Rh antigen, Rh_o or D, on their red cells. Rh-negative people do not have it. If Rh-positive blood is given to an Rh-negative person in a transfusion, the Rh-negative person can make antibodies to the Rh_o factor and there is the risk of a serious transfusion reaction. Somewhat similarly, Rh-negative mothers who have Rh-positive babies can sometimes develop antibodies against the major Rh factor, and these can do considerable harm to Rh-positive babies in subsequent pregnancies. Actually, the Rh system is more complicated than indicated so far. Instead of just one Rh factor, there are five common Rh antigens which can be typed. If all of them are tested for, quite a few different Rh types can be distinguished in different people. Some of them are shown in Table 9-2. Because of the number of different types, the Rh system is one of the most useful in distinguishing people on the basis of blood type.

The MNSs system consists of four major antigens, M, N, S, and s. The inheritance of the M and N factors is closely related to that of the S and s factors. The MN and Ss types must be considered together, therefore, if all of the factors are typed. If tests are done for all four antigens, the population can be divided into nine different types, as shown in Table 9-2.

The Kell system consists of two major antigens, called K and k. If both are typed, the population can be divided into three Kell types (Table 9-2). These are far from being evenly distributed, though. Most people are kk, and only a very few people are KK.

The Duffy system has two major antigens, called Fy^a and Fy^b. The abbreviation Fy for the antigens comes from the last two letters of the name Duffy, primarily for historical reasons. There are three main Duffy types in white people. In the black population there is a large fourth group of Fy(a-b-) people who lack both antigens, as indicated in Table 9-2.

Red Cell Isoenzymes

Enzymes are proteins found in all living organisms. They serve as catalysts for the chemical reactions that take place in living things. *Catalysts* are substances which speed up chemical reactions without being changed or consumed in the process, as

TABLE 9-2
BLOOD-GROUP SYSTEMS OTHER THAN ABO

System	Types	Approximate occurrence, %, in U.S. populations	
		White	Black
Rh	Rh_o	2	48
	Rh_1rh	34	20
	Rh_1Rh_1	18	2
	Rh_2rh	12	14
	Rh_2Rh_2	3	1
	Rh_1Rh_2	13	3
	rh	14	6
	Rarer types	4	6
MNSs	MS	6	2
	MSs	14	6
	Ms	9	15
	MNS	3	3
	MNSs	24	12
	MNs	24	35
	NS	1	2
	NSs	5	5
	Ns	14	20
Kell	KK	<1	<1
	Kk	9	2
	kk	91	98
Duffy	Fy(a+b−)	17	9
	Fy(a+b+)	51	4
	Fy(a−b+)	32	23
	Fy(a−b−)	—	64
Kidd	Jk(a+b−)	27	55
	Jk(a+b+)	52	38
	Jk(a−b+)	21	7

noted in Chapter 3. Many of the reactions that go on in living things would be too slow to sustain life if it were not for the enzyme catalysts, which speed them up. Enzymes are generally very specific for the reactions which they catalyze. They catalyze only one reaction or a few closely related ones. There are tens of thousands of different enzymes. Every cell contains many of them; and red blood cells, like other cells, contain large numbers of enzymes.

All the enzymes necessary for life are present in the cells of all individuals. Many known enzymes have only a single form in the cell, but in many cases the same enzyme has several different forms. The forms are not the same in every person because different genes must be inherited in order to make the different forms. The particular forms of an enzyme in one person's cells can be used to distinguish that person from others who have different forms of the enzyme. Enzymes which have these different forms are called *isoenzymes.* In some cases, isoenzymes are the same in everybody, and these are not useful as genetic markers. These isoenzymes sometimes have different forms in different body tissues or organs, and they can be useful in diagnosing various diseases. The human red blood cell contains a number of isoenzymes that do show variation in form from person to person, however.

Using a technique called *electrophoresis* (Chapter 3), many different isoenzymes in a person's red cells can be separated, and the forms which are present determined. Just as the population can be divided into different segments on the basis of blood groups, so too it can be divided up on the basis of the different isoenzymes present. The forms of the isoenzymes present are, as we have said, inherited. The pattern of isoenzymes seen in a particular person is called the *isoenzyme type.* Determining the isoenzyme type is called isoenzyme typing in the same way that determining someone's blood type is called blood typing. Isoenzymes are very different from the blood-group antigens, and the typing is done very differently. However, the terminology is similar because in both cases it is a matter of determining which of several possible sets of inherited characteristics (genetic markers) is present in the person's blood.

The main red cell isoenzyme systems are listed in Table 9-3, along with their usual abbreviations and the number of common types that exist in the population. The abbreviations of the names are often used because the names are quite long and cumbersome.

Serum-Group Systems

In the serum there are a number of proteins which show the same kind of inherited variation in different people that is seen in the blood groups and in the red cell isoenzymes. Different people have different forms of these proteins. Using electrophoresis or sometimes serological methods, the forms of the proteins that are present in a person can be determined.

A number of different serum proteins are known which exhibit various types in different individuals. The different ones are often called *systems,* such as the *haptoglobin system.* The major serum-group systems are shown in Table 9-4. Not all these have been successfully applied to bloodstain analysis as yet.

Hemoglobin

Hemoglobin, as noted in the discussion of blood above, is the major protein of the red blood cell. Hemoglobin itself is red, and it gives the red cells their color (and their name!). Hemoglobin is the oxygen-carrying protein for many air-breathing animals, including ourselves.

Sometimes, hemoglobin shows variation from its usual form within the same species. Two types of variant human hemoglobin are important in forensic serology. The first occurs in fetuses and in very young children. *Fetal hemoglobin,* as it is called, is different from the adult kind, and the two can be distinguished from one another by electrophoresis.

The second kind of variation occurs almost exclusively in black and some Hispanic

TABLE 9-3
RED-CELL ISOENZYME SYSTEMS

System [usual abbreviation]	Types	Approximate occurrence, %, in U.S. populations	
		White	Black
Phosphoglucomutase*·† [PGM]	1	59	66
	2-1	35	29
	2	6	5
Adenylate kinase* [AK]	1	93	99
	2-1	7	1
	2	<1	<1
Acid phosphatase* [ACP; EAP]	A	12	7
	BA	42	32
	B	40	58
	CA	2	1
	CB	4	2
	C	<1	<1
Glyoxalase I* [GLO]	1	18	14
	2-1	52	41
	2	30	45
Esterase D* [ESD]	1	79	84
	2-1	20	15
	2	1	1
Adenosine deaminase* [ADA]	1	90	97
	2-1	10	3
	2	<1	<1
Glutamate-pyruvate transaminase [GPT]	1	29	67
	2-1	49	29
	2	22	4
Uridine monophosphate kinase [UMPK]	1	91	98
	2-1	9	2
	2	1	<1
6-Phosphogluconate dehydrogenase* [PGD]	A	96	93
	AC	4	7
	C	<1	<1
Carbonic anhydrase II*·‡ [CA]	1	100	81
	2-1	—	18
	2	—	1
Glutathione reductase‡ [GSR]	Usual	100	75
	Usual-variant	—	23
	Variant	—	2
Glutathione peroxidase‡ [GPX]	Usual	100	94
	Thomas variant	—	6
Peptidase A‡ [PEPA]	1	100	90
	2-1	—	8
	2	—	2

*Can be typed in dried bloodstains.
†Shows 10 types if isoelectric focusing or electrophoresis under special conditions is employed.
‡Significantly polymorphic only in black populations.

TABLE 9-4
SERUM GROUP SYSTEMS

System [usual abbreviation]	Types	Approximate occurrence, %, in U.S. populations	
		White	Black
Haptoglobin*·† [Hp]	1	17	29
	2-1	48	39
	2	35	19
	2-1M	<1	10
	0	<1	3
Group-specific component*·‡ [Gc]	1	50	76
	2-1	42	22
	2	8	2
Transferrin*·§ [Tf]	C	99	95
	CB	1	—
	CD	<1	5
Protease inhibitor or α_1-antitrypsin¶ [Pi]	Many		
Immunoglobulin markers [Gm and Km]	Many		

*Can be typed in dried bloodstains.
†Hp 2-1M and Hp 0 cannot be diagnosed reliably in bloodstains. Hp 1 can be subtyped but not routinely in stains;
‡Gc 1 can be subtyped, but this is not done in stains.
§Tf C, the common electrophoretic type, can be subtyped by isoelectric focusing, but this is not done in stains.
¶Pi has many electrophoretic variants; the common electrophoretic type Pi M can be subtyped by isoelectric focusing.

people. The most common variant form, called *hemoglobin S,* is responsible for sickle cell disease. It is possible for a person to have half normal hemoglobin, and half hemoglobin S. Such a person is said to have *sickle cell trait* and is usually healthy. People who have all hemoglobin S suffer from *sickle cell anemia,* a serious anemia that requires constant medical attention. Another variant form of hemoglobin is called *hemoglobin C.* Usual adult hemoglobin (called *hemoglobin A*) can be distinguished from hemoglobin S, hemoglobin C, and hemoglobin F by electrophoresis. When these forms of hemoglobin are present, they provide another genetic marker in human blood.

RULES OF INHERITANCE

The individualizing characteristics of blood—the blood groups, the serum groups, the isoenzymes, and hemoglobin—are all inherited. Because they are inherited and because they are inherited in such a way that not everyone has the same types, all are useful as individualizing characteristics. A brief understanding of the rules of inheritance helps in understanding how the genetic markers can be a powerful tool in the individualization of blood specimens. The science of inheritance is called *genetics.*

Everyone starts life as a single cell. From this one cell develops a complete individual with a unique set of characteristics. The single cell—the fertilized egg—from which each person develops contains all the information necessary to specify the development of the complete individual. The information is coded in a complicated chemical form, called deoxyribonucleic acid, or DNA, in the cell's nucleus. The unit of information responsible for a particular characteristic is called a *gene*. There are tens of thousands of genes in each cell. They are located in threadlike structures in the cell nucleus called *chromosomes*. Chromosomes can be seen under the microscope under certain conditions. Human beings have 46 chromosomes. Forty-four of them occur in pairs (22 pairs), and the remaining two are the sex chromosomes. Women have two X chromosomes in addition to the other 22 pairs; men have an X and a Y. It is actually the chromosomes that are inherited. They are in the nuclei of the sperm and the egg which combine to form the fertilized egg. The chromosomes contain all the genes. So, when we say "blood groups are inherited," for example, we really should say "the chromosomes containing the genes for particular blood groups are inherited."

At conception, each individual receives 23 chromosomes from the mother in her egg cell, and 23 chromosomes from the father in his sperm cell. The 23 that are received from each parent represent a random selection of one chromosome from each pair, plus one of the sex chromosomes. There are more than 8 million combinations of chromosomes that can wind up in any given sperm or egg cell from a single parent! Because of this, the same parents can have several children with quite different characteristics.

All but two chromosomes are paired in every person. For most characteristics, therefore, each individual has two genes controlling the trait, one on each chromosome. The genes, too, are therefore paired. When considering the rules of inheritance for a particular characteristic, it must be remembered that a pair of genes is responsible for the characteristic. A parent passes on only one of the two genes to each child, and there is a 50:50 chance of passing either gene of a pair.

A child therefore inherits one of the members of the gene pair from one parent while inheriting the other member from the other parent. As an example, the MN blood-group system can be considered. There are three possible types: MM, MN, and NN. These types are controlled by two genes, *M* and *N*. People who are MM have two *M* genes, people who are NN have two *N* genes, and those who are MN have an *M* and an *N* gene. Parents who are MM can make only *M*-containing sperm or egg cells, and so can pass only *M* along to their children. Similarly, NN parents can only pass *N* along to their children. But what if both parents were MN? The father could make both *M* sperm and *N* sperm. Likewise, the mother could make both *M* eggs and *N* eggs. The *M* sperm could fertilize an *M* or an *N* egg, and so could the *N* sperm. Therefore, these parents *could* have MM, NN, or MN children. Statistically, it is expected that they will have MN children twice as frequently as MM or NN children, and there is an equal chance that they will have an MM or an NN child.

Even though most physical characteristics are inherited from parents, some of them show an almost continuous variation in the population. Their inheritance is complicated and controlled by many genes. Examples are height, build, and eye color. In addition, characteristics such as height can be influenced by nutrition, hormonal conditions, and other nongenetic factors. As a result, these characteristics cannot give precise information about a person's genetic makeup. Some characteristics, though, are inherited in a simple, straightforward way. Determining these characteristics can disclose the genetic makeup of the person. In some cases, everyone has the same characteristic. Thus, even though we may be able to find out the genetic makeup of the person by determining the characteristic, it is not helpful in individualizing the person because everyone is the same. In a few cases, though, simply inherited traits occur in several different forms in different people. These are commonly referred to as *polymorphic*. In such cases, testing for the characteristic gives us the genetic makeup of the person and also distinguishes the person from some of the other people in the population. Forensic serologists concentrate on polymorphic characteristics in blood. Quite a few useful genetic markers have now been discovered in blood. All the blood groups, serum groups, isoenzymes, and hemoglobin variants belong to the group of useful genetic markers in blood.

If a large number of people is examined for an individualizing blood characteristic, the percentage of people in the population having each of the various types can be discovered. In the ABO blood-group system, for example, a large sample of the white population would have about 45 percent O, 41 percent A, 10 percent B, and 4 percent AB people. A large sample of the black population would have about 50 percent O, 25 percent A, 20 percent B, and 5 percent AB people.

If the MN blood-group system were considered, the white population would show about 30 percent MM, 50 percent MN, and 20 percent NN people. In the black population, about 25 percent MM, 50 percent MN, and 25 percent NN would be found. The reason these figures are known, and can be quoted, is that many different investigators have actually typed many different people. For most of the blood-group, isoenzyme, and serum-group systems, at least some information is available about the distribution of the types, and more is being accumulated all the time.

This kind of information can be very useful in forensic serology. If a sample is typed for a number of different genetic marker systems, only part of the population is expected to have the combination of types found. The more systems that are typed, the fewer the number of people that will be expected to have the particular combination found. This concept is simply illustrated in Figure 9-3 for the ABO and MN systems. The reason it works this way is that the inheritance of one system does not influence the inheritance of the others. Thus, although we cannot actually individualize blood, we can approach individualization as a goal by trying to type more and more systems.

Although it is not possible to show that two different blood specimens came from the same person (which would be a true individualization), it *is* possible to show that they could *not* have had a common origin. This is called *exclusion,* and it is an important aspect of forensic serology. If a bloodstain on a piece of carpet were typed, for example, and the types compared with those of a suspect, the finding of different types in the two samples would show for sure that the suspect was not the source of the stain on the carpet. Failure to exclude a person after successive applications of

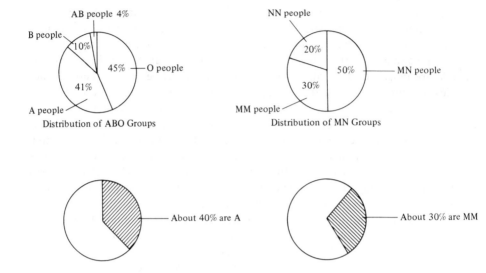

AB people 4%

B people
10%

45% —O people

41%

A people
Distribution of ABO Groups

NN people

20%

50% — MN people

30%

MM people
Distribution of MN Groups

— About 40% are A

— About 30% are MM

Only about 12% of the population
will be both A and MM
(0.4 × 0.3 = 0.12 or 12%)

FIGURE 9-3
Discrimination by ABO and MN blood types in the general population. Circles represent total population.

several systems (although not a true individualization) can supply important information.

Some forensic serologists carry out blood typing in cases of disputed parentage (usually disputed paternity). The simplest cases involve a mother, a child, and a man suspected of being the father. The bloods of all the people are typed, and the results are examined to see whether the rules of inheritance have been followed. If they have, it means that the man *might* be the father. But if they have not, the man is excluded, and cannot be the father of the child by the particular mother.

COLLECTION, PRESERVATION, AND PACKAGING OF BLOOD EVIDENCE

The ability to perform a successful forensic analysis of blood recovered at a crime scene depends very much on what kinds of samples are collected and how they are preserved and transported. The ideal situation for the collection of blood evidence is one in which a crime-scene searcher and a laboratory examiner work closely together at a crime scene. At minimum, there should be communication and agreement between laboratory personnel and crime-scene searchers as to how best to collect this kind of evidence.

Blood which is still wet, or even which has clotted, is much easier to type than dried blood. It is important for crime scene searchers to realize, however, that collecting wet blood requires that the laboratory be set up and ready to handle it, and that it be kept cold and submitted quickly. Another important consideration is bloodstain patterns. These will be discussed in some detail in Chapter 11. Often the blood patterns can give considerable information about what took place at the scene (reconstruction). Sometimes, the information that can be obtained from the patterns is more important than the information that will be obtained from the blood groups. Care should be taken, therefore, not to alter or obliterate blood patterns in a hurried effort to collect wet blood specimens. Wet blood samples if they are to be collected, must be preserved in a suitable anticoagulant solution, and they must be put into a refrigerator as soon as possible after collection. Failure to collect and preserve wet blood correctly can cause the samples to become putrefied. Putrefaction is brought about by the growth of bacteria in the specimens. These bacteria get into the blood from the environment. Low-temperature storage inhibits the growth of the degradative bacteria. Frequently, little or no information can be obtained from badly degraded samples because the putrefactive processes can cause the test results to be negative or unreliable. Garments bearing wet or moist bloodstains should **never** be sealed in airtight containers, such as plastic bags. Under such conditions, the specimens retain their moisture, encouraging bacterial growth.

Sometimes, it may be better to air-dry blood samples before collecting them or packaging them for transportation to the laboratory. The decisions about how best to collect blood evidence should be made by crime-scene searchers in consultation with laboratory analysts. Laboratory analysts are in the best position to know what they are or are not equipped to do and what kinds of samples they are set up to handle. Careful documentation of a crime scene is essential before beginning to collect evidence. Without documentation of what samples came from where, the serological results will not be of much help in reconstructing the event. All samples should be placed in appropriate containers and carefully labeled. Blood evidence should be taken to the laboratory as soon as possible after it is collected. The older a dried stain becomes, the fewer are the individualizing characteristics that can be tested for in the samples, and the less information will be obtained. Storage of dried blood samples at refrigerator or freezer temperatures often greatly extends the period of stability (and thus typability) of the genetic marker systems.

Collection of blood evidence and proper packaging of it requires an appreciation of many factors involved in investigation and reconstruction of what took place at the scene. Greater cooperation between crime-scene searchers and laboratory analysts is desirable. In this way, the maximum amount of information can be obtained from the available evidence. It is worth repeating that investigators have only one chance to process a crime scene correctly. Once the scene has been disturbed or evidence ruined, there is no way to put it right. Whatever information might have been acquired has been lost. The best practice, therefore, is to take the time and effort to process the scene with care and in consultation with experienced laboratory personnel.

LABORATORY EXAMINATION AND INTERPRETATION OF BLOODSTAIN EVIDENCE

In many situations, blood that is found in connection with criminal investigations is dried out. The blood may be found on practically any object, and it may be contaminated with a variety of things. It may have been subjected to changes in temperature or humidity. Bloodstained objects can be found outdoors where they were exposed to weather. As a rule, neither investigators nor the laboratory analyst knows very much about the history of a bloodstain. The testing of such specimens requires great skill and care, not only in carrying out the tests themselves but in interpreting the results. Even in the best laboratories, satisfactory results cannot always be obtained from dried blood specimens.

There are three main aspects to the testing of dried blood samples: (1) identifying the sample as blood, (2) determining whether the dried blood is of human or animal origin, and (3) typing the bloodstain for as many genetic markers as possible, if it is human.

IDENTIFICATION OF BLOOD

The first job to be done with suspected dried blood evidence is to identify it. The sample must be proved to be blood. A variety of chemical tests are used for this purpose. All the tests have one thing in common: in one way or another, they all detect *hemoglobin*. Strictly speaking, the tests detect the *heme* part of hemoglobin. No other material except blood contains hemoglobin, and if it is certain that hemoglobin is present, then it is also certain that the material is blood.

The kinds of tests that are used to detect the presence of blood may be divided into two categories: (1) preliminary, or presumptive, tests and (2) confirmatory, or conclusive, tests. Preliminary tests are generally quick, easy to do, and very sensitive. But they are not specific for blood. These tests are useful as searching devices to locate spots and stains that require further, more involved testing. They are also used to do quick, preliminary examinations of stains submitted to the laboratory. A positive result indicates that it is worthwhile to continue with further tests; a negative test strongly suggests (but does not absolutely prove) that blood is absent. Since the tests are quick and easy, their use as preliminary screening devices saves a lot of analytical time.

Preliminary or Presumptive Tests Most presumptive tests are based on the same principle. Hemoglobin is really made up of two different parts: the *heme* and the protein part, called *globin*. It is the heme that is detected in these blood tests. Heme can cause a number of chemicals to undergo a reaction with peroxide (or other similar oxidant) to give a color change. The heme acts as a *catalyst* in these reactions. All the reactions are *oxidation* reactions. The peroxide is the oxidizing agent, and the heme is the catalyst. The chemical used for the test is oxidized, and its oxidized form is colored, resulting in the color change that is seen.

A number of compounds have been used for the tests, and the particular test is often named after the chemical compound that is used. Some of the compounds are: benzidine, phenolphthalein, leucomalachite green, *ortho*-tolidine, tetramethylbenzidine, *ortho*-dianisidine, and luminol. Thus, people speak of the *benzidine test,* the *phenolphthalein test,* and so forth. One of the compounds, luminol, is a little different from the others. It reacts with peroxide in the presence of blood to give off *light.* Chemically, this process is called *chemiluminescence.* In it, some of the energy of the chemical reaction is converted to light energy.

All the chemicals have slightly different sensitivities for blood, and they are subject to interference by different things, not the same in every case. There are advantages and disadvantages to be considered in deciding which test to use for a particular application. Luminol, for instance, has to be used in the dark. For years, benzidine was the most popular and widely used of the preliminary test substances, but the discovery that it causes cancer has resulted in most laboratories switching to one or more of the other, apparently safer, chemicals.

There are several different ways of doing the preliminary tests. The method chosen depends on whether the test is being done in the field or in the laboratory and on what is being tested. It also depends on whether one is searching an area or object for possible dried blood or doing a preliminary test on a visible stain to decide whether further testing is necessary.

The testing solutions and the peroxide can be successively applied or sprayed directly onto suspected dried blood. This technique may have the advantage of outlining a stained area which was not visible to the naked eye. Generally, this procedure is not useful on dark or brightly colored backgrounds because the color changes are masked. However, luminol could be used on such backgrounds. The test solutions can interfere with some of the subsequent tests (species tests and typing), though, and this is probably the biggest disadvantage of direct application. If a stained area can be seen, direct application could be used on a portion of the stain. Alternatively, an extract of the suspected stain can be made and the extract tested. Still another technique is to apply a wetted piece of filter paper onto the suspected stain, press, and then test the filter paper. This last technique has the advantages of being nondestructive to the stain and of indicating its boundaries.

These tests are extremely sensitive. Some of them can detect as little as one part of blood in 1 million parts of water! But they are not specific for blood. Other things besides hemoglobin can cause the color changes. Applying the reagent and the peroxide solution separately helps to increase the specificity. Chemical oxidants, which will cause the color change in the absence of peroxide, are detected in this way. Another possible cause of false positive results is the presence of certain plant enzymes, the vegetable peroxidases. These are rapidly destroyed by heat, however, whereas heme is heat-stable. Thus, heating samples which have given positive tests and retesting the heated samples can distinguish between a blood reaction and a false one caused by plant peroxidases.

Most authorities agree that positive presumptive tests *alone* should not be taken to mean that blood is definitely present. A positive test suggests that the sample could be blood and indicates confirmatory testing. On the other hand, a *negative* presumptive test is a reasonably certain indication that blood is absent, although in rare circumstances an inhibiting chemical could be present.

Confirmatory or Conclusive Tests　A number of different tests have been used to confirm the presence of blood in stains. These include: (1) microcrystal, (2) chromatographic, (3) spectral, and (4) immunological tests with anti-human hemoglobin serum.

There are three microcrystal tests in use. All involve treating some of the suspect material with chemicals which cause the formation of distinctively shaped microscopic crystals with heme or one of its derivatives or degradation products. The *hematin* test is the oldest crystal test, having been first used by the Polish scientist Teichmann in 1853. The *hemochromogen* test was perfected for dried blood testing by Takayama in Japan in 1912. The *acetone chlorhemin* test was devised by Wagenaar in 1935 in Germany. The crystals one obtains with these tests are microscopic, and the specimens have to be looked at under the microscope to see the crystals (Figure 9-4).

The *chromatographic test* is nothing more than the use of paper or thin-layer chromatography (Chapter 3) to detect the presence of hemoglobin. It is the same technique that is used to detect and help to identify a variety of drugs (Chapter 5).

The spectral tests are based on the careful measurement of the way in which hemoglobin, or one of its derivatives, absorbs light. Spectrophotometers operating in the ultraviolet and visible ranges (Chapter 3) are used to make these measurements.

The immunological tests with anti-human hemoglobin are based on the principles of immunology that were discussed briefly in Chapter 3. Human hemoglobin injected into an animal causes the animal to make specific antibodies to it. The animal's

FIGURE 9-4
Takayama crystals from blood.
*(Courtesy of Philip C.
Langellotti, John Jay College,
City University of New York.)*

serum can then be collected and is used as an anti-human hemoglobin serum. This antiserum can be used to detect human hemoglobin in dried stains and hence to establish the presence of human blood. The techniques used to perform the test are the same as those used to do *species* tests and are discussed next.

Most of the confirmatory tests are not nearly as sensitive as the presumptive tests. As a result, quite a bit more material is usually required for them. There are things, too, which can interfere with the confirmatory tests and which may not interfere with the presumptive tests. Negative confirmatory tests, therefore, should not necessarily be interpreted to mean that blood is absent. But a positive confirmatory test is virtually certain evidence of the presence of blood.

Species Tests—Determining Whether Dried Blood is Human or Animal

Once a specimen has been identified as blood, it is necessary to find out whether it is human or not. If the blood is from an animal, it might be necessary in some cases to find out which one. Determining the species of origin of the blood specimen is done by an immunological test called a *precipitin test*.

If human serum is injected into an animal, the animal makes specific antibodies to the human serum proteins. After a time, the animal's blood can be collected and the serum removed. This animal serum is now an *anti-human serum*; that is, it contains specific antibodies to human serum proteins. If some of this antiserum is put into contact with some human blood, a visible precipitate will form, indicating that an antigen-antibody reaction has taken place. Human serum proteins are soluble and so are the specific antibodies to them, but the human serum protein–antibody complexes (antigen-antibody complexes) are not soluble and come out of solution as white precipitates. Antibodies which cause precipitation when they react with antigens are called *precipitins*. For this reason, the species tests that use these kinds of antibodies are known as precipitin tests.

An antiserum for identifying an animal blood can also be made, just as is done for human blood. Suppose, for example, some *anti-dog serum* was needed. Dog serum would be injected into a rabbit, and after several days or weeks of waiting while the rabbit developed antibodies, the rabbit blood could be collected and the serum separated. This rabbit serum would now contain antibodies to the proteins in the dog serum and could be regarded as an anti-dog serum. Several commercial laboratories prepare antisera against a number of animal bloods, and these can be purchased.

The precipitin test was perfected for forensic use by Uhlenhuth and independently by Wassermann and Schuetze in 1901. There are a number of ways of doing precipitin tests. No matter what the procedure, though, the idea is to get a suitably diluted bloodstain extract into contact with the antiserum and to see whether a precipitate then forms. The test can be done in tubes simply by layering the stain extract over the denser antiserum. This is usually called a *ring test* because in a positive test a visible ring (or disk) of precipitate forms in the tube at the junction between stain extract and antiserum (Figure 9-5).

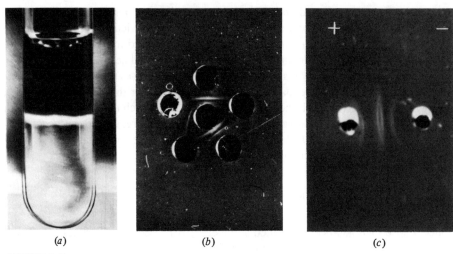

(a)   (b)   (c)

FIGURE 9-5
(a) Precipitin reaction—ring test. *(Courtesy of Suzanne Ehart, University of New Haven.) (b)*
Precipitin reaction—Ouchterlony immunodiffusion. *(Courtesy of Robert Adamo and W. Reid Lindsay, Forensic Science Laboratory, Office of the Medical Examiner, Westchester County, New York.) (c)* Precipitin reaction—crossed-over electrophoresis. *(Courtesy of Joy Carroll, University of New Haven.)*

The test can also be done in agar, or agarose, gels. These gels are semisolid and semitransparent, and they allow the antigen (serum protein) and antibody molecules to move freely within the substance of the gel. Small wells (little round holes) can be punched into one of these gels fairly close together. The stain extract is then put into one of the wells and the antibody into the other one. The antigen and antibody will move in the gel toward one another by a process called *diffusion*. At the point where they come into contact with each other, a precipitation line will form in the gel. The precipitation line can be seen with the naked eye, and this procedure is called *immunodiffusion* (Figure 9-5). It is also possible to do *electrophoresis* (Chapter 3) in these gels. An electric field can be applied across the gel, causing antigen and antibody molecules to move toward one another faster than they would by themselves (by diffusion alone). This kind of antigen-antibody species test procedure is called *crossed-over electrophoresis*. In this case, as in the others, a visible precipitation line indicates that the reaction has taken place (Figure 9-5).

Questioned samples are usually tested primarily to find out whether they are human. Occasionally, though, it is important to try to identify animal blood. For example, a suspect accused of poaching deer might claim to have cut himself and that the bloodstain is his own. Using the precipitin test, it would be possible to find out whether the blood was human or deer.

Precipitin tests are fairly easy to do, but they must be done properly if the results are to have meaning. There are features of antigen-antibody reactions that must be appreciated in order to do the precipitin tests correctly. There are two potential problems with these tests: (1) false reactions, positive or negative, because of incorrect dilutions of the antigen or antibody solutions or both and (2) cross-reactivity of antisera in which antibodies raised against one species also react with the blood of a closely related species. Problems arising from incorrect dilutions can be avoided by carefully titrating each serum and determining the correct dilutions to be used for the forensic tests. Antisera are not all the same by any means, and tests must be done with every different batch to find out how they react with various human and animal bloods at various dilutions. It is also essential to include proper controls (for example, various knowns and blanks) with every precipitin test.

Cross-reactivity of antisera among closely related species can present a more difficult problem. The reason the antibodies cross-react in the first place is that the antigens of the two species are similar in structure. Anti-human serum can cross-react with the bloods of other primates such as monkeys and apes. This is not a serious problem in the United States because monkeys and apes are not found here very often outside of zoos. In some other countries, it can be a serious problem, and forensic serologists there have to resort to more complicated immunological and serological tests in order to discriminate among the bloods. Cross-reactivity between animal bloods is usually not a problem either, although it could be in certain specific kinds of cases. Anti-dog serum, for example, might cross-react with the blood of coyotes or wolves. In a case where the illegal killing of coyotes is being investigated, this could be a problem. But these cases are not very common. What is most important is to make sure that the anti-human sera being used do not cross react with the bloods that might occur fairly commonly, such as those of farm animals, horses, dogs, cats, and other common pets. Carefully selected known controls must be run in every test so that the results of the tests with the questioned samples can be interpreted.

Blood Typing in Dried Bloodstains

Once a sample has been shown to be blood and to be human, the next task in analysis is to attempt to type it. The more systems that can be typed, the smaller the number of people expected to have the combination of types found. The number of systems that can be typed in any given specimen depends on many factors, including: (1) the age of the sample, (2) the condition of the sample, (3) the amount of sample available, and (4) the capabilities of the laboratory doing the work. In general, older samples can be typed for fewer systems. The more recent the bloodstain, the better for typing. Contamination and adverse environmental conditions decrease the chance of getting satisfactory typing results. Different systems require different amounts of stain sample for typing. If a limited amount of sample is available, the analyst must decide which systems would be most profitably typed for the particular case. Not every laboratory is set up to type every system.

More time and effort is required for the typing of dried blood than of fresh, or whole, blood. When blood dries, one of the things that happens is that the red cells break open. There is no way of getting those cells back again in their intact, original condition. Because of this, dried blood cannot be typed simply and directly like fresh, whole blood containing intact cells. With fresh blood cells, the sample can be typed by adding specific antiserum and looking for agglutination. But in dried blood there are no intact cells, so that there is nothing that can agglutinate. Under certain circumstances, it may be better for investigators to try to collect whole blood at crime scenes when it is found because it is so much easier to analyze. But there are a number of considerations, apart from ease of analysis, in deciding upon the best way of collecting blood evidence. These were discussed above. In the case discussed at the beginning of the chapter, a blood clot was found in the suspect's car. The circumstances were such that the blood clot turned out to be an important piece of evidence. One of the reasons was that this blood could be typed for a number of genetic marker systems, thus giving very good population discrimination.

Typing ABO Blood Groups in Dried Stains   Bloodstains can be typed for ABO in two ways: (1) by detecting the antibodies of the serum and (2) by detecting the antigens of the red cells. Detection of the antibodies is the older method. This procedure was first extensively employed by Lattes in Italy in 1913, and has been modified and improved over the years.

Detecting the Antibodies (Lattes Procedure)   It will be recalled from the discussion of ABO earlier in the chapter that people who are blood group A have the A antigen on their red cells and anti-B in their serum; B people have B antigen on cells and anti-A in serum; AB people have both red cell antigens, but no ABO antibodies in their serum; and O people have neither A nor B antigen, but have both anti-A and anti-B in serum (Table 9-1).

To find out which antibodies are present in a dried blood specimen, two portions of the stain are placed onto microscope slides. Type A red cells are added to one, and type B red cells to the other. If anti-A antibodies are present in the specimen, the added A cells will agglutinate; if anti-B antibodies are present, the B cells will agglutinate. Agglutination of the A cells indicates that anti-A is present, and therefore, that the stain is of group B. Similarly, agglutination of the B cells indicates that the sample is group A. If both kinds of cells agglutinate, the sample is indicated to be group O, and if neither of the kinds of cells agglutinates, group AB is indicated (but see qualifications below). Figure 9-6 shows the results of the Lattes procedure and their interpretation.

There are many variations of the test, and there are certain problems with it too. One of the problems is that results are difficult to obtain with older stains. Even stains a few weeks old may fail to give a result. Another problem is that there can sometimes be other antibodies in the stain (from the serum) which cause agglutination of the test cells and give a misleading result. The use of additional controls can help with the problem of unusual antibodies to some extent but cannot eliminate it altogether. The fact that older stains may fail to give results raises the important question of how to interpret negative results. If a specimen causes agglutination of the A cells, for example, it contains anti-A, and this result should mean that the specimen is of group B. But it could be the case that the specimen was really group O, originally containing both anti-A and anti-B, and for some reason the anti-B deteriorated faster than the anti-A. Results with the test have to be interpreted very carefully because of these problems. Negative results with both A and B cells is usually considered an inconclusive result.

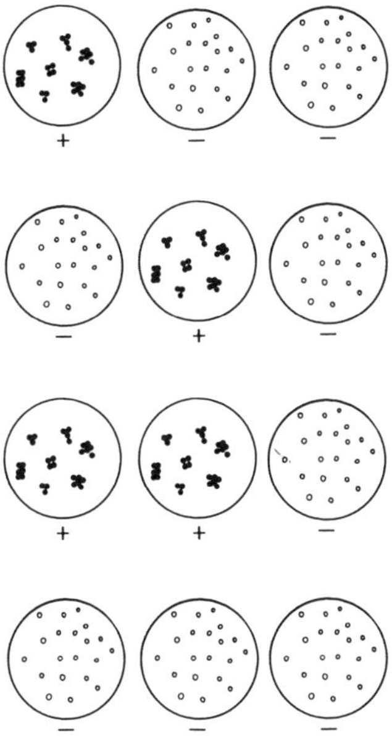

Micrographs of tests of blood crusts with			Agglutination results				Blood type indicated
A cells	B cells	D cells	A cells	B cells	D cells	Interpretation	
+	−	−	+	−	−	Anti-A is present	B
−	+	−	−	+	−	Anti-B is present	A
+	+	−	+	+	−	Anti-A and anti-B are present	O
−	−	−	−	−	−	No antibodies are present	No conclusion possible

FIGURE 9-6
Lattes test and its interpretation. O cells are used as a test control. The results with O cells must be negative or the test cannot be interpreted. The degree of agglutination (clumping) will actually vary considerably, with the cell groups sometimes being quite large.

Detecting the Blood-Group Antigens. The other approach to typing dried blood is to detect the blood-group antigens remaining on the ruptured cell membranes. They can be detected using indirect testing methods. The two major methods that have been used are absorption-inhibition and absorption-elution.

Absorption-Inhibition Method. Antisera vary in their strength. Some antisera have more antibodies in them than others do. By doing a procedure called *titration* of the antiserum, an estimate of the amount of antibody present in the antiserum can be obtained. The absorption-inhibition method depends on being able to estimate the amount of antibody present in an antiserum before and after exposure to a stain extract containing a possible antigen.

Suppose, for example, that a sample of dried blood is to be tested to see whether it has group A antigen. Anti-A serum is added to a portion of the bloodstain. By doing a titration, the amount of antibody present in the anti-A which was added to the stain can be determined. If the dried stain does have A antigen in it, some of the anti-A in the added antiserum will bind to the A antigen in the stain. As the A antigen in the stain absorbs (binds) anti-A from the antiserum, the strength of the original antiserum is being decreased. By doing careful titrations of the antiserum both before and after absorption, reductions in the strength of an antiserum can be detected. If the dried blood does contain A antigen, the anti-A antiserum will be weaker after absorption than it was to begin with. The stain material inhibits the strength of the antiserum. And, if inhibition is seen, it means that the stain did contain A antigen and that it is therefore group A. The very same thing can be done with anti-B to find out whether B antigen is present and with anti-H to test for group O. The test is called absorption-inhibition because it is designed to find out whether the dried blood will *absorb* some of the specific antibody in the antiserum, thereby *inhibiting* its strength. A diagram of the way the test works is shown in Figure 9-7.

The inhibition test for ABO typing of dried blood was used as long ago as 1923 by Siracusa in Italy. The procedure was improved somewhat and made more popular by Holzer of Austria in 1931, and it has been modified many times over the years by various workers.

Absorption-Elution Method   Dried bloodstains, as we have noted, still contain the blood-group antigens even though the red cells are broken. It has been known for a long time that blood-group antibodies can bind to their specific red cell surface antigens in bloodstains. The antigen-antibody complex can then be dissociated and the antibodies recovered. One of the ways of breaking antigen-antibody bonds is to increase the temperature. Removing specific antibodies from complexes with their antigens in this way is called *elution.*

An A bloodstain will absorb anti-A antibodies. They will bind specifically to the A antigens present in the stain material. Suppose that an excess of anti-A is added to some A bloodstain and allowed to sit for a time while the stain absorbs as much anti-A as it can. If the stain fragment is then washed with *cold* water or saline solution, only the excess *unbound* anti-A will be washed away. The specifically bound anti-A will stay bound to the A antigen as long as the washing solutions are kept cold (refrigerator temperature). Once all the excess unbound anti-A has been washed

FIGURE 9-7
Absorption-inhibition test.

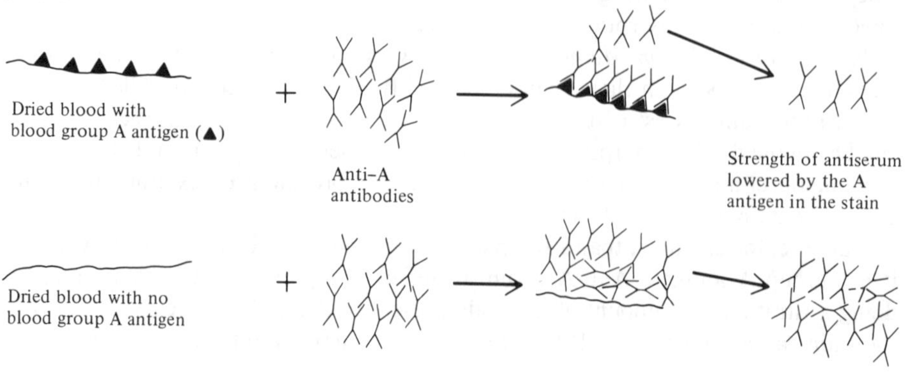

Dried blood with
blood group A antigen (▲)

+

Anti-A
antibodies

Strength of antiserum
lowered by the A
antigen in the stain

Dried blood with no
blood group A antigen

+

away, the temperature can be raised to about 55°C. At the higher temperature, the specifically bound anti-A will be broken apart from the A antigen and can be removed and detected. The way it is detected is by adding fresh, red blood cells (test cells) of group A and observing agglutination. A diagram of the absorption-elution process is shown in Figure 9-8.

The same test can be done with anti-B, with B cells used to detect the eluted antibody. Dried blood can, therefore, be tested with anti-A and anti-B to see whether A or B antigen is present. In an O stain, neither A nor B antigen is present, and the agglutination results will be negative with both anti-A and anti-B tests. O cells do contain a blood-group antigen which is called H, as discussed above. An elution test can be done with anti-H to prove that a bloodstain is really of group O. With an AB stain, both antibodies will be absorbed, and both will be eluted and subsequently detected. The absorption-elution procedure for dried blood typing dates back to Siracusa's experiments in 1923, but it has become more popular since 1960 when Kind in England first published his results with the method.

Experience has shown that the blood-group *antigens* are far more stable than the blood-group *antibodies*. Bloodstain grouping by the inhibition and elution procedures which detect the antigens, therefore, are frequently more successful than grouping by the Lattes procedure, particularly with older stains. In the absence of harmful environmental influences, age alone does not appear to be a serious problem with ABO antigens. Bloodstains many years, and even decades, old have been successfully typed for ABO. Most laboratories today, use one of the antigen detecting procedures for bloodstain grouping; some labs combine one of these techniques with the Lattes procedure in routine work.

There are differences between absorption-inhibition and absorption-elution. The

FIGURE 9-8
Absorption-elution test.

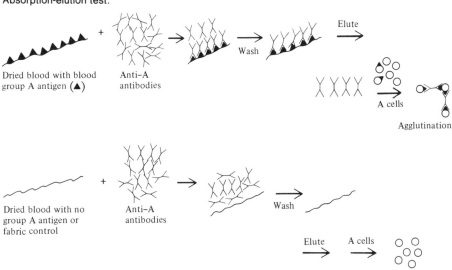

major one is sensitivity. The elution technique is very much more sensitive than the inhibition technique. It will detect blood-group antigens in a much smaller sample. The sensitivity is a big advantage in some ways. First, very small amounts of sample can be typed, and thus more tests can be done with less sample material. Second, and closely related, it is often possible to obtain a blood grouping result from a sample that is of very limited size. But sensitivity can be a disadvantage as well. There are many things besides red cells that contain A and B antigen-like substances. These things could be present as contaminants of dried blood samples. If they were present, their ABO-like antigens could be detected by these tests, thus giving incorrect and misleading results. If such contaminants are present in small amounts, there is a greater chance of detecting them with a very sensitive technique than with a less-sensitive one. The possibility that a contaminating material may be present which may react with anti-A or anti-B, giving a false positive result, is probably the biggest single problem with ABO typing in bloodstains.

Inhibition procedures, being less sensitive, require more bloodstained material than elution tests. Certain inhibition procedures are also more involved than the usual elution procedure, but both techniques have their place in bloodstain grouping. Selection of a technique must be based upon the size and nature of the sample and the circumstances of the case. Most laboratories in this country use elution techniques for most bloodstain samples.

Typing Other Blood Groups in Dried Bloodstains Most of the other blood-group antigens that were discussed above can be typed in dried bloodstains. The earlier workers all used inhibition procedures for typing these factors, but at present almost everyone uses elution procedures. During the past 20 years or so, techniques have been reported for typing Rh, MNSs, Kell, Duffy, and Kidd antigens. The procedures for typing these other antigens are somewhat more complicated and require more serological skill than is the case for ABO. Antisera having the necessary characteristics are not always easy to get, and they require more careful evaluation before use than do the usual ABO antisera.

Sample age and deterioration are much more serious problems with these systems than with ABO. The prospects of typing stains a year or more old for antigens other than ABO are not very good. There are far fewer antigens per red cell to begin with for the other systems, and thus more stained material is required for testing the antigens. With M and N typing in dried bloodstains, there are some particular problems which are complicated and require further investigation.

Antigens of systems other than ABO can be reliably typed by experienced forensic serologists in many case samples, provided the bloodstains are not too old and are in reasonably good condition. However, because of the various difficulties and complexities of these other systems, most laboratories do not type these antigens in bloodstains. There are a number of specialized forensic serology laboratories where good results are obtained on a relatively routine basis.

Typing Red Cell Isoenzymes in Dried Bloodstains Red cell isoenzymes are frequently typed by a procedure called *electrophoresis* (Chapter 3). The technique brings about the separation of different proteins based primarily upon differences in net charge, and it is usually done on some kind of gel or on a cellulose acetate support. In the past 25 years or so, procedures have been devised for typing a number of the red cell isoenzymes in dried bloodstains. The procedures are not very different from those used for the typing of the enzymes in fresh blood, but there have been a number of modifications. Most of the early work was done at the Metropolitan Police Forensic Science Laboratory in London. As new isoenzymes are discovered and their patterns of inheritance established, efforts are made to devise suitable techniques for typing them in dried bloodstains. The isoenzymes which can be typed in bloodstains at present are indicated in Table 9-3.

The actual techniques for isoenzyme typing are not very complicated, but skill and experience are required to obtain consistently reliable and readable results, even with fresh blood. Dried blood does not always give exactly the same kind of results as fresh blood. Sometimes the reasons for the differences are understood, and sometimes they are not. Interpretation of the patterns of isoenzymes must be done with care and requires experience. Figure 9-9 shows the kind of results obtained from typing the red cell isoenzyme phosphoglucomutase (PGM) by starch gel electrophoresis.

Recently, a somewhat different technique called *isoelectric focusing* has been applied to the typing of red cell isoenzymes. This procedure brings about the separation of proteins in a mixture on the basis of differences in their isoelectric points (Chapter 3); it can be regarded as a different kind of electrophoresis. As a result, isoelectric focusing gives different isoenzyme patterns than those obtained with electrophoresis. Occasionally, the use of both methods of typing and comparison of the results reveals additional information about a system. A noteworthy example is the PGM system. The typing of red cell PGM by isoelectric focusing shows 10 different

FIGURE 9-9
(a) Photograph of PGM polymorphic types on starch gel. *(Courtesy of Robert Adamo and W. Reid Lindsay, Forensic Science Laboratory, Office of the Medical Examiner, Westchester County, New York.)* *(b)* Diagram of PGM polymorphic types. Letters refer to bands, and numbers refer to types.

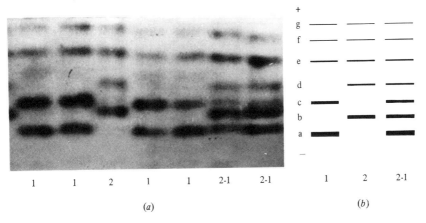

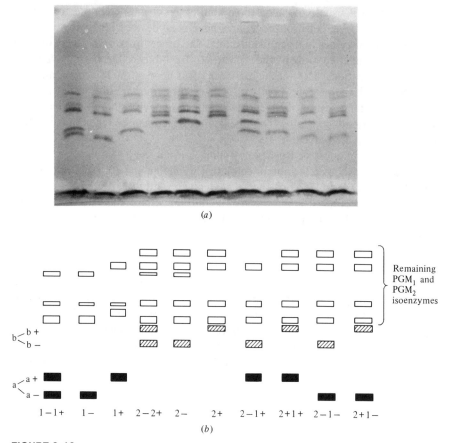

(a)

(b)

FIGURE 9-10

(a) Photograph of PGM patterns with isoelectric focusing. *(b)* Diagram of PGM patterns with isoelectric focusing. *(Courtesy of Dr. P. H. Whitehead, Central Research Establishment, Aldermaston, Great Britain.)*

patterns instead of the 3 types seen with electrophoresis. The explanation lies in the fact that there are more genes controlling the expression of PGM than was first thought. The additional polymorphism was not observed by the original electrophoresis procedure. Bloodstains can be typed by isoelectric focusing, and some laboratories are now using this technique. The PGM patterns seen with it are shown in Figure 9-10. The major difficulty with it is cost: isoelectric focusing requires additional equipment in the laboratory, and the cost of materials is considerably higher than for conventional electrophoresis. It has been found that the PGM system can be typed for all 10 phenotypes using conventional electrophoresis under special conditions.

The red cell isoenzymes vary in their stability in dried stains. The most stable one is probably adenylate kinase (AK). Generally though, bloodstains older than a few months cannot be expected to give very satisfactory enzyme typing results.

Typing Serum Proteins in Dried Bloodstains   The serum proteins which can be typed in dried bloodstains are shown in Table 9-4. The major ones are haptoglobin (Hp) and group-specific component (Gc). Hp and Gc show stability patterns quite similar to those of many red cell isoenzymes. The results obtained from a haptoglobin typing are shown in Figure 9-11. Haptoglobin is typed by electrophoresis. Gc may be typed by conventional electrophoresis or isoelectric focusing. Hp is somewhat easier to detect on gels than is Gc.

The Gm and Km systems that were shown in Table 9-4 are different. The Gm and Km factors are antigens and are typed by means of specific antibodies by serological procedures. The typing procedure is more complicated than that for red cell antigens. Specific antisera for the Gm factors are also difficult to get, and although the system is a good one for discriminating among individuals, only a few laboratories have the appropriate materials and skill to do the typing. Gm factors have the advantage of being very stable in dried blood. They have been reportedly typed in bloodstains several decades old. Should the antisera become more widely available and the techniques better known, Gm typing will probably find greater use in forensic science laboratories.

Typing Hemoglobin in Dried Bloodstains.   Hemoglobin variants are typed by electrophoresis, and the procedure is the same for fresh blood or for bloodstains. The results of typing several common hemoglobin variants are shown in Figure 9-12. Hemoglobin typing can be useful in discriminating fetal from adult blood. Hemoglobins S and C are found in black people on occasion and less frequently in Hispanic people. They are almost never found in other ethnic groups.

Value of Different Genetic Marker Systems in Forensic Serology   As indicated in the foregoing sections, there are many different blood-group, isoenzyme, and serum-group systems (as well as hemoglobin variants) that can be typed in bloodstains. Not all of them, however, are equally valuable as genetic markers. The value of a system as a genetic marker depends on how well its types are distributed in the population.

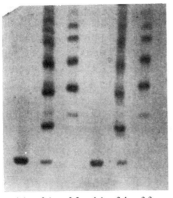

FIGURE 9-11
Haptoglobin electrophoresis patterns. (*Courtesy of Mark D. Stolorow, Illinois Department of Law Enforcement.*)

1-1   2-1   2-2   1-1   2-1   2-2

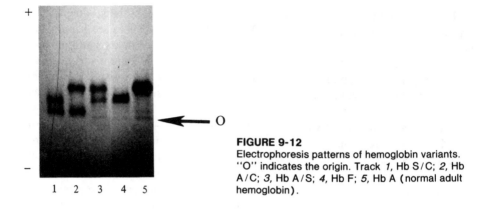

FIGURE 9-12
Electrophoresis patterns of hemoglobin variants.
"O" indicates the origin. Track *1*, Hb S/C; *2*, Hb
A/C; *3*, Hb A/S; *4*, Hb F; *5*, Hb A (normal adult
hemoglobin).

Let us illustrate this point using two different isoenzyme systems: glyoxalase I (GLO) and adenylate kinase (AK). There are three major GLO types. GLO 1 is found in about 20 percent, GLO 2-1 in about 50 percent and GLO 2 in about 30 percent of American whites. There are also three AK types, and they are found in approximately the following frequencies in the same population group: AK 1, about 93 percent; AK 2-1, about 7 percent; and AK 2, less than 1 percent. Thus, we have two isoenzyme systems here, each with three types. But the distributions of the three types in the population are very different. If we picked out two people at random, there would be a greater chance of their having different GLO types than of their having different AK types, simply because the GLO types are more widely distributed. Stated another way, we would have a better chance of distinguishing two randomly selected people on the basis of GLO than we would on the basis of AK. In general, the more widely distributed the types of a system are, the better are the chances of distinguishing between individuals on the basis of that system.

It is possible to calculate a numerical quantity which gives a measure of the value of all the various systems discussed in the chapter. In order to do the calculation, the distribution of the types in a population has to be known. In other words, a representative number of people have to have been typed for the system. The numerical quantity that is often used is called the *discrimination index*. It is actually a probability value and tells the chances that two randomly selected people will have different types in a particular system. The higher the discrimination index for a system, the better the chances of distinguishing between members of a population by typing that system. Going back to the two systems used as examples above, you would expect that GLO would have a higher discrimination index than AK, and this is indeed the case. The value for GLO is about 0.6 and for AK is about 0.13. Thus, with two people selected at random from the white American population, we would have about a 60 percent chance of finding different GLO types, but only about a 13 percent chance of finding different AK types.

Discrimination index values can be calculated for all the systems discussed in the chapter. The approximate values for the white and black populations in the United States for many of the systems discussed are shown in Table 9-5.

TABLE 9-5
DISCRIMINATION INDEX VALUES FOR GENETIC MARKER SYSTEMS

System	Discrimination index	
	White population	Black population
Blood-group systems		
ABO	0.62	0.64
Rh	0.79	0.69
MNSs	0.83	0.78
Kell	0.15	0.04
Duffy	0.62	0.56
Kidd	0.61	0.55
Isoenzyme systems		
PGM	0.52	0.47
ACP	0.66	0.54
AK	0.13	0.04
ADA	0.18	0.10
ESD	0.35	0.27
GLO	0.61	0.62
Serum-group systems		
Hp	0.62	0.72
Gc	0.57	0.33
Tf	0.02	0.09
Pi	0.36	0.06
Hemoglobin variants	—	0.20

Other Characteristics of Dried Bloodstains

There are certain other pieces of information that can sometimes be obtained from dried bloodstain analysis. One of these is the sex of the individual from whom the blood came. The procedures for testing for the sex of origin in dried bloodstains are complicated and do not give accurate results in every single case. Only a few laboratories can do these tests, but in cases where reliable results are obtained the information can be very useful.

The age of a bloodstain would be a useful piece of information. Over the years, many methods have been proposed for estimating the age of bloodstains. None of them gives a very accurate estimate of the age, however. Sometimes it is possible to tell that the stain is months old, rather than days old, but there are not any methods which allow for greater precision than that.

There has been some promising research in England on profiling the allergy antibodies that people have and detecting them in dried blood. It would be expected that an allergy profile, if it could be obtained, would be quite individualistic and would be of help in individualizing dried bloodstains. Further work will be needed before these tests are used in routing blood analysis, however.

Other recent research indicates that the presence of certain specific drugs can be diagnosed in dried bloodstains. The finding of particular drugs in a bloodstain could yield information about the person responsible for the stain (such as in the case of a drug addict, or of a person being treated for a particular clinical condition with a certain drug). Although the techniques appear to be quite reliable, very few laboratories are equipped for these tests or experienced with them at the present time.

STUDY QUESTIONS

1 What steps does the forensic serologist follow in examining a questioned blood specimen?
2 What are the different kinds of blood cells found in human blood?
3 What is plasma? What is serum? How are these different?
4 What is the importance of bloodstain patterns at crime scenes?
5 What are the five main categories of individualizing characteristics of blood?
6 What is meant by the term "genetic marker"?
7 What is agglutination? What kind of test involves agglutination?
8 What is a blood-group system? What is a blood group?
9 What are the blood types in tbe ABO system? For each type, list which antigens are on the red cell and which antibodies are in the serum.
10 What are some of the blood-group systems besides ABO?
11 What are red cell isoenzymes? What is an isoenzyme type?
12 What is electrophoresis? What is it used for in forensic serology?
13 What is genetics? Why is knowledge of genetics important in forensic serology?
14 How are blood groups and other genetic markers in blood used to help in individualizing blood samples? Can blood be individualized?
15 What are the principles involved in proper collection and preservation of blood evidence?
16 What are some of the problems with blood evidence that is improperly collected or stored?
17 How is blood identified in a bloodstain?
18 What is a presumptive test? What are the main presumptive tests for blood?
19 What is a confirmatory test? What are the main confirmatory tests for blood?
20 What are the principles involved in species testing of blood specimens?
21 What are some of the problems associated with species tests?
22 Describe three methods for typing bloodstains for ABO type. Explain briefly how each method works and describe the underlying principle for each.
23 What is meant by "discrimination index"? Of what value is the discrimination index in forensic serology?

REFERENCES AND FURTHER READING

Boorman, K. E., B. E. Dodd, and P. J. Lincoln: *Blood Group Serology,* 5th ed., Churchill Livingstone, London, 1977.

Culliford, B. J.: *The Examination and Typing of Bloodstains in the Crime Laboratory,* U.S. Government Printing Office, Washington, D.C., 1971.

Gaensslen, R. E.: "Blood, Sweat and Tears . . . and Saliva and Semen," *Law Enforcement Communications,* February 1980.

Gaensslen, R. E.: *Sourcebook in Forensic Serology, Immunology and Biochemistry,* U.S. Government Printing Office, Washington D.C., 1983.

Gaensslen, R. E., and F. R. Camp, Jr.: "Forensic Serology," in C. H. Wecht (ed.), *Forensic Sciences,* vol. 2, chaps. 29 and 30, Matthew Bender, New York, 1981.

Giblett, E. R.: *Genetic Markers in Human Blood,* Blackwell Scientific, Oxford, England, 1969.

Lee, H. C.: "Identification and Typing of Bloodstains," in R. Saferstein (ed), *Forensic Science Handbook,* Prentice-Hall, Englewood Cliffs, N.J., 1982.

Metropolitan Police Forensic Science Laboratory: *Biology Methods Manual,* Metropolitan Police, London, 1978.

Prokop, O., and G. Uhlenbruck: *Human Blood and Serum Groups,* Interscience-Wiley, New York, 1969.

Race, R. R., and R. Sanger: *Blood Groups in Man,* 6th ed., Blackwell Scientific, Oxford, England, 1975.

Sensabaugh, G. F.: "Uses of Polymorphic Red Cell Enzymes in Forensic Science," *Clinics in Haematology,* vol. 10, pp. 185–207, 1981.

Sensabaugh, G. F.: "Biochemical Markers of Human Individuality," in R. Saferstein (ed.), *Forensic Science Handbook,* Prentice-Hall, Englewood Cliffs, N.J., 1982.

CHAPTER 10

BODY FLUIDS

INTRODUCTION

The body fluids other than blood most often encountered in connection with criminal investigations are semen and saliva. Urine, perspiration, nasal mucus, and even human milk may be seen on occasion. These materials are frequently present as dried stains. Fecal matter, which, strictly speaking, is not a body fluid, can occur at scenes and in stains on articles of clothing in certain cases. Forensic serologists, who examine blood and bloodstains (Chapter 9), also examine body-fluid and secretion evidence in the laboratory. The purposes of their analyses are: (1) identification of the fluids present, (2) use of genetic markers in the fluids to associate them with particular people or to prove that they could not be associated, (3) interpretation of patterns of stains as a means of reconstructing the events leading up to the deposition of evidence, and (4) recovery of any other trace evidence that might be present. The tests and procedures used for these purposes are discussed below.

Body-fluid analysis is most frequently associated with sexual assault cases. The number of cases of forcible rape which come to the attention of the police has been increasing for a number of years. There are other kinds of cases that can involve body-fluid evidence. Cigarette butts may have traces of saliva on them. So may envelope flaps or postage stamps. Perspiration and urine stains are common on undergarments; it is sometimes necessary to investigate them in some detail, and it is always necessary to take their possible presence into account. The ABO blood-group substances in these body fluids can be helpful in association or in exclusion. Just as often, though, it is important to know about the presence of such substances so as not to be misled about the blood type of a bloodstain on a garment which also has body-fluid stains. Saliva material can sometimes be collected from around the area of a bitemark (see Chapter 12) on a human body. Urine or urine stains can be found under many different circumstances.

It is essential that suspected body-fluid stains be *identified*. Frequently, more than one fluid is present in a stain, and grouping results cannot be interpreted unless the nature of all the body fluids present in the stain is known. Each of the body fluids is identified by a different procedure. The nature and circumstances of each case and the article being examined help the examiner decide which body fluids may be present. It is not always necessary to do tests to prove that body fluids are human, although species tests are sometimes done on body fluids. Common sense has to be used in looking at a particular case exhibit in trying to decide what may have happened. Saliva found on a cigarette butt filter, for example, is probably human. On the other hand, a saliva stain on the sleeve of a jacket owned by a man who had three large dogs might call for more caution before concluding that the saliva was human. Once body-fluid residues or stains have been identified, the analysis can be directed toward individualizing genetic markers.

There are not as many useful genetic markers in body fluids as there are in blood, and it is thus not possible to obtain the degree of individualization that is possible with blood. Different body fluids do contain genetic markers, though, and they can sometimes be very useful. If a body fluid contains a genetic marker that is not present in the person suspected of depositing it, then that person is excluded from consideration. Many of the genetic markers found in body fluids are also found in blood. These were discussed in Chapter 9. There are some genetic markers that are unique to one or more body fluids, and these will be mentioned in this chapter.

ABO BLOOD-GROUP SUBSTANCES IN BODY FLUIDS— SECRETOR SYSTEM

The most important and common genetic markers in all body fluids are the ABO substances. The substances present correspond to the person's blood type. It has been known since the mid-1920s that saliva, semen, and other body fluids and organ material (stomach lining, bile, muscle, etc.) can have ABO substances in them. These substances are usually detected by the absorption-inhibition technique discussed in Chapter 9. An antiserum of known strength is reduced in strength by a body fluid which contains the corresponding antigen; that is, the antiserum strength is inhibited. The antigens in the fluid combine with the antibodies in the antiserum to form antigen-antibody complexes. When the antiserum is then tested for its strength in agglutinating red blood cells, the strength will be much lower. The strength of an antiserum is measured by titration, and serologists use the term *titer* to describe how potent an antiserum is. The titer of an agglutinating antiserum is actually the highest dilution of the antiserum, in multiples of two (1:2, 1:4, 1:8, 1:16, etc.), that will still agglutinate red cells having the corresponding type. Thus an anti-A serum with a titer of 256, for example, would still agglutinate A cells when the antiserum is diluted to 1 part in 256 parts of saline. There are several different ways to carry out inhibition tests. But the principle is always the same: if the fluid being tested significantly reduces the titer of the antiserum, then it is normally concluded that the fluid contains the antigenic substance.

In 1932, it was discovered that the presence of ABO substances in body fluids and tissues was an inherited characteristic. People who have the substances are called *secretors;* people who do not are called *nonsecretors.* The characteristic is controlled by a single gene pair, and the secretor gene *Se* is dominant to the nonsecretor gene *se.* Thus, people with the genetic makeup *SeSe* or *Sese* are secretors, and people who are *sese* are nonsecretors. The easiest way to determine someone's secretor status is by testing saliva because this fluid is so easy and convenient to obtain. In most populations, 75 to 85 percent of the people are secretors. Thus, the presence of the ABO substances in body fluids can be a valuable marker in the majority of people. The body fluids of nonsecretors, incidentally, do not lack ABO substances altogether. A very small amount of group substance in a different form is present in tissues and fluids, but the usual tests for secretor status are not sensitive enough to detect them. The tests thus allow the classification of people into two groups, secretors and nonsecretors.

COLLECTION, PACKAGING, AND PRESERVATION OF EVIDENCE

Many of the same principles that apply to blood evidence also apply here. Ordinarily, body-fluid evidence will be in the form of dried stains, and these stains may be found on any imaginable object or surface. If possible, the entire piece of evidence containing the stain should be submitted for examination. If not, the area containing the stain can be cut out, labeled and submitted; a *control* area that is not contaminated by the stain must be cut out and submitted as well. Any article having a suspected body-fluid stain should be collected, dried completely, and placed in a paper container that is not airtight. These fluids are particularly susceptible to bacterial contamination, and airtight containers tend to make this problem worse, especially if the stain is not completely dry and/or if the humidity is high. Some of the bacteria which can infect these stains have ABO receptors in their cell walls and can cause misleading results in grouping tests. Spurious reactions for A, B, and H may all be seen, separately or in any combination, as the result of bacteria in stains. Careful workers use techniques designed to help detect these bacterial reactions as distinct from those of the body fluids, but even the most careful techniques cannot always distinguish the difference. It is best, therefore, to try to avoid any bacterial contamination in the first place. Unless the laboratory has given explicit instructions for the collection of wet stains, it is best to air-dry the material completely before packaging. This practice helps not only in preventing bacterial growth but also in avoiding the transfer of the moist material to other parts of the stained object or fabric. Even fully dry stains suspected of containing semen should be handled with care and not crushed, wadded up, folded, and so on. Rough handling of the stain area causes more destruction of the sperm cells which the laboratory needs intact to make the identification of the stain.

It is very important, as has been emphasized over and over again, to document and record every detail of the crime scene before disturbing it to collect pieces of evidence. Containers must be labeled carefully, and the name(s) of the people who have had custody must be recorded.

Investigators and scene personnel should never handle evidence bearing blood or body-fluid stain evidence with their bare hands. They should wear disposable gloves or use clean tools. Even a minute and unseen amount of perspiration from someone's hands can deposit blood-group substances onto the evidence, and this will thoroughly complicate or make impossible interpretation of the grouping results. Nothing is more wasteful than to spend dozens of hours of laboratory time only to discover that unstained control areas of the evidence are giving ABO reactions, making interpretation of the grouping results impossible. We have had more than one occasion to wonder what the ABO groups and secretor status of the crime-scene personnel in a case were!

It is sometimes necessary to collect saliva from a person for the determination of secretor status. Saliva should be collected in a clean glass container or tube after the subject has rinsed out his or her mouth with water. The container should then be placed in a boiling water bath for 5 min. If this cannot be done, the material can be frozen immediately. As another alternative, the saliva can be collected on clean cotton cloth or filter paper and rapidly dried to a stain.

Almost any kind of biological evidence is more stable in the cold than at room temperature. Low to moderate humidity is better for the material as a rule than high humidity. The best procedure is to store evidence in a refrigerator if possible. The environment in frost-free-type refrigerators is usually very dry.

EVIDENCE COLLECTION IN SEXUAL ASSAULT CASES

Collection of this type of evidence deserves special comment. Sexual assault victims are always examined by doctors, whose first concern is the patient's health and well-being. The doctor then collects the evidence which will be used to establish the elements of the crime. The most important consideration is cooperation and communication between police investigators, examining physicians, and laboratory personnel. Unfortunately, the lack of such cooperation is a problem in many jurisdictions. In places where the problem has been addressed, there are special police teams and special medical teams, and they often work in cooperation with personnel from a rape crisis center.

Only physicians or other qualified medical personnel can collect the necessary evidence in these cases, and many are not well versed in handling forensic cases. The physician should document the physical (and emotional) state of the victim. The victim's clothing should be collected in separate containers after all stains have dried, and the containers should be labeled carefully. The doctor may collect vaginal swabs, washings, or both. These should be delivered to the laboratory as soon as possible. Several swabs should be taken from different areas of the perineum and vaginal vault and labeled appropriately. Combings of pubic hair may be collected to try to locate transferred hairs from the perpetrator. If this is done, pubic hair that is known to be the victim's must also be taken for comparison (Chapter 8). Anal and/or oral swabs may be taken if anal or oral sexual contact is reported. Blood and saliva samples must *always* be collected from the victim if any grouping results are expected to be interpretable. A number of "rape kits" are now commercially available. These provide the doctor with containers, labels, slides, pubic hair combs, and so forth (Figure 10-1). The kits can be a convenience, but the choice of such a kit, like the choice of examination and collection protocol, should be a collective decision of all the persons involved in the investigation. More was said about these kits in Chapter 8.

In some jurisdictions, examining physicians may prepare slides from the swabs or washings and do the microscopical examination for sperm cells. In a few places, the doctors also perform the remainder of the required tests on the evidence. More commonly, however, the articles are turned over to the forensic laboratory. It is very important that the investigator obtain a history from the victim and make its essential facts known to the laboratory examiner. A detailed account of the incident is essential, including such information as how long ago it took place and what the victim did in the meantime. Having changed clothes, showered, and other such activities will greatly affect the interpretation of the analytical results. The doctor should determine whether the victim is menstruating and her most recent sexual activity prior to the incident. The police investigators can also help in providing some of these details. The presence of any vaginal infections should be noted and the diagnosis made known to the evidence examiner. These facts are important not for their own sake but because all of them affect the way the findings will be interpreted. The more

FIGURE 10-1
Rape kit components. *(Sirchie Laboratories, Raleigh, North Carolina.)*

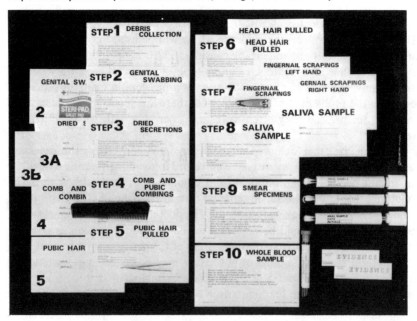

the serologist knows about what occurred, the more intelligently the analytical results can be used to help solve the case.

Coordination is the most important factor in these cases because by their very nature they involve a number of different specialists. Many cases are ruined by poor evidence collection procedure or by the failure to collect needed samples. A disrupted chain of custody with an important piece of evidence can lead to inadmissibility and loss of the entire case. Working together, however, the police, the examining physicians, and the forensic laboratory can ensure that forensic serology and legal medicine provide the maximum assistance to the solution of these difficult criminal cases.

LABORATORY EXAMINATION OF SEMEN AND SEMINAL STAINS

Semen, or seminal fluid, is the fluid produced by the reproductive organs of the male; the name *semen* is applied to the fluid which is ejaculated. It is a thick, milky white to off-white fluid which normally contains spermatozoa and the secretions of the seminal vesicles, the prostate gland and the bulbourethral gland. The prostate contributes the greatest volume of material to the semen. A normal ejaculate is about 2 to 5 mL in volume and ordinarily contains from 100 million to 150 million sperm cells per milliliter of semen, although this varies considerably from one individual to another. Seminal fluid is chemically complex, containing hundreds of different substances.

Identification of Semen

Semen must be identified in two types of situations: in seminal *stains,* which may be found on any object, but are often found on clothing and bedding; and in vaginal *swabs,* or *washings,* from the victims of sexual assault. Depending upon the case, and especially the victim's account of what took place, anal and/or oral swabs may be collected and submitted to the laboratory as well.

Most evidence submitted to forensic serologists in crime laboratories is from criminal cases. A few forensic serologists may examine items of evidence from civil cases relating to body fluids. Most of these cases involve divorce proceedings, and articles of evidence are submitted because one of the parties is attempting to establish evidence of adultery.

Spermatozoa Human spermatozoa are very small cells and must be looked for under the microscope (Figure 10-2). Suspected seminal stains cannot be examined directly for spermatozoa. One of a number of different techniques must be used to prepare the questioned material for microscopical examination. Ordinarily a cutting is made first. It is then wetted with water, saline, or a buffer solution in order to extract the seminal-fluid components into the liquid. Some authorities then examine this extract of the suspected stain. Others may use a scraping procedure to remove the seminal material from the object or cloth to which it is adhering. Some have used ultrasonic oscillation devices (high-frequency sound waves) to try to dislodge the sperm cells from the fabric into the extract. Others centrifuge the extract to try to

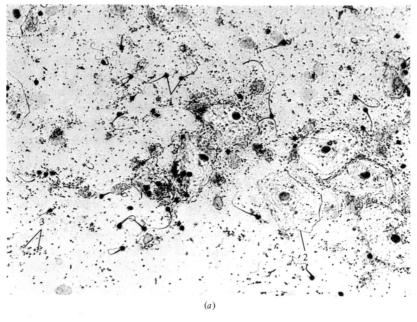

(a)

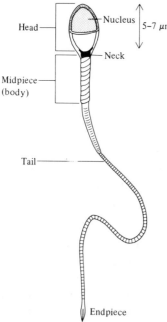

(b)

FIGURE 10-2

(a) Photomicrograph of spermatozoa. The sample was from a vaginal swab obtained in a rape investigation. In addition to spermatozoa (1), vaginal epithelial cells (2) and bacteria (3) are also seen in the photomicrograph. (Courtesy of Frederick C. Drummond and W. Reid Lindsay, Forensic Science Laboratory, Office of the Medical Examiner, Westchester County, New York.) (b) Diagram of a mature spermatozoon; total length 50–70 μm. (Courtesy of Kevin McMahon, University of New Haven.)

collect the cells together at the bottom of a test tube. Ultimately, the material is placed on a microscope slide as a droplet or smear. It may then be examined directly, or it can be stained with any of a variety of biological stains (dyes) designed to make the cells more evident against the background. Phase contrast and dark-field microscopy have been employed to look at unstained preparations. Vaginal washings are treated very much like suspected seminal-stain extracts although they are usually quite a bit more dilute. Swabs may be used to make smears on microscope slides, or they, too, may be extracted into a liquid medium and then treated like suspected seminal-stain extracts.

The finding of sperm cells constitutes proof of the presence of semen. Sperm cells on vaginal swabs or in washings is taken as proof of penetration, which is one of the elements of the crime of rape. Spermatozoa are fragile, especially in dried semen stains; the heads of the cells can break off from the rest of the cell. Older stains tend to have much larger percentages of broken cells. Intact sperm cells are generally difficult to find in stains that are more than a few months old. Some authorities have said that sperm-cell heads can be unequivocally identified in stain extracts. However, many will not make an identification based upon the finding of heads alone and insist that intact cells must be found to be certain of the stain's identity.

There are a number of reasons why seminal fluid (and seminal stains) may lack sperm cells. Some men have little or no sperm for a variety of different physiological reasons. Men who have undergone vasectomies lack sperm cells in their semen, and many men have lower than average sperm counts. The chances of recovering sperm from a stain or swab will depend to some extent on the number of cells deposited initially. Since only a fraction of the cells are expected to survive in a stain, the chances of finding cells in a seminal stain are reduced if the initial number was low. Seminal stains may come about in a number of ways: direct deposition, drainage from the vagina, filtration through layers of cloth, and even transfer from one area to another because of fabrics coming into contact before the semen has dried. Each of these circumstances will produce somewhat different kinds of stains in which sperm density will vary greatly.

Another factor in determining the presence of sperm is sampling. It cannot be assumed that sperm cells are uniformly distributed throughout a seminal stain, because semen is a mixture of several fluids, only one of which contains spermatozoa. Thus, a cutting from one part of the stained area may have a large number of cells, while a cutting from another part may have few or none. The way that vaginal swabs are taken will greatly affect the chances of finding sperm cells; serologists have no control over this process as a rule, since swabs are taken by examining physicians or other hospital personnel. Experienced examiners take all these factors into account before deciding upon the best course of action in the examination.

Other Identification Techniques   The identification of semen by finding spermatozoa has long been regarded as the best and most certain means of identification. It is a reality, though, that sperm cannot always be found. The failure to find sperm cells cannot be taken as evidence that semen is absent because there are a number of reasons for seminal stains not having sperm cells present. Over the years, a number of procedures have been devised to identify semen in the absence of sperm. All of them are based on the finding of some other component of semen. The difficulty arises from the fact that most of these other components are *not unique* to semen; they may occur in other body fluids or even in other living organisms. In most cases, semen contains a relatively large amount of the component being used as the basis for the test. It is usually the presence of a large amount of a component, therefore, that is diagnostic, and not its mere presence. With fresh whole semen, quantitative tests would be a relatively simple matter. We could measure the amount of a component and express it as a concentration (for example, so many milligrams per milliliter of semen). But forensic samples are not fresh semen samples. They are stains, or swabs, or washings. And it is impossible to know how much semen is represented in the sample. It is thus very difficult to know how much of a component is a "large" amount, using fresh semen as a basis of comparison, even if quantitative tests are used.

Three different types of tests which may aid in the identification of semen will be discussed: microcrystalline tests, the acid phosphatase test, and immunological tests. Other tests have been suggested but have not been used much.

There are two microcrystalline tests, and they are still employed in some laboratories. In one procedure, suspected samples are treated with an iodine solution to detect a seminal component called *choline*. In a positive test, characteristic choline iodide crystals can be seen under the microscope (Figure 10-3). The test is variously called the *Florence test* or the *choline test*. A second crystal test, the *Barberio test*, employs saturated picric acid solutions as a reagent. A seminal component called *spermine* is detected, and crystals of spermine picrate are seen in a positive test. Spermine and choline can be detected by thin-layer chromatography as well. Neither

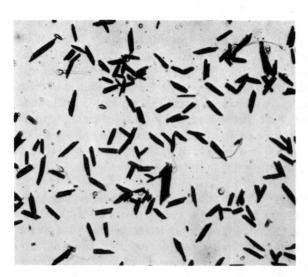

FIGURE 10-3
Florence crystals from seminal fluid. A few spermatozoa can be seen among the crystals. *(Courtesy of Robert Adamo and W. Reid Lindsay, Forensic Science Laboratory, Office of the Medical Examiner, Westchester County, New York.)*

of these components is unique to semen. The finding of either or both of them, therefore, is only an indication of the presence of semen.

The acid phosphatase test is much more widely employed. A number of factors complicate its interpretation, however. These include:

1 How the test is done, whether qualitatively or quantitatively, what reagents are used, and so on.

2 The nature of the samples (stains, swabs, etc).

3 The age of a stain being tested.

4 The presence of vaginal material in the sample (it is always present in swabs or washings and may be present in certain kinds of stains as well).

5 The time since intercourse in the case of swabs or washings.

It has been known for more than 40 years that human semen has a large amount of the enzyme acid phosphatase. It is produced in the prostate gland, which contributes it to the semen. In the mid-1940s forensic scientists began to take advantage of the acid phosphatase as a basis for the identification of human semen. An *acid phosphatase* is an enzyme (biological protein catalyst) which accelerates the splitting of a number of different phosphate compounds and does so best under mildly acidic conditions (at pH values of approximately 4 to 6—see Chapter 3). The test may be done qualitatively ("yes" or "no"), or quantitatively ("how much"). Because it is not the presence or absence of acid phosphatase but the relatively large amount of it that is characteristic of semen, many investigators prefer a quantitative test. However, even a qualitative test determines the amount of acid phosphatase in a certain way: every test has a lower limit of sensitivity; that is, there has to be a certain minimum amount of material present before the test will detect it. Thus, whereas qualitative tests are designed to say yes or no to the presence of a substance, what a positive test actually says is that the substance is present and that it is present in *at least* a certain amount. It does not tell how much more than the minimum is present. These tests can often be adjusted to different levels of sensitivity; that is, the amount of material required for the test to say yes can be adjusted to some extent. Regardless of the procedure chosen, however, it is often difficult to decide how much acid phosphatase is enough for it to be interpreted as a positive test for semen.

The difficulties that arise in interpreting an acid phosphatase test vary, depending on what is being tested. Seminal stains, like other biological fluid stains, tend to deteriorate with time. Among other things, this means that the enzymes in the stain will become less active as the stain ages, and acid phosphatase is no exception. The amount of acid phosphatase activity in the stain decreases as the stain gets older, although much more slowly if the stain is dry. The rate of decrease is not easy to relate to stain age because so much depends on the conditions under which the stain ages. After a time, the stain will not contain detectable acid phosphatase activity even though semen is present. With vaginal swabs or washings, or stains contaminated with vaginal material, the problem is a little bit different. The vagina does not *secrete* any fluids in the strict sense. Fluids from the tissues lining the organ do find their way into the vaginal canal; this fluid is called a *transudate*. Mucus produced by the cervix and even by the uterine tissues may also be present. In addition, the normal, healthy vagina is inhabited by a balanced population of microorganisms. Besides these normal resident organisms, there are a number of fairly common organisms which can infect the vagina, including various yeasts and fungi. Thus, what is often called *vaginal secretion* is not a secretion at all, but a complex mixture of fluids, mucus, mircoorganisms, and cells. The epithelial cells which line the vaginal canal are shed over the course of time, and new cells replace them. The technical term for these shed cells is *exfoliated epithelial cells.*

Swabs or washings thus contain many different cells and fluids, and it is known that these can have acid phosphatase activity. It has been found that the *amount* of acid phosphatase is usually much less than what would be found in semen. Once in a while, however, a relatively high value is observed. And it is also the case that, occasionally, a semen sample has a comparatively low value. The concern among experts may be expressed, therefore, by this question: Could a particular semen-free vaginal swab or washing sample give an acid phosphatase value sufficiently high to be interpreted as a positive test for semen? There is no definite answer to the question.

In order to try to make the test as specific as possible for *seminal* acid phosphatase, experts have introduced into the test additional steps which help distinguish the acid phosphatase of semen from other acid phosphatases from other sources. One of these is inhibition of the enzyme by an ion called L-tartrate. This substance inhibits seminal acid phosphatase, but it also inhibits vaginal acid phosphatase and hence cannot be used as a means of differentiating the two. The failure of tartrate to inhibit the acid phosphatase activity, however, indicates that the enzyme is not of seminal or vaginal origin. Another approach is to try to separate the seminal and vaginal acid phosphatases by electrophoresis or by isoelectric focusing. There is no doubt that separation can be achieved, and this fact can be useful in trying to show that the acid phosphatase in a sample is seminal, rather than vaginal, bacterial, etc. It can be useful, too, in showing that vaginal material is indeed present. Recent studies indicate that seminal and vaginal acid phosphatase are essentially the same enzyme. The different cells in which the two enzymes find themselves after initial assembly, however, modify them slightly differently so that, in most cases, they can be separated. It should also be noted that the presence and the amount of vaginal acid phosphatase seen in an individual is highly variable and that its *absence* does not prove that vaginal material is absent.

The last method for identifying sperm-free semen that will be discussed is the immunological one. Antisera can be produced in rabbits for almost any human protein or proteins, as was discussed in Chapter 9 in connection with the precipitin test. Just as antibodies can be produced against blood proteins by injecting blood into a rabbit, so antibodies against seminal proteins can be produced by injecting seminal fluids into the animal. Under such conditions, the rabbit will make antibodies to *all* the proteins of semen. Semen shares a number of proteins with other body fluids. Albumin, for example, is found in blood serum, and lactoferrin, another seminal protein, is found in mothers' milk. The end result is that the anti-human semen serum produced is not specific for semen, but it can react in varying degrees with other body fluids. Indeed, it is well known that antiserum prepared against blood serum (anti-human serum) reacts with human semen, showing that they share some proteins in common.

Recently, a protein has been found that seems to be specific to seminal plasma. It has not been found in other body fluids or organs nor in vaginal material. The protein has been called *p30*. Antisera against this seminal fluid component should provide the basis for an entirely specific immunological test for semen, regardless of whether the semen contains any sperm or not. Once anti-p30 becomes more widely available, the immunological test should come into much wider use and forensic scientists will have an unequivocal test for sperm-free semen.

Screening and Searching Techniques   There are several reasons for wanting to have screening tests for the presence of semen on articles of evidence. In busy laboratories, many hundreds of articles are submitted for examination. In the interest of economy of examiner and case turnaround time, it pays to have relatively quick, presumptive tests which can be used to decide whether further, more time-consuming analysis is in order. These tests can also be used to locate the areas of a garment or other object where stains have been deposited.

It has been known for years that seminal stains usually fluoresce brightly under ultraviolet (UV) light, and that they have a starchy feel. These properties form the basis of methods used to help locate stained areas for further examination. Many things will fluoresce under UV light, and this search procedure is in no way a test for semen. But it is helpful in looking at articles of evidence. Modern synthetic fabrics as well as modern detergents and other laundry products often contain brighteners which can fluoresce brightly under UV light. These brighteners are added to make fabrics look whiter in sunlight. Their fluorescence under UV light can make it difficult to use this searching technique on fabrics which contain them, and which are also suspected of containing seminal stains. The intensity of fluorescence of the optical brighteners can be so much stronger than the weak fluorescence due to the seminal stain that the presence of the stain may be detected by the appearance of a darker spot or a brighter background.

The acid phosphatase test can be used as a searching device as well. Quick, qualitative acid phosphatase tests are easy to devise. In this way acid phosphatase-positive areas of an object or garment can be located quickly and then subjected to more rigorous tests. Acid phosphatase test papers can be prepared as well. These can be placed into contact with an article of evidence, and acid phosphatase–positive stained areas will leave a kind of "image" on the paper.

Individualizing Characteristics of Semen

The most commonly used individualizing characteristic of semen is its ABO substance content, as discussed above. In secretors, who make up 75 to 85 percent of the population, all the body fluids, including semen, have water-soluble ABO substances corresponding to the ABO blood group of the individual. It is a standard practice to test seminal stains and vaginal swabs or washings for ABO. An inhibition test is used for this purpose, as noted previously. In an uncontaminated seminal stain deposited by a secretor, it is possible to determine the ABO blood group of the person who left the stain. If the stain came from a nonsecretor, no ABO substances will be detected in the seminal stain with the tests ordinarily used. This information can be used to include, or especially to exclude, suspects. If a suspect does not have the ABO substances which are found in the stain, he is excluded. Further, if ABO substances are found in the stain, but the suspect is a nonsecretor, he is excluded. These conclusions may be drawn only if the stain is pure semen not contaminated with body fluids from others which can furnish the ABO substances of the contaminating fluids. In swabs or washings, therefore, the grouping results can never be interpreted unless we know the ABO type and secretor status of the victim from whom they were obtained. Only by knowing what group substances to expect from the victim's secretions can any conclusions be drawn about which of the observed substances might be from someone else.

The group substances expected in the body fluids of secretors of all four blood groups are shown in Table 10-1. In Chapter 9, it was noted that type O red cells have a surface antigen called H, and that anti-H reacts with O red cells. In body fluids of secretors, the A, B, and H substance relationships are a little different from those in blood. Notice that all secretors ordinarily have H substance in their body fluids even if they are not type O. Type O secretors have only H in their body fluids. Substance H is present in the fluids of secretors of the other groups because A and B are made in the body from H and the conversion of H into A, or H into B, or H into A and B is not complete.

Because of these properties of the ABO-secretor systems, there are always some circumstances under which we are unable to sort out mixtures of body fluids from different people on the basis of ABO grouping. Obviously, if there are two people involved, both having the same blood group, and both secretors, we cannot tell the difference. But there are less obvious cases too. Suppose a rape victim is an A secretor. Her fluids will have A and H. Suppose that the suspect is an O secretor. He will have H in his semen. In testing the swabs or washings and finding A and H, we cannot tell whether the H is from the victim or the suspect. He is thus not excluded. At the same time, a different man, who was a nonsecretor, could have committed the crime, and the body-fluid grouping results would be the same.

TABLE 10-1
ABO SUBSTANCES IN THE BODY FLUIDS OF
SECRETORS

Secretors of blood group	ABO group substances in the body fluids
O	H
A	A + H
B	B + H
AB	A + B + H

There are some other individualizing characteristics of semen which could be used to help individualize it. These include the isoenzymes of the PGM, PGD, ESD, and PEPA systems (Table 9-3) as well as the Gm, Km, and Tf plasma protein markers (Table 9-4). There are various problems with all of them, and very few laboratories carry out analyses of these other genetic markers. Some laboratories are now typing the PGM isoenzymes in seminal-fluid stains, swabs, and washings. Since the genetic markers are or may be present in the victim's fluids too, it is necessary to know the victim's type(s) for the system(s) before the results of typing on swabs or washings can be interpreted. There is an isoenzyme system called *diaphorase,* or DIA (it was originally called *sperm diaphorase,* but it is now known that it is not limited to sperm), which may be typed in sperm cells. It is not found in sperm-cell-free semen, and thus has no value in such samples. This system, like many of the others, is potentially valuable in the individualization of semen, but some of the problems with its typing in stains will have to be worked out before it can be used in routine casework.

LABORATORY ANALYSIS OF SALIVA AND SALIVA STAINS

Identification of Saliva

The most widely used method of identifying saliva is based on the presence of *amylase* in this fluid. Amylase is an enzyme which catalyzes the breakdown of starch to simple sugar (glucose). The amylase, like the other components of saliva, is secreted by the three pairs of salivary glands. Saliva samples may also contain exfoliated epithelial cells from the inner lining of the mouth.

Many variations of the test for amylase are in use. Quantitative tests for amylase for saliva identification are preferred because amylase is present in other body fluids and organs, too. Saliva usually has a lot of amylase by comparison. Thus, it is better to do a test that gives a measure of the amount of enzyme present than one which simply indicates that it is there. The considerations are no different in principle from those discussed above in connection with the use of the acid phosphatase test for semen identification.

Other substances in saliva have been used as the basis of identification tests, including thiocyanate ion, nitrite ion, and the enzyme alkaline phosphatase. Tests based on amylase are by far the most common, however. Amylase tests can be used not only as analytical tests for the identification of saliva in stains but also as ways of searching for possible saliva stains, especially on garments. Relatively rapid qualitative tests can be done on stain extracts or on wetted filter papers that have been pressed onto suspected stains to see whether there is any evidence of saliva. Test papers which contain starch have been devised too. These can be used to help locate stains on garments for further analysis. Saliva stains can be fluorescent under UV light, and this property is sometimes helpful in searching for stains on articles of evidence. However, fabric and laundry brighteners can cause problems with this procedure, as pointed out above in connection with the search for seminal stains using UV light.

Individualizing Characteristics of Saliva

The only individualizing property of saliva that is used at present is the ABO system. Saliva specimens and saliva stains can be typed for ABO if they come from secretors. Saliva from a person is used as the fluid of choice for the determination of secretor status because it is so easy to obtain. It is important to know whether saliva is present as a contaminant in a stain being examined in a case sample because of the presence of the ABO substances if it comes from a secretor.

There are a number of proteins in saliva which are controlled by polymorphic genetic loci, and they can thus be used as genetic markers. There are quite a few different systems known, each having a number of different types. The amylase which is used to identify saliva shows genetic variation, and there are thus several types of amylase isoenzymes. At present, however, suitable procedures have not been worked out for the use of these markers in saliva stains.

LABORATORY ANALYSIS OF OTHER BODY FLUIDS AND SECRETIONS

Besides semen and saliva, urine and sweat are the most commonly encountered fluids other than blood. Urine contains a large amount of a substance called *urea,* which is used as a basis for identifying the fluid, especially in stains. There are a number of methods for testing for urea. The presence of another compound, *creatinine,* is also used for identification. Creatinine forms a red compound with picric acid (Jaffe test). Urine also has a distinctive odor which can be helpful in recognizing its presence. Gentle heating of urine-stained material generates the characteristic odor.

Sweat is often present on garments that come directly into contact with the skin. It is seldom necessary to identify sweat as such, but it is very important to keep its possible presence in mind when examining clothing, bedding, etc. The salt content of sweat has been used as a means of identifying it when necessary.

Both urine and sweat may contain ABO substances. The presence of these fluids can thus cause difficulty in the interpretation of grouping results. In testing articles for ABO substances, it is essential to test an "unstained" control area of the sample near the stained area. This practice is necessary to disclose the presence of ABO substances which may appear as contaminants and thus to prevent errors in the interpretation of grouping results. Common sense must be used in deciding which articles to test for the various body fluids so as not to be misled by the presence of an unsuspected contaminating fluid. Communication between the submitting officers and the laboratory is extremely important in this regard. Knowing the circumstances of the case is extremely helpful in trying to decide what fluids may be present, how different people may be involved, and so forth.

STUDY QUESTIONS

1 What is meant by a person's being a secretor or a nonsecretor?
2 What important principles should be kept in mind in collecting body-fluid evidence?
3 What special procedures should be used in collecting evidence in rape and other sexual assault cases?

4 Name the different kinds of evidence that should be collected from a sexual assault victim, state how each should be collected, and give the reasons for collecting each one.

5 What is the single, most unequivocal method for identification of semen?

6 Describe some of the methods for extracting spermatozoa from a seminal stain.

7 Describe several methods other than identification of spermatozoa with the microscope for the identification of semen.

8 Discuss the meaning of a positive qualitative acid phosphatase test. Of a "positive" quantitative acid phosphatase test.

9 What kind of serological test is used to determine which ABO substances are present in body fluids?

10 Which blood-group substances would be detected by an absorption-inhibition test in the body fluids of a nonsecretor?

11 Which blood-group substances would be detected by an absorption-inhibition test in body fluids of an A secretor? Of an O secretor?

12 Why is it necessary to test the body fluids of the victim in a rape case if typing results are to be conducted on and interpreted from vaginal swabs?

13 How is saliva usually identified in a questioned sample?

14 How is urine identified in a questioned sample?

15 Why does a serologist always include an unstained cloth control in grouping tests conducted on body-fluid stains? What would be wrong with the test if this cloth control were not included?

16 What is the best way of choosing a rape kit and who should be involved in this decision?

17 Describe the methods for collecting saliva from a person and preserving it for secretor status determination.

REFERENCES AND FURTHER READING

Blake, E. T., and G. F. Sensabaugh: "Genetic Markers in Human Semen: A Review" and "II. Quantitation of Polymorphic Proteins," *Journal of Forensic Sciences,* vol. 21, pp. 784–796, 1976, and vol. 23, pp. 717–729, 1978.

Gaensslen, R. E.: "Blood, Sweat and Tears . . . and Saliva and Semen," *Law Enforcement Communications,* February 1980.

Gaensslen, R. E.: *Sourcebook in Forensic Serology, Immunology and Biochemistry,* U.S. Government Printing Office, Washington, D.C., 1983.

Gaensslen, R. E., and F. R. Camp: "Forensic Serology," in C. H. Wecht (ed.) *Forensic Sciences,* vol. 2, chap. 29, Matthew Bender, New York, 1981.

Kind, S. S.: "The Acid Phosphatase Test," in A. S. Curry (ed.), *Methods of Forensic Science,* vol. 3, pp. 267–288, Interscience-Wiley, New York, 1964.

Metropolitan Police Forensic Science Laboratory: *Biology Methods Manual,* Metropolitan Police, London, 1978.

Pollack, O. J.: "Semen and Seminal Stains," *Archives of Pathology,* vol. 35, pp. 140–196, 1943.

Sensabaugh, G. F.: "Isolation and Characterization of a Semen-Specific Protein from Human Seminal Plasma; A Potential New Marker for Semen Identification," *Journal of Forensic Sciences,* vol. 23, pp. 105–115, 1978.

Sensabaugh, G. F.: "The Quantitative Acid Phosphatase Test. A Statistical Analysis of Endogenous Postcoital Acid Phosphatase Levels in the Vagina," *Journal of Forensic Sciences,* vol. 24, pp. 346–365, 1979.

Sensabaugh, G. F.: "Biochemical Markers of Individuality," in R. Saferstein (ed.), *Forensic Science Handbook,* Prentice-Hall, Englewood Cliffs, N.J., 1982.

CHAPTER 11

PHYSICAL PATTERNS

INTRODUCTION

Physical pattern evidence is used in a variety of ways in crime investigations. Patterns may contain both class and individual characteristics and can thus form the basis for identification and for individualization. In addition, patterns of one kind or another make up the basis for most reconstructions. The varieties and applications of physical patterns in identification and individualization can be appreciated by examining Table 11-1. Descriptions and examples of the uses of physical patterns in reconstruction will be also discussed in this chapter. Physical patterns are described and discussed here according to whether their principal application is for identification, individualization, or reconstruction. The distinction between the detailed descriptions of different physical patterns and their forensic science applications on the one hand and what might be called the laboratory examination of physical patterns on the other is not always clear.

The following cases illustrate some of the uses of physical pattern evidence.

Several years ago, a man was found murdered in a wooded area of a county bordering a large city. The victim had been released from prison several months earlier. An investigation revealed that he had often been in the company of another man who had been released at the same time. The police also discovered that the two had often rented automobiles from car rental agencies together.

The second man became a suspect in the case, and the police learned that he and the victim had rented a car a short time before the murder. The car had not yet been returned, and it was located in the nearby city, parked near the suspect's apartment house. Blood, trace evidence, and other investigative information provided evidence that the murdered man's body had been transported in this car. In addition, bloodstains were found under three plastic trash bags in the back seat of the car.

TABLE 11-1
PHYSICAL PATTERN COMPARISONS

Purpose	Description	Examples	Comparison process	Documentation and collection	Requirement for exemplar
Identification	Morphological identifications: size, shape, color	Marijuana leaf, species of animal hair, pollen	Comparison with known specimen or known mental image	Collection	No; reference samples in lab used if necessary
Individualization	Physical match Direct match (physical fit; jigsaw fit)	Torn paper, broken wood, plastic or glass	Physical fit	Collection and careful packaging	No; known and questioned samples compared
	Indirect match	Plastic film bags, wood grain	Juxtaposition and evaluation of pattern continuities	Collection	No; known and questioned samples compared
	Comparison of markings Imprints	Two-dimensional; fingerprints, typewriting, shoeprints	Point-by-point; side by side or overlay	Collection; photography; lifting	Yes; produced in the laboratory
	Indentations	Three-dimensional; firing-pin impressions, bitemarks	Point-by-point	Collection; photography; casting	Yes; produced in the laboratory
	Striations	Land and groove markings on bullets, sliding toolmarks	Continuity of pattern	Collection; photography; casting	Yes; produced in the laboratory
	General shape and form comparisons	Handwriting, morphological comparison of hair	Subjective; pattern recognition	Collection; photography	Yes; multiple samples

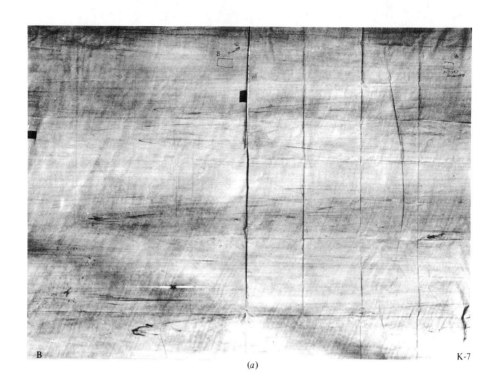

B   K-7

(a)

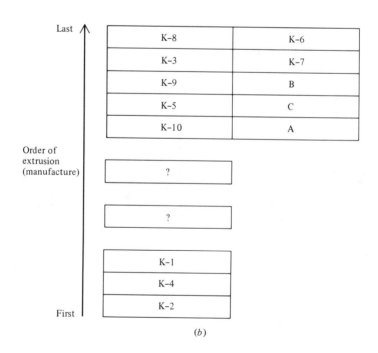

(b)

A preliminary evaluation of the bags, combined with information about their manufacturing process (provided by the manufacturer), allowed the development of a means of comparing the bags. The plastic film from which the bags were made had a random pigmentation pattern which could be seen when the bags were taken apart at the seams and held up to the light. In comparing bags from newly purchased control boxes, it was found that these patterns would allow the bags in the box to be uniquely matched to show that they had all been made from a single continuous piece of plastic in a specific sequence. Thus, the order of manufacture of sequentially made individual bags and packages of bags could be determined if no bags in the sequence were missing.

In this case, it was possible to show that the three bags from the car had originally been packaged in a box of bags in the suspect's apartment (Figure 11-1). The plastic bag evidence linked the suspect to the car, while other evidence linked the car to the victim (blood clot in the seat hinge molding—see Chapter 9).

This case illustrates the importance of pattern evidence such as may be encountered in a variety of manufactured articles. Plastic film bags, such as trash bags, have become increasingly frequent as evidence in recent years. They are often used to dispose of tools, bloody clothing, or even body parts. They are also used in drug traffic and other illegal activities. Such pattern evidence as was found in this case could be encountered in many different types of cases.

Not long ago in a quiet, rural area in the northeastern part of the country, a man was awakened from his sleep in the middle of the night by the sounds of an intruder. As he awoke more fully and started to get up, he realized that the intruder was in his bedroom. The intruder was startled, apparently frightened, and he swung at the homeowner with a sticklike object, and then quickly fled, dropping the weapon as he did so. The object turned out to be a broken axe handle. The broken end was ragged, and several nails had been driven through it so that their sharp ends protruded outward.

The axe handle looked quite new, and the police conducted an investigation of local hardware outlets to try to find the purchaser. This task was made easier because the area was rural and there were not many stores that handled such items. One of the recent

---

FIGURE 11-1
(a) Photograph illustrating an indirect physical match of known and questioned plastic trash bags. The bags have been opened up and illuminated from behind to reveal the pigmentation patterns. The photograph illustrates a portion of the match between the questioned bag B (left) and K-7 (right) [see *(b)*]. *(Courtesy of Vincent Crispino and W. Reid Lindsay, Forensic Science Laboratory, Office of the Medical Examiner, Westchester County, New York.)* *(b)* A diagrammatic representation of a plastic bag match in a homicide case. The indirect physical matching of 10 plastic trash bags is shown. Each rectangle represents a plastic bag opened flat. Those labeled K-1 through K-10 were found in a box of new bags (originally containing 15) in the suspect's apartment. Bags A–C were found concealing bloodstains in the car. Contact between rectangles in the diagram indicates an indirect physical match along the line of contact. The rectangles with the "?" represent bags that were unaccounted for. They may have been used for some other purpose either before or after the incident. The missing bags made it impossible to associate K-1, K-2, and K-4 with the "block" of 10 bags although they could be associated with each other. The overall indirect physical match and knowledge of the manufacturing process made it possible to state that the three questioned bags were once adjacent to seven from the box in a continuous piece of plastic film and that they had been packaged in the same box (that is, the one found in the suspect's apartment).

purchasers identified in the investigation was a suspected burglar, and the police obtained a warrant to search his home. The search was fruitful and turned up what appeared to be the other part of the axe handle, still attached to the chopping head. Both parts of the axe were carefully examined in the laboratory. A jigsaw fit match between the two pieces was not possible because of the splintering and raggedness of the broken ends. However, the two pieces appeared to be quite similar in shape, size, structure, and longitudinal wood-grain markings.

After the initial comparisons and documentation, the examiners made careful cross-sectional cuts on the two pieces, so as to produce smooth ends for detailed comparison (Figure 11-2). The two pieces compared in wood type, grain, growth ring structure, microscopic wood cell structure, longitudinal grain, and markings. It was possible to establish, after careful comparison, that the two pieces had originally been part of a single, complete axe.

This case illustrates an indirect physical match in a situation where a direct physical match (jigsaw fit) could not be achieved. Even though a direct physical match could

FIGURE 11-2
Photograph demonstrating an indirect physical match of cut and polished ends of an axe handle. *(Courtesy of Marshall Robinson, Connecticut State Police Forensic Science Laboratory.)*

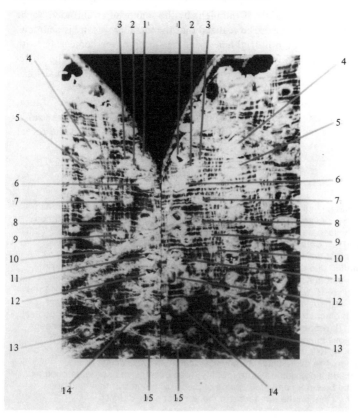

not be obtained, a conclusive and informative result was possible. Direct and indirect physical matches are described below.

> In a recent hit-and-run case, a car hit a pedestrian with great force and then left the scene. The victim was taken to the hospital, but his injuries were so severe that he died shortly afterward. The hit-and-run scene was carefully searched. Among the debris and broken parts from the car, several fairly large pieces of glass from the headlight reflector were found, along with a piece of the grill.
>
> The police conducted a search of auto body repair shops in the area in a search for the suspected car. Before long, a suspect car was located; luckily it had not yet been repaired. The car was impounded and checked carefully. The pieces of headlight reflector found at the scene could be physically matched directly with the remaining pieces in the car headlight (Figure 11-3). In addition, the piece of grill could be fitted exactly onto the missing portion still on the car. A fabric imprint of the victim's clothing on the bumper, along with blood and hair consistent with the victim, added further weight.

This case illustrates the great value of direct physical matching in the solution of certain types of cases. In the material which follows, physical patterns of many kinds will be discussed in detail. The material is organized according to whether the physical patterns relate primarily to identification, individualization, or reconstruction.

PHYSICAL PATTERNS IN IDENTIFICATION

Morphological identification (identification based on structural features) is nothing more than the recognition of a physical pattern. Such identifications are accomplished by comparing the questioned pattern with a known one. In some cases, the known pattern used for the comparison may be only a mental image in the mind of the examiner. This process of identifying an item (or individual) by recognition of a physical pattern is widely used, often unconsciously.

Pattern recognition identification is common in everyday life. A shopper in a

FIGURE 11-3
Direct physical matches between fragments of a reflector from a broken automobile headlamp.
(Courtesy of Deborah Baughn, Connecticut State Police Forensic Science Laboratory.)

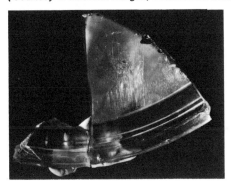
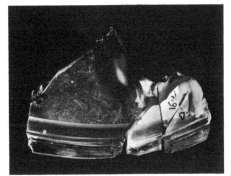

supermarket unconsciously utilizes the process to identify different items, such as fruits or vegetables. An apple is identified as an apple by comparing the general pattern of its visual image with a pattern stored in the brain. The same process is used by bird watchers in identifying a certain species of bird, or by entomologists in identifying insects, although more detailed criteria may also be involved.

In the forensic laboratory, the morphological examination of marijuana and the determination of species of origin of animal hairs are two examples of identifications using physical patterns. In some cases, such a morphological identification is sufficient; in other circumstances, a follow-up or confirmatory test may be required. The human mind is particularly adept at evaluating physical patterns, especially visual ones. In fact, many chemical and biochemical comparisons directed toward identification or individualization are facilitated by techniques which convert the chemical information into a physical pattern prior to the time the comparison is made. Different types of chemical spectra (Chapter 3) are examples.

PHYSICAL PATTERNS IN INDIVIDUALIZATION

Physical patterns are even more important in problems of individualization. In fact, the examination and comparison of physical patterns is probably the most widely used and easily the most effective approach to many individualizations. Individualizations based upon physical pattern matches are often possible and are both persuasive and easily intelligible to juries. Three more or less different applications of physical patterns to individualizations can be distinguished: (1) physical matching, (2) comparison of markings, and (3) general shape or form comparison. Examples of these different pattern comparisons are discussed and illustrated in more detail below, and examples are also shown in Table 11-1.

Physical Matching

Physical matching methods are used in attempts to uniquely associate pieces of materials with articles from which they are thought to have been separated. This approach is preferred in demonstrating common origins with appropriate types of physical objects. If no physical features are present for comparison, an approach to individualization based on chemical composition would be indicated. As has been pointed out, however, compositional comparisons do not allow absolute individualizations. The possibility of obtaining a physical match should *always* be considered before any samples are taken for chemical analysis.

Two types of physical matches can be distinguished, direct and indirect. The *direct* method is used when it is possible to demonstrate common origin conclusively by fitting the known and questioned pieces together in a unique fashion. The process is similar to fitting together the pieces of a jigsaw puzzle. The direct method is also sometimes called the *physical fit* or *jigsaw fit* method. For a variety of reasons, direct physical matches are not always attainable. The causes range from limitations in the properties of the material to damaged or missing pieces. In such cases, an *indirect* method must be considered.

Direct Physical Matches   Physical fit or jigsaw fit pattern comparisons are applicable to certain situations in which an article has been broken, torn, cut, or otherwise separated into two or more pieces. If the separation process is random and the material is of a suitable type, it is likely that the separated pieces can be fitted together in a unique fashion to demonstrate conclusively a common origin. Such a uniquely individualizing physical fit is made possible by the involvement of random processes, and the particular separation would not be expected to occur again in exactly the same way. As a practical matter, such matches are easier to accomplish in situations where an article has been separated into relatively few but larger pieces. Fractures of wood, glass, many plastics, paint, and metals are often sufficiently random and detailed to allow convincing direct physical matches. (Figures 11-4 and 11-5).

As an instructional exercise, the reader can take 10 identically sized squares of the same type of paper. Have a friend label each half of these with a number and letter code, and then tear them in half. The pieces should then be mixed or shuffled before being returned to you. Even if great care is taken to tear all the pieces uniformly in half to produce nearly equal sized fragments, it is usually a simple matter to examine the general shape of the pieces and the details of the torn surfaces to find

FIGURE 11-4
(a) A revolver and a piece of the plastic grip broken from it. The revolver was dropped by the suspect at the scene of a robbery. He picked up the weapon but left the piece of plastic at the scene. *(b)* Demonstration of a direct physical match between the piece of grip remaining with the revolver in the suspect's possession and the piece found at the robbery scene. *(Courtesy of Detective Nicolas Petraco, Crime Laboratory, New York City Police Department.)*

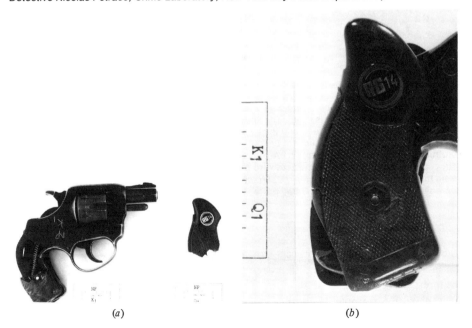

(a)   *(b)*

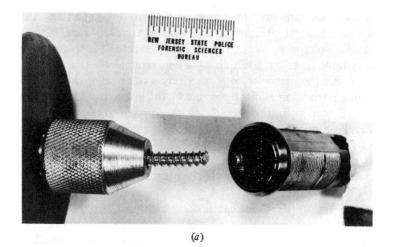

(a)

(b)

FIGURE 11-5
(a) An inertial puller (slap hammer) with a broken screw tip and a lock cylinder from a burglar alarm system. The slap hammer was found in the possession of a burglary suspect, and the lock cylinder was removed from the scene by investigators. A piece of broken screw can be seen protruding from the lock cylinder. (b) An enlarged photograph showing a direct physical match between the screw from the lock and that protruding from the chuck of the slap hammer. (Courtesy of George Neighbor, Forensic Science Bureau, New Jersey State Police.)

the matching halves. This process can be repeated with other types of materials or surfaces, and it will be found that each piece can be conclusively associated with its counterpart in a matter of minutes. The exercise can be carried out with broken toothpicks, for example. Here, the examiner might want to use a magnifier or stereo-microscope to aid in observing the details of the fracture surfaces and the fit.

Matches obtained by physical fits, although usually not difficult, often produce individualizations that are among the most definitive attainable. Fitting a glass fragment into a broken headlamp or a paint chip into the damaged portion of an automobile fender are examples of commonly encountered situations in which physical fits can be used. Even though direct physical matches are ordinarily easy to accomplish, they should not be attempted in the field, because (1) the value of any trace evidence present may be compromised, and (2) the mating surfaces can be damaged in the process.

Indirect Physical Matches   Indirect physical matches may be attempted under circumstances in which an article has been separated into two or more pieces but in which a direct physical match is not possible. Such a situation may arise in several ways. If a very smooth cut separated the two pieces being compared or if an intervening piece is missing, a physical fit may not be possible. The same would be true if the surface that separates the pieces is featureless. In addition, a direct physical match may not be possible if the fracture or separation takes place in a soft or elastic medium which distorts or deforms as the separation occurs. Indirect physical matching takes advantage of both surface and internal characteristics of the separated pieces. Figures 11-1 and 11-2 illustrate good examples of indirect physical matches from case situations.

Indirect physical matches utilize a number of properties. Generally, the continuity of patterns of surface markings, inhomogeneities, and other internal features are employed in the comparison process. Such matches can be almost as definitive as direct physical matches under favorable circumstances. This point may be illustrated by the example of matching pieces of wood. If the pieces of wood have been broken apart, a direct physical match would probably be attempted after observing proper precautions to preserve trace evidence. It would be done by fitting the pieces together carefully. If an exact fit were obtained, it would be documented photographically. An examiner would probably not pursue a match like this beyond this point. Further careful examination would probably reveal, however, that other features of the two pieces correspond: wood grain, surface markings, surface contours, and external dimensions. These features would have to be relied on exclusively in an *indirect* match if one or both of the fracture surfaces had been damaged. The same would be true if the pieces had been separated by sawing. If these indirect match features lined up perfectly and if only a modest amount of the intervening material were missing, a persuasive match could be obtained. Better indirect matches would be obtained more easily with larger pieces of wood, where a larger number of rings of wood grain and other features are present. Here, the inability to match the pieces directly by a physical fit would be of little consequence; the indirect match would be a virtual certainty.

Comparison of Markings

Some types of evidence are produced when two surfaces come into contact and one or both of them receive distinctive marks in the process. If the acquired marks are detailed and accurately record information about the other surface, the potential for individualization exists. These markings can be classified into three types: imprints, indentations, and striations.

Imprints Imprint evidence consists of *two-dimensional* contact markings. These marks are made when material is transferred as a result of contact and subsequent separation. An imprint may represent a transfer of material to the marked surface or, occasionally, the removal of material from it. In either case, the pattern produced is in some measure a record of features of the object that made the mark. These features are essentially two-dimensional, and can be adequately documented by photographic techniques. The distinction between imprint and indentation (the next category) evidence may become somewhat blurred at times. Some imprints may have a slight three-dimensional character. In such cases, some of the documentation techniques described below for indentations (for example, casting) might be appropriate. In most cases, however, photography and lifting methods are used for the documentation and preservation of imprint evidence. It is preferable to collect the actual imprint itself whenever possible.

Typewriting and fingerprints are common examples of imprint evidence. These are discussed separately and in more detail in Chapters 13 and 12, respectively. Other types of essentially two-dimensional contact pattern evidence would include certain footprints or shoe prints, palm prints, tire prints, fabric pattern imprints, and lip prints.

Surfaces that have remained in contact for long periods of time, and have then been separated, may bear unique markings which can be used to demonstrate their prior association. Some marks of this type may have a low-relief, three-dimensional character but can still be handled as imprints. Case examples of various types of imprint evidence are shown in Figure 11-6 through 11-8.

In the laboratory, imprint evidence is usually individualized by comparing the questioned mark to an exemplar mark made by a known object which is suspected of having made the questioned mark. A point-by-point comparison process is used. The questioned and exemplar marks may be placed side by side, or a transparency overlay of one of the marks, which can be superimposed over the other mark, may be prepared. The overlay procedure greatly facilitates a rapid checking of the correspondence of points. For court purposes, a display showing both marks side by side, with points of comparison numbered, is often prepared.

Indentations Indentations are *three-dimensional* contact patterns. They are generally produced when a harder material leaves an impression of its surface features and contours in a softer one. There need not be any transfer of matter from one surface to the other for the production of an indentation; material is transferred in producing an imprint marking (as noted above). The three-dimensional indentation is itself the evidence.

Examples of indentation evidence are breech-face markings on the head of a cartridge case, firing pin indentations, certain pry marks (Figure 11-9), footprints in soft mud or soil, plastic fingerprint impressions (Chapter 12), teeth impressions (bite-

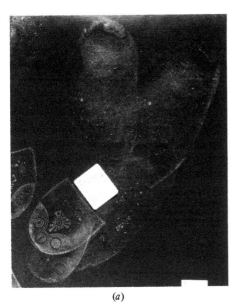

(*a*)   (*b*)

FIGURE 11-6
(*a*) Shoe prints in dust on the surface of a vinyl chair at a burglary scene. (*b*) Shoes taken from the burglary suspect. (*Courstesy of George Neighbor, Forensic Science Bureau, New Jersey State Police.*)

FIGURE 11-7
A cloth imprint on the bumper of an automobile suspected of being involved in the hit-and-run killing of a pedestrian. (*Courtesy of Stanley Zaniewski, Forensic Science Laboratory, Connecticut State Police.*)

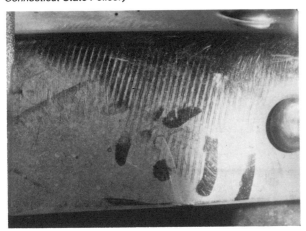

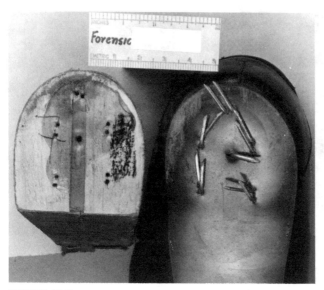

FIGURE 11-8
Imprint evidence used to associate the heel of a shoe with a shoe
worn by a suspect thought to have fled the scene of a robbery.
The association was proved by comparing the individual
characteristics of the glue and nail hole patterns. A corresponding
wood-grain pattern was also present on the glue. *(Courtesy of
Vincent Crispino and W. Reid Lindsay, Forensic Science
Laboratory, Office of the Medical Examiner, Westchester County,
New York.)*

FIGURE 11-9
A pry mark indentation in a painted wood door frame and a
screwdriver taken from a burglary suspect. Trace evidence in
the form of paint was found in the grooves on the surface of the
screwdriver blade. *(Courtesy of George Neighbor, Forensic
Science Bureau, New Jersey State Police.)*

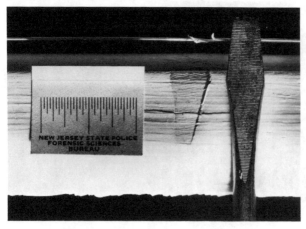

marks) and certain fabric impressions. Bitemarks and their comparison make up part of the special field called forensic odontology, and are discussed further in Chapter 12.

Striations Striation marks are produced by dynamic processes, whereas those in the imprint and indentation categories can occur without the receiving surface having to undergo any relative lateral motion. Striations can be described as sliding contact patterns. The degree of individualization possible with such evidence depends on the number and types of features present in the mark and on the relationship of the mark to the case. The matching of detailed striation markings on a questioned bullet to those of an exemplar bullet fired from a suspect's gun, for example, could prove conclusively that the questioned bullet had been fired by a particular gun. This finding would normally be a significant piece of evidence. On the other hand, the matching of two pieces of drawn wire by the correspondence of equally detailed die marks on their surfaces would show only that the two pieces of wire had been drawn through the same wire-making die during manufacture. Since thousands of feet of wire could bear these same marks, this finding would ordinarily have less significance than would being able to say that the two pieces came from the same original piece of wire. Only direct physical matching techniques would allow a conclusion as to whether two pieces of wire had a common origin. Die marks on wire may be considered toolmarks (Chapter 14). Bitemarks in certain materials, such as cheese or fruit, may exhibit striation characteristics which can be useful in comparisons.

Unusual examples of striation markings can be important in cases where contact between two surfaces has taken place. Even if a slight amount of sliding contact is suspected, the possibility of striation mark evidence ought to be considered. In one case, a car fleeing a liquor store robbery was driven over a short metal post that was part of a parking lot divider. The post contacted the car's oil pan and tore a small hole in it. The resulting oil trail was followed for several miles before it ended. A suspected car was found broken down a few miles from the end of the oil trail. This car had a hole in its oil pan, and the engine had seized from lack of oil. Proof that this was indeed the car that had been driven by the robbery suspects was obtained by comparing striation marks on the oil pan with exemplars made in soft lead using the metal post. Striation marks can be useful in reconstructions as well as in individualizations. Striation markings are compared using a comparison microscope. The technique is further discussed in Chapter 14 in connection with toolmarks and firearms.

General Form Comparisons

Pattern individualizations by comparisons of general shape or form are subjective in nature. An example of this type of comparison was discussed in Chapter 8: the individualization of hair by the microscopical morphological approach. It was pointed out that these comparisons, although intrinsically subjective, can yield valuable information when they are carried out by skilled and experienced individuals. Facial recognition is an example of an everyday use of this basic process that is widely recognized as being valid. Mistakes in facial recognition are rare when the face in question is familiar to the observer. Most errors in eyewitness identification occur when the witness is not familiar with ths suspect.

A further example of this process is handwriting comparison (Chapter 13). The comparison of a questioned handwriting sample with known standards is a distinctly different process from the one used for typewriting. Typewriting is an example of an imprint. Handwriting is not amenable to the kind of point-by-point comparison process used for imprints. Two signatures written at the same time by the same individual are rarely, if ever, exactly alike. In fact, if two signatures were found to be superimposable, it would suggest that one had been traced from the other, a crude forgery attempt. Because of this intrinsic signature-to-signature variation, a document examiner focuses on the general features and forms of letters that are valuable in individualization. The individual forms selected depend on the extent and nature of the writing and on the experience of the examiner. A considerable amount of training and experience is necessary before this particular degree of shape and form recognition can be developed.

Two additional examples of general form comparisons may be mentioned. One is the comparison of dental x-rays for the identification of a person. These comparisons are a part of forensic odontology. The second is voiceprint comparisons. Voiceprints are graphic displays of variations in the sound patterns of an individual's voice. Comparisons of these chart records may be considered an example of general form comparison.

Despite the general validity of the shape and form comparison approach and the great skill of qualified examiners, it remains fundamentally a subjective process. Generally, comparisons of this kind are not as definitive as those with most other physical patterns used for individualization, although every case must be evaluated upon its own merits.

PHYSICAL PATTERNS IN RECONSTRUCTION

Certain types of physical patterns are particularly useful in the reconstruction of the events which caused them. In addition to identification and individualization, reconstruction is a very important part of the forensic scientist's work. Attempts at reconstruction require a careful, coherent approach to all the facts in a case. Identification and partial or complete individualization of evidence can be important to an overall reconstruction.

Crime-scene reconstruction techniques are employed to learn what actually took place in a crime. Knowledge of what took place and how or when it happened can be more important than proving that an individual was at a scene. A defendant may admit being at a scene but deny responsibility for the criminal act. Or the defendant may admit being involved but only in a way that is favorable to his or her defense. A skilled reconstruction can be successful in sorting out the different versions of the events and helping to support or refute them. The interpretation of physical patterns is central to reconstruction. Several fundamentally different types of patterns may have to be examined and studied in order to arrive at the overall reconstruction.

Certain types of physical pattern evidence are particularly useful in contributing to reconstructions. A few of them are discussed below. Bloodstain, glass fracture, and gunshot discharge and trajectory patterns are covered in detail later in this section. Fire patterns were discussed in Chapter 4.

Various specialized patterns can be exploited for limited purposes in reconstructions in particular cases. Some are obvious; others are more subtle. Some examples are: (1) markings indicating that a body has been dragged, (2) cut or scratch marks on a leather holster which could be used to indicate the position of the weapon it contained when force was applied to remove it, and (3) marks on the hood and/or roof of a car consistent with those characteristic of accidents in which pedestrians are struck.

There are other examples of more subtle patterns which can be used in reconstruction. A tire skid mark, for example, is such a pattern. Interpretation of tire skid marks is often more complex and potentially informative than many investigators realize. Details of skid marks, such as shape, spacing, and position on the roadway, are often as important as the length of the mark in reconstructing a traffic accident. Other, more general patterns are difficult to discuss in detail. Often, they are not even thought of or recognized as patterns. Proper interpretation of these patterns depends more on experience than on training. An example would be a pattern of evidence indicating activities which can be used to develop a *modus operandi* (MO). This knowledge could link crimes together at the investigative stage. Another example would be overall patterns of disturbance of the condition or position of objects or articles, such as furniture. These patterns can be of help in an investigation.

At times, track or trail patterns may be encountered at outdoor scenes. Proper interpretation of them may yield information about the class characteristics of the individual responsible for producing them, such as stature, weight, shoe size, stride length, or abnormalities of the foot or stride. These interpretations are more difficult than they might appear. They can be of great help in producing investigative aids, but caution should be exercised when facts for use in court are being sought. There is a real danger of overinterpreting patterns of this type.

A reconstruction of an actual case might well employ several of the techniques discussed here and some that have not been discussed as well. Reconstruction is a complex process, requiring both knowledge and experience in order to obtain accurate and meaningful results.

Reconstructions from Bloodstain Patterns

Bloodstain pattern evidence is often more valuable in solving a case than serological analysis, even in the favorable circumstances when blood can be individualized to a significant degree (Chapter 9). A situation like this could arise when a defendant does not deny having contact with a victim. Consider a case in which a woman is found murdered and her husband reports the crime, claiming that an unknown assailant was responsible. His version of the facts may include an innocent explanation for the presence of the victim's blood on his clothes. He could say, for example, that upon discovering his injured wife, he tried to revive her and acquired the bloodstains in the process. Extensive typing of the blood on his clothing and of both people's bloods, and demonstrating that it could have come from the victim but not the husband, would be of little value here. If, however, a forensic scientist, after a study of the clothing and the crime scene, was able to offer the opinion that the bloodstains on the clothing were consistent with a bludgeoning but inconsistent with a mere contact, it could be crucial to the outcome of the case.

Reconstruction from bloodstain patterns has been a long-neglected area but has received more attention during the past 20 years or so. The increased awareness of its importance can be attributed partly to recent growth and interest in forensic sciences, partly to an increase in the skill and educational background of investigators, and partly to the widely publicized advocacy of its importance by Paul Kirk, Herbert MacDonell, and others.

Much can be learned from a careful consideration of bloodstain pattern evidence. Failure to consider it where it is present can be a serious omission in the investigation. Investigators should be familiar with the rudiments of bloodstain pattern interpretation. However, extensive knowledge of physics and a good deal of experience are necessary before expert opinions can be offered. It is true that there are general guidelines in the interpretation of these patterns and that the basic principles can be taught, but the need for experience cannot be circumvented. Extensive bloodstain patterns may be present at scenes of violent crimes. Careful examination and documentation of them can make detailed reconstruction possible in certain cases. The approximate speed and direction of individual blood droplets can be learned from an examination of the stains they leave. In addition, the size of the stains can yield information about the nature of the force that produced the droplets. This information can then be combined with that obtained from studying the overall pattern to yield a reconstruction.

Falling, Projected, and Impacting Blood Droplets   The dynamics of blood drops as projectiles and falling bodies have not been studied in detail, although such work has been done with drops of water and milk. Milk has often been selected for this kind of experimental work because its opaque white color makes it an easy subject for high-speed stroboscopic photography.

The published work with blood to date has involved studies of the pattern records left by such drops after they have impacted a surface. These studies have established some basic facts and helped to create an awareness of the potential of bloodstain pattern interpretation in crime-scene reconstruction. However, the results of these studies should be used only as guidelines or indicators. A forensic scientist involved in a reconstruction should actually carry out tests and do so under conditions which approximate those in the case situation as closely as possible. When a drop strikes a surface, it undergoes a series of shape changes as a result of the impact itself as well as complex wave motions and interactions which are set up in the drop during impact. High-speed stroboscopic photos of falling and impacting liquid drops have been obtained and studied by Dr. Harold Edgerton of the Massachusetts Institute of Technology (Figure 11-10). Work of this type with blood droplets would help us in gaining a clearer understanding of blood-drop dynamics.

Falling drops are more or less spherical (Figure 11-11). This fact comes as a sur-

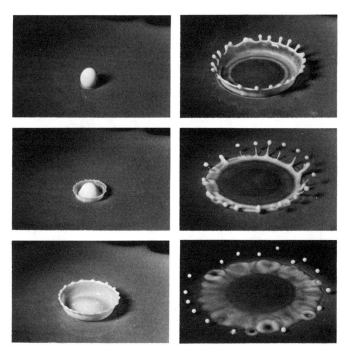

FIGURE 11-10
High-speed stroboscopic photographs of a drop of milk impacting a surface. *(Courtesy of Dr. Harold E. Edgerton, Massachusetts Institute of Technology and The MIT Press, Cambridge, Mass.)*

prise to most people, who have been influenced by the cartoonist's "teardrop" perception. The smaller a drop, the more spherical it will be during its fall. For larger drops, deviations from sphericity are caused by oscillations and air resistance. The oscillations decrease as the drop falls, and air resistance increases with increasing speed. The latter effect causes a falling drop to be squatter and flatter, quite the opposite of the teardrop. A drop falling in air will accelerate under the influence of gravity until it reaches a certain velocity at which the effect of air resistance offsets the acceleration. It then falls at a constant velocity known as its *terminal velocity*. Blood drops that form as a result of dripping have an average volume of 0.05 mL (50 μL). A drop of this size has a terminal velocity of about 25 ft/s which is attained after a fall of about 15 ft. For smaller drops, the terminal velocity is lower and is attained after falling a shorter distance. The opposite is the case for drops that are larger than average volume.

Interpretation of Individual Droplet Stain Patterns Individual blood droplet patterns can give several kinds of information: (1) an indication of the droplet's speed at the time of impact, (2) an indication of its direction of travel, and (3) an indication of the kinds of forces or actions that produced it.

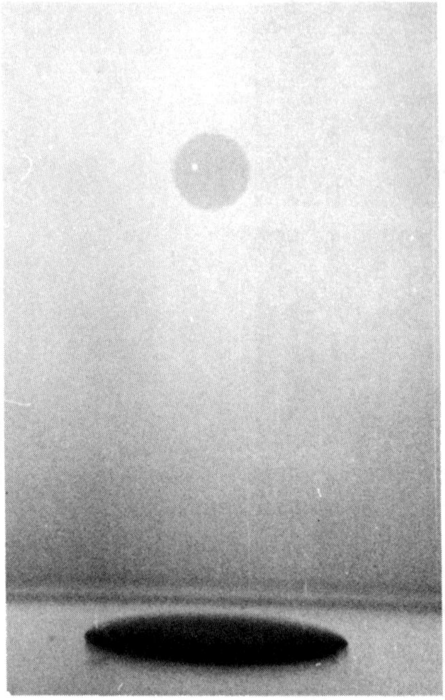

FIGURE 11-11
A high-speed stroboscopic photograph of a
blood drop falling in air. *(Courtesy of Peter
Pizzola, Forensic Science Laboratory, Police
Department, Yonkers, New York.)*

Speed   When a drop of blood strikes a surface normal to it (that is, straight on,
at a 90° angle from the surface), the shape of the spot deposited will be approximately circular, or at least relatively symmetrical (noteworthy exceptions can be
caused by target surface irregularities). In addition to the size of the original droplet,
the size of the pattern will be influenced by four other important factors: surface
texture, surface resilience, surface porosity or absorbency, and speed at the moment
of impact. The nature of the edge configuration of the spot and the extent to which
the shape varies from a simple circular one also depend upon these four factors (Figure 11-12). In general, higher velocities and rougher surfaces produce a more ragged
edge configuration. In some cases, "satellite" droplets are ejected and fall outside the
main area of the stain. Normal, or straight-on, impacts with hard, smooth surfaces
(such as glass) produce a spot which is almost perfectly circular with a smooth edge.
Droplets striking more resilient surfaces have a lower impact and therefore may leave
somewhat smaller spot patterns. With some absorbent surfaces, the blood can diffuse
(spread) laterally immediately after impact, yielding a larger stain. In other cases,
diffusion into the surface may occur more rapidly than along the surface. If such a

FIGURE 11-12
Patterns left by drops of blood falling from various indicated heights onto several different
surfaces. The angle of incidence is 0° in each case. *(Courtesy of Robert Adamo, Forensic
Science Laboratory, Office of the Medical Examiner, Westchester County, New York.)*

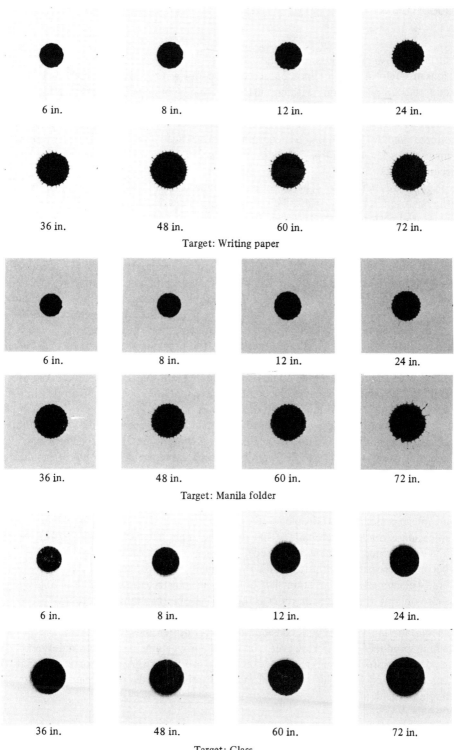

6 in.   8 in.   12 in.   24 in.

36 in.   48 in.   60 in.   72 in.

Target: Writing paper

6 in.   8 in.   12 in.   24 in.

36 in.   48 in.   60 in.   72 in.

Target: Manila folder

6 in.   8 in.   12 in.   24 in.

36 in.   48 in.   60 in.   72 in.

Target: Glass

surface is also resilient, smaller-than-usual stains may be produced. These observations are helpful as guidelines, but it would be unwise to apply them literally to stains in actual case situations without further testing. Nothing can substitute for actual experiments with the surface in question. When it is not possible to do so, a similar surface may be used for such control experiments, but the strength of the opinion offered should be qualified accordingly. The need for investigators to obtain unstained, known-control surfaces whenever possible is emphasized by these requirements.

Angle of Incidence The definition of angle of incidence used here conforms to the one used in optics to describe reflection and refraction of light rays. The angle is measured with respect to the normal to the surface, rather than to the surface itself. The *normal* is an imaginary line perpendicular (90°) to the plane of the surface. Thus, a straight-on impact (along the normal) is said to have an angle of incidence of zero. Some other writers on this subject describe an *impact angle* measured with respect to the plane of the surface itself. In that system, a straight-on impact would have an impact angle of 90°. The angle in the system we are using can be found from that in the other system by subtracting it from 90°. It is important to know what definition is being used when reading discussions of blood patterns.

Mechanisms similar to those described in the previous section are involved when a drop strikes a surface at an angle. The five factors cited must be considered here, along with the new variable, angle of incidence. Here, blood that is projected away from the surface as a result of the complex wave motions set up in the drop at impact may travel further and land ahead of the main pattern.

Aside from this blood which falls ahead of the main drop, the remainder (or bulk) of the pattern can be viewed as corresponding roughly to the shape (although not necessarily size) of the droplet's projected area at a particular angle of incidence. The *projected area* corresponds to the shadow cast on the surface by a nearly spherical drop if the suspended drop and the surface could be illuminated by a distant point source of light. If the light were to fall on the surface parallel to the normal, an interposed spherical droplet would cast a circular shadow. As the angle of illumination is made more oblique (that is, as the angle between the illuminating beam and the surface normal is increased), this drop would cast a shadow which would become increasingly elliptical. This rough analogy can be used to explain the generally elongated shape of stains left by drops which strike a surface at an angle. The more oblique the angle, the more elongated will be the stain (Figure 11-13). With actual blood droplets, particularly at smaller angles of incidence, impact results in the production of stains with considerably larger dimensions than those of the droplet which produced them. However, the rough proportionality holds, and the crude model is helpful in visualizing how the stains are formed. A trigonometric equation can be derived from this simplified model to relate the degree of elongation to the angle of incidence.

The equation is

$$\cos \theta = \frac{d}{D}$$

where d is the minor diameter (or width) of the elliptical stain, and D is its major

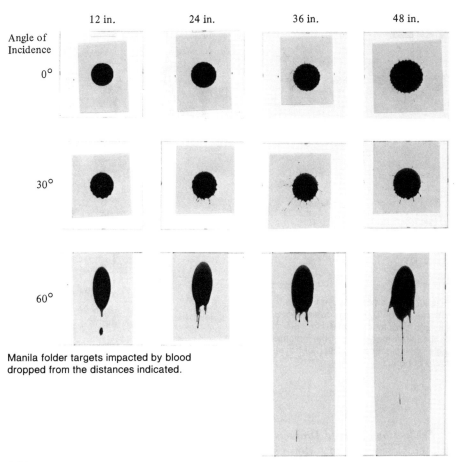

Manila folder targets impacted by blood dropped from the distances indicated.

FIGURE 11-13
Patterns left by droplets of blood impacting several target surfaces at different angles of incidence measured from the normal to the surface. (Continued on pages 302, 303.) *(Courtesy of Robert Adamo, Forensic Science Laboratory, Office of the Medical Examiner, Westchester County, New York.)*

diameter (or length). Since we usually want to know θ and can measure d and D, the inverse form of this equation

$$\theta = \arccos \frac{d}{D}$$

is of more practical significance. This formula is useful for determining the approximate angle of incidence from measurements of the ellipticity of the stain. A simple trigonometric table or scientific calculator can be used to find the values of the arccosine once the d/D ratio has been computed. Since this equation is only an approximate description of the behavior of actual blood droplets, the abbreviated table presented here (Table 11-2) is quite suitable for field investigation purposes.

Angle of Incidence

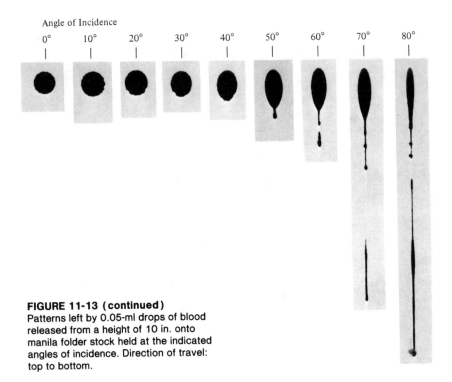

FIGURE 11-13 (continued)
Patterns left by 0.05-ml drops of blood
released from a height of 10 in. onto
manila folder stock held at the indicated
angles of incidence. Direction of travel:
top to bottom.

Production of Blood Droplets Blood droplets can be produced in several ways. If a droplet is allowed to form slowly, it will have a volume close to the 0.05-mL average mentioned above. This average volume is typical of dripping blood. More rapid formation, taking place during more energetic interactions, such as in beatings, results in the production of smaller droplets. The extremely rapid and energetic interactions that occur during a shooting can yield very small droplets, the smallest of which are similar to the fine droplets produced by an aerosol spray can. When stains resulting from such mistlike droplets are seen, it is a good indication that they resulted from a gunshot discharge or other highly energetic event such as an explosion. However, the context and overall pattern of such small stains must be taken into account before a conclusion is drawn. A reconstruction should not be based on one or a few isolated stains. Other phenomena can produce such tiny droplets, and on occasion stains from such a source might be encountered in an investigation. Caution and experience are necessary to avoid pitfalls in interpretation.

Types of Bloodstain Patterns Different forces and activities result in the production of different kinds of bloodstain patterns. Analysis of the patterns can yield important information about their manner of production and thus be of value in reconstruction.

FIGURE 11-13 (continued)
Patterns left by 0.05-ml drops of blood released from a height of 10 in. onto smooth white writing paper held at the indicated angles of incidence. Direction of travel: top to bottom.

TABLE 11-2
COSINES AND ANGLES

Width/length ratio d/D ($\cos \theta$)	Angle of incidence θ (arccos d/D)	Width/length ratio d/D ($\cos \theta$)	Angle of incidence θ (arccos d/D)
1.00	0°	0.71	45°
0.99	5°	0.64	50°
0.98	10°	0.57	55°
0.97	15°	0.50	60°
0.94	20°	0.42	65°
0.91	25°	0.34	70°
0.87	30°	0.26	75°
0.82	35°	0.17	80°
0.77	40°	0.09	85°

Radial Spatter Patterns from Blows A weapon striking pooled blood causes it to fly out in a radial pattern, much like spokes of a wheel. A single blow is generally not sufficient to cause blood spatter. But after blood pools in the wound as a result of a first blow, subsequent blows will produce spatter. The scene, and probably the perpetrator, will be stained with the spattered blood. Sometimes, a sector of the pie-shaped radial pattern will be missing. Such a finding indicates that some object, which is no longer present, intercepted part of the spattered pattern. Often, this "object" is the assailant. The pattern of spattered blood on the person and clothing should correspond to the missing "piece of the pie". This information can be used to fix the position of the perpetrator at the time the blows were being administered.

Arc Patterns from Swinging Weapons Swinging a blood-covered bat, pipe, or other similar weapon causes accumulated blood to be thrown off. This blood will travel tangentially to the arc of the swing until the effect of gravity causes it to begin to fall or until it encounters surfaces such as ceilings, walls, or furnishings. The pattern of bloodstains on these surfaces can be used to define the plane of the arc of the weapon swing. This information can be used in locating the position of the assailant as well as in indicating how the weapon was swung. The pattern may also indicate whether the assailant was right- or left-handed, but such a deduction drawn from swinging weapon arc patterns can easily be wrong. Such conclusions should be reached with considerable caution.

Patterns from Artery Spurts If an individual is wounded and an artery is severed, the pressure of the blood in the artery may cause blood to spurt from the wound. Since the pressure in the artery is produced by the pulsating contractions of the heart, it rises and falls with each heartbeat. Thus, the force with which blood is projected from such a wound will also fluctuate. As more blood is lost or as the victim gets weaker from other wounds, the force of each succeeding artery spurt lessens until the spurting ceases. A moving victim of such a wound can leave a very distinctive pattern on floors or nearby walls. Although these patterns are not very often encountered, they can be helpful in reconstructing the spatial (geometric) and temporal (time or sequence) relationships of the event when they are found and recognized.

Trail Patterns Bloody trails are quite commonly seen in the investigation of crimes of violence, but they may also occur in crimes of stealth. It is not uncommon for a burglar to get cut in the process of breaking and entering through a window, for example. If the wound is significant and not immediately bandaged, a trail of blood may result. Such trails can be useful in reconstruction. They may yield information about the movements of both victim and perpetrator. The dripping blood need not come from a wound. A blood-covered weapon can drip blood for a limited distance as it is being carried from a scene.

Flow Patterns and Pools Stain patterns indicating the direction of flow of shed blood on the body or clothing of a victim are a record which can be interpreted to yield reconstructions concerning postmortem disturbance or movement of the body. In addition, a study of the degree of clotting or drying involved can help in the estimation of the time lapse from bloodshed to alteration of the body's initial position. Time is required for shed blood to separate into cells and serum. This time can vary with conditions but can be estimated if the conditions are known.

The extent and nature of blood patterns at crime scenes can be used to estimate the volume of blood shed. Such estimates can be important in scene interpretation. For example, if the estimate of the volume of blood shed at the scene plus that remaining in the body is considerably less than the victim's expected blood volume during life, this can suggest that the scene may be a *secondary scene*. Such information would indicate that the body has been moved to this location from the place where the killing took place, that is, the *primary crime scene*. This knowledge could profoundly affect the reconstruction and prompt investigators to search for the primary crime scene and perhaps uncover considerably more evidence in the process.

Contact Patterns and Transfers A bloody object coming into contact with a surface can produce a useful and distinctive bloodstain pattern. Such a contact pattern would not normally be confused with a pattern produced by falling projected blood. The pattern may reveal class or individual characteristics of the bloody object (fingerprints, footprints, fabric imprints, etc.) or may yield important information about how the event took place. In some cases, both kinds of information can be derived from the same pattern. Further information regarding the time or sequence of events can also be obtained from such a pattern. For example, if such a pattern revealed that the blood had started to clot when the transfer took place, this finding would indicate that the pattern was not produced immediately after the blood was shed. Some interval of time (perhaps 10 min depending on environmental conditions) must have elapsed. Carefully conducted controlled experiments can sometimes help in pinpointing this interval. Details of the shape of patterns can also be quite important. Patterns such as those produced by bloody hair, for example, are often quite distinctive and can indicate the position of a victim's head at some point (in both space and time) during a crime.

Blood Patterns from Shootings Shooting wounds caused by weapons that fire a single projectile (handguns, rifles) or multiple projectiles (shotguns) may be of two types: perforating or penetrating. In a *perforating* (through-and-through) wound, blood droplets of various sizes along with some tissue will be expelled from the exit wound and travel in a conical pattern in the general direction of the bullet or shot (forward spatter). The amount of forward spatter resulting from a perforating wound (particularly from a shotgun) can be rather extensive, and a good deal of tissue will be carried out of the wound. In addition, a smaller amount of blood may be projected back toward the weapon from the entrance wound. This is known as back spatter. Figure 11-14 shows forward and back spatter in a laboratory experiment. In a *penetrating* wound (one in which there is entrance, but no exit), there will clearly be no forward spatter.

The blood droplets produced by shooting wounds have a range of droplet sizes, regardless of the direction in which they are projected. This range may include some very large ones, particularly in the case of perforating shotgun wounds. Other droplets will be very small, unlike those found in most other blood patterns. These fine,

FIGURE 11-14
The blood pattern left on a target surface placed near a blood-soaked sponge which was struck by a 0.22 caliber bullet traveling parallel to the plane of the target surface. The direction of bullet travel was from right to left (arrow). Notice the smaller amount of back spatter compared with forward spatter. *(Courtesy of Robert Adamo, Forensic Science Laboratory, Office of the Medical Examiner, Westchester County, New York.)*

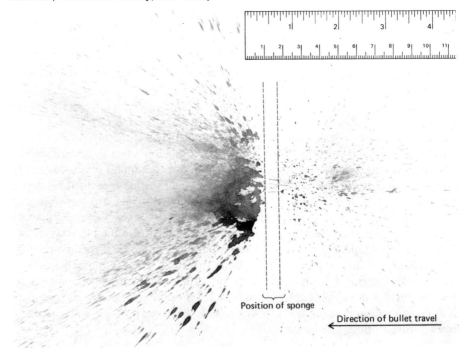

Position of sponge

Direction of bullet travel

mistlike droplet patterns are characteristic of highly energetic interactions between objects and liquid blood, such as in shootings. As noted above, however, the possibility of events other than shootings having produced such patterns must be considered when they are observed. If a shooting takes place near a wall or other vertical surface, the fine droplets may produce a pattern on this surface. If no vertical surface is near enough to the victim, these droplets will drift to the ground or floor. Very fine droplets do not travel very far in air—rarely more than a yard horizontally—even if they had high initial velocities. The distance which they are able to travel is influenced, of course, by other factors, such as the height at which they were produced and wind or air currents. People who have observed the discharge from an aerosol spray can in a shaft of sunlight can easily appreciate how rapidly the velocity of the mist droplets decreases with distance from their source. The presence of very small (submillimeter) droplet stains on a floor or on an object on the ground outdoors indicates that a highly energetic event, such as a shooting, took place in the vicinity. The precautions we have indicated must be considered in arriving at an interpretation of these patterns, however, since there are other interactions that can produce them.

A firearm can produce fine droplets of blood without actually ejecting them from a wound. A bullet impacting a bloody surface can produce spatter with droplet sizes in this range, as can the discharge of a blood-covered weapon. In the latter case, blood which has found its way into recesses around the cylinder of a revolver, for example, can be sprayed out when the revolver is subsequently discharged.

Close-range shootings provide the opportunity for some of the back-spattered blood (from the entrance wound) to be projected onto the shooter and the weapon. Small droplets may even be deposited inside the muzzle of the weapon after the expansion of gases from the explosion of the cartridge has ceased. An investigator should be alert to the possibility of finding bloodstains on a weapon and even in the barrel. The presence of these blood droplets can be important in the reconstruction of the distance between weapon and target and of the sequence of shots if more than one were fired. The weapon should not be test fired (Chapter 14) until these points have been carefully checked and documented by a criminalist.

Precautions in Preserving and Interpreting Bloodstain Patterns Fairly detailed reconstructions are sometimes possible from careful and thoughtful analyses of bloodstain patterns. Reconstruction of the geometry and spatial relationships between people and objects can be learned from their examination. Reconstruction of the temporal relationships and the sequence of events may also be possible. Much of this potential information can be lost, however, if there is a lack of awareness of the value of bloodstain pattern evidence on the part of investigators. It is important that bloodstain patterns be documented carefully prior to evidence collection. Experience, thoughtfulness, and careful observation during the initial investigation can yield good dividends later on.

Reconstruction hypotheses that are developed must take all the facts and observations into account. Facts cannot be ignored because they fail to fit the hypothesis. Interpretation by the investigator and the criminalist should be a true scientific endeavor, and not mere guesswork. An ongoing objective reevaluation and testing of one's hypotheses is necessary. This process should involve actual experiments where possible and appropriate. There is always a potential for overinterpretation of stain pattern evidence because of inexperience (or even outright unscrupulousness). In cases where the scene has been well documented and evidence properly collected, however, such problems are less likely to arise.

Reconstructions from Glass Fracture Patterns

Glass as physical evidence was discussed in Chapter 7. Broken glass at a scene can sometimes aid in reconstructions and thus provide useful information about the events which took place. In order to understand how this type of analysis can be done, it is necessary to know something about the way glass fractures. If we take a window pane as an example, we can analyze the way an applied force produces a fracture. Consider a slowly increasing force applied at a point near the center on one side of the pane until slight deformation takes place. At this time, the surface opposite the point of contact will be under tension. If the force is increased until the tension exceeds the tensile strength of the glass, a crack will start at this point. The crack or cracks will proceed in two directions: it will propagate from the side *opposite* the point of contact toward the surface where the force was applied; at the same time, it will spread outward from the point of contact (Figure 11-15). This type of crack or fracture is commonly called a *radial fracture* because it appears to radiate outward from the center. The important point to remember about a radial fracture is that the crack starts on the side opposite the applied force. Radial fractures result in the production of several nearly triangular or pie-shaped sectors of glass. If the force does not continue, these pieces of glass are held in place by the third side of the "triangle," an imaginary line connecting two adjacent radial fractures.

Continuation of the force would be expected to produce a fracture along the third side of the triangle, thus separating the triangular piece from the main body of the glass. This fracture is different from the radial types that form the other two sides of the triangle. Just before this fracture takes place, the glass in the area of the third side is under tension on the same side as the applied force. Thus, unlike the situation with the radial fracture, the crack starts on the same side as that on which the force was exerted. This type of fracture is known variously as a tangential, spiral, or concentric fracture. Radial and tangential fractures are illustrated in Figure 11-16.

When a piece of glass from a broken pane is examined, it is usually easy to tell which edges represent radial and tangential fractures. A closer examination of a broken edge can reveal the direction of travel of a break. This is done by studying and interpreting irregularities known as rib marks (Figure 11-17). These are curved lines on the fracture surface that resemble rib bones. The rib mark is perpendicular to the glass surface where the crack was initiated and is nearly parallel to the surface where it terminates. The direction of propagation along the length of the crack is *from* the concave side of the rib mark pattern *toward* its convex side.

This kind of information can be used to determine whether a window was broken inward or not. In order to do it, however, investigators must have certain critical parts of the window. With isolated pieces, it may not be possible to distinguish

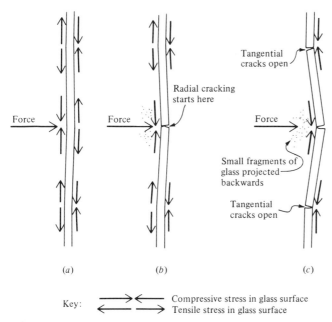

Key: $\longrightarrow \longleftarrow$ Compressive stress in glass surface
       $\longleftarrow \longrightarrow$ Tensile stress in glass surface

FIGURE 11-15
Steps in the fracture of sheet glass. The figure shows a side view
of the glass as progressively greater force is applied normal to one
surface. *(a)* Slight deformation or bending takes place as the
force is first applied. This deformation is exaggerated for clarity in
the drawing. *(b)* Continuing force opens radial cracks on the side
of the glass opposite the force. *(c)* Finally, additional force opens
tangential cracks which start on the same side of the glass as the
applied force. Also note small fragments of glass are projected
rearward from the area where the force is applied. This latter
observation often accounts for the presence of glass fragments in
a burglar's clothing.

between the inner and outer surfaces unless the investigator has marked them. In
situations where the need to mark them has been overlooked, clues at the edge of a
nearly complete pane, such as the presence of putty, or a certain color or sequence
of colors of paint, can be very helpful. Once a determination of inner-vs.-outer surfaces has been made, it is a simple matter to examine the rib marks on either a
tangential or radial fracture surface and reach a conclusion. It is always a good idea
to double-check the conclusion reached by making another determination on a different fracture surface.

Other reconstructions are also possible from an examination of broken glass from
crime scenes. One well-known and rather simple example is the determination of the
sequence of shots from an examination of bullet holes in windows. Radial fractures
which end abruptly at a fracture line associated with another hole must be from a
later shot. This type of reasoning can be applied to pieces of glass containing multiple
bullet holes. A determination of spatial relationships, such as bullet trajectories and

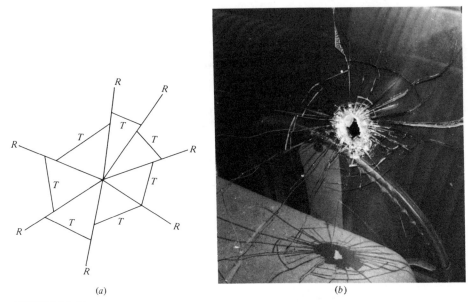

FIGURE 11-16
(a) Radial (R) and tangential (T) fractures in glass. *(b)* Radial and tangential fractures associated with a bullet hole in an automobile windshield. The pattern is complicated somewhat by the fact that this is laminated (one layer of plastic between two of glass) safety glass. *(Courtesy of Paul Hebert, Connecticut State Police Forensic Science Laboratory.)*

blood patterns, can also be aided by reconstruction work with glass. Figure 11-18 shows the patterns left by sequentially fired bullets which have pierced a pane of glass.

Reconstructions in Shooting Cases

Gunshot Residue Patterns Gunshot residue patterns are useful in reconstructing shooting events. The size, shape, and distribution of the pattern can also provide valuable information in estimating the distance from which a shot was fired. The methods normally used to determine the pattern involve placing chemically impreg-

FIGURE 11-17
Rib and hackle marks. The large curved lines are rib marks. The smaller lines perpendicular to these are the hackle marks. In the illustration the crack first opened on side A, moved toward side B, and then progressed from left to right (arrow).

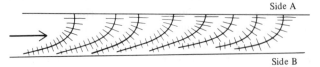

Side A

Side B

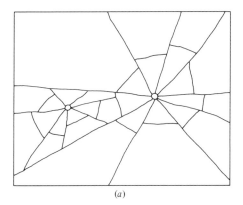

(a)

(b)

FIGURE 11-18
(a) Reconstruction of the sequence of bullet holes in window glass. The sequence of
shots fired through a pane of glass is usually obvious from an examination of the
fracture lines. When this information is combined with that from a determination of
direction, it should be possible to tell which of two shooters on either side of the
glass fired first. *(b)* Three bullet holes in a windshield. *(Courtesy of Theodore
Yarusewicz, Connecticut State Police Forensic Science Laboratory.)*

nated papers in contact with the surface and then applying heat and other chemicals. The end result is a pattern of colored spots on the paper, each representing areas where residue particles were present. A number of chemicals not present in gunshot residues can give false-positive results with these techniques, but this is normally not a serious problem with pattern determinations on cloth because the pattern of a gunshot discharge is usually quite distinct and difficult to duplicate by accident. If the unknown surface yields a positive result and the pattern is consistent with that produced by a firearm discharge, then it is usually correct to interpret the pattern as produced by gunshot residues.

Distance Estimation　In a shooting case, it is frequently necessary to try to estimate the distance of the gun muzzle from the target at the time of firing. This determination can be important in cases of suicide or when there are claims of self-defense. A shot fired under either of these circumstances would not have originated from any great distance.

Distance determination generally involves the identification of gunshot residues and the interpretation of both shot and powder patterns. In close-range shots, gunpowder or other discharge residues are deposited around the entry hole. Microscopical examination of the victim's garments and the target surface reveals the presence of gunpowder residue. These particles are readily identifiable by their characteristic shape, color, and pattern. If black soot and smoke particles are found around the bullet hole, it generally indicates that the discharge occurred close to the target. The presence of scattered gunpowder particles without black carbonaceous deposits indicates that the discharge occurred at medium range (approximately 18 to 30 in., depending upon the weapon, the ammunition, the load, and so on). If a weapon was fired from a distance fairly far away from the target, no powder residue is usually found.

The patterns of discharged residues are often circular in shape. A noncircular shape indicates that the shot was fired at some angle with respect to the normal to the surface. The spread of the pattern is directly related to the distance, given the same weapon, target surface, and ammunition. When the target is close to the muzzle, the pattern is relatively small and dense. The farther from the gun the target is placed, the more spread out and sparsely distributed the discharge pattern grows. The precise distance between a weapon and its target, however, must be determined by careful comparison of powder patterns produced by the suspect gun using similar ammunition and a similar target surface. Figure 11-19 shows a series of infrared photographs of powder residue patterns from a .32 caliber revolver with a 2-in. barrel, illustrating the effects of different muzzle-to-target distances.

The entry pattern on the target surface may also give an indication of the distance from which a shot was fired. If a muzzle impression is found, it usually indicates a contact shot.

Projectile Trajectory Patterns　Knowledge of bullet and shot trajectories can be used to help establish specific facts or to aid in an overall reconstruction. This discussion focuses on rifled bullets from handguns and rifles, but most of the prin-

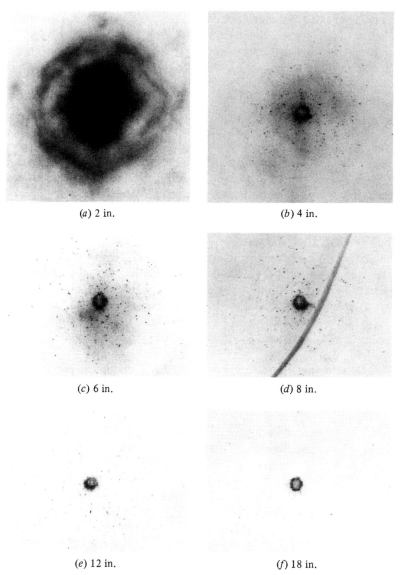

(a) 2 in.

(b) 4 in.

(c) 6 in.

(d) 8 in.

(e) 12 in.

(f) 18 in.

FIGURE 11-19
(a) to (f) Powder patterns from a .32 caliber revolver (shown half size). The six infrared photographs depict the density and distribution of carbonaceous material in the discharge residue from a .32 caliber revolver with a 2-in. barrel. The shots were fired normal to the surface from the indicated distances. Comparison of these known patterns with an unknown one produced by the same weapon would make it possible to estimate the distance the muzzle was from the receiving surface when the shot was fired. (*Courtesy of Joseph Reich, BCI, Westchester County Police and W. Reid Lindsay, Photographer, Forensic Science Laboratory, Office of the Medical Examiner, Westchester County, New York.*)

ciples are equally applicable to shotgun pellets or other projectiles where penetration has been sufficient to produce a well-defined record of the trajectory.

Whenever it appears that determination of trajectories would be useful, every attempt should be made to recover, or at least to account for, all of the projectiles involved. A cursory search is not sufficient. Unaccounted-for bullets can greatly complicate a reconstruction and leave room for raising doubts about its significance or validity later on. There will be occasions when even thorough searches by skilled and experienced investigators will fail to turn up a sought-after bullet or shell casing. Experience and judgment are necessary to decide when an unproductive search should be called off. In actual practice, these searches tend to be disorganized and too hurried. A search should not be called off until the investigator in charge is satisfied that the search was well planned and executed in a thorough, systematic, and methodical manner. As much information as possible should be available to investigators during the search. Accurate information about the number of shots fired is essential. The stories told by witnesses should be compared with the physical evidence. It is necessary to correlate the number of bullet holes with the number of recovered casings and projectiles. It may be desirable to maintain control of the scene until a final determination of the number of projectiles recovered from or remaining in the body of a victim has been obtained from the hospital or medical examiner's office. It is advisable to exercise caution before acting on the basis of preliminary information.

Methods of Determining Trajectory Patterns The tools necessary for trajectory determinations can be quite simple. For short trajectories, probes such as metal rods or wooden dowels can be used. They can be aligned with the holes and photographed from a few selected angles to document the trajectory. Probes are not practical for delineating trajectories which extend over long distances. String or twine can be used to trace out and illustrate trajectory patterns over moderate distances. For most situations, a gray or tan string will show up best in photographs. White or black string may be preferred in special cases where the background is all of a uniform contrasting color. The string method is unsuitable for long distances because the string sags too much under the influence of gravity. Here, optical methods such as sighting with the naked eye or a surveyor's transit or the use of a small low-power laser are of a more practical value. The laser method can be used for intermediate-range trajectories as well. It is more rapid for quick trials at establishing trajectories but requires the presence of some fog or smoke in its path for overall visualization and photographic documentation of the trajectory path. The laser beam is not visible as it passes through clean air. When a case is encountered in which several shots have been fired, a large number of possible trajectories may have to be studied and eliminated before the correct ones are found. The speed and ease of the laser method may be a distinct investigative advantage in these circumstances, despite the difficulty of photographic documentation.

Each of the above methods for delineating and documenting trajectories has tangible advantages in specific situations. No single one is best under every circumstance. The different methods are complementary. They are all based on the assumption that projectiles travel in straight lines. For projectiles traveling at high velocities over moderate distances in open space, this assumption is reasonably accurate. Over longer distances, or at relatively lower velocities, this straight-line approximation is not strictly valid. Here, a parabolic arc would more accurately describe the projectile path. Under these conditions, the effect of gravity on the projectile becomes more apparent, and the distance the bullet falls toward earth during the course of its flight becomes more significant. Of course, neither parabolic nor straight-line approximations apply to a bullet which strikes or penetrates some object and is deflected in the process.

In cases where several shots have been fired, a determination of individual bullet trajectories can be difficult. Careful application of trajectory determination methods may be helpful, however. Accurate alignment of corresponding pairs of holes can exclude some otherwise confusing possibilities. In addition, other evidence can be used to clarify certain points. For example, markings and residues on a recovered bullet, if noticed and documented, are helpful in determining what materials and surfaces the bullet has contacted or penetrated before coming to rest. Suppose that a distinct fabric impression were found on the nose of one bullet. If the pattern impression matches the weave pattern in the area of the bullet hole in a victim's garment, this finding strongly suggests that this was the particular bullet that passed through the body. Deformations of a bullet and scuff marks on its surface can often be used similarly to distinguish among two or more alternative trajectories.

Residues found on recovered bullets are often equally valuable. In a recent case, several members of a motorcycle gang fired numerous shots into an occupied building. One of the occupants was killed by a single shot that passed through his body and embedded itself in a wall. He had no other wounds. Standard firearms identification techniques ultimately allowed all the recovered projectiles to be matched to particular weapons in the possession of the gang members. These data did not, however, provide an answer to the question of which was the fatal bullet, and thus who had fired the fatal shot. The question was answered in this case because a knowledgeable, alert investigator found what appeared to be a bloodstain in the concave recess at the base of one of the bullets. Had this small stain not been noticed, it might have been washed away when the bullet was being cleaned in preparation for examination by the comparison microscope. Laboratory analysis confirmed the stain as human blood of the same type as the victim.

In another case, bullets traveling similar trajectories might be distinguished on the basis of residues adhering to or imbedded in them. Three bullets fired at a door containing glass windows could acquire different residues depending on what part of the door or surrounding area was pierced. One bullet might bear wood fragments, whereas another might contain glass particles. A third bullet, which just misses the door but passes through an adjacent wall might carry plaster particles with it. Such residues could be extremely valuable in sorting out the exact trajectories. An investigator should always be aware of these possibilities so that this kind of evidence will be recognized and preserved when it is available.

Applications of Trajectory Analysis as an Aid in the Recovery of Projectiles One of the simplest uses of bullet trajectories is to assist in locating and recovering projectiles. In some cases, determination of the trajectory will lead to the immediate recovery of a bullet. The final impact site may be located in a direct line with other parts of the trajectory. At other times, knowledge of the trajectory will help only in limiting the areas to be searched. Consider, for example, a bullet which has gone out through a window. It would be inefficient to search a large, poorly defined area outside the window. On the other hand, if the trajectory within the room were accurately known, it should be possible to predict the direction of travel outside with reasonable accuracy. However, estimating the distance of travel can present more of a problem. It would depend on the height and initial angle of elevation of the projectile trajectory upon leaving the room. It would also depend on the type of weapon (barrel length, etc.), the ammunition, and the amount of energy lost in passing through surfaces in the room. The last of these would be the most difficult to assess accurately. It is easy to see that accurate knowledge of the trajectory within the room could limit the region of search to a rather narrow angular area out of doors, but a degree of uncertainty as to distance might remain. Even this factor, however, might be limited by careful consideration of some of the variables affecting it.

If a bullet passes through only one fixed surface before exiting the room through an open window, it may be difficult or impossible to obtain an accurate trajectory. However, even in this case a careful interpretation could yield a limited range of angles for the possible trajectories. If the *known fixed point within the room* is some distance from a rather small open window, the angular uncertainty is relatively small compared with that when the only fixed point is near a large window opening. A similar amount of uncertainty can exist even when a bullet passes through a closed window if the broken fragments fall from the frame. In this case the determination of an accurate trajectory is possible if the window fragments can be reassembled so that the exact position of impact can be located.

Range Determinations Range determinations are a major aspect of the general problem of determining the position of the weapon or the shooter. Other aspects of this problem are discussed below.

One of the ways in which questions of range can be answered was discussed above in connection with close-range gunshot residue discharge patterns. Shot pellet patterns can also be interpreted to yield fairly accurate range determinations. The approach is very much like that used with gunshot residue discharge patterns, except that it requires no special chemical or photographic visualization methods and can be applied to moderately long ranges as well. In both cases, the determination will be more accurate and valid if the original weapon and ammunition are available for comparison testing.

Information obtained from studying the trajectory of a shot can often be used to set a limit on the maximum range from which the shot could have been fired. Once the trajectory is known, range determination can sometimes be quite straightforward and at times even simple. For example, if an undamaged wall were in the path of a line extending toward the original source of the shot from the first point in the known trajectory, it would be obvious that the shot had been fired from a point between the wall and the first known trajectory point. Less often, similar facts and reasoning can be used to establish minimum muzzle-to-target distances.

Special angular relationships can also be important. Consider a case where a bullet entry hole is found in a wall at a point 4 ft above the floor. Suppose that measurements made on the exit hole on the other side of the wall, combined with that of wall thickness, allow the conclusion that the trajectory is downward at a 45° angle. From this information, it can be concluded that the shot could not have been fired from any appreciable distance from the wall unless the shooter were suspended from the ceiling or at least positioned well above the floor level. Even in the unlikely event that the shot was fired from a height of 8 ft above the floor, the weapon could not have been more than 4 ft horizontally from the wall in this case.

Determining the Position of the Shooter Study of a bullet trajectory combined with knowledge of the scene geometry can yield information which is helpful in establishing the position of the shooter. The determination of range (discussed above), combined with the geometry of the trajectory, can often be used to fix the position of the weapon and thus of the shooter at the moment the shot was fired.

The geometry of a trajectory can be simple in cases where only a single shot was fired. Here, two or more holes which line up can be used to define the trajectory path accurately. Such an alignment, in and of itself, does not, of course, indicate which direction the bullet was traveling along the well-defined trajectory. Studying the trajectory in the context of scene geometry can be helpful in deciding the direction. If a careful examination and comparison of both sides of each hole allows entry and exit holes to be clearly distinguished, the direction of fire along the trajectory can be confirmed. Entry- and exit-hole determinations should never be based on the examination of only one side of a hole. Appearance can be deceiving. An entrance hole may resemble an exit hole, and vice versa, when it is viewed in isolation. The determination is valid only when both sides of each hole have been compared carefully.

When several shots have been fired in approximately the same direction, establishing the exact trajectory for any particular bullet can be complicated. In favorable circumstances, however, it may be accomplished by a careful application of the methods detailed above. Complications can also arise when one or more of the projectiles break apart or produce secondary projectiles. When a bullet fragments, it is difficult to predict the paths the individual fragments may take. If some of the fragments are not recovered, it will be impossible to determine the trajectory of the bullet prior to fragmentation unless other evidence is available. Secondary projectiles are fragments of an intermediate target material that acquire some of the bullet's energy when it impacts and fractures the material. Most of the fragments travel away from the impact site in the approximate direction of the bullet travel. As was the case with blood spatter produced by firearms, a range of fragment sizes may be produced. The effect of air resistance will be greatest on the smallest of these. Thus, the smallest fragments will slow most rapidly and will not travel as far. Larger fragments with high initial velocities may travel for considerable distances and may even have sufficient energy to embed themselves to other surfaces.

Additional sources of complication in trajectory determinations would include ricochets and other kinds of projectile deflections. It is probably safe to assume that a projectile will be deflected to some degree whenever it perforates a surface. The actual amount of deflection can vary considerably, however. Deflection for heavy, higher-velocity projectiles at small angles to less resistant surfaces would probably be very slight. On the other hand, large deflections could occur for lighter, low-velocity projectiles impacting or entering harder surfaces at larger angles of incidence. The possibility of deflection should always be considered. Prediction of the degree of deflection expected in a given situation is difficult and should not be attempted unless it is based on experiments under conditions which closely duplicate those of the shot in question.

Determining the Position of Movable Intermediate Targets When a trajectory through two or more fixed surfaces is known, the information can be used to fix the location and orientation of movable objects (including bodies) through which the bullet is known to have passed. This determination is easier in situations involving a single shot, but can sometimes be done in cases where several shots have been fired. However, even in cases where it cannot be done, an investigator can often limit the possibilities by ruling out certain positions and trajectories.

It is necessary to distinguish between entry and exit holes if the correct orientation of the intermediate target is of concern. The holes in both sides of the object and in the fixed surfaces should be examined and compared before a determination is made. As noted earlier, determinations should not be made on the basis of an examination of only one side of any one of the holes.

Lining up the bullet track in an object with the known trajectory at the scene is the first step in locating the position of the object at the moment the shot was fired. The next step is the determination of the orientation of the object with respect to the scene, using entry- and exit-hole information as noted. Even after these steps have been taken, some uncertainty may remain concerning the position of the body or other object along the path of the trajectory. In favorable circumstances, the geometric relationships of the trajectory and scene may limit this uncertainty. In other cases, it may be necessary to rely on the presence or absence of residues around bullet holes and the patterns of these residues where they are present. We have already seen that patterns of gunshot discharge residues around bullet holes can be used to estimate muzzle-to-target distances. These residues could include particles derived from the primer and the propellant as well as lead fragments from the bullet and contaminants in the barrel.

Intermediate targets (fixed or movable) through which a bullet has passed can also serve as sources of patterns which are useful in distance determinations. One example of this behavior is blood and tissue spatter patterns projected from a wound. A blood pattern can also result from a bullet impacting or passing through a blood-soaked object. Patterns can also be produced by the passage of bullets through other types of objects. A nearby surface is, of course, necessary to receive and retain the pattern. The receiving surface can be fixed or movable. As long as either the object which is the source of the pattern or the nearby receiving surface is fixed, a distance determination may be possible. If not, only a relative positioning is possible. Other examples of residue patterns are glass fragments from a window, building material particles from a wall, or fibers from clothing or other textiles. These can be carried into bullet holes (including wounds). They may be found even when no obvious pattern is evident around the hole. Without a pattern, an accurate distance determination may not be possible, but the identity of the particles themselves can be helpful in deciding the nature of the intermediate target as an aid in reconstructing the trajectory.

DOCUMENTATION, COLLECTION, AND PRESERVATION OF PATTERN EVIDENCE

Documentation

The major methods of documenting pattern evidence are notes, sketches (along with measurements), and photography. The purpose of and need for notes and sketches are discussed in Chapter 2 and Appendix 2. Both are particularly valuable for pattern evidence to be used in reconstructions. They serve to correlate the details of the scene with patterns documented by other methods.

Locations of patterns and evidence bearing patterns should be determined as precisely as possible and thoroughly documented before any collection or preservation methods are employed. Information about the type, shape, and directionality of patterns should be documented in notes and sketches, along with appropriate measurements. Various photographic techniques are then used for additional and detailed documentation of the patterns.

Photographs need to be taken both at a distance from the pattern and close to it. Distance photos should reflect the general locations and orientation of the patterns, indicate their number, and show their positions relative to other evidence and landmarks. Close-up photos are taken to record the details and should, therefore, indicate size, shape, and any irregularities. To avoid distortion, close-up pictures should be taken with the camera film plane parallel to the plane surface containing the pattern. A tripod is recommended for most close-up pattern photography. Careful attention to focusing is essential if all the pertinent details are to be captured for future examination. Lighting should be directed obliquely at the indentation-type patterns to enhance and highlight the detailed characteristics. With the camera kept stationary in relation to the indentation, additional shots should be taken while moving the light source in 90° increments along a horizontal arc, from one compass point to another, until an almost complete orbit has been completed. The exact angles selected depend on the nature of the indentation. Shots at different camera settings should be taken along with the different illumination angles to ensure that the best possible results will be obtained. Case number, time, location, type of camera used, film, settings, photographer's name, and any other appropriate data should be recorded for each shot taken. (Appendix 3 supplies some basic information on the use of photography in forensic science.)

Collection and Preservation

Many different types of materials can contain or be a part of pattern evidence. It is preferable, whenever possible, to collect items containing pattern evidence intact and to transport them to the laboratory. This procedure should ordinarily be possible with items of evidence which can be examined by direct or indirect physical matching techniques. It also may be possible in some cases with items bearing imprints, indentations, or striations. However, these markings are often deposited in or on surfaces which cannot be transported. Examples are permanent fixtures, objects too large or cumbersome to move, or indentations in soft surfaces like mud, clay, wet sand, packed snow, or fresh tar. Sometimes, attempts to move or collect markings could result in their destruction. In these situations, lifting and casting techniques have to be employed in addition to photographic documentation.

Lifting of Imprint Patterns   Photography is the first step in the documentation and recording of a mark-impression-type pattern. After photographs are taken, an investigator should record all the detailed information about the pattern including the measurements. If the pattern is a mark such as a two-dimensional imprint on a readily movable object like glass, paper, floor tile, or a piece of wood, the entire item should be collected, marked and labeled appropriately, and transported to the laboratory. It is far better for a forensic scientist to be able to compare an item suspected of making the mark with the original questioned imprint, rather than with a photograph or lift. If an imprint is on a surface that cannot be removed, however, it should be lifted using a sheet of commercially available imprint lifting film. Fingerprint tape is sometimes useful if the mark is not too big, and this operation is exactly the same as the lifting of a developed fingerprint (Chapter 12). Following the lifting, the tape with the residue imprint is carefully placed on a colored rubber or plastic backing sheet. The color of the backing is chosen to provide maximum background contrast for the imprint pattern. If the imprint were a dark color, for example, a white lift-backing would be used, whereas a light colored imprint would be placed onto a black lift-backing. These lifts, as well as the one-to-one photographs of the imprints, can then be compared with inked imprints of the suspected shoe, tire, or other object suspected of having made it. Laboratory examination generally consists of a two-stage comparison. The first stage is a *class characteristic* identification. The size, width, and general pattern design of the imprint are compared with the suspected pattern. If all of these are found to match, then a class identification has been made. Following a class identification, the patterns are compared for flaws and irregularities. If all of these individual characteristics match perfectly, then a positive conclusion can be drawn.

Lifting tape can also be applied to the problem of documenting and collecting blood spatter pattern evidence after it has been photographed. This technique has the advantage of allowing blood evidence to be collected while preserving the pattern and the spatial relationships.

Casting Procedures for Indentation and Striation Patterns When a three-dimensional indentation pattern such as a footprint or tire track is encountered, a positive cast of it should be made. Several types of casting materials are available commercially. The procedure for casting with the most common casting material— plaster of paris—is shown in Figure 11-20. Detailed steps involved in a casting are as follows:

1 After photography of the indentation pattern with and without a scale present, the area to be cast should be carefully examined. Any precautions that seem to be necessary to protect the integrity of the indentation should be taken.

2 Large, loose pieces of foreign matter should be carefully removed, but without disturbing the surface of the mark. Any accumulated water or liquid can be removed with a pipette or plastic syringe.

3 The indentation is prepared for casting if necessary. When the three-dimensional impression is in loose, dry sand or soil, the surface must be prepared by spraying shellac or lacquer onto a cardboard deflector held above the indentation at a 45° angle so the sprayed liquid falls onto the pattern surface by gravity, rather than being propelled by a potentially disruptive jet of gas. The shellac or lacquer will harden the surface of the indentation once it has dried, making it suitable for casting. If the pattern is in very dry, firm dirt, it should be sprayed with a light oil.

4 A physical barrier to restrict the flow of the plaster must be set up around the indentation. Commercially manufactured metal frames are available for this purpose, but any material (cardboard, wood strips, metal frame) that will retain plaster and confine it to the immediate area of the mark will suffice. A little ingenuity with commonly available materials will solve most containment problems.

5 A rubber mixing bowl should be used for mixing the plaster. If the plaster is lumpy, it should be sifted through a screen to make the powder homogeneous. An amount of water sufficient for the area to be cast is placed in the mixing bowl. Plaster is slowly added to the water with constant, gentle stirring until the mixture has the consistency of pancake batter.

6 The plaster mixture is then poured into the indentation by holding the bowl close to the mark and deflecting the pouring liquid off a spatula just before it reaches the surface of the mark. The pour should be continued around the area of the indentation until the plaster reaches a depth of ½ in.

7 Wire or screen is placed on top of the poured plaster as a reinforcement device. The pour is now continued until the cast is 1 in. thick.

8 After allowing the cast to dry for about 10 min, identification data are scratched into the top of the cast which is allowed to dry completely. When the cast is completely dry, it can be removed from the indentation. No attempt should be made to clean soil or debris clinging to the cast because they may be valuable samples for future trace evidence comparisons.

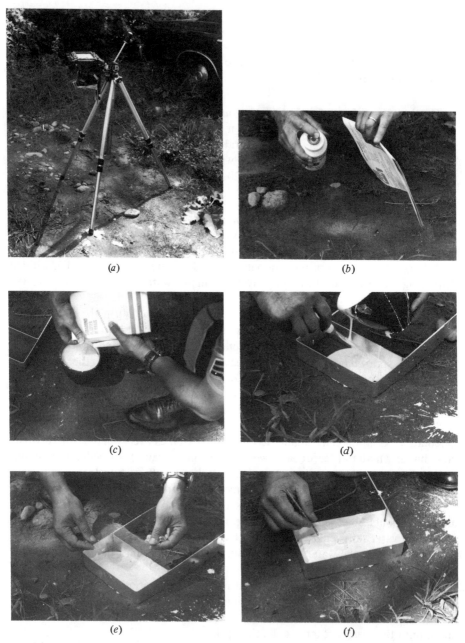

(a)

(b)

(c)

(d)

(e)

(f)

FIGURE 11-20

(a) Photography prior to casting an indentation in soil. The indentation is carefully photographed as found and with loose debris removed. A scale should be included in some of the photographs. Two scales at right angles are preferable. Lighting conditions should be varied if possible.

(b) Spraying a protective coating on the indentation. After loose debris has been removed, the heel mark indentation is carefully coated with a protective lacquer. The jet of spray is deflected before being allowed to fall on the indented mark. (c) Mixing the casting plaster. After a frame has been placed around the sprayed print, the plaster is mixed. A special-purpose frame is shown here, but the plaster can be retained by dams constructed from readily available materials (for example, wood, cardboard). (d) Pouring the plaster. The plaster is poured into the indentation carefully. A putty knife, spatula, or other device is used to break the fall of the

9 The finished cast should be wrapped in paper or other cushioning material, placed in a firm container, and sent to the laboratory.

Casting Materials The most common casting material used in the field is plaster of paris because it is inexpensive and easy to use. Plaster of paris is partially hydrated calcium sulfate. However, since ordinary plaster of paris has a greater expansion factor (0.25 percent) than dental plaster (0.19 percent), dental plaster is considered a slightly better casting medium for size comparisons.

Other casting materials, such as silicone rubber, moulage, wax, modeling clay, thermoplastic materials, and synthetic resins, can also be used for three-dimensional pattern reproductions. They are most commonly used to reproduce fine structure and microscopic detail in patterns, such as in fine striation marks, fabric indentations or bitemarks. They are seldom used to cast footprints or tire tracks.

Liquid silicone rubber is probably the most popular material for reproducing fine striation marks. Commercial liquid silicone rubber consists of two basic ingredients, a liquid silicone rubber base and a catalyst. The catalyst causes a polymerization reaction in the rubber base material (polymerization was discussed in Chapter 8). The catalyst and rubber base are mixed carefully and poured into the indentation. The catalyst causes the rubber base material to harden, after which the cast can be removed from the mark.

In the early part of this century, moulage was a very popular process for making face masks for identification purposes. Even today, it is occasionally used for casting detailed patterns. There are two basic types of materials used in the moulage technique, moulage positive and moulage negative. Moulage negative is a colloidal substance based primarily on agar, which is used to make negative casts or molds, from which a positive cast can then be made using moulage positive. The cast made with moulage negative is not designed to be permanent and will dry out. Permanent replicas require the production of the positive cast soon after the negative mold is ready. The negative material can be broken up after use and stored for future use. Heating in a boiling water bath will melt it so that is can be poured to make a new mold. Moulage positive is normally a wax-based material which can be liquified by heating, although sometimes plaster of paris may be used to make the positive. Where reproduction of fine detail is of primary importance, the wax-based casting material is better.

Special Casting Conditions Some situations call for special techniques if casting an indentation-type impression is necessary. Marks in snow are difficult to cast with plaster because of its exothermic properties during setting. The heat given off

---

plaster and to distribute it evenly over the entire indentation. *(e)* Reinforcing the plaster. Wire screen, gauze, cheesecloth, sticks, or similar materials can be added to reinforce the plaster. After this step, more plaster is added. *(f)* Labeling the cast. The cast is labeled before the plaster has set completely by scratching the case number, date, location, investigator's initials, etc., into the soft plaster using a stick, knife point, or similar device. *(Courtesy of Marius Venclauskas and David Paige, Connecticut State Police Forensic Science Laboratory.)*

by the plaster as it sets can melt the snow and destroy the detail. Such an indentation should be photographed and then cast with sulfur. In this procedure, flowers of sulfur is heated to reduce it to a liquid state. The sulfur should be stirred constantly during the melting process, and burning must be avoided. Once the sulfur has liquefied, it is allowed to cool while the constant stirring is continued. When it is sufficiently cool but still liquid, the sulfur can be poured into the indentation. The sulfur will harden immediately. The technique is very similar to that used in preparing the mark for plaster casting. Sulfur is useful for casting indentations in snow, because the solidification of sulfur, although exothermic, evolves less heat per gram than many other substances. The heat of fusion of sulfur is considerably less than that of water/ice. A newer method for casting marks in snow has been proposed. A commercial product known as Snow-Print-Wax has been developed for this purpose (Figure 11-21). The product is packaged in spray cans, and is used to coat the surfaces of the indentation. After the sprayed-on layer has dried, plaster of paris is employed in the usual fashion to cast the prepared indentation.

Indentation marks in mud, which are partly filled with water, are also commonly encountered. The water in the indentation should first be removed with a pipette or syringe, care being taken not to disturb the surface of the mark. Dry plaster is then sifted into the indentation until all the remaining water is absorbed. The cast can then be completed by pouring plaster in the usual way.

Marks in sand or soft powdery earth should first be sprayed with a dilute shellac or lacquer to harden the surface. The indentation can then be cast with plaster of paris.

LABORATORY EXAMINATION OF PHYSICAL PATTERN EVIDENCE

The simplest type of physical pattern examination is physical matching. Techniques were discussed above in connection with direct and indirect matches.

Different markings are compared on a point-by-point basis. The procedures and principles involved in these comparisons for several specific types of evidence are discussed in the chapters which follow. Examination and comparison of indentation or striation patterns can be accomplished by comparison of originals and exemplars or casts. The procedures involved and some of the principles which apply in obtaining appropriate exemplar markings are discussed below.

The cast of an indentation generally yields both class and individual characteristics. Class characteristics are those general properties which allow the object to be put into a certain category. Examples are the general size, type, and perhaps brand of a shoe, or the size, type, pattern design, and perhaps manufacturer of a tire. This information can be valuable to an investigator as a lead, or as an aid in locating a suspect or a particular kind of object. In addition, indentations may capture some of the individual characteristics of the object that made them. These will differ for each object, such as a shoe, tire, tool, etc. By comparing these individualizing irregularities in indentations, the marks can be traced to an original object.

Laboratory examination of a cast proceeds from the general to the specific, from

(a)

(b)

(c)

FIGURE 11-21
Casting indentations in snow. Casting indentations in snow poses special problems. A new product, Snow-Print-Wax, makes it possible to use plaster for casting indentations in snow. The inner surface of the indentation is coated with the spray before the plaster is used. (*Kjell Carlsson Innovation, Sundbyberg, Sweden. Distributed in the United States by Kinderprint Co., P.O. Box 16, Martinez, Calif.*)

class characteristics to individual ones. Class features are length, width, dimensions, pattern designs, distances between patterns, flaws, shape, length-to-width ratio, angles, numbers of lines in a pattern, and degree of bending. In a tire track imprint or indentation, the zigzag patterns, their number and dimensions, the number per unit length, and the degree of zigzag angle are important class characteristics.

Individual features of a pattern are those specific characteristics which indicate a particular individual object. These characteristics are developed as a result of wear, cuts, damage, irregularities, and other accidental or intentional marks. Such features are unique to a particular shoe, tire or other object. The probability is extremely low that two shoes of exactly the same brand and size will be worn in exactly the same way and damaged to exactly the same extent in precisely the same locations. Similarly, the chances of finding two different tires which have the same class and individual characteristics is very small indeed. Therefore, if the cast of an indentation bears exactly the same class and individual characteristics as a known object, it can be concluded that the object was responsible for the mark.

When making comparisons, allowance must be made for the shrinkage of the casting material and for abnormalities that result from making the cast. A plaster of paris cast is usually slightly smaller than the original imprint because of shrinkage of the plaster during dehydration, which occurs during hardening. Certain abnormal conditions must also be considered. If a person whose shoe made an impression was struggling, carrying a heavy object, or wounded, then the shape of the shoe indentation may be changed. Such circumstances could affect the comparison results and must be taken into consideration.

Another factor that plays an important role in comparisons of casts with known objects is whether the known object is recovered in essentially the same condition as when it is thought to have made the imprint. Continued wear and possibly additional damage or markings on the original object, if it is not recovered for some time, could greatly affect a comparison. The sooner a suspected tire or shoe or other object is recovered, therefore, the better for obtaining useful comparison results.

It is important that known shoes thought to have made the mark be used in making comparisons with a shoe impression cast. A known print of a suspect shoe must be used in comparison with photographs or with lifts. Known exemplar tire impressions (either imprint or indentation) should be made with the weight of the vehicle bearing upon the tires. A laboratory examiner must try to duplicate the conditions thought to have been prevailing when the questioned mark was made in making the known standard marks.

Tire track comparison is similar to footprints or shoe print comparison. When a tire track is compared with a known tire, class characteristics such as width, arrangement of land width, number of lands, land and groove patterns, and land and groove location are first compared. If the questioned track shows all these features, then the known tire can be placed in the same class of tires which made the track. Individual characteristics are compared next. These develop according to the types of surfaces on which the vehicle is commonly driven, the vehicle's mechanical and physical condition, inflation pressure, and the driver's driving habits.

These wear markings are valuable in individualizing a suspected tire, and as a result, a suspect vehicle. Accurate measurement of tire tracks can yield information about the manufacturer and possibly the year of production and model of a suspected vehicle. There are three important parameters for such identifications: wheelbase, front track width, and rear track width. Wheelbase is the distance between the front and rear axles of a vehicle. The track width relates to the length of an axle and is defined as the distance between centerlines of tread imprints on the ground. Track measurements can result in identifying a suspect vehicle. For example, a track with a 63.75-in. rear track width, 64-in. front track width, and 120-in. wheelbase could

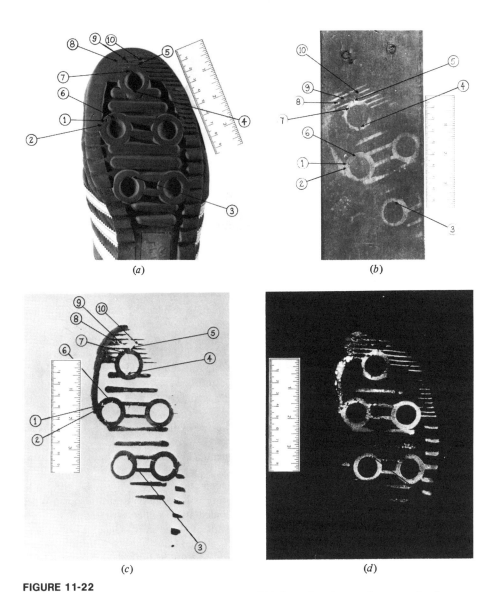

(a)   (b)

(c)   (d)

FIGURE 11-22

(a) Class and individual characteristics of a shoe. This is a mirror image of a suspect's shoe. The image reversal was obtained by printing the negative backwards. *(b)* A questioned shoe print found in dust at the crime scene. *(c)* An inked exemplar imprint of the shoe in *(a)*. *(d)* A talcum powder exemplar imprint of the shoe in *(a)*. *(Courtesy of Frederick C. Drummond and W. Reid Lindsay, Forensic Science Laboratory, Office of the Medical Examiner, Westchester County, New York.)*

have been made only by domestic vehicles in the 1974 and 1975 Chrysler Imperial line.

Figure 11-22 shows the class and individual characteristics of a shoe print.

STUDY QUESTIONS

1 Discuss some different types of cases in which physical pattern evidence would be important and why.
2 How are physical patterns used in identifications?
3 What is meant by physical matching?
4 What is a direct physical match? An indirect physical match? Give examples of each.
5 What is an imprint? What is an indentation? How are they different?
6 What is a striation? Give some examples of striation marks.
7 What is meant by a general form comparison? Give some examples of general form comparisons.
8 Explain how patterns can be used to assist in reconstructions.
9 What information can be obtained from bloodstain droplet patterns? Name several different general types of bloodstain patterns.
10 What information can be obtained from broken glass evidence? Discuss ways in which glass fracture patterns can help in reconstructions.
11 How can gunshot discharge residue patterns be used in estimating distances between shooter and target?
12 Discuss different aspects of determining projectile trajectory patterns. Of what value in an investigation is knowledge of a trajectory pattern?
13 Discuss the role of photography in documenting different types of physical pattern evidence.
14 What types of physical patterns should be collected by lifting techniques? Under what circumstances should lifts be used?
15 What types of physical patterns must be documented by casting techniques? Under what circumstances should casting techniques be used?
16 Discuss the general procedure for casting an indentation.
17 What special procedures are required for casting indentation patterns in snow? What procedures are needed in wet mud, where the indentation is filled with water?
18 What is the moulage process? What components are used in it? Under what circumstances is it used in forensic science?
19 What principles are involved in comparing physical patterns in the laboratory?
20 What are some of the special considerations in comparing casts with objects suspected of having made the indentation?
21 What kinds of exemplar markings are required for the comparison of imprints, indentations, or striations? What are some of the precautions that have to be considered in obtaining the different kinds of exemplars needed?

REFERENCES AND FURTHER READING

Abbott, J. R.: *Footwear Evidence,* Charles C Thomas, Springfield, Ill., 1964.
Auten, J. H.: *Traffic Crash Investigation,* Charles C Thomas, Springfield, Ill., 1972.
Baker, J. S.: *Traffic Accident Investigator's Manual,* 4th ed., Traffic Institute, Northwestern University, Evanston, Ill., 1963.

Bulbulian, A. H.: "A Professional Looks at Plaster Casts," *FBI Law Enforcement Bulletin,* September 1965.

Dolan, D. N.: "Vehicle Lights and Their Use As Evidence," *Journal of the Forensic Science Society,* vol. 11, p. 69, 1971.

Fawcett, A. S.: "The Role of Footmark Examiner," *Journal of the Forensic Science Society,* vol. 10, p. 227, 1970.

Given, B. W., R. B. Nehrich, and J. C. Shields: *Tire Tracks and Tread Marks,* Gulf, Houston, Tex., 1977.

Grogan, R. J., and T. R. Watson: "Tyres and Crime," *Journal of the Forensic Science Society,* vol. 11, p. 3, 1971.

Kirk, P. L.: "Identification by Patterns—Paper Separation Methods," *Journal of Forensic Medicine,* vol. 3, pp. 169–176, 1956.

Loughran, J. H., J. B. F. Lloyd, and T. R. Watson: "Murder Involving Discovery and First Application of Tyre Prints," *Nature,* vol. 256, p. 762, 1974.

"Tips on making casts and tire prints," *FBI Law Enforcement Bulletin,* October 1963.

CHAPTER 12

FINGERPRINTS AND OTHER PATTERNS FOR PERSONAL IDENTIFICATION

In 1892, a woman named Rojas living in La Plata, Argentina, murdered her two sons and in the process cut herself. She then blamed her neighbor for the attack. Bloody fingerprints on a doorpost were identified by Juan Vucetich, an Argentinian police officer, as belonging to the woman. This evidence led to her confessing to the crime. The case involved one of the first official criminal identifications by means of fingerprints left at the scene of a crime.

INTRODUCTION

Today, fingerprints are one of the most valuable types of physical evidence in criminal investigations. The fingerprints of the offender are often found at scenes in connection with a variety of crimes ranging from larceny to burglary to homicide. Besides their use in identifying suspects, fingerprint comparisons also make possible the apprehension of fugitives, determination of previous arrests, and identification of unidentified bodies, amnesia victims, missing persons, and mass disaster victims. Fingerprints are also used in various kinds of social and business activities as a means of personal identification.

In addition to fingerprints, a number of other types of patterns which could be used for individualizing persons could be encountered in the course of criminal investigations. The process of individualizing human persons is commonly known as *personal identification*. Examples of other individualizing patterns are palm prints, sole prints, voiceprints, and bitemarks. These patterns can yield considerable information about the identity of an individual. In many cases, these patterns if properly compared with known standards by qualified experts can result in an identification. Foot-

330

prints of infants have long been used in hospitals for identification. Other types of markings and patterns, such as ear prints, lip prints, tattoos, caste marks, and skeletal material forms have also been used in investigations.

FINGERPRINTS

There are two definite periods in the history of fingerprinting. The first period began when human beings became aware of fingerprints and utilized them as a means of of individual signature. The second period is much more recent and began with the development of fingerprint coding and filing systems and techniques of searching for latent prints.

The question of who was the first person to recognize fingerprints as valuable individualizing characteristics will probably remain unanswered. Unquestionably, however, the ancient Chinese and the Babylonians used fingerprints on business contracts, although it is not clear whether they realized that these were truly individual.

The development of fingerprinting as a means of individualization can best be described through accounts of the efforts of the pioneers in the field. William Herschel, Henry Faulds, Sir Francis Galton, Juan Vucetich, and Edward Henry have all been credited with contributing to the development of modern fingerprint identification procedures.

Sir William Herschel, British Chief Administrative Officer for the Hooghly District, Bengal, India, was the first known official to use fingerprints on a large scale. In 1858, Herschel was having trouble with natives impersonating others, and he required them to affix their fingerprints, as well as signatures, to contracts. Later, in 1877, he proposed the fingerprint system as a means of identifying prisoners as well as parties to civil contracts.

At the same time, Dr. Henry Faulds, then at Tsukiji Hospital in Tokyo, Japan, began his observations on fingerprints. In 1880, he published an article in *Nature,* a respected scientific journal, about his studies and suggested the application of fingerprints to criminal identifications. He discussed fully the potential for identifying criminals through fingerprints which had been left behind at the scenes of crimes. In 1892, Sir Francis Galton published the first text on fingerprints, simply entitled *Finger Prints.* Galton's studies established the individuality and permanence of fingerprint patterns. He made another important contribution by divising the first scientific method of classifying fingerprint patterns.

In 1891, Juan Vucetich, an Argentinian police official, set up a classification system based upon his own studies and Galton's pattern types. He was the first to set up fingerprint files to be used as an official means of criminal identification. As we mentioned at the beginning of the chapter, Vucetich has also been credited with the solution of the first case based on fingerprint evidence left at the scene of a crime. In 1901, Sir Edward Henry, then Inspector-General of Police in Bengal, India, and later Commissioner of London's Metropolitan Police, introduced fingerprinting as an official method for criminal identification in England. He simplified fingerprint classification and made it applicable to criminal identification. His system forms the basis of most modern 10-digit fingerprint identification systems.

There are three fundamental facts that have made fingerprints a superlative method for personal individualization and accepted by the courts as such:

1 An individual's fingerprint ridges are formed during fetal life, between 100 and 120 days of development, and remain unchanged for the remainder of a person's lifetime.

2 It has been shown empirically, with theoretical support, that fingerprints are unique. No two persons, even identical twins, possess identical ridge characteristics.

3 Fingerprint classification systems permit the development of files of systematically classified fingerprints and the ability to retrieve a particular file rapidly.

Fingerprint Classification Systems

Types of Patterns The fingerprint ridges, which can be observed on the inner surfaces of the hands, are known as *papillary ridges* (or *friction ridges*). These ridges occur in certain definite formations, and they can be classified into specific types of patterns. There are three basic fingerprint patterns from which are derived the fingerprint classification system. These are: *arches, loops,* and *whorls.* These basic patterns can be further subdivided into eight types:

1 Plain arch   **2** Tented arch
3 Ulnar loop   **4** Radial loop
5 Plain whorl   **6** Central pocket loop
7 Double loop   **8** Accidental

All the pattern types are formed by a series of lines, corresponding to ridges (hills) and grooves (valleys) on the skin of the fingertip. The skin is composed of two major types of cell layers. The outer layer (the surface) is known as the *epidermis.* The inner layer is known as the *dermis* (Figure 12-1).

By their relationship to one another the ridges form definite designs, and these are called fingerprint patterns. The area which displays the patterns of the fingerprint, and is surrounded by the type lines, is called the *pattern area. Type lines* are the two innermost ridges which run parallel and then diverge and surround the pattern area. The approximate center of the pattern is called the *core.* The outer, terminal, point of the pattern, nearest the type line divergence, is known as the *delta.* The pattern area contains all the ridge detail necessary to classify the print, although features outside this area may be useful in comparing latents with knowns. The eight basic types of fingerprint patterns are shown in Figure 12-2.

The *plain arch* is the simplest pattern. The ridges enter on one side, rise to form a wave in the center, and exit smoothly on the opposite side.

The *tented arch* is a variation of the plain arch. Ridges at the center are thrust upward in a more abrupt manner similar to the appearance of a tent pole.

The *radial loop* is a pattern in which one or more ridges enter on the side toward the thumb (the side on which the radius bone of the forearm lies), recurve, and then exit on the same side.

The *ulnar loop* is a pattern in which one or more ridges enter on the side toward

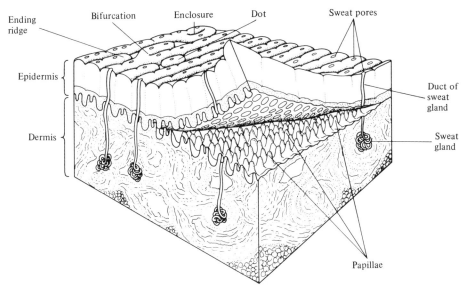

FIGURE 12-1
Cross-sectional view of the structure of friction skin. *(The Federal Bureau of Investigation.)*

the little finger (the side on which the ulna bone of the forearm lies), recurve, and then exit toward the same side.

The *plain whorl* is a pattern in which one or more ridges form a complete revolution around the center. Whorls generally have two or more deltas.

The *central pocket loop* is a variation of the plain whorl pattern. Some ridges tend to form a loop pattern, which recurves and surrounds a whorl at the center.

The *double loop* (*twinned loop*) is another type of whorl. In it two separate loop formations are present and may surround each other.

The *accidental* is a relatively rare type of pattern. This category is used to accommodate those patterns that do not conform to the patterns previously described, such as the lateral pocket loop of Figure 12-2.

Modified Henry System The goal of a classification system is to assign a working formula to a set of fingerprints which will enable the set of prints to be classified readily and/or located in a file. In South America, most police departments use a system devised by Juan Vucetich. In much of the rest of the world including Asia, law enforcement agencies have generally adopted a modified Henry system. The formula used by the FBI and by most police departments in this country consists of letters and numbers written above and below a horizontal line. It consists of the following subdivisions: key, major, primary, secondary, subsecondary, and final. The formula and its description are shown in Table 12-1. It will be helpful to refer to Table 12-1 often while reading through the discussion of fingerprint classification.

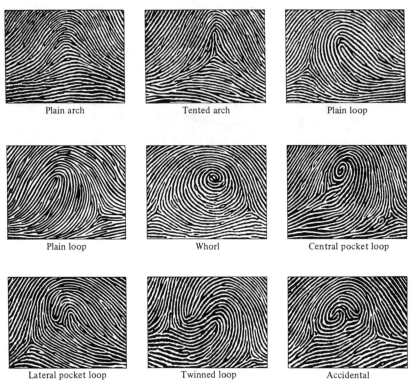

Plain arch   Tented arch   Plain loop

Plain loop   Whorl   Central pocket loop

Lateral pocket loop   Twinned loop   Accidental

FIGURE 12-2
Basic fingerprint patterns. *(Faurot Inc., Elmsford, New York.)*

The original Henry system consisted only of primary, secondary, subsecondary, and final subdivisions. Major and key subdivisions are used in modified systems which are discussed below.

Primary Classification This is the first classification step in the Henry system. Using primary classification alone, all fingerprints could be classified into 1024 groups.

1 The first step is to assign numerical values to the whorl patterns. (Arches and loops have no numerical value in the primary classification.) The value to be assigned to each finger is given in Table 12-2. If a whorl is found in No. 1 (R thumb) or No. 2 (R index), it is assigned a value of 16. On the second pair of fingers, No. 3 and No. 4, the value is 8. On the third pair, No. 5 and No. 6, it is 4; on the fourth pair, No. 7 and No. 8, the value is 2; and on the fifth pair, No. 9 and No. 10, the value is 1.

2 The second step in establishing the primary classification is to find the sum of the values assigned to even fingers and the sum of the values assigned to odd fingers. The even fingers are R index, R ring, L thumb, L middle, and L little; the odd fingers are R thumb, R middle, R little, L index, and L ring.

TABLE 12-1
FINGERPRINT CLASSIFICATION

Classification	Formula	Description
Primary	$\dfrac{17\ L\ \ 10\ U\ IOM}{19\ W\ OII\ \ \ 10}$	Obtained through the summation of the value of the whorls as they appear in the various fingers (see Table 12-2)
Secondary	$\dfrac{17\ L\ \ 10\ U\ IOM}{19\ W\ OII\ \ \ 10}$	The type of pattern appearing in the index fingers
Subsecondary	$\dfrac{17\ L\ \ 10\ U\ IOM}{19\ W\ OII\ \ \ 10}$	The value of the ridge counts of loops or tracing of whorls of index, middle, and ring fingers (detail, see text)
Final	$\dfrac{17\ L\ \ 10\ U\ IOM}{19\ W\ OII\ \ \ 10}$	The ridge count of loops of little fingers (detail, see text)
Major	$\dfrac{17\ L\ \ 10\ U\ IOM}{19\ W\ OII\ \ \ 10}$	The value of the ridge counts of loops or tracing of whorls of thumb
Key	$\dfrac{17\ L\ \ 10\ U\ IOM}{19\ W\ OII\ \ \ 10}$	The ridge count of the first loop appearing in fingers other than the little finger

3 After values for all fingers have been determined and totaled, the quantity 1 is added to each sum. The numerator and denominator of the primary classification are then formed as follows:

$$\frac{\text{Numerator}}{\text{Denominator}} = \frac{\text{even finger (No. 2, 4, 6, 8, 10) values} + 1}{\text{odd finger (No. 1, 3, 5, 7, 9) values} + 1}$$

Suppose, for example, a person's R thumb, R ring, L index, and L little fingers showed whorl patterns, and all the other fingers showed loop patterns. The primary classification would be determined as follows:

$$\frac{\text{Numerator}}{\text{Denominator}} = \frac{(0+8+0+0+1)+1}{(16+0+0+2+0)+1} = \frac{9+1}{18+1} = \frac{10}{19}$$

TABLE 12-2
VALUES ASSIGNED TO WHORLS FOR PRIMARY CLASSIFICATION

No. 1 (R thumb)	No. 2 (R index)	No. 3 (R middle)	No. 4 (R ring)	No. 5 (R little)
16	16	8	8	4

No. 6 (L thumb)	No. 7 (L index)	No. 8 (L middle)	No. 9 (L ring)	No. 10 (L little)
4	2	2	1	1

Notice in Table 12-1 how this fits into the overall classification formula. The extreme values of primary classification are $\frac{32}{32}$ (when all 10 fingers have whorl patterns) and $\frac{1}{1}$ (when no whorls are found on any finger). About 60 percent of the population falls into the $\frac{1}{1}$ category.

Secondary Classification The secondary classification is based on the types of patterns appearing on the index fingers. Each pattern is represented by a capital letter (as shown below). The letter representing the pattern on the right index finger is entered in the numerator, and that of the left index finger in the denominator. Designations for the patterns are

$$W = \text{whorl}$$
$$U = \text{ulnar loop}$$
$$R = \text{radial loop}$$
$$A = \text{plain arch}$$
$$T = \text{tented arch}$$

If, for example, the right index finger showed an ulnar loop, and the left index finger showed a plain whorl pattern, the secondary classification would be $\frac{U}{W}$. The way in which this portion of the overall classification formula fits into the whole can be seen in Table 12-1.

Small-Letter Groups These classifications require prints in which an arch or tented arch pattern appears on any finger or prints with a radial loop pattern on a finger other than the index fingers. An arch is represented by a, a tented arch by t, and a radial loop by r. If an a, t, or r appears on fingers other than the index fingers and thumbs, the subsecondary classification can be eliminated.

Subsecondary Classification Subsecondary classification is based on the ridge count for the index, middle, and ring fingers. Since arches do not have ridge counts, they are not considered in subsecondary classification. The ridge count of loops is represented by letters, I or O, according to the number of ridges on a particular finger, as follows.

	I	O
Index finger	1 to 9	10 and over
Middle finger	1 to 10	11 and over
Ring finger	1 to 13	14 and over

Ridge tracing of whorls is represented by I (inner), O (outer), or M (meeting). The inner trace is one in which the end of the tracing ridge of the left delta passes over the right delta and three or more ridges intervene between the end of the tracing ridge of the left delta and the right delta. An outer trace is one in which the end of the tracing ridge of the left delta passes under the right delta and three or more ridges intervene between the end of the tracing ridge of the left delta and the right delta. A meeting trace is one which is neither inner nor outer. As in secondary classification, the right-hand designation goes into the numerator and the left-hand one goes into the denominator.

Suppose a person has the following print characteristics: index and middle finger of the right hand have ulnar loop patterns with ridge counts of 7 and 12; right ring finger has a whorl pattern with a meeting trace; left middle and ring fingers are ulnar loop patterns with ridge counts of 9 and 8; and left index finger has a whorl pattern with an outer trace. The subsecondary classification is then $\frac{IOM}{OII}$.

Final Classification The final is the ridge count of the loop pattern on the right little finger, and it is entered in the numerator. If the right little finger does not have a loop pattern, a ridge count is made of the left little finger and the value entered in the denominator.

If, for example, the right little finger is an arch and the left little finger is a radial loop with 10 ridges, the final classification would be $\frac{}{10}$. Note in Table 12-1 how this fits into the overall formula.

Major Classification The major classification represents an extension of the classical Henry system. It is the ridge count or whorl tracing of the thumb patterns.

Key Classification The key is the ridge count of the first loop pattern appearing on the fingerprint card, beginning with the right thumb and omitting little fingers. If there are no loops, there is no key classification.

The major and key classifications are used primarily for large filing systems. There are also other extensions of classification, such as the secondary subsecondary, WCDX, special loop extensions, and so forth. These allow further subdivisions of large files.

Other Classification Systems There are some other methods of classifying fingerprints. These are often modifications and variations of the Henry system, and include the following:

NCIC System: The classification used by the National Crime Information Center (*NCIC*) amounts to a conversion of a modified Henry classification into a form suitable for computer coding.

American or NYSIIS System: This method is used by the New York State Identification and Intelligence System (NYSIIS) for filing inked fingerprints. It, too, represents a modified Henry system.

Vucetich System: This system was developed by Juan Vucetich and is used in most countries in South America.

Battley System: This system is used to file and retrieve single fingerprints. It was developed by Henry Battley of Scotland Yard.

FINDER System: This is a computerized fingerprint reader system (*fin*gerprint rea*der*). It was developed by the FBI.

Of the systems mentioned, Battley's single-print filing system and the computerized automated latent print system will be discussed more fully. The Battley system was devised by Henry Battley, former Chief Inspector, Fingerprint Bureau, at New Scotland Yard in England. In this system, each finger is considered separately. Each finger is printed on its own 3 × 5 in. card. In addition to space for the print, space is provided for: (1) name of the person printed, (2) full 10-finger classification, (3) name of print type, (4) name of the hand and finger involved, (5) general pattern type, and (6) core and other special information. In Battley's system, the name of the hand and finger involved are recorded first. Next, the general pattern type of the print is established. Then, the Battley core is located and classified. Battley delta and ridge counting in loops and ridge tracing in whorls are also employed. For examination, a special disk or reticle attached to the magnifier is employed. The combined Henry-Battley reticle has also been used for ridge counting and ridge tracing.

Single-digit fingerprint classification systems have particular importance in criminal investigations. Since complete prints of all 10 fingers are rarely found at crime scenes, 10-digit classification systems are often of little value in identifying a suspect from latent prints. If no example of the questioned suspect print is in the file, of course, then a search for and comparison of the single prints will be impossible. Further development and implementation of single-digit fingerprint classification systems should expedite and facilitate searching these files and help to make subsequent comparison possible.

In the past, single latent prints have been regarded as almost worthless without known suspect prints for comparison. Since manual searches of all the fingerprint cards in a file are almost impossible, the development of automated fingerprint identification systems has been a subject of considerable interest. By combining the accuracy and speed of computers with single-digit fingerprint files, automated latent print search systems could be a valuable aid in criminal investigations.

Over the years, a number of systems have been proposed and evaluated: the Automatic Fingerprint Identification System, the Videfile Information System, the FBI Automatic Fingerprint Identification System, the California Automated Latent Print System, and others.

In general, a questioned latent print from the crime scene should be in excellent condition and have a significant number of points of minutiae (ridge details and relationships). A 1:1 photo of the latent print is then submitted for automatic search. Minutiae from the fingerprint are coded and entered into the system by latent print analysts. The minutiae of the latent print are compared with those of the fingerprints stored in the data base by the computer. The computer system compares relative positioning of minutiae characteristics in the questioned latent print as well as other search factors, such as description data, to data base fingerprints and search factor data and produces a candidate list in rank order of probable matches. The known prints of those on the candidate list are then compared with the unknown latent print by latent fingerprint examiners. With computerized automated latent print systems, it should be possible to solve many previously unsolvable crimes.

Search, Preservation, and Collection of Fingerprint Evidence

Fingerprints are fragile, and may be destroyed by contamination or improper handling. Both the quality and quantity of latent fingerprints are usually affected by the methods of searching, preservation, and collection. In every case, the primary concerns are preventing the addition of fingerprints to the evidence and preventing the destruction of the ones that are already present. In one homicide case, 23 sets of fingerprints were discovered by the fingerprint specialist who examined the scene. All those prints, unfortunately, were identified as belonging to police officers present at the scene! Thus, the first step to be taken upon reaching a crime scene is to exclude all unauthorized persons and to protect the scene. This matter is discussed further in Appendix 2. Police personnel entering a scene should be required to sign a log and provide elimination prints. This practice, apart from its avowed purpose, usually has the added benefit of reducing the number of such people.

Searching A systematic search plan should be used for locating fingerprints at a scene. The search should begin with the area surrounding the actual scene. The next logical places to search are points of possible exit and entry. The search should continue in a logical way, trying to follow the possible path of the criminal. All suspected areas should be checked. Any item that has been moved or displaced should be searched for fingerprints. One house burglary was solved when the complainant told the investigator that a beer can had not been on her kitchen table when she left her home. Examination of the can yielded the burglar's fingerprints. A strong, oblique light or flashlight is a great aid for the investigator in discovering latent prints on reflective surfaces. The following areas and objects may be expected to yield latent prints:

1 The pathway traveled by the criminal, including doors, windows, hallways, staircase handrails, window sills, walls, and possible points of entry and exit.

2 Objects or materials touched by the criminal, such as light switches, tables, drawers, safes, mirrors, closets, telephones, refrigerators, liquor cabinets, or counter tops.

3 Weapons or tools used by the criminal, such as knives, screwdrivers, credit cards, flashlights, or vehicles.

4 Target locations of the crime, such as wallet or pocketbook, cash register, safe, cabinets used to keep records, bonds, jewelry, or guns, or other locations where valuables might be kept.

5 Objects or materials destroyed by the criminal, such as broken glass, broken doorknobs, drawer handles, or torn letters or notes.

6 Articles or materials left at the scene, such as bottles, cans, cigarette butts, empty cigarette packages, matchbooks, notes, or other personal property.

In general, in the case of an indoor crime scene, the investigation should be started at the point of entry. Fingerprints should be searched for on the door, lock, doorknob, windows, broken glass, and other objects and surfaces in the immediate surroundings. Special attention should be given to the target area where the criminal activity occurred. The paths of the criminal to the target area, and the path away from it to the point of exit, as well as the point of exit, should also be checked. In the case of searching a vehicle, the investigation is started from the exterior. All doors, side mirrors, and windows should be checked. Other areas, such as trailer hitches, luggage racks, hood release levers, license plates, and trunk areas should also be searched.

Interior areas around rearview mirrors, door handles, brake release levers, steering wheels, shifting levers, seat adjustment levers, and seat belt buckles are likely places for the possible discovery of latent prints.

Occasionally, a latent fingerprint found at a scene may give some idea about a person's size or other characteristics. Small fingerprints, for example, are likely to have been made by a person with small bones and delicate body structure. Prints on a wall may provide an indication of the person's height. Construction workers, farm workers, mechanics, and manual laborers tend to have rough hands which result in unclear ridge patterns.

If no latent prints are found at a scene, several explanations are possible. The criminal may have worn gloves or may have wiped surfaces clean after touching them. Such information can provide leads in the investigation. They are, however, just hints or investigative aids and should not be treated as facts nor relied on too heavily by investigators.

Preservation When a latent print is located, the first thing that must be done is to photograph it. Various techniques have been used to bring about maximum contrast and the best results. With visible or plastic prints, photographing them (and collection, if possible) is the only thing needed since they do not have to be developed.

A data card should be prepared: it should contain the case number, date, location, name of the officer who discovered the print, and the name of the photographer. The photographs should then be taken again, with the data card. The objective of this procedure is to produce a photograph with clear ridge patterns along with documentation containing the necessary identifying information. It is good practice to sketch the object on which a latent print was found and indicate the exact location of the print and the orientation of the finger on the sketch. The sketch can be made on the fingerprint lift card.

Collection Once a fingerprint has been visualized (developed), as discussed in the following section, and photographed, other methods of preserving and collecting it may be attempted. With small objects, such as paper or glass, the entire object can be retained as evidence. The object should not be handled with bare fingers. It can be picked up with gloves or a handkerchief, although it should be handled and touched as little as possible. Avoiding bare fingers eliminates the possibility of leaving additional prints, while minimizing handling reduces the chance of wiping or smearing prints that may be present.

If the print appears on a movable object, such as a bottle or a weapon, it may be advisable to cover the print with fingerprint tape, and then transfer the entire item to the laboratory. Care must be taken in applying the tape, however, so as not to destroy the ridge details. All such evidence should be placed in proper containers, secured, labeled, and sealed, before transporting it to the laboratory (Appendix 2).

If a fingerprint appears on an immovable object, such as a wall or countertop, the print can be lifted after it has been photographed. In applying the lifting tape, the end is placed a little distance away from the print and the tape carefully smoothed out over it. Air bubbles should be avoided by using a gradual but deliberate technique. The tape is then carefully removed and placed on the backing paper, as described below. All lifted, developed prints should be labeled and sealed into marked envelopes along with the data card.

Methods for Developing Latent Prints

There are three basic types of fingerprints that occur at crime scenes, visible, plastic, and latent.

1 *Visible prints:* Visible prints are made by fingers stained with colored materials, such as blood, ink, paint, grease, or dirt. Ordinarily, a visible print does not require further treatment to be fully visualized.

2 *Plastic prints:* A plastic print is actually an indentation. This type of pattern is formed by pressing the friction ridges of the fingers onto a soft surface, such as wax, putty, tar, soap, butter, or clay. Plastic prints generally do not require additional development to be fully visualized. They are usually photographed and sometimes may be cast (Chapter 11). However, plastic as well as visible prints should be saved if at all possible.

3 *Latent prints:* Latent prints are normally not visible. Some means of development is generally required for their visualization. Occasionally latent prints can be visualized and photographed by controlling the lighting, especially if they lie on smooth, reflective surfaces (Figure 12-3). The residue left behind by the finger which

FIGURE 12-3
An undusted latent on a knife blade visualized with with oblique illumination. Note the detail present including pore structure. Dusting often obscures such detail. *(Courtesy of Christopher P. Chany, Forensic Science Laboratory, Office of the Medical Examiner, Westchester County, New York.)*

forms the latent print can be oily if the fingers have contacted oil sources such as sebaceous secretions on nonfriction-ridge skin (forehead or nose, for example). The secretions from the pores (sweat glands) in friction-ridge skin may be the basis of most latents, and these are not oily. Under normal conditions, the secretion from a sweat pore in friction-ridge skin contains 98.5% water and 1.5% dissolved solids. The composition of normal sweat secretion is indicated in Figure 12-4.

Various methods for the visualization of latent fingerprints have been devised. Table 12-3 summarizes the major approaches to date. Generally, all the techniques can be classified into one of two broad categories, physical methods and chemical methods.

Physical Methods Physical methods depend on the adherence of inert materials to fingerprint residue. The most common method for developing latent prints is dusting with fingerprint powder. Other techniques, such as argon laser, x-ray, and vacuum coating, have been suggested.

Powder Dusting Fingerprint powders are available in a wide range of colors, including black, white, gray, red, bronze, and aluminum, from many manufacturers. The selection of a powder is extremely important for obtaining good latent prints. The following factors are usually considered in selecting a fingerprint powder.

1 The color of the powder should be selected to give maximum contrast with the background.

2 The powder must adhere to the deposits left by the friction skin ridges, and yet not adhere too readily to the surface on which the latent prints are located.

FIGURE 12-4
Composition of sweat secretion.

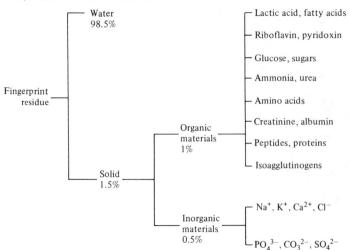

TABLE 12-3
METHODS OF VISUALIZING LATENT FINGERPRINTS

Technique	Principle	Surfaces to which applicable
Physical		
Powder dusting	Adherence of inert material to fingerprint residues	Smooth, nonporous surfaces, such as metals, glass, plastics, tile, and finished woods
Oblique lighting and photography	Natural residues of fingerprints	Smooth and nonreflective surfaces
Laser	Luminescent material in fingerprint residue	Smooth, nonporous, or slightly porous surfaces, such as plastic and paper (nonfluorescent)
X-ray	Adherence of lead powder to fingerprint residues	Smooth, nonporous, and slightly porous surfaces, such as human skin
Vacuum coating	Adherence of gold, silver, or cadmium to fingerprint residues	Smooth surfaces, such as plastic films, polyethylene, and paper
Chemical		
Iodine fuming	Chemical interaction of iodine with fatty acids and lipid in residue	Smooth surfaces, such as paper, human skin
Ninhydrin	Chemical interaction with amino acids, peptides, and proteins of residue	Paper, cardboard
Silver nitrate	Chemical interaction with chloride in residue	Paper
Fluorescamine, o-phthalaldehyde, dansyl chloride	Chemical interaction with amino acids in residue	Paper, multicolored absorbent surfaces (nonfluorescent)
Nitric acid, hydrofluoric acid	Chemical interaction with surfaces without destroying residues	Glass, cartridge cases

3 The powder should have sufficient wetting characteristics and adhesiveness to keep the developed ridges from being broken by the brushing action.

4 The particle size of the powder should be fine enough to give good, clear ridge lines.

When applying powder with a brush, extreme care must be taken to avoid damaging the latent print. The most serious errors are the use of too much powder and the application of too much force in the brush strokes. Since various powders may not always behave the same way on different surfaces, it may be wise to run a "control test" by trying out the brush and powder on a known, experimentally produced print on a "clean" area of the questioned surface. The keys to successful powder development are the use of a small amount of powder and a delicate touch. A small amount of the fingerprint powder should be poured from its container onto a sheet of paper. The brush should never be put directly into the container. There are several different types of fingerprint brushes, including nylon fiber, camel hair, and ostrich feather. Choice of a suitable brush depends on the conditions. The ends of the brush bristles are touched to the powder lightly, and the excess powder is then shaken off. A smooth stroke is used to apply powder over the suspected area. When sufficient ridge detail has developed, the brushing stroke should then follow the ridge flow. After development and photographing, the latent print may be lifted using transparent lifting tape, hinged fingerprint lifters, or rubber fingerprint lifters. A sketch of the object upon which the latent print was found should be made on the back of the fingerprint lift card. The sketch should indicate the exact location and orientation of the print. Procedures for developing latent fingerprints with powder are shown in Figure 12-5. This method works best on smooth, nonporous surfaces, such as metals, glass, plastics, tile, and finished wood.

Several special kinds of fingerprint powders are available for special applications, including fluorescent powders and the magnetic powder used with the Magna brush. Fluorescent powders are made of special chemicals, such as zinc orthosilicate and anthracene. They can be used for the development of latent prints on multicolored objects. A source of ultraviolet (UV) light is required for visualization of the prints treated with these powders. By photographing the fluorescence pattern of the developed fingerprint under UV light, the obscuring effect of the multicolored surface is greatly reduced. The Magna brush is a specially designed magnet. The magnet picks up the finely divided metallic powder. The brush has no bristles, so only the powder touches the surface containing the latent print. This characteristic reduces the chance of destroying or damaging the ridge detail of a print, which can happen with a bristle brush. This method also permits the use of the same powder over and over again. This conserves the powder and leaves cleaner surfaces. Excellent latent prints have been developed on paper, wood, leather, and other slightly porous surfaces using the Magna brush.

Laser, X-Ray, and Vacuum Coating   In recent years, new techniques have been reported for visualizing latent prints.

The argon laser is a source of very intense, highly collimated, monochromatic light. This means that the light is of a single wavelength (see Chapter 3) and that the beam is very small and concentrated. When used with the proper kind of optical system, the laser light can induce fluorescence in various components of the latent print secretion material (such as riboflavin and pyridoxin). This fluorescent pattern, when documented with suitable photographic techniques, can be used for the detection of latent prints. The method is nondestructive, but it requires expensive equipment and specialized technique.

Electron emission radiography has been used for the detection of latent prints on various objects and on human skin. The electron emission is induced by filtered high-energy (hard) x-rays, which are capable of passing through most objects. Hard x-rays, passing through the film, will strike the object, which has been dusted with fine lead powder, without having any direct effect on the film. In response to the x-ray

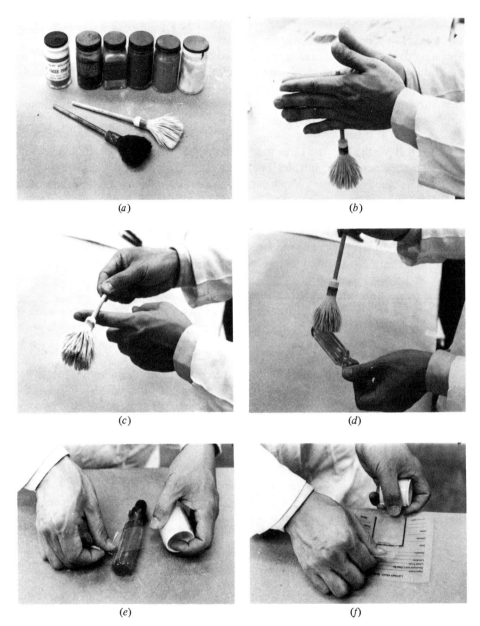

(a)   (b)

(c)   (d)

(e)   (f)

FIGURE 12-5
Powder dusting procedure. *(a)* Selection of brush and powder; *(b)* distributing powder; *(c)* removing excess from brush; *(d)* dusting latent print; *(e)* applying lifting tape to dusted latent; *(f)* transferring lifted print to card. *(Courtesy of Thomas McMullen and Ronald Luneau, Forensic Science Laboratory, Connecticut State Police.)*

bombardment, the lead powder adhering to the latent print ridges produces photo-electrons, to which the photographic film is highly sensitive, and an image corresponding to the dusted pattern is thus formed on the film.

The vacuum coating method involves the development of latent prints by deposition of a thin film of metal from the vapor of a metal like gold, silver, or cadmium in a vacuum onto the latent print. This method may be used for visualizing latent prints on paper, fabrics, or polyethylene.

Chemical Methods　The three most common chemical methods are iodine fuming, ninhydrin, and silver nitrate. They rely upon the chemical interaction of the detection reagent with some component of the secretions which form the latent print. More recently, fluorescamine, o-phthalaldehyde, dansyl chloride, and radioactive sulfur have also been reported as useful for the development of latent prints.

Iodine Fuming　The iodine fuming method of developing latent fingerprints does not result in a permanent chemical change. Iodine crystals can yield iodine vapor upon mild heating (sublimation), which forms a reversible complex with the fatty acid and lipid components of oily type prints. For this reason, some latent print experts refer to this procedure as a *physical* method.

When iodine crystals are warmed, they produce violet fumes, which consist of iodine vapor. The fumes are absorbed by the latent print secretions to give yellowish-brown prints with good ridge detail. There are two ways of applying iodine fumes to latent prints to develop them.

The *iodine fuming gun* can by made from either glass or plastic tubing, about 1.5 cm in diameter. Iodine crystals are introduced into the tube and held in place by glass wool. A small quantity of calcium chloride should also be introduced into the tube, at the end into which the breath is to be blown. The calcium chloride is a drying agent and serves to absorb moisture from the breath. An iodine fuming gun is shown in Figure 12-6(*a*). The heat of the breath causes the iodine crystals to produce vapor and cover the suspected area with iodine vapor. This technique is generally used for developing latent prints on articles or in searching crime scenes.

The *iodine fuming cabinet* is employed when a large number of specimens have to be treated. The fuming cabinet is box-shaped, as shown in Figure 12-6(*b*.) It has glass sides and a removable top, which permits observation of the development of the latent prints inside the cabinet, and control of the amount of vapor in the cabinet. The iodine crystals are placed in an evaporating dish, which is placed on a heating block. The heating block is heated, in turn, by a burner or by electricity.

Since iodine-developed prints are not permanent and will fade within a few hours, it is necessary to photograph the prints as soon as they have developed. The prints can be made permanent, however, in several ways:

1 The developed prints can be fixed with a 1% starch solution (1 g starch in 100 mL water). This procedure will yield blue-colored print patterns. Prints on papers containing starch sizing can be made permanent by "breathing" moisture on them. Here, the iodine print is placed close to the mouth and exposed to a slow flow of warm, moist breath until the pattern turns from brown or yellow to blue.

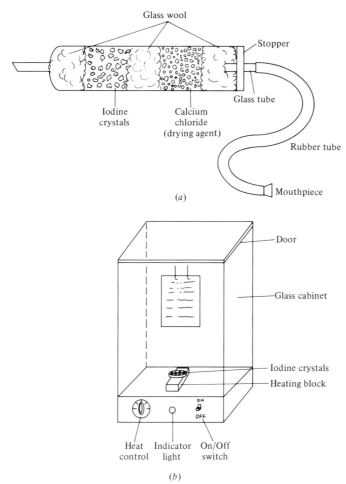

FIGURE 12-6
(a) and *(b)* Iodine fuming devices.

2 Developed prints can also be fixed with a solution of 0.3% 7,8-benzoflavone in cyclohexane. Prints treated in this way are a purple-blue color.

3 Alternatively, developed prints can be made permanent using photographic film. The film, after being completely exposed and developed, is moistened until the emulsion becomes tacky. The film is then pressed against the iodine print for a few minutes and then dipped into chrome alum and nitric acid solution. The resulting print can be made permanent in this way.

4 Iodine prints can be lifted by means of a thin silver plate. The polished silver plate is placed against the iodine print for a few seconds and then exposed to a photoflood lamp. The ridge details, where the iodine was in contact with the silver, will turn black. This method has been used for lifting prints from human skin.

Iodine stain can be removed from a print by placing the specimen in a current of air from a vent or a fan.

Ninhydrin The development of latent prints with ninhydrin is based on the reaction between triketohydrindene (ninhydrin) and amino acids, peptides, urea, and proteins of the latent secretions. There are many different ways of preparing ninhydrin solutions. Generally, a 0.6% solution in acetone (0.6 g ninhydrin in 100 mL acetone) appears to be effective, although this may cause running or bleeding of some inks, particularly ball-point. The solution may be applied to the suspected surface by spraying, brushing, or dipping. Spraying with a fine mist of solution to cover the surface is the preferred method. Prints usually take about 24 h to develop after spraying with ninhydrin, though development can be speeded up with heat, and moisture or humidity also have an enhancing effect. Ninhydrin can be dissolved in solvents other than acetone. Ethyl ether, petroleum ether, ethyl acetate, methyl alcohol, ethyl alcohol, hexane, and naphtha are examples. Hexane-, petroleum ether-, and naphtha-ninhydrin mixtures exhibit no evidence of bleeding or running on documents written with most inks. Heating of ninhydrin-treated latent print specimens can be achieved by heating the item in a 100°C oven, with a hot steam iron or a mounting press or by blowing hot air onto the surface with a hair dryer.

The ninhydrin method works extremely well with old prints on paper. There are reports indicating that latent prints more than 9 years old on documents still yield excellent results when treated with ninhydrin. Before treating with ninhydrin, however, special attention should be given to the possibility of damage to the specimen surface and to the dissolution of ink on the document by the solvent. As noted above, different solvents can be used, and solvent selection is an important consideration when there is a possibility that inks on a document will bleed or run.

Most of the unwanted ninhydrin stain can be removed by wetting the surface with 3% ammonium hydroxide, after which the surface is washed in running water. Use of such a procedure assumes, of course, that the surface in question is compatible with water and ammonium hydroxide.

Silver Nitrate The visualization of latent prints by silver nitrate is possible because of the reaction of the chloride (primarily in the form of sodium chloride) in the latent secretions (Figure 12-4) with the silver nitrate to form silver chloride:

$$AgNO_3 + NaCl \rightarrow NaNO_3 + AgCl$$

When silver chloride (AgCl) is exposed to light, it decomposes to form metallic silver and chlorine:

$$2AgCl \rightarrow 2Ag + Cl_2$$

The areas containing the metallic silver are thus made more visible.

Ridges of a latent print developed by this method have a reddish-brown color. The required 3% silver nitrate solution is prepared by dissolving 3 g $AgNO_3$ in 100 mL distilled water. The solution is light-sensitive, and it should be kept in the dark to prevent deterioration. Development of a latent print with silver nitrate can be achieved by immersing the specimen in the solution for 5 min in the dark. When the surface of the specimen is completely moistened, it can then be taken out and dried. When dry, the sample can be exposed to a photoflood light (or direct sunlight, or UV light) until ridge detail is visible. If the surface is too large for immersion, it may be treated with silver nitrate by brushing the solution onto the specimen surface. Prints developed with silver nitrate can be made permanent by applying photographic fixer solution after the prints have been visualized by exposure to light. The fixer removes unreduced silver chloride and excess silver nitrate.

Removal of unwanted silver stain can be brought about by placing the specimen in a 2% mercuric nitrate solution. Normal precautions should be observed in the handling of all these chemicals, and special care ought to be exercised when solutions of them are to be sprayed.

Other Chemical Methods Fluorescamine, *o*-phthalaldehyde, and dansyl chloride are newer reagents for the detection of latent prints. They react sensitively with primary amines in the range of picogram to nanogram amounts. Their reaction with amines is almost instantaneous, and the products are highly fluorescent. These chemicals are especially useful for developing latent prints on absorbent multicolored surfaces.

Nitric acid etching has been used for the detection of latent prints on cartridge case surfaces. The heat generated when a cartridge is fired has been found not to affect the latent prints on the casing. Consequently, usable prints can sometimes be developed by exposing the cartridge casing to the fumes of heated 20% nitric acid for a short time. This nitric acid etching method sometimes produces clear ridge details. Nickel casings are usually more difficult to obtain clear latent prints from than are brass casings.

Radioactively labeled sulfur dioxide (labeled with ^{35}S) has been used for the detection of latent prints on fabrics. Radiolabeled sulfur dioxide gas is absorbed by the lipid components of the latent secretions; subsequent autoradiography will resolve the ridge pattern. Autoradiography is a procedure in which photographic film is placed in contact with the test surface and allowed to be exposed by the radiation from a radiolabeled substance which is part of the test surface. The film is then developed.

Identification and Comparison of Fingerprints

After a latent print has been located, developed, and photographed, it should then be transferred for actual comparison. Several steps are required prior to the actual comparison:

1 All prints and data cards should be marked for identification. The information should include the case number, date, location, and name of the investigator.

2 All elimination prints should be collected and properly labeled for identification.

3 All photographs of developed prints should be labeled and marked for identification.

Comparison of latent prints with known ones begins with the overall pattern. The ridge detail of fingerprints, including the ends of ridges, their separations, and their relationships to one another, constitute the bases for the comparison of fingerprints. These ridge details and their relationships are collectively known as *minutiae*. The use of minutiae in fingerprint comparison is illustrated in Figure 12-7.

The following individual ridge characteristics are valuable for comparison purposes:

1 *Bifurcation (fork)*

This is a single ridge, splitting or forking into two branches.

2 *Island (enclosure)*

An island is formed by a single ridge which, after bifurcating for a short distance, reconverges and continues as a single ridge. An enclosure usually refers to a larger island.

FIGURE 12-7
Comparison of latent and known inked prints. (*Courtesy of Detective Nicolas Petraco, Crime Laboratory, New York City Police Department.*)

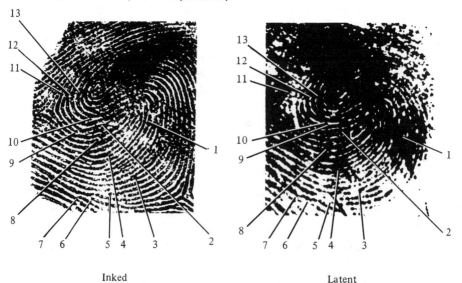

Inked   Latent

3 *Dot*

A dot is a very short ridge and means exactly what the word *dot* implies.

 4 *Short ridge*

A short ridge is a relative term, and is used to denote a ridge that is not as long as the average ridge in that specific print.

 5 *Ridge ending*

A ridge ending is the point of the ridge's termination. It is considered an ending ridge only if it terminates within the pattern area.

 6 *Trifurcation*

This is one single ridge splitting into a three-pronged, fork-shaped pattern.

 7 *Bridge*

A bridge is a short ridge which interconnects two other parallel ridges.

 8 *Angle*

An angle results from two or more ridges converging with one another at a point.

 9 *Converging ridges*

Two or more ridges which meet at a point are converging, and the point at which they meet is called the point of convergence.

 10 *Diverging ridges*

Diverging ridges are ridges which are parallel for some distance but then swing out away from each other.

In checking for similarity, most experts require from 10 to 12 matching points. In the past, different countries used different standards. In Spain, 10 to 12 points were required; in Switzerland, 12 to 14; in Austria, 12; in England, 16; in France, 17; in Germany, 8 to 12; and in most Asian countries, 12. In 1973, the International Association for Identification, after a three-year study of the question of the minimum number of points which should be required for matching, concluded that no valid basis existed for requiring any predetermined minimum number of points to be present before a positive identification could be made.

As a general rule, if two prints have the same pattern and enough matching point ridge characteristics and there are no unexplained differences, they are considered to match and a positive identification is made. In testifying on fingerprint identifications, experts sometimes prepare charts similar to Figure 12-7. These visual presentations are very helpful to a jury in understanding the basis for a fingerprint identification.

OTHER PAPILLARY OR FRICTION-RIDGE PATTERNS

Introduction

Palm prints and sole prints can occasionally be found at crime scenes. Because of their comparative rarity at scenes, and the difficulty in building files, palm and sole prints have not received as much attention and emphasis as fingerprints. Since the structure of the skin of the palm and sole is the same as that of the skin of the fingertip, it also exhibits characteristic ridge patterns. In addition, many lines or creases appear on palms and soles. All these parameters can be useful in the individualization of persons. If a palm or sole print is collected properly, a latent fingerprint examiner can compare such a print with known palm or sole prints from suspected persons. If sufficient ridge information is available, an examiner can make a positive identification.

Palm Prints

Palm prints generally appear at crime scenes in three different forms: visible print, indentation (plastic) print, and latent print. The definition and nature of these different forms of prints was discussed above. Since the size of palm prints is much larger than that of fingerprints, experienced investigators expect to find appreciable segments of them only on large, smooth surfaces. Examples of such extensive surfaces include counter tops, desk tops, smooth walls, refrigerator surfaces, washers, dryers, metal cabinets, motor vehicle exteriors, and bottles. If visible or three-dimensional forms of palm prints are found, they can be photographed and documented according to the procedure discussed in the fingerprints section above. Latent palm prints are generally developed in the same fashion as latent fingerprints. Methods of collection or documentation are likewise similar to those used for fingerprints, except for the larger size of the media used (such as lifting film).

Sole Prints

Sole prints are generally found at indoor scenes and on smooth surfaces such as kitchen or bathroom floors or bathtubs. Occasionally they may be found outdoors, especially in warmer climates where people are likely to be barefooted. Frequently, sole prints at crime scenes are in a visible form, such as a bloody footprint. Sole prints at crime scenes should be photographed and properly documented. If the surface containing the sole print is removable, the surface should be collected intact and sent to the laboratory for possible comparison.

Comparison of Palm and Sole Prints

Laboratory comparison of palm prints and sole prints follows the same general principles as fingerprint comparison. There are several areas on palms and soles, generally referred to as *zone* areas, which contain the ridge patterns and deltas. The thick part of the palm on the radial (thumb) side makes up the *thenar* zone, whereas that of the ulnar (little finger) side is the *hypothenar* zone. The area near the wrist is referred to as the *carpal delta* zone. The elevated area just behind the fingers and above the center of the palm is the *palmar* zone. The raised areas between each pair of fingers, running from thumb to little finger, are designated by the roman numerals I, II, III, and IV. The lines on the center of the palm are called *creases*. Comparison of palm prints found at scenes with known palm prints can be made in some instances through a detailed examination of the delta and ridge characteristics just described. A detailed discussion of formulations for and pattern classifications of palm prints can be found in the reference by Cummins and Midlo cited at the end of this chapter.

There are also zone areas on the foot. The proximal area of the sole is the *calcar* zone, the name being derived from that of the heel bone. The center of the sole is the *tread area*. The *ball pattern* zone is located on the ball of the foot on the big toe side; the remainder of this area is called the *plantar pattern* zone. There are two other zones as well. The *tibial pattern* zone is located in the center of the tread area at the medial portion of the arch. This area is reproduced in a print only if the individual has flat feet. Near the distal end of the tread area is the *fibular pattern* zone. The ball, plantar, and calcar zones are the most important portions for sole print comparisons. They contain not only well-delineated ridges, deltas, and patterns, but also large areas with details that can be used to make positive comparisons.

ODONTOLOGICAL PATTERNS

Bitemark Evidence

Bitemark evidence can have particular value in investigations of sexual assaults, homicides involving homosexuals, and cases involving battered or abused children. Bitemark evidence results from an impression of the teeth being left in food products, on the skin of victims, or even in chewing gum and other objects such as pencils.

As we noted in the introductory chapter, the application of dentistry to bitemark comparisons and to the identification of persons based on dental characteristics is called *forensic odontology*. This field has gained much recognition in both civil and criminal cases in recent years.

Bitemark comparison is a special area of forensic odontology (or forensic dentistry). When a bitemark is deep, pronounced, clearly visible, fresh, and well preserved, and when it contains some unusual characteristics, a match with an exemplar bite mark from a suspect is possible. Most odontologists believe that no two mouths have exactly the same dental structure. Bitemarks made by different persons are expected, therefore, to have different individualizing characteristics (Figure 12-8). By comparing alignments of teeth and their positions, relationships, and irregularities in a questioned bitemark with the same characteristics in a known mark, an odontologist may be able to make a definite individualization. The difficulties in examining and evaluating bitemarks are many, however. One of the most important is that the marks change their shape and size depending upon the amount of time that has elapsed and the nature of the material bearing the impression. A bitemark discovered at a crime scene or on a victim's body can be an important piece of evidence. A one-to-one photograph should be obtained if possible. An odontologist should be consulted as quickly as possible to perform further examinations. With a living victim, it is a good idea to photograph a bitemark periodically during the healing process. The mark may become accentuated during this period of time.

Other Odontological Examinations and Comparisons

Besides bitemark comparisons, the other important application of this field is establishing the identities of dead bodies which cannot be identified in other ways (such as by fingerprints, physical characteristics, clothing, etc.) because of severe damage from fire, putrefaction, or destruction. Because teeth and various types of dental work (fillings, bridgework, dentures, etc.) are highly resistant to damage, heat, and decomposition, the teeth and dental work of a victim can sometimes be discovered among bodily remains, even when the rest of the body is almost totally destroyed. Forensic odontologists can compare the teeth, dental characteristics, and/or dental appliances with x-rays of the teeth and a known person's dental records, which may be available from dentists who have worked on the person's teeth. If the location, shape, and type of fillings, the structure and configuration of the teeth and roots, the orientation of adjacent teeth to one another, the number and location of extracted, original, and replaced teeth, and other such dental characteristics are identical, then it is often possible to establish with certainty the identity of a victim. These types of identifications become very important in cases of badly burned or decomposed bodies and in mass disasters.

VOICEPRINT INDIVIDUALIZATION

The comparison and individualization of human voices from magnetic tape recordings of speech made directly or by telephone or radio is called *voiceprint individu-*

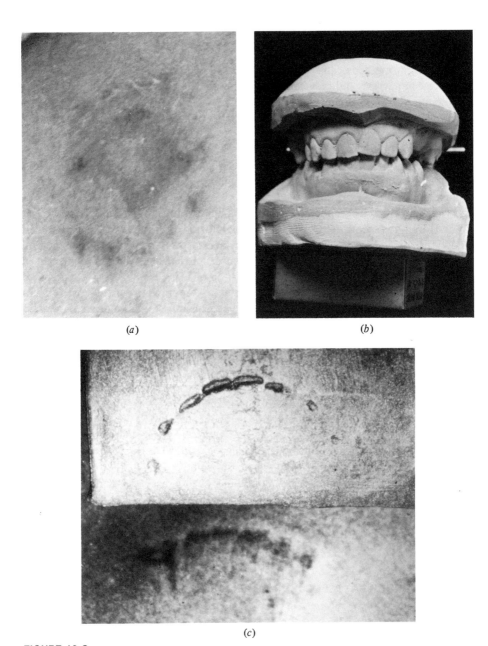

FIGURE 12-8.
(a) A bitemark on skin. *(b)* A plaster replica cast of a set of teeth. *(c)* Comparison of exemplar (top) and bitemark (bottom). *(Courtesy of C. P. Karazulas, D.D.S., Bridgeport, Connecticut and Joseph Scalise, Office of Chief Medical Examiner, Nassau County, New York.)*

alization. This technique utilizes the results of sound spectrography and the findings of aural analysis.

Voiceprint methods can transform human voice patterns into a visual form suitable for comparison, and they can convert the sounds of dialing a telephone mechanically into a form suitable for determining what number was dialed. The visual display relates variations in pitch and loudness to time. Voiceprint analysis has been utilized in many different situations, such as telephoned bomb threats, undercover investigations, obscene telephone calls, telephoned ransom messages from kidnappers, decoding of recorded messages, and telephone number tracing from rotary dial or touch-tone telephone pulses. The instrument used in voiceprint comparisons is called the *sound spectrograph.*

The sound spectrograph was first developed at Bell Laboratories during World War II by Lawrence Kersta. The basic principle underlying voiceprints is that each individual's voice has its own unique quality and characteristics. These characteristics arise from individual variation in the vocal mechanism, which is controlled by the size of the vocal cavity and the coordination of the movements of its parts, such as lips, tongue, and teeth. The different parts and interactions of the vocal mechanism are often referred to as *articulations.* The probability that voice characteristics will be exactly the same in two different individuals is remote. Thus, each person's voice is thought to be unique in some respects. Voice spectrograms are produced by the voice spectrograph, which converts the sounds into a visual graphic display, or voiceprint (Figure 12-9). By comparison of voice prints, an examiner may be able to make a determination as to whether a particular suspect made a particular phone call or recording. In order to draw a useful conclusion, an examiner must make a positive comparison of 10 or more words or phonemes (the smallest units of spoken sound).

The quality of the recording and the known standard are the two most important factors in determining the success of voiceprint comparisons. A known standard has to have a similar context and set of conditions to the questioned sample. A known sample should be repeated three times on the recording so that a more natural sample of the suspect's voice can be obtained. The tape recording should be prefaced with identifying information such as the speaker's identity, who is present, and the date and time of the recording.

MISCELLANEOUS PATTERNS FOR HUMAN IDENTIFICATION AND INDIVIDUALIZATION

Besides fingerprints, palm prints, sole prints, bitemarks, and voiceprints, there are other types of patterns which have been used for individualization purposes. In some cases, however, only limited information is available about the variations of the patterns and few studies have been conducted.

In the past, tattoos, caste marks, and branding marks were used for identifying persons in many countries. In the 19th century, Alphonse Bertillon (Figure 1-3) developed the first systematic method for personal identification. This method, based upon body measurements (see Chapter 1), was called Bertillonage (or anthropome-

(a)

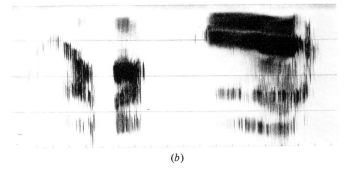

(b)

FIGURE 12-9
(a) A voiceprint instrument. (b) Two voiceprints of the same
individual. The phrase "Hello Angels" was used for each. (*Courtesy
of David Paige, Forensic Science Laboratory, Connecticut State
Police.*)

try). Bertillon also developed a methodical system of detailed personal descriptions, known as *portrait parlé*. Today, artist's drawings, composite drawings, and composite photo kits are still used by many law enforcement agencies as aids in facial identifications.

Bone and bone materials have also been used for identification. From skeletal remains, a forensic anthropologist may be able to determine the sex, possible age, race, and size of the unknown person. The more complete the skeleton is, the more that can be learned. If an x-ray of the person taken prior to death is available, a positive comparison can sometimes be made with those of the skeletal parts.

Other patterns like the prints made by lips and by ears have been used in investigations. Published studies on lip prints have indicated that they are individual. Ear prints have not been as thoroughly investigated, but if sufficient detail is present in such a print, it is probably unique to a particular individual. The patterns of parallel lines or ridges (striations) in fingernails also appear to be different in different individuals. We assume that every aspect of the human body in some way reflects the individual's unique makeup, even though we may be unable to recognize the unique features and utilize them to individualize the person. This is the case with hair, where the pattern of microscopic morphology is heavily relied upon in making comparisons (Chapter 8). Although hair is undoubtedly individual, we are unable to individualize it at this time. Fresh bloodstains, with their many discrete, genetic marker characteristics, can be individualized to a much greater degree (Chapter 9).

STUDY QUESTIONS

1 Discuss reasons why fingerprints are so valuable as physical evidence.
2 What are the eight basic types of fingerprints? Briefly describe each pattern.
3 Describe how each of the following fingerprint classifications is determined: primary, secondary, subsecondary, final, major, key.
4 Describe the procedures for searching for latent fingerprints at a crime scene.
5 What procedures should be followed in photographing latent prints?
6 What procedures should be followed in collecting and preserving latent prints?
7 What are elimination prints and why are they necessary?
8 What characteristics are used in making fingerprint comparisons? Why are some of them more valuable than others? What characteristics are used in making palm- and sole-print comparisons?
9 What is a visible print?
10 What is a plastic print?
11 What procedures and precautions should be followed in dusting for latent fingerprints at a scene?
12 What is iodine fuming? Under what circumstances should it be used to look for latent prints?
13 How can a latent print revealed by iodine fuming be made permanent?
14 What is ninhydrin? How should it be used in searching for latent prints?
15 What is the silver nitrate method and when should it be used in looking for latent prints?
16 What is forensic odontology? What are the most important applications of forensic odontology in forensic science?
17 What is a voiceprint?

REFERENCES AND FURTHER READING

Alexander, H. L. V.: *Classifying Palmprints,* Charles C Thomas, Springfield, Ill., 1973.

Allison, H. C.: *Personal Identification,* Holbrook Press, Boston, 1973.

Battley, H.: *Single Fingerprints,* H. M. Stationery Office, London, 1930.

Beckstead, J. W., R. D. Rawson, and W. S. Giles: "Review of Bitemark Evidence," *Journal of the American Dental Association,* vol. 99, p. 69, 1979.

Cowger, J. F.: "Moving Towards Professionalization of Latent Print Examiners," *Journal of Forensic Sciences,* vol. 24, pp. 591–595, 1979.

Cummins, H., and C. Midlo: *Fingerprints, Palms, and Soles,* Research, South Berlin, Mass., 1976.

Dalrymple, B. E.: "Case Analysis of Fingerprint Detection by Laser," *Journal of Forensic Sciences,* vol. 24, pp. 586–590, 1979.

Dinkel, E. H.: "The Use of Bite Mark Evidence As an Investigative Aid," *Journal of Forensic Sciences,* vol. 19, p. 535, 1974.

Federal Bureau of Identification: *The Science of Fingerprints,* U.S. Government Printing Office, Washington, D.C., 1977.

Field, A. T.: *Fingerprint Handbook,* 2d ed., Charles C Thomas, Springfield, Ill., 1971.

Harvey, W.: *Dental Identification and Forensic Odontology,* Henry Kempton, London, 1976.

Kerley, E. R.: "Forensic Anthropology," in C. H. Wecht (ed.), *Forensic Sciences,* vol. 2, chap. 27, Matthew Bender, New York, 1981.

Larson, J. A.: *Single Fingerprint System,* Appleton, New York, 1924.

Lee, H. C., and A. E. Attard: "The Comparison of Fluorescamine, *o*-Phthalaldehyde and Ninhydrin in Latent Print Detection," *Journal of Police Science and Administration,* vol. 7, p. 330, 1979.

Menzel, E. R., and K. E. Fox: "Laser Detection of Latent Fingerprints," *Journal of Forensic Sciences,* vol. 25, pp. 150–153, 1980.

Moenssens, A. A.: *Fingerprint Technique,* Chilton, Philadelphia, 1974.

National Academy of Sciences: *On the Theory and Practice of Voiceprint Identification,* Washington, D.C., 1979.

Reichardt, G. J., J. C. Carr, and E. G. Stone: "A Conventional Method for Lifting Latent Fingerprints from Human Skin Surfaces," *Journal of Forensic Sciences,* vol. 23, pp. 135–141, 1978.

Sobel, M. N.: "Forensic Odontology," in C. H. Wecht (ed.), *Forensic Sciences,* vol. 2, chap. 28, Matthew Bender, New York, 1981.

Sperber, N. D.: "Bitemark Evidence in Crimes Against Persons," *FBI Law Enforcement Bulletin,* July 1981.

Tosi, O.: *Voice Identification: Theory and Legal Applications,* University Park Press, Baltimore, 1979.

Vickery, K.: "California's Automated Latent Print System," *FBI Law Enforcement Bulletin,* August 1981.

CHAPTER 13

QUESTIONED DOCUMENT EXAMINATION

INTRODUCTION

The examination of questioned documents is one of the oldest activities in the field of forensic science. Forgery and fraud involving documents evolved almost simultaneously with the development of writing systems.

Today, the term *document* refers to any written, printed, or typed material. If the authenticity of a document is doubtful, its source unknown, or its origin questionable, it becomes a questioned document. The subdivision of forensic science involved with the identification and analysis of questioned documents is called *document examination* or *questioned document examination.* Questioned document examination may be directly or indirectly connected with a variety of different kinds of criminal and civil cases, such as contested wills, forgery, embezzlement, breaches of contract, extortion, robbery, suicide, homicide, and kidnapping.

In a recent kidnapping case, the ransom note appeared to have been prepared with letters cut out of newspapers. The style of the letters and the printer's ink corresponded to the type and ink used by a small underground newspaper. This information helped the investigators to limit the range of suspects.

Further, the typewritten name and address on the envelope which had contained the note allowed a document examiner to determine that the typing had been done on a Smith-Corona portable typewriter. Finally, the ransom note had a torn edge. When a suspect was found, it became possible to connect the note to the suspect by physically matching the torn edge of the ransom note to the remaining edge of the paper on a writing pad recovered from his apartment. In addition, a document examiner was able to conclude that the envelope had been typed on the Smith-Corona typewriter which was also found in the suspect's apartment.

This case illustrates the potential value of document evidence and document examination in one type of criminal case.

Types of Questioned Document Examinations

Document examination is not limited to handwriting comparison. A document examiner may be called upon to examine a variety of types of physical evidence besides handwriting. Several types of examinations are sometimes necessary in the comparison of two documents. Any of the following examinations may be carried out by a document examiner:

1 Examination, comparison, and determination of types of writing materials, such as pens, ink, paper, typewriters, or photocopying or printing devices, to establish class characteristics

2 Examination of documents or other articles to disclose the presence of alterations, erasures, eliminations, or obliterations

3 Determination of the age of writing and/or materials used to construct a particular document

4 Determination of the order or sequence in which writing or typing was entered onto a document

5 Examination and comparison of papers and inks to determine the manufacturer and to establish evidence of a common origin

6 Identification of authorship and comparison of signatures or other markings

7 Examination of charred, indented, or obliterated writing to try to reconstruct the original writing

8 Examination of typed, photocopied, or printed material and comparison of it with material produced by a particular typewriter, photocopying device, stamp, or printing press

Basic Principles of Document Examination

The basic philosophy behind document examination is similar to that of other forms of physical evidence examination and evaluation in forensic science. Characteristics which vary most from one sample to another, and least within a particular sample, are used as a primary basis of examination. The class and the individual characteristics of a given sample, in other words, are often the most important aspects of the comparison. Reconstructions can also play a crucial role.

A major difference between document examination and many other types of comparison lies in the significant extent of variation within samples from a single source. These must be taken into account, and they complicate the comparison. In the comparison of a bloodstain type with that of a given individual or of refractive index of a glass chip with that of a particular window glass, for example, the variation in a sample from a given source is very small or nonexistent. The variation in a person's handwriting, however, can be very great, and it can occur naturally or be deliberately caused. Accordingly, conclusions reached by document examiners are relatively subjective and cannot be backed up by a firm, objective data base such as would be the case in blood-group comparisons. In Chapter 8, we noted that the intraindividual differences in hair contributed to the subjectivity of hair comparisons.

The equipment necessary for document examinations includes such items as magnifying lenses, stereomicroscopes, infrared microscopes, microcomparators, photographic devices, special lighting equipment, some chemical reagents, and sometimes other instrumentation.

COLLECTION AND PRESERVATION OF DOCUMENT EVIDENCE

An investigator's responsibility for the successful pursuit of investigations involving document evidence is as great as a document examiner's. An investigator's activities can be as important to the outcome of the case as those of the examiner. Unless an investigator realizes that the document is suspicious in some way, it will never become questioned. Like other types of evidence, the integrity and value of a document is always dependent upon its proper recognition, collection, and preservation.

Each document submitted to the laboratory should be in its original condition and be accompanied by a sufficient number of standards and an explanation of the case detailing the reasons for the requested examination. Any type of change may destroy the potential value of document evidence and make an examination more difficult. Some documents contain fingerprints or other valuable trace evidence. Investigators should be alert to these possibilities. Latent prints on documents can be developed by various physical and chemical methods, as described in Chapter 12. If a fingerprint is found, it can increase the evidential value of the document immeasurably. Trace evidence, such as hairs, fibers, pollens, blood, semen, or saliva, can also significantly increase the value of the evidence. Therefore, tweezers should be used or gloves worn when handling questioned documents. Excessive handling of documents should be avoided; it may damage the writing, latent prints, or other evidence. Care should be taken to avoid contamination and loss of trace evidence. A questioned document should be placed in a clean envelope of proper size. If an identification mark has to be placed on the document, it should be put in one corner, preferably on the back if this is blank. No mark should ever be placed on the front of a document, and document evidence should never be folded, stapled, or taped.

WRITING INSTRUMENTS AND MATERIALS

A written or printed document is usually constructed from three different articles or materials: a writing surface, an ink or inklike material, and a writing instrument. The most common specimens received for examination in forensic science laboratories are written on paper, with ink, by a pen. However, questioned document examination may involve writing or markings found on walls, mirrors, doors, or other surfaces; they can be made by pencils, crayons, fiber-tip markers, lipstick, chalk, spray paint, and even blood. It should be noted that the habitual characteristics of the writer may be significantly modified in writing or markings made with some of these materials. Special care is necessary if they are used in comparisons.

Writing Instruments

Many things can be used as writing instruments, including quills, sticks, paint brushes, steel pens, fountain pens, pencils, crayons, lipstick, chalk, ball-point pens, fiber-tip pens, and Chinese brushes. The most commonly available writing implement, however, is the ball-point pen. At present, about 80 percent of the handwriting material submitted to forensic science laboratories for analysis is done with ball-point pen. About 15 percent is done with fiber-tip pens, and the remainder is done with other types of writing instruments.

Identification of different types of writing instruments based upon class characteristics is usually relatively simple. The general class characteristics of a particular type of writing implement can be determined by visual inspection and stereomicroscopical examination.

Ball-point pens generally leave a single, rounded line. Many worn or poor quality ball-points accumulate ink on the side of the ball housing, and when the direction of movement is reversed, this ink is picked up by the ball and deposited as a smudge on the line. Ball-point ink itself, and the way it goes onto the paper, can also be distinguished from that of other types of pens. Since it is not a true liquid, it does not flow into the paper fibers and spread in the same way as fountain pen inks. The inks from "erasable" ball-point pens are even more unusual in this respect.

Modern fountain pens ordinarily have a more or less rounded point, but when pressure is increased, there is a separation of the nib, producing two marks which can be readily detected. Compared with steel pens, which often scratch the fiber surface of the paper and periodically run low on ink, fountain pens yield a relatively uniform ink flow and do not leave a sharply cut line or indentation at the edge of the line.

Fiber-tip pens often give a thicker line compared with ball-point pens. The ink flow is uniform and constant unless the ink supply is running low or the tip of the pen has been exposed to the air for too long a time. They usually do not leave indentation marks like other pens, and there are no nib marks or any cut appearance. However, since the ink is a true liquid, it sometimes does spread and may show diffuse edges or "bleeding" and accumulation between letters.

Pencil markings can easily be determined by their appearance. The "lead" of a common pencil is essentially a mixture of graphite and clay, the proportion determining the hardness of the pencil. Because of the very simple composition of pencil lead, pencils have a very limited degree of individuality. Some polymeric binders are now being used which may contribute to increased comparison value.

Individualization of ball-point and fiber-tip pens is also very difficult. Steel pens and fountain pens, because of wear or damage to the tip of the pen through use, do develop individualizing characteristics, and writing with one of these instruments can sometimes be traced to a particular pen. Occasionally, useful striation marks may appear in ball-point pen writing. These may have an individual character which develops as a result of wear.

Paper

A variety of materials are used in manufacturing paper, but most paper is made from wood pulp. Wood pulp paper may be either mechanical or chemical, depending upon the method used to break down the wood into isolated fibers.

Other, nonwood, fibers may be introduced to impart special characteristics in producing certain special types of paper. Bond paper used for legal documents, for example, contains a relatively high percentage (25 to 50 percent) of cotton fiber. Sometimes known as rag paper, it has more permanence than papers made solely from wood fibers. The percentage of cotton fiber, or rag, is generally indicated in the watermark. The mechanical and chemical pretreatments to which wood is subjected in being reduced to pulp for paper-making produce certain effects which can be detected using microscopical and microchemical techniques. Fibers found in papers in which mechanical methods have been used to produce the pulp show distinctive damage and are generally shorter. Paper made from mechanically produced pulp is known as *ground wood*. Newsprint is an example of such paper. Wood pulp used in making writing papers is generally treated with sodium sulfite. The resulting product is usually called *sulfite* paper. Bond papers contain both rag and wood fibers. By using special stains which dye these two types of fibers different colors, each type of fiber can be recognized and counted in the mixture, and the rag content of a small paper fragment can thus be estimated. A sulfate process is used to produce so-called *kraft* papers. The term *kraft* is derived from a German word that implies strength. Kraft papers are among the strongest of wood pulp papers and are used for making paper bags and brown wrapping paper.

In addition to determinations on the nature of the raw material of the paper, there are other properties used by document examiners in paper identification: (1) color; (2) size and shape; (3) inclusions; (4) pattern design, ruling and framing; (5) watermarks; (6) thickness; (7) weight; (8) bleaching, dyeing, or other special processes, including sizing and loading, and (9) surface appearance and fluorescence.

Many of these properties can be determined by simple nondestructive tests. The color of a paper can be compared with a color chart; the size can be measured with a suitable ruler; thickness can be checked using a micrometer, or paper caliper; fluorescence can be seen by exposing the paper to ultraviolet (UV) light; and watermarks are easily visible by transmitted visible light. Although these tests are empirical, the properties they reveal are quite characteristic.

Some tests, such as weight determination, require that the paper be cut and dried before the measurement. With other examinations, such as raw material identification, the paper must be completely disintegrated by chemical or mechanical means and the fibers examined microscopically and/or instrumentally. The dye used in colored papers may be identified by thin-layer chromatography (TLC), and trace inclusions may be identified by various microscopical and instrumental methods. Sizings and clays, used for "loading" to make the paper heavier and slicker, can also be studied by microscopical and instrumental methods. These methods can also be employed to detect specialized fillers, such as titanium dioxide, which are used to make papers whiter and more opaque.

Inks

The most common writing material is ink. Ink is made by incorporating a mixture of pigments or dyes into a carrier substance. Although there are many different formulas used by different manufacturers, the colored components of ink include only a few types of basic substances which give the ink its class designation. The most common kinds of ink are described in the following paragraphs.

India ink: The oldest form of ink, also referred to as Chinese ink, it is a fine suspension of carbon black in water and gum, or other binder, or in a solution of shellac and borax with a wetting agent. It gives the most permanent of all ink colors.

Logwood ink: An extract of wood chips of the logwood tree, its chief color ingredients are hematoxylin and potassium chromate. These inks were used to a considerable extent in the past.

Iron gallotannate ink: Consisting of tannic acid, gallic acid, ferrous sulfate, and often an aniline-based dye, this ink is not merely deposited on the surface but can penetrate and react within the paper fibers. It has been used for a long time, and still is, as the basis of many commercial writing inks. The aniline dye provides the immediate, or short-term, pigment; the other components react as they age on the paper to produce the permanent mark.

Nigrosine ink: One of the early black dye inks, the dye in this ink is a synthetic compound prepared from aniline and nitrobenzene. Because of its water solubility and the weathering effects of writing made by this ink, it is now used infrequently.

Dye inks: Consisting of some type of basic, acidic or neutral organic dye, largely derived from coal tar or petroleum, these are the chief source of color in most inks. The dyes can be readily removed from an ink line and separated by TLC. The separation pattern of component dyes is distinctly different for different preparations and thus provides a basis for the determination of whether a known or questioned document was prepared with the same type of ink.

Methods of ink analysis and comparisons of unknown samples with known ink standards are generally straightforward. The initial approach to a comparison between known and questioned inks utilizes nondestructive techniques, such as color comparison, determination of the type of ink (ball-point, fiber-tip, fountain pen, etc.), infrared absorption, infrared luminescence, and UV fluorescence properties. If the unknown ink differs from the known in any of these properties, then the inks could not have had a common origin. If the questioned ink exhibits the same properties as the known standard, further analysis is required to try to establish a basis for possible common origin.

The most generally applicable technique for the chemical analysis of ink is TLC. This technique makes use of a solid stationary phase and a moving liquid phase to separate various constituents of a mixture (Chapter 3). There is a variety of commercially available TLC plates that have different stationary phase coatings. The sample is spotted (applied) at one end of the plate, which is then placed into a closed chamber containing a mixture of solvents selected according to what is to be separated. The end to which the samples were applied is dipped into the solvent so that the solvent can wet this end of the support layer and migrate across the plate. When the solvent front has migrated a sufficient distance, the plate is dried. The TLC technique makes possible the separation (and comparison) of both colored and many noncolored components used in ink formulations. Colored substances which have separated can be seen under normal room light, and UV illumination will reveal any separated fluorescent components. Infrared luminescence may also be useful in detecting certain components. The pattern of separation for an unknown can easily be compared with that of known standards, and the R_f values of each component can be determined.

Ink can be removed from a document with a special tool made from a hypodermic needle having a sharp, squared-off point to punch out a microdot from a written line or simply by removing the middle portion of a written line with a sharp scraper. The ink is then extracted out of the microdot with a solvent suitable for chromatographic analysis. Two of the most popular TLC solvent systems used for ink analysis are ethyl acetate:ethanol:water, 70:35:30, and n-butanol:ethanol:water, 50:10:15.

Differences between two inks can often be observed easily by comparison of the patterns of the colored components. Those inks with similar visible chromatograms can be further compared by observing any differences or similarities in fluorescent components on the TLC plate under UV illumination. Once a questioned ink has been identified, the first date of its production can sometimes be determined from information supplied by the manufacturers.

HANDWRITING COMPARISON

Handwriting comparison is the most frequently requested type of document examination. Handwriting occurs in many phases of human activity and throughout life. As children, we are taught a system of handwriting. Throughout the early years of learning, children are urged to copy the system as closely as possible. During later years, we gradually drift away from the standard forms, and consciously or unconsciously experiment with new letter forms and unique combinations of designs. With maturity and adulthood, an individual becomes more concerned with the content of a written message and pays less attention to the actual letter forms. Although there is still variation in a person's writing, the wide fluctuations and experimentation with forms that tend to characterize the adolescent years are no longer evident. Throughout the process of development of writing, personal habits contribute their own characteristics, and writing becomes as individualistic as speech and mannerisms.

Handwriting comparisons and the identification of the writer of a document are thus predicated on the assumption that certain deeply ingrained habits develop over the lifetime of a writer, and that they are consistently and unconsciously reproduced in a person's handwriting. Even where there is a marked effort to disguise the writing, some of the peculiarities continue to show up in it. Through careful comparison, analysis, and interpretation of the individual and class characteristics of questioned and known writing, a document examiner can usually determine whether the questioned document and the known standards were written by the same individual. Many factors must be considered, but it is primarily through a comparison of individualistic writing habits that an association between a sample of writing and its author is established. Handwriting comparison has no connection with the field of graphology, or so-called character reading through handwriting. The methods used and the purposes are distinctly different.

Class and Individual Characteristics

The gross features of writing are called *class characteristics*. This group generally refers to the gross features of letters, relative dimensions of letters, connections, capitalization, punctuation, and other such features of the writing. Some of the class characteristics of writing are derived from the particular writing system learned early in life. Figure 13-1 shows some of these features. The unusual *T*, the distinctive *L*, and the Greek *e* are examples. Class characteristics are ordinarily easier to reproduce than are individual characteristics.

The *individual characteristics* are those less-conspicuous special features in writing. In Figure 13-1, for example, in the top frame (genuine signature), the *o* is open at the top, the *m* and *n* have pointed humps, and there is a tendency to end with an exaggerated upward upstroke. Individual characteristics are usually developed by the writer over a long period of time. Those distinct and particular letter forms which characterize an individual's handwriting are more difficult to duplicate and therefore more significant in handwriting comparison.

Handwriting comparisons are based on the premise that no two individuals produce exactly the same handwriting. Two pieces of writing may look very much alike and yet have been written by two different persons. Two such grossly similar pieces of handwriting could be differentiated on the basis of their individual characteristics.

Some individual and class characteristics are undoubtedly affected by the speed of writing and the condition of the writer. Greater writing speed, for example, generally increases slant, and introduces a marked simplification of letters, a greater

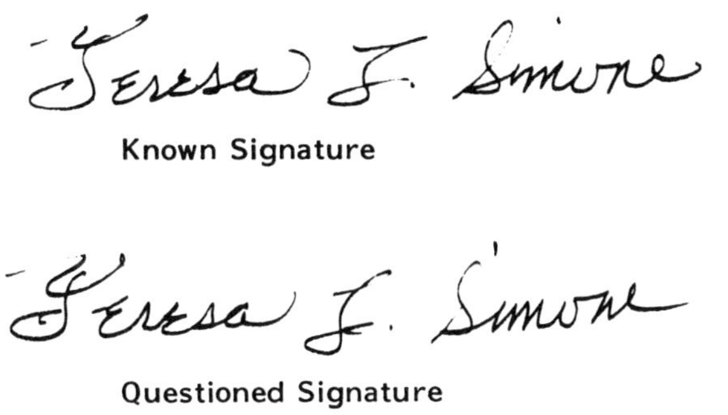

FIGURE 13-1
Characteristics of handwriting.
(Courtesy of Patricia Hatch, University of New Haven.)

Known Signature

Questioned Signature

difference in emphasis, and increased illegibility toward the end of words. Document examiners have to consider such factors when carrying out their examinations.

There are some key suspicious signs that may indicate spuriousness. Examples are broken strokes, wavering lines, retouching of parts of letters, contradictory signs of writing speed, accentuation at the end of words, and overemphasis on initial strokes. These signs can have significant value in comparisons.

Standards for Comparison

As mentioned earlier, the writing of an individual will contain a certain amount of variation. Some people show relatively little variation, whereas others display a considerable amount. In order to arrive at a correct and valid interpretation, therefore, a document examiner must have an adequate quantity of sample writing, a good representative sample of standards, and samples of a directly comparable nature for comparison. Any limitation or restriction of these basic criteria can adversely affect the outcome of a handwriting comparison.

Handwriting standards for comparison are generally obtained from two sources, collected writing and requested writing.

Collected Writing   This type of standard consists of material written before any investigation began and at a time when the writer would have no reason for thinking that the writing was eventually to be employed as a standard for handwriting comparison. Such materials will have been written in the normal course of life activities and are expected to exhibit the normal writing habits and individualities of the particular author. Collected writing standards are most useful if they were written at a time as close to that of the questioned writing as possible. In addition, the standards should contain writing of the same form as that of the questioned sample, that is signatures, extended writing, or perhaps printing. There are a number of different possible sources of collected writing, and it is generally advisable to obtain samples written by a suspected author, even in cases where it will be possible to obtain requested standard writing (see below). It is imperative that the authenticity of collected writing standards be verified. Without such proof, the samples are useless as standards and will not be admissible in a court. Some examples of possible sources of collected standard writings are: business and personal correspondence; cancelled checks and bank records; school records; library records; written applications for jobs, credit or loans, insurance coverage, certificates, and various types of licenses.

Requested Writing   This type of standard consists of materials written by specific request during an investigation to be used as comparison standards for questioned writing samples. A sufficient quantity of writing should be obtained to enable an examiner to determine the specific writing habits of the individual and the individual characteristics of the writing. There are no hard-and-fast rules establishing what constitutes a sufficient sample, since different individuals may or may not write in a consistently individualistic manner. However, many document examiners would agree with the following general guidelines, subject to necessary modifications in particular situations. (1) Standards for writing on the faces of checks or for check endorsements consist of 10 to 15 comparable writings or signatures, using the same text and similar blank check forms if possible. If blank check forms are unavailable, the paper should be of a similar size and quality to that of the questioned checks. (2) Standards for questioned miscellaneous notations or signatures should be collected in a similar manner, 10 or 15 separate samples being generally regarded as adequate. (3) Standards for questioned extended writing samples (such as letters or notes) usually consist of two to five samples of the same text written on separate sheets of similar paper.

In collecting requested writing sample standards, the type of paper, its size, the writing instrument, and the ink should be duplicated as closely as possible. These standards are often collected by having the investigator or examiner dictate the text to the subject. If this procedure is followed, the subject should be made comfortable and put at ease, seated at a desk or table, and the text dictated with no suggestion as to spelling, punctuation, capitalization, arrangement of the material, and so forth. The speed of dictation may have to be varied depending upon the individual's writing speed. Each collected sample should be taken by the examiner when it is completed and before the subject begins to prepare the next sample. Questioned samples are not shown to such subjects until after the requested writing standards have been collected. In cases where the text of the questioned writing is not to be disclosed to the subject for some reason, a similar text with similar characteristics may be substituted to obtain the standards. If there is evidence of deliberate disguise in the collected specimens, it may be necessary to collect requested samples at different times. Experience indicates that handwriting samples secured early in an interview with a subject are more likely to reflect ordinary writing habits than those obtained after a great deal of discussion.

Various law enforcement agencies have developed several different kinds of handwriting standard forms. Some of them have limitations and are undesirable as the sole sources of standards. Investigators should not utilize such forms exclusively and should look upon them as aids.

Other Individualities

Handwriting is a unique, complex, and exclusively human activity. It reflects a number of the writer's individual characteristics, including manipulative dexterity, learning experience, and exercise of muscular control and neuromuscular coordination. All these factors affect not only the style of the letters in handwriting but also the arrangement of the writing. Spacing, alignment, margins, and insertions are the result of personal habits. Spelling, grammar, punctuation, and phraseology are the result of one's education, cultural background, knowledge of the language being written, and habits. All these characteristics are important in handwriting comparisons. When one person traces or otherwise copies another's writing or signature, the forger attempts to omit his or her own writing habits and to adopt those of the original author of the document. On the part of the individual doing the copying, this activity is really drawing rather than writing. In cases of this kind, it is often possible to recognize the copied signature as a forgery; but it is seldom possible to identify the author of the copy by comparing the copied writing with normal writing samples of the forger. Hand printing and numerals produced by an individual can often be identified as that person's work as well, using essentially the same principles as those which apply to handwriting comparisons.

In handwriting analysis, all the characteristics and special features of both the known and questioned documents must be considered and compared. Differences between the two give a strong indication of two different writers, unless the differences can be accounted for by the facts known to surround the preparation of the documents. The uniqueness of characteristics is an important factor, but no single handwriting characteristic can, by itself, be taken as the basis for a positive comparison.

Document examiners are occasionally called upon to examine materials written under awkward or unusual circumstances. In some cases, these conditions are obviously responsible for the exaggerated letter forms and special features. Since normal handwriting is the product of neuromuscular coordination, any condition which affects central nervous system function, and/or fine muscle control, will affect normal handwriting. It is known that various drugs, alcohol, and various physical and mental conditions can contribute to many unusual features being reflected in handwriting.

Before a positive opinion of identity can be stated, there must be a sufficient number of individual characteristics present in both questioned and known writing. When considered in combination with each other, these characteristics are sufficient to establish that both writings were prepared by the same individual. In some cases, the amount of evidence available to support such a positive opinion will be more than adequate. In other instances, however, the evidence may be less convincing for any number of reasons. The questioned writing sample may be too limited; it may be too distorted or disguised; there may be insufficient standards, or improper ones; a questioned document may have been prepared under some unusual circumstances which for some reason causes failure to exhibit sufficient individual characteristics. In cases like these, an examiner may be unable to reach a positive opinion, and an opinion that the comparison was inconclusive may be offered.

MECHANICAL IMPRESSIONS

Mechanical impressions are impressions placed on a document by a machine or tool. It is often possible to determine the type of mechanical device used to produce the markings on a certain document. It is also possible to determine whether or not different documents were produced by the same device.

Many types of mechanical devices are used to produce all different sorts of documents. Most mechanical impressions are produced on paper, and the most common types of mechanical impression devices are typewriters, checkwriters, printing presses or machines, stamps (rubber or steel), and copying machines. Less common types of machines include plate makers, microfilm or microfiche reader-printers, transparency makers, and facsimile machines.

Typewriting Comparisons

Typewriting is the most common kind of mechanical writing encountered by document examiners. Four different kinds of typewriting examinations are commonly requested:

1 Determination of the type, make, and model of typewriter which produced the questioned typing
2 Determination of whether a particular typewriter produced the questioned typing
3 Determination of when the questioned typing was produced
4 Determination of whether the typed material was produced continuously

To attempt the first of these determinations, a document examiner must have access to a complete reference collection of typefaces used by different manufacturers. In the past, typewriter companies in the United States designed and manufactured their own typefaces. At present, many companies purchase type styles from other companies which specialize in typeface design and manufacture.

Two of the most popular type pitches are pica and elite (Figure 13-2). Pica type has 10 characters to the inch; elite type has 12. It is not too difficult for a document examiner to identify the make and model of a typewriter used to produce a questioned typing sample, using the style and shape of the typeface and the horizontal and vertical spacing between characters. Today, however, since many typewriter manufacturers purchase typefaces from other companies, different brands of typewriters may use identical type styles. At the same time, it is also possible for some examples of the same brand of typewriter to have different type styles. These developments limit a document examiner's ability to make a positive identification of the typewriter manufacturer simply by a comparison of typefaces.

Typewriter manufacturers may periodically purchase a different typeface from a different supplier, change a type design for a certain brand of typewriter, or discontinue a certain model. All this information, if it is available, can be very helpful to a document examiner in establishing the backdating of a questioned sample of typewriting.

Each typewriter has its own individual characteristics that enable differentiation of characters typed on it from those typed on other machines. These differences are easy to see on typewriters with different characters and different type styles. Differences are apparent even between similar machines of the same manufacturer, although they are not so pronounced. These differences come about in two ways: manufacturing imperfections and wear due to usage.

When a new typewriter comes out of the factory, it already has some "personality" of its own in terms of the typewriting it will produce. Misalignment of the type, irregular impression of the typebars, cavity and accidental defects on the characters, and other mechanical imperfections are the common defects. These defects combine to give the typewriter its own individuality. And they can be detected, regardless of how slight they may be, by carefully conducted visual and microscopic comparisons.

Like other mechanical devices, typewriters are subject to wear and develop indi-

10 PITCH TYPEFACES

Forensic science is the .... Prestige Pica
application of natural .... Courier
sciences to matters of .... Delegate
THE LAW. FORENSIC SCIENCE .... ORATOR

12 PITCH TYPEFACES

is the application of natural sciences .... Artisan
to matters of the law. Forensic .... Letter Gothic
science is the application of .... Prestige Elite
natural sciences to matters of .... *Light Italic*

PROPORTIONAL SPACING TYPEFACES

the law. Forensic science is the .... Boldface
application of natural sciences .... *Boldface Italic*
to matters of the law. Forensic .... Thesis
science is the application of natural .... **Title**
sciences to matters of the law .... Modern

(*a*)

SCALE (in twelfths of an inch)

This is an example of 15.00 pitch.

This is an example of 13.33 pitch.

This is an example of 12.00 pitch. (Elite)

This is an example of 10.91 pitch.

This is an example of 10.00 pitch. (Pica)

This is an example of 09.23 pitch.

This is an example of 08.57 pitch.

This is an example of 08.00 pitch.

This is an example of 07.50 pitch.

This is an example of 07.06 pitch.

This is an example of 06.00 pitch.

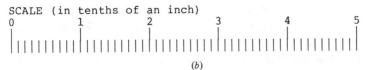

SCALE (in tenths of an inch)

(*b*)

FIGURE 13-2
(*a*) Typeface and (*b*) pitch variations.

vidual characteristics through use. In addition, individual characteristics present when the machine was new may become accentuated through use. These characteristics are developed over the course of time due to bending of typebars, chipping of typefaces, damage to characters, and wear on certain parts. All of these minor alterations will affect the vertical and horizontal alignment of characters, the pressure of the impression of each character, the relative spacing and location of each character, and the condition and deformation of the typeface.

In 1961, a new type of machine, the Selectric typewriter, was introduced by IBM. This typewriter does not use conventional typebars. The typing is done by a typing element, a nickel-plated plastic ball, bearing the typeface, which is mounted on the type head. The platen of a Selectric typewriter does not move from left to right as characters are typed; instead, the platen remains stationary and the type head moves on a special carriage. Today, with the expiration of the IBM patent, several other manufacturers have produced similar typewriters. The examination of documents typed on Selectric typewriters is similar to the examination of conventional typewriting. The Selectric's principles are also employed in a number of word processor devices. There still can be many individual characteristics, such as typeface imperfections, letter defects, improper line spacing and misalignment, and letter spacing misalignments, which can be used for comparison. Since the typing elements of Selectrics are interchangeable, however, the comparison of typeface is actually a comparison of individual typing systems, machine and element together, and not so much the typewriter itself. Certain characteristics of the typewritten product, such as line spacing, are products of the typewriter rather than of the typing element.

With the newer self-correcting Selectrics and their electronic successors, typing errors can be corrected using correctable film ribbons and an auxiliary lift-off tape. The pitch of these machines can be changed to either 10 or 12 characters per inch, and the newer electronic models have a proportional spacing feature (Figure 13-2). In addition, spacing, margins, and strike pressure can be controlled by the operator within certain limits, depending upon the machine. All these features have created some new problems in typewriting comparisons.

With many of the printers used with modern word processors, the positioning of letters is controlled electronically by computer programs rather than by the mechanical escapements used in electric and mechanical typewriters. The pitch of type may be different from the standard pica and elite and may vary from line to line. In addition, proportional spacing can be used on these devices, and, as mentioned above, is available on the newer IBM electronic typewriters. Here, the spacing between letters is varied according to the size of the letter.

The same techniques used for typewriting comparisons can be used to compare machine printing or stamped impressions on documents.

Copying Machines

A great variety of chemical, thermal, and electrostatic office copying machines have been introduced in the past two or three decades. Electrostatic types, led by Xerox, have largely supplanted the earlier types. Today, document examiners are encountering photocopies rather than originals with increasing frequency. Document examiners are now often called upon to determine: (1) the type of process used to make the copy, (2) the manufacturer and model of the machine used to make the photocopy, (3) whether a particular copier was used to make a particular photocopy, and (4) whether two or more copies can be shown to have been produced by the same copying machine.

Photocopier Processes Photocopier machines generally use one of three types of copying processes: chemical, thermal, or electrostatic. The electrostatic process is gradually replacing the other two.

Chemical Copier Processes Chemical copiers use light-sensitive papers to receive the image of the document being copied. In a simplified version of the photographic process, the exposed light-sensitive paper is placed in contact with another type of special paper. Both are processed through a wet chemical solution and then pulled apart to reveal a positive image on the second sheet.

Thermal Copying Processes The thermal copying process uses heat to form the image. This process, developed by the Minnesota Mining and Manufacturing (3M) Company (Thermofax) uses a sensitized paper treated with special chemicals. When subjected to varying degrees of heat, these chemicals form visible images. The sensitized paper is placed in direct contact with the document to be copied. They are both introduced into the machine where they are exposed to radiant heat from an infrared lamp. The characters (writing) on the original absorb more heat than the reflective surrounding surface and directly heat the appropriate areas of the sensitized paper to form the image.

Electrostatic Processes This process is the most common in modern photocopiers. The first commercial electrostatic photocopier equipment was introduced by the Haloid Company (now Xerox Corporation) in 1950. The equipment was called a xerographic machine. Today, there are about 40 different manufacturers of such equipment, and nearly 200 different models are available. Electrostatic processes are based on physical and electrical phenomena where static electricity attracts small particles having an opposite charge onto a photoconductive surface. There are basically two similar electrostatic processes in use for copy reproduction. The first is *xerography,* which employs a selenium coating on a metal plate as the photoconductor. The image, first formed on this metal plate, is used to attract toner particles which are then transferred to a sheet of plain paper. The second type of process is called *electrofax.* Here, a thin coating of zinc oxide on paper is used as the photoconductor. Since this type of process requires special zinc oxide–coated paper instead of plain paper, the two basic types of processes can be readily distinguished.

Examination of Photocopies and Photocopier Identification Determination of the manufacturer and model of the photocopy machine which produced the copies is generally the primary concern when examining photocopy documents. Each type of photocopier usually imparts some class characteristics to its products. To distinguish whether a photocopied document was produced by an electrostatic or thermal copying process, the photocopy itself can be examined. A copy produced by a xerographic process is on plain paper; electrofax process copies are produced on a paper coated with zinc oxide; thermal process copies are produced on papers coated with heat-sensitive chemicals. The texture, weight, color, tone, and trademarks of these papers are different. Through careful observation and comparison, a document examiner can arrive at a correct conclusion.

Many photocopiers also yield other class characteristics. Copies may have observable physical markings which can be associated with a particular make and model of machine. Some copiers, for example, cause characteristic marks on the paper from the rollers and gripping devices used to feed the paper. These marks can be helpful in identifying the possible make and model of a copier, based upon their shape, design, and position. Many copiers also impart various types of black streaks or lines on the front and reverse sides of the paper because of the design and positioning of the rollers in the transport system within the machine. These lines can also serve as identifying marks. Sometimes, however, these lines are not consistent from one machine to another in the same model group. The types of toners and the papers can also serve as parameters for identification.

Besides the class characteristics, photocopiers may also yield individual characteristics on their products. These are produced by dirt, marks, or other features on the drum, the glass cover, and the protective cover. They are transmitted to the copy and can help identify a particular copying machine. Some of these marks are permanent and represent imperfections in certain parts of the machine. Others, however, are transient and may be due to dirt or certain temporary defects. An examiner must be extremely cautious in basing a comparison on this type of "trash" mark. Service records and repair information can be very helpful in interpretation in this respect.

In addition to copier classification and individual characteristics, questions sometimes arise concerning other aspects of photocopies. These can have to do with enlargement or reduction in cases of copies from machines that have such capabilities, for example. Another example might be the determination of the "generation" of the copy in question from the original document (that is, the question of whether the questioned document is a copy of a copy).

Frauds involving photocopies sometimes involve the preparation of a copy from parts of one or more original documents. For example, the heading and signature of a letter may come from one document, and the text from another source. Examiners, therefore, have to be very careful in examining photocopies of documents.

Standards from suspected photocopying machines are very important for comparisons. The proper procedure for obtaining comparison standards is to activate the suspected machine without a document to be copied in place. The copy produced will then be a blank but will contain all the class characteristics such as streaks, lines, grab marks, and the individual trash marks produced by dirt or defects. At least seven samples should be obtained from a suspected machine and submitted to the laboratory. The glass cover and drum should never be cleaned before obtaining the standards, and the make and model of the copier should be noted, preferably on a separate sheet of paper. The front of the standard samples, as well as the questioned sample, should not be marked or written on. Any recent repair information or service records should be noted and included along with the submission.

Other Printing Machines

Occasionally, document examiners are called upon to examine documents produced by a variety of business machines, such as adding machines, checkwriters, rubber stamps, steel stamps, stencil cutters, and printing presses. It is often possible to determine: (1) the basic type of machine which produced the document, (2) the make of the particular machine used to produce the document, and (3) the possibility that a particular machine produced a particular document.

The same general principles using class and individual characteristics apply to the examination of adding machine tapes, checkwriter impressions, and documents produced by various printing presses. There are many different types of printing machines available. The process of identifying the type of machine is similar to that used with typewriters. The individual characteristics resulting from slight defects and malfunctions can be used to help individualize a particular machine. Sometimes, the ink and paper can be helpful in identification. It is still sometimes difficult to distinguish a genuine printed document from a forged copy. Document examiners must compare the plates, artwork, and original documents which have been copied.

Checkwriters are designed to perforate, print, or make a grooved number in the check. There are several different types of checkwriters available. They can be differentiated by the design, shape, and size of the type fonts. Checkwriters may also produce individual characteristics. If at all possible, the suspected machine should be submitted to the laboratory in a case involving a questioned document produced on a checkwriter. If this cannot be done, approximately 10 impressions of each questioned combination should be obtained using the same type of paper.

With rubber or steel stamps, it is often possible to determine whether a certain stamp was used to make a particular impression. It is important to submit the original stamp in its original condition, along with the questioned specimens. It should not, for example, be cleaned.

RECONSTRUCTIONS

Erasures

A change in the existing writing on a document may be accomplished by alteration of one or more original letters or by erasure of an original entry and substitution of a false one. In either case, the questioned document examiner must show that a change has taken place, and, if possible, try to reveal the nature and content of the original writing.

Erasures can be made by simple mechanical removal of the writing or by chemical bleaching. A mechanical erasure can be done with different rubber erasers or by scraping. Microscopical examination under low-power magnification will certainly detect the disturbance of the paper fibers and the traces of rubber eraser residue. Mechanical erasures may also be revealed by dusting the suspected area with a fine fingerprint powder or dyed lycopodium powder, which adheres to the areas that were erased. Infrared microscopy and/or infrared photography can occasionally be employed to reveal the original writing and make it legible (Figure 13-3). A chemical erasure is generally made with acidic oxidizing solutions (similar to household bleach) which bleach the dyes and dissolve the iron salts of the ink. Examination under UV light will generally reveal such erasures as patches of altered fluorescence. The use of powders to detect mechanical erasures is not a truly nondestructive technique and should not be attempted by inexperienced examiners.

Alterations

The most commonly altered documents are checks, books of account, wills, lottery tickets, certificates, and official records. An alteration may be made by a simple addition. For example, a check for $6 may be changed by adding a zero after the *6* to make it read *60* and writing *ty* after the *six* to make it *sixty*. Alterations may also be made by combinations of erasures and additions. Figures in account books may be erased and changed, for example, and numbers may be substituted on lottery tickets. Alterations may also be carried out simply by cutting off or otherwise removing the unwanted part of the document.

Simple alteration by addition can be detected by careful inspection of the document under magnification. Generally, the differences in writing materials, shade, spacing between letters, and appearance of letters or numbers will be apparent under low-power magnification (Figure 13-4). Infrared and UV photography can sometimes reveal such alterations as well. Alterations carried out by cutting away parts are difficult to do. The person altering the document needs both luck and skill; the part to be removed (and parts to be added) must fall in the right places and possess

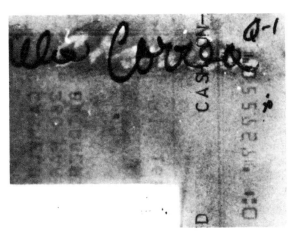

FIGURE 13-3
An infrared photograph of a document with obliterated printing. (*Courtesy of James Behrendt, Forensic Science Laboratory, Connecticut State Police.*)

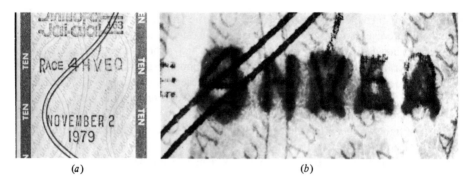

(a)   (b)

FIGURE 13-4

(*a*) A gaming ticket. (*b*) Alterations detected by magnification and UV light. (*Courtesy of Marius Venclauskas, Forensic Science Laboratory, Connecticut State Police.*)

similar writing styles. Visual inspection of the document and reading of the contents often suffice to detect these changes.

Indented Writing and Charred Documents

Indented writings are marks (indentations) which are left on a sheet of paper (or other surface) underneath the one on which the visible writing was done. Such indentations are caused by the pressure on the paper exerted by the writing instrument (Figure 13-5). In many instances, indented writing has proved to be valuable evidence, and it can often be deciphered simply by viewing it with oblique light. This evidence can remain long after the original document has been lost or destroyed. The oblique lighting method of deciphering indented writing is the oldest and best-known technique. The amount, quality, and angle of the lighting are all important. Usually, a high-intensity or fiber-optics light with a rheostatic control and adjustable focal system and held at an angle of about 5 to 10° with respect to the paper or surface will yield a good result. A linear slit source is also valuable for this purpose.

A fluorescent powder method has also been used by document examiners for deciphering indented writing. In this procedure, a fluorescent powder is blotted over the suspect surface. After removal of the excess powder, the document is viewed under UV illumination. Some papers, however, may contain brighteners which also fluoresce under UV light, causing some problem with this technique. Accordingly, a selection of powders that are sensitive (fluorescent) at a number of different excitation wavelengths can be quite helpful.

A new instrument called an electrostatic detection apparatus (ESDA) was recently made available for detecting indented writing. ESDA employs some of the principles of xerography (see above, in connection with copying machines) to produce a transparency of indented impressions on documents. The method is nondestructive.

Another technique for revealing indented writing involves the use of iodine vapor and is based on the fact that these vapors are absorbed more readily by the fibers in

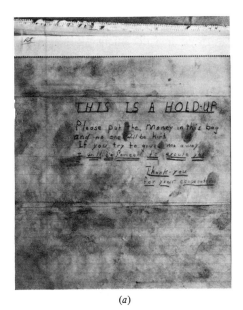

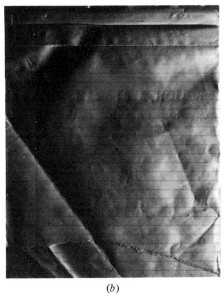

(a)   (b)

FIGURE 13-5
(a) A hold-up note left at a bank by a bank robber. (b) A note pad from a bank robbery suspect's residence. This note pad shows indented writing brought out by oblique illumination. The indented writing corresponds to the hold-up note shown in (a) indicating that the note was written on the suspect's pad. (*Courtesy of Sergeant First Class Richard Tidey, Forensic Science Bureau, New Jersey State Police.*)

the compressed (indented) portions of the paper. The iodine fuming cabinet used for raising latent fingerprints (Figure 12-6) gives good results. Other methods which have been reported include dusting the document with a lead powder followed by examination by radiographic technique, the gelatin gel method, infrared retroreflection technique, differential evaporation of benzene, and instrumental techniques.

Sometimes, criminals attempt to destroy incriminating documents by burning them. In other cases, important documents can be involved in accidental fires. It is sometimes possible for a document examiner to decipher documents that have been in a fire. If the paper or surface is merely "toasted," the writing can be rendered legible by viewing or photography under infrared light.

Determination of the Age of Documents

Document examiners are often asked to try to determine the age of a document. Cases involving age determination might include false entries in account books, suspicious papers in connection with contested wills, fraudulently antique or old documents, and many others. Some knowledge of paper, ink, watermarks, and other document components is necessary before an estimation of a document's age can be attempted.

The age of the ink is considered the most useful indicator for determining the approximate age of a document. The presence of comparatively fresh markings on old, faded paper is usually an indication of a fraudulent document. With iron gallotannate and some dye inks, the colors undergo a series of orderly changes with age, first reaching a maximal intensity and then generally fading out. The phenomenon is due to light and oxidation effects. The acidity or alkalinity of most paper will also affect the rate at which ink color fades.

There are several chemical tests for the determination of the age of inks. One of the most popular is the chloride migration test. It is based on the assumption that chlorides in the writing move away from the ink stroke at a constant rate and the distance moved is a linear function of time. The extent of chloride migration on a questioned document is compared with known standards, providing a means of determining the approximate age of the questioned ink writing. Although this test is the best currently available for the purpose, many factors such as storage conditions and humidity affect the rate of chloride migration. In addition, many modern inks do not contain sufficient amounts of chloride for the migration test to be feasible.

The ball-point pen was introduced in this country in 1945. A document prepared prior to that date, therefore, should not contain any ball-point ink. Determination of the age of ball-point ink itself is based on periodic changes in formula by the manufacturers. The pigment and dye composition of ball-point ink can be analyzed using TLC, spectrophotometry, microspectrophotometry, UV fluorescence, and infrared luminescence techniques.

The Bureau of Alcohol, Tobacco and Firearms (ATF) has an extensive collection of inks in its ink library. For many years industry has cooperated with ATF in providing samples of inks on a periodic basis. When a change is made, or a new formula introduced, a sample is sent to ATF for the ink library. By comparing the TLC patterns, composition, and other properties of a questioned sample with knowns, the manufacturer and approximate age of the ink can be determined. In recent years, some manufacturers have begun cooperating with ATF in an ink taggant program. Nontoxic but chemically detectable tags are added to ink formulas. These tags are valuable in determining the age of more recent inks containing them.

The use of watermarks is one of the most reliable methods for determining whether a document is as old as it is purported to be. The watermark is a distinctive mark or design placed in the paper at the time of manufacture. Some manufacturers change their watermark annually, or include codes that are changed more frequently. This practice provides a very nice method for determining the approximate date of production of a paper. In some instances, the watermark alone is sufficient to establish a document's validity or lack of it. For example, a document dated November 22, 1938, but written on paper bearing a 1970 watermark is obviously fraudulent.

The components of paper fibers, brighteners, pigments, and sizings have also been used to some extent in estimating the age of documents. In the past, for example, the most common type of paper whitener was China clay, but more recently titanium dioxide has been used. A document's authenticity is obviously questionable if it contains chemicals which were not in use at the time of its alleged preparation!

STUDY QUESTIONS

1 What is a questioned document?
2 Describe several different situations which would require questioned document examinations.
3 Why is a questioned document examination of handwritten materials more subjective than a forensic comparison of blood, glass, or typewritten material?
4 Describe the characteristics of writing impressions made by ball-point pens. By fiber-tip pens. By pencils.
5 What is the "rag" content of paper?
6 Name several properties of papers that can be used for comparisons.
7 Name several different varieties of ink, and explain how they differ from one another.
8 What is the most common technique for the comparison of inks?
9 What are the basic principles in handwriting comparison? Name and discuss some of the characteristics of handwriting used by document examiners for comparison.
10 What are the basic features of typewriting used by document examiners in making comparisons?
11 What does pitch mean in connection with typewriting?
12 What kinds of problems has the IBM Selectric typewriter introduced for the document examiner in terms of making typewriting comparisons?
13 What are the basic types of copy production used in copying machines? Briefly describe each one.
14 What characteristics can be used by document examiners in comparing copies of documents?
15 What are the most common types of erasures and how are they detected on a document?
16 Name some of the different kinds of alterations of a document other than erasures and explain how they might be detected.
17 What are several methods used to reconstruct indented writing?
18 How can the age of a document be estimated?
19 Discuss the principles that should be followed in collecting and preserving document evidence.
20 Discuss the principles and mechanics of obtaining known standards for handwriting comparison, for typewriting comparison, and for the comparison of copies.

REFERENCES AND FURTHER READING

Attenberger, D. W., and W. G. Kanaskie: "Examination of Typewritten Documents," *FBI Law Enforcement Bulletin,* June 1981.

Bates, B. P.: *Identification System for Questioned Documents,* Charles C Thomas, Springfield, Ill., 1970.

Brunelle, R. L.: "Questioned Document Examination," in R. Saferstein (ed.), *Forensic Science Handbook,* Prentice-Hall, Englewood Cliffs, N.J. 1982.

Brunelle, R. L., and A. A. Cantu: "Ink Analysis—A Weapon Against Crime by Detection of Fraud," in G. Davis (ed.), *Forensic Science,* American Chemical Society, Washington, D.C., 1975.

Conway, J. V. P.: *Evidential Documents,* Charles C Thomas, Springfield, Ill., 1959.

Envall, K. R., and E. J. Shangold: *Survey of Photocopier and Related Products,* U.S. Department of Health, Education & Welfare, Rockville, Md. 1978.

Gayet, J.: "Identification of a Typewriter by the Defects of the Stroke," in F. Lundquist (ed.), *Methods of Forensic Science,* vol. 2, pp. 79–126, Interscience-Wiley New York, 1963.

Harrison, W. R.: "Erasures," in A. S. Curry (ed.), *Methods of Forensic Science,* vol. 3, pp. 289–336, Interscience-Wiley, New York, 1964.

Harrison, W. R.: *Suspected Documents; Their Scientific Examination,* Praeger, New York, 1976.

Hilton, O.: *Scientific Examination of Questioned Documents,* Callaghan, Chicago, 1956.

Hilton, O.: "History of Questioned Documents Examination in the United States," *Journal of Forensic Sciences,* vol. 24, pp. 890–897, 1979.

Osborne, A. S.: *Questioned Documents,* 2d ed., Boyd, Albany, N.Y., 1929; *The Problem of Proof,* Essex, Newark, N.J. 1926.

Osborne, A. S., and A. D. Osborne: *Questioned Documents Problems,* Boyd, Albany, N.Y., 1944.

Witte, A. H.: "The Examination and Identification of Inks," in F. Lundquist (ed.), *Methods of Forensic Science,* vol. 2, pp. 35–77, Interscience, New York, 1963.

CHAPTER 14

TOOLMARKS AND FIREARMS

INTRODUCTION

The examination of toolmarks has certain similarities to the examination of firearms. In many laboratories, toolmark and firearms cases are handled in the same section by the same examiners. This combination may not seem very logical at first glance until one realizes that a substantial part of firearms examination consists of the study and comparison of toolmarks left on bullets and cartridge cases by various parts of firearms. Recognition of the similarities in firearms and toolmarks examinations is further evidenced by the fact that the major professional association of specialists in this area is the Association of Firearms and Toolmark Examiners. Despite the parallels and similarities in examining firearms and toolmarks, there are some laboratories in which these two kinds of casework are carried out by specialists in different sections.

A well-known case which has historical significance and in which an unusual type of toolmark evidence figured prominently is the Lindbergh kidnapping case. In March of 1932, kidnappers broke into the home of Colonel Charles Lindbergh through a second-story window and kidnapped his infant son. Lindbergh was a national hero, having made the first solo flight across the Atlantic 5 years earlier. A ransom was paid, but the victim was killed.

A government wood expert, Arthur Koehler, was instrumental in solving the case. A ladder was found outside Lindbergh's home at the time of the kidnapping, and it had obviously been used in the crime. It was homemade and put together in sections. Both Carolina pine and Ponderosa pine had been used in its construction, along with some dowels of birch and a single piece of fir. Koehler studied the wood in the ladder in great detail, and he found faint but recognizable grooves in certain pieces which had been made by a lumber mill planer. By carefully examining the grooves in the piece of fir, he found that the planing machine cutter head had contained eight knives. In addition, a slight imperfection in the grooves revealed that one of the knives had had a slight irregularity. Koehler set out to trace the planing machine and found that only two firms made this type of machine. He obtained and studied samples of lumber from every mill which used such machines. One sample, from the Dorn Company in South Carolina, contained the same imperfections as the fir plank in the ladder.

Koehler examined the records of the company to try to find out if he could trace the lumberyard from which the lumber in the ladder had come. After extensive searching, he found a similar sample in a Bronx, New York, lumberyard. It bore the telltale planing machine marks, and it had been supplied by the Dorn Company. The lumberyard dealt only in cash transactions, however, and there was no way of finding out who might have purchased the wood from this batch.

Meanwhile, the police were keeping a careful eye out for any trace of the ransom money, which had been paid. All the serial numbers had been recorded. One day, a man named Bruno Hauptmann was found trying to pass some of the ransom money. He denied any knowledge of or involvement in the kidnapping. It was soon found out, however, that he had worked in the Bronx lumberyard which Koehler had identified as the supplier of the piece of fir in the ladder.

Hauptmann was arrested, and his house was searched. In the attic, investigators found another plank of fir. Koehler examined it and found it to be identical to that used in the ladder on the basis of the wood dimensions and grain (indirect physical match) and the unusual planing marks on the cut surfaces. Koehler was able to decide that the wood in the ladder, the wood found in Hauptmann's attic, and that found in the lumberyard where the suspect had worked all came from the same batch. In addition, there were clean, regularly spaced nail holes in some pieces of the ladder as well as in the piece found in Hauptmann's attic. These markings also matched perfectly.

Hauptmann was convicted of the crime and later executed. The toolmark evidence which Koehler had patiently gathered was very important evidence against Hauptmann.

Although the planing machine knife mark imperfection is not a commonly exploited kind of toolmark, it was extremely important in this case.

TOOLMARK COMPARISONS

A *toolmark* is a mark resulting from contact between a tool and the surface of some object. When two surfaces are brought into contact with sufficient pressure, the harder one (usually the tool) will scratch or make an impression of itself on the softer surface (usually the object). The "tool" need not be an object that was designed to be used as a tool; thus, objects that would not normally be thought of as tools in the conventional sense can be responsible for toolmarks. Both class and individual characteristics are commonly found in toolmarks, and much can be learned from their examination. The impression left by a screwdriver used to pry open a window, for example, may reveal the width and outline of the head of the tool and the shape of the shaft and the manner in which the shaft was joined to the head, in addition to individual characteristics. Tools in the possession of criminals are often extensively used or abused and may be damaged. The damage or use characterstics of a tool may be reflected in the toolmark it leaves, and this becomes an important element for individualization of the tool. Even with new tools, particularly those which have been finished by grinding, individual characteristics may be present in the toolmark. Knowledge of how tools are manufactured can be important in certain investigations.

Types of Toolmarks

Toolmarks are basically of two major types, indented and striated, The difference between these types of markings was discussed in Chapter 11.

An *indented mark* is generally made by forcing a tool against the surface of an object and applying sufficient pressure to leave a negative impression of some aspect of the tool in the surface. This type of indentation resembles a footprint, tire track, or breech-face impression on a cartridge case. Indentations are also sometimes called *impression* or *compression* marks. This type of toolmark can reproduce the form of the tool quite accurately, as for example in the case of an old, used hammer with irregular edges leaving its impression in a soft wood surface. Many of the characteristic irregularities of the hammer edge can be reproduced in the mark. The material in which an indentation mark is made is very important in determining its quality. Certain woods, painted soft surfaces, and soft plaster can yield good clear marks. Concrete, wood with a texture that causes easy chipping, or other surfaces that are easy to break, often yield indentations of much less value. Certain metal and other hard surfaces are unlikely to show good impressions unless the tool is harder than the surface material and a great deal of force has been applied. If an indentation mark is found at a scene, an investigator should never place a suspected tool into the mark to see if it fits since the indentation can be irreparably altered by this contact. There is also a danger of jeopardizing the value of transfer and trace evidence, such as paint, wood, fibers, or metal, on the tool itself. Questions may later be raised as to whether such evidence was transferred to the tool by the criminal's actions or by the investigator's.

The second main type of toolmark is a *striated mark*. It is produced when a tool is placed against an object surface that is softer than the tool, pressure is applied, and the tool is moved across the surface. Since these marks are made by the sliding or lateral movement of a tool like a crowbar, prybar, or screwdriver, they are also sometimes called *sliding* or *scrape* marks. The edge of a tool is usually rough and irregular, at least when looked at on a microscopic scale. These irregularities produce parallel striations aligned with the direction of the movement. Using a comparison microscope, these striation marks can be compared with known marks produced by the suspected tool, as shown in Figure 14-1. The value of striation marks, like that of indentations, varies with the surface on which they occur. Unfinished or soft wood surfaces rarely give useful sliding mark patterns, whereas finished or painted surfaces are better in this respect. The best striation marks are usually found on metal surfaces. Other descriptive terms sometimes used to indicate striation marks are *friction, abrasion,* and *scratch* marks.

Sometimes a combination of the two types of toolmarks is present on the same surface. In a glancing tool blow, for example, a striation mark is generated, but a final negative impression of the tool surface (indentation) is also left. Another example might be a crowbar used on a metal-wood double door. Striation marks could be generated by the pushing action of the crowbar, whereas an impression mark could

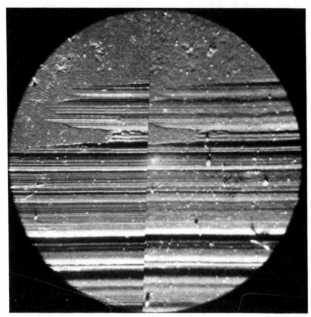

FIGURE 14-1
Striation-type toolmarks under the comparison microscope. The illustration actually shows a comparison of casts of toolmarks made with two different casting materials. The replica on the left was made with a new material known as Mikrosil. *(Kjell Carlsson Innovation, Sundbyberg, Sweden. Distributed in the United States by Kinderprint Co., P.O. Box 16, Martinez, California.)*

be left as the result of the final prying action. Other types of marks which may be seen include cutting marks, saw marks, shearing marks, and pinch marks. These may also be made up of both indented and striated components. Wire or bolt cutters, for example, can leave both types of marks. The edges normally slide along the metal being cut and compress it as well.

Collection of Toolmark Evidence

Toolmarks are generally found on doors or windows at points of entry. They may also be found on and around crime target areas, such as safes, locked drawers, closets, or other places where valuables might be kept, and on objects or containers that were forced during the commission of a crime. Occasionally, unusual situations may be encountered. A getaway car, for example, might acquire toolmarks (as well as transferring trace evidence) as a result of a minor collision with an object near the scene (pipe, post, etc.). A case involving such a mark was given in Chapter 11 in connection with the discussion of striation markings.

When toolmarks are discovered at a scene, they should be photographed to record their location, size, pattern, and arrangement. If the object bearing the toolmark is movable, it is better to submit the entire object to the laboratory. If it is immovable, then the portion containing the toolmarks may be removed or the marks may be cast using one of the techniques described in Chapter 11. If a suspected tool is found, investigators should not try to fit it into the toolmark, as pointed out above. Such action could damage the mark and could compromise the value of any trace evidence. Information about a tool may be obtained from trace materials left behind in impressions or on the surface around the toolmark. This information can be as important as that represented by the mark itself. Similarly, trace evidence can be transferred from a surface to a tool in the course of making a toolmark.

Laboratory Comparison of Toolmarks

Laboratory examination of toolmark evidence can yield information about: (1) the type of tool used, (2) the size of the marking portion of the tool, (3) any unusual features of the tool, (4) the action by which the tool made the marks, and (5) a conclusion as to whether a particular suspected tool made the specific marks.

Original evidence (the toolmark itself) is more useful for laboratory examination and evaluation than a reproduction of the toolmark, such as a cast or a photograph. Comparison of a questioned toolmark with a known one is generally done with a comparison microscope. Several examples of known marks are produced with the suspected tool. These are then compared with the questioned mark found at the crime scene.

The way in which a tool is applied to make the mark in the receiving surface can greatly influence the character of the mark and must be taken into consideration in any comparison work. The known, or exemplar, mark should be made in a way that closely duplicates that by which the questioned mark is thought to have been produced. Achieving this goal may require some careful thought as well as ingenuity. Investigative information can help to limit the possibilities which must be considered. Striation marks made by a tool can be very different, depending upon the portion or surface of the tool used and the angle it makes with the surface of the receiving material. In addition, both the angle of the tool with respect to the direction of movement and the direction of movement itself can have a profound effect on the character of the mark produced. One of these effects is illustrated in Figure 14-2.

The basic elements in a toolmark examination and comparison are: (1) reproduction of test marks in a manner resembling the questioned mark as closely as possible (as noted above, test marks produced at slightly different angles or directions can result in marks that are completely dissimilar) and (2) comparison of the striations, damaged areas, and other characteristics of the test mark with those of the questioned mark. There is no specific number of matching lines which examiners require in order to conclude that test and questioned marks match. Successful determinations depend on the quality of the original toolmarks, that of the standard mark, the nature and quality of the tool, and the experience of the examiner.

Besides being instruments for the production of toolmarks, tools can be a source of trace evidence materials, such as paint, oil, grease, hairs, fibers, and soil. These trace materials can also be very important in an investigation (see in Chapter 6).

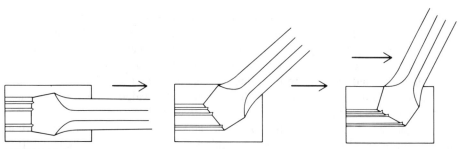

FIGURE 14-2
The effect of tool angle on toolmarks. The way in which a tool is applied can affect the resulting mark. One factor is the angle of the tool with respect to the direction of movement. Motion in a direction normal to the cutting surface and at two other angles is illustrated. *(Courtesy of Francis X. Sheehan, John Jay College of Criminal Justice, The City University of New York.)*

FUNDAMENTALS OF FIREARMS

Introduction

Homicides and felonious assaults are regarded as being among the most serious crimes committed in our society. Firearms are used in a large percentage of these cases. Statistical data for the United States indicate that firearms are used in more than 60 percent of all homicides, more than 20 percent of all assaults, more than 35 percent of all robberies, and in almost half of all suicides. Thus, the identification and examination of firearms is often an integral part of the forensic investigation in cases of this kind. Although examinations of toolmarks on bullets and cartridge cases is an important part of a firearms examiner's work, firearms examination is not limited to identifying and individualizing bullets and cartridge cases. The work may also include identifying weapons by class characteristics, serial number restorations, functional testing, gunshot residue detection, powder and shot pattern interpretations, and distance estimations.

A well-known case, which has a great deal of historical interest, and which was also of significance in the development of methods for firearms and toolmark examinations, is the Sacco-Vanzetti case. It involved a robbery and murder incident, and the firearms evidence became central in deciding its outcome.

On the afternoon of April 15, 1920, five armed men held up a paymaster named Parmenter and a payroll guard named Berardelli in South Braintree, Massachusetts. The paymaster and guard had the payroll for a shoe factory in their custody. Both Parmenter and Berardelli were shot and killed in the incident. The five robbers escaped in a car, and the $16,000 payroll was never recovered. On May 5, 1920, Sacco and Vanzetti were charged with the crime.

The firearms evidence was extensive. There were .32 caliber ACP bullets taken from the bodies of the two victims for which a matching automatic pistol was never found. From the right twist markings found on some of the bullets and from the cartridge case markings, it is thought that some were fired in a Savage automatic pistol, which was never located. Further, a .38 caliber Harrington and Richardson revolver, very similar to that carried by Berardelli, was taken from Vanzetti. It was never possible to tie this revolver definitely to the victims, however. A total of thirty-two .32 caliber ACP cartridges similar to those used in the crime were taken from Sacco at the time of his arrest.

The clinching evidence was a .32 caliber Colt pocket automatic pistol taken from Sacco at the time of his arrest, a single .32 caliber bullet from the body of Berardelli, and one cartridge case found at the scene of the crime.

Captain van Amburgh and Lieutenant Proctor of the Massachusetts State Police indicated in their original testimony that the pistol, the bullet, and the cartridge case all matched, although they later seemed less convinced about the match.

Every imaginable aspect of the groove width, pitch, manufacturing procedures, bullet cannelures, and so forth was discussed in this case. Almost every expert in the East was called, including some with no profound knowledge of what they were talking about. At one point, there was even an unsuccessful attempt by one of the defense experts to substitute a different barrel in the Colt automatic.

Later examination of the pertinent evidence by more up-to-date and modern procedures showed that there can be no doubt that Sacco's pistol fired one of the cartridge cases and one of the fatal bullets.

The defendants in the case held socially unpopular political views, and students of the case have noted the difficulty in separating the substance of the legal proceedings from the intense public feelings that surrounded them. After considerable turmoil surrounding the trial, unprecedented publicity and public feeling, and even riots both here and abroad, both Sacco and Vanzetti were convicted of the crime and were executed August 23, 1927, more than 7 years after the crime had occurred. Much of the controversy and unpleasantness might have been avoided had firearms examination techniques been as advanced as they are today. Three other men who were thought to have participated in the robbery were never apprehended.

This case gained notoriety at a time when toolmark and firearms examination was in its infancy. Undoubtedly, the case fostered progress and development in this field.

Rifling and Rifled Barrels

The barrel of a firearm is, in essence, nothing more than a metal tube. There are two types of barrels: smooth and rifled. A shotgun has a smooth-bored barrel, but almost all modern handguns and rifles have rifled barrels.

A *rifled* barrel contains grooves cut into its inner surface; the uncut, raised area between the grooves is called the *land*. The lands and grooves together constitute the rifling. The lands "bite" into the bullet and cause it to rotate on its longitudinal axis as it passes along the barrel. This rotation gives the bullet stability in flight and prevents it from tumbling end-over-end. The lands and grooves leave significant markings on a bullet; the markings contain both class and individual characteristics. It is these which make firearms identifications and individualizations possible from a study of projectiles.

The diameter of a gun barrel, measured between opposite lands, is known as the *caliber* of the weapon. Figure 14-3 shows interior views of three gun barrels in which the lands and grooves can be seen. In general, caliber denotes the nominal diameter of a barrel. In the United States and other English-speaking countries, the caliber is

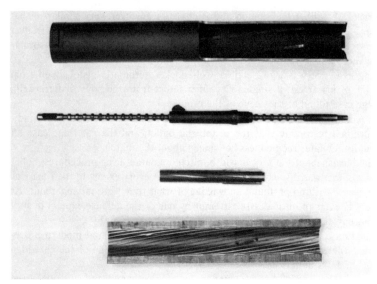

FIGURE 14-3
Interior views of three sectioned gun barrels. A rifling broach is also shown.
(*Courtesy of Marshall Robinson, Forensic Science Laboratory, Connecticut State Police.*)

measured in hundredths or thousandths of an inch, for example .22, .38, .45, .220, .357, or .405 caliber. In other countries, the caliber may be designated in millimeters, for example, 6.5, 8, or 9 mm. The designation 7.65 mm is equivalent to .30 or .32 caliber (depending on the means of measurement), whereas 9 mm is equivalent to .38 caliber.

There are several methods of rifling in which tools are forced through the barrel with slight rotation: (1) the *broach* method in which all grooves are cut simultaneously with a series of progressively larger cutters; (2) the *hook (scraper)* method in which a single cutter is dragged from one end of the barrel to the other repeatedly until the helical grooves are cut; (3) the *button swage* method in which the metal on the surface of the bore is displaced (pushed and compressed) by a hardened swage until all the grooves are formed; (4) the *hammer* method in which a positive rifling tool is made and forced through the bore, leaving negative rifling inside it. The rifling tool, like any other tool, leaves its signature in the form of toolmarks inside the barrel. When a bullet passes through the barrel, these toolmarks combined with the effects of wear and corrosion will produce distinctive marks on the bullet.

Types of Firearms

There is an almost countless number of different makes and models of firearms. The term *firearms* includes not only common and easily recognizable types of weapons like revolvers, automatic handguns, shotguns, and rifles, but other weapons such as machine guns, artillery, and many kinds of homemade weapons. Indeed, any instrument or device assembled from some type of barrel and some type of action from which a projectile is propelled by the products of the explosion of gunpowder is considered a firearm.

Weapons other than pistols, rifles, and shotguns are not commonly encountered in routine casework. Occasionally, an obsolete weapon like a smooth-bore musket, a homemade pipe gun, nail gun, or cane gun is employed in the commission of a crime.

Rifles A rifle is a shoulder-held weapon normally having a long, rifled barrel. Although all modern pistols also have rifled barrels, the term *rifle* is now applied only to long arms with rifled barrels. The basic components of a rifle are the rifled barrel, a firing chamber, a shoulder stock, and provision for loading and unloading. In old-fashioned muzzle loaders, the chamber could not be opened, and the powder and projectile charges were introduced through the muzzle end of the weapon. Modern rifles open at the other end of the barrel (the *breech* end) for loading and unloading. The mechanism used for this purpose is sometimes referred to as the *action*.

Rifles may also be categorized as single-shot, repeating, or semiautomatic, according to the nature of their reloading mechanisms. Single-shot rifles require that cartridge case removal and reloading be done singly by hand. In repeating weapons, by contrast, the cartridge cases are removed and fresh ones loaded by a mechanism built into the manually operated action. Repeating rifles may use a bolt action or a movable breech block. The breech block may be operated by a lever to the rear of the trigger (lever action), or by a slide on the fore stock (pump action). Semiautomatic rifles improve on these repeating rifles by eliminating the need to operate the action manually. These are sometimes called *autoloading* rifles. Here, the action is actuated automatically after each shot by forces liberated during the explosion (gas or recoil), so that a fresh cartridge is in place, ready to be fired, when the trigger is next pulled. Fully automatic weapons are designed for military use. Unlike the semiautomatic types, a separate trigger pull is not required for each shot. These weapons are more like machine guns, and will continue firing as long as the trigger is depressed and ammunition remains. The ammunition in repeating rifles and semiautomatics is held and specially positioned so that a new cartridge is ready to be chambered each time the action closes. The cartridges may be held in carefully ordered rows in various kinds of so-called magazines. A spring-loaded follower mechanism is used to assure a continuous feed until the magazine is empty. Magazines may be of the stack (straight or staggered), tubular, or drum (coiled or "snail") types. The last type is restricted to fully automatic military weapons, such as submachine guns.

The principal feature of rifles is the long, rifled barrel. Rifles are designed to fire a single projectile at a time. The velocity of projectiles fired from rifles is generally higher, and the accuracy and range are greater, than for other types of firearms. It is the long, rifled barrel that accounts for the high velocity, stability, and range.

Pistols A pistol or handgun consists essentially of a barrel, a firing mechanism, and a grip, or handle. There are three general types: single-shot, revolver, and semiautomatic. Figure 14-4 shows some of the different types and models of firearms, including handguns.

(a)

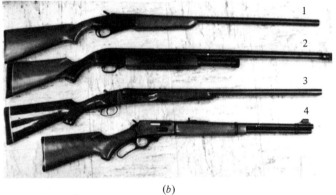

(b)

FIGURE 14-4
(a) Pistols: *1,* High Standard .22 caliber long rifle automatic; *2,* Butler
.22 caliber short; *3,* Smith & Wesson model 292, .44-caliber revolver;
4, vest pocket Saturday night special, .22 caliber revolver; *5,* Colt
Agent .38 Special; *6,* Smith & Wesson model 59, 9 mm automatic; *7,*
Astra 380 automatic; *8,* Colt .25 caliber automatic. *(b)* Shoulder
weapons or "long arms": *1,* Sears single-shot 12 gauge shotgun; *2,*
Sears, Ted Williams 12 gauge pump-action shotgun; *3,* Connecticut
Valley Arms 12 gauge double-barrel shotgun; *4,* Marlin .35 caliber
lever-action rifle. *(Courtesy of Robert Hathaway, Forensic Science
Laboratory, Connecticut State Police.)*

A *single-shot* pistol is limited to one shot per firing cycle and has no reloading
mechanism of its own. It must be emptied and reloaded by hand like the single-shot
rifle. Often, these weapons are of the break style, in which the chamber is accessed
by means of a hinged barrel, the muzzle of which is depressed during the breaking
operation. Modern single-shot pistols are used largely for competition target
shooting.

A firearm which utilizes a revolving cylinder containing multiple firing chambers is a *revolver.* It is a repeating weapon with a rifled barrel. At one time, a few long arms or shoulder-held weapons of this kind were made. All the more modern revolvers, however, are designed to be hand-held and are thus pistols. The revolving cylinder may contain up to nine firing chambers, each able to accommodate a single cartridge. After a shot is fired, the next chamber in the cylinder is aligned with the barrel for the next shot. This cylinder rotation and alignment takes place when the hammer is pulled back (cocked) in *single-action* revolvers. In some revolvers, pulling the trigger raises the hammer and aligns the cylinder if the hammer has not already been cocked. This mode of firing is referred to as *double action.* Most modern revolvers can be fired in either single- or double-action modes. Normally, a heavier trigger pull is required to fire the weapon in double-action mode.

Cartridge cases are not automatically ejected by a revolver. This operation is carried out by hand, usually after the cartridges in all the chambers have been discharged. For this reason, cartridge cases are not commonly found at shooting scenes involving the exclusive use of revolvers. Revolvers can be divided into four general types, based upon the loading-unloading mechanism employed: (1) solid frame–detachable cylinder, (2) solid frame–nonremovable cylinder, (3) top-break design, and (4) solid frame–swing-out cylinder.

The first type has a solid frame with a detachable cylinder which can be removed by withdrawing a cylinder pin. The cylinder pin is a large-diameter pin upon which the cylinder rotates. With the cylinder pin removed, the cylinder can be removed for unloading and reloading.

The second type of revolver also has a solid frame, but the cylinder is not removed for loading or unloading. The cases are removed one at a time by pushing a rod into the appropriate chamber of the cylinder from the front. The spent case is pushed out through the back through an aperture in the flange in the frame which covers the rear of the cylinder. The chamber to be loaded or unloaded must be aligned with this aperture. The ejector rod is normally affixed to the weapon in the proper position so that it can be actuated by pushing a tab or lever. It is returned to the resting position by spring action. This design is retained in some modern revolvers which are patterned after certain "frontier" models. In inexpensive versions of the basic design, a rod which is not actually part of the weapon may be used to push out spent cartridges.

The so-called top-break design is the third type of revolver. Here, a latch at the top of the frame allows the hinged barrel to be bent downward, exposing the rear of the cylinder. The breaking action may actuate a rod attached to a star-shaped extractor at the rear of the cylinder which lifts all the cartridges from their chambers simultaneously. The top-break mechanism was common on weapons made for a few decades at the turn of the century. Although this type of revolver allows relatively rapid loading and unloading, the hinge and latch mechanisms make it somewhat weaker than comparable solid-frame designs.

In part for reasons of strength, the fourth type of revolver, which employs a solid frame with a swing-out cylinder, has largely replaced the top-break type in modern premium-quality revolvers. Top-break designs may still be encountered, however, in so-called Saturday night specials. In the swing-out design, the rod on which the cylinder revolves is mounted on a hingelike device known as a *crane*. When the cylinder is swung out on the crane, a rod, much like the extractor rod in the top-break type, is manually activated to extract all the spent cartridges at one time.

The last general type of pistol is the *semiautomatic*. Such a weapon can fire several shots without reloading, and reloading is effected by a mechanism built into the weapon. This type of weapon has several additional components. A vertical spring-activated magazine, commonly located in the handle grip, holds the extra ammunition and helps in the automatic loading of fresh ammunition into the firing chamber. An extractor removes the expended cartridge case from the chamber as the breech block moves rearward after firing and an ejector expels the spent case from the gun. Semiautomatic pistols normally utilize recoil actions for automatic reloading. Cartridge cases will be found at shooting scenes most frequently when semiautomatic weapons of this kind have been involved.

Shotguns   A shotgun is a smooth-bore shoulder weapon with an external construction very similar to that of a rifle. The major difference in the weapon itself is in the barrel. Shotguns generally have barrels with larger bore diameters than rifle barrels, and shotgun barrels are not rifled. Another difference between shotguns and other types of firearms is the type of ammunition used. Shotguns normally fire a load consisting of a number of lead pellets (shot), instead of a single bullet, although ammunition containing a single bullet (commonly referred to as a *rifled slug*) is available. For this reason, it is usually not possible to identify the shotgun which fired a particular load by examining the fired pellets. Even if a slug has been fired, the absence of barrel rifling makes identification of the weapon from an examination of the projectile very difficult.

Shotguns may be classified as single-barreled and double-barreled, according to the number of separate barrels the weapon possesses (Figure 14-4). Double-barreled shotguns allow a single shot to be fired from each of the barrels before reloading. The reloading mechanisms of shotguns resemble those of rifles. Some shotguns employ a break action for reloading, which is comparatively rare with rifles. Slide or pump actions are very common, and weapons that have automatic reloading mechanisms, (semiautomatic) are quite popular with sports shooters.

The size of a shotgun (its *gauge*) is expressed by quoting the *number* of lead shot balls, each of which would fit exactly inside the shotgun barrel bore and which would weigh 1 lb in the aggregate. A 10 gauge shotgun, for example, would exactly accommodate a lead ball weighing 0.1 lb. The most common types of shotguns are 12, 16, and 20 gauge and .410 caliber. This original meaning of gauge is illustrated in Table 14-1. Notice that the figures given in the "number of balls per pound" column correspond to the gauge of the shotgun. The principal shotgun which does not use this gauge scheme is the "410" shotgun which is specified by the diameter of its bore in inches. It would take approximately 70 lead balls of 0.410 inch diameter to make up one pound. Thus, the equivalent "gauge" of the .410 shotgun is about 70.

Ammunition

A live round of ammunition is also called a cartridge, and it may consist of the following basic components: projectile(s), wads (shotgun), primer, gunpowder, and car-

TABLE 14-1
MEASUREMENTS OR PROPERTIES OF LEAD BALLS JUST FITTING BORE

Gauge	Approx. diameter		Weight or mass		No. of balls	
	in.	mm	grams	grains	per pound	per ounce
4	1.05	26.7	113	1750	4	.250
8	.84	21.2	57	875	8	.500
10	.78	19.7	45	700	10	.625
12	.73	18.5	38	583	12	.750
14	.69	17.6	32	500	14	.875
16	.66	16.8	28	437	16	1.000
20	.62	15.6	23	350	30	1.250
24	.58	14.7	19	292	24	1.500
28	.55	14.0	16	250	28	1.750
32	.53	13.4	14	219	32	2.000
"70"	.41	10.3	6	100	70	4.375

tridge case. Figure 14-5 shows the typical components of cartridges. The bullet (projectile) is generally made of lead, sometimes with alloys, and may be encased partially or wholly in envelopes (jackets) of a harder metal. Fully encased bullets (base to tip, where the base may be open) are called *fully jacketed*; those that are only partially encased (tip or nose exposed) are called *semijacketed*. Jacketed bullets are more resistant to external distortion than ordinary ones. Bullet diameter is generally somewhat larger than the bore diameter of the gun in which it is intended for use. There are various bullet designs, including flat nose, wadcutter, roundnose, and hollow point. Some of them are shown in Figure 14-6.

The shot used in shotgun ammunition consists of small lead balls, or pellets. Elongated, hollow rifled slugs may also be used in shotgun ammunition. Shot is classified by number. Each number corresponds to a specific shot size, usually the diameter of the pellet (Table 14-2). Note that numbers decrease with increasing size.

Cartridge cases are used to contain the ignition system, powder charge, and projectile(s). The case itself is usually made of brass. Shotgun shells are made of brass or a combination of paper, plastic, and metals. A cartridge case may be rimmed, semirimmed, rimless, or belted, depending upon the type, design, and manufacturer. Generally, revolver and shotgun ammunition is rimmed, although some rifle ammunition may also be of this kind. Cartridge cases may be stamped at the factory to indicate make and type. These stamped markings, sometimes referred to as cartridge designations, can be used to determine the manufacturer of the ammunition.

Cartridge designations are expanded from basic caliber groupings in a variety of ways. Each designation denotes a specific cartridge case size and configuration. Although some cartridges can be interchanged, most are specific for a weapon of a particular cartridge designation. The variety of cartridge designations and their

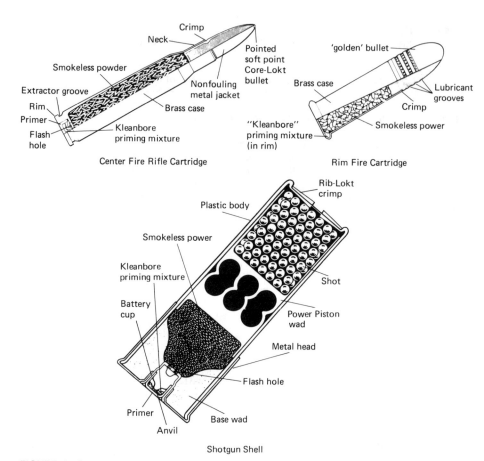

FIGURE 14-5
Cutaway views of cartridges. *(Remington Arms Company, Inc., Bridgeport, Connecticut.)*

origins are illustrated in the following list (in each case the first number refers to the caliber):

1 Descriptive words: .38 Special; .41 Magnum; .380 Auto; 9 mm Parabellum (Luger)
  2 Original powder charge: .25-20; .30-30; .30-40 Krag; .45-70 Government
  3 Manufacturer's name: .30 Remington; 6 mm Remington
  4 Designer's name: .257 Roberts
  5 Velocity: .250-3000
  6 Year of adoption: .30-06 Springfield
  7 Length of case in millimeters: 8×57; 7×57

Some examples of cartridge designations on the base (headstamp) are shown in Figure 14-7.

FIGURE 14-6
A variety of cartridge types. *(Courtesy of David Paige, Forensic Science
Laboratory, Connecticut State Police.)*

TABLE 14-2
SHOT COMPARISON TABLE

Shot number	Diameter, in.	Diameter, mm	Mass, g	Weight, gr	Approximate number of pellets			
					per gram	per grain	per pound	per ounce
12	0.05	1.27	0.012	0.188	83	5	37,300	2330
11	0.06	1.52	0.021	0.324	48	3	21,600	1350
10	0.07	1.78	0.033	0.515	30	2	13,600	850
9	0.08	2.03	0.050	0.769	20	1	9.100	570
8	0.09	2.29	0.071	1.09	14	1	6,400	400
7½	0.095	2.41	0.083	1.29	12	1	5,400	340
7	0.10	2.54	0.097	1.50	10	1	4,700	290
6	0.11	2.79	0.130	2.00	8	—	3,500	220
5	0.12	3.05	0.168	2.60	6	—	2,700	170
4	0.13	3.30	0.214	3.30	5	—	2,100	130
2	0.15	3.81	0.328	5.06	3	—	1,400	86
Air rifle	0.175	4.44	0.521	8.04	2	—	870	55
BB	0.18	4.57	0.567	8.76	2	—	800	50
#4 buck	0.24	6.10	1.34	20.7	—	—	340	21
#3 buck	0.25	6.35	1.52	23.5	—	—	300	19
#1 buck	0.30	7.62	2.63	40.5	—	—	170	11
#0 buck	0.32	8.13	3.19	49.2	—	—	140	9
#00 buck	0.33	8.38	3.50	54.0	—	—	130	8

FIGURE 14-7
Views of bases of cartridges showing headstamps. *(Courtesy of Louis Kapitulik, Forensic Science Laboratory, Connecticut State Police.)*

The primer is a mixture of chemicals detonated by the crushing impact and force of the firing pin. Two common types of priming are rim fire and center fire (Figure 14-7). Rim fire design was common in several older types of cartridges but now is found only in .22 caliber ammunition.

There are two types of gunpowder: black powder and smokeless powder. Before 1886, black powder was the only type. It consists of potassium nitrate, sulfur, and charcoal. The only type used in modern ammunition is smokeless powder, and there are two different kinds: single-based smokeless powder, made of nitrocellulose, and double-based smokeless powder, made of nitrocellulose and nitroglycerin.

COLLECTION AND PRESERVATION OF FIREARMS EVIDENCE

When firearms evidence is discovered at a scene, its location should be recorded and it should be photographed to show the item itself and its relationship to the scene as a whole. Any weapon must be handled with great care. Surfaces that might bear latent fingerprints should not be touched. The weapon should be handled only by surfaces that would not normally yield fingerprints, such as checkered grips, edges of the trigger guard, or roughly machined surfaces. A weapon should never be lifted by placing a pencil or other object in the end of the barrel. If trace evidence, such as blood, hair, tissues, or fibers, is present in or on the muzzle of the firearm, a small bag should be secured around the muzzle area to protect it. The firearm should be labeled with an evidence tag containing information such as the serial number, make and model of the weapon, the date, time, and location of recovery, the investigator's name, and the case number. When dealing with revolvers, the cylinder should be marked so that it can be determined later which chamber was under the hammer at the time of recovery. After the weapon is recovered, secured, and labeled properly, it should be forwarded to the laboratory.

When bullets or cartridge cases are recovered at a scene, they too must be labeled for identification. Bullets should be marked on the base, or on top of the nose. However, when marking a bullet, extreme care must be taken so as not to destroy any critical trace debris, such as fibers, hairs, or blood, any impressions on the bullet, such as of cloth fabric or a screen, or any other indications of the bullet's trajectory. Sometimes, it may be wise to place each bullet in a separate small cardboard box with separate labeling, rather than to risk loss of evidence by attempting to mark them. Under no circumstances should bullets be marked anywhere along the striation mark patterns.

A shell casing is best marked on the inside of the open end of the case. The marked cases and bullets should be placed in individual containers (envelopes or cardboard boxes), which are then sealed, labeled, and forwarded to the laboratory for examination.

FIREARMS COMPARISON

Basic Principles of Firearms Examination

The basic function of a firearm is to launch a projectile. A cartridge containing the projectile is placed into the firing chamber for firing. The cartridge is supported by the chamber on all sides and at the rear by the breech-face portion of the bolt, the frame of a revolver, or the breech lock of an automatic weapon. When the trigger is pulled to fire the weapon, the hammer is driven down onto the firing pin, which in turn strikes the primer of the cartridge. The primer mixture explodes, and this event in turn causes ignition of the powder. The powder burns rapidly, generating an enormous amount of gas pressure within the confined space of the cartridge. The pressure forces the bullet out of the cartridge, through the barrel, and out of the muzzle of the weapon.

There are many different makes and models of firearms. The evidence presented for examination in a shooting case, however, usually consists of a questioned firearm, a bullet, and sometimes a cartridge case. Ordinarily, the toolmarks on questioned bullets or cartridge cases are to be compared with those on known samples fired from the suspect weapon to determine whether or not the particular weapon fired the questioned bullet(s) or cartridge case(s).

The principles involved in this type of examination are the same as those used in toolmark comparisons, as discussed above. The questioned weapon is usually test-fired several times, and the test-fired bullets are compared with one another and with the questioned bullet. Similar methods are used for comparing cartridge cases. For the examiner, the barrel is an important part of the weapon, because it makes the characteristic marks on the bullet. The firing mechanism may be important as well, because the firing pin and breech face make characteristic marks on the primer and the cartridge case. Extractor and ejector marks may also be present. Most firearms examinations are based on the detailed comparisons of these "toolmarks". A full understanding of the significance of these comparisons requires knowledge of the basic features of firearms and their functions and firing mechanisms. Comparison of the different markings is discussed in detail below.

One of the most important objectives of a firearms examination is to link a specific weapon to a fired bullet or cartridge case. Often, a bullet can be recovered from a crime scene or from a victim's body. Less frequently, cartridge cases may be found at scenes. They should be expected and searched for if it is known that an automatic weapon was involved.

By examining and comparing the different types of class and individual characteristic markings on bullets and cartridge cases, a firearms examiner (Fig. 14-8) can determine the kind of ammunition used, the kind of weapon used to fire a bullet or cartridge, and whether a particular weapon fired a particular bullet or cartridge case.

Generally, the following information may be obtained from laboratory examination of the types of firearms evidence noted:

1 Bullet recovered from the scene or victim
   a List of possible manufacturers, caliber, type, and make of weapon from which fired

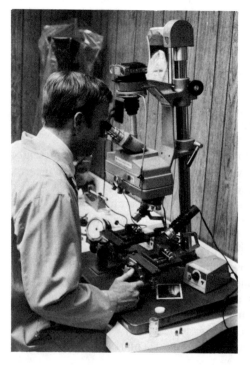

FIGURE 14-8
A firearms examiner conducting a bullet comparison. *(Courtesy of Robert Hathaway, Forensic Science Laboratory, Connecticut State Police.)*

    b Whether sufficient markings are present for individualization

    c Whether fired from a particular weapon, assuming sufficient markings present and depending on whether the weapon is available for test firing

    d Shot pellet size or slug load gauge for shotgun projectiles

2 Fired cartridge case or shotshell casing from the scene

    a Specific caliber or type

    b Possible make of the weapon from which fired

    c Gauge of shotgun in the case of a shotshell casing and whether it was an original factory load or a hand load

    d Whether a cartridge case or shotshell was fired by a particular weapon, assuming the weapon is available for test firing

    e Manufacturer in cases of a factory load

3 Weapon

    a Manufacturer, specific caliber (or gauge), and type

    b Whether it is functional and has been recently fired

    c Whether it was used to fire a particular bullet or cartridge case or shotshell casing

    d The amount of pressure necessary to fire the weapon (trigger pull)

    e Whether the weapon is capable of being fired accidentally

    f Identification of gun parts as to the type of weapon from which they originated

Bullet Comparisons

When a bullet travels through a gun barrel, distinctive markings are impressed onto it. These are referred to as *striation*-type toolmarks, and they result from the forced movement of the bullet against the lands and grooves of the barrel. As mentioned above, all rifled firearms have a specific number of lands and groves. The number and dimension of the lands and grooves are usually characteristic of particular makes and models of weapons. The direction and pitch of rifling twist are also important characteristics. The number and dimensions of lands and grooves, their direction, and their pitch are class characteristics, and they are valuable in firearms identification. Diameter, length, weight, and shape of a bullet may also be valuable in identifying caliber and type. Some bullets have additional features called *cannelures,* which serve to hold grease for lubrication. The number, design, and dimensions of the cannelures can be valuable in identifying the ammunition manufacturer and determining the possible date of manufacture.

    A firearms examiner uses class characteristics to determine what possible types or makes of weapons could have been used to fire a particular projectile. However, it is rarely possible to state with absolute certainty the exact make and model of weapon, because the class characteristics of similar weapons from different manufacturers may be quite similar. Sometimes, a bullet is mangled or damaged, but an experienced examiner may still be able to determine the caliber and type of the gun from which it was fired. The greater the damage to the bullet, however, the less information one can hope to obtain. When extensive deformation of the bullet has occurred or when only fragments of it have been recovered, instrumental analysis to determine metal composition may yield useful information. Based on metal composition and on the total weight of the fragments, an examiner may be able to eliminate all bullets which are lower in weight and those which differ in chemical composition.

The detailed rifling striations on the bullet are a result of individual characteristics of a weapon's barrel. At the time of manufacture, many minute marks are imparted to the barrel by the rifling process. These marks are unique to each gun barrel. Extensive use and abuse of a weapon after manufacture can also result in further individualizing characteristics which may be reflected in the markings on bullets fired through the barrel. Thus, the striation marks serve to link any bullet fired through the barrel of that firearm to the particular firearm. The questioned bullet is usually compared with a test bullet which has been fired from the suspected gun, by comparison microscopy (Chapter 3). The comparison microscope is one of the most important tools in firearms examination. Test and questioned bullets are mounted on the holders of the stage. Both are then viewed simultaneously through the eyepiece. The examiner adjusts the position of one bullet until a clear, well-defined land and groove pattern comes into view. Then the other bullet is rotated until the striation marks are matched, if they can be, with those of the first one. Figure 14-9 shows a typical photomicrograph of two bullets which match, as seen under the comparison microscope. Two bullets can be said to match if the major portions of their striations are identical around the periphery, and it can thus be concluded that the two were fired from the same weapon. If the bullets do not match, several explanations are possible. They may have been fired by different weapons, the barrel of the weapon may have been altered (wear, abuse, or even intentional alteration) between the time the questioned and test bullets were fired, or one of the bullets may have been damaged or some of its markings obliterated. Besides rifling striations, some bullets fired by revolvers show slippage (skid) marks, and these can have value in bullet comparisons as well. Silencers can also impart characteristic marks.

FIGURE 14-9
Comparison of (left) questioned and (right) test or exemplar bullets as seen with a comparison microscope. *(Courtesy of Anthony Gura, Forensic Science Laboratory, Connecticut State Police.)*

Cartridge Case Comparisons

The barrel markings from a firearm are not the only characteristics that can be used to link a specific weapon to a specific crime. When a weapon is fired, markings can be impressed and scratched onto the cartridge casing by various parts of the gun's mechanism. As with striation marks on bullets, these markings will be reproduced on a test cartridge fired by the same gun. A firearms examiner can compare those markings and link a cartridge case to a specific weapon. The most characteristic marks expected on a fired cartridge case are outlined below.

Firing Pin Indentations The primer must be struck by the firing pin in order to cause the projectile to be fired. The negative impression of the firing pin is thereby pressed into the relatively soft metal of the primer on the cartridge case. Firing pins vary in size, shape, and location and may also contain imperfections, finishing marks, and other individual characteristics. Sometimes, a firing pin undergoes changes in shape through use or abuse. It is rare, therefore, that two different weapons would leave identical firing pin impressions. These indentations are compared by means of the comparison microscope. The questioned cartridge case is mounted vertically with the base up on the stage and compared with a standard which has been fired in the suspected weapon. Figure 14-10 shows a comparison photomicrograph of firing pin impressions.

FIGURE 14-10
Comparison of (left) questioned and (right) test or exemplar primer indentations as seen with a comparison microscope. The marks being compared are those around the firing pin impression. These are caused by machining marks on the breech face of the weapon. (*Courtesy of Robert Hathaway, Forensic Science Laboratory, Connecticut State Police.*)

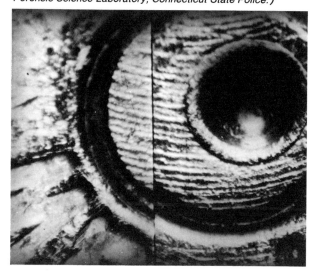

Breech-Face Marks   At the time of firing, the base of a shotshell or cartridge case is forced backward against the breech-face. The surface of the breech-face is usually finished with a file, milling machine, or other cutting tool, leaving a large number of individual striation marks on its surface. These striation mark patterns are impressed on the base of the fired cartridge case or shotshell, particularly in the soft primer metal around the firing pin indentation. Questioned breech-face marks can be compared with those on a standard cartridge case using a comparison microscope, and can serve as a means of positive matches.

Extractor and Ejector Marks   Virtually all modern repeating firearms have some form of extractor or ejector, although ejectors are not used in revolvers. An extractor is a mechanism in a firearm by which a cartridge or fired case is withdrawn from the chamber. An ejector is the mechanism in a firearm that throws (ejects) the cartridge or fired case from the weapon after it has been withdrawn from the chamber. The surfaces of these extractor and ejector mechanisms also contain many individual characteristics which are impressed or scratched on the cartridge or shotshell when it is removed from the weapon. The size, shape, and location of extractor and ejector marks are also valuable in making identifications of weapon type.

Other Marks   At the time of firing, part of the force of the explosion is exerted on the cartridge case itself, causing its sides to expand. The expansion causes close contact with the internal surfaces of the chamber. Since most firearms have irregularities in their chambers, the pattern of these markings can be impressed onto the fired cartridge case. In a weapon with an irregularly worn chamber, the case may swell and assume a characteristic shape. All of these types of marks can be important in making comparisons.

Automatic and repeating weapons always have some type of loading mechanism or magazine which may be of the stack, tube, or drum type. Insertion of the unfired cartridge into the mechanism, removal of the fired cartridge case, and reloading of a fresh one will all involve pressure, scratching, or scraping on the sides of the cartridge case. These magazine and/or feeder marks are sometimes very distinctive and reproducible and as such can be useful in comparisons.

RECONSTRUCTIONS IN SHOOTING CASES AND GUNSHOT RESIDUE ANALYSIS

Reconstructions in Shooting Cases

In the investigation of shooting cases, forensic analysis can help in answering a number of questions. (1) What was the muzzle-to-target distance? (2) What was the trajectory of the fired bullet(s)? (3) Has the suspected individual recently fired a weapon? Trajectory analysis and distance estimations make up part of the reconstruction effort in this type of case. Collection and analysis of suspected gunshot residue from a suspected person's hands can help to decide whether the individual has recently fired a weapon.

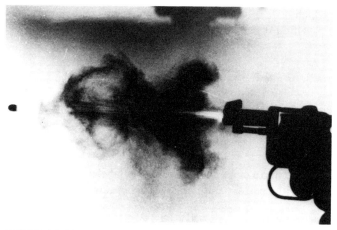

FIGURE 14-11
High-speed photograph of a revolver during discharge. Note the expanding cloud of residue. Leakage around the cylinder, although undoubtedly present, is not readily apparent in this photograph. (*Crime Laboratory, New York City Police Department.*)

When a firearm is discharged (see Figure 14-11), unburned and partially burned particles of gunpowder, in addition to smoke and residue particles, are propelled out of the barrel along with the bullet toward the target. At the same time, some of the residue of the gunpowder and primer is blown backward, and can be deposited on the hands of a shooter. The discharge patterns and bullet paths can be analyzed to help in reconstructing the distances involved and the relative positions of shooter and target. These matters were considered in detail in Chapter 11 in connection with the use of pattern evidence in reconstructions. The collection and analysis of gunshot residues is considered in the sections which follow.

Collection of Gunshot Residue

The detection of gunshot residue on the hands of a shooter is based upon microscopical, chemical, and instrumental identification of various components of gunpowder, primer, lubricants, metals from bullets or their jackets, and traces from the cartridge case and the gun barrel. There are many tests available, and their basic objective is to demonstrate the presence of characteristic chemicals such as lead, barium, antimony, nitrates, nitrites, or actual particles of gunshot residue. Determination of the presence of these materials, and in some cases the amounts of each present on a suspect's hand, may indicate whether or not the person has has recently fired a gun. Many techniques are available for collecting gunshot residue from a suspect's hands. Residue on clothing and other target surfaces is often examined in place (without removing or transferring it), whereas suspected residue on a person's hands is sampled first by one of several lifting or swabbing techniques.

Two of the methods which have been used for sampling residue on hands for elemental analysis are the paraffin lift method and the cotton swab method.

1 Paraffin lift method

   a Warm, melted paraffin is allowed to flow from a brush and onto the suspect's hands.

   b The liquid paraffin is allowed to cool to a solid glovelike cast. (Several reinforced layers may be used.)

   c The cast is carefully removed. (The gunshot residue, if present, is embedded in the paraffin.)

   d The paraffin cast is placed into a clean container, sealed, labeled, and submitted to the laboratory along with control paraffin lifts (usually from the other hand).

2 Cotton swab method

   a Four drops of 5% nitric acid (reagent grade) are applied to each of two clean cotton swabs.

   b Using both swabs simultaneously, the back of a suspect's hand and fingers are thoroughly swabbed.

   c The swabs are placed into a clean plastic bag which is sealed and labeled.

   d The procedure is repeated for other portions of the hand (left palm, right palm, and right back) with fresh pairs of swabs.

   e All the swabs are submitted, along with control swabs, to the laboratory for analysis.

Other procedures have involved (1) dipping the suspect's hand into a plastic bag containing dilute nitric or hydrochloric acid, (2) lifting the residues from the hand with double-stick tape, and (3) spraying 4% cellulose acetate in acetone onto the hand, waiting until a hard film forms, and then removing the film for submission to the laboratory.

Laboratory Examination of Gunshot Residue

Detection of gunshot residue is based on the identification of certain chemical compounds and elements, which are present in gunpowder and primer, and traces of metals from bullets and casings. When a gun has been fired, gunshot residue may arise from primer, propellant, lubricants, metals (bullet, projectile), bullet jacket, cartridge case, gun barrel, and gunpowder. Any of the following chemical elements, ions, or compounds may be present in residue: nitrate, nitrite, nitrocellulose, nitroglycerin, nitric oxide, lead, barium, copper, and antimony. Several types of tests are available for the identification of these chemical materials, including (1) microscopical examination, (2) chemical tests for the presence of nitrates and nitrites, and (3) methods for the detection of trace elements in gunshot residue.

Microscopical examination is employed for examination of the area surrounding a bullet hole, or for examination of swabs from such an area. An examiner looks for gunshot residue particles and other gunshot residues as well as for smudging and soot marks.

Chemical tests for the presence of nitrate on the skin (hands) are known as *dermal nitrate* or *paraffin* tests. The term *paraffin test* is derived from the method used to sample the hands (described earlier). The hand surface is painted with successive layers of molten paraffin until a "glove" is built up. After cooling, it is cut away from the hand, and chemical tests can be performed on its inner surface. The technique has a major advantage which has not been matched by later ones, namely, that it is possible to obtain a fairly detailed picture of the *distribution* of gunshot residue particles over the surface of the hand. The paraffin test can be used solely as an investigative aid when no subsequent test for use in court is envisioned. Nitrates can be found in many other materials, including cigarette smoke, urine, fertilizers, and so on. In addition, other kinds of chemicals such as oxidizing agents can be expected to yield positive results. Because of these problems, these tests for residues on skin were challenged in the courts and fell into disfavor and disuse.

The third type of method for gunshot residue detection is based on the detection of trace elements. Primers commonly contain antimony sulfide as a fuel and barium nitrate as an oxidizer. The residues produced after firearm discharge, therefore, contain trace amounts of antimony and barium.

The theoretical validity of this testing approach is based on the expectation that barium and antimony should be relatively uncommon on the hands of nonshooters. The techniques used for detection of these trace elements have included microchemical methods, neutron activation analysis (NAA), and atomic absorption spectroscopy (AA). The latter two are extremely sensitive for both trace elements. Very low concentrations of either one can be detected in samples from the hand's surface. Traces of copper from the ammunition may also be detected in this way. AA, but not NAA, can be used to detect low levels of lead as well. Anodic stripping voltammetry has also been used for this purpose. There are two major shortcomings of these trace elemental techniques as applied to the detection of gunshot residues. (1) They are bulk analysis techniques. In other words, they yield little or no information about the *distribution* of gunshot residue particles over the hand surface. (2) The basic assumptions upon which the methods are predicated, namely, that antimony and barium are seldom found on the hands of nonshooters, are not completely correct.

So-called hand blank studies have shown that very high levels of both antimony and barium can be found on the hands of nonshooters on occasion. Thus, in order to interpret measurements on unknown samples, it is necessary to establish some kind of threshold level below which a case specimen will be interpreted as negative or inconclusive. This threshold level must be established somewhat arbitrarily. As a result, the hands of a nonshooter may contain antimony and barium levels above the threshold, or more commonly, the amounts of these trace elements on the hands of an actual shooter may be below the threshold value. In the first case, a false-positive result is obtained, and in the second case, a false-negative or inconclusive result.

In recent years, a method for the definitive identification of gunshot residue particles has been developed and applied to actual investigations in some cases. This particle analysis procedure employs the scanning electron microscope (SEM), which was discussed in Chapter 3. An SEM used for gunshot residue particle analysis must be outfitted with an x-ray spectrometer, so that both the *micromorphology* and the *elemental composition* of the particles can be studied simultaneously. No other particles have been found which have both the characteristic morphology and the particular elemental makeup. When these particles are found on evidence removed from the hand of a suspected shooter, there is little question that they are in fact derived from gunshot residues. The present state of development of the technique, however, does not provide information about the distribution of the particles on the surface of the hand. Under these circumstances, a defendant could explain their presence on his hand by claiming to have been in the vicinity when a gun was discharged or having handled a recently discharged weapon. It would even be possible for gunshot residue particles to be transferred to a defendant's hands from the hands of a police officer as a result of postarrest activities such as handcuffing. The particle analysis method is ultimately capable of giving both a definitive identification of gunshot residue and a record of their distribution. With present techniques, however, it would be prohibitively expensive and time-consuming to obtain this information. We may anticipate that, in the future, the automation or computerization of SEM/x-ray spectrometer systems may allow such information to be obtained from an analysis with relative ease.

NUMBER RESTORATIONS

Introduction

Manufacturers often stamp serial numbers, other specific letters and numbers, or combinations of these onto products like firearms, valuable tools, cameras, watches, automobile engines, and other machinery. These numbers or marks have important value in investigations for establishing ownership or the identity of a manufacturer. Criminals sometimes attempt to alter or obliterate these numbers, and firearms and toolmark examiners are often asked to try to restore them.

When an identifying number is stamped or pressed into a metal surface, the underlying structure of the metal is compressed and deformed. The deformation carries deeper than the depth of the markings themselves. Thus, although such a number may appear to have been obliterated, evidence of it may still remain. In some cases, the number can be restored and made visible by chemical etchants, electrolytic methods, ultrasonic cavitation, magnetic particle methods, or a combination of these.

In addition to numbers on guns and tools, forensic science laboratories may be asked to try to restore identifying numbers on automobiles, bicycles, motorcycles, engines, motors, television receivers, and many other metal articles.

Methods of Obliterating Numbers

A variety of techniques have been used by criminals to obliterate serial numbers, thereby concealing evidence or original ownership. The simplest ways are to scratch the serial number with a sharp tool or file it down with a metal file. These crude techniques are very effective on softer metals, particularly aluminum alloys. The surface is usually in a rough condition and may require considerable smoothing before restoration. Grinding the serial number with a power grinder or peening with a hammer are also common techniques used by professional criminals.

The amount of metal removed by grinding and the degree of metal deformation caused by peening can vary and with it the difficulty encountered in an attempted restoration. Other methods include overstamping, in which a false serial number is applied over the area of a previously obliterated one. Welding may be used as well, where fresh metal is added to an obliterated surface. Occasionally, a criminal may reapply the original finish to a previously obliterated surface. All of these processes can complicate restoration efforts.

Methods of Restoration

The choice of the best method to restore obliterated serial numbers depends on the particular metal and the method which was used to obliterate the number. In 1978, the National Aeronautics and Space Administration Lewis Research Center and Chicago State University conducted detailed studies evaluating the different restoration methods. Some of their findings are summarized in Table 14-3.

Chemical Methods The chemical etching method is the simplest and most effective method used in the forensic science laboratory for restoring obliterated numbers. It is simple to apply and requires no expensive equipment. In addition, it works well on any size or type of object.

Use of proper reagents and techniques can often bring about a restoration of the number. The procedure is as follows:

1 Examine the obliterated area for visible or partially visible symbols, the extent

TABLE 14-3
METHODS OF NUMBER RESTORATIONS ON VARIOUS METALS

	Method		
Metal	**Chemical**	**Electrolytic**	**Other**
Steel	Fry's reagent: 90 g $CuCl_2$, 120 mL HCl, 100 mL water	Turner's reagent: 2.5 g $CuCl_2$, 40 mL HCl, 24 mL ethyl alcohol, 30 mL water	—
Cast iron	Fry's reagent	Turner's reagent or 10% HCl in methyl alcohol	Indirect heat
Aluminum alloys	Acid ferric chloride: 25 g $FeCl_3$, 25 mL HCl, 100 mL water	Ferric chloride: 25 g $FeCl_3$, 100 mL water; or hydrofluoric acid in glycerol	Indirect heat
Brass	Acid ferric chloride	Acid ferric chloride; or 25% nitric acid	Ultrasonic cavitation
Zinc alloys	Chromic acid: 20 g CrO_3, 1.5 g Na_2SO_4, 100 mL water; or 25% nitric acid	Chromic acid; or 10% NaOH	—

of grinding or punching, any additional stamping, and metal or finish added over the original area. Identify the type of metal from which the object is made.

2 Photograph the entire item, and record details of the obliterated area by close-up photography.

3 Clean and polish the obliterated area. First, remove grease, paint, and debris from the surface by application of suitable solvents, such as paint remover, mineral spirits, or penetrating oil. Next, polish the surface to a smooth, mirrorlike finish with emery cloth, polishing rouge, a jeweler's cloth, or other fine abrasive. It is best to use a series of progressively finer abrasives.

4 Clean the area with a solvent, such as acetone or other grease solvent.

5 Apply a thin film of chemical etchant (Table 14-3) to the polished surface with a cotton swab, medicine dropper, or glass stirring rod. Occasionally, a clay retaining well can be built around the area and the etching solution placed within it. The time required for restoration may vary from a few seconds to an hour, depending upon the chemical reactivity of the specimen.

6 The chemically etched surface must be carefully observed throughout the etching process since restoration can occur at any time and may be lost if etching is prolonged. Once the symbols or partial symbols appear, they should be noted. Low-power magnification is sometimes helpful.

7 Photograph the final observation, recording the restored numbers.

8 Remove the etching solution to preserve the evidence. The surface should be washed thoroughly and treated with oil to preserve the restored number.

Electrolytic Method   The electrolytic method is a combination of electropolishing and electrochemical etching techniques. In this method, the obliterated surface is first polished with fine abrasives and cleaned with acetone. A variable dc voltage source (commonly a 6-V battery and sometimes a 1.5-V flashlight battery) is connected to the specimen. The specimen is connected by wire to the positive (+) terminal. A wire from the negative (−) terminal is connected through a metal clamp to a piece of cotton dipped in the electrolytic etching solution. The type of solution depends on the type of metal from which the specimen was made (Table 14-3). To accomplish restoration, the obliterated area is continuously swabbed with cotton containing the etching solution. Observation of the progress of restoration is made a regular intervals. The remainder of the procedure is the same as that used for chemical etching.

Ultrasonic Cavitation Etching Method   *Cavitation* is the formation of vapor bubbles in a liquid due to localized reduction in pressure. A solid object moving rapidly through a liquid can create the reduction in pressure necessary for cavitation. This phenomenon can be used to restore obliterated serial numbers. In the process, a specimen is first polished and cleaned prior to treatment. The specimen is then immersed in an ultrasonic cavitation bath filled with water. This kind of bath will create vibrational cavitation. The number may be restored by the etching action of the cavitation bubbles. Experiments indicate that this method works well with some steel and brass surfaces. It is partially successful on aluminum surfaces, but no number restoration is obtained with heavily obliterated and restamped cast iron items.

Magnetic Particle Method   The specimen subjected to this method must be a ferromagnetic metal such as iron or steel. As with the other methods, the specimen is first polished and cleaned. It is then placed in a strong magnetic field in contact with a vibrator. Finely divided magnetic powder suspended in a light oil such as kerosene is applied to the surface of the magnetized specimen in the area of interest. The powder particles migrate on the surface, accumulating at the point where the obliterated number or other discontinuity exists. If the restoration is successful, the magnetic particles outline the obliterated number. Since this method is nondestructive to the specimen surface, it can be used first without in any way affecting the possible success of restorations by subsequent methods.

Other Methods   Many other methods for number restoration have been used. The heat etching method involves heating the specimen to a high temperature in a vacuum. The heating process enables the metal microstructure to be observed. The cold-frost method has also been used for number restorations. The specimen is first polished and then wiped with dry ice. If restoration is successful, the number is made visible by the frost pattern. Other methods include radiography, liquid penetrants, and electroplating techniques. None of them, however, shows any great advantages over the chemical etching technique.

STUDY QUESTIONS

1 Name the different types of firearms and describe the main characteristics of each one.
2 Describe the series of events which occurs inside a weapon when it is fired.
3 What is rifling? What types of firearms have rifled barrels? What is the significance of rifled barrels for the forensic scientist?
4 What does the caliber of a rifle or handgun mean?
5 Name several methods used for rifling barrels.
6 What is an indented toolmark: What is a striated toolmark? How do they differ? What types of actions produce them?
7 On what types of surfaces might you expect to find indented toolmarks? Striated toolmarks?
8 Why are the markings on bullets and cartridge cases considered toolmarks?
9 What principles should be followed in documenting and collecting toolmark evidence? Are there actions which should be avoided in this process?
10 What properties are used in the laboratory for comparing toolmarks? What types of information can be obtained from these comparisons?
11 What are the basic components of a round of ammunition?
12 How does shotgun ammunition differ from handgun and rifle ammunition?
13 What is a primer and what is its function?
14 Outline the proper method of documenting and collecting firearms evidence at a scene. What actions should be avoided? How should firearms evidence be preserved?
15 What information can be obtained from a bullet? From a cartridge case? From a weapon?
16 What characteristics are used in bullet comparisons?
17 What characteristics are used in cartridge case comparisons? To what extent does the presence of these different characteristics depend on the type of weapon used?

18 What is gunshot residue? What types of information can be obtained from gunshot residue analysis?
19 What is the underlying principle behind methods used to detect and identify gunshot residue?
20 Name several methods for collecting samples from a suspected shooter's hands for gunshot residue analysis. What are the advantages and drawbacks of each? How do they relate to the methods used for analysis?
21 What are the disadvantages of bulk analysis techniques in testing for gunshot residue?
22 Why is the SEM particle analysis technique a superior method for gunshot residue identification?

REFERENCES AND FURTHER READING

Barnes, F. C., and R. A. Helson: "An Empirical Study of Gunpowder Residue Patterns," *Journal of Forensic Sciences*, vol. 19, p. 448, 1974.

Biasotti, A. A.: "The Principles of Evidence Evaluation as Applied to Firearm and Toolmark Identification," *Journal of Forensic Sciences*, vol. 9, p. 428, 1964.

Burrand, G.: *The Identification of Firearms and Forensic Ballistics*, Barnes, New York, 1962.

Davis, J.: *Toolmarks, Firearms and the Striagraph*, Charles C Thomas, Springfield, Ill., 1958.

Goleb, J. R., and C. R. Midkiff: "Firearms Discharge Residue Sample Collection Techniques," *Journal of Forensic Sciences*, Vol. 20, p. 701, 1975.

Hatcher, J. S., F. J. Jury, and J. Weller: *Firearms Investigation, Identification and Evidence*, Stackpole, Harrisburg, Pa., 1957.

Joling, R. J., and W. W. Stern: "An Overview of Firearm Identification Evidence for Attorneys," *Journal of Forensic Sciences*, vol. 26, p. 142, 1981.

Josserand, M. H., and J. A. Stevenson: *Pistols, Revolvers and Ammunition*, Bonanza Books, Crown Publishers, New York, 1972.

Krishnan, S. S.: "Detection of Gunshot Residue on the Hands by Trace Element Analysis," *Journal of Forensic Sciences*, vol. 22, p. 304, 1977.

Matricardi, V. R., and J. W. Kilty: "Detection of Gunshot Residue Particles from the Hands of a Shooter," *Journal of Forensic Sciences*, vol. 22, p. 725, 1977.

Seamster, A., et al.: "Studies of the Spatial Distribution of Firearms Discharge Residues," *Journal of Forensic Sciences*, vol. 21, p. 868, 1976.

Stone, I. C., V. J. DiMaio, and C. S. Petty: "Gunshot Wounds: Visual and Analytical Procedures," *Journal of Forensic Sciences*, vol. 23, p. 361, 1978.

Wilhelm, R. M.: "General Considerations of Firearms Identification and Ballistics," in W. U. Spitz and R. S. Fisher (eds.), *Medicolegal Investigation of Death*, Charles C Thomas, Springfield, Ill., 1973.

Wolten, G. M., R. S. Nesbitt, A. R. Calloway, G. L. Loper, and P. F. Jones: "Particle Analysis for the Detection of Gunshot Residue," *Journal of Forensic Sciences*, vol. 24, p. 409, 1979.

SCIENTIFIC MEASUREMENT— METRIC SYSTEM

For our purposes, the three most useful metric units of measurement are: the *gram*, the basic unit of mass; the *meter*, the basic unit of length, and the *liter*, the basic unit of volume. One gram equals approximately 0.035 ounce. One meter equals approximately 39.4 inches, a little longer than a yard. A liter is a little bigger than a quart. There are approximately 3.78 liters in a gallon.

Quantities larger or smaller than the basic metric units are always expressed in tenfold multiples of them. Prefixes which have their roots in Greek or Latin are used along with the basic unit terms to indicate the multiples. The most important of these prefixes are: *kilo-*, meaning 1000 (10^3); *centi-*, meaning one hundredth, or 0.01 (10^{-2}); *milli-*, meaning one thousandth, or 0.001 (10^{-3}); *micro-*, meaning one millionth, or 0.000001 (10^{-6}); and *nano-*, meaning one billionth, or 0.000000001 (10^{-9}). Thus, a milliliter is one thousandth, or 0.001, of a liter; a centimeter is one hundredth, or 0.01, of a meter; and a kilogram is 1000 grams.

Metric units are so common in scientific writing and usage that standard abbreviations have been adopted for them, as well as for some of the prefixes: g = gram; m = meter; L or l = liter. Prefixes are abbreviated: n = nano; m = milli; c = centi; μ (Greek mu) = micro; k = kilo.

The abbreviations for the units generally appear without periods. The following examples illustrate the unit abbreviations: μg = microgram(s); mg = milligram(s); nm = nanometer(s); cm = centimeter(s); μL or μl = microliter(s); mL or ml = milliliter(s); kg = kilogram(s). In denoting microscopic lengths, the unit *micrometer* is still often called by its old name *micron* and abbreviated μ instead of μm. The unit for one-tenth of a nanometer, or 0.0000000001 (10^{-10}) meter, has the special name *angstrom unit*, abbreviated Å.

Table A1-1 illustrates many of the metric units and their relationships to one another and gives some conversions to the more familiar English system units.

Scientists usually measure and express units of temperature on the Celsius scale, instead

413

of on the more familiar Fahrenheit scale. Pure water freezes at 0°C (32°F) and boils at 100°C (212°F). Temperatures on one scale may be converted to the other using the formulas

$$°C = \frac{5}{9}(°F - 32) \qquad °F = \frac{9}{5}°C + 32$$

TABLE AI-1
METRIC MEASUREMENTS AND CONVERSIONS

Mass

$$\begin{array}{rll}
1 \text{ mg} = & 0.001 \text{ g} = 0.000001 \text{ kg} \\
1000 \text{ mg} = & 1 \text{ g} \quad = 0.001 \text{ kg} \\
1,000,000 \text{ mg} = & 1000 \text{ g} \quad = 1 \text{ kg}
\end{array}$$

1 mg =	0.000035 oz		1 oz = 28.35 g =	0.028 kg	
1 g =	0.035 oz	= 0.0022 lb	1 lb = 16 oz	= 453.6 g = 0.45 kg	
10 g =	0.35 oz	= 0.022 lb			
100 g =	3.53 oz	= 0.22 lb			
1 kg =	35.27 oz	= 2.2 lb			

$$\begin{array}{l}
1 \text{ ton} = 2000 \text{ lb} = 907,200 \text{ g} = 907.2 \text{ kg} \\
1 \text{ metric ton} = 1000 \text{ kg} = 2,204.6 \text{ lb} = 1.1 \text{ ton}
\end{array}$$

Length

$$\begin{array}{l}
1 \text{ Å} = 0.1 \text{ nm} = 0.0001 \text{ µm} = 0.00000001 \text{ cm} = 0.0000000001 \text{ m} \\
10 \text{ Å} = 1 \text{ nm} \quad = 0.001 \text{ µm} \quad = 0.0000001 \text{ cm} \quad = 0.000000001 \text{ m}
\end{array}$$

$$\begin{array}{rll}
10,000 \text{ Å} = & 1000 \text{ nm} = 1 \text{ µm} = & 0.0001 \text{ cm} = 0.000001 \text{ m} \\
& 10,000 \text{ µm} = & 1 \text{ cm} \quad = 0.01 \text{ m} \\
& 1,000,000 \text{ µm} = & 100 \text{ cm} \quad = 1 \text{ m}
\end{array}$$

1 µm = 0.00000394 in		1 in = 2.54 cm	= 0.0254 m	
1 cm = 0.394 in	= 0.033 ft	1 ft = 30.48 cm	= 0.305 m	
1 m = 39.37 in	= 3.28 ft = 1.094 yd	1 yd = 91.44 cm	= 0.914 m	
1 km = 39,370 in	= 3,280.8 ft	1 mi = 1760 yd	= 160,934 cm	
	= 1,093.6 yd = 0.621 mi		= 1609.3 m = 1.61 km	

Volume

$$\begin{array}{rll}
1 \text{ µL} = & 0.001 \text{ mL} = 0.000001 \text{ L} \\
1,000 \text{ µL} = & 1 \text{ mL} \quad = 0.001 \text{ L} \\
1,000,000 \text{ µL} = & 1000 \text{ mL} \quad = 1 \text{ L}
\end{array}$$

1 µL = 0.000034 fl oz	1 fl oz = 29,600 µL	= 29.6 mL = 0.0296 L	
1 mL = 0.034 fl oz	1 pt = 473.2 mL	= 0.473 L	
1 L = 33.8 fl oz = 0.264 gal	1 qt = 946.4 mL	= 0.946 L	
	1 gal = 3785.4 mL	= 3.785 L	

GENERAL CRIME-SCENE PROCEDURE

INTRODUCTION

Throughout this book we have attempted to point out that every crime scene is unique and that there is no single "right way" to process crime scenes. Each scene must be evaluated individually. There are no hard-and-fast rules for successful crime-scene processing. This appendix is designed to provide a general discussion of crime-scene procedure; its purpose is to supplement the discussions and suggestions applicable to specific types of evidence that were presented in individual chapters. Some of the more general activities (for example, documentation methods) were discussed in Chapter 3. Certain chapters where details pertaining to specific evidence types are covered will be cited in this appendix. In some instances the appropriate chapter for finding these details will be obvious. It is hoped that, by integrating the present discussion of general crime-scene procedure with the ideas and information presented in individual chapters, the student will develop an appropriately flexible approach to crime-scene processing. Nothing can substitute for experience, but the discussions in the individual chapters plus some of the following guidelines should be helpful while this is being gained.

PROTECTION OF THE SCENE

It is obvious to almost everyone that a crime scene must be protected and that access to it must be strictly limited; however, certain problems exist, and serious mistakes are commonly made. Such mistakes are most often irreversible and can compromise or thwart an investigation, jeopardize a prosecution, or effectively deny a defendant due process. Of course, perfection in this or any other human endeavor is never achieved. It is probable that no crime scene has ever been processed in such a way that hindsight would not allow someone else to criticize the work at a later date. However, investigators must learn from their mistakes and strive for continuous improvement. No attempt should be made to cover up these mistakes or offer excuses for them. Responsibility for mistakes should be faced squarely. In addition, guidance should be sought (from supervisors or knowledgeable laboratory personnel) to assure that the occurrence of such errors will be minimized in the future. Although it seems that commonsense rules should be adequate for the protection of a crime scene, it is still worthwhile discussing certain general points and offering suggestions.

All unauthorized personnel should be excluded from the scene after it has been secured. This is a commonsense but essential rule that is often ignored or sidestepped in practice. The scene can be considered to have been secured when it has been ascertained that suspects (armed or otherwise), witnesses, and living victims have been removed, and an adequate staff has been deployed to safeguard it. It is clear that the search for a dangerous suspect or the securing of medical attention for a wounded victim must take precedence over physical evidence concerns for the moment. However, such activities should not be carried out with careless abandon and a complete disregard for physical evidence. In fact, these activities should be carefully monitored and recorded by the first responding officer or other responsible individual. Seemingly insignificant details such as initial positions of doors, windows, and light switches and any subsequent alterations of these should be noted and documented.

There is normally no need to remove a body until after the scene has been completely processed and thoroughly documented. In fact, it is preferable that the body be left undisturbed throughout the entire scene investigation even though the medical examiner or coroner may be in a hurry to remove it. Crucial evidence on the body or information regarding its relation to the scene may be lost if it is removed hastily. Of course, if there is any chance that the victim is still alive, first aid and/or an examination by a physician or other qualified medical professional is certainly necessary and should be arranged for as soon as possible. Notes describing the activities of those rendering aid to the victim should be made at the time the activities are being monitored. In this way the notes are taken when the details are fresh in the observer's mind. Objects moved and paths taken should be noted. It is not improper for the officer responsible for the scene to instruct paramedics regarding paths to follow which will minimize damage to potential physical evidence as long as this does not impede timely aid to the victim. Considerable judgment on the part of the officer in this and many other crime-scene decisions is required. If a victim is obviously dead (decapitated, putrefied, etc.) or has been pronounced dead at the scene, the body should be left alone.

Those admitted to the scene after it has been secured should only be persons who are capable of making a contribution to the physical evidence aspects of the investigation and whose presence is actually necessary. This means that the simply curious among the detectives and police "brass" should be excluded as well as the members of the public and the press. This may be difficult at times. Such exclusion is more readily accomplished in departments where there is a clearly enunciated policy which is regularly enforced. If the department's policy is unclear or ignored, it may be embarassing for the officer in charge of the scene to exclude higher-ranking individuals or influential politicians. However, even in this case some fairly effective tactics can be adopted and utilized. These tactics have two purposes. The first of these is merely to discourage entry by nonessential personnel rather than risk confrontation in attempting to prohibit it. This eases the burden on the officer in charge. The second purpose is to minimize the damage caused by the entry of curious officials.

The following tactics used singly or in combination will be found to be useful in controlling access to the scene. Personnel may be admitted only if they agree to sign in and out on a log sheet kept by the first officer. In addition, each individual may be given a form to take into the scene upon which to record details of his activities within the scene. Blanks or spaces to be filled in should deal with the path taken and any objects touched or handled. The act of carrying the form and filling it out fosters an awareness of proper crime-scene procedure and serves as a constant reminder to make these individuals more careful while they are in the scene area. At the end of the investigation, the first responder's report should account for all the forms issued and those returned. Such records can prove very valuable later when questions concerning scene integrity arise. Knowledge of these documentation requirements also makes a person think twice about requesting permission to enter.

An additional condition for nonessential admission can also be used. Each individual entering can be requested to supply a set of "elimination" prints prior to being admitted. This has the direct value of allowing the convenient on-the-scene comparison of any latents discovered with the prints of those at the scene so that time is not needlessly spent on the documentation, collection, and preservation of extraneous fingerprints. Perhaps more important, it is similar to the above-cited tactics in serving as a deterrent to capricious and frivolous entry to the scene. This is accomplished without producing the "ruffled feathers" that a direct confrontation or denial of permission might entail. In summary, the accountability aspect and the time required to keep records and produce the elimination set of prints create a reluctance to submit to the procedures unless the motivation is very strong. It should also be noted that the messy fingerprint ink serves as its own deterrent. This is particularly true if a suitable hand cleaner is not provided. Once established, these requirements should reduce or even eliminate unjustified requests from curious officials in the future.

Many individuals have what is apparently an almost irresistible urge to clean up a disorderly residence or office. It is not uncommon to find housewives, maids, or secretaries cleaning up a crime scene when the police arrive. This, of course, cannot be allowed to continue. At this point it is important for the first officer to document what has been done and elicit as much information as possible about the conditions existing prior to the cleanup, in addition to putting an end to the cleanup and rearranging.

Under no circumstances should a suspect be led back to or be allowed to enter the scene. If this were to happen, it would compromise all evidence which might be developed later to attempt to associate the suspect with the scene and could also be used to great advantage by a knowledgeable defense attorney. Such an admonition would seem to be unnecessary, but cases where a suspect is apprehended at some remote location and then led back to the scene for questioning are not uncommon.

In a number of cases the laboratory results may prove "inconclusive" and the care exercised in protecting the crime scene may seem to have been wasted. It should be remembered that, at our present state of the art in forensic science, the field is not sufficiently developed to allow a definitive solution in every case or perhaps even a majority of cases. However, recognition of this fact should not make the investigator less meticulous and vigilant. Care and thoroughness will pay off in a worthwhile number of cases. It should also be remembered that the exclusion of a particular suspect, although it may sometimes complicate the investigation, is also a useful result.

In some departments the first responder's responsibilities end once the investigators arrive and assume control of the scene. Although it is true that the bulk of this individual's work and the hardest part have been done, he or she can still serve a useful purpose and perform valuable functions. The presence of the first responder at the scene during the entire investigation adds continuity. This officer can serve as a readily available resource to be consulted about certain initial conditions that were not specifically considered earlier. The first responder should be allowed to continue maintaining a watch over the security of the scene and work with the investigator in charge, or *crime-scene coordinator,* to help document entry and exit of individuals and changes in conditions. For the duration of the scene investigation the first officer reports to the crime-scene coordinator rather than the patrol supervisor.

It is normally not within the scope of the first officer's responsibility to decide which items of evidence are significant. It is wise to assume that everything is significant and protect the scene accordingly. Recognition of evidence is normally an investigator's responsibility. Investigators processing the crime scene should also assume that everything is significant, at least initially. There are many cases in which seemingly unimportant evidence gains importance as the investigation proceeds. It is very unfortunate if such evidence is destroyed before its importance is recognized.

RECOGNITION

Recognition of evidence is not as easy a job as might be supposed. It is, in fact, a complex and difficult task. The crime-scene investigator must be able to sort the relevant and significant evidence from irrelevant and insignificant articles that may be present. Since every case is different, what is insignificant in one case may prove to be crucial in another. This places difficult demands on the investigator. To be successful requires experience at crime scenes, a knowledge of what can be done in the laboratory, and an imaginative approach. It is also necessary that careful observation and adequate time be devoted to this task. As long as proper precautions regarding possible perishable evidence are being observed, the job should not be rushed. The investigator should take his or her time—and think!

For evidence to be recognized as being significant, its relationship to the act under investigation must be understood. Mental reconstructions greatly facilitate a recognition of such relationships. Other factors to be considered are often quite obvious but less often fully appreciated. This is true of signs of disturbance. The investigator should recognize normal vs. abnormal conditions. Where possible the investigator should try to establish initial conditions existing at the scene prior to the crime as accurately as available information will allow. Ideally, detailed notes made by the first officer regarding conditions observed on arrival will be available and are indispensable to the investigator. If there is an indication that the scene had been disturbed prior to the official response, these notes should reflect this. Such notes should also contain statements relative to its initial condition by persons present at the scene.

Recognition of evidence extends into the laboratory investigation. Good communication between field investigators and laboratory investigators may result in important evidence being recognized on articles collected and submitted to the laboratory. A good criminalist knowledgeable about details of a case can be far more effective than one acting solely in response to a routine request for analysis. If the right questions are posed to the laboratory investigator, the most useful answers will be forthcoming. Comprehensive documentation techniques are most effective in helping to communicate details of a case to the criminalist who is unable to be at the crime scene.

DOCUMENTATION

The importance of documenting physical evidence has been stressed in Chapter 3 and in particular chapters dealing with specific evidence types. In addition to individual items of evidence, the overall scene must be documented. Signs of disturbance and both missing as as well as found objects and their relation to the scene should be noted and documented.

The type of documentation appropriate for the first officer is different from the detailed documentation required of the investigator. The first officer notes conditions of the scene and its perimeter and makes written notes and rough sketches as the observations are made. The main value of these is to help establish the initial conditions at the scene. Evidence may be altered by weather and activities during the investigation. Even when *no* alteration takes place, these records are helpful in removing any lingering doubts and establishing that this is, in fact, the case. Such records can be extremely valuable during the progress of the investigation as well as later on when the case reaches court. On certain occasions the first officer may want to go beyond notes and rough sketches to make measurements and employ a simple camera. This is rather unusual, but there is no reason why it should be discouraged as long as it is understood that such records and photographs do not lessen the need for those made by the investigator. Photographs taken by the first responder or another patrol officer have decidedly different purposes than those taken by the investigator. The quality of the former does not have to be as good. Their value is as overall records of general features of the crime scene early in the investigation. These photographs can serve as a useful point of reference and a valuable adjunct to the first responder's written notes. Later pictures taken by skilled investigators will normally contain more detail.

Crime-scene sketches need not be works of art. An investigator's lack of drawing skills should not be viewed as a handicap. The sketch made at the scene is normally a rough sketch. Its purpose is the recording of objects, positions, and relationships in sufficient detail to allow a finished or smooth sketch or even an architect's drawing to be made at a later date. The investigator is usually responsible for producing the finished sketch from his or her own rough sketch, but a professional draftsman or architect would be consulted to produce an architectural drawing or model. A notebook containing graph paper is a great aid in producing a rough sketch. The rulings on the paper facilitate the drawing of right-angle corners and help maintain approximate proportions. Even if this sketch is done carefully, it will look rather sloppy because it will contain records of all the measurements made. The finished sketch will be drawn to scale from this. The rough sketch should be retained after the finished sketch is completed. Examples of a crime scene depicted in both rough and finished sketches are presented in Figure A2-1.

The finished sketch can be one of two main types, depending on the nature of the crime scene. The simplest of these is the *plan* sketch. This is basically a floor plan of the crime scene designed to depict the scene as it would appear as viewed from above. For complex scenes where evidence or marks on the walls or ceilings may be present, such a sketch is inadequate. The most universally applicable type of sketch is the *cross-projection* sketch. This sketch depicts the room as if the walls had been pushed out from the top and folded down flat in the same plane with the floor. Most recommendations on cross-projection sketches do not take the ceiling into account. This can be a serious omission in some cases where ceilings can be very important. The most obvious ones are those that involve blood spatter and bullet holes, but dents, scuffs, and other marks can be equally important. An example of a cross-projection sketch for the crime scene depicted in Figure A2-1 is shown in Figure A2-2.

The role of photography in crime-scene documentation was discussed in Chapter 2. Additional references should be consulted for certain details. The advantages of audio and video documentation methods were outlined and discussed in Chapter 2, where a case was made for their increased utilization at crime scenes. Specialized methods for documenting certain kinds of pattern evidence such as casting and lifting were presented in Chapters 11 to 14.

SEARCHES

Certain evidence may not be discovered in the recognition phase discussed earlier. In fact, the mental reconstruction done during this phase may suggest that certain items are missing and should be sought. Weapons, tools, and expended cartridge cases are obvious examples

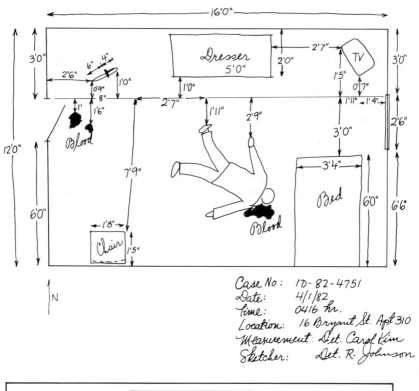

Case No: ID-82-4751
Date: 4/1/82
Time: 0416 hr.
Location: 16 Bryant St. Apt 310
Measurement: Det. Carol Kim
Sketcher: Det. R. Johnson

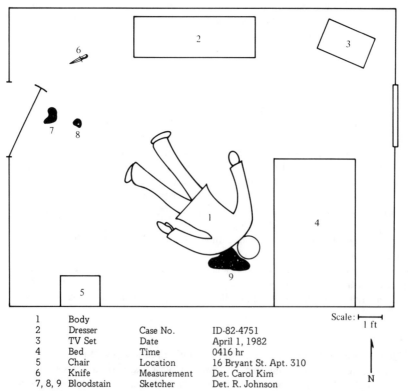

1	Body			
2	Dresser	Case No.	ID-82-4751	
3	TV Set	Date	April 1, 1982	
4	Bed	Time	0416 hr	
5	Chair	Location	16 Bryant St. Apt. 310	
6	Knife	Measurement	Det. Carol Kim	
7, 8, 9	Bloodstain	Sketcher	Det. R. Johnson	

Scale: |—————| 1 ft

N

FIGURE A2-1
(a) Rough and (b) finished sketches. (Courtesy of Leo Blanchette, Forensic Science Laboratory, Connecticut State Police.)

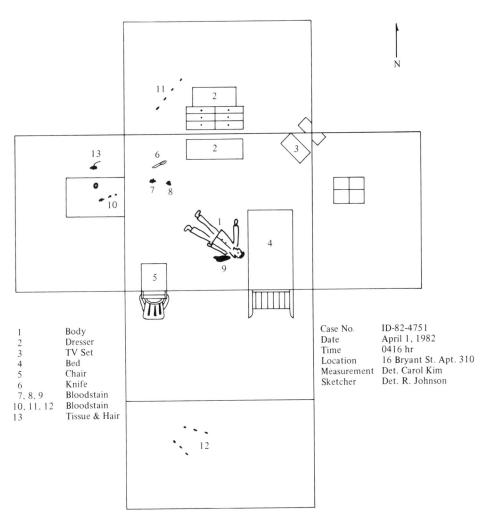

1	Body		Case No.	ID-82-4751
2	Dresser		Date	April 1, 1982
3	TV Set		Time	0416 hr
4	Bed		Location	16 Bryant St. Apt. 310
5	Chair		Measurement	Det. Carol Kim
6	Knife		Sketcher	Det. R. Johnson
7, 8, 9	Bloodstain			
10, 11, 12	Bloodstain			
13	Tissue & Hair			

FIGURE A2-2
A cross-projection sketch. This is based on the same hypothetical crime scene as the plan or
finished sketch shown in Figure A2-1. *(Courtesy of Eugene Ozerhoski, Forensic Science
Laboratory, Connecticut State Police.)*

of evidence that might fall into this category. Others would include broken fragments of
potential value in physical matches. A search for the latter type suggests itself when an
object thought to have been involved in an event under investigation exhibits a freshly fractured surface and the missing piece is not at hand. Searches may also be prompted by information obtained from preliminary reports from the medical examiner and from witnesses.
Timely investigative aid from the criminalistics laboratory may also be helpful in this regard.

When knowledge of the case and reconstruction has suggested particular things to be
looked for, it is appropriate to consider instituting a search. However, the search itself should

not commence until other evidence has been documented and/or collected. Searchers should know what they are looking for. It would certainly not be good to complete an extensive search and then think of something else to seek. This would be a waste of time and worker resources, and worse, the desired evidence might be destroyed in the process. In searches of large outdoor areas it may be necessary to enlist the help of large numbers of individuals. Ideally, such individuals should have some crime-scene experience, but at times one may have no alternative to the use of inexperienced personnel. These auxiliary searchers should be carefully instructed as to what *not* to do as well as how to proceed. A search should never be carried out by more than the minimum number of personnel necessary. Large-scale search operations are normally done only as a last resort after careful selective searches of key areas have been carried out by a small number of knowledgeable and skilled personnel.

The use of *search patterns* can be an aid in searching crime scenes. Several different search patterns have been recommended. These include spiral, grid, strip, and quadrant or zone patterns. These search patterns are depicted in Figure A2-3. The nature of the crime scene must be considered in choosing one of these methods. The decision as to which particular method to follow is less critical than the manner in which the search is conducted. It should be executed in a logical, systematic, and methodical fashion. In general, the spiral, grid, and strip methods are used for outdoor scenes. In other outdoor scenes the search may be conducted along a path, stream bed, or road. In a large indoor area such as a factory, it may not be practical to search the entire premises. Instead, attention should be focused on points of entry and exit and target areas (for example, a safe or vault) within the building. The probable paths taken by the criminals between these areas should also be checked. The decision concerning the most appropriate method to employ is left to the investigator.

Scenes of suspected arson are somewhat like other indoor crime scenes, especially if breaking and entering was involved. They have the added complexities of fire damage and

FIGURE A2-3
Search patterns. *(Courtesy of Elaine Pagliaro, Forensic Science Laboratory, Connecticut State Police.)*

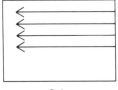

Strip

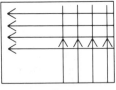

Grid

Spiral

Quadrant or zone

the need to search for a cause and origin. Specific points concerning tracing fire patterns to their origins and the search for accelerants and incendiary devices were discussed in Chapter 4.

The searching of suspects for useful physical evidence is normally not a difficult task. The clothing is taken, marked for identification, and packaged separately as noted in Chapters 6 to 8 and in the sections to follow. The individual should be checked for wounds and marks, and if any are found, they should be properly documented. Suspects in sex crimes should be examined for trace evidence which might indicate contact with the victim. The search for and collection of hairs and fibers were covered in Chapter 8. Blood and body-fluid stains should be dealt with according to the suggestions given in Chapters 9 and 10. Many of these considerations also apply to the collection of evidence from victims. Here bitemark evidence, which was discussed in Chapter 12, might also be encountered. It is very important that this be documented photographically and immediately brought to the attention of a qualified forensic odontologist. It is sometimes valuable to photograph such evidence over a period of days as the wound heals. Different contrast may be obtained, and different features may become apparent during this interval.

COLLECTION

It is difficult to generalize about the collection of physical evidence. Different kinds of evidence require different collection methods. For this reason details of collection methods appropriate to specific evidence types were discussed in the individual chapters pertaining to those evidence types. The only general comments that are applicable to all types of evidence are rather obvious commonsense precautions. These are reviewed briefly here. Evidence should not be disturbed and collected until it and the surrounding area have been inspected and thoroughly documented.

Care is necessary to minimize the chances of altering the evidence during collection. Certain specific types of evidence require specialized collection methods. For example trace evidence, physiological stains, and imprints are not collected in the same way. With respect to this point, the discussions in the individual chapters (that is, 6, 9, and 11) should be particularly helpful. With certain types of evidence consideration needs to be given to the need for control (known or blank) samples. Controls can be particularly important with respect to fire investigation, trace evidence, blood and body-fluid stains, and questioned documents.

It is occasionally appropriate to document details of the collection process. For example, with certain kinds of evidence it might be a good idea to photograph the collection in progress and note the time and other details such as the weather. Of course, the continuity of the chain of possession of the evidence must be maintained as well as the integrity of the evidence itself. These points should be kept in mind in reading the following sections dealing with marking, packaging, and transportation of evidence.

MARKING OF EVIDENCE

The marking of evidence is necessary to assure its unambiguous identification later on. In certain cases it is difficult to decide how best to mark particular items. Knowledge and experience on the investigator's part are required. Some consideration must be given to the way in which the evidence is relevant to the investigation and how it will be examined in the laboratory before a decision is made concerning how and where it should be marked. If areas containing marks or other important information are obliterated by the marking process, the evidence may be rendered valueless. Guidelines can be offered for dealing with commonly encountered evidence types, but nothing can substitute for forensic science knowledge and experience in nonroutine situations.

The decision regarding proper marking is generally easier when relatively large items of evidence are encountered. With small items which present no clearly unimportant or non-critical sites, the decision might be made not to mark them at all. If it is decided that such an object cannot be marked, an identifying sketch or photograph depicting unique features should be made so that the object can be recognized later. In other cases there may be available space, but it may be so limited that it is not possible to include much information. Perhaps only the investigator's initials and a single digit number can be accommodated. In this case it is particularly important to have the marking process and any code used thoroughly documented in the notebook. With very small items such as trace evidence, it is obviously impossible to mark the evidence itself. Here only the packaging can be marked.

Garments can usually be marked by securely affixing a tag or label to them or by writing in indelible pen on some inside surface such as the pockets, waistbands, and linings. These surfaces are often not dyed and offer good contrast to dark inks. Care must be exercised so that bullet holes, cuts, and stains are not disturbed. Many other relatively large items of evidence can be handled in a similar fashion. In addition to the markings applied to the evidence to identify it so that it can be recognized later, other markings may also be necessary. Thus, in some cases markings which indicate the orientation of articles of evidence as found may also be included. This is particularly true of pieces of window glass remaining in a frame. Suggestions concerning the marking of moderate-sized fragments of glass were given in Chapter 7. The difficulties peculiar to the marking of firearms, projectiles, and ammunition were discussed in Chapter 14.

PACKAGING

The primary purpose of packaging is protection of the evidence and the preservation of its integrity. Secure packaging is essential. Evidence should not be allowed to escape from the container or be exposed to the risk of contamination from the exterior. In general packaging must be robust enough to allow the evidence to survive the rigors of transportation (see next section). However, the exact type of packaging which is appropriate will depend on the nature of the evidence. Details of packaging suitable for various evidence types were given in the individual chapters. Volatile evidence such as accelerant residues collected from the scene of a suspected arson must be hermetically sealed so that they will not evaporate and become lost. Suitable containers and collection methods for volatile residues were discussed in Chapter 4. Different items of evidence should not be lumped together in a common package as this would allow the transfer of evidence to take place between items from different sources. Similarly, folding of clothing could allow the transfer of evidence from one part of a garment to another. This could compromise the value of the evidence in certain reconstructions. The packaging of items bearing possible trace evidence was the subject of parts of Chapters 6 to 8. Fresh bloodstains can also be transferred by folding which can destroy bloodstain pattern information. For this reason, wet bloodstained garments should never be folded. Wet bloodstains are also subject to deterioration from microbial action. For this reason bloodstained garments should never be sealed in airtight containers such as plastic bags. Even stains that appear to be dry may contain enough moisture to allow putrefaction to take place. Paper bags and wrappings are a much wiser choice for this type of evidence. The paper will retain trace evidence but is porous and can "breathe" allowing water vapor to escape. The reader should refer to Chapters 9 and 10 for more details.

TRANSPORTATION

Two major considerations are important in the transportation of evidence. The evidence must be packaged and transported in such a way that fragile items are not damaged. Handling during transit is important, but equally important is adequately secure packaging with proper mounting and cushioning of items where necessary. Thus, when evidence is being packaged some thought should be given to the way in which it will be transported to the laboratory.

The second major consideration is time. The investigator must think about the nature of the evidence and the time involved in getting it to the laboratory. Perishable items such as wet or moist physiological stains must be given special consideration to avoid deterioration and the loss of evidential value. If the laboratory is remote, different preparation, packaging, and transmittal methods would be used from what would be used if it is being sent to a local or nearby regional laboratory. When a local laboratory is being utilized, rapid delivery and refrigeration during transit are possible. Thus if proper arrangements have been made, wet samples can be submitted. Perishable samples must *never* be sent to remote laboratories in this condition. In fact they should not even be sent to local laboratories unless they are rushed there under refrigeration. Time, temperature, and moisture all play critical roles. When in doubt, moist biological stains should be carefully dried prior to packaging. See Chapter 9 on blood and Chapter 10 on body fluids for specific details.

THREE

FUNDAMENTALS OF
PHOTOGRAPHY

INTRODUCTION

Photography is an important documentation technique in forensic science. It is an essential part of general crime scene documentation and is also used to document details of particular items of evidence at the scene and in the laboratory. In addition, it is often used in the laboratory to visualize patterns and phenomena that might not be detectable visually. Photography in different spectral regions (for example, ultraviolet and infrared) is one instance of this latter application of photography in forensic science.

The uses of photography in forensic science are examples of scientific photography. Here we are concerned with recording and possibly accentuating specific features and details in a realistic manner. The primary focus is the extraction of information from evidence and its documentation. We are not preoccupied with matters of artistic expression or the production of aesthetically pleasing photographs.

Many investigators seem to have a fear of photography or at least see it shrouded in some type of incomprehensible mystique. In reality technical or scientific photography is quite straightforward. An investigator can start producing useful photographs as soon as he or she knows a few basic facts. Continued utilization of and practice with photography will allow skills to be honed and additional techniques to be developed. One can produce useful results and continue learning at the same time.

This appendix is designed to give the reader an overview of basic photographic theory and techniques and their application in forensic science. It is hoped that the information and philosophy presented here will be sufficient to get a number of readers started along the road to acquiring essential photographic knowledge and useful skills. The references listed at the end of the appendix have been carefully selected to supplement the information given here and provide details of specific techniques that can be useful in forensic science.

The word *photography* is derived from two Greek roots, *photos,* meaning "light," and *graphos,* "pertaining to drawing or writing." Thus, literally translated, photography means to write or draw with light. Recording with light is closer to the modern meaning of the word.

LIGHT AND LIGHTING

Light

Some knowledge of the nature and behavior of light is necessary for a working understanding of photography. In Chapter 3 we saw that what we commonly refer to as light is a narrow region of the electromagnetic spectrum (see Figure 3-6). Electromagnetic energy with wavelengths within the range of 400 to 700 nm is capable of stimulating receptors (rods and cones) in the retina of the eye and for this reason is known as visible light. Normal photographic films are sensitive to visible light and some shorter wavelength regions. Certain specialized films are also sensitive in the near-infrared region, where the wavelengths are somewhat longer than those of visible light. Thus, some films are designed to mimic the sensitivity of the eye and duplicate its response, while others are designed to extend vision into other wavelength regions.

Visual and photographic images are produced by gathering a portion of the light emitted or reflected by an object and reassembling it to form an image. The light from a typical object is light that has interacted with it by being transmitted through it (transparent objects) or reflected off its surface (opaque objects). The way in which the light has interacted with the object determines the type of information that can be learned about the object by reassembling this light to form an image.

Choice and Control of Illumination

Lighting can make the difference between a good photograph and an unsatisfactory one. The photographer can choose from among several different types of illumination. There are generally more options when *artificial* illumination rather than *available* light is used. Sources of artifical illumination include arc light, floodlights, flashbulb, and electronic flash. These sources can be moved and positioned so that various angles of illumination can be used. This can be very important with subjects which have a small amount of three-dimensional relief. Control of the illumination angle is difficult when available light such as sunlight or normal room light is being relied upon for the exposure. Thus, artificial illumination is preferable when control of the angle of illumination is important. Whenever there is any doubt about which illumination angle to use, several different angles should be tried.

Lighting and Contrast

Angle is only one of several illumination parameters that can be varied. Thus far we have only considered *unidirectional* light sources where the light is directed at the subject from essentially only one direction. There are times when this type of illumination will produce too much contrast and shadowing. In these situations a source of *diffuse illumination* should be used. This is softer light which will result in a reduction of shadow contrast. Diffuse lighting is commonly obtained by placing a translucent material, such as thin white paper or ground glass, between the source and the subject to scatter the light and act as a diffuser. Light can also be scattered and softened by reflection from flat white surfaces such as white walls, ceilings, or cardboard. This method is the basis of so-called bounce lighting. A third means of obtaining somewhat softer illumination is the use of two or more light sources aimed at the subject from different directions.

Suitable illumination, although very important, is not as difficult to achieve as it may sound. With a little thought and practice, almost anyone can get good results.

Filters and Contrast

When black-and-white film is being used to photograph a subject containing different colors, colored filters can be placed over the light source or the camera lens to enhance the contrast for details of a selected color. At the same time details of certain other colors may be de-emphasized. In principle, objects of a given color will appear darker in the final photograph if a filter of a complementary color (see Table 3-1) is used. A filter of the same color would cause the object to appear lighter. Filters used with black-and-white film to modify contrast are called *color contrast* filters. If the filter is placed over the lens of the camera it must be of high optical quality. This high quality is not necessary with filters designed to be placed over the light source.

Color Temperature and Color Balance

Color contrast filters must not be used for color photography. The "color" of the "white" light used in color photography is critical. We know that white light is made up of all the colors of the visible spectrum. However, all white light sources are not the same. The light given off by a candle contains a higher proportion of the longer wavelengths (yellow, orange, and red) and thus appears yellowish or yellow-white. The light from a tungsten filament in a normal incandescent lamp bulb also contains a preponderance of longer wavelengths, although to a lesser degree. This light appears whiter than that from the candle flame but is distinctly yellow compared to sunlight. The tungsten filament is hotter than the candle flame.

In general, the hotter an incandescent source, the whiter the light it produces. This relationship between the color of the source and its temperature allows one to numerically specify "the degree of whiteness" of the source by comparing it to the color of the light emitted from a theoretically perfect standard source. When the colors of the two sources have been matched by adjusting the temperature of the known standard source, the physical temperature of the standard source in kelvins is a measure of the degree of whiteness of the unknown source. This numerical value is called the *color temperature* of the source. The manufacturers of color films very carefully specify the color temperature of the light source to be used with the film. So-called daylight films are designed to be used outdoors or with an artificial source which has the same color temperature as natural daylight (6000 K). Electronic flash is designed to have a color temperature close to 6000 K. Photoflood bulbs have color temperatures of either 3200 or 3400 K. Sources with color temperatures other than 6000 K can be utilized with daylight films if special filters are used to change the color temperature to 6000 K. Filters of this type are known as *color correction* filters. Poor results can be expected if a color film is used with a source whose color temperature is significantly different from that for which the film was designed. The term *color balance* is often used in describing the color correction built into color films.

LENSES

Introduction

The subject of lenses was reviewed in Chapter 3. The formation of both real and virtual images was discussed. The image projected onto film in a camera is a real image (Figure

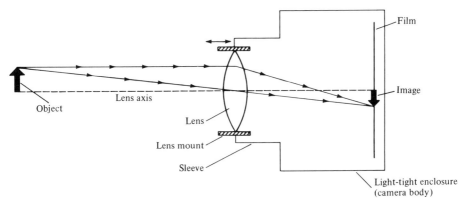

FIGURE A3–1
Image formation in a camera.

A3-1). The spatial variation of intensity in this image affects the film, producing a *latent image*. Following treatment with a developer and other chemicals, the latent image is made visible and permanent. The chemistry of photography and film developing will be discussed in a later section. For the present we direct our attention to factors that affect the selection and use of photographic lenses.

Focusing

Focusing of a camera is accomplished by altering the distance that separates the lens and the film. For a distant subject this separation should be just slightly more than the *focal length* of the lens. If the subject being photographed is so far away that it can be considered to be at an infinite distance in comparison to the focal length of the camera lens, the proper lens-to-film separation will be equal to the focal length. This is true because, by definition, light from infinity (parallel light) is brought to focus at the *principal focus* of the lens. For objects closer to the camera, the lens must be moved farther from the film to produce an in-focus image. Lenses supplied for 35-mm cameras are generally focused by rotating a ring on the lens barrel. This rotary motion is translated into linear motion by a helical screw mechanism that allows the lens-to-film distance to be altered in a smooth continuous fashion. A lens-to-subject distance scale is inscribed on the lens barrel in both feet and meters.

Helical lens mounts on most lenses provide enough range of movement to allow correct focus to be obtained for objects from a few feet to "infinity." For extreme close-ups this range of movement or *extension* is not sufficient. With 35 mm cameras, the requisite extension can be achieved in several ways. A fixed amount of extension can be obtained by affixing *extension tubes* between the camera body and the lens. Tubes of various lengths may be used singly or stacked in various combinations to allow the range of focus desired. However, they must be removed to photograph distant subjects. This can be troublesome when a mixed series of close-ups and distance shots is being taken, and is an intrinsic limitation of the fixed extension provided by extension tubes. The extreme-range continuous extension possible with mounts of specially designed *macro* lenses gets around this difficulty. Macro lenses are particularly well suited for use in taking extreme close-ups. Limits of a 1:1 image:object ratio are typical of such lenses. Macro lenses can also be focused on distant subjects but are not ideally suited to such use. As a practical matter, the compromises involved in such an application will probably not be apparent in the resulting photograph. Greater range continuous extension can be obtained by the use of *bellows* attachments for the camera. With specially designed lenses on such a bellows the range of focus can cover extreme close-ups and distant shots. With normal lenses the bellows often cannot be "collapsed" or shortened enough to allow images of distant objects to be formed in the film plane. However, a wide range of image:object ratios in close-up photography would be possible with such an arrangement.

Selection of Photographic Lenses

Lens Types—Focal Length   Lenses designed for use with better quality cameras are often quite complex. They are made up of a combination of a number of individual lenses known as *elements* mounted and/or cemented together. These assemblies are called *multielement lenses*. The additional elements are necessary to make the lens perform more closely to a hypothetical *ideal lens*. For our purposes we do not need to consider details of lens design and construction. We can treat photographic lenses as though they were ideal single-element lenses.

In Chapter 3 we mentioned that the focal length of a lens was its primary descriptive parameter. Recall that this was defined as the distance from the lens to the point where parallel light is brought to focus. The particular use to which a lens will be put determines which focal length lens is most appropriate. A photographer will generally have a selection of lenses with different focal lengths to use in specific situations. Three general classes of lenses can be distinguished on the basis of focal length. These are the wide-angle, normal, and telephoto.

A *normal lens* is one that has a focal length that is approximately equal to the length of a diagonal line drawn between opposite corners of the picture area on the film. For a 35-mm camera the film is 35 mm wide, including the sprocket holes. The picture area or frame size is 24 × 36 mm (see Figure A3-2). In this case the calculated length of the film diagonal is slightly more than 43 mm. In actual practice, lenses with focal lengths in the range of 50 mm are used as normal lenses for 35-mm cameras. Most macro lenses available for 35-mm cameras use a normal focal length of about 50 mm. The main difference between a macro lens and a normal lens is the range of movement of the focusing mount. The focusing mount of a macro lens can be extended a considerable distance from the camera and thus the film

FIGURE A3-2
35-mm film format (full frame).

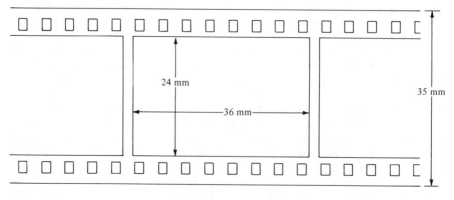

24 mm

36 mm

35 mm

plane. In addition, these lenses are better corrected for use close to the subject and relatively far from the film plane. Lenses with focal lengths substantially less than 45 mm are known as *wide-angle lenses* when they are used on 35-mm cameras. These lenses provide a wider angle of view than a normal lens. *Telephoto* lenses, or lenses with longer than normal focal lengths, have narrower angles of view but yield larger images of distant objects. There is a noticeable difference in perspective when lenses with different focal lengths are used to produce photographs which are designed to be viewed from a standard distance. Longer focal length lenses produce a distinct foreshortening of distance. Distant objects appear to be closer to objects in the foreground. The opposite is the case when a wide-angle lens is employed. Here the distance between closer objects and more distant ones appears to be exaggerated when the resulting photograph is viewed at a normal distance from the eye. If the photograph produced by a wide-angle lens is viewed at a distance closer than normal, the exaggerated perspective is reduced. The foreshortening of perspective characteristic of longer focal length lenses is diminished at longer-than-normal viewing distances.

In crime-scene work, wide-angle lenses are particularly useful for making overall photographs in the cramped quarters that are typical of many indoor scenes. When using a normal lens under these conditions it is often not possible to step back far enough to include much of the interior of the room in the photograph. The wide-angle lens alleviates this difficulty. The normal and wide-angle lenses will suffice for most crime-scene situations. Telephoto lenses are less commonly used for this type of work. Occasionally, a telephoto lens may be used to produce an enlarged image of a remote or inaccessible object from a reasonable or more convenient distance.

So-called zoom lenses are available for most 35-mm cameras. These are complex lenses with provision for moving certain groups of internal elements so that the focal length can be varied continuously. The image quality produced with zoom lenses is generally not as good as it is with high-quality fixed-focus lenses. However, with recent computer-aided designs, coupled with advances in lens coating technology, the difference is very slight. If only one lens is to be purchased, the photographer might consider a zoom lens with a focal length range extending from wide-angle to mildly telephoto. Of course this should be chosen from the product line of a reputable manufacturer. In addition, this lens should have macro capabilities so that close-ups of evidence at crime scenes can also be taken.

Lens Types—Lens Speed We have just seen that photographic lenses can be characterized and classified on the basis of focal length. The second major descriptive parameter of a photographic lens is its speed. *Lens speed* is a measure of the light-gathering power of a lens. Two lenses of the same focal length may have very different speeds. When both are used under identical conditions, the faster lens will be capable of producing a brighter or more intense image on the film. Alternatively, the faster lens will have the advantage of producing an image of a given intensity on the film (for example, the minimum exposure for the production of a negative) at a lower level of illumination than would be required for the slower lens. The speed of a lens is related to the maximum size of its opening or *aperture*. The larger the maximum aperture, the faster the lens. Better quality photographic lenses have adjustable apertures. In this case it is the largest usable aperture that characterizes the speed of the lens. Lens aperture is expressed numerically as the focal ratio or *f-number* (*f/*#), which is calculated by dividing the focal length of the lens by the diameter of the aperture as shown in the following equation:

$$\text{f-number } (f/\#) = \frac{\text{focal length}}{\text{diameter}} = \frac{f}{d}$$

TABLE A3-1
COMMON f-NUMBER PROGRESSION BASED ON POWERS OF 2

Power of 2	2^0	2^1	2^2	2^3	2^4	2^5	2^6	2^7	2^8	2^9	2^{10}	2^{11}	2^{12}
Reciprocal of relative area of lens aperture	1	2	4	8	16	32	64	128	256	512	1024	2048	4096
$f/\#$ in one-stop increments*	1	1.41	2	2.83	4	5.66	8	11.31	16	22.63	32	45.25	64
$f/\#$ for half-stops		1.19	1.68	2.37	3.36	4.76	6.73	9.51	13.45	19.03	26.91	38.05	53.82

*Square root of above row, rounded to two places.

Note that the $f/\#$ is inversely proportional to the diameter of the aperture. Thus, a large numerical value for the $f/\#$ implies a small-diameter aperture and vice versa. The smallest usable $f/\#$ (the largest opening) is the $f/\#$ that is used to specify the speed of a lens.

Lenses in which the $f/\#$ can be varied employ adjustable-iris diaphragms to change the size of the opening. It is useful to be able to vary the size of the opening by certain standard increments. The most useful increments have been found to be those which change the amount of light passing through the lens by a factor of 2. Thus, each adjustment of the $f/\#$ ring either halves or doubles the amount of light falling on the film. These standard-size increments are referred to as *stops* or *f-stops*.

The amount of light reaching the film is directly related to the area of the opening, whereas the $f/\#$ is inversely related to the diameter. Doubling the area of the opening is equivalent to reducing the $f/\#$ by one stop. Keep in mind, however, that one does not double the diameter to double the area. The area and the diameter are related by the formula for the area of a circle: $A = \pi \times d^2/4$. Doubling the diameter would increase the area by a factor of 4. To merely double the area (for example, increase the exposure by one stop), we need to increase the diameter only by a factor of the square root of 2 (~ 1.414). This is the same factor that adjacent f-stops differ by. Table A3-1 lists the most common progression of f-stops in use today. It is based on a progression obtained by raising the base 2 to integral powers. The numbers obtained by doing this are reciprocals of the relative area of the lens opening and thus are inversely proportional to the relative area of the lens opening. Taking the square root of each of these numbers yields the most common progression of f-stops. Aside from the fact that each $f/\#$ is equal to the square root of the number representing the reciprocal of the relative area above it in the table, each $f/\#$ differs from its immediate neighbors by a factor of $\sqrt{2}$.

Many lenses have detents or click stops at half-stop increments to allow the photographer a little finer control over the exposure. Usually, however, only the full f-stop positions are labeled with an $f/\#$. The numerical values of the intervening half-stops are shown at the intermediate positions in the last row of the table. The term *stopping down* is commonly used to describe the act of decreasing the size of the lens opening.

FILM AND ELEMENTARY PHOTOGRAPHIC CHEMISTRY

Historical Background

In photography the term *film* is used to refer to the image-recording medium. Originally, specially treated metallic or glass plates were used to record the image. Glass plates coated with a light-sensitive layer known as the *emulsion* are still used for certain specialized sci-entific applications where there is a need to make extremely accurate measurements directly on the photographic image. For general photographic use, glass plates are heavy, bulky, fragile, and cumbersome. About 100 years ago George Eastman sought a replacement for glass plates that would overcome these difficulties. His solution was to coat sheets of cellulose nitrate (celluloid) with the light-sensitive emulsion. Once the emulsion layer had dried, long strips of this film could be made into compact rolls capable of recording a large number of images. Eastman also made inexpensive cameras for use with his film. The introduction of these two innovations revolutionized photography by making it available to almost anyone. Eastman's success led to the founding of the Eastman Kodak Company. This revolution in photography was much like the one Henry Ford's Model T produced in the automotive industry.

Celluloid (cellulose nitrate or nitrocellulose) is no longer used as the backing or support for film emulsions, because it is extremely flammable (or even explosive). The material first used in the so-called safety film that replaced celluloid was cellulose acetate, which is diffi-cult to burn. This is still the most commonly used film backing or *base,* although more recently polyester films similar to Mylar have been introduced for special-purpose films. Kodak's trademark for one of these bases is Estar.

The Photographic Emulsion and the Latent Image

The light-sensitive emulsion basically consists of grains of silver (Ag) salts suspended in gelatin. Film is prepared by coating the base with a hot suspension or emulsion of Ag salts and then letting it cool so that it gels. After this the gelatin is allowed to dry to form a thin, relatively hard layer. The silver salts used are silver chloride ($AgCl$), silver bromide ($AgBr$), and silver iodide (AgI). In a given emulsion these salts may be used singly or in combination. The atoms combined with the Ag to form these salts (chlorine, bromine, and iodine) are members of the halogen family (see the periodic table, Figure 3-2). Salts of halogens are collectively known as halides. The letter X is commonly used to symbolize a halogen. We can simplify the description of a photographic emulsion in our discussions by referring to it as a suspension of silver halide (AgX) grains in gelatin. When a small quantity of light falls on a single grain of AgX this grain becomes activated. During exposure light intensity vari-ations across the image produced by the lens result in selected grains receiving light and becoming activated. The activation of some of the AgX grains in the emulsion and not others produces what is called the *latent image.*

As the name implies the latent image is not visible. Exposure of the film to daylight at this point would activate all of the AgX granules so that those that had received light when the picture was taken could not be distinguished from those that had not. This would result in the destruction of the latent image. The latent image needs to be treated chemically before it can be exposed to light, viewed, and preserved. The first step in this process is known as *development.*

Development of the Negative

Photographic developers are relatively mild chemical reducing agents. Their action is mild enough to be selective. The proper developer will act only on the activated AgX grains, reducing them to elemental or metallic silver. The unexposed and therefore nonactivated grains will remain unchanged. The finely divided grains of elemental Ag will appear black, whereas the unreduced AgX will appear white or gray. The contrast between these two types of particles results in what is sometimes called the "silver image." If the film is washed free of developer, the silver image will be stable for a limited amount of time in subdued light. However, exposure to intense light would soon turn all of the remaining AgX to Ag. In order to become permanent the silver image must be fixed. A photographic *fixer* solution is used for this purpose. (Fixer was formerly commonly referred to as *hypo*, a term still used by some photographers.) The job of the fixer is to dissolve AgX and remove it from the emulsion without affecting the Ag. Once this has been done and the fixer has been thoroughly washed out of the film, the image is permanent. A commonly used ingredient in fixers is sodium thiosulfate. This is the chemical that dissolves the AgX. Other chemicals may be included in commercial fixer formulations to harden the gelatin in the emulsion.

In actual practice a *stop bath* containing acetic acid may be used to arrest development prior to fixing. In other cases a water rinse may suffice. It is also necessary to have an extensive washing step following the fixing to remove residual fixer before the film is dried. Traces of fixer remaining in the emulsion after washing can shorten the storage life of the negative. Thus, the following basic sequence of five steps or solutions is commonly used in processing photographic emulsions: developer, stop bath, fixer, washing, and drying.

Development of the Film as a Positive Transparency

The image on the film after this chemical processing is a photographic negative. This is because the areas that received light are now dark, whereas those that received little or no light are transparent. In order to get a positive image, additional steps or procedures must be used. Occasionally, one may wish to process the film to produce a positive transparency directly. This can be done by developing the silver image and then "bleaching" it rather than fixing it. In the bleaching step a chemical is used which dissolves the Ag grains and removes them from the emulsion leaving the AgX behind. The areas which once contained the Ag are now transparent. In the next step the remaining AgX is exposed to light to activate it so that it can be developed to yield a dark silver image in the areas that received no light during the original exposure. A positive transparency is the result.

Printing

The more common means of producing photographic positives is through *printing*. Printing is much like rephotographing the negative. Since the second photographic process will produce a negative of the negative, the result is a positive. The simplest printing process is *contact printing*. Here the negative is placed in contact with an unexposed light-sensitive material such as film (if a transparency is desired) or an emulsion-coated paper as the first step in producing a contact print. The light-sensitive material is then exposed by shining light through the negative onto it. The areas that receive the most light will be those that lie under the clearer areas of the negative. These will be the darker areas in the print and will correspond to the darker areas in the original subject. Processing the exposed material results in the production of a positive.

If one wishes to have a print with an image larger than that on the negative, a process known as *enlarging* is used. Here the negative is placed in a special projector known as an *enlarger*. The enlarged image of the negative is projected onto a piece of sensitive material, such as photographic paper, which is then developed to produce a print. The size of the projected image and thus the degree of enlargement is determined by the projection distance and the focal length of the enlarger lens.

The chemistry of the process used in developing and fixing black-and-white prints is very similar to that used for producing negatives. However, the emulsion on the printing paper is generally substantially slower (requires more exposure) than the typical emulsions used with films. In addition, different developers are normally used. With the exception of these minor differences, the process is pretty much the same.

A selection of printing papers is available in different contrast grades. This allows the photographer to exert control over contrast during printing. Additional control of contrast is possible by careful selection of exposure and development times during printing. A nearly infinite number of combinations of exposure and development times can be used to produce an image of normal density (degree of darkness) in the print. However, the contrast can vary markedly depending on the particular combination used. In general, short exposure times coupled with longer development times will result in increased contrast, whereas longer exposure and shorter development times will produce the opposite effect. The use of this means of controlling contrast coupled with the use of different strength developers and the availability of a selection of papers with different contrast grades provides the photographer with the means of controlling contrast over a considerable range.

FILM SPEED, GRAIN SIZE, AND CONTRAST

The term *film speed* is used to indicate the particular emulsion's sensitivity to light. A slow emulsion requires more light for exposure than a fast one. Two numerical systems are commonly used to describe film speeds. These are the ASA and the DIN systems. The first of these is used more commonly in the United States, whereas the second is more common in Europe. The ASA system consists of three overlapping progressions in which each number differs from its neighbor by a factor of 2. These progressions are reminiscent of the f-stop scale discussed earlier. In fact, it is common to refer to one film as being a certain number of stops faster or slower than another. The ASA and DIN systems are illustrated in Table A3-2. Note that the three progressions in the ASA system are offset from each other by about one-third of a stop and that one DIN "degree" is equal to one-third of a stop. Rating film speed in stops or one-third stops makes it easy to determine the correct exposure for one film from that known to be correct for another by a simple mental calculation.

Fast films make it possible to take photographs at low light levels. However, they are not the best for all purposes; their speed is achieved at a price. In general, fast films are "grainier" than slower films. The term *grain* refers to the granules of AgX in the emulsion. The smaller these grains are the finer the detail the film will be capable of recording. Slow films are usually a better choice for documenting fine details and will generally produce negatives which can be enlarged to a greater degree. Fast, coarse-grained films have limited utility in forensic photography. In general, fast films should be used only for recording the overall relationships in dimly lit outdoor scenes or in large indoor scenes with poor available light conditions. It should be remembered, however, that the use of a tripod to support the camera can make it possible to use slower, finer-grained films under low light conditions. There is no justification for using coarser-grained films when electronic flash is being used with modest-sized interior scenes or for close-ups outdoors.

The general relationship between film speed and grain size can readily be appreciated by referring to a simple example. Consider two hypothetical films, one with uniform grains of AgX which are one arbitrary unit in diameter, and the other with grains one-fifth as large. The area occupied by a single grain in the first film would accommodate 25 grains of the size employed in the second. In our earlier discussion of latent image we pointed out that a unit of light could activate a single grain of AgX. This is true without regard to the size of the grain. Thus, far less light is required to activate all of the grains within a given area of

TABLE A3-2
FILM SPEED SCALES*

	8		16		32		64		125	
ASA	10		20		40		80		160	
progressions		12.5		25		50		100		200
DIN degrees	10	11	12	13	14	15	16	17	18	19	20	21	22	23	24

*Two of the ASA progressions have been rounded off at the fast film speed end. The DIN and ASA scales can be related by the equation: $DIN = 1 + 10 \log_{10} ASA$

the coarser grained film. In the simplified example just given, 25 times as much light would be required to activate all the grains in an equivalent area of the fine-grained film. The speed disadvantage of this hypothetical slow film would be offset in many applications by this film's ability to record details about five times as fine as those recorded by the faster film.

Within a particular range of exposure (that is, light levels incident upon the film coupled with exposure duration), an increase in the exposure will produce a result showing a proportional increase in density (or blackness) of the silver image on the developed film. A curve representing a generalized relationship between exposure and image density, which is typical of photographic emulsions, is shown in Figure A3-3. This type of curve is known as an H-D curve. Each type of film or emulsion will have its own characteristic H-D curve. The range where the density of the silver image is directly proportional to the logarithm of the exposure is illustrated by the distance on the exposure scale which corresponds to the straight-line portion of the H-D curve. This range is wide with some films and narrow with others. It is commonly referred to as *exposure latitude* or simply *latitude*. Films with wide latitudes can faithfully record subtle differences in light intensity in a scene as distinct differences in density of the silver image. A narrow-latitude film might record all these slightly different levels of intensity as either black or white, depending on whether they exceeded a certain intensity level. This inability to faithfully portray a range of subtle differences in scene brightness as shades of gray is characteristic of high-contrast films. Contrast is expressed in terms of gamma, which is equal to the slope of the straight-line portion of the H-D curve. A high-gamma emulsion (steep slope) has a correspondingly narrow latitude and what is called a narrow *tonal range*. Wide-latitude films have wide tonal ranges and are characteristically low-contrast films. Thus, in general. exposure errors are much less critical with low-contrast films. Conversely, with a very high contrast film a small error in determining the exposure can result in the production of an unusable negative. Properly used, high-contrast film can accentuate subtle low-contrast features such as imprints in dust and latent fingerprints on smooth surfaces.

THE CAMERA

The camera in its simplest form is a light-tight enclosure in which a lens and a light-sensitive emulsion are mounted. If the lens and the emulsion are positioned properly with respect to each other, excellent photographs can be obtained with such a rudimentary device. The quality of the photographs need depend only on the quality of the two major components of the camera, the lens and the film. Many early cameras were no more elaborate than what we have just described. The additional refinements which are found on more modern cameras

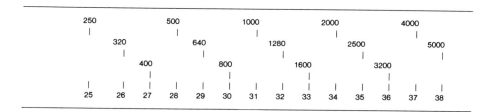

are not absolutely necessary. They are fundamentally convenience features, although they do eliminate the need for a great deal of trial and error and thus make photography much more practical as a documentation tool.

Early photographers used relatively insensitive or slow emulsions and controlled their exposures by uncovering and then recapping the lens after a predetermined time interval. This would be difficult with today's faster emulsions or with higher light levels where the

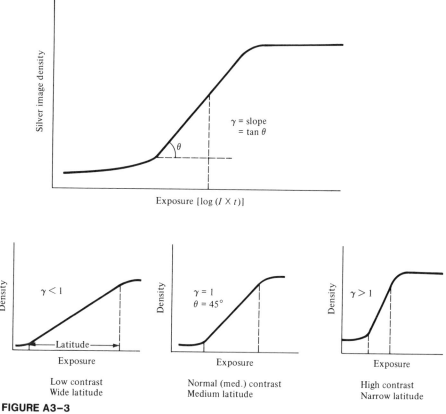

FIGURE A3–3
H-D Curves (also known as characteristic curves).

exposure durations are fractions of a second. Automatic control of short-duration exposures is provided by mechanically or electronically timed *shutters* in modern cameras.

Two distinct types of shutters are used, the *leaf* (or *between-the-lens*) shutter and the *focal plane* shutter. The leaf shutter is situated between elements of the camera lens and is thus essentially part of it. This design is relatively quiet and fairly easy to synchronize with flash illumination. The focal plane shutter is capable of faster speeds than the leaf shutter but is generally somewhat noisier. It is located just in front of the film plane and is the preferred type when cameras featuring interchangeable lenses are being designed. This is because with the between-the-lens type a separate shutter would be needed for each accessory lens, adding to the expense of each lens. It would also be necessary to take special precautions to avoid exposing the film each time a lens containing the shutter was exchanged for another. Since the film is not exposed when the lens is removed from cameras with focal plane shutters, this is another of the reasons that they are commonly used with cameras with interchangeable lenses. Certain larger-format interchangeable lens cameras may be provided with a manually operated opaque slide (that is, "dark slide") which can be inserted in front of the film when lenses containing the shutter are being changed.

The drawbacks of the focal plane shutter are related to its relatively greater mass and to the fact that at faster shutter speeds all areas of the image plane are not receiving light at the same instant of time. This latter characteristic is seldom a serious difficulty but can cause some distortion problems when rapidly moving objects are photographed at fast shutter speeds. In addition, it restricts X synchronization flash photography to relatively slow ($\frac{1}{60}$ to $\frac{1}{125}$ s) shutter speeds. As long as the photographer is aware of this characteristic it will not cause a problem. It should be clear that the massiveness of a focal plane shutter is related to the size of the film format. This accounts for this design being restricted to use with small- and medium-format cameras. Most better quality 35-mm (2.4 × 3.6-cm format—see Figure A3-2) cameras use focal plane shutters, but these shutters may be used with larger formats (for example, 6 × 7 cm) as well.

The relative massiveness of focal plane shutters also accounts for their somewhat greater noise and vibration problems, although special mechanical damping can reduce this in well-designed cameras. In summary, the drawbacks of the leaf shutter are primarily its effective incompatibility (or at least awkwardness and excessive expense) with interchangeable lens systems as well as its limited speed—that is, difficulty obtaining exposure durations shorter than about $\frac{1}{250}$ s. With respect to high-quality cameras, leaf shutters find their greatest use with large-format designs.

Unless the camera has been designed to be used at some predetermined fixed distance from the subject, some type of focusing mechanism is necessary. In addition, there should be some provision for a simple means of changing plates or advancing the film between exposures. Other desirable features would include a viewing device to aid in aiming the camera and composing the picture, a built-in meter to aid in exposure determinations, electrical contacts for triggering synchronized flash illumination, and a provision for interchangeability of lenses. A number of other minor refinements can also be included with the camera or its accessories to provide simplicity and versatility of operation. However, the photographer should never lose sight of the fact that the essential items are the lens and the film.

CONTROL OF EXPOSURE

Let us consider the factors which can affect the density of the silver image on a piece of developed film. These include the film speed, the manner and length of development, the illumination level, the reflectance of objects in the field of view, and the exposure settings on

TABLE A3-3
COMMON SHUTTER SPEED PROGRESSION BASED ON POWERS OF 2

Power of 2	2^0	2^1	2^2	2^3	2^4	2^5	2^6	2^7	2^8	2^9	2^{10}	2^{11}	2^{12}
Relative shutter speed	1	2	4	8	16	32	64	128	256	512	1024	2048	4096
Shutter speed duration*	1	½	¼	⅛	$1/15$	$1/30$	$1/60$	$1/125$	$1/250$	$1/500$	$1/1000$	$1/2000$	$1/4000$

*One-stop increments, rounded.

the camera. At times the photographer may exercise control over all of these with the exception of subject reflectance. More commonly, the choice of film and its development has already been made. In this case the photographer may have control over the illumination levels (flash or flood) and the exposure settings on the camera. In other situations, particularly with outdoor scenes, the preexisting illumination or *available light* may be used. Here when single film is used the primary control of image density of the film is provided by the exposure settings on the camera—the lens opening ($f/\#$) and the exposure duration. We have already discussed the f-stop scale that is used to standardize lens openings. We have also mentioned that exposure duration is normally controlled by selecting a shutter speed.

Modern shutter speed scales are designed to be most compatible with $f/\#$ and film speed scales. Thus, these are also based on a power-of-2 progression. Each setting changes the exposure by one stop from the previous adjacent setting. A typical shutter speed scale is shown in Table A3-3. The use of lens opening, shutter speed, and film speed scales based on one-stop increments greatly facilitates mental exposure calculations and conversions. The example of equivalent exposures for three different film speeds given in Table A3-4 illustrates this point. Do the mental calculations necessary to satisfy yourself that these are in fact equivalent exposures.

Table A3-5 lists equivalent exposures for 21 light levels spanning a relative intensity

TABLE A3-4
EQUIVALENT EXPOSURES FOR THREE DIFFERENT FILMS

All of the following examples would yield the same exposure under a single fixed set of lighting conditions.

For ASA 32 film	For ASA 64 film	For ASA 125 film
$f/16$ at $1/15$	$f/16$ at $1/30$	$f/16$ at $1/60$
$f/11$ at $1/30$	$f/11$ at $1/60$	$f/11$ at $1/125$
$f/8$ at $1/60$	$f/8$ at $1/125$	$f/8$ at $1/250$
$f/5.6$ at $1/125$	$f/5.6$ at $1/250$	$f/5.6$ at $1/500$
$f/4$ at $1/250$	$f/4$ at $1/500$	$f/4$ at $1/1000$
$f/2.8$ at $1/500$	$f/2.8$ at $1/1000$	$f/2.8$ at $1/2000$
$f/2$ at $1/1000$	$f/2$ at $1/2000$	
$f/1.4$ at $1/2000$		

TABLE A3-5
EXPOSURE VALUE (EV) AND EQUIVALENT EXPOSURES FOR A GIVEN FILM SPEED

Relative light intensity →

Increasing depth of field ←

Relative Illumination level
←Dimmer Brighter→

Better stopping of movement →

Relative light intensity	1	2	4	8	16	32	64	128	256	512	1,024	2,048	4,096	8,192	16,384	32,768	65,536	131,072	262,144	524,288	1,048,576
Exposure value	0	1	2	3	4	5	6	7	8	9	10	11	12	13	14	15	16	17	18	19	20
Shutter speed (sec)																					
480	22	32																			
240	16	22	32																		
120	11	16	22	32																	
60	8	11	16	22	32																
30	5.6	8	11	16	22	32															
15	4	5.6	8	11	16	22	32														
8	2.8	4	5.6	8	11	16	22	32													
4	2	2.8	4	5.6	8	11	16	22	32												
2	1.4	2	2.8	4	5.6	8	11	16	22	32											
1	1	1.4	2	2.8	4	5.6	8	11	16	22	32										
1/2		1	1.4	2	2.8	4	5.6	8	11	16	22	32									
1/4			1	1.4	2	2.8	4	5.6	8	11	16	22	32								
1/8				1	1.4	2	2.8	4	5.6	8	11	16	22	32							
1/15					1	1.4	2	2.8	4	5.6	8	11	16	22	32						
1/30						1	1.4	2	2.8	4	5.6	8	11	16	22	32					
1/60							1	1.4	2	2.8	4	5.6	8	11	16	22	32				
1/125								1	1.4	2	2.8	4	5.6	8	11	16	22	32			
1/250									1	1.4	2	2.8	4	5.6	8	11	16	22	32		
1/500										1	1.4	2	2.8	4	5.6	8	11	16	22	32	
1/1000											1	1.4	2	2.8	4	5.6	8	11	16	22	32
1/2000												1	1.4	2	2.8	4	5.6	8	11	16	22
1/4000													1	1.4	2	2.8	4	5.6	8	11	16

*f numbers as a function of shutter speed for equivalent exposures.

440

range of from one to over one million (namely, $1:2^{20}$). This is a wider range than would normally ever be encountered. The f numbers in a particular *exposure value* (EV) column combined with the indicated shutter speeds all result in the same exposure. Thus, under one set of lighting conditions, even when only one film is being used, the photographer may still have a rather wide range of equivalent exposure settings from which to choose. In practice, the range of equivalent exposures is limited by the range of possible lens and shutter settings and by properties of the particular film being used. At either extreme (that is, small lens opening, long duration; large lens opening, short duration) the film may not respond in exactly the same fashion to such "equivalent exposures." The failure of the film to respond equally to the extremes of the calculated equivalent exposures is known as *reciprocity failure.* Reciprocity failure is more likely to become apparent at extremes of light levels (that is, low or high EV's) requiring either very long or very short exposures.

Within the range where the reciprocity relationship holds, the exposure choices available to the photographer may range from a relatively wide lens opening combined with a fast shutter speed to a narrow lens opening and slow shutter speed. Since each of these combinations of settings would provide the "correct" exposure, one might properly wonder if the choice could be made randomly. Although it is true that the resulting exposure would be equivalent, the overall results obtained may not be the same. Two factors must be considered in making a choice (Table A3-5). The first of these is relative movement of camera and subject. Where movement is possible, a relatively rapid shutter speed is desirable. This is true, for example, if the subject is not fixed in one position and/or the camera is not rigidly mounted on a tripod. The second factor is *depth of field,* the distance measured from the point nearest the camera that is in acceptable focus to the farthest point that is in acceptable focus. The point the camera was focused on (the *nominal* or exact focus) is between these two but is closer to the nearest point of acceptable focus. In other words, the range of acceptable focus extends farther behind the nominal focus than it does in front of it. Depth of field varies with focal length and lens aperture. Wide-angle lenses generally have greater depths of field than longer focal length lenses. Greater depth of field is also characteristic of small-aperture lenses or lenses used at a small aperture setting. When a photograph is about to be taken it is convenient for the photographer to anticipate the depth of field that will exist in the photograph. The depth-of-field scales provided on many lenses or focusing mounts are helpful in this regard. Figure A3-4 depicts a typical depth-of-field scale and illustrates how it is used. With certain types of cameras it is also possible to "preview" the depth of field. (Camera types will be discussed shortly.) When depth of field is the major consideration, the photographer would select a combination of small aperture and slow shutter speed which would yield the desired exposure. On the other hand, when stopping camera movement (for example, with a hand-held camera) or action in the subject is of primary concern, a wider lens opening coupled with a faster shutter speed would be selected.

One important exception to the case of exposure duration being controlled by shutter speed must be noted. This is the case where so-called X-synchronization flash illumination is used. In this case the shutter opens before the flash is triggered and closes after the output of the flash has ceased. Even though the shutter is open for a relatively long period of time (for example, $1/60$ s), the exposure time is determined primarily by the duration of the pulse of light from the flash. In this situation the ambient light level is too low to have an appreciable effect on the film at the lens opening used. With electronic flash the pulse typically lasts $1/1000$ s or less. The modern thyristor-controlled units, which sense the level of light reflected from the subject during the flash and shut it down when the desired exposure is achieved, can have appreciably shorter flash durations where close-ups are taken with relatively fast films. In some newer systems the duration of the flash is controlled by a sensor

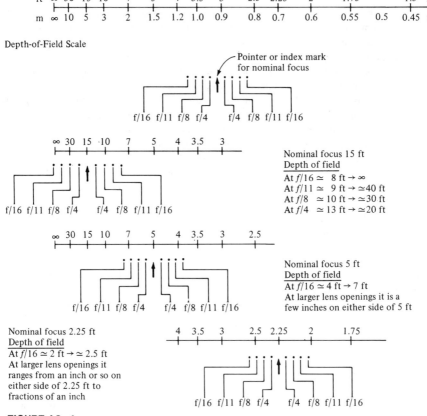

FIGURE A3–4
Depth-of-field scale and examples of its use.

placed behind the camera lens. This sensor measures light reflected from the film surface during exposure.

THE CAMERA—VIEWING AND FOCUSING SYSTEMS

The simplest way of determining exactly what the film will "see" when the picture is taken is to place a ground glass viewing screen in the position where the film will be placed at the moment of exposure. This method of focusing and composing was used in some of the earliest cameras and is still used in modern *view cameras*. The mental image one has of a photographer huddled under a black cloth is commonly associated with old-fashioned cameras. However, this procedure may still be necessary today when view cameras are used outdoors. The cloth serves the purpose of shielding the ground glass so that the relatively bright ambient light will not wash out the fainter image on it. Once the desired image is obtained on the ground glass the camera is locked in position and the ground glass is replaced with the photographic plate or film. This is still the most accurate way of ensuring that the film sees exactly what is desired. The disadvantages of this system are that it cannot be used unless both the subject and the camera are in fixed positions. In addition, it is rather slow and cumbersome. However, for photographing details of certain pattern evidence at crime scenes such as extended area blood spatter, tire tracks, and footprints, there is no better method.

After the view camera, the most accurate focusing and composing system is provided by the *single-lens reflex* (SLR) design. Here a movable mirror is used to divert the light passing through the lens to a ground-glass viewing screen placed at right angles to the film plane. If the ground glass and the mirror are properly positioned, the image on the ground glass should be the same as that in the film plane when the mirror is swung out of the way for the exposure. With proper positioning this design can be as accurate as the view camera. The main drawback of the SLR design is the noise and vibration caused by swinging the mirror out of the way at the moment of exposure. Special mechanical damping devices minimize this vibration and that caused by the focal plane shutter. The SLR is the most prevalent system used in modern high quality 35-mm cameras. It is also used in a few medium-format cameras. Cameras of the SLR design are useful for both crime-scene and evidence photography. The fact that the image formed on the ground glass by the picture-taking lens can be studied prior to making the exposure allows the photographer to preview the depth of field as well as to compose and focus. Of course, this important advantage extends to the view camera also.

Other focusing and viewing designs are less exact. In the *twin-lens reflex* design, two closely matched lenses are provided. One is for viewing, while the other is for taking the picture. Focusing the camera causes both lenses to move in unison. Thus, when the image in the viewer is in focus it should also be in focus on the film when the shutter is tripped. This, of course, assumes that the lenses are exactly matched and properly mounted with respect to the viewing screen and the film plane. Aside from the increased bulk and extra expense due to the inclusion of the extra lens, this design has other drawbacks. When a design incorporating interchangeable lenses is used, the expense of the extra lens becomes even more significant. However, the main technical shortcoming with the twin-lens design is the fact that the two lenses view the world from slightly different positions. This is not much of a problem for moderate-range to long-distance photography. However, it does become a problem for close-ups. Here the difference in viewing position results in the film seeing a somewhat different scene than is displayed in the viewfinder.

This is known as *parallax*. The closer the subject is to the camera, the more pronounced the parallax problem is. The only camera viewing systems that are free of parallax problems during close-up photography are those that use the picture-taking lens for viewing (that is, the SLR and the view camera).

Some camera designs use even more indirect means of focusing. Rather than using the picture-taking lens or one like it to form the image on a viewing screen, proper focus is determined by making a measurement or estimate of the subject-to-camera distance and adjusting the distance settings on the lens accordingly. This may be done fairly precisely in one operation by using a built-in range finder which is coupled mechanically to the focusing mount of the lens. In other cases the approximate focus is obtained by measuring or estimating the distance and then setting the lens. Some cameras may only have provision for gross focusing such as settings for portrait, group, or landscape. With still simpler cameras, the focus is fixed; it cannot be adjusted. Such cameras cannot produce sharp photographs under all conditions. They may be of reasonably acceptable sharpness for a range of from about six feet to infinity. This range is obtained by using a small-aperture, relatively short-focal-length lens to increase depth of field. Such cameras are obviously unsuitable for even modest close-up photography.

Certain more expensive range-finder versions of adjustable-focus cameras may allow close-ups to be taken but have to incorporate elaborate mechanical parallax-correction devices to ensure that the intended subject is recorded on the film. For extreme close-ups or *macrophotography* even these refinements are not sufficient. With one notable exception, true macrophotography of physical evidence can be carried out only with the view camera or SLR designs. The exception pertains to the use of special-purpose fixed-focus cameras which are designed to be used exclusively at one lens-to-subject distance. A common example f such a device is the fingerprint camera. Here the lens is fixed at a distance of exactly twice the focal length from the film so that 1:1 photographs are possible. The lens-to-subject distance is also fixed at twice the focal length by incorporating a housing or frame that is designed to be placed in contact with the surface on which the fingerprint lies. Some variations of this basic design may use attachment lens-and-frame combinations which allow a selection of other fixed image:object ratios such as 2:1, 3:1, etc. Adapters of this type can even be made available for attachment to cameras which normally have variable focus. The Polaroid CU-70 (see Figure 2-2) is an example of a variable-focus camera that can be supplied with such fixed-focus attachment lens-and-frame combinations to be used as accessories. With this particular example the frame also incorporates a close-up flash adapter.

In summary, view cameras, SLRs, and special-purpose fixed-focus cameras such as fingerprint cameras are the only types suitable for close-up evidence photography.

EXPOSURE DETERMINATION METHODS

There is no sure-fire means of always ascertaining the correct exposure before the picture is taken, although many refined methods will give an exposure that is approximately correct. The results so obtained will probably be adequate for most purposes. For critical work with narrow-latitude films, it may be necessary to use a method of trial exposures. Here, refined exposure-determination methods are used as a guide. The pictures are taken and the film is developed and evaluated as an aid in deciding on the settings for the next series of exposures. This approach is rarely practical in the field but can be very useful in the laboratory. Some of its advantages can be realized in field use if a modification known as *bracketing* is used. With this method the approximate exposure is determined using a meter. Then a series of exposures which includes the indicated nominal exposure and ones on each side of it is taken. In the next paragraph we will discuss sophisticated metering systems for determining exposures. However, it is important to remember that for very critical work the methods of trial exposures and bracketing are best.

Two distinct types of light-level metering are available to photographers. One of these measures incident light and the other, reflected light. In the first case the level or intensity of the light *falling on* the subject is measured, whereas in the second case the amount of light being *reflected from* the subject is measured. Some hand-held light meters are capable of making both incidence and reflectance measurements. The meters built into cameras are designed for making reflectance measurements only. Neither type of measurement is ideal in all photographic situations. The advantages and disadvantages of both types will be discussed separately below.

Incident light meters generally incorporate a hemispherical diffuser over the sensing element. This is sometimes known as an *integrating sphere*. A major disadvantage of incident light metering is that the meter must be placed in the area of the subject so that the light falling on this area can be measured. For remote or difficultly accessible subjects or in situations in which the illumination level is changing fairly rapidly this can be awkward. A further drawback is that the incident light meter cannot compensate for certain accessories such as filters that may be added to the camera. To be fair, neither hand-held nor certain built-in reflectance meters are capable of automatically compensating for the presence of such accessories either. Here the correct exposure must be calculated using the appropriate "filter factor" for each filter used. However, behind-the-lens meters measure the light reflected off the subject through devices such as filters that are added to the lens and thus automatically compensate for their presence.

Reflectance light meters are undoubtedly more rapid and convenient to use than incidence meters. Specialized types of these offer two distinct advantages. The first was mentioned above in connection with the behind-the-lens design. Here the meter sees the light that the film will be exposed to. The second advantage is offered by so-called spot meters. The most precise of these are hand-held devices that can be used to measure the light reflected from a relatively small selected area of a remote subject. Despite the sophistication of specialized versions, all reflectance meters suffer from one major shortcoming which requires a rather detailed explanation.

The readings of both incidence and reflectance meters clearly depend on the level of illumination. However, the readings of the reflectance type also depend on an additional factor. Lack of knowledge of this can result in inaccurate exposure determinations being made. The reflectance of the subject can profoundly influence the reading. Consider an example where both incidence and reflectance measurements are being used to determine the proper exposure for two subjects placed side by side in the same light. One of the subjects is primarily white and the other is primarily black. Since the incident light meter reading will only depend on the illumination level, which is the same for each, the same exposure will be indicated for each. This is as it should be. However, the reflectance readings in this extreme example will be very different. The level measured for the black object will be lower than that for the white one. A combination of slower shutter speed and wider lens opening would be indicated for photographing the black object than was indicated using the incident light meter. The opposite would be the case with the white object, the reflectance reading indicating the use of a faster shutter speed or smaller lens opening than that suggested by the incident light measurement. If the reflectance readings were to be believed, the black object would be overexposed so that in the final print it would be rendered as a gray rather than as a black. The white object would be underexposed and would also appear gray in the final black-and-white photograph. In order for a reflectance meter to be designed, an assumption concerning the reflectance of the scene or subject must be made. The subject must exhibit average reflectance. The average value decided upon by meter designers is 18 percent reflectance. For most photographic situations this is a workable solution. However, subjects with substantially higher reflectances will inflate the meter reading, resulting in some degree of underexposure. Similarly, low-reflectance objects lead to overexposed photographs when reflectance meter readings are taken at face value. Variations in subject reflectance present problems for reflectance meters. This is an inherent limitation of such meters. Reliance on readings from such meters in situations where the scene reflectance is abnormal will result in poor or even unacceptable exposures. The experienced photographer recognizes such abnormal scenes and interprets the exposure indicated by the meter and adjusts it accordingly. Such subjective judgments will usually produce exposures that are reasonably accurate.

There is one way of obtaining a result with a reflectance meter which should agree exactly with that obtained with an incident light meter. Here a standard scene is substituted for the actual one for the purpose of exposure determination and is then removed prior to taking the photograph. This standard scene is an *18 percent gray card*. Its reflectance is the same as that for which the meter was designed. In addition, it is *neutral*. That is, its reflectance is 18 percent for all the wavelengths in the visible region of the electromagnetic spectrum. This method of exposure determination is particularly useful for evidence photography in the laboratory where a fixed setup such as a copy stand can be used. However, it should also be used in the field for critical photography with abnormal scenes. Arson scenes with extensive charring present a commonly encountered example of a low-reflectance subject. At certain limited angles the char can be highly reflective. This is normally recognized and does not contribute to metering problems. However, unanticipated glare from this source can be a problem in flash photography of fire scenes. The main problem with metering exposures at such scenes is the low overall reflectance of extensively charred areas. Examples of high-reflectance scenes are not uncommon in forensic photography and would include subjects such as fine drops of blood spatter on a white wall and documents written on white paper. In these examples the characters on the document or the fine spots on the wall make up only a small fraction of the total surface area in the scene. The bulk of the scene is white. Such a scene (white paper or paint) has a reflectance of about 90 percent. If a gray card is not available, an exposure which will be approximately correct can be calculated from a reading taken from a piece of white paper.

Let us determine how many stops separate 90 percent reflectance from 18 percent reflectance. We will start with the standard 18 percent reflectance. If we consider a scene with double this reflectance, that is 36 percent, a one-stop exposure correction would need to be made. If we now consider a scene where the reflectance is again doubled (72 percent), a two-stop adjustment would be required. A three-stop adjustment would compensate for a scene with an impossibly high 144 percent reflectance. Thus, the proper exposure correction for a white surface with a reflectance of 90 percent is between two and three stops greater (that is, open lens or lengthen exposure), or about two and a half stops.

The gray card has an additional use in color photography. It can be of value when it is actually placed in a noncritical area of the scene and photographed with it. Comparison of the color of the gray in the gray card reproduced in the final photograph with the neutral gray of the test card itself will facilitate detection of errors in the color balance caused by both the illumination and the processing. Examination of this color can also reveal the magnitude and nature of the color balance problem. Bluish, reddish, or other nonneutral grays are readily recognizable. Having the ability of pointing to a properly rendered gray card in a color photograph can be a considerable advantage in a court situation. This allows the witness to demonstrate that the color balance of the film, processing, and illumination was correct. Inclusion of a *gray scale* in a photograph adds to this the capability of detecting density and tonal differences in the photographic rendition as well.

COLOR PHOTOGRAPHY

The image which is formed by the camera lens and falls on the film exhibits spatial variations of intensity, as pointed out earlier. These produce different degrees of exposure in different areas of the emulsion, leading to the formation of the latent image. Normally, the image formed by the lens exhibits spatial variations of wavelength as well as intensity. In other words, the image would be in color as perceived by the normal human visual complex. A black-and-white film is capable of recording only the intensity variations. The information concerning color is rendered as shades of gray in the final black-and-white image. This is a less-than-ideal record of what the normal human being sees under conditions of adequate illumination. To overcome this difficulty, color films have been developed.

The earliest work with color photography dates from the turn of the century. The first commercially successful color films became available around 1930. Two fundamentally different approaches to color photography have been used. The first of these, based on the combination of additive primary colors, utilizes a single black-and-white photographic emulsion. This emulsion is then coated with a suspension of dyed starch granules in gelatin. If a mixture containing equal quantities of red, green, and blue granules is used, these will be distributed randomly over the surface of the emulsion. When the gelatin has dried, the film is ready for packaging and use as a positive transparency film. During exposure, areas of the AgX emulsion will receive quantities of light which will depend on the intensity and color of the light in that area of the image as well as the color of the starch granule which overlies that area. If a red area of the image falls on a red granule, the area of the emulsion below the granule will be exposed. When the film is developed as a positive transparency, this area of the silver image will be clear or of low density. The developed film emulsion would transmit a large amount of light at this location. The presence of the red granule would cause the light to be red corresponding to the color of the original image at this location. Green light falling on a red granule would be absorbed, causing little exposure of the AgX emulsion below the red granule. This would be a dense area in the positive transparency. Little or no light would pass through this particular red granule. Thus, little or no red light would be contributed to the overall image at this point. However, an adjacent green granule would have allowed the green light to expose the AgX beneath it, so that a clear area would exist at this location in the developed positive. Green light would be contributed by this granule when the final positive transparency was viewed. The eye would interpret the overall pattern of colored granules in the final positive as a colored image of varied densities and subtle hues. This is very much like the way in which the collection of red, green, and blue spots of light on a color TV screen blend together when seen from a moderate distance to form a color picture. The color photographic process just described and color TV both depend on the combination of additive primaries to produce the image containing various shades of color. The fact that the image in each case is made up of differently colored dots adjacent to each other results in the fine detail in the image being considerably less than it would be in the case of a comparable black-and-white image. For this reason this system is no longer used in most color films, although Polaroid Corporation has recently introduced an instant slide film that makes use of additive primaries.

Most modern color films are based on a system of combining subtractive primaries. Each of the subtractive primaries is the color that results when a particular additive primary is removed from white light. Removing red produces a blue-green color known as *cyan*. Taking blue away yields yellow, whereas the removal of green results in a bluish-red called *magenta*. It might seem strange to the reader that neither the additive primaries (red, green, and blue) nor the subtractive primaries (cyan, magenta, and yellow) are the primary colors we were all taught about in grade school art. This seeming contradiction can be resolved when it is realized that these "primary" colors (blue, red, and yellow) are actually, and more strictly speaking, the subtractive primaries cyan, magenta, and yellow. When one mixes pigments in inks or paints to obtain the desired color, one is taking advantage of the properties of subtractive primaries. When all the subtractive primaries are combined in the proper proportions, black is obtained. However, such a combination of the additive primaries produces white light. The subtractive primaries are appropriate for use in mixing individual pigments which each absorb particular colors of light, whereas the additive primaries are appropriate when colors of light are being mixed. For example, if red, green, and blue spotlights were directed at a performer on stage, the area where all three overlapped would be white. Areas where only two of the lights overlapped would produce the subtractive primaries (see Figure A3-5). Mixing cyan, magenta, and yellow paints together would produce a muddy brown or black. Similarly, stacking dense cyan, magenta, and yellow filters together would block nearly all of the light, producing black. For a stack of equally balanced, less-dense filters, some of the light would be blocked to yield a neutral gray. With the yellow filter removed

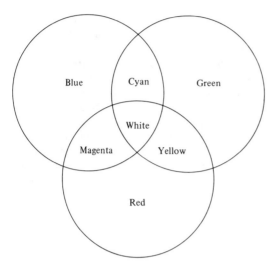

FIGURE A3–5
Additive and subtractive primaries.

Additive primaries: red, blue, green
  Red + blue + green = white
  Blue + green = cyan ⎫
  Red + blue = magenta ⎬ Subtractive primaries
  Red + green = yellow ⎭

Subtractive primaries: cyan, magenta, yellow
  White − yellow = blue ⎫
  White − magenta = green ⎬ Additive primaries
  White − cyan = red ⎭

from this stack, the overall effect would be a blue color. The depth, or *saturation,* of the blue color would depend on the density of the magenta and cyan filters remaining in the stack, whereas the shade, or *hue,* would depend on the relative balance between the densities of these two filters. Other colors would be obtained with different filter combinations as shown in Figure A3-5. An infinite number of subtle hues can be obtained by replacing individual filters in the stack with ones of the same color but slightly different densities.

Present-day color films are much like this stack of three filters. The film consists of three separate AgX emulsions with different color sensitivities. Filter layers may be placed over or between emulsion layers to control the color sensitivities of individual layers. Further details of film construction are beyond the scope of this discussion. In the case of a developed positive transparency, one layer may reflect different degrees of exposure by ranging from transparent for an overexposure to a deep cyan for underexposure. The effect in another layer would range from transparent in areas which were exposed to a deep magenta in those areas that were not. Similarly, in the third layer the effects would range from transparent to deep yellow. Thus, in the developed film each small region acts like a stack of these three filters. The density in each of these layers in one small area of the developed image is dependent on the amount and color of the light falling on this region during the exposure. This is, of course, determined by the intensity and color of the light in this region of the real image formed by the lens as well as by the duration of the exposure. Exposure reciprocity ranges may be different for each of the three emulsions. Thus, under extremes of exposure times with color films, reciprocity failure may result in shifts of color balance as well as exposure error. This is more difficult to correct for than the mere exposure shift that was the only problem due to reciprocity failure with black-and-white films.

CONCLUSION

The fundamental knowledge outlined in this appendix combined with reading about and practice with specific techniques should prove very valuable in developing expertise as a forensic photographer. The following references are offered to supplement this appendix.

REFERENCES

Blaker, Alfred A.: *Photography for Scientific Publication,* Freeman, San Francisco, 1965.
————: *Field Photography—Beginning and Advanced Techniques,* Freeman, San Francisco, 1976.
————: *Handbook for Scientific Photography,* Freeman, San Francisco, 1977.
Kodak Publications:

B-3	*Kodak Filters for Scientific and Technical Uses*	N-9	*Basic Scientific Photography*
M-1	*Copying*	N-12A	*Close-Up Photography*
M-2	*Using Photography to Preserve Evidence*	N-12B	*Photomacrography*
M-27	*Ultraviolet and Fluorescence Photography*	P-52	*Microphotography*
M-28	*Applied Infrared Photography*	R-19	*Color Dataguide*
		R-27	*Neutral Test Card*
		R-28	*Professional Photoguide*

Larmore, Lewis: *Introduction to Photographic Principles,* Dover, New York, 1965.
Sansone, Sam J.: *Modern Photography for Police and Firemen,* Anderson, Cincinnati, 1971.

REFERENCES

Blaker, Alfred A.: *Photography for Scientific Publication,* Freeman, San Francisco, 1965.
————: *Field Photography—Beginning and Advanced Techniques,* Freeman, San Francisco, 1976.
————: *Handbook for Scientific Photography,* Freeman, San Francisco, 1977.
Kodak Publications:

B-3	*Kodak Filters for Scientific and Technical Uses*	N-9	*Basic Scientific Photography*
M-1	*Copying*	N-12A	*Close-Up Photography*
M-2	*Using Photography to Preserve Evidence*	N-12B	*Photomacrography*
M-27	*Ultraviolet and Fluorescence Photography*	P-52	*Microphotography*
M-28	*Applied Infrared Photography*	R-19	*Color Dataguide*
		R-27	*Neutral Test Card*
		R-28	*Professional Photoguide*

Larmore, Lewis: *Introduction to Photographic Principles,* Dover, New York, 1965.
Sansone, Sam J.: *Modern Photography for Police and Firemen,* Anderson, Cincinnati, 1971.

INDEX